D1000536

BUSINESS LAW GUIDE TO SWITZERLAND

BUSINESS LAW GUIDE to SWITZERLAND

Pestalozzi Gmuer & Heiz

Zurich Law Firm

CCH Europe Inc.

TAX, BUSINESS AND LAW PUBLISHERS

DISCARD

Pfeiffer Library
Pfeiffer College
Misenheimer, N. C. 28109

132105

Published by CCH Europe Inc.
Parkstr. 71–73, D-6200 Wiesbaden, Germany
Tel. (0611) 564331, Facsimile (0611) 560140.

UNITED KINGDOM	CCH Editions Limited, Bicester, Oxfordshire.
USA	Commerce Clearing House, Inc., Chicago, Illinois.
CANADA	CCH Canadian Limited, Toronto, Ontario.
AUSTRALIA	CCH Australia Limited, North Ryde, NSW.
NEW ZEALAND	CCH New Zealand Limited, Auckland.
SINGAPORE	CCH Asia Limited.
JAPAN	CCH Japan Limited, Tokyo.

This publication is designed to provide accurate and authoritative information in regard to the subject-matter covered. It is sold with the understanding that the publisher is not engaged in rendering legal or other professional services. If legal advice or other expert assistance is required, the services of a competent professional person should be sought.

Ownership of Trade Marks

The Trade Marks

CCH ACCESS, COMPUTAX and **COMMERCE, CLEARING, HOUSE, INC.,**

are the property of Commerce Clearing House, Incorporated, Chicago, Illinois, USA

British Library Cataloguing in Publication Data
Business law guide to Switzerland.
 I. Pestalozzi Gmuer & Heiz (*Firm*)
 344.940666

ISBN 3-928947-00-1

©**1991 CCH Europe Inc.**

All rights reserved. No part of this work covered by the publisher's copyright may be reproduced or copied in any form or by any means (graphic, electronic or mechanical, including photocopying, recording, recording taping, or information and retrieval systems) without the written permission of the publisher.

Produced in Great Britain by CCH Editions Limited.
Typeset in Great Britain by Quorum Technical Services, Cheltenham.
Printed in Great Britain by Hartnolls Ltd, Bodmin, Cornwall.

Preface

Business executives of the 1990s think and act globally: the world is their oyster. They must spot quickly all legal aspects, domestic and foreign, of an international transaction.

To them and their advisers this comprehensive book on Swiss business law is destined. Sometimes we may generalise and simplify, but all we hope is to create awareness of Swiss legal and tax issues, not to replace professional advice.

We wish to express our gratitude to Ms Takemi Ueno for numerous suggestions given in good cheer, and to our secretaries for their valuable support.

Pestalozzi Gmuer & Heiz
Zurich, 1 August 1991

About the Publisher

CCH Editions Limited and CCH Europe Inc. are part of a world-wide group of companies that specialises in tax, business and law publishing. The group produces a wide range of books and reporting services for the accounting, business and legal professions. The CCH premises in Oxfordshire, England, and Wiesbaden, Germany, are the centres for all UK and European operations.

All CCH publications are designed to be practical and authoritative and are written by CCH's own highly qualified and experienced editorial team and specialist outside authors.

In the UK and Europe CCH produces a comprehensive series of reporting services on UK, European and international tax, business and law, and many books covering specific areas of interest for accountants, lawyers and businessmen. Irrespective of the subject matter being discussed or the depth and scope of its treatment, the material is always dealt with in the same clear and concise manner.

CCH is committed to you and your information needs, and this commitment is reflected in the constant updating and development of our reporting services and the growth and expansion of our range of publications.

If you would like to know more about our books or loose-leaf services please call (0869) 253300 in the UK or (0611) 564331 in Germany.

Contents

Contents

Contents

4 Agency and Distribution 69

Contents

Contents

Contents

Contents

Contents

Contents

Contents

Contents

Contents

1 Introduction

CONSTITUTIONAL SYSTEM

¶101   Legal and constitutional history

(1)   The beginnings of Switzerland: independence, diversity, neutrality
The Swiss Confederation traces its history to the late-thirteenth century, traditionally to 1 August 1291. During that period the Holy Roman Empire, which extended from Germany to Italy across much of what is now Switzerland, was without an emperor, and regional lords were seeking to solidify their power. In central Switzerland, a more direct route across the Alps had just opened, the Gotthard pass. The original cantons in the area united their forces against outsiders who might try to dominate their newly opened alpine crossing. With the blessing of a distant emperor, they wished to run their own affairs and did not want foreign judges to interfere.

Over the years, a number of neighbouring towns and valleys joined or associated themselves with this alliance. Now a regional power, the cantons acquired buffer territories in the surrounding areas and won victories against the rising Habsburgs (1315, 1386, 1388), the Dukes of Burgundy (1476, 1477), and even against the emperor (1499). By the end of the fifteenth century, the cantons had gained *de facto* independence from the Holy Roman Empire. They controlled various German-, French- and Italian-speaking regions.

After 1515, following an unsuccessful foray into northern Italy, Switzerland no longer fought wars to expand its territory. The policy of neutrality that was so initiated was confirmed by the Congress of Vienna in 1815 and is followed by the Swiss Confederation to this day.

Switzerland's independence was legally recognised by the European powers in the Treaty of Westphalia of 1648. By that time, the Reformation had been successful in Zurich, Geneva and other parts of Switzerland, but other cantons remained Roman Catholic. Consequently, the cantons became deeply divided by religious strife.

Despite this and other tensions among the cantons, the Swiss Confederation survived for another 150 years as a loose alliance. Its neighbours were too weak and involved in their own conflicts to conquer it.

(2)   Switzerland after the French Revolution: the federal structure takes shape

In 1798, in the aftermath of the French Revolution, Switzerland's *ancien régime* was finally overthrown by the armies of France. Under French influence, a constitution providing for central government was enacted, but in 1803, Napoleon granted Switzerland a Federal Constitution which appeared better suited to the character of the country. The constitution was influenced by the recently enacted Constitution of the United States of America.

The Napoleonic period, and with it the French domination of Switzerland, ended with the Congress of Vienna in 1815. Thereafter Switzerland once more became a loose confederation of cantons (Restoration period, 1815–30).

The liberals ('liberals' in the classic nineteenth-century sense) gained power in a majority of the cantons (Regeneration period, 1830-48). After putting down a brief secession by the Roman Catholic cantons with little bloodshed (1847), Switzerland once more adopted a Federal Constitution.

(3)   Since 1848: the Swiss Confederation

The Federal Constitution of 1848 embodied liberal ideas. It was re-enacted in 1874. Substantially amended since, it survives to this day.

As required by the Federal Constitution, Switzerland stayed neutral in World Wars I and II. It defended its borders and remained unoccupied. See also ¶112(1).

¶102   Sources of law – Federal Constitution

(1)   Fundamental rights

The Federal Constitution guarantees several fundamental rights. The equal rights provision of Article 4, which has been made concrete in abundant cases, reads as follows:

> 'All Swiss citizens are equal before the law. In Switzerland, there shall be no subjects, nor privileges of place, birth, person or family.
>
> Men and women have equal rights. The statute shall provide for equality, in particular in the areas of family, school and work. Men and women have the right to equal pay for equivalent work.'

Other fundamental rights include the guarantee of privacy (unwritten), property, the freedom of trade and industry, and numerous other freedoms.

Switzerland is a party to the European Convention for the Protection of Human Rights and Fundamental Freedoms (¶1801).

¶102

(2) Federal and cantonal law; courts; municipalities

Switzerland is a federal republic with democratic rights on the federal, cantonal and municipal levels.

The 26 Swiss cantons and half-cantons, although equally autonomous in law, vary considerably in size, population, language(s), and per capita income. The most populous canton is Zurich, which had 1,157,000 inhabitants and SFr 52,807 per capita income in 1990. The smallest is Appenzell-Innerhoden, which had 13,800 inhabitants and SFr 30,942 per capita income in 1990.

Each canton has a republican form of government with separate legislative, executive, and judicial branches.

Cantonal parliaments are unicameral and have between 50 and 200 members. In a few mainly rural cantons, they take second place to the still existing People's Assemblies (*Landsgemeinden*), where the voters meet annually to decide on various questions and to elect officials. The voters play an even greater role in the cantons than in the Confederation, because all laws, even appropriation bills, may be submitted to them.

Each canton has a complete judicial system with a trial court and an appellate court. The cantonal courts apply both federal and cantonal law. Judges are elected by either the Parliament or the people and must stand periodically for re-election.

Each village, town and city is organised as a municipality (*commune/ Gemeinde*). The municipalities differ greatly in size and in autonomy according to the canton; they all have their own executive and legislative authorities.

Separation of legislative, executive and judicial power is thus a fundamental principle of Swiss political life, as is direct influence by voters on political affairs.

As a rule, federal laws and programmes are administered by the cantons under the supervision of the federal authorities.

The cantons and municipalities have the right to levy their own individual and corporate income taxes, estate and inheritance taxes and net-worth taxes. The Federal Government may levy only those taxes provided for expressly by the Federal Constitution (¶1002(1)).

(3) Re-enacting and amending the Federal Constitution and statutes

The adoption of a constitutional amendment and adhesion to international collective security organisations (such as the United Nations) or to supranational communities (such as the EC) require an affirmative vote of the majority of cantons (the six half-cantons counting only half) and a majority of the popular vote.

The constitutional initiative is a petition of at least 100,000 eligible voters to change the Federal Constitution.

By optional referendum, the adoption of a federal statute and of important international treaties may be put to the vote of the electorate upon the demand of 50,000 eligible voters filed within 90 days after publication.

¶102

The involvement of the people in the law-giving process – so-called 'direct democracy' – is one of Switzerland's characteristic traits and, at the same time, a major obstacle to Switzerland's joining the European Community (EC).

¶103   Federal Parliament

(1)   House
The 200 members of the House (*Conseil national/Nationalrat*) represent the Swiss population at large.

(2)   Senate
The Senate (*Conseil des Etats/Ständerat*) has 46 members, two representatives each from 20 cantons and, for historical reasons, one representative each from the other six cantons (called half-cantons for this reason and because they count only half in constitutional votes).

(3)   Federal Assembly
The Federal Assembly (*Assemblée fédérale/Vereinigte Bundesversammlung*) consists of all House members and senators. It convenes only to elect the members of the Federal Government and of the Federal Supreme Court.

(4)   Political parties
The main political parties are:

- *Parti radical démocratique*, PRD/ *Freisinnig-Demokratische Partei*, FDP – market-economy oriented.

- *Parti socialiste*, PS/*Sozialdemokratische Partei*, SP – social democratic.

- *Parti démocrate-chrétien suisse*, PDC/*Christdemokratische Volkspartei*, CVP – Roman Catholic.

- *Union démocratique du centre*, UDC/*Schweizerische Volkspartei*, SVP – agrarian conservative.

All these are represented in the Federal Government.

(5)   Pressure groups
The main pressure groups are:

- *Union suisse du commerce et de l'industrie/Schweizerischer Handels- und Industrie-Verein* – employers (¶116).

- *Union syndicale suisse/Schweizerischer Gewerkschaftsbund* – labour unions.

- *Union suisse des paysans/Schweizerischer Bauernverband* – farmers.

- *Association suisse des banquiers/Schweizerische Bankiervereinigung* – banks (¶1110).

- *Union suisse des propriétaires/Schweizerischer Hauseigentümerverband* – landlords.

- *Union suisse des locataires/Schweizerische Mietervereinigung* – tenants.

- *Touring Club suisse/Touring Club der Schweiz* – traffic lobby.

- *Société suisse pour la protection de l'environnement/Schweizerische Gesellschaft für Umweltschutz* – environmentalists.

¶104 Federal Government

The Federal Government (*Conseil fédéral/Bundesrat*) is a panel of seven members, presently representing four different political parties (¶103(4)).

Members are elected for a period of four years and may stand several times for re-election. Decisions emanate from the body as a whole. Each member serves as a Minister. There is no Prime Minister. The Chairman's largely ceremonial function of President of the Swiss Confederation rotates each year among the members of the Federal Government.

LEGAL SYSTEM

¶105 International organisations – multilateral and bilateral treaties

Switzerland is not a member of the United Nations (this was turned down by popular vote in 1986) but is quite active in all its special organisations. The following have their headquarters in Geneva:

- International Atomic Energy Agency/*Agence internationale de l'énergie atomique* (AIEA),

- Economic Commission for Europe/*Commission économique pour l'Europe* (CEE),

- United Nations Conference on Trade and Development (UNCTAD)/ *Conférence des Nations Unies sur le commerce et le développement* (CNUCED),

- United Nations Centre for Human Settlement (UNCHS)/*Centre des Nations Unies pour les établissements humains (Habitat)* (CNUEH),

¶105

- Office of the United Nations Disaster Relief Co-ordinator (UNDRO)/ *Bureau coordinnateur des Nations Unies pour les secours en cas de catastrophes,*

- United Nations Research Institute for Social Development (UNRISD)/*Institut de recherche des Nations Unies pour le développement social* (IRNU),

- Technical Assistance Recruitment and Fellowship Office (TARFO) /*Bureau de recrutement pour l'assistance technique et des bourses* (TCD),

- United Nations Children's Fund (UNICEF)/*Fonds des Nations Unies pour l'Enfance,*

- United Nations Institute for Training and Research (UNITAR) /*Institut des Nations Unies pour la formation et la recherche,*

- General Agreement on Tariffs and Trade (GATT)/*Accord général sur les tarifs douaniers et le commerce,*

- Office of the United Nations High Commissioner for Refugees (UNHCR)/*Haut commissariat pour les réfugiés* (HCVR),

- International Trade Centre (ITC)/*Centre du commerce international* (CCI),

- Interagency Procurement Service Unit (IAPSU)/*Groupe des services d'achats interorganisations,*

- International Computing Centre (ICC)/*Centre international de calcul (CIC).*

Switzerland is a member of the Council of Europe (Strasbourg) and of the European Free Trade Association (EFTA), but not (yet) of the European Community (EC) (¶102(3)). It is presently seeking to create a European Economic Area encompassing EFTA and EC and does not exclude the possibility that it may join the EC one day. See ¶112(3).

Switzerland is party to numerous multilateral and bilateral treaties (including numerous double-taxation treaties). See ¶1073(2) and ¶1902 et seq.

As soon as they are approved by the Federal Parliament and the instruments of ratification have been deposited, international treaties become federal law and are applicable as such if they are self-executing.

¶106   Sources of law – the Federal Constitution and federal statutes

(1)   The Federal Constitution

The Federal Constitution (*Constitution fédérale*/*Bundesverfassung*) leaves all law-making power to the cantons, except as expressly delegated to the federal authorities by the Federal Constitution itself. Even where the federal authorities have the power to enact a statute, this power may be – and often is – limited to the enactment of guiding principles, leaving the detailed regulation to the cantons. However, the federal law takes precedence over cantonal law.

(2)   Order of priority of federal law
Statutes are the most important sources of law. The order of priority is as follows:

- the Federal Constitution,
- international conventions or treaties (*convention internationale/ Internationales Abkommen*),
- federal statutes (*loi fédérale/Bundesgesetz*),
- administrative regulations or ordinances (*ordonnance/Verordnung*) based on a formal statutory or constitutional delegation of power which specifies the content, purpose, and scope of the authority so granted.

(3)   Publication of federal laws
Federal statutes and administrative regulations are published in the official German, French and Italian languages (which are all equal; none takes precedence) in the 'Official Collection of Federal Law' (*Recueil officiel des lois et ordonnances de la Confédération suisse*, RO/*Amtliche Sammlung der eidgenössischen Gesetze*, AS) in chronological order of their entry into force.

With a delay of some six months, the legislative texts are also published in the loose-leaf 'Systematic Collection of Federal Law' (*Recueil systématique du droit fédéral*, RS/*Systematische Sammlung des Bundesrechts*, SR), where they stay as long as they are in force; texts which are not introduced into the systematic collection or which are removed from it by a supplement are deemed to be repealed. This collection also contains the international treaties entered into by Switzerland in the Swiss official languages. It is cited according to a code consisting of three to 12 digits (e.g., Federal Constitution – RS 101; Civil Code – RS 210). International treaties and conventions are preceded by the sign '0' (e.g., Convention between Switzerland and the United States of America for the Avoidance of Double Taxation with Respect to Taxes on Income RS 0.672.933.61). Finally, an annual systematic index, published as an appendix to the collection of laws, supplies a complete list of the legislative provisions in force, with references to the systematic as well as to the chronological collection.

The 'Official Gazette' (*Feuille fédérale*, FF/*Bundesblatt*, BBl) contains, among other texts, minor federal enactments that are not included in the Official Collection cited above, in particular the government reports on draft legislation (*message/Botschaft*).

Each canton has a similar system of publication for its legislation in its official language(s). German is the official language in Zurich, Lucerne, Uri, Schwyz, Unterwalden, Glarus, Zug, Solothurn, Basel, Schaffhausen, Appenzell, St Gallen,

¶106

Aargau and Thurgau; French in Geneva, Vaud, Neuchâtel and Jura; and Italian in Ticino. Berne, Fribourg and Valais have two official languages: German and French. Graubünden has three: German, Italian and Rumantch.

The published *travaux préparatoires* for federal and cantonal legislation usually consist of a government report and the minutes of the deliberations of Parliament. The minutes of parliamentary committee meetings and hearings usually remain unpublished.

¶107   Public law and private law distinguished

Public law (*droit public/öffentliches Recht*), as distinguished from private law (*droit privé/Privatrecht*), is that part of the law that deals with the organisation of the State and other public bodies and their relations as holders of public authority, among themselves and with individuals.

The major branches of public law are constitutional law (*droit constitutionnel/ Verfassungsrecht*), administrative law (*droit administratif/Verwaltungsrecht*), tax law (*droit fiscal/Steuerrecht*), criminal law (*droit pénal/Strafrecht*), criminal procedure (*procédure pénale/Strafprozessrecht*), and public international law (*droit international public/Völkerrecht*). Civil procedure (*procédure civile/Zivilprozessrecht*), including the law of collection of debts (*droit des poursuites/Zwangsvollstreckungsrecht*) and bankruptcy (*droit de faillite/ Konkursrecht*), also come under the classification of public law in Switzerland.

The most important federal statutes on public law are:

- Federal Constitution of 29 May 1874, as amended (*Constitution fédérale de la Confédération suisse/Bundesverfassung der schweizerischen Eidgenossenschaft* – RS 101). The Federal Constitution has been translated by the Federal Department of Foreign Affairs, 1980; by Blaustein, Flanz and Siegenthaler, 1979 in *Constitutions of the Countries of the World*; by Hughes, 1954.

- Federal Statute on Collection of Debt and Bankruptcy (*Loi fédérale sur la poursuite pour dettes et la faillite/Bundesgesetz über Schuldbetreibung und Konkurs* – RS 281).

- Swiss Penal Code (*Code pénal suisse/Schweizerisches Strafgesetzbuch* – RS 311; abbreviated in this book 'CP').

- Federal Statute on the Organisation of the Federal Judiciary (*Loi fédérale d'organisation judiciaire/Bundesgesetz über die Organisation der Bundesrechtspflege* – RS 173.11); excerpts translated by Pierre A. Karrer and Karl W. Arnold, *Switzerland's Private International Law Statute of December 18, 1987 – The Swiss Code on Conflict of Laws and Related Legislation 1988/1989*.

¶108   Private law

(1)   History of codification

Switzerland has always been a civil law country. From the fifteenth century onwards, Swiss scholars studied Roman law in the universities of northern Italy and Germany and in Basel. Although some aspects of Roman law found their way into local laws, Roman law was never considered the law of the land.

In the nineteenth century, the example and university teaching of neighbouring countries influenced private law and conflict of laws in Switzerland. The cantons enacted civil codes of their own. Some cantons in the west and south modelled their civil codes after the French *Code Civil*. Some cantons in the east followed the Austrian Civil Code (*Allgemeines Bürgerliches Gesetzbuch*, ABGB). Other codes were the original work of local scholars seeking to reflect local traditions.

In the latter half of the nineteenth century, under the influence of the Swiss (centralist and populist) 'democratic' movement, Switzerland became more centralised. The federal powers were extended to all areas of private law.

The most important federal private law statutes are civil law-type codes. Such codes attempt to cover an entire area of the law in a systematic fashion by stating rules and exceptions of varying, but usually broad, scope of application. Any given question of law is seldom answered by just one code provision.

(2)   Federal Civil Code (CC)

This code, encompassing persons, family, inheritance and property, was enacted in 1912. *Code civil suisse*, CC/*Schweizerisches Zivilgesetzbuch*, ZGB – RS 210 – Swiss Civil Code (abbreviated in this book 'CC').

Translated by:

- Ivy Williams, 1925,

- Ivy Williams, Siegfried Wyler and Barbara Wyler, 1987.

Excerpts translated by:

- Swiss-American Chamber of Commerce, 1974, in *Swiss Corporation Law* (Arts 52 to 59, Legal Entities, General Provisions),

- Bruno Becchio, Allan D. M. Phillips and Urs Wehinger, 1984, in *Swiss Company Law* (Arts 52 to 89bis, Legal Entities),

- Jean Russotto and Frank E. Samuel, Jr, 1965, *Swiss Family Law* (Arts 22 to 38, Persons; 90 to 177, Marriage; 252 to 456, Parents and Children, Guardianship).

(3) Federal Code of Obligations (CO)

The Federal Code of Obligations was enacted in 1881, adapted in 1912 and substantially revised in 1938. *Code des obligations*, CO/*Schweizerisches Obligationenrecht*, OR-RS 220 (abbreviated in this book 'CO').

Translated by:

- Georg Wettstein, 1928 and 1939,

- the Foreign Tax Law Association, *Commercial Law of Switzerland*, 1958,

- Simon L. Goren, 1984.

Excerpts translated by:

- Hans Henrik Lidgard, Claude D. Rohwer and Dennis Campbell, *Survey of Commercial Agencies*, 1984 (Arts 394 to 424, Mandate),

- Bruno Becchio, Allan D. M. Phillips and Urs Wehinger, 1984, (Arts 458 to 465, *Prokura and other Commercial Mandates*, and 530 to 964, *Partnerships and Corporations*),

- Swiss-American Chamber of Commerce, 1984 (Arts 1 to 238 *Obligations, Sales*; 253 to 343, *Lease, Employment Contracts*; 356 to 362 *Labour Contracts*; 394 to 439, *Mandates*,

- Swiss-American Chamber of Commerce, 1974 (Arts 620 to 763, *Share Corporation*; 927 to 944, *Register of Commerce, etc.*; 950 to 952, *Name of Corporations*; 956 to 964, *Accounting*).

(4) Federal Private International Law Statute (PIL Statute)

This major codification enacted in 1987, effective since 1989, covers all areas of conflict of jurisdictions, private international law, recognition and enforcement of foreign decisions, international bankruptcy and international arbitration. *Loi fédérale sur le droit international privé*, LDIP/*Gesetz über das internationale Privatrecht*, IPRG – SR 291 (abbreviated in this book 'PIL Statute').

Translated and annotated by Pierre A. Karrer and Karl W. Arnold, *Switzerland's Private International Law Statute of December 18, 1987 – The Swiss Code on Conflict of Laws and Related Legislation 1988/1989.*

¶108

¶109   The court system – source of case law

(1)   Cantonal and federal courts of general jurisdiction

In contrast to the dual system of parallel federal and state courts that exist, for example, in the United States, the civil, criminal and administrative courts at the trial level in Switzerland are cantonal (*tribunal d'arrondissement* or *tribunal de district/Bezirksgericht*); so are the intermediate appellate courts (*tribunal cantonal* or *cour de justice/Obergericht* or *Kantonsgericht*).

The highest court is federal. The Federal Supreme Court (*Tribunal fédéral/ Bundesgericht*) is the court of last resort on federal constitutional matters. The Federal Supreme Court may not, however, declare a federal law unconstitutional. Article 113(3) of the Federal Constitution precludes judicial control of the constitutionality of federal statutes and international treaties approved for ratification by the Federal Parliament. The Federal Supreme Court further hears civil appeals (reviewing both the facts and the law) and criminal pleas in nullity (where only the law is reviewed) against decisions of the cantonal intermediate appellate courts. It also acts as the highest federal administrative court.

(2)   Reporter of the Federal Supreme Court (ATF)

Since the establishment of the Federal Supreme Court in 1874, its most important decisions have been published in the 'Official Collection of the Decisions of the Federal Supreme Court' (*Recueil officiel des arrêts du Tribunal fédéral suisse*, ATF/ *Amtliche Sammlung der Entscheidungen des schweizerischen Bundesgerichts, BGE*). Six volumes are published each year: Ia (constitutional law), Ib (administrative law), II (private law), III (debt collection and bankruptcy), IV (criminal law) and V (social security). Throughout this book the French abbreviation 'ATF' is used when judgments of the Federal Supreme Court are cited. Accordingly, 'ATF 116 Ib 217' means a judgment of the Federal Supreme Court rendered in 1990 (i.e., 1874 + 116) in the area of administrative (*in casu* tax) law, starting at page 217.

(3)   Statutory, customary and case law, doctrinal writing

While statutory law is the primary source of law, it is often expressed in extremely general terms, and the courts must give it content and apply it to a particular case.

Article 1(2) CC recognises customary law (*droit coutumier/Gewohnheitsrecht*) as a secondary source of law in the absence of an applicable statutory provision. A custom must be recognised as a binding rule of law in all parts of Switzerland in order to become customary law.

Article 1(3) CC recognises case law as a further (in practice second most important) source of law: when both a statutory provision and customary law are lacking, it instructs the court to decide 'as if it were acting as legislator'. In doing that, 'it must follow recognised case law and doctrinal writing'.

Doctrinal writing may thus be considered a fourth source of law.

¶110   The legal profession

(1) Legal training
Legal training differs from canton to canton, but may be described in general terms as follows:

After several years of elementary school, most future lawyers attend a special university preparatory school (*gymnase* or *collège/Gymnasium* or *Kantonsschule*), which leads, around the age of 18 to 20, to the *maturité/ Maturität*, a demanding federal examination similar to the French *baccalauréat* and British A levels. (The closest American equivalent would be taking Advance and Placement examinations in several related subjects.)

Students then enter one of the eight cantonal universities (Basel, Berne, Fribourg, Geneva, Lausanne, Neuchâtel, St Gallen, Zurich) and study law, with some courses in legal history, philosophy of law and Roman law in the early stages. There may be one or more intermediate examinations, and after roughly four years a student graduates as a *licentiatus iuris* (*licencié en droit/lic. iur.*). Some students continue for a doctorate in law (*Dr en droit/Dr iur.*) and write a doctoral dissertation.

After at least one year of clerkship with a court and/or apprenticeship in a law firm, some law graduates take the cantonal bar examination which allows them to practise law. They are called *avocat/Fürsprecher/Advokat/Rechtsanwalt/ avvocato*. In French, male and female attorneys are addressed as *Maître* (abbreviation *Me*). Swiss lawyers are bound by strict codes of ethics. Their confidentiality obligation extends to the names of their clients. They may not work on a contingency fee basis. The legal profession is partly self-regulated, partly subject to government disciplinary supervision.

Some persons with legal training prefer a career in judicial administration, staying on in legal clerkship until they are elected as a lower court judge, then rising in the judiciary. There is no barrier between the judiciary and private practice, but few lawyers cross over.

The majority of persons trained in the law go into public administration and business without taking the bar exam.

(2) Lawyers' organisations

- *Fédération suisse des Avocats/Schweizerischer Anwaltsverband* (FSA/SAV); Swiss bar association, Lavaterstrasse 83, CH-8002 Zürich.

- *Verein Zürcherischer Rechtsanwälte* (VZR); Zurich cantonal bar association, Sekretariat, Talstrasse 20, CH-8001 Zürich.

- *Ordre des Avocats de Genève*; Geneva cantonal bar association, Secrétariat, Place du Bourg-de-Four 1, CH-1204 Genève.

- *Association suisse d'arbitrage* (ASA); Swiss arbitration association, PO Box 4182, CH-4002 Basel.

- *Association suisse de droit international* (ASDI)/*Schweizerische Vereinigung für Internationales Recht* (SVIR); Swiss association of international law, 4 rue de la Serre, CH-2000 Neuchâtel.

- *Association suisse de droit fiscal*/*Schweizerische Vereinigung für Steuerrecht*; Swiss national group of the International Fiscal Association (IFA), Löwenstrasse 1, CH-8001 Zürich.

- *Association genevoise du droit des affaires*; Geneva business law association.

(3) Role of notaries public and public registers

A Swiss notary public (*notaire/Notar*) does not have necessarily a university degree but has taken some courses at a university. In some cantons (e.g. Zurich), a notary public is a cantonal public official; in other cantons (e.g. Geneva), a self-employed professional (as in France, Italy, Spain, etc.). Other cantons combine the two systems.

Switzerland has a highly developed system of public registers for inhabitants, companies (¶702), land (¶1706), cattle mortgages (¶904(3)), ships (¶904(3)), aircraft (¶904(3)), retention of title in movables (¶904(4) and ¶1704(2)), collection of debt (¶904(3)), etc. Some are open to the public. Some can be consulted only if a justified legal interest is shown. See ¶901.

SWITZERLAND AND INTERNATIONAL BUSINESS

¶111 Switzerland's economy

Originally one of the poorer agrarian emigration countries of Europe, Switzerland today is modern and prosperous. Of its (1990) 6.8 million inhabitants more than one million are foreign immigrants.

The economic system of Switzerland is based on the principle of freedom of trade and industry guaranteed by the Federal Constitution. However, numerous exceptions have been introduced in some areas, particularly agriculture which is heavily subsidised and regulated.

Industry, which largely manufactures high-quality products, sells almost half – in some industries more than 90 per cent – of its output abroad. Total exports of merchandise in recent years (in 1990: SFr 88,260 million) equalled one-quarter of the country's gross national product (GNP) (in 1990: SFr 331,100 million).

Export of services is important as well (tourism, telecommunications, and the financial sector: banks and insurance).

The country has greatly strengthened its financial potential in widely varying fields of international capital transfer. It is one of the world's leading financial centres and a major international investor. The Swiss balance of payment on current account tends to close near the equilibrium point.

The banks account for a substantial portion of the country's foreign assets and liabilities. For example, at the end of 1989 all financial institutions subject to the Banking Statute (¶1122) – not taking into account the Swiss National Bank – held SFr 382,177 million in assets abroad, and additionally SFr 296,800 million in fiduciary deposits.

The three leading big banks are:

● Union Bank of Switzerland, UBS (*Union de Banques Suisses*, UBS/ *Schweizerische Bankgesellschaft*, SBG),

● Swiss Bank Corporation, SBC (*Société de Banque Suisse*, SBS/ *Schweizerischer Bankverein*, SBV),

● Swiss Credit Bank, CS (*Crédit Suisse*, CS/*Schweizerische Kreditanstalt*, SKA).

They maintain close business relations with other countries.

Cantonal banks (*banque cantonale/Kantonalbank*) exist in all cantons. A few are active universal banks, and many have an important savings and loans business.

At the end of 1989, the Swiss banking system included 631 banks and investment companies subject to the Banking Statute, with total assets of SFr 1,036 thousand million and a domestic network of 4,245 banking offices in Switzerland, a density matched by few other nations.

¶112 Switzerland's foreign trade

(1) Neutrality

In the year 1815, Swiss neutrality, which had been the basis for its foreign policy since 1515, was solemnly recognised by the Congress of Vienna as 'being in the political interest of all Europe'. Ever since then Switzerland has pursued a policy of armed neutrality linked with a willingness to co-operate with all nations.

(2) OECD and GATT
Switzerland is a member of OECD and GATT. See also ¶304.

(3) Switzerland and the European Community
Switzerland was one of the founding members of the European Free Trade Association (EFTA) in 1959/60. In July 1974 it signed a Free Trade Agreement with the EC. On the basis of these treaties, customs duties on industrial goods traded among the EFTA nations and the European Community have largely been eliminated. However, Switzerland is not a member of the EC, and is unlikely to become one in the near future. Neutrality and the system of direct democracy are perceived as possible obstacles to full EC membership. On 22 October 1991, the EC and EFTA states reached agreement to create the European Economic Area encompassing 19 countries, among which was Switzerland. It is intended that this treaty will have effect as from 1 January 1993, provided that the Swiss voters accept it in a public referendum scheduled for December 1992.

(4) Switzerland and the United States of America
Several bilateral treaties exist between the United States and Switzerland:

- Treaty of friendship of 25 November 1850 (11 Bevans 894; 11 Stat. 587; TS 353; RS 0.142.113.361). In this treaty, each country agreed to give the citizens of the other country equal treatment with its own citizens. It contains provisions relating to jurisdiction and applicable law in inheritance matters and provisions for consular services on the basis of the 'most favoured nation clause'.

- Treaty of 11 November 1937 on liability for military service of certain persons possessing the citizenship of both countries (RS 0.141.133.6).

- Treaty of extradition of 14 May 1900 (11 Bevans 904; 31 Stat. 1928; TS 354; RS 0.353.933.6).

- Treaty of arbitration and conciliation of 16 February 1931 (11 Bevans 920; 47 Stat. 1983; TS 844; 129 LNTS 465; RS 0.193.413.36).

- Convention for the avoidance of double taxation with respect to income taxes of 24 May 1951 (2 UST 1751; TIAS 2316, 127 UNTS 227; RS 0.672.933.61).

- Convention for the avoidance of double taxation with respect to estates and inheritances of 9 July 1951 (3 UST 3972; TIAS 2533; 165 UNTS 51; RS 0.672.933.62).

- Interim agreement relating to air transport services of 3 August 1945 (11 Bevans 946; 60 Stat. 1935; TIAS 1576; 51 UNTS 233; RS 0.748.127.193.36).

- Treaty concerning co-operation in field of peaceful use of atomic energy of 30 December 1965 (17 UST 1004; 594 UNTS 55; RS 0.732.933.6).

- Treaty between International Atomic Energy Organisation, the United States and Switzerland of 28 February 1972 on measures of control in regard to material and equipment (23 UST 184; RS 0.732.011.933.6).

- Treaty on social security of 18 July 1979 (32 UST 2165; TIAS 9830; RS 0.831.109.336.1). Each country grants the benefits of its federal old age and dependants insurance and disability insurance to citizens of the other country.

- Treaty on assistance in criminal matters of 25 May 1973 (27 UST 2019; TIAS 8302; RS 0.351.933.6). It also permits the two countries to give assistance against organised crime and, under certain conditions, to pierce Swiss bank secrecy.

There is no convention between the United States and Switzerland on service of process abroad or on the taking of depositions in civil and commercial matters. Switzerland and the United States (the latter on 24 December 1980) adhered to the Hague Convention of 5 October 1961, exempting foreign public deeds from legalisation. The United States has published a list of authorities competent to apply the special stamp called 'Apostille'.

(5) Switzerland and Japan
The following bilateral treaties exist:

- Treaty between Switzerland and Japan on establishment of diplomatic relations and commerce (with signing protocol)/*Traité d'établissement et de commerce du 21 juin 1911 entre la Suisse et le Japon (avec procès-verbal de signature)/Niederlassungs- und Handelsvertrag vom 21. Juni 1911 zwischen der Schweiz und Japan (mit Unterzeichnungs-protokoll)*, RS 0.142.114.631.

- Treaty between Switzerland and Japan on judicial settlement of disputes/ *Traité de règlement judiciaire du 26 décembre 1924 entre la Suisse et le Japon/Vertrag vom 26. Dezember 1924 zwischen der Schweiz und Japan zur gerichtlichen Erledigung von Streitigkeiten*, RS 0.193.414.63.

- Declaration of reciprocity between Switzerland and Japan on judicial assistance in criminal matters/*Déclaration de réciprocité des 16 avril/12 mai 1937 entre la Suisse et le Japon concernant l'entraide judiciaire en matière pénale/Gegenrechtserklärung vom 16. April/12. Mai 1937 zwischen der Schweiz und Japan über die Rechtshilfe in Strafsachen*, RS 0.351.946.3.

- Treaty between Switzerland and Japan on the avoidance of double taxation in the area of income taxes (with exchange of notes)/*Convention du 19 janvier 1971 entre la Suisse et le Japon en vue d'éviter les doubles impositions en matière d'impôts sur le revenu (avec échange de notes)/Abkommen vom 19. Januar 1971 zwischen der Schweiz und Japan zur Vermeidung der Doppelbesteuerung auf dem Gebiete der Steuern vom Einkommen (mit Notenwechsel)*, RS 0.672.946.31.

- Treaty on scheduled air traffic between Switzerland and Japan/*Accord du 24 mai 1956 relatif aux services aériens entre la Suisse et le Japon/Abkommen vom 24. Mai 1956 über Luftverkehrslinien zwischen der Schweiz und Japan* and exchange of letters of 30 June 1989, RS 0.748.127.194.63.

¶113   Foreign investment in Switzerland

Swiss businesses have traditionally been solid and heavily self-financed. There is only limited potential for investment in manufacturing or physical facilities in Switzerland. In general, there are no special tax incentives for this type of investment except in a few remote or economically depressed areas. Incentives for major projects may be negotiated with the cantonal and municipal authorities on a case-by-case basis; they could include accelerated depreciation, a tax holiday for a few years, and low-interest loans.

SOME USEFUL ADDRESSES

¶114   Federal and cantonal printing offices

(1)   Confederation

Office central fédéral des imprimés et du matériel/Eidg. Drucksachen- und Materialzentrale
Bundesverwaltung
CH-3003 Bern
Tel.: (41) (31) 61 39 16
Fax: (41) (31) 61 39 75
Telex: 91 15 15 edmz ch
(For all federal statutes, regulations, and legislative materials, including international treaties adhered to by Switzerland – all materials are available in German, French and Italian.)

¶114

(2) Zurich

Kant. Drucksachen- und Materialzentrale
Räffelstrasse 32
CH-8030 Zürich
Tel.: (41) (1) 461 34 10
Fax: (41) (1) 461 30 56
(For Zurich cantonal legal materials.)

(3) Geneva

Administration cantonale genevoise
Chancellerie d'Etat
Service de la législation et des publications officielles
Rue de l'Hôtel-de-Ville 2
Case postale 164
CH-1211 Genève 3
Tel.: (41) (22) 27 22 17
(For Geneva cantonal legal materials.)

¶115   Federal Institute of Comparative Law

Institut suisse de droit comparé
Dorigny
CH-1015 Lausanne
Tel.: (41) (21) 692 43 11
Fax: (41) (21) 692 43 43
Telex: 454 711 dvoc ch
(Source of information for Swiss, comparative and non-Swiss law.)

¶116   Some important trade associations

Union suisse de commerce et de l'industrie/Vorort des schweizerischen
Handels- und Industrievereins
Börsenstrasse 26
CH-8001 Zürich
Tel.: (41) (1) 221 27 07
Fax: (41) (1) 211 90 92
Employers.

Union centrale des associations patronales suisse/Zentralverband Schweiz
Arbeitgeber-Organisationen
Florastrasse 44
CH-8008 Zürich
Tel.: (41) (1) 383 07 58
Fax: (41) (1) 383 39 80
Employers.

Office suisse d'expansion commerciale/Schweiz Zentrale für
Handelsförderung (Osec)
Stampfenbachstrasse 85
CH-8035 Zürich
Tel.: (41) (1) 365 51 51
Fax: (41) (1) 365 5221
Swiss office of trade development.

¶117 Important chambers of commerce

Zürcher Handelskammer
Bleicherweg 5
CH-8001 Zürich
Tel.: (41) (1) 221 07 42
Fax: (41) (1) 211 76 15

Berner Handelskammer
Gutenbergstrasse 1
Postfach
CH-3001 Bern
Tel.: (41) (31) 26 17 11
Fax: (41) (31) 26 17 15

Chambre de commerce et de l'industrie de Genève
Boulevard du Théâtre 4
CH-1204 Genève
Tel.: (41) (22) 21 53 33
Fax: (41) (22) 20 03 63

Chambre vaudoise de commerce et de l'industrie – Association des industries
vaudoises
Avenue d'Ouchy 47
CH-1006 Lausanne
Tel.: (41) (21) 617 72 91
Fax: (41) (21) 617 73 03

Basler Handelskammer
St Alban-Graben 8
CH-4051 Basel
Tel.: (41) (61) 23 18 88
Fax: (41) (61) 23 62 28

Camera di commercio dell'industria e dell'artigianato del cantone Ticino
Corso Elvezia 16
CH-6900 Lugano
Tel.: (41) (91) 23 50 31
Fax: (41) (91) 22 03 41

Swiss-American Chamber of Commerce
347 Fifth Avenue, Suite 1008
New York, NY 10076, USA
Tel.: (212) 481-7792
Fax: (212) 481-7969

Swiss-American Chamber of Commerce
Talacker 41
CH-8001 Zürich
Tel.: (41) (1) 211 24 54
Fax: (41) (1) 211 95 92

British-Swiss Chamber of Commerce
Freiestrasse 155
CH-8032 Zürich
Tel.: (41) (1) 55 31 31
Fax: (41) (1) 55 32 44

Schweiz-Japan Wirtschaftskammer
Hallwylstrasse 71
CH-8004 Zürich
Tel.: (41) (1) 291 04 04
Fax: (41) (1) 291 03 83

¶118   Bar associations and other professional associations

Fédération suisse des avocats/
Schweizerischer Anwaltsverband
Lavaterstrasse 83
CH-8002 Zürich
Tel.: (41) (1) 202 56 50
Fax: (41) (1) 201 33 28

Verein Zürcherischer Rechtsanwälte (VZR)
Sekretariat
Talstrasse 20
CH-8001 Zürich
Tel.: (41) (1) 211 48 61

Ordre des avocats de Genève
Secrétariat
pl. du Bourg-de-Four 1
CH-1204 Genève
Tel.: (41) (22) 20 50 65

Association suisse d'arbitrage (ASA)/Swiss arbitration association,
PO Box 4182
CH-4002 Basel

Association suisse de droit international (ASDI)/Schweizerische Vereinigung
für Internationales Recht (SVIR)/Swiss association of international law,
4 rue de la Serre
CH-2000 Neuchâtel

Association suisse de droit fiscal/Schweizerische Vereinigung für Steuerrecht/
Swiss national group of the International Fiscal Association (IFA),
Löwenstrasse 1
CII-8001 Zürich

¶119   Swiss consulates abroad

Australia:
Swiss Embassy in Sydney
'Edgecliff Center', 203-233 New South Head Road
Edgecliff NSW 2027, PO Box 82
Tel.: (612) 328 7511 / 328 7925
Fax: (612) 327 7097

United States of America:
Swiss Embassy in Washington
2900 Cathedral Ave, NW
Washington, DC 20008-3499
Tel.: (1) (202) 745-7900
Fax: (1) (202) 387-2564

Swiss Consulate in New York
665 Fifth Avenue
New York, NY 10022-6881
Tel.: (1) (212) 758-2560
Fax: (1) (212) 207-8024

Swiss Consulate in San Francisco
235 Montgomery Street
San Francisco, CA 94104-1233
Tel.: (1) (415) 788-2272
Fax: (1) (415) 788-1402

Swiss Consulate in Los Angeles
3440 Wilshire Boulevard
Los Angeles, CA 90010-2176
Tel.: (1) (213) 388-4127/29
Fax: (1) (213) 385-4514.

Swiss Consulate in Atlanta
1275 Peachtree Street NE
Atlanta, GA 30309-3533
Tel.: (1) (404) 872-7874
Fax: (1) (404) 874-6655

Canada:
Swiss Embassy in Ottawa
5, avenue Marlborough
Ottawa, ON K1N 8E6
Tel.: (1) (613) 235-1837 / 235-0958
Fax: (1) (613) 563-1394

Hong Kong:
Swiss General Consulate in Hong Kong
3703 Gloucester Tower, 11 Pedder Street
Hong Kong
Tel.: (852) (5) 227 147/8
Fax: (852) 845 26 19

India:
Swiss Embassy in New Delhi
PO Box 392, New Delhi 110021
Tel.: (91) (11) 60 42 25/6/7
Fax: (91) (11) 687 30 93
Swiss Consulate in Bombay
400 020 Manik Mahal Vir Nariman Road 90
Tel.: (91) (22) 204 35 50 /204 25 91 /204 30 03
Fax.: (91) (22) 202 99 36

Japan:
Swiss Embassy in Tokyo
Minato-ku
Azabu P.O. Box 38
5-9-12 Minamiazabu
Tokyo 106-91
Tel.: (81) (3) 3473 0121
Fax: (81) (3) 3473 6090

Swiss Consulate in Osaka
Central P.O. Box 413
Volkart-Building
1-2-5 Dogima, Kita-Ku
Osaka 530-91
Tel.: (81) (6) 344 7671/73
Fax: (81) (6) 344 7678

Nigeria:
Swiss Embassy in Lagos
PO Box 536
Lagos
Tel.: (2341) 61 38 48 / 61 39 18

Brazil:
Swiss Embassy in Brasilia
Caixa postal 04 0171
70000 Brasilia D.F.
Tel.: (55) (61) 244 55 00 / 244 56 11
Fax: (55) (61) 244 57 11

¶119

Argentina:
Swiss Embassy in Buenos Aires
Casilla de Correo, Central No 4895
RA-1000 Buenos Aires
Tel.: (541) 311 6491/5
Fax: (541) 313 2998

¶120   Holidays

1 January	New Year's Day
2 January	Berchtoldstag (partly observed)
3 January	Instauration de la République (Neuchâtel)
4 January	Epiphany (partly observed)
varying	Carnival (Basel)
19 March	St Joseph's Day (partly observed)
varying	Good Friday (except Ticino and Valais)
varying	Easter Sunday
varying	Easter Monday (partly observed)
Third Monday in April	Sechseläuten (Zurich, afternoon)
1 May	Labour Day (partly observed)
varying	Ascension Day
varying	Whit Sunday
varying	Whit Monday
30 May	Corpus Christi (partly observed)
1 August	National Day (partly observed)
15 August	Assumption (partly observed)
5 September	Jeûne genevois (Geneva)
Second Monday in September	Knabenschiessen (Zurich, afternoon)
varying	Jeûne fédéral/Eidgenössischer Bettag (Neuchâtel and Vaud, also following Monday)
1 November	All Saints Day (partly observed)
8 December	Immaculate Conception (partly observed)
25 December	Christmas
26 December	St Stephen's Day (partly observed)
31 December	Restauration de la République (Geneva)

Even if observed, not all these days are holidays for federal and cantonal legal purposes.

SELECTED LITERATURE

(A highly arbitrary list of helpful books)

American Women's Club of Basel, *Living in Basel* (1985)
American Women's Club of Berne, *Welcome to Berne Booklet* (1989)
American Women's Club of Geneva, *Living in Geneva* (1988)
American Women's Club of Zurich, *Hints for Living in Zurich* (1986)
Dianne Dicks, *Ticking along with the Swiss* (Basel, 1988)
René Hildbrand, *Tell me a Swiss joke* (Bern, 1987)
John McPhee, *La Place de la Concorde suisse (The Swiss Army)* (1985; 1986)
George Mikes, *Switzerland for Beginners* (1975)

2   Sales and Other Contracts

PRINCIPAL LEGISLATION

Code des obligations/Obligationenrecht/Code of Obligations (CO), RS 220.

CONTRACTS

¶201   Sources of law

Swiss contract law is found in the Code of Obligations (see ¶108(3)), Arts 1 to 529. These provisions fall into two parts: the first part (Arts 1 to 183) on general contractual principles governing, for instance, the creation and discharge of a contract. The second part (Arts 184 to 551) contains provisions pertaining to specific types of contracts, such as sales of goods, lease agreements, employment contracts, construction contracts and mandates. Unlike other continental European legal systems, Switzerland does not have a separate body of law applying exclusively to merchants. In a few instances, the Code of Obligations contains some specific provisions governing dealings among merchants.

Lawyers with an Anglo-American background are often astonished at how succinctly agreements are drafted in countries whose legal tradition goes back to Roman law. This relative brevity does not leave open any more questions than an extensive common-law style agreement. Many issues that are regularly agreed upon specifically in common-law contracts are covered in civil law statutes. For example, the Code of Obligations addresses such fundamental questions as the definition and the consequences of error by a party, authority of agents, place and time of performance and modalities of payment. Moreover, the Code of Obligation regulates the effects of such legal concepts as the assignment of rights arising from a contract, the substitution of parties to a contract, prerequisites and effects of late performance, the Statute of Limitations, and joint and several obligations.

Within the limits of freedom of contract (¶202), the parties may depart from the statutory framework. The need to deal with a specific issue arises only if the parties want to contract out of that framework. In order to secure proof of their opting out, the parties are advised to do so expressly and preferably in writing.

¶202   Freedom of contract and its limits

(1)   Freedom of contract

The contents and the type of the contract, as well as the contractual partner(s), may be chosen freely. The would-be parties to a contract can limit themselves to agree only on the terms that are essential for the contract to come into being. The parties can also enter into a type of contract not regulated by statute.

Nobody may be forced into making a contract. Once a contract is made, it must be performed by the parties. The parties are free to cancel the contract again if they agree to do so.

(2)   Limits on freedom of contract

There are only minor exceptions to the principle of freedom of contract. First, the Code of Obligations contains some provisions that impose the duty to enter into a contract on a party. Such provisions are found in particular in the field of labour law.

Secondly, the contents of a contract must not violate mandatory statutory provisions. Such provisions essentially fall into three categories:

(a) One sometimes needs a permit before entering into a contract. For instance, Swiss immovable property or shares of companies owning substantial immovable property may not be sold to foreigners without a government permit (see ¶1709 et seq.).

(b) In several fields, such as labour, banking or environmental law, there are many provisions providing contractual terms which the parties to a contract have to follow. Any deviation is legally impossible.

(c) Further, contracts stipulating immoral clauses are forbidden.

Contracts that overly restrict the personal freedom of one of the parties are immoral. Thus, contracts that bind an individual for an unspecified period of time without giving a possibility of termination will be invalid.

Contracts that refer to an impossibility, have an illegal content, or violate *bonos mores* or basic personal rights are null and void. If only a single clause of a contract suffers from such a defect, this clause alone will be deemed null and void. The remainder of the contract will be enforceable, unless the parties entered into the contract only because of the clause in question (partial nullity: Art. 20 CO).

A distinction must be made between contracts that are void and those that are voidable. Voidable contracts have only a latent defect and are enforceable until the aggrieved party elects to have the contract annulled. Contracts that are unconscionable as a result of the patent disparity between the considerations given by the parties, or contracts entered into by coercion are voidable at the election of the aggrieved party.

Contractual provisions that are void have no effect from the beginning (*ab initio*). Voidness must be taken into account at the court's own initiative, i.e., even if the parties fail to assert it. However, if time has passed and the parties have already partly or entirely performed the contract, it may be unsatisfactory to hold the contract void; in such cases the courts can uphold even a void transaction. The parties may not be aware of the defect or try to pass over it. Such contracts remain in jeopardy forever. For instance, if immovable property has been bought without the required government permit, the lack of the permit may be invoked years later. If a party performs under such a contract, the judge may refuse restitution for such undue performance, assuming that the performing party waived its rights. This may happen in situations where immovable property is purchased with a public deed recording only parts of the price, so that fees and taxes are assessed only on the disclosed portion of the price.

Moreover, unusual contract terms are void if they are so different from legal provisions that they cannot reasonably be expected by the other party under the rules of good faith.

(3)   Liquidated damages/contract penalty

It is quite common for parties to provide for liquidated damages in case of non-performance or improper performance of a contract. In such cases, the aggrieved party is relieved from the burden of proving the amount of damages. If the actual damage exceeds the amount of liquidated damages, the aggrieved party may recover the excess amount but must prove it. In employment contracts, clauses providing for liquidated damages must meet certain requirements, such as reasonableness, in order to be valid.

Drafters of distributorship and employment agreements often reinforce a non-competition clause with a contractual penalty in case of breach. Contract penalties are perfectly legal.

Excessive contractual penalties may be reduced by the courts.

FORMATION OF CONTRACTS

¶203   Formal requirements

(1)   No Statute of Frauds: most oral agreements are valid

The concept of the Statute of Frauds does not exist in Swiss law. This holds true for both substantive and procedural law. The existence of an agreement may be proven in court by all means receivable in evidence, including witnesses. It is, however, desirable to have a written contract available that contains all essential provisions and is signed by the parties involved. On the basis of a written contract, the parties can enforce their rights in a summary and inexpensive legal procedure. Most oral contracts are valid regardless of the amount involved. Some agreements must, by statute, be evidenced in writing.

(2) No consideration required

The requirements that there must be a bargained-for exchange between the parties and that this exchange must have legal value do not exist in Swiss law. Any contractual obligation that has been properly promised is valid. An acknowledgement of debt is valid regardless of whether or not it mentions consideration (e.g., the underlying transaction). Further, an offer, limited in time in the offer or by statute, is binding without consideration (see ¶204). Finally, the substitutes that under Anglo-American law make executory bilateral agreements at least partially enforceable even in the absence of consideration, do not exist in Swiss law. If under Swiss law certain promises must be in writing in order to be binding, this is based on an express statutory provision and has nothing to do with absence of consideration. The concept of a sealed promise does not exist.

(3) Contractual formal requirements

A contract has been validly formed if there has been mutual assent (i.e., offer and acceptance) and if no defence to formation exists. If a contract specifies a form that is not required by law, the parties are not bound until the contracted-for form is satisfied (Art. 16 CO). If the parties provide that the contract shall be in writing, the contract must bear the signatures of all persons bound by it. Signatures must be handwritten. A letter or facsimile message is deemed to meet the writing requirement, provided that the letter or the message bears the signatures of the persons binding themselves. However, a facsimile of a signature produced by mechanical means is recognised as sufficient only if its use is customary as, for example, in the case of signatures on financial instruments which are issued in large numbers.

In contrast to United States law, a party's contractual reservation that future modifications of a contract must be in writing has only limited effect. Under certain circumstances it is possible to modify such a contract by a mere oral agreement, or even by conclusive action.

(4) Statutory formal requirements

The creation of most contracts does not depend on the observation of formalities of any kind. Contracts can be entered into by oral agreement. It is even possible to enter into a contract by mere actions implying the intention to do so. Examples of contracts that can be concluded freely are contracts for the sale of goods, lease agreements, partnerships, employment agreements, mandates and commissions.

¶203

For certain categories of contracts that typically imply high personal risks for the obligor, the statute requires that they be in writing in order to be binding. The same applies to important legal transactions that must be provable a long time after conclusion. Promises to make gifts, insurance contracts and assignments fall within this category. In addition, a suretyship must be in writing and mention the amount of the undertaking (¶902).

Some contracts require not only conclusion in writing but also recording in a public deed. Such contracts include mortgages, contracts for the sale of immovable property, and the organisation of share corporations and limited liability companies. Moreover, if an individual undertakes a suretyship, the undertaking must be recorded in a public deed and signed before a notary public.

If a formal requirement established by statute is not met, the contract is void as a matter of substantive law. The requirement of form cannot be waived by the parties. The court must take the voidness of the transaction into account on its own initiative. If the formal requirements are not met, a contract simply does not exist despite the full agreement of the parties on all essential terms. Hence, in the context of the undertaking of a suretyship, the prospective surety may at the last minute refuse notarisation, thus 'killing' the transaction. In this case the prospective surety would not be liable for any damages. It is possible that in cases where this volte-face violates the principle of bona fides, *culpa in contrahendo* (detrimental reliance) may be invoked to recover damages.

¶204 Offer and acceptance

In order to conclude a contract, the parties must manifest their mutual assent. The manifestation can be either express or implied (Art. 1 CO). The process by which parties reach a meeting of the minds is generally some form of negotiation during which one party makes an offer and the other accepts it.

(1) Offer

A communication, in order to be an offer, must create a reasonable expectation in the offeree that the offeror is willing to enter into a contract on the basis of the offered terms. Offerors have no obligation if they add to the offer a declaration that they decline to be bound, or if such a reservation arises from the nature of the transaction or the circumstances. Sending of price lists and the like does not constitute an offer. Rather, it is a mere invitation to make an offer (Art. 7 CO).

If the offeror fixes a time limit for the acceptance of the offer, the offeror remains bound by the terms of the offer until the expiration of the time limit. The offeror is released if a declaration of acceptance arrives after the expiration of the time limit. If an offer without a time limit for acceptance is extended to a party who is present, or if it is made by phone, the offer lapses immediately unless the offeree accepts it during the conversation.

In contrast, if the offer is made to an absent offeree without setting a time limit, the offeror remains bound until a reply could be reasonably expected. If a merchant transmits via facsimile an offer that is not limited in time to another dealer, the offer will probably not remain open more than a day. The offer will lapse automatically. If the dealer accepts belatedly, it is certainly advisable for the offeror to inform the offeree that he will disregard the belated acceptance.

If the dealer accepts in time, but the acceptance reaches the offeror late, the offeror must inform the dealer that the acceptance arrived belatedly; otherwise the offer will be deemed to have been accepted (Art. 5(3) CO). A contract concluded among persons that are not present takes effect at the time when the declaration of acceptance is dispatched (Art. 10 CO).

An offer can be terminated by express revocation. The power of offerees to accept the offer ends when they learn of the revocation prior to acceptance.

(2) Acceptance

An offer creates a power of acceptance in the offeree. The offeree can accept as long as the offer is open. Acceptance must be unequivocal. Where the acceptance is not consistent with the terms of the offer, there is no acceptance. Rather, the offeree has made a new offer which the original offeror may accept or not. Incomplete offers are likely to lead to counter-offers. Unless the terms of the offer and the acceptance are certain, definite and consistent, there is no contract.

The terms of the offer need not necessarily spell out all the characteristics of the envisaged transactions. Ancillary missing terms are supplemented by the terms of the applicable contract type regulated by the Code of Obligations. If the parties agree with regard to all essential points, there is a legal presumption that a reservation of ancillary points is not meant to affect the binding nature of the contract. If the parties declare at the conclusion of a meeting that they have a hand-shake deal and have only to hammer out some technical details at a subsequent meeting, there is a valid contract.

In addition, a contract does not necessarily require an express acceptance. Where, due to the particular nature of the transaction, express acceptance is not expected, the contract is deemed concluded unless the offer is declined within a reasonable time. If, for example, a distributor has for years taken delivery of one shipment each month, the offer by the supplier to ship 'as usual' creates a binding agreement unless the distributor declines the offer within a time period deemed reasonable considering the means of communication used by the parties.

Acceptance is possible by declaration or, depending upon the nature of the transaction, by performance.

¶205   Rules of contract construction

(1)   True intent of parties

Courts have developed a number of rules concerning the validity of contracts. They seek to establish the bona fide intent of the parties when entering into the contract. This applies to both the form and the contents of the contract. An incorrect statement or method of expression used by the parties, whether due to error or with the intention to conceal the true nature of the contract, will be discharged by the court. In their endeavour, the courts consider the circumstances surrounding each individual case. The parties' way of acting, the various stages of the negotiations, and earlier drafts of the contract may help the court to understand the true meaning of the contractual provisions.

The courts prefer to construe contracts in a way that upholds their validity and enforceability. They will take into account custom and usage existing in the particular line of business and in the particular place where the contract was made or is to be performed. Further, they will also construe the words according to their ordinary meaning. If a contract contains unusual or technical language, the particular meaning is disregarded if the other party could reasonably be expected to understand the language in its ordinary sense. Proponents of a clause cannot insist upon their own reading if the other party could reasonably understand them differently. In extreme cases, the court may find that there is no contract at all since the parties did not agree on essential points.

(2)   No parol evidence rule

When construing a contract, the courts are not limited by the parol evidence rule that exists in Anglo-Saxon law. Under Swiss law, the concept of this rule is not accepted. Even if the parties declare that a written instrument is the complete embodiment of their intention, the courts are not barred from considering preliminary drafts or other extrinsic evidence. This is true for extrinsic evidence varying, contradicting or adding to an 'integration', and applies even more strongly to evidence regarding defects in formation or conditions precedent.

(3)   Supplementing ancillary points

If the parties reached a contract but left agreement on some ancillary points for further discussion, a valid and enforceable contract exists (Art. 2 CO). Where the parties subsequently fail to reach an agreement with regard to the ancillary points left open, the courts will determine these points. Since the parties left open these terms, the courts' determination of the missing points is not a construction of the contract properly speaking; the courts, rather, supplement the contract. However, courts apply similar principles both in construing and in supplementing the contract. The nature of the transaction, customs and usages, the principle of good faith and the hypothetical intent of the parties provide guide-lines on how to complement the missing ancillary terms.

¶206   Defences to formation

(1)   Unilateral mistake

If only one of the parties is mistaken about facts relating to the agreement, the mistake will not prevent formation of a contract. Similarly, where a party after the conclusion of the contract discovers that the terms of the contract do not correspond to her or his real intention, the formation of the contract is not affected. However, if this party acted under a material error at the conclusion of the contract, he or she may void the contract (Art. 23 CO). An error is deemed to be material, for example, if a party intended to enter into a different contract or wanted to contract with a different party. These categories stem from the fact that the mistaken party made a declaration that did not correspond to the actual intention.

The most important category of mistake is an error related to facts which the party in error could, in good faith, consider to be a necessary basis of the contract. An error of subject matter, e.g., the suitability of goods sold for a special purpose, does not constitute a material error. Only if the seller knew, or should have known in good faith, that the purchaser was buying the goods for a special purpose, may the contract be voidable at the option of the aggrieved purchaser if the goods are not fit for this purpose.

Errors merely affecting the motives for entering into the contract are not considered to be material. Errors in calculation do not invalidate the contract, but their correction can be requested (Art. 24 CO).

The party who is entitled to invoke a material error is free to void the contract within one year after discovery of the error. In practice, the impact of the statutory provisions regarding unilateral errors is limited by the obligation for the rescinding party to make compensation for the damage resulting from the avoidance of the contract.

(2)   Voidability on other grounds

If a party has been induced to enter into a contract by the wilful deception of the other party, the contract may be voided, even though the deception involved the party's motives only (Art. 28 CO). Similarly, the conclusion of a contract under duress or coercion entitles the aggrieved party to void the contract. The same applies to contracts that are unconscionable or were concluded through one party's exploitation of the stress, inexperience, or improvidence of the other (Art. 21 CO).

¶207   Conditions precedent and subsequent

Almost any contractual duty may be undertaken conditionally. However, declarations of intention cannot be subject to a condition. This means that declarations such as the giving of notice of termination or the exercise of an option must be made unconditionally. Once the declarations are given, they cannot be revoked unless the other party gives his or her assent.

Conditions precedent and subsequent are of particular importance. As a practical matter, there is no fundamental substantive difference between the two categories. The distinction is relevant, however, in regard to burdens of pleading and proof.

In case of a condition precedent, the time when the condition materialises determines the commencement of the validity of the agreement unless there is an agreement to the contrary (Art. 151 CO). So long as the condition is pending, the obligor who is liable subject to that condition is not allowed to do anything to impair the proper fulfilment of his or her obligation. If this obligor attempts to prevent the condition from materialising, the condition, consistent with the principle of bona fide, is deemed to occur. If the rights of the beneficiary of the conditional contract are in jeopardy, he is entitled to ask for securities.

A contract whose termination is made dependent upon the occurrence of a condition becomes ineffective when the condition materialises. The occurrence of a condition subsequent renders the contract invalid *ex nunc*. If the occurrence of the condition has been avoided, it is deemed to have materialised.

¶208   Contracts of adhesion

(1)   Requirement of acceptance
Standardised printed form contracts often contain provisions that do not leave the buyer the option to procure goods without signing the form. Such contracts frequently contain fine print that shifts the risk for many aspects of the transaction to the buyer. Such standardised contracts are widely used. They usually contain 'General Conditions of Business'.

Like other jurisdictions, Switzerland had to decide whether contracts of adhesion bind the party with inferior bargaining power under all circumstances. In contrast to other jurisdictions, Switzerland does not have specific statutory rules dealing with this issue, except Art. 8 of the Unfair Competition Statute, the application of which is limited (¶1210(3) and ¶602). Rather, case law and legal writers have developed a certain number of rules governing the enforceability of adhesion contracts.

Fine print, like other items of the agreement, becomes formally binding only if it is accepted by both parties. For General Conditions of Business to become effective, the parties must manifest mutual assent that the conditions are integrated into the contract. The acceptance can be expressed or implied. It occurs if the party with the inferior bargaining power knew or should have known when signing the contract that fine print existed. It is irrelevant whether he or she actually perused the fine print. According to the principle of good faith, the party signing an instrument without concerning him- or herself with its contents must accept the contents of such text.

(2) Lack of enforceability

Even after the fine print has become binding as part of the agreed-upon contents of the contract, this does not necessarily mean that each and every contract provision is enforceable. It is possible for the party with inferior bargaining power to challenge specific provisions. If the courts are called upon to rule on such a dispute, they will proceed to analyse the contents of the challenged provision and the circumstances under which the contract was entered into.

According to case law, provisions that are surprising inasmuch as they contain unexpected risk-shifts will not be enforceable on the grounds of unconscionability. The line between risk-shifting provisions that will be upheld and those that will not is not always easy to draw. In sales and construction contracts, for instance, the purchaser or the principal has several remedies if the other party does not perform correctly or in a timely manner. Fine print may restrict the array of remedies. Such limitations are basically valid. In contrast, clauses violating statutory law or allocating the rights and duties in a way that is essentially contradictory to the nature of the contract are not valid.

Thus, the enforceability of 'add-on' clauses, that subject all of the property purchased from a seller to repossession if the newly-purchased item is not paid for, is doubtful. If a court is called upon to construe an adhesion contract, it will regularly construe the contract against the party that drafted the instrument.

As a matter of constitutional law, a debtor residing or having its corporate domicile in Switzerland must be sued at the place of domicile or seat. According to case law, a waiver of this right by contract is enforceable only if the waiver is printed conspicuously. From this case law it is possible to infer that provisions printed in bold or upper case (capital) letters are more likely to be deemed enforceable than those that are not, although the provisions might disadvantage the party with inferior bargaining power. This holds true as long as the provisions are not blatantly unconscionable.

(3) Battle of the forms

When a prospective purchaser receives an offer containing fine print from a seller, he may respond with his own standard acceptance form that includes terms and conditions not found in the original offer. In this context the question arises whether an agreement was reached, and if so, on what terms.

¶208

If the parties agreed on the essential terms of the contract, such as the nature of contract, price and quantity, a binding agreement exists. Is the fine print of the seller or that of the purchaser binding? Case law is silent on this issue, and the most distinguished legal writers disagree. According to the rule of the last word, the fine print of the purchaser is binding since the offeror impliedly waived his own conditions by accepting those of the counter-offer. According to what appears to be the prevailing opinion, the fine print of neither party is binding, and courts will instead use statutory provisions to supplement any terms that are missing as a result of the inapplicability of both General Conditions of Business.

THIRD PARTIES

Contracts affect only the concluding parties. Third parties get involved only if they either assume contractual duties with the assent of the existing parties or obtain rights. Third parties may also guarantee a contractual duty of an existing party.

¶209   Assignment of rights

An obligee may assign the claim to a third party without the consent of the obligor, unless the law, the agreement or the nature of the legal relation prohibits such assignment (Art. 164(1) CO). Claims that by express statutory provision cannot be assigned include wages. Contracts that by their nature usually cannot be assigned include personal service contracts involving a confidential relationship between the parties. Rights expected to arise in the future can be assigned. However, in order not to infringe on the personal freedom of the assignor, such rights must be specifically identified and cannot comprise 'all rights' the assignor may ever have.

   In order to be valid, an assignment must be in writing (Art. 165(1) CO). As soon as the debtor is notified of the assignment, performance for the benefit of the assignor no longer validly discharges the debtor's obligation. Only if the debtor performs in good faith before being notified, will the debtor be validly discharged. The question of whether the assignor or an alleged assignee is entitled to the claim may sometimes be disputed; in order to avoid having to perform twice, the debtor is in such cases well advised to refuse payment. The debtor can obtain discharge by making a deposit in court (Art. 168(1) CO).

   The defences that a debtor has against the assignor may also be raised against the assignee. Privileges and ancillary rights (e.g., accrued interest or bankruptcy privileges) pass together with the claim to the assignee. Those rights which are inseparably connected with the person of the assignor are excepted. In case of an assignment against payment, the assignor warrants the existence of the claim at the time of the transaction. Still, the assignor does not warrant that the indebtedness can eventually be collected unless he expressly says so.

Claims may be assigned individually or collectively. They may be in existence already or may exist only in the future (if they are exactly identifiable). It is also possible to assign a claim silently, i.e., without notifying the debtor. This happens frequently when a business entity assigns future receivables to a bank in order to secure a loan. If the company defaults on the loan, the bank will ask for a list of customers and notify them that they may perform only by paying to the bank.

¶210   Assumption of indebtedness

The assumption of the obligor's duties by a third party does not automatically release the obligor from these duties. Such a release presupposes the assumption of the debt by the third party and the discharge of the obligor by the obligee. Usually, a release of the obligor takes place by the obligee's entering into an agreement with the assuming third party, by the terms of which the third party assumes the indebtedness. There is a legal presumption that such an agreement comes into being when the obligee accepts without reservation a payment from the assuming third party. Therefore, a creditor receiving a payment from a third party must be careful either not to accept the payment or to make a reservation; otherwise the original party, the obligor, may be discharged from his duties.

Pledges and mortgages provided by third parties, as well as guarantees, will continue to constitute a security for the obligee only if the pledgor or guarantor consents to the assumption of the obligations. Such a party will usually withhold its consent if the assuming third party constitutes a worse risk than the obligor.

¶211   Third-party beneficiary contract

If a party acting in his or her own name stipulates in the contract a performance in favour of a third person, he or she can enforce such a performance. Depending upon whether the third party is an incidental or intended beneficiary, the third party can also ask that the obligor perform. The line of demarcation between the two categories is not always easy to draw. If a foreign parent company acts on behalf of its subsidiary, for example, it is advisable to be clear about whether the subsidiary company can request performance in its own right. The rights vest with the intended beneficiary when he or she declares to the obligor that he or she claims the right. Once the rights have vested, the original obligee can no longer release the obligor, and the obligor has an absolute duty to perform.

¶212   Contract to the detriment of a third party

Contracts to the charge of third parties are not possible. To be bound, the third party must have participated in the making of the contract or ratified an obligation undertaken by an agent.

SALES AND CONSTRUCTION CONTRACTS

¶213   Domestic contracts

(1)   Sources of law; missing terms; no formal requirements
Switzerland joined the United Nations Convention on contracts for the international sale of goods ('Vienna Convention') on 1 March 1991. The Convention applies to sales agreements between parties whose places of business are in different states (see Arts 1 to 6 of the Vienna Convention). Otherwise internal law applies.

Internally, contracts for the sale of goods are regulated in Arts 184 to 215 of the Code of Obligations. They are, basically, comparable to Art. 2 of the United States Uniform Commercial Code. There is no separate body of law governing the commercial relationship between merchants. Still, Arts 184 et seq. contain some statutory provisions that apply specifically to merchants. These rules include, in particular, provisions facilitating the computation of damages.

The parties can conclude a contract for sale even though the price is not settled. It is presumed that the goods were bought at the fair market price at the time and place of performance (Art. 212(1) CO). A contract need not be in writing regardless of price. Since the concept of the Statute of Frauds is unknown in Swiss law, an oral contract for the sale of movable goods is enforceable.

Contracts, in order to be binding, require at least that:

(a) the parties agree to enter into a contract for sale;

(b) the price be determinable; and

(c) the goods be determined.

(2)   Passage of title
Passage of title and passage of risk of loss (see (3) below) must be distinguished. They may pass to the purchaser simultaneously, but this is not necessarily the case.

Passage of title is not automatically triggered by the conclusion of a contract for sale. This is so because the conclusion of such a contract merely implies the seller's promise to convey title to the purchaser. Similarly, the question of whether and when the price is paid does not have any bearing on passage of title. Rather, passage of title occurs at the point in time when the seller, in discharge of the promise made, conveys possession to the purchaser.

Usually, title to goods passes once the goods are handed over to the purchaser. If the seller has to deliver a document of title (e.g., bill of lading), title passes with the delivery of the document. The very moment of passage of title is usually defined in the purchase contract. Among merchants, provisions contained in general conditions of sale normally regulate the issue. It is quite common to refer to the Incoterms of the International Chamber of Commerce. In cases involving immovable property, the conveyance takes place with the recording of the deed in the appropriate register.

(3) Passage of risk

The issue of when title passes to the purchaser has no bearing on when the risk of loss passes to the purchaser. As a rule, the risk of loss passes to the purchaser upon the conclusion of the contract. Fungible goods must be segregated and shipped in order to let the risk of loss pass.

If the seller, for any reason, fails to deliver or tender the goods in accordance with the contractual terms, the regular allocation of risk of loss does not apply. The situation is instead governed by the provisions on non-performance. Similarly, if the seller was responsible for creating the risk, the purchaser's liability is not triggered.

The allocation of risk is usually regulated in the contract by express stipulation, in general conditions of sale or by reference to the Incoterms of the International Chamber of Commerce. If such an express agreement provides that the seller bears the costs of delivering the goods at the domicile of the purchaser, there is a presumption that the parties intended the risk to pass only at the time of due tender. For the warranty of the seller see ¶501 et seq.

(4) Warranty of seller and guarantee distinguished

The parties to a contract are free to determine their respective contractual obligations. Not only are they allowed to restrict their liability, but they may also extend it beyond statutory limits. The seller may, for instance, assume an obligation to repair any defects, although under the Code of Obligations the buyer has no claim for repairs (¶503(6)).

The promise to assume an obligation extending beyond the statutory warranty must be distinguished from a separate guarantee contract attached (e.g., to a sales contract where a seller guarantees future qualities of the goods).

¶213

¶214   Consignment stock

By establishing a consignment stock in the country where the goods will eventually be sold, the manufacturer or seller secures speedy delivery of the goods to the end buyer. It is also cheaper to go through customs with bulk goods than to undergo the necessary formalities in connection with every single delivery.

The foreign manufacturer or seller usually contracts with a Switzerland-based agent, who will be entitled to withdraw from the consignment stock the quantities of goods needed in the course of business. In most instances, the agent sells the goods based on an agency or commission agreement on behalf of the foreign manufacturer or seller. In such instances, there is no advantage for the principal in retaining title to the goods. The principal remains, as a matter of agency, owner of the consignment stock up to the moment the sale occurs. The sale occurs between the purchaser and the principal, with the Switzerland-based agent acting as an intermediary.

In contrast, if the Switzerland-based party is the purchaser intending to resell or, in case of a buffer stock, to process the goods, the foreign seller may want to retain title to the goods. However, there are obstacles to a postponement of passage of title. First, the seller's retention or retainer of title might be interpreted as a sign of mistrust *vis-à-vis* the purchaser. Secondly, under Swiss law, retainer of title is valid only if the reservation is entered into the appropriate register at the purchaser's domicile. In addition, for the reservation to be valid, the goods involved must be described specifically. Therefore, for practical reasons, the protection of title regarding goods transiting through a buffer stock is not possible. In practice, the potential liabilities of the purchaser tend to be secured by suretyships, bank guarantees on first demand, or mortgages.

¶215   Construction contracts

Under this kind of contract, a contractor typically undertakes to build an entire building according to the plans of the owner or the owner's architect. If he provides all the work or co-ordinates the work of various subcontractors, he is called the main contractor. The owner makes a contract only with the main contractor and pays only him. The various subcontractors have their own subcontracts with the main contractor. Alternatively, it is possible to have the owner's architect co-ordinate all the work and have the owner make a contract with each of the individual contractors.

If the contractor's work is defective, the owner has remedies similar to those available for breach of contract for sale (see ¶222): he may cancel, reduce the price or ask for corrective measures. In many instances the contractor stipulates the right to first take corrective actions himself.

The Association of Swiss Architects and Engineers (SIA) has prepared standard contracts that, to some extent, take the owner's interest into account.

The statutory provisions applying to construction contracts govern more than just the construction of buildings. Any legal relationship where a party has to furnish an end product is a construction contract. The preparation of building and engineering plans is deemed to constitute a construction contract.

SECURED TRANSACTIONS

¶216 Suretyship and guarantee

Swiss law distinguishes between two kinds of undertakings securing the performance of a third party: the suretyship (*cautionnement/Bürgschaft*) and the guarantee (*porte-fort/Garantieversprechen*). There is no requirement of form for a guarantee. In contrast, a suretyship must be in writing and, if the undertaking party is an individual, be executed in a public deed. In addition, the maximum amount of the undertaking must always be fixed in writing in the instrument.

Furthermore, the guarantee is an undertaking independent of the validity of the basic obligation between debtor and creditor; it is a primary and autonomous obligation. The suretyship, in contrast, is a secondary obligation that depends on the validity of the underlying contract. The surety (i.e., the person providing the suretyship) has the same defences and objections as the principal.

A true guarantee exists where a third party agrees to be bound financially, regardless of all formal and substantive particularities of the debt of the main debtor, and waives all defences and objections that the debtor may have. An example is a foreign parent company of a subsidiary that guarantees to the subsidiary's bank to cover all unpaid balances. Why such balances are unpaid would be irrelevant.

Because a guarantee is an unconditional undertaking, its general requirements are more stringent than those of a suretyship. Performance or tender guarantees extended by banking institutions are usually guarantees rather than suretyships. It is up to the courts to decide the nature of a given undertaking. If an undertaking that is labelled a guarantee is found to be a suretyship because of its import, it may be invalid if the stringent formal requirements of a suretyship are not met. Hence, when signing an undertaking, the parties have to be careful about choosing the type of security that suits their needs best.

There is no statutory regulation of letters of intent, comfort letters and similar instruments. Any such document must be interpreted on its own terms. Often they are neither a suretyship nor a guarantee and only require the issuer to negotiate in good faith how to hold the creditor harmless. They are mere moral obligations of large enterprises not to leave their subsidiaries' creditors,

¶216

particularly banks, unpaid, even though this would be possible because of the lack of legal identity between the parent and the subsidiary company.

The mandatory nature of the legal provisions regarding the form of the suretyship is meant to be a safeguard to protect a guarantor from assuming excessive commitments. It is not possible to opt out of these provisions. Instead, it might be advisable to have a guarantee agreement governed by a foreign law which is less rigorous than Swiss law. Provided that the guarantee is given in an international context, courts will enforce such a choice-of-law provision.

See ¶902 for protection of creditors' rights.

¶217   Retention of title

For practical reasons, a seller is interested in retaining title to goods sold until the purchaser has paid the full price. In many jurisdictions the seller can freely contract to retain title to the goods until such point in time. If the purchaser fails to pay the price in full, the seller simply repossesses the purchased item.

Swiss law restricts the seller's opportunities to retain title to goods delivered to the purchaser. The statutory scheme aims at preventing an individual or a company from possessing a number of perhaps expensive items that in reality do not properly belong to the possessor. The rationale is that creditors must not be misled by an individual's or a company's apparent wealth into extending credit not warranted by the actual financial situation of the borrower.

Retention of title is possible if agreed upon by seller and buyer, and if the seller enters the reservation on a public register at the purchaser's domicile. The register is kept by the debt collection office. In order to constitute an enforceable retainer of title, the entries must specifically identify the goods delivered. An identification by serial number is admissible, but not one by quantity only (e.g., three tons of crude oil). The retainer of title is enforceable *vis-à-vis* the debtor but not *vis-à-vis* third parties who acquire the goods bona fide.

As a practical matter, it is not possible to enter each and every item sold or delivered on the register. Often companies stipulate in the sales contract that the seller may proceed to the recording of the reservation at any time he chooses. As soon as there are signs casting a doubt on the purchaser's willingness or ability to pay the price as due, the seller proceeds to the recording of the retainer of title. Timing is crucial. Recording must occur prior to the opening of bankruptcy or composition proceedings in order for the purchaser to derive any privilege from the recording.

¶218   Pledges and mortgages

Mortgage of immovable property is far more common than the pledging of movable property to secure a claim. This situation is largely due to the means by which the two types of security are achieved. Mortgage of immovable property requires the signing of a public deed before a notary public and a subsequent recording on the land register at the site of the immovable property.

In contrast, the pledge of immovable property requires the physical transfer of the pledged asset. Reservation of title is not possible by means of a contractual stipulation of the reservation. The legislature aims at preventing the appearance that an individual or company is in possession of goods whose actual proprietor is a third party. Since the transfer of collateral is often impracticable, pledges are rarely used. A notable exception is the pledging of securities to the bank where they are deposited.

To facilitate the pledging of some categories of movable property, the legislature has created certain public registers. If such a register exists, the physical transfer of collateral to the creditor is not necessary for the pledge to be valid. Since third parties are free to inspect the appropriate register, the debtor is not required to dispossess himself of the pledged item. As a result, some assets of particular importance, such as livestock, railway stock, aircraft and ships, can be pledged even though the debtor continues to use them.

What kinds of securities can a company put up within the limits of the law? If the company owns immovable property, it can take out a mortgage on the premises. The mortgaged items will include not only the immovable property properly speaking but also the buildings and fixtures such as permanently installed machinery. In contrast, items that can be removed, such as light machinery, furniture, inventory and supplies, are not subject to the mortgage. Neither are they capable of being pledged, for they are needed where they are and cannot be physically transferred to the creditor. Pledging of items such as inventory is allowed only if the creditor is the only one who has access to these items; i.e., the debtor has no possibility to make use of them without the consent of the creditor. In practice, such arrangements seldom work out satisfactorily.

For enforcement of pledge and mortgage, see ¶904(5).

¶219   Liens

Where a creditor is in possession of movable property or securities with the debtor's consent, he can retain possession of them until his claim is satisfied. A creditor can exercise this right of retention if his claim is enforceable and closely connected with the transaction involving the asset in question. The required nexus is always deemed to be met in dealings between two merchants. Consequently, a manufacturer of machinery may retain machinery returned by a customer for repair if the customer, for this or any other machinery previously purchased, has not settled an open account (mechanic's lien). Agreements for forfeiture of movable property are void: if the realisation of the retained item yields more than the outstanding claim, the surplus belongs to the owner. No lien can be exercised over things which have no sale value.

The general provisions contained in the Code of Obligations governing the exercise of liens are complemented by some more specific statutory provisions. Workmen or contractors who are employed in building or other works on a property, and who have supplied material and labour or labour alone can request the courts to grant them a lien on the immovable property whose value they have helped to increase with their labour. The party entitled to such a lien cannot renounce his or her rights in advance. The statutory lien to which workmen and contractors are entitled can be registered in the land register at any time after they have undertaken to carry out the work. But the registration must take place at the latest within three months after the completion of the work.

The right to such a lien can be exercised regardless of whether the owner of the immovable property or a contractor has failed to settle an open account. If a contractor for one reason or another fails to pay the wages of his or her workmen, the owner of the immovable property runs the risk of paying twice for the services and materials provided by the workmen: although he may have paid the contractor in advance, he has still to pay the workmen in order to satisfy their preferential claim that is secured with a lien.

In order to avoid this risk, the proprietor is well advised to pay the contractor only after having made sure that he or she in turn has paid his or her workmen. Alternatively, the proprietor is free to agree with the contractor that he or a third party (e.g., a bank) will pay the workmen directly.

In addition, public bodies on the municipal, cantonal and federal level can exercise, as provided in different statutes, a right of lien some kinds of taxes and other public levies due (mostly immovable property transfer and capital gains taxes).

OTHER CONTRACTS

¶220   Contracts not specifically regulated by the Code of Obligations

(1)   In general

The parties are free to define their contractual relationship in a way that does not fit into the classifications provided by the Code of Obligations. The legal requirements of modern life often cannot be met by the limited number of statutorily defined types of contracts. A variety of new contract types emerged over the years. Such contracts include leasing, franchising, factoring, travel organisation and hospitalisation contracts, as well as licensing agreements for patents or software. As long as the parties to such contracts regulate exhaustively each and every aspect of their relationship, the need for well-defined statutory rules does not arise. However, for contingencies that were not foreseen and thus not regulated, the parties must be able to turn to settled legal principles governing their relationship.

To meet this requirement, trade usages regulating the different types of contracts have emerged. Legal writers and case law have taken up these usages, refining and developing them. For certain types of these contracts a well-settled body of case law exists today. With respect to other contracts case law is still vague.

A court that has to judge contracts not regulated by statute first looks which type of regulated contract is closest in concept to the contract under examination. The court then takes inspiration from the statutorily regulated contract to find an equitable rule applying to the unclassified contract.

(2) Leasing

The concept of leasing as applied in Switzerland is similar, but not identical, to a rental agreement. Since leasing is not specifically regulated in the Code of Obligations, the courts have developed legal principles governing this contract. Leasing is considered to have some of the features of a rental agreement, a mandate and an instalment sale.

Leasing has become an important corporate financing instrument, regarded in a similar way to bank borrowing or tapping new sources of capital. There are two types of leasing: operating and finance leasing. Typically, the lessor authorises the lessee to use movable property for a certain period of time. In consideration of the granted use, the lessee makes monthly payments corresponding to the depreciation of the movable property over the life of the contract, plus financial and administrative expenses incurred by the lessor. Leasing normally is not terminable during the life of the contract. The lessor remains owner of the subject of the leasing; courts have held, for example, that the lessor can claim a leased car in the bankruptcy of the lessee even if no retainer of title, necessary for preventing passage of title, had been entered on the appropriate register.

Leasing of immovable property is also known but is not the traditional form of investment in immovable property. Immovable property is leased above all by foreign branches or foreign-owned subsidiaries. Usually, about 20 to 40 per cent of the value of the immovable property is amortised. This type of amortisation is permitted only to a very limited extent for tax purposes.

Amortisation is tantamount to a down payment for the possible purchase of the immovable property by the lessee. If the lease is not extended and the immovable property is not purchased, the lessor is often left with immovable property that is geared to special needs, and this reduces the saleability of the property. It is, therefore, economically justified to amortise the investment over the leasing period. For the lessee, the advantage of leasing real property is that the use of the property may be paid out of profits; hence, capital does not have to be invested and immobilised in high-priced Swiss real property.

¶220

(3) Licensing agreement

The purpose of a licence agreement is to enable the licensee to use a right that is the property of somebody else. The subject matter of such agreements includes both actual industrial property rights, such as patents, copyrights, designs, and trade marks, as well as property which embodies a licensor's position of *de facto* exclusivity, such as know-how.

Statutes contain only a few provisions governing licence agreements. Basically, it has been up to the courts to develop the legal principles applicable to such agreements.

Though rules governing rental agreements and leasing have been deemed applicable to licence agreements, features of corporate law have also to be taken into account. As a result of the confidential relationship between the licensor and the licensee, the latter is barred from challenging the validity of the licensed patent. In addition, if the relationship of trust between the parties is seriously shaken, the contract can be terminated despite contractual provisions to the contrary.

The parties should agree expressly upon the basic provisions of the contract, preferably in writing. The licensor should give the licensee guarantees that the object of the licence in fact exists. If the licensee develops the object of the licence further, there should be rules for licensing the additional rights back. The parties should define exactly whether the licence is exclusive or not. Exclusivity may be granted for a particular territory only.

It is still disputed whether computer software may be copyrighted and a licence given (see ¶1319 et seq.). Here royalties are regularly claimed, but the licensor rarely takes back the software at the end of the licensing period. Violations of licensing agreements usually lead to difficult litigation. Licensors of valuable objects often tend to secure themselves by stipulating liquidated damages if there is a breach of contract.

(4) Distributorship agreement

See ¶418 et seq.

PERFORMANCE AND OTHER DISCHARGE OF CONTRACT

¶221 Place of performance

Like the time of performance, the place of performance is regulated by the Code of Obligations. Hence, unless the parties have expressly departed from the statutory provisions, the rules laid down in the Code of Obligations govern the issue of where performance must take place.

The place of performance is determined by the express or implied agreement of the parties. As a rule, financial obligations are payable at the place where the obligee has his domicile at the time of performance. Where a certain object is due to be delivered, delivery has to be made at the place where the object was located at the time of the conclusion of the contract. Other obligations, such as goods described only generically (e.g., a particular quantity of a commodity) or still to be manufactured (e.g., machinery or equipment), have to be performed at the place where the obligor had his domicile at the time when the obligation originated (Art. 74 CO).

¶222 Time of performance

The Code of Obligations contains special rules on when contractual duties must be discharged. Accordingly, and as long as the parties do not depart from the statutory framework, there is no need to include provisions addressing these issues in a contract.

Where neither the contract nor the nature of the legal relationship determines the time of performance, performance can be effected and claimed at any time (Art. 75 CO). In contrast, where the contract defines a maturity date, performance must be made on this date. Unless there is an express or implicit agreement to the contrary, the debtor is entitled to perform prior to the maturity date (Art. 81(1) CO). The debtor may not claim a discount for performing early, unless this is stipulated or corresponds to business custom. In any case, performance does not have to be accepted outside normal business hours (Art. 79 CO).

If both parties have to perform, it is good practice to specify who must perform first. Otherwise, only a party who has already performed or who offers to perform may claim performance.

The terms 'beginning', 'middle' and 'end' of a month are statutorily defined. If a time-limit is specified by days, the first day is not counted. Time limits specified in weeks, months and half months are similarly defined. Performance that is due within a certain period of time must take place prior to the expiration of the period. If the contractual period of time has been extended, the new period begins on the first day following expiration of the old period, unless the contract provides to the contrary. If the time of performance or the last day of a period is a Saturday, Sunday or public holiday at the place of performance, the relevant day is the following working day.

Under Swiss law, declarations of intent between parties to a contract such as notices of termination are effective on receipt only. Therefore, dispatch of such a declaration on the last possible day is not advisable: the declaration of intent has to be received within the relevant period. Contingencies such as vacations must be taken into account. If the mails are used and the addressee is absent, the postal clerk issues a notice asking the addressee to pick up the letter at the post office within seven days. If the addressee fails to do so, the letter is deemed to have been received on the last day of the seven-day period.

Timely performance may be crucial in light of statutory provisions that shift the risk for *force majeure* and other contingencies to the defaulting party (Art. 103 CO). See ¶231(1).

¶223   Methods of payment

Monetary claims must be discharged in Swiss Francs. Even if a contract provides for payment in a foreign currency, payment of the equivalent in Swiss Francs is allowed. The debtor has the option of paying either in the contractually agreed-upon foreign currency or in Swiss Francs unless, through the use of the term 'effective' or a similar expression, payment in Swiss Francs has been ruled out (Art. 85 CO). If the creditor causes the debt collection office – an official body – to initiate collection of a claim pursuant to the Federal Statute on Collection of Debt and Bankruptcy, any amount in a foreign currency must be converted into Swiss Francs. The debt collection office only handles requests for collections that involve monetary claims in Swiss Francs. The exchange rate used to compute the amount in question is usually the rate listed on the day the request is filed.

Partial payments are first applied to outstanding interest claims, then to the principal. If a debt is secured by pledge, mortgage or a similar instrument, any partial payment is first used to reduce the unsecured debt (Art. 85 CO).

If the obligor must pay several debts to the same obligee, the obligor has the right, when making the payment, to declare which debt he wishes to discharge. In the absence of such a declaration, the debt that matures first is reduced first (Art. 87 CO). If payment is made, the debtor is entitled to a receipt. Moreover, if the debt is entirely discharged, he or she may ask for the return or cancellation of the document evidencing the debt, if applicable (Art. 88 CO).

¶224   Refusal by obligee of performance tendered by obligor

An obligee is in default if he refuses, without justification, to accept duly tendered performance (default of obligee, *demeure du créancier/Gläubigerverzug*; Art. 91 CO). In this case the obligor is entitled to discharge his contractual duties by depositing the goods, usually with approval of a court, at the obligee's risk and expense (Art. 92 CO). On petition of the offering party, the court may order the sale of perishable goods (Art. 93 CO). In the event that one party to a contract becomes insolvent, the other party may withhold his performance until the other party's performance is secured (Art. 83 CO).

¶225   Types of breach of contract

Several cases of non-performance are considered under Arts 97 to 109 CO: failure of performance and defective performance on the one hand (Arts 97 to 101 CO), and delay in performance on the other (Arts 102 to 109 CO).

¶226   Failure of timely performance

If a certain due date for performance was stipulated, or if such a date arises from a stipulated and duly exercised notice of termination, the obligor is in default after the expiration of such date. If the obligor is in default, the obligor must pay the damages that the obligee sustains as a result of the delayed performance. The legal rate of interest payable by the debtor is 5 per cent unless a higher interest rate is stipulated or the creditor establishes that he sustained higher damages. It is payable from the first day of default. Among merchants, the applicable rate corresponds to the usual bank discount rate at the place of payment.

As a result of being in default, the obligor is liable for any risk of loss. The obligor can relieve himself from these liabilities if he proves that the delay occurred without any fault on his part or that the loss would have taken place even in the event of timely performance (Art. 103(2) CO).

¶227   Non-performance as breach of contract

Any kind of performance inconsistent with the contractually agreed upon performance is tantamount to a breach of contract. Thus, no performance at all certainly constitutes a breach of contract that will trigger damages and possibly release the obligee from the contract. The same applies to defective or incomplete performance and delivery of an item that is not consistent with the subject matter of the contract.

¶228   Liability for non-performance

General contractual liability depends on the obligor's negligence. In contrast to the rules governing extracontractual liability (i.e., liability in tort), negligence is always presumed in the event of non-performance of contract; the burden of proof shifts to the defaulting party who, in turn, has to prove that non-performance, or defective or delayed performance, was not due to his or her negligence.

The debtor is liable for any negligence, whatever its degree (Art. 99(1) CO). The degree of negligence may be taken into account in determining to what extent the defaulting party has to pay for damages.

In some cases, the law provides for strict liability. If the obligor performs the obligation, with the assistance of an auxiliary (not necessarily an employee), the obligor is strictly liable for any damage caused to the other party by the auxiliary

(Art. 101(1) CO). The defaulting party is liable even if recourses to the auxiliary was authorised and regardless of whether the auxiliary was chosen with due care and trained and supervised adequately. This strict liability may be limited or excluded by agreement (Art. 101(2) CO).

The parties may limit or exclude their contractual liability under the principle of freedom of contract. However, there are some statutory restrictions. The most important restriction provides that any agreement excluding in advance liability for intent or gross negligence is void (Art. 100(1) CO). Exclusions or limitations of liability are enforceable only for slight negligence.

¶229   Remedies for breach of contract

There is no automatic discharge of a contract as a result of breach. Unless the obligee undertakes certain steps stated in the Code of Obligations, the contract continues to have binding effect.

Faced with a breach of a bilateral contract caused by non-performance or defective performance, the obligee must cause the obligor to fall into 'qualified default' (*demeure du débiteur/Schuldnerverzug*) by setting an additional time limit for subsequent performance (Art. 107(1) CO). The granting of an additional time limit is, in certain cases, not required (for example, if an exact performance day was stipulated, or if the performance has become useless because of the delay).

If the contract is still not performed within this additional time limit, the obligee basically has two options. Depending upon the option pursued, the amount of damages awarded is different. In either case there will be no damages at all if the party who failed to perform proves that he or she is not at fault for the encountered difficulties.

Under the first option, the obligee seeks damages so as to be put in as good a position as if the other party had performed the contract. The obligee is free to seek expectation damages, regardless of whether he or she chooses to meet his or her own contractual duties or to be released from the contract. Under this hypothesis, the obligee can only claim the difference between the value of his or her own performance and the expected performance of the other party.

Alternatively, the obligee may choose to have his own contractual duties discharged. To achieve this, he must fix a time limit for the non-performing party to perform properly. If performance is not offered, he can then declare that he wants to be released from the contract. The damages that are awarded are meant to put the party who was willing to perform in as good a position as he was before entering into the contract (reliance damages).

The mechanism that eventually leads to the award of damages is unnecessarily complicated. The statutory provisions governing the sale of goods, in particular those involving merchants, contain rules that are more straightforward. These specific rules, if applicable, prevail over the general rules.

If in a commercial setting a fixed date for delivery has been agreed upon, in case of default on the part of the seller, the purchaser is presumed to waive delivery and to claim compensation for damages arising from non-performance. The purchaser may claim as damages the difference between the purchase price and the price he had to pay in good faith for a substitute. In the case of goods that have a market price or are quoted on an exchange, the buyer may, without having to purchase a substitute, claim as damages the difference between the contract price and the price at the date fixed for performance (Art. 191 CO).

Conversely, if the seller has transferred the goods to the buyer before payment of the purchase price, the seller may rescind the contract in the case of the buyer's default if he has expressly reserved that right (Art. 214 CO). In order not to fall back on the more complicated and less favourable general conditions, it is advisable for a seller selling goods on credit to reserve the right to rescind the contract if the purchaser defaults.

¶230   Discharge of payment obligation by set-off

If debts of an identical kind are mutually owed, a party may set off his or her obligations against the counter-claim, provided that both claims are due (Art. 120 CO). In practice, this possibility arises mostly in cases involving monetary claims in the same currency. Set-off is possible even though the counter-claim is in dispute. A party desiring to set off must declare so; set-off does not intervene automatically. Once such a declaration has been made, the set-off takes effect at the earliest possible moment when the two claims could be set off.

Privity of contract is required. Set-off occurs only in so far as the claims compensate each other. If the opposing claims are not identical, the difference between the two amounts is not affected by the set-off.

¶231   Discharge of contract by unforeseen circumstances

(1)   Subsequent impossibility/*force majeure*
Contractual duties will be discharged if performance has become impossible. If an obligor's performance becomes impossible because of circumstances for which he or she is not responsible, the obligation is deemed to be extinguished (Art. 119 CO). For this rule to operate, the impossibility must be 'objective', i.e., the duties cannot be performed by anyone. *Force majeure* such as an act of God is a sufficient ground for triggering discharge. In contrast, mere 'subjective' impossibility will not suffice, i.e., where the duties could be performed by someone but not the promisor.

The impossibility must arise after the contract has been closed. If the fact giving rise to impossibility already existed when the contract was formed, the question is not really one of 'discharge of contractual duties'. Rather, it is a 'contract formation' problem, involving the question of whether the contract is voidable because of mistake. Where a contract is discharged because of impossibility, a promisor who has been released from a bilateral contract is thereafter liable for any counter-performance already received because of the principle of unjust enrichment. Such promisor shall also lose his or her claim for any counter-performance still outstanding (Art. 119 CO).

If the subject matter of the contract or the designated means to perform the contract have been destroyed, the claim for counter-performance depends upon the passage of risk. If the risk has passed to the promisee prior to performance, due to a statutory or a contractual provision, the promisor loses his or her claim for counter-performance.

(2) Hardship/frustration

Courts are reluctant to discharge contractual duties on the grounds of impracticability or frustration. Under Swiss law, the equivalent of the common-law doctrine of frustration does not exist; the discharge of a contract by performance is either possible or not possible. The concept of 'subjective' impossibility is not really acknowledged, and in most cases does not lead to the discharge of the contract. However, situations that, under common law, are dealt with by the doctrine of frustration, are, under Swiss law, analysed pursuant to the principles of unilateral mistake. If the mistake is deemed material, such contracts can be discharged.

The attitude of the courts to the doctrine of impracticability properly speaking is reserved. In rare instances, courts have discharged contracts if the party who had to perform encountered extreme and unreasonable obstacles and/or expenses, provided that this could not be anticipated. Under the concept of *clausula rebus sic stantibus*, courts have discharged contractual duties if holding a party to the contract would violate the principle of good faith.

Alternatively, a contract can be deemed to contain an implied condition that the parties do not want to be bound if outside conditions change drastically. Thus, a delivery contract with a long life that does not provide for adjustment of terms in response to a fundamental modification of market conditions might be altered by the courts. However, contracts are to be performed on the stipulated terms (*pacta sunt servanda*).

¶232   Statute of Limitations

Under Swiss law, the concept of the Statute of Limitations (*prescription/verjährung*) belongs to substantive rather than to procedural law. All contractual claims for which there is no express statutory provision to the contrary are time-barred after ten years because of the Statute of Limitations (Art. 127 CO). Claims arising from everyday life activities, such as claims for rent, interest payments and other periodic performances, are barred by statute after five years. The same applies to claims arising from retail sale of goods and the professional work of lawyers and employees (Art. 128 CO).

The Statute of Limitations begins to run when the claim becomes due. This is usually achieved by putting the debtor on notice following the contractual maturity date. In this case, the Statute of Limitations will start to run on the day when notice is given. The statutory provision addressing the issue of when a claim becomes barred cannot be altered by the agreement of the concerned parties. Instead, the running of the Statute of Limitations can be tolled or waived retrospectively. For example, interruption occurs if the obligor acknowledges the claim, or if he or she makes an interest or instalment payment. The running of the Statute of Limitations is also interrupted if the creditor files a petition, pursuant to the Statute on Debt Collection and Bankruptcy, that an order to pay be served on the debtor. Similarly, the filing of a suit against the debtor also tolls the Statute of Limitations.

If an interruption occurs, the Statute of Limitations starts to run again. If its running is interrupted by bringing a suit or raising a defence during the course of litigation, the time period will start anew with any such act of the parties and with any ruling or decision of the judge.

The court is not allowed to consider the Statute of Limitations on its own initiative. It is up to the debtor to assert that his or her debt is barred by the Statute of Limitations. Therefore, it is possible to waive the defence that a claim is barred.

In practice, a creditor often has an order to pay served on the debtor in order to prevent the debt from becoming barred by the Statute of Limitations. If the service of an order to pay is made essentially for the sake of tolling the Statute of Limitations, the creditor, prior to his or her doing so, often prefers to ask the debtor to waive the Statute of Limitations. Usually the debtor agrees.

SELECTED BIBLIOGRAPHY

Eugen Bucher, *Schweizerisches Obligationenrecht, Allgemeiner Teil*, 2nd edn (Zürich, 1988)

Pierre Engel, *Traité des obligations en droit suisse (Dispositions générales du Code des obligations)* (Neuchâtel, 1973)

Peter Gauch, *Der Werkvertrag*, 3rd edn (Zürich, 1985)

¶232

Theo Guhl, Hans Merz, Max Kummer, Alfred Koller and Jean Nicolas Druery, *Das Schweizerische Obligationenrecht mit Einschluss des Handels- und Wertpapierrechts*, 8th edn (Zürich, 1991)
Heinrich Honsell, *Schweizerisches Obligationenrecht, Besonderer Teil* (Bern, 1991)
Pierre Tercier, *La partie spéciale du Code des obligations* (Zürich, 1988)
Andreas von Tuhr and Hans Peter, *Allgemeiner Teil des schweizerischen Obligationenrechts*, vol. 1 (Zürich, 1979)
Andreas von Tuhr, Arnold Escher, *Allgemeiner Teil des schweizerischen Obligationenrechts*, vol. 2 (Zürich, 1974)

3   Importing into Switzerland

PRINCIPAL LEGISLATION

Loi fédérale sur les douanes/Zollgesetz/Customs Statute, RS 631.0.

Loi fédérale sur le tarif des douanes/Zolltarifgesetz/Customs Tariff Statute, RS 632.10.

Loi fédérale sur les mesures économiques extérieures/Bundesgesetz über aussenwirtschaftliche Massnahmen/Foreign Trade Statute, RS 946.201.

SOURCES OF CUSTOMS LAW

¶301   Treaties and statutes

Importing into Switzerland is regulated by constitutional and statutory provisions and, most importantly, by international treaties.

Switzerland is a member of the European Free Trade Association (EFTA, RS 0.632.31), which has historically been a counterpart to the European Community (EC). Customs law has been, and most likely will continue to be, strongly influenced by EC law in this area.

Furthermore, Switzerland is a member of the General Agreement on Tariffs and Trade (GATT, RS 0.632.21). It is also a party to the multilateral International Convention on the Harmonised Commodity Description and Coding System (SR 0.632.11) and numerous other multi- and bilateral treaties regarding customs and tariffs.

Under the Federal Constitution, the regulation of imports serves the dual purpose of providing fiscal revenue for the federal treasury and protecting certain economic activities. The Customs Duty Act, the Customs Tariffs Act, the Foreign Trade Act, and a number of related regulations and decrees deal with the details of customs law.

Switzerland does not levy export duties.

DIFFERENT CUSTOMS TREATMENTS

¶302   Customs treatment rules

Goods imported are, as a general rule, subject to customs duties. The goods must be accompanied by a customs declaration, which is examined before the goods are cleared, and released upon payment of the customs duties. The amount of the customs duties is based on weight: the gross weight of the imported goods is multiplied by the applicable tariff. The Appendix to the Customs Tariff Act states in detail whether goods are subject to customs duties and the applicable tariff.

¶303   EFTA/EC

Goods originating in member states of the EC are cleared under the preferential treatment applied to the European Free Trade Zone. To qualify for preferential treatment, goods must fall within the scope of the EFTA Treaty or the Free Trade Agreement between Switzerland and the EC (RS 0.632.401). The goods entering Switzerland must not have left the European Free Trade Zone on their way from the exporting country to Switzerland (except for Greece), and documentary proof of the goods' origin within the European Free Trade Zone is necessary. Furthermore, the customs declaration must contain a specific request for preferential treatment. Other rules apply for postal delivery and 'free pass clearance'.

¶304   GATT

Since 1 August 1966 Switzerland has been a party to the General Agreement on Tariffs and Trade. Therefore, it basically grants most-favoured-nation status to foreigners and equal treatment to foreign and Swiss nationals in the application of customs law.

¶305   Special treatment

(1)   Developing countries

Special customs treatment is granted to imports from most developing countries. The prerequisites for preferential treatment are that the goods are listed in the Customs Preference Regulation (RS 632.911), that they are accompanied by the necessary certificate of origin, that the goods have remained under customs supervision while being shipped, and that preferential treatment is explicitly requested in the customs declaration.

(2) Insufficient supply
In situations where there is a shortage of certain goods, or where the prices of foodstuffs and other indispensable items increase significantly, the Federal Government may lower the customs tariffs for these goods or exempt them from customs duties altogether.

(3) Agricultural products
The import of agricultural products is restricted in various ways, including import prohibitions, import monopolies, government distribution of import quotas, seasonal import quotas for fruits and vegetables, requirements that the importer buy certain quantities of domestic products of the same kind, increased import duties, and special fees for the allocation of import quotas.

CUSTOMS PROCEDURE

¶306 Customs authorities

The customs authorities are federal authorities and are under the general supervision of the Federal Finance Department. The Federal Customs Administration supervises the district customs offices, which, in turn, are subdivided into customs clearance offices and the border control corps. The respective responsibilities and levels of competence of these units of customs administration range from the issuance of rulings and quasi-judicial decisions regarding most aspects of customs law through simple instructions, to information about customs tariffs and procedures. Based on the customs declaration or the revised findings of the customs clearing office, a customs officer determines the amount of duties to be paid. It is possible to appeal this decision to the district customs office.

The system of administrative review of decisions of first instance is described in Art. 109 of the Customs Act. In many cases an administrative decision can be appealed to the Federal Supreme Court.

¶307 Obligations of the foreign exporter

(1) Before and after customs clearance
Foreign exporters must file a customs declaration and pay customs duties if they transport goods across the border or bring about the import of goods. If the importers have assumed responsibility for filing the customs declaration, or if the goods are transported for their account, they become jointly and severally liable with the exporter for the payment of customs duties. If the importer fulfils

all of the above functions, the exporter should merely co-operate in providing proper and complete documentation for customs clearance. Statutory requirements concerning quality and specification of goods should be observed.

Goods which have passed customs clearance may subsequently be subject to other controls by cantonal or federal authorities. Foodstuffs and drugs are often subject to further scrutiny. Of course, false declaration of origin, misuse of registered trade marks, and non-compliance with the obligation to indicate specific data on packages (e.g., for purposes of consumer protection) are unlawful, and may have legal consequences even if the goods have already passed customs clearance.

(2) Documentation

For goods which fall under customs control, a customs clearance request must be submitted, and the necessary documents and permits must be presented. For imports from EC or EFTA countries, the '*document unique*' must be used as a form for customs declaration. Detailed instructions as to the use of this form are available from the customs authorities in German, French and Italian. The information contained in this form includes the names of the exporter, importer and persons applying for customs clearance, the country from which the goods are shipped, the countries of origin and destination, a description of the goods, and their prices, measurements and weight.

The regulation on certification of origin (RS 946.31) contains the forms and criteria for certificates and declarations of origin. The origin of the imported goods is important when preferential treatment is sought. The legal requirements and forms to be used for certificates of origin are also specified in the regulation concerning the rules that determine the origin for customs preference of developing countries.

¶308   Presentation of goods

As a general rule, traffic across the customs border is restricted to certain streets, harbours, and airports specifically designated by the Federal Customs Administration. Customs inspection of commercial goods is limited to regular business hours. All goods which cross the customs border must be presented to the responsible customs authorities and prepared for customs control and clearance. Special rules for the presentation of goods apply for transportation by train (RS 631.252.1), ship (RS 631.253.1), aircraft (RS 631.254.1), and mail (RS 632.255.1).

The goods must be' presented at the nearest customs office; pertinent instructions given by the border guards must be followed. For goods delivered by mail, the customs authorities proceed with customs clearance on their own.

The sender only has to comply with the requirements for postal customs applications.

The person who brought the goods into the territory is responsible for the presentation of the goods to the customs authorities. In the case of commercial imports, the documentation concerning the goods is presented to the customs authorities. Tourists will usually pass in person by a customs official and present any goods imported. If the customs office to which the application is submitted does not consider itself to be competent, the importer may either take the goods back across the border or apply to the nearest competent customs office. The person presenting the goods to the customs office is entitled to obtain customs declaration forms, have the customs authorities verify the nature of the imported goods, and receive information on the applicable tariffs.

¶309 Customs application

After submission to a competent customs office, the customs declaration becomes binding, and customs treatment procedures are initiated by stamping the customs declaration. The type of customs clearance to which an application is subjected may be chosen by the applicant.

¶310 Customs declaration

As a general rule, the customs declaration is in writing and is signed. In tourist traffic and in frequent cross-border traffic, oral declarations of the imported goods are accepted. Every person issuing a customs declaration is responsible for its content. If the person who is required to complete the customs declaration form is unable to do so, a customs official may be asked to give assistance.

The bills of lading, the waybills, the original forms of declaration and similar transportation documents, as well as official certificates on the quality and condition of the goods and all accompanying documents issued by the exporter, must be presented together with the customs declaration. Imports on highways or streets must be declared to the customs authority within 24 hours after the goods have been presented at the border. If the goods are to be cleared inside the country, the customs declaration must be completed within six days after the goods have come under customs control. For goods imported by train or ship, different time limits apply. If the declaration is not completed in time, the customs authority will either return the goods across the border or store them in a customs warehouse and require the obligated persons to pay customs duty.

False customs declarations, such as false indications of weight (i.e., more than 3 per cent lower than the actual weight), are subject to a fine of up to 20 times the amount of customs duties evaded and imprisonment of up to six months. Negligent violations of customs law are also punishable.

¶311   Customs duty assessment

Unlike most EC countries, Switzerland uses the weight, not the economic value, of the imported goods as the basis for the assessment of customs duties. However, the domestic value of goods is relevant in determining the amount of wholesale tax owed on imported goods (¶1066 et seq.).

The assessment of the customs duty payment is based on the declaration of the person responsible for paying the import duties, as long as no official inspection has found the declaration to be incorrect. The inspection of a customs declaration allows customs officials to take all actions necessary to verify the declaration. Losses of value and costs incurred by the importer during the inspection procedure are generally not reimbursed, but custom officials are required to mitigate possible damages.

Once the imported goods have been so qualified, the amount of import duty to be paid is calculated at the rates stated in the import tariff appended to the Customs Tariff Act (¶314).

If goods of different categories are packaged together and their weight is not specified separately, the highest tariff applicable to one of the goods included is used for the whole package.

¶312   Clearance for home use

The clearance procedure consists of the examination of the customs declaration, and possibly an inspection procedure, including the taking of samples, weighing of the goods, personal search, search of vehicles used for transportation, and even the seizure of certain goods.

If the customs declaration is accepted or the inspection procedure is finalised, the customs office will issue a customs certificate stating the amount of customs duties owed. After payment of this amount a receipt is issued, and the goods may be reclaimed from customs control. Enterprises clearing several shipments daily may (with the prior permission of the Federal Customs Administration) pay the customs duties within certain delays if they provide sufficient security for the maximum amount of customs duties owed. Interest at the rate of 5 per cent per annum is charged as of the day of customs clearance on deferred secured payments. The holder of the customs duty receipt is entitled to receive the goods released from customs control.

¶313   Customs treatment without clearance

Samples of merchandise up to the gross weight of one kilogram, photographs for publication and newspapers do not fall under customs control. They may be imported without clearance if delivered by mail.

If imported goods are to be re-exported or forwarded to another customs office or a customs warehouse, an accompanying customs warrant must be attached to them against payment or securities for the customs duty calculated at the highest tariff. By presenting the customs warrant and the goods in their unchanged condition under seal, this accompanying customs warrant is cancelled. Failing such cancellation within the time limit given, the customs duties secured become due.

Goods of Swiss origin temporarily shipped through foreign territory to a final destination in Switzerland may, under certain conditions, be exempt from customs clearance; they receive a 'free pass' or are sealed. If this treatment is not requested before the goods leave the country, or if the seal is broken when the goods re-enter Swiss customs territory, the normal customs procedures ensue.

¶314 Customs tariff

The customs tariff is based on the classification of goods stated in the Customs Act, which is in compliance with the International Convention on the Harmonised Commodity Description and Coding System (RS 0.632.11). The tariffs are stated in Francs per hundred kilograms gross weight of the classified item and indicate separate rates for normal imports and imports originating from EC or EFTA countries. The Federal Customs Administration has issued a three-volume loose-leaf publication which contains rulings and interpretations of the Swiss Customs Tariff Act – the so-called *Notes explicatives du tarif 1986*.

¶315 Refund of customs duties

Customs duties are refunded if the goods had been paid for but are subsequently re-exported because of rejection by the buyer, rescission of the contract or unfitness of the goods for the market.

Refunds may also be requested if the goods are forwarded to a third party abroad or if they are destroyed under the supervision of the customs authorities. The re-export or destruction of such goods must take place within two years after their importation. If the foreign exporter replaces unfit goods free of charge, no customs duties are levied for their replacement within three years after return of the unfit goods.

Requests for the refund of customs duty must be submitted together with the export clearance or separately in writing no later than 60 days thereafter, provided the identity of the goods can be proven.

¶316 Customs rulings

The Federal Customs Administration issues rulings concerning the classification of goods not explicitly listed in the Customs Statute. Such rulings may be requested on an official form, together with a sample of the material to be qualified. If a sample cannot be supplied, pictures and an exact description can be presented instead. The costs for technical examinations, transportation and other expenses incurred are charged to the person requesting the ruling. A ruling by the Federal Customs Administration may be appealed to the Federal Government.

If a prior ruling is subsequently changed, or if customs authorities come to a different conclusion after actual clearance, and the new ruling is disadvantageous to the person responsible for paying the import duties, the original ruling may be applied, provided the import takes place within three months after the publication of the prior ruling. Oral information by customs officials, however, is not binding.

¶317   Import wholesale tax

A wholesale tax is levied on imported goods (¶1068). The legislative policy behind this tax on imports is to treat domestic and foreign sellers equally. A wholesale tax is levied on domestic transfers when the goods are sold from the wholesaler to the retailer; the same tax is, therefore, levied on imports. It amounts to 9.3 per cent of the goods' value for wholesalers and 6.2 per cent for retailers. The person who must pay import duties (¶307) must also pay the import wholesale tax, which is assessed by the customs authorities under rules analogous to those of regular customs procedure. The import wholesale tax is also levied on goods exempt from customs duties. If, however, the importer is a wholesaler, or if goods of minimal value are imported, this tax is not levied.

An importer qualifies as a wholesaler if its deliveries to third parties are in excess of SFr 35,000 per annum. Goods for which the wholesaler did not pay the import wholesale tax will be subject to the domestic wholesale tax at a later stage before reaching the consumer.

The status of a wholesaler must be specifically requested on an official form (No. 419). It is available for importers and fiduciaries acting in their own name but for a third party's financial account. Agents and carriers do not qualify as wholesalers, but they may present the wholesaler declaration (¶1066(6)) on behalf of their principal.

The calculation of the wholesale tax is based on the purchase price of the goods, including delivery costs up to the border. The following *deductions* can be made from the invoice price: foreign value added taxes, rebates granted without reciprocal consideration, freight from the border to the domestic destination, payments made to acquire industrial property rights (e.g., trade marks), late payment interest, fuel, customs duty, and the wholesale tax itself. The following items are *added* to the price invoiced: freight costs up to the border, foreign export levies, down payments, the value of goods exchanged in return (barter), contractual interest payments, interest and fees owed to the customs authorities, warehouse deposit fees, etc. The customs office may estimate the value of the goods if it has reasons to doubt that the prices shown in the invoice are accurate.

For details of wholesale tax on imports, see also ¶1066 et seq.

¶318   Excise taxes

The importation of alcoholic beverages and tobacco is subject to a special excise tax. For alcoholic beverages the Federal Government has a monopoly on import rights, which it grants to private importers for a monopoly fee. The excise tax is charged in addition to the customs duty.

¶319   Agricultural products

Regulations concerning the importation of agricultural products are dispersed among a number of decrees and statutes. For various political and social reasons, legislation aims at providing a guaranteed income to farmers which is at least equal to that of a middle-level employee. The different means of providing such an income include seasonal and constant protection of the agricultural market from foreign low-priced products, as well as quota allocations, e.g., for wine importers.

The importation of agricultural products, such as meat, dairy products, vegetables and produce listed in Art. 28 of the General Decree on Agriculture (RS 916.01), is restricted in various ways (¶305(3)). Goods which may serve as substitutes for the products explicitly listed may be subject to restrictions to the extent that the Federal Government deems necessary and so orders.

Animal feed may be imported only by the Co-operative Company for Cereals and Animal Feed, which has a monopoly on reselling animal feed. The Co-operative is obliged to sell at the prices decreed by the Federal Government. Furthermore, animal feed must meet certain quality requirements which are periodically modified.

Agricultural imports competing with domestic production may be subject to seasonal import quotas in order to protect the price level of Swiss products. The Federal Government requires importers to purchase certain quantities (set every year) of domestic production. Butter and flour may be imported only through the Federal Government.

¶320   Judicial review of customs rulings

An importer whose legal interests are infringed by an order (quasi-judicial decision) of the customs authorities may appeal to the Federal Customs Administration. Decisions of first instance rendered by the Federal Customs Administration can be appealed to the Federal Department of Finance. Other decisions of the Federal Customs Administration can be appealed first to the Customs Court and finally to the Federal Supreme Court. Judicial review through the Federal Supreme Court is possible for most aspects of customs law, but is not available against administrative orders regarding the determination of the tariff applied and the weight of imported goods. The Federal Supreme Court may review the customs authorities' assessments and orders only as to their compliance with federal law and the correctness of the factual findings, but not as to whether the customs authorities have adequately used their discretion.

The request for judicial review of decisions of first instance must be made in writing within 60 days (30 days for questions concerning the import turnover tax); it must indicate the reasons for which the order is challenged. The review procedure is governed by the general rules of administrative procedure.

PRODUCT ORIGIN

¶321   Country of origin

For the purposes of preferential treatment granted to developing countries, product origin is defined as the place where production of the imported item is completed. For imported raw materials, the country of origin is more easily defined than for semi-finished and finished imports. The country of origin is the place where the goods have been finished or processed if the processing caused the goods to be qualified differently under the Treaty on the Harmonised System of the Description and Codification of Goods.

Activities like storing, preserving, cleaning, repackaging, labelling, mixing, etc. do not affect the origin of the goods. For goods listed in Appendix 2 to the Decree on Customs Preference Granted to Developing Countries (RS 946.39), certain percentages of value added to the product in the country of origin and other processing requirements are stated in detail. Production steps that do not comply with these criteria do not change the determination of the origin of the product.

According to Art. 4 of the EFTA Treaty, the portion of the value of raw material of non-EFTA country origin must be less than 50 per cent of the FOB export price if EFTA country origin of the goods is claimed.

STRATEGIC GOODS

¶322   Switzerland and COCOM

Although Switzerland (as a neutral country) does not directly adhere to the COCOM group, it effectively prohibits unauthorised re-exports of goods which

¶321

figure on the COCOM list. Strategic goods from COCOM countries can therefore be imported. The so-called 'pink list' (RS 946.221), a regulation issued by the Federal Government, contains an exhaustive enumeration of the goods which can be re-exported only with special permission. Changes in the COCOM list are usually soon followed by corresponding changes in the 'pink list'. The next change can be expected to follow COCOM's general tendency toward liberalisation in 1991.

PROCESSING AND CONVERSION

¶323 Inward and outward processing

Goods which are imported solely for the purpose of processing or repair and are re-exported after inward processing (*trafic de perfectionnement actif/aktiver Veredlungsverkehr*) are exempt from customs duties. When processing and repair are combined, special permission must be obtained from the Federal Customs Administration, which will grant it under the conditions of Art. 39(2) of the Customs Ordinance (RS 631.01).

For outward processing (*trafic de perfectionnement passif/passiver Veredlungsverkehr*), i.e., export of goods followed by re-importation after the goods have been processed or repaired, permission for reduction of, or exemption from, customs duties can be obtained from the Federal Customs Administration. If, however, it can be proved that the foreign processor is the only one capable of completing the repair needed, or if the processing falls within a treaty provision, the customs offices may grant duty exemptions. The burden of proving the identity of processed goods rests on the party requesting the advantages of inward and outward processing.

In frequent cross-border traffic, customs offices may grant exemptions for the processing of specific goods depending on local conditions.

SPECIAL ZONES AND BONDED WAREHOUSES

¶324 Special zones

The customs border is almost identical with the political border. In order to facilitate neighbourly cross-border traffic, an economic zone, which extends 10 km on both sides of the border, has been created. However, certain foreign territories are considered to be Swiss for customs purposes, most notably the principality of Liechtenstein. On the other hand, some municipalities that belong politically to Switzerland are considered to be outside the Swiss customs territory because of their topographic location (e.g., Samnaun).

¶325   Bonded warehouses

The Federal Finance Department may grant permission to store imported goods in bonded warehouses (*port franc/Zollfreilager*) without payment of customs duties if the goods are to be re-exported or their destination is not yet defined. A special bond must be posted before such permission is granted. Bonded warehouses may be considered foreign territory for purposes of customs law; still, they are under the control of the customs authorities and, for example, as far as the protection of industrial property rights is concerned, the bonded warehouses are considered to be Swiss, and the goods stored therein remain subject to Swiss jurisdiction (ATF 110 IV 110).

Bonded warehouses may be private or public; storage in private bonded warehouses is permitted only for wholesale goods in certain minimum quantities. The keeper who stores the goods in the bonded warehouse will issue a storage bill, which serves the purpose of transferring possession of the goods stored but is not an official customs document. The duration of storage in public bonded warehouses may not exceed two years. The liability of the keeper for damage to the stored goods is basically defined by Arts 482 et seq. of the Code of Obligations. Insurance for theft and other damage done to the goods is mandatory in public warehouses, and the customs authority will automatically enter into the respective insurance contracts on behalf of and for the account of the importer. If goods are withdrawn from the warehouse for home use, normal customs procedures apply, and the goods must be declared within 24 hours.

CUSTOMS EXEMPTIONS

¶326   Duty-free list

Persons entering Switzerland may import certain goods for home use; these goods are exempted from customs duties. Duty-free goods are not subject to any taxes if they are imported in certain limited amounts. Brochures specifying the types of goods and quantities allowed may be obtained from the customs authorities and from Swiss embassies.

Under certain circumstances specified in Arts 9 to 29 of the Customs Statute the following goods, among others, may be cleared for use inside Switzerland without import duties:

- instruments and materials used by artists and artisans,

- personal belongings,
- furniture,
- personal property of people taking up domicile in Switzerland,
- inherited goods,
- gifts for needy persons,
- sample merchandise which cannot be resold,
- objects for exhibition or use for teaching purposes or medical treatment,
- prizes and souvenirs,
- war materials used by the federal army, and
- certain packaging materials.

ANTI-DUMPING AND COUNTERVAILING DUTIES

¶327   GATT and stand-by legislation

International dumping law is set forth in the General Agreement on Tariffs and Trade (GATT) and in the 1980 Anti-Dumping and Subsidies Code (Agreement on Implementation of Art. VI of GATT and Agreement on Interpretation and Application of Arts VI, XVI and XXIII of GATT).

GATT defines dumping in Art. VI(1) as a trade practice by which products of one country are introduced into the commerce of another country at less than the normal value of the products. Such dumping is unfair, according to GATT, if it causes or threatens material injury to an established industry in a territory of the contracting party, or materially retards the establishment of domestic industry. GATT allows the country whose industry is affected to impose anti-dumping duties on the dumped products. Anti-dumping duties may only neutralise the dumping effect, they may not lead to a domestic price above the normal value.

According to Art. VI(3) of GATT, the term 'countervailing duty', means a special duty levied for the purpose of offsetting any bounty or subsidy bestowed, directly or indirectly, upon the manufacture, production, or export of any merchandise.

According to Art. 7 of the Swiss Customs Tariff Act, the Federal Government may as an extraordinary measure change the customs tariffs or introduce new customs duties for a certain period of time if measures taken by foreign countries, or other extraordinary conditions abroad, negatively affect foreign trade relations and have a substantial impact on Swiss economic interests.

As there is almost no published case law or administrative practice in the areas of anti-dumping and subsidies, details further clarifying the above generalisations are not available.

SELECTED BIBLIOGRAPHY

Administration Fédérale des Contributions, *Instructions à l'usage des grossistes* (Bern, 1982)
Direction Générale des Douanes, *Notes explicatives du tarif*, 3 vols (Bern, 1986)
Direction Générale des Douanes, *Le traffic des marchandises dans la zone européenne de libre échange* (Bern, 1988)
Dieter Metzger, *Handbuch der Warenumsatzsteuer* (Muri/Bern, 1983)

¶327

4 Agency and Distribution

PRINCIPAL LEGISLATION

Code des obligations/Obligationenrecht/Code of Obligations (CO), RS 220.

PRINCIPAL AND AGENT

¶401 Sources of law

The Code of Obligations contains general provisions which apply to all contracts and special provisions which apply only to certain types of contracts. While the general part of the Code of Obligations regulates the power of attorney in general, the special part contains provisions about the power to act on behalf of another person and other powers of attorney, acting without authority, the ordinary mandate, the commercial agency agreement, the brokerage agreement and the commission agreement.

The specific provisions on the commercial agency agreement were introduced into the special part of the Code of Obligations in 1950. Until then, the provisions on the ordinary mandate and brokerage and commission agreements were applied to the commercial agency agreement. The special part of the Code of Obligations does not contain express provisions on the exclusive distributorship agreement. Depending on the specific circumstances of a case, the provisions on ordinary mandate, sales, and/or ordinary partnership may be applicable by analogy.

¶402 Power of attorney – legal basis

A power of attorney (*procuration/Vollmacht*) is the unilateral authorisation by a principal to an agent to perform legal acts on his or her behalf (Art. 32 CO). The legal basis for a power of attorney may be contractual or statutory.

¶403 Form of power of attorney

In general, there is no special formal requirement for a power of attorney. However, an authorisation to enter into a suretyship agreement (*cautionnement/*

¶403

Bürgschaft) on behalf of the principal must meet the special formal requirements prescribed for the suretyship itself (Art. 493 CO). See ¶902.

¶404   Content of power of attorney

An agent must obtain a mandate (*mandat/Auftrag*) from the principal to be able to bind the principal. Further, the agent must act implicitly or explicitly in the other party's name (Art. 32 CO). If the agent does not disclose the agency relationship when entering into a contract with a third party, the party who is represented receives direct rights or incurs direct obligations only if the third party, under the circumstances, would have accepted the agency or does not care about the identity of the contracting counterparty. If this is not the case, a formal assignment of the rights, or an assumption of the obligations, is necessary (Art. 32 CO). An agent who acts without a mandate is liable to the principal. The persons so 'represented' are bound only if they ratify the contract (Art. 38 CO). If the principal refuses to ratify it, the person who acted as an unauthorised agent may be liable for damages to the third party (Art. 39(1) CO).

Bona fide third parties are protected if they reasonably relied on the power of attorney. If the principal who has granted the power does not request the return of the document containing the power of attorney, the principal remains liable for damages to third parties.

¶405   Special powers of attorney

Companies usually act through their officers or managers or employees with collective signing authority, i.e., two signatures are required. In particular, large enterprises very seldom authorise officers or managers to sign individually.

Those employees having power of procuration for a company (*par procuration/Prokura*) are authorised to conduct business and sign contracts on behalf of the company they represent. The power must be entered in the Register of Commerce, but its validity does not depend on entry (Art. 458 CO). *Vis-à-vis* bona fide third persons, the holder of this power may perform any legal act within the purpose of the enterprise except conveying real estate, authority for which must be granted expressly (Art. 459 CO). A power of procuration may be restricted to a branch office or may be restricted so as to require a signature from another agent of the business (joint or collective procuration). Further restrictions on the power of procuration are invalid *vis-à-vis* bona fide third parties. The cancellation of the power of procuration must also be entered in the Register of Commerce. As long as it has not been cancelled, the power of procuration remains effective with respect to bona fide third persons.

An employee may have the power to conduct transactions for a business, without having the right to sign *par procuration*. This authority of a commercial representative (*mandataire commercial/Handlungsbevollmächtigter*) cannot be entered in the Register of Commerce. The holder of this power is authorised to perform all legal acts normally connected with the conduct of the enterprise, and special transactions. Acts under this power require no special mandate. Signing bills of exchange or loan contracts or instituting legal proceedings require express authorisation (Art. 462(2) CO).

An agent with power of procuration and a commercial representative who has been appointed manager of a whole enterprise, or who is an employee of the enterprise, are prohibited by law from competing with the principal (Art. 464 CO). The power of procuration and the power to conduct transactions for a business may be revoked at any time. These two special powers of attorney do not expire upon the death or incapacity of the principal (Art. 465 CO).

¶406 Termination of power of attorney

A power of attorney may be revoked and limited at any time by the principal and, unless otherwise provided in the contract or implied by the conduct of the business, automatically expires upon the death, declaration of absence, incapacity, or bankruptcy of the principal or the agent (Arts 34 and 35 CO). Powers of attorney drawn up so as not to expire upon the death of the principal are common.

ORDINARY MANDATE

¶407 Sources of law

The ordinary mandate (*mandat proprement dit/einfacher Auftrag*) is regulated in the special part of the Code of Obligations (Arts 394 to 406). These articles provide the basic rules for one person who acts for another. The parties are free to arrange their contractual · relationship individually. If they do not state otherwise, the provisions of the ordinary mandate apply.

The ordinary mandate is a contract according to which the agent agrees to carry out the business or service entrusted (Art. 394(1) CO). If the extent of the mandate is not expressly determined, it depends on the nature of the business or service to be performed. The mandate implies authority for all legal acts necessary to carry out the function involved (Art. 396(1) and (2) CO).

¶408 Form of ordinary mandate

No special form is required for the ordinary mandate.

¶409   Content of ordinary mandate

An agent entrusted with an ordinary mandate is responsible to the principal for
the proper and careful performance of the mandate. The agent must perform
personally unless the principal has authorised recourse to a substitute (Art. 398
CO). Compensation is due if agreed upon or customary in the business. The
principal is required to reimburse the agent for out-of-pocket expenses incurred
in performing the mandate, plus interest thereon, and to comply with any
contractual duties arising out of the agent's dealings with third parties in the
interest of the principal (Art. 402 CO). The mandate expires upon the death,
incapacity or bankruptcy of either the principal or the agent, unless otherwise
agreed (Art. 405 CO).

¶410   Examples of ordinary mandates

According to Swiss law, the contractual relationships between the following are
considered ordinary mandates:

- an attorney-at-law and a client,
- a physician and a patient,
- a dentist and a patient,
- a trustor and a trustee,
- a general insurance agent and an insurance company.

¶411   Termination of ordinary mandate

There is one important – although somewhat controversial – mandatory
provision. According to Art. 404 CO, a mandate may be terminated at any time
by revocation or notice by any party. If a mandate is terminated at an
unreasonable time, the terminating party is required to indemnify the other party
for the resulting damage. Recent case law shows a tendency to limit the
application of this provision.

ACTING WITHOUT AUTHORITY

¶412   Sources of law

The special part of the Code of Obligations contains provisions on acting without
authority (*negotiorum gestio* of Roman law; *gestion d'affaires/Geschäftsführung
ohne Auftrag*).

¶409

If the business which has been conducted without a mandate is subsequently ratified by the principal, the provisions governing the ordinary mandate apply (Art. 424 CO).

¶413 Obligations of the parties

(1) Obligations of the 'agent'

A person who acts for another without the latter's request is bound to carry out the transaction thus undertaken for the benefit of, and in accordance with, the presumed intention of the other party (Art. 419 CO).

The person conducting the business is liable for negligence. The fact that the would-be 'agent' acted in order to avert a danger threatening the principal is taken into consideration as a mitigating circumstance. If 'agents' act contrary to the express or otherwise perceptible intention of the principals, they are responsible in case of accident, unless they prove that the accident would have happened even without their interference (Art. 420 CO).

(2) Obligations of the principal

Where the would-be 'agent' acted in the principal's interest, the principal is required to indemnify the 'agent' for all expenses which were necessary or useful and reasonable under the circumstances, plus interest. Further, the principal must discharge the would-be 'agent' to the same extent from the obligations incurred and compensate the 'agent' at the discretion of the court for other damages (Art. 422(1) CO).

Where the would-be 'agent' does not act in the principal's interests, the principal may nevertheless avail him or herself of the benefits resulting from the agent's acts. The principal need indemnify or discharge the would-be 'agent' only to the extent of the benefits received (Art. 423 CO).

COMMERCIAL AGENCY

¶414 Sources of law

In a commercial agency (*agence/Agentur*), the commercial agents undertake to act on a continuous basis as intermediaries on behalf of one or several principals in business transactions. They may conclude these transactions in their name and for their account without being in an employment relationship with the principals (Art. 418a(1) CO). The commercial agents perform their work independently. They are entitled to organise their work and to dispose of their time freely (ATF 99 II 313, 104 II 114). For part-time commercial agents, the provisions on commercial agency agreements apply to the extent that the parties have not agreed otherwise in writing. However, the provisions of the law on guarantee of outstanding debts of customers (*delcredere*, Art. 418c(3) CO), on prohibition of competition (Art. 418d(2) CO) and termination of contracts for cause (Art. 418r CO) may not be waived to the detriment of the commercial agent (Art. 418a(2) CO).

In addition to the provisions of Arts 418a to 418v CO, the provisions concerning brokerage contracts (Art. 412 et seq. CO) apply to the commercial agent who acts as an intermediary for third persons in business transactions, and those provisions regarding the commission contract (Art. 425 et seq. CO) also apply to the commercial agent who concludes business on behalf of third persons.

¶415   Form of commercial agency agreement

The commercial agency contract may be concluded orally. The complexity of the relationship between the commercial agent and the principal, however, makes a written contract desirable. If the commercial agent works only on a part-time basis, the provisions concerning commercial agency agreements are applicable unless the parties have stipulated otherwise in writing (Art. 418a(2) CO).

¶416   Content of commercial agency

(1) Obligations of the commercial agent

Commercial agents must safeguard the interest of the principal with the care of ordinary merchants. Unless otherwise agreed upon in writing, they may act on behalf of other principals. The commercial agent's guarantee of customers' payments or suppliers' deliveries, or undertaking to defray the costs of enforcing claims (*delcredere*), must be agreed upon in writing to be valid. In such a case, the commercial agent has an inalienable right to special and adequate indemnification (Art. 418c CO). Commercial agents may neither personally exploit, nor disclose to others, business secrets of which they have obtained knowledge in the course of their business relationship. They must not use or disclose business secrets after termination of the contract. The rules prohibiting competition in employment contracts (Art. 340 et seq. CO) apply by analogy to commercial agency agreements (¶1603(5)). If a prohibition against competition is stipulated, the agents have an inalienable right to a special indemnity upon termination of the agency contract (Art. 418d CO). Agents can claim this compensation even if they have terminated the contract themselves (ATF 95 II 149). 'Inalienable' means that the agent cannot waive this right in advance.

(2) Authority of the commercial agent

The commercial agent has authority to act as an intermediary in business transactions and to receive notices and other legally relevant declarations of default or non-performance from a customer who alleges faulty performance by the principal. The agent may exercise the principal's rights to secure evidence. In contrast, the agent does not have the authority to accept payments, grant terms of payment, or agree with the customer upon other alterations of the contract (Art. 418e CO).

(3) Obligations of the principal in commercial agency

The principal must perform all acts necessary to enable the commercial agent to perform all functions successfully. In particular, the principal must put the necessary documents at the commercial agent's disposal. The principal must immediately inform the commercial agent if it is anticipated that a considerably lower volume of sales can or should be achieved than was agreed or expected under the circumstances.

A commercial agent is entitled to the agreed-upon or customary brokerage fee or signing commission (*provision/Provision*) on all business transactions in which he or she acted as an intermediary or which were concluded during the term of the commercial agency contract, including transactions originally initiated by the agent but concluded by the principal (Art. 418g(1) CO).

Unless otherwise agreed, the commercial agent to whom a certain territory or clientele is exclusively allocated is entitled to the customary commission on all business which is concluded with customers within the scope of the commercial agency contract in this sector. Unless otherwise agreed in writing, a claim for a commission arises as soon as a business transaction is concluded with a customer (Art. 418g(2) and (3) CO). The commercial agent has no claim for a commission if the non-performance of a business transaction was caused by reasons beyond the control of the principal. There is no claim for a commission if the performance by the third party, in consideration of the principal's completed performance, does not take place or fails to such a substantial extent that the principal cannot reasonably be expected to pay the commission (Art. 418h CO). Unless otherwise stipulated or customary, the commission becomes due at the end of each six-month period (January–June; July–December) during which the business was concluded (Art. 418i CO).

The principal, upon the request of the commercial agent, must disclose the company books and vouchers relevant to the statement of account on the commission due to the agent. The agent may not waive this right in advance (Art. 418k(2) CO).

Commercial agents charged with collecting amounts due to the principal have a right to a special collection commission unless otherwise agreed or otherwise customary (Art. 418l CO).

The principal must pay a fair and adequate compensation to the commercial agent if the principal is in breach of legal contractual duties by preventing the

¶416

agent from earning the agreed upon or expected commission. Any agreement waiving this provision is invalid (Art. 418m(1) CO).

Commercial agents who work exclusively for one principal and who are prevented from performing their functions because of illness, compulsory Swiss military service or other incapacitating reasons, are entitled to compensation for the period of their absence or disability, provided that the commercial agency has lasted at least one year. The commercial agent may not waive this right in advance (Art. 418m(2) CO).

Unless trade customs or the contract are to the contrary, the commercial agent has no claim for reimbursement of costs and out-of-pocket expenses incurred in the ordinary course of business, with the exception of those costs incurred under special instructions of the principal (Art. 418n(1) CO). The reason why commercial agents are generally not entitled to claim compensation for the expenses and outlays which arise from the regular pursuit of their business is that they are not integrated into the enterprise of the principal; rather, they pursue an independent economic activity (ATF 104 II 114).

As security for claims due arising under the commercial agency relationship, and in the event of insolvency of the principal for claims not yet due, commercial agents have a lien on property and on securities which have come into their possession pursuant to the agency contract and on amounts received from third parties pursuant to their authority to collect for the principal. The agent may not waive this right to lien in advance (Art. 418o(1) CO).

(4) Exclusivity of commercial agency
Unless otherwise agreed upon, the commercial agency agreement is not exclusive.

¶417 Termination of commercial agency

(1) Advance notice requirement
If the commercial agency contract specifies a certain duration, the lapse of this period automatically terminates the agency. If the commercial agency contract does not specify a certain duration and if this period cannot be deduced from the purpose of the agreement, the contract can be terminated by either party during the first year of the contract period with one month's notice, the termination notice being effective at the end of the calendar month following the month during which the notice was given. Any agreement for a shorter notice must be made in writing. If the contractual relationship has lasted longer than a year, it may be terminated at the end of a calendar quarter with two months' prior notice (Art. 418q CO).

Both the principal and commercial agent may immediately terminate the contract with cause (Art. 418r CO). This provision is mandatory (ATF 89 II 33).

The commercial agency contract terminates upon the death or incapacity of the commercial agent or the bankruptcy of the principal. The agency terminates upon the death of the principal if the contract was essentially for personal services for the particular principal (Art. 418s CO).

(2) Special indemnity for termination of the commercial agency
Unless trade customs or the contract are to the contrary, the commercial agent has a claim for a commission only for orders received prior to the termination of the agency relationship, and only for transactions with customers who were actually solicited by the agent during the agency relationship. All of the agent's claims for commissions or reimbursements become due upon termination of the agency relationship (Art. 418t CO).

Commercial agents who, through their activity, have substantially increased the principal's clientele, have a right to fair compensation if the principal substantially benefits from the business relations with this clientele after the termination of the commercial agency contract. The compensation may not exceed the amount of net earnings for one year derived from the contract, computed on the average of the last five years, or, if the relationship has not lasted so long, on the average of the total of this period. The compensation is not deemed a commission for the agent's performance during the contractual period, but rather an indemnification for a business value which can be exploited by the principal after the termination of the agency contract (ATF 84 II 531). No compensation is due if the commercial agency is terminated for a reason for which the agent was responsible (Art. 418u CO). Compensation may be totally refused only under very specific circumstances: if the commercial agent has brought about the termination of the contract by fault or if the agent has terminated the contract without special reason (ATF 110 II 282), no compensation is due.

Upon termination of the commercial agency, each contracting party shall make full restitution to the other party for everything received during the contract period from the other party or from third parties for the account of the other party. The rights of lien of the contracting parties remain unaffected (Art. 418v CO).

EXCLUSIVE DISTRIBUTORSHIP AGREEMENT

¶418 Sources of law

The exclusive distributorship agreement (*concession exclusive de vente/ Alleinvertriebsvertrag*) is not regulated by statute. Case law defines the rights and obligations of the supplier and distributor.

¶418

In this contract, there is a continuous mutual relationship: the supplier sells to the distributor and the distributor resells the supplier's products in a particular territory on an exclusive basis. The distributor undertakes to promote the sale of these products actively (ATF 107 II 223). The supplier is obliged to deliver the products to the distributor, and the distributor is obliged to take delivery of these products and pay for them (ATF 78 II 81). An exclusive distributor acts in his or her own name and sells and delivers the products for his or her own account and risk.

The legal independence of the distributor is considered to be the major element which distinguishes a distributorship from a commercial agency where the commercial agent only brings about sales by the principal.

¶419   Form of distributorship agreement

Like most other contracts, the distributorship agreement can be concluded orally. However, the complexity of the relationship between the supplier and the distributor makes a written contract desirable, especially since the Code of Obligations does not contain specific provisions governing the distributorship agreement.

¶420   Content of distributorship agreement

(1)   Obligation of the supplier
In a distributorship agreement, the supplier undertakes:

(a) to sell the products to the distributor on the agreed-upon terms and conditions for resale by the distributor on an exclusive basis in a given territory; and

(b) to support the distributor's efforts to promote sales by providing the distributor with the necessary information and promotional materials concerning the products.

(2)   Obligation of the distributor
The distributor purchases the products from the supplier on the terms and conditions stated in the contract in order to resell them in the specified territory. The contract commonly provides for a minimum quantity. By fixing minimum sales quotas, the marketing risk is transferred to the distributor; this would not be possible under a commercial agency contract. The parties may agree that the distributor shall have further specific obligations concerning sales promotion, e.g., to maintain an inventory, to do market research, to use special equipment and to employ specialists. In addition, the distributor may be subject to various restrictions, such as export bans and prohibitions on selling in specific market segments.

¶421 Termination of distributorship agreement

(1) Advance notice requirement

If the distributorship agreement specifies the duration of the relationship, the lapse of this period automatically terminates the contract. Where the agreement does not provide for a fixed period, the duration of the notice of termination is disputed by legal commentators. Under the prevailing opinion, the contract may be terminated in accordance with the provisions pertaining to the commercial agency contract, i.e., Art. 418q CO: if the contract has lasted less than one year, it can be terminated at the end of the month following the month in which termination notice is given (see ¶417(1)). If the contractual relationship has lasted longer than one year, the provisions concerning ordinary partnerships are applied by analogy: the contract may be terminated by giving six months' notice (Art. 546(1) CO). See ¶712.

With cause, both the supplier and distributor may terminate the contract immediately (Art. 418r CO; ATF 89 II 30). Article 418r CO mandatorily applies to the exclusive distributorship agreement. Insolvency of the distributor is considered cause for immediate termination (ATF 78 II 36).

Article 418s CO, which pertains to the commercial agency contract, applies to the termination of the distributorship: the contractual relationship terminates upon the death or incapacity of the distributor and the bankruptcy of the supplier; the contract is terminated upon the death of the supplier only if the agreement was mainly for personal services for the particular supplier.

(2) Indemnity for termination of the exclusive distributorship

Considering the relative independence of the distributor and supplier, most commentators think that the distributor has no claim for compensation for loss of clientele if the distributorship agreement is terminated (ATF 88 II 170). Several legal writers, however, believe that the indemnity provision of the agency agreement is applicable to the distributorship agreement as well (Art. 418u CO). It is advisable to stipulate the consequences of termination expressly in the contract; but even if an indemnity is excluded altogether, under the present state of the law one cannot rule out the possibility that a court will award an indemnity to a terminated distributor.

If the agreement restricts the freedom of the distributor substantially, i.e., where it limits the distributor's discretion in such a way as to make him or her dependent upon the supplier, the distributorship agreement may be characterised as an agency agreement, and the distributor will be entitled to receive clientele compensation according to the applicable agency rules.

BROKERAGE AGREEMENT

¶422   Sources of law

A brokerage contract (*courtage/Mäklervertrag*) is an agreement according to which the broker or middleman (*courtier/Mäkler*) is charged with acting as an intermediary or with providing the principal with an opportunity to conclude a contract. Except for the specific provisions of Arts 412 to 418 CO, the brokerage contract is subject to the provisions governing the ordinary mandate (¶407 to ¶411).

¶423   Form of brokerage agreement

The law does not require a specific form for the brokerage contract. It may be concluded orally or in writing, explicitly or implicitly. A brokerage contract is deemed to have been entered into if a 'principal' tolerates the action of a broker – especially a professional broker – on his or her behalf. Lack of objection by the 'principal' will be construed as acquiescence in a contract even if the 'principal' has rejected the services of the broker before (ATF 72 II 87).

> **Example**: an owner of a house is approached by a professional real estate broker who knows persons interested in buying the land. If a sale of the land is concluded, the real estate broker may require payment of the usual commission from the previous owner (e.g., 2 per cent of the price).

¶424   Content of brokerage agreement

(1)   Obligation of the broker

Brokers have no general duty to be active in the interest of the principal. However, if they accept a specific task, they must do so in the best interests of the principal (ATF 110 II 277). There is an important exception to this general rule: the Federal Supreme Court has held that the brokers have an obligation to act if they enjoy exclusivity, which prevents the principals from appointing other brokers (ATF 103 II 133).

In particular, brokers must inform the principal of all circumstances of which they become aware and which may frustrate the principal's goals. If, for example, the achievement of the principal's goal is dependent on the solvency of the third party with whom a contract is about to be concluded, the broker must disclose everything he or she knows about the financial condition of the third party (ATF 110 II 277).

An unsuccessful broker need not inform the principal unless otherwise provided in the contract. If he or she is successful, he or she must inform the principal or bring the potential contractual parties together (ATF 84 II 527).

Brokers have a general obligation to act in good faith. They are liable to the principals for all damage caused by their negligence.

(2)   Obligation of the principal

The principal must pay the brokerage fee (*salaire du courtier/Mäklerlohn*) as soon as a contract is concluded with a third party either because the broker arranges the opportunity or because the broker acted as an intermediary (Art. 413 CO). Subsequent performance of the contract by the third party is not necessary (ATF 106 II 224). In contrast, the principal is not compelled to enter into a contract with the third party presented by the broker. In general, the brokerage fee is due only if the conclusion of the contract was the direct result of the broker's action (ATF 84 II 524, 76 II 381, 72 II 421).

Unless otherwise agreed, the principal is not required to reimburse the broker's costs and out-of-pocket expenses.

If, however, the contract provides for reimbursements, they become due even if the expected transaction does not materialise (Art. 413(3) CO).

(3)   Exclusivity of brokerage agreement

Unless otherwise agreed, the relationship between broker and principal is non-exclusive. Brokers must avoid any conflicts of interest, but they may collect brokerage fees from both parties to a contract if they have been instrumental in bringing them together (ATF 111 II 368).

¶425   Termination of brokerage agreement

The brokerage agreement may be terminated by either party at any time without prior notice. In general, the rules on the termination of the ordinary mandate are applicable (Art. 404 CO). See ¶411.

COMMISSION AGREEMENT

¶426   Sources of law

Persons who, in consideration of payment of a commission (*provision/Provision*), undertake to buy or sell tangible assets or securities in their own names but for the account of another (the principal) are commission agents (*commissionnaire/ Kommissionär*) (Art. 425(1) CO). Unless Arts 425 to 439 CO provide otherwise, the rules governing the ordinary mandate are applicable (Art. 425(2) CO; see ¶407 et seq.). A commission agent may not sell real estate.

¶426

¶427   Form of commission agreement

No specific form is required for a commission contract.

The statutes of the cantons of Basel and Zurich require a permit for dealers in securities. See ¶1123.

¶428   Content of commission agreement

(1) Obligations of commission agent

Commission agents provide the principals with all necessary information and, in particular, notify them immediately of the performance of the mandate (ATF 59 II 251). At the principal's request, the commission agent must insure the goods on commission (Art. 426 CO).

If the goods consigned for sale on commission are delivered in an obviously defective condition, the commission agent must safeguard the principal's remedies against the carrier, by:

(a) securing the necessary evidence of the defective condition;

(b) notifying the principal without delay; and

(c) taking whatever action is necessary to preserve the goods (Art. 427 CO).

A commission agent who sells below the price fixed by the principal must pay the difference to the principal unless the sale of the goods was to avert a loss and circumstances prevented the commission agent from obtaining the principal's consent in advance. The commission agent is liable for any damage caused by his or her breach of contract. A commission agent who buys at lower prices than expected, or who sells at higher prices than those fixed by the principal, is not allowed to keep the profit but must remit it to the principal (Art. 428 CO).

Generally, commission agents are not responsible for the payment or other performance of obligations by third parties unless they have assumed such an obligation or it is common commercial practice at their place of business (Art. 430 CO).

(2)   Obligation of the principal

The principal must reimburse the commission agent for all advances, disbursements, and other out-of-pocket expenses made in the principal's interest (Art. 431 CO).

Upon completion of the transaction, or if the transaction is not completed for reasons attributable to the principal, the commission agent is entitled to the commission fee (Art. 432 CO). This fee does not become due if the commission agent has acted dishonestly, e.g., has deceived the principal by exaggerating purchase prices or understating sale prices (Art. 433(1) CO).

(3)   Dealings by commission agents for their own account
Commission agents who are entrusted with the purchase or sale of goods or securities for which a market value exists are allowed, unless specifically prohibited by the principal, to sell their own goods or securities to the principal and to acquire the principal's goods or securities for their own account. In such cases, commission agents are obliged to account for the goods or securities at the market price, and are entitled to the ordinary commission fee and the reimbursement of the expenses which normally occur in connection with the transactions (Art. 436 CO).

(4)   Exclusivity of commission agreement
Since a commission contract by its nature involves only a single transaction, exclusivity is implied. As the commission contract is not a continuous contractual relationship between the principal and the commission agent, exclusivity ends with the conclusion of that particular transaction.

¶429   Termination of commission agreement
The commission agreement may be terminated by either party without prior notice. In general, the provisions of the ordinary mandate apply (Art. 404 CO). See ¶411.

SELECTED BIBLIOGRAPHY

Martine Bénédict, *Le contrat de concession de vente exclusive* (Lausanne, 1975)
Heinrich Honsell, *Schweizerisches Obligationenrecht, Besonderer Teil* (Bern, 1991)
Hans Hendrik Lidgard, Claude D. Rohner, Dennis Campbell, *A Survey of Commercial Agency* (Deventer, 1984), pp. 329 et seq.
Walter R. Schluep, 'Innominatverträge', in *Schweizerisches Privatrecht*, vol. VII/1 (Basel, 1979), pp. 83 et seq.
Pierre Tercier, *La partie spéciale du Code des obligations* (Zürich, 1988)

5 Breach of Warranty, Torts, Product Liability and Unjust Enrichment

PRINCIPAL LEGISLATION

Code des obligations/Obligationenrecht/Code of Obligations (CO), RS 220.

Convention des Nations Unies sur les contrats de vente internationale de marchandises/Übereinkommen der Vereinten Nationen über Verträge über den internationalen Warenkauf/The United Nations Convention on Contracts for the International Sale of Goods, RS 0.221.211.1.

WARRANTIES IN DOMESTIC SALES AGREEMENTS

¶501 International and domestic sales

Switzerland joined the United Nations Convention on Contracts for the International Sale of Goods ('Vienna Convention') on 1 March 1991. The Convention's rules apply to the warranties in sales agreements between parties whose places of business are in different states (see Arts 1 to 6 of the 'Vienna Convention'). Otherwise internal law applies.

Internal contract law provides for general rules on the non-performance of a contract (¶225 et seq.), as well as specific rules on the seller's warranty (¶502 et seq.). These rules regulate the seller's obligations if the goods sold are not in conformity with the contract.

Internal sales law distinguishes two cases of lack of conformity. The first case is when the seller does not comply with the obligation to deliver goods free from any right or claim from a third party. In that case, the seller is in breach of warranty with regard to the title transferred (¶502). The second case is when the seller delivers goods which do not conform to the quality agreed on. Here, the rules on the seller's warranty of the object sold are relevant (¶503).

¶501

¶502   Warranty of title

(1)   Practical importance

In general, the seller warrants the title, i.e., that ownership and possession of the goods can be transferred to the purchaser. The seller must deliver goods free from any right or claim from a third party.

However, since Swiss law provides for bona fide acquisition of rights *in rem* with respect to movables and immovables (Arts 714(2), 933, and 884(2) CC), the rules on warranty of title are of minor importance in practice. The reason is that the bona fide purchaser becomes the lawful owner even though the seller had no legal right to dispose of the goods. Therefore, the bona fide purchaser is not exposed to a claim from a third party unless the goods left the latter's sphere of control without his or her consent (for example, if they had been stolen). In that case the seller's warranty of title is relevant and can be invoked by the purchaser.

(2)   Prerequisites of warranty of title

According to Art. 192 CO, warranty of title is subject to three conditions:

- the goods must have been transferred to the buyer;
- a third party has a claim of title at the time the contract was concluded; and
- the buyer did not know of the existence of the third party's claim at the time of the contract.

The seller's negligence is no condition to the warranty of title.

The seller may exclude or limit the warranty. However, agreements excluding or limiting such warranty are void if the seller intentionally conceals the existence of third-party claims (Art. 192(3) CO).

(3)   Remedies in event of breach of warranty of title

In case of total deprivation, the sales agreement is deemed to be rescinded, and the buyer is entitled to restitution of the purchase price (Art. 195 CO; ¶503(6)).

In case of partial deprivation, the sales agreement is generally not rescinded, but the purchase price is reduced (Art. 196 CO).

In both cases, the buyer is entitled to compensation for the damage caused by the deprivation (¶503(6)).

¶503   Warranties against defects

Practically, the most important provisions of sales law pertain to the buyer's rights in case the goods sold contain defects that existed before the risk passed to the buyer. According to Art. 197 CO, the seller warrants the quality of the goods sold and their fitness for the intended purpose.

(1) Quality of the goods sold
Pursuant to Art. 197 CO, goods sold are deemed defective if they lack the quality which the buyer was entitled to expect in good faith, or if certain attributes necessary for the utility and value of the goods are missing. In other words, while the agreed upon goods have been delivered, they are not of the agreed upon quality. Usually, the defect is of a material, physical nature. However, the defect can also be legal or economic.

Sales law distinguishes between the absence of a promised quality and the absence of an implied quality.

(2) Express warranty
Article 197(1) CO refers to cases where the seller expressly warrants certain features of the sold goods. In some cases, the seller expressly warrants that the goods sold are of a certain specified quality. This may be done:

(a) positively, by asserting that the goods have certain qualities, or

(b) negatively, by declaring that certain defects are absent.

In the latter case, the seller also has a liability for the defects that the buyer could have ascertained by exercising reasonable care (Art. 200(2) CO).

The warranty of certain qualities must be distinguished from mere puffing. It is generally admitted that simple advertising claims by the seller with obviously exaggerated promises ('miracle claims') are not legally binding warranties (promised qualities under the law).

The principle of interpretation is that of good faith: the seller's promise has the meaning that the buyer can reasonably attribute to it in good faith. The warranty is given only if the seller's express undertaking has been instrumental in the buyer's decision to enter into the contract.

(3) Implied warranty
Although the seller has not made an express promise as to the quality of the goods sold, the goods are defective if they do not present the quality which one may normally expect. The goods must be fit for the purpose for which they are ordinarily used.

The implied qualities are determined, again, according to good faith and with respect to all the circumstances, in particular the relevant commercial practices.

(4) Defects known to the purchaser
The seller is relieved of responsibility if the purchaser was actually aware of the existence of the defect at the time the contract was concluded. The same holds

¶503

true if the purchaser could have discovered the defect through customary examination, unless the seller has made an express warranty as to the absence of this defect.

(5) Limitation of warranty

The parties may exclude or limit the warranty for defects (Art. 199 CO). However, there are certain statutory limits on contract terms that restrict an exclusion of warranty. Some of them are general and apply to all contracts (¶228). Others are specific to sales agreements. With regard to warranty against defects, Art. 199 CO provides that agreements excluding or limiting warranties are void if the seller has fraudulently concealed the defects from the buyer.

(6) Remedies for breach of warranty

The Code of Obligations grants specific remedies to buyers in the event of breach of warranty. They may demand either:

- rescission of the whole transaction (Arts 205(1) and 208 CO); or
- reduction of the contract price (Art. 205(1) CO); or
- in case of fungible goods, delivery of goods in conformity with the contract (Art. 206(1) CO).

All these remedies are available to the purchaser irrespective of the seller's negligence.

Under statutory law, the buyer has no right to ask for the repair of the defective goods. However, contract terms which provide for repair of defective goods and at the same time exclude all other remedies are frequent. The courts have upheld such terms if they have been found to be clearly formulated (¶506).

In addition to these remedies, under certain circumstances, the buyer may also claim damages under either the specific provisions of sales law or the general provisions applying to the non-performance of contractual obligations (¶225 et seq.). The latter apply only if the seller is negligent.

(a) Rescission of the contract

Under Art. 205(1) CO, the buyer may elect to sue for rescission of the sale in case of a breach of warranty (the *actio redhibitoria*). The same remedy is available to the buyer in case of total deprivation (Art. 195(1) CO).

However, the buyer's remedy of rescission of the contract is limited to situations where the defect of the goods is material, so that the buyer cannot reasonably be expected to keep the defective goods (Art. 205(2) CO).

In case of rescission, the buyer returns the goods and the benefits derived therefrom to the seller in exchange for return of the purchase price (Art. 208(1) CO). In addition, the seller has the following obligations (Art. 208(2) and (3) CO):

(i) refund of the purchase price together with interest accrued and, in accordance with the provisions on total deprivation, refund of the costs of legal action and of all related expenses;

(ii) compensation for damages directly resulting to the buyer following the delivery of defective goods (Art. 208(2) CO);

(iii) payment of indirect further damages. Unlike the foregoing remedies, indirect damages cannot be awarded unless the seller was negligent. There is, however, a presumption of negligence which can be overcome by opposing evidence from the seller (Art. 208(3) CO).

The distinction between direct and indirect damages is important. While, according to the Code of Obligations, the seller is subject to strict liability in case of direct damages, the seller is liable for indirect damages only in case of negligence (although, in a contract, such negligence is presumed). However, this distinction is controversial under Swiss law. The Federal Supreme Court has decided that the damages resulting directly from the delivery of defective goods are those damages actually endured (*damnum emergens*), whereas the additional or indirect damages cover the lost profits (*lucrum cessans*). Some writers have proposed a distinction between direct and indirect damages which depends upon the degree of causal connection. In relation to product liability, it is also disputed whether consequential damage qualifies as direct or indirect damage (¶512(1)).

(b)   The reduction of the purchase price
Instead of rescinding the contract, the buyer may elect to maintain the contract, retain the defective goods and demand a reduction of the contract price (the *actio quanti minoris*). This choice may be exercised only within the limits of the principles of good faith. Hence, if the reduction in value claimed is equal to the purchase price, the buyer can only sue for rescission (Art. 205(3) CO).

Furthermore, the Federal Supreme Court has decided that the buyer may claim damages under the general provisions of the Code of Obligations governing the non-performance of a contract (¶225 et seq.). This right may be exercised either together with the claim for reduction of the purchase price or independently.

(c)   Substitution of the goods sold or delivery of goods in conformity with the contract
In case of a fixed quantity of fungible goods, the buyer may, instead of suing for rescission of the contract or reduction of the price, demand the delivery of merchantable goods of the same kind (Art. 206(1) CO). Except in cases of long-distance sales, the seller may likewise preclude all further claims by the buyer by immediately delivering merchantable goods of the same kind and by paying for any damage (Art. 206(2) CO).

¶503

(7) Notice requirements

(a) Inspection of the goods
Upon receipt of the goods, the buyer must inspect them to see if they conform to the contract. The buyer may also have the goods examined by a third party. The examination must take place within a reasonable period of time (Art. 201(1) CO). Defects which cannot be detected by customary examination must be announced immediately upon later discovery (Art. 201(2) CO).

(b) Notice of defect
The notice of non-conforming delivery must specify the nature of the defect. Although there is no compulsory form, notice is preferably and customarily given by registered letter.

The buyer who discovers a lack of conformity must give notice without delay. In case of hidden defects, notice thereof must be given immediately after discovery.

The time limit for notice of non-conformity can be modified by agreement. A longer, or more commonly a shorter, time limit may be agreed on.

If the buyer gives no notice of non-conformity, the goods are deemed to have been accepted (Art. 201(2) and (3) CO). The buyer loses his or her rights under the warranty. However, if the seller wilfully deceives the buyer (e.g., in case of deceptive concealment of a defect), lack of notice or belated notice by the buyer does not affect the seller's warranty (Art. 203 CO).

¶504 Statute of Limitations

Claims based on a warranty are time-barred one year after delivery (Art. 210(1) CO). The parties to the contract may provide for a longer or a shorter period.

If the seller undertakes a more extensive warranty, the majority of legal writers deem this to be not only an extension of the time during which defects discovered are subject to warranty, but also an extension of the time during which action may be brought by the buyer.

The one-year Statute of Limitations may not be invoked if the seller wilfully deceived the buyer. The ordinary time limit governing contractual obligations – ten years – is then relevant (Arts 210(3) and 127 CO).

WARRANTIES IN OTHER CONTRACTS

¶505   General and specific rules

Besides the specific rules on the seller's warranty, the Code of Obligations also provides rules concerning the warranty for other types of contracts, such as construction contracts, rental agreements, or mandates. It must be stressed that these rules apply only in case of defective performance. All other cases are subject to the general rules governing the consequences of contractual non-performance laid down in Arts 97 to 109 CO. The general rules are thus, generally speaking, subsidiary to the specific rules.

¶506   Warranties in construction contracts

The special provisions concerning warranty in construction contracts apply only if the construction itself is defective. Like a purchaser in a sales contract, the principal must inspect the construction immediately after delivery and notify the contractor of defects, if any. Both parties can, at their own cost, have the construction inspected by experts and have the result put on record.

If the contractor's work is defective, the principal's remedies are similar to those available for breach of a sales contract. The principal is, firstly, entitled to refuse acceptance. This remedy is limited to situations where the construction is materially defective (i.e., if it is of no use to the principal or its acceptance cannot reasonably be expected) (Art. 368(1) CO). The refusal of acceptance causes the contract to be rescinded. A rescission is not possible if the construction has been erected on the real estate of the principal and could be removed only at disproportionate expense (Art. 368(3) CO).

If the construction is not substantially defective, or if it has been erected on the real estate of the principal, the principal may reduce the price. The reduction must correspond to the reduced value of the construction (Art. 368(2) CO).

In contrast to the rules concerning sales contracts, Art. 386(2) CO also provides for the principal's right to demand the improvement of the construction without cost, unless this causes undue expense to the contractor.

If the contractor cannot prove that the defects are not due to negligence, the principal is also entitled to claim damages. This claim refers to all damage (including consequential damage) that is caused by the defective construction.

Claims based on warranty are time-barred one year after delivery of the construction. If, however, the construction is an immovable construction, the claim is barred five years after the date of acceptance.

¶507 Warranties in rental agreements

The remedies for breach of warranty in rental agreements are similar to those for construction contracts. The statutory provisions distinguish non-performance or defective performance of the contract at the time the object was transferred and defects arising during the rental period.

In case the lessor does not transfer the object at the agreed time, or transfers it with defects that exclude or significantly impair its suitability for the pre-determined use, the lessee may proceed according to the general provisions in Arts 107 to 109 CO (¶225 et seq.).

If the defect arises after the transfer of the leased object, or if the defect does not exclude or significantly impair the suitability of the object for the pre-determined use, the lessee may request that the lessor:

(1) remedy the defect;

(2) proportionately reduce the rent; and

(3) compensate for damages (Art. 259a CO).

In addition, if the lessor is aware of the defect and does not remedy it within an adequate period of time, the lessee may give notice of termination with immediate effect. If the object concerned is immovable, the defect has to prevent or significantly impair its pre-determined use. The lessee may also remedy the defect at the lessor's expense, as long as the defect is not substantial (Art. 259b CO).

Defects that may be cured by minor cleaning or repairs necessary for ordinary maintenance in accordance with local custom must be remedied by the lessee at his own expense (Art. 259 CO).

¶508 Warranties in other statutory contract types

A number of statutorily regulated types of contracts, such as the brokerage contract (Arts 412 to 418 CO), the commission (Arts 425 to 439 CO), or the contract of carriage (Arts 440 to 457 CO), refer to the rules concerning the ordinary mandate (Arts 394 to 406 CO). However, since the statutory rules of the ordinary mandate do not provide for specific remedies, the general rules concerning breach of contract apply (¶225 et seq.).

¶509 Statute of Limitations

In contrast to, for example, the American legal system, the Statute of Limitations (prescription/*Verjährung*) under Swiss law is substantive, not procedural in nature. It does not extinguish the obligation; rather, it is a defence enabling the debtor to oppose the creditor's claim.

Unless stated otherwise, the general time limit for claims is ten years (Art. 127 CO). This time limit may not be modified or restricted by agreement. The Code of Obligations provides for several specific time limits. The law provides for a one-year time limitation (for claims based on sales warranty (¶504), extracontractual liability (torts) and unjust enrichment (Arts 60 and 67 CO).

The general rule is that the Statute of Limitations starts to run from the date when performance was due under the contract (Art. 130(1) CO). There are, however, several exceptions, among which the following are noteworthy:

(1) if a claim matures upon notice, the Statute of Limitations will start to run on the earliest day on which notice may be given (Art. 130(2) CO);

(2) for claims resulting from extracontractual liability (i.e., torts; ¶517), the Statute of Limitations will start from the date the injured party received knowledge of the damage and of the liable person (Art. 60(1) CO);

(3) for claims stemming from unjust enrichment (Art. 62 et seq. CO), the period of limitation commences on the day the aggrieved party discovers the claim (Art. 67 CO).

The day on which the period of limitation commences is not counted when calculating the time limit.

The Swiss Code of Obligations also provides for some rules concerning the extension or suspension of the time limit:

(1) The time limit does not begin to run and, if it has already begun to run, is suspended in the cases described in Art. 134(1) CO, e.g., as long as a claim subject to Swiss law cannot be asserted before a Swiss court for objective reasons.

(2) The Statute of Limitations starts running anew if the debtor acknowledges the debt (Art. 135(1) CO) or if the creditor starts judicial or debt collection proceedings (Art. 135(2) CO). However, in order for the time period to start anew, it is not sufficient to send a registered letter requesting performance.

As mentioned above, the running of the Statute of Limitations allows the debtor to refuse performance. However, this defence must be pleaded expressly and may not be considered by the judge *sua sponte* (Art. 142 CO). A claim that is barred by the Statute of Limitation may nevertheless be subject to set-off if it had not been barred when set-off could have been invoked (Art. 120(3) CO).

¶509

LIABILITY FOR UNLAWFUL ACTS (TORTS)

¶510 Definition – delimitation – sources

Like many other legal systems, Swiss law distinguishes between contractual liability (warranty) and extracontractual liability (torts). The first pertains to liability for damage caused by breach of contract. The latter refers to a person's liability for damage caused in the absence of any contractual relationship.

Sometimes, an unlawful act is both a breach of contract and a tort (e.g., medical malpractice that causes the death of a patient, or a product sold that is defective and injures the buyer). The question arises whether the injured party can claim compensation according to the rules of contractual liability in addition to those of extracontractual liability. The victim may claim damages under both contract and tort rules. This does not, however, mean cumulation of damages, but only alternative claims.

In many respects (e.g., proof of negligence, ¶228; liability for an auxiliary's act, ¶228 and ¶506; or statute of limitations, ¶232 and ¶509), a claim based on contract will be more favourable to the injured party than one based on tort. In certain cases, however, the time limit may have run on the contractual claim, but a claim in tort may still exist (for instance, when the buyer has failed to give timely notice of defects, see ¶503(7)).

Where the parties do not enjoy privity of contract, the provisions on extracontractual liability are relevant. The general rules are contained in Arts 41 to 61 of the Code of Obligations.

In addition, there is an increasing number of special provisions that deal with specific types of extracontractual liability. These provisions are laid down in the Civil Code, in the Code of Obligations, and frequently also in special statutes. They usually provide for particular conditions of liability, but the remedies are subject to the general rules of the Code of Obligations.

¶511 Different forms of liability

Traditionally, Swiss law distinguishes between three types of liability:

The oldest ground of liability is the defendant's intent or negligence (Art. 41 CO).

A second form of liability is based on an objective set of facts. The defendant is liable, not because of fault, intent or negligence, but because the activity itself implied an objective lack of diligence. For example:

- the liability of an employer or principal (Art. 55 CO),
- the liability of the keeper of an animal (Art. 56 CO),
- the liability of the owner of a building (Art. 58 CO),

- the liability of the head of a family (Art. 333 CC),
- the liability of a landowner (Art. 679 CC).

The third category of liability considered is strict liability in tort, where the defendant is liable on the ground that his or her activity is inherently dangerous.

In practice, the most important case of strict liability is governed by the Federal Road Traffic Statute (*loi sur la circulation routière*, LCR/*Strassenverkehrsgesetz*, SVG – RS 741.1) of 19 December 1958, which renders the holder of a car liable for damage caused by the car irrespective of the owner's or the driver's fault (Art. 58 Road Traffic Statute). Other statutes deal with the liability of common carriers (trains, ships and aircraft) and the liability for electrical power plants and, more recently, nuclear power plants.

Even though liability based on the defendant's negligence is still important, the modern Swiss law of torts increasingly leans towards different forms of strict liability linked to an unprecedented growth of insurance and social security. For further details, see ¶514.

¶512   Common features

There are two common prerequisites for all grounds of liability: damage and causal connection.

(1)   Damage

Under Swiss law, damage is the involuntary diminution of one's net worth. Such damage must be distinguished from non-pecuniary damage (so-called *tort moral/immaterielle Unbill*), namely the pain, suffering and emotional distress arising out of injury or death. A claim for *tort moral* arises only if there is a specific provision to that effect (¶516).

Several types of damage can be distinguished, e.g.:

- actual loss and lost profits,
- personal injury and death as opposed to damage to things (mainly damage to chattels),
- other damage, mainly invasion of privacy.

As a rule, all these types of damage are recoverable under Swiss law.

Another distinction must be made between direct damage and subsequent (indirect) damage. An example is a person who breaks a leg in a traffic accident and who subsequently falls down the stairs of the hospital and also breaks the other (so-far healthy) leg. The recovery for such damage depends on the causal connection and remoteness of damage (see (2) below).

Less classic is the distinction drawn between the victim's own loss and the indirect loss of a third party (so-called reflective loss or loss by *ricochet*). For example, the electric cable belonging to a power plant is cut, causing a manufacturing plant to be shut down. The damage to the power plant is direct, while the damage to the manufacturing plant is indirect. While courts in the past used to deny compensation in such cases, today case law has become more flexible.

(2) Causal connection (adequate causation)
Under tort law, damages can usually be recovered only for the harm caused by the tortfeasor's conduct or by the act or state of some person, animal or thing for whom or which the tortfeasor is responsible.

To decide whether the tortfeasor's conduct or a related event played a sufficient part in bringing about the harm, the courts, applying the theory of adequate causation, examine the course of events as a whole. An act or event is considered relevant for that purpose only if everyday experience shows that such events normally lead to the type of harm that occurred. This theory differs from the theories followed in Anglo-Saxon jurisdictions, in particular the theory of 'proximate cause', although the result is often the same.

The theory of adequate causation allows a Swiss court to set limits to liability. It implies, *inter alia*, that the chain of causation has not been interrupted by independent causes or by events for which the tortfeasor need not assume responsibility, such as *force majeure* (Acts of God). If the harm results from an extraneous cause of this kind, the effect under Swiss law is to exonerate the alleged tortfeasor in whole or in part.

¶513 Liability for unlawful and negligent acts

Article 41(1) CO reads as follows: 'Whoever unlawfully injures another, whether wilfully or negligently, shall be liable for damages.'

In addition to the general prerequisites for liability (¶512), Art. 41 specifically requires unlawfulness and negligence before damages can be awarded.

(1) Unlawfulness
An act is deemed unlawful if it violates a rule of conduct designed to protect, directly or indirectly, private individuals' rights. The relevant rules of conduct are derived from both written law (federal, cantonal; public or private law) and from unwritten law.

An act is unlawful if it infringes an absolute right, such as the right to life, bodily integrity, property, or personality. In addition, a violation of a rule of conduct which, although not protecting an absolute right, requires or forbids certain conduct, is an unlawful act. These rules are relevant in case of harm to one's economic situation which, as a rule, is not absolutely protected. For example, the law forbids certain kinds of conduct, such as unfair competition, which damages a person's economic situation.

¶513

Swiss courts have considerably extended the scope of unlawfulness in recent years. One of the most important unwritten rules developed by the courts states that whoever has brought about a dangerous condition must take affirmative steps to ensure that injury to persons and things is avoided.

(2) Negligence

Negligence is the main ground on which tortious liability is based. It also has other functions, such as determining the extent of liability (Arts 43 and 44 CO; ¶516). In addition, negligence plays a part in contractual warranty (¶506).

Negligence is defined as a lack of due diligence by the tortfeasor. It is the subjective aspect of liability, whereas unlawfulness constitutes the objective side.

Negligence implies the capacity of an individual to make a reasonable judgment (Art. 16 CC). The capacity to make a reasonable judgment depends on specific circumstances (e.g., a young person who has not reached the age of majority) which are examined on a case-by-case basis.

Legal entities can also be held liable for negligent acts through the conduct of their officers, managers or agents (Art. 55(2) CC).

A distinction is drawn between intent and negligence. The former requires the tortfeasor to be aware of the harmful result of his or her act; he or she desires or approves it, or is at least indifferent to the result of the act (reckless disregard). The latter implies that the tortfeasor, without intending the harmful consequences of the act, does not take the measures appropriate under the circumstances to prevent injury.

Whether conduct is negligent is determined by an objective standard. The court compares the tortfeasor's conduct with the conduct of a reasonable person under similar circumstances.

Liability does not require a particular degree of fault: slight negligence is enough. However, the degree of negligence and the distinction between gross and slight negligence are relevant for the amount of damages (Art. 44(2) CO).

¶514   Strict liability in tort

As mentioned above (¶511), there are several kinds of liability based on objective facts. In practice, the most important are the principal's or employer's liability under Art. 55 CO, and the liability of the holder of an automobile pursuant to Arts 58 to 89 of the Federal Road Traffic Statute.

(1) Liability of a principal or an employer

Article 55(1) CO reads as follows:

'The principal shall be liable for damage caused by his employees or other auxiliary persons in the course of their work unless he proves that he has taken all precautions appropriate under the circumstances in order to

¶514

prevent damage of this kind or that damage would have occurred in spite of application of such precautions.'

In addition to the general conditions (¶512), three other specific conditions must be met in order to render the principal liable:
The first deals with the principal's relationship to the auxiliary. Article 55 CO is limited to acts of subordinate auxiliaries. This relation exists whenever the employer has the duty to supervise and give instructions to the auxiliary.
The second concerns the auxiliary's act. The principal is liable only if the auxiliary committed an unlawful act in the normal course of his or her work.
The third condition deals with the failure of the principal to supply evidence that he or she has acted diligently. This defence is not a general one but is limited to three elements: the principal has to prove that he or she diligently chose, instructed and supervised the auxiliary. This defence is commonly referred to as *cura in eligendo, instruendo et custodiendo*. In practice, the courts are rather strict in applying these *curae* and, in connection with the manufacturer's liability, the Federal Supreme Court has considerably extended the diligence required of the principal (¶515 and ¶228).

(2) Liability of the holder of an automobile

The liability of a person who operates a motor vehicle is governed primarily by Arts 58 to 89 of the Road Traffic Statute of 19 December 1958. For international claims based on traffic accidents, the Hague Convention of 4 May 1971 on the Law Applicable to Traffic Accidents applies.
Article 58(1) of the Road Traffic Statute states the general rule on liability as follows: 'If, as a consequence of using a motor vehicle, a person is killed or injured or property is damaged, the holder is liable for damages.' In addition to the general prerequisites of liability (¶512), this provision requires two specific conditions to be fulfilled:
The first deals with the person who is liable: the so-called 'holder' of the automobile, by whom is meant the person (mostly but not necessarily the owner) who exercises effective control over the vehicle and uses it for his or her own purposes and at his or her own risk. The law extends the concept of 'holder' to some other persons, in particular to anyone who has unlawfully taken possession of the vehicle (Art. 75(1) Road Traffic Statute).
The second condition is that the vehicle concerned must have been in motion and not merely stationary. A vehicle is considered to be in motion whenever the accident is due to a specific risk resulting from some mechanical part of the vehicle.
The holder of an automobile is obliged to have third-party liability insurance. This insurance covers the holder's liability as well as the liability of persons for whom he or she is responsible. This insurance has two important features. First,

¶514

the injured third party is the beneficiary of the insurance policy and has a direct claim against the insurer according to Art. 55(1) of the Road Traffic Statute. Second, the insurer may not use the defences that it has against the insured if the injured third party brings suit (Art. 65(2) Road Traffic Statute).

¶515   Product liability in particular

The question of the manufacturer's liability arises where a defective product turns out to be dangerous and causes damage. Product liability is not intended to cover direct damage to the product itself; rather, it is intended to cover consequential damage caused by products which are defective, unhealthy or otherwise unsafe.

There is no specific statutory provision governing product liability, with the exception of Art 135 of the Private International Law Statute governing the applicable law in international matters. There are only a few court decisions dealing with product liability, but their importance cannot be overstated.

(1)   Defect
As under other legal systems, there are several types of defect:

(a) A *design defect* is due to faulty conception or planning and has consequences on the whole production line, so that products are dangerous or unfit for their purpose from the beginning. An example is an error in designing the brakes of a motor vehicle.

(b) A *manufacturing defect* concerns an individual product which has been improperly manufactured. This defect could have been discovered if appropriate care had been taken.

(c) A *failure to warn* may make a manufacturer liable, even though the product itself exhibits neither manufacturing nor design defects. The manufacturer has to warn against possible dangers and misuses of the product.

(d) Growing importance is attached to the *surveillance defect*. The manufacturer is responsible for monitoring products. If the manufacturer concludes, through observation or receipt of new information, that its product is no longer safe, it must arrange for the subsequent improvement or recall of its product.

(e) *Development risks* are defects which could not be discovered because of the state of the art and technical knowledge at the time the product was put into circulation and which cause damage afterwards.

(f) *Unknowable defects* (runaways) are defects which are known to exist in a few batches of otherwise useful products and which are undetectable.

(2) Damages

Product liability deals essentially with consequential damages (¶512).

Unlike the EC Directive on product liability, the Code of Obligations does not set a maximum limit in case of personal injury. As a rule, the whole damage must be compensated. Furthermore, unlike the EC Directive, Swiss law allows the plaintiff to ask for fair compensation for pain and suffering (¶516).

(3) Contractual versus extracontractual liability

The starting point of many product liability cases lies in the purchase of a defective product. In that case the victim of the damage caused by the defective product may sue under contractual warranty, possibly combined with the rules on extracontractual liability (¶510). Where contractual remedies are available to the plaintiff, product liability may be considered under two aspects: warranty claims in specific types of agreements (e.g., sales contracts, ¶503), or general contractual liability pursuant to Art 97 et seq. CO. As seen above (¶506), the latter applies to any contracting party that is in breach of its contractual obligations, and is based on the defendant's presumed negligence.

A claim based on contractual liability presents not only advantages but also some disadvantages for the consumer, in particular the following: a short Statute of Limitations in the case of sales contracts, the possibility that the seller may limit his or her liability by contract, and the difficulty of knowing whether consequential damage qualifies as direct or indirect damage according to Art. 208(2) CO (¶512(1)). Although there are no court decisions to this effect, it seems that consequential damages will mostly qualify only as indirect damage. Thus, the plaintiff will not be able to invoke contractual strict liability. However, if the product is immediately examined and the seller is notified, the plaintiff will benefit from the presumption of the seller's negligence, which means that the burden of proof lies on the seller.

If the victims of a defective product qualify as bystanders (e.g., unrelated third parties), they cannot invoke contractual remedies which apply only to persons in privity of contract. They must base their claims on extracontractual liability. Since Swiss law contains no specific provisions dealing with damage caused by defective products, the courts rely on existing general rules, mainly Art. 41(1) CO on liability for unlawful and negligent acts and Art. 55 CO on the principal's strict liability.

(4) Liability for unlawful and negligent acts according to Art. 41 CO

Since Art. 41 CO prescribes a general duty of care (¶513), it may constitute the basis for product liability. The general duty of care encompasses the manufacturer's duty to take the necessary steps to protect third parties against harm if a dangerous situation is created by putting defective products on the market. Taking precautionary measures implies, *inter alia*, that products are designed and manufactured safely and the ultimate consumer is informed (by means of a specific warning which will be deemed part of the product) of the danger involved in using a particular product. It follows from the objective standard of the duty of care and the concept of negligence that a manufacturer acts negligently if it fails to take all the precautionary measures necessary to ensure the safety reasonably expected with regard to the intended and foreseeable use of a product.

Nevertheless, Art. 41(1) CO is not the ideal basic product liability provision, because it is up to the plaintiff to prove the tortfeasor's negligence. The plaintiff must prove that the manufacturer omitted to take all necessary measures which could reasonably be expected. This is a serious obstacle which limits the usefulness of Art. 41(1) CO to the injured party. Product liability cases will often be brought against a highly diversified, multinational manufacturer who employs several thousand people, and it will be almost impossible for the plaintiff to show where a negligent act was committed in such a huge organisation. In addition, Art. 41(1) CO is not applicable in cases where no negligence can be attributed to the manufacturer, as for instance, in the case of development risks or runaways (see (1) above).

(5) Strict liability according to Art. 55 CO
For the time being, Art. 55 CO is the main statutory provision for product liability under Swiss law. Recently, two important decisions of the Federal Supreme Court considerably extended the sphere of application of strict liability of principals, by limiting the defence that the principal acted diligently in choosing, instructing and supervising the auxiliary person. (The first decision has been published in ATF 110 II 456; the second one has been published only partly in *Journal des Tribunaux* 1986 I 571.) The Federal Court basically established that the principle of due care extended to adequate organisation of the enterprise, in particular to adequate end-control of the products in order to prevent injury to third parties. Under this recent case law, if the defects cannot be detected by appropriate examination of the product, the manufacturer must choose a safer design. If the manufacturer puts the product on the market and someone is injured, the manufacturer is deemed to have violated its duty of care and is therefore liable. In other words, under Swiss law there is now strict liability for the whole production process, ending only with the marketing of the product. Certain types of defects, such as development risks, would still not entail the manufacturer's liability since, in such a case, the manufacturer can successfully establish the defence of adequate organisation.

(6) Trends
The strict liability for defects which has been developed by recent cases of the Federal Supreme Court is similar to the manufacturer's liability of the EC

Directive. For the time being, the question remains open whether this case law will be upheld, since a majority of legal writers have criticised its theoretical background and still prefer a specific statutory solution.

¶516 Remedies for unlawful acts

The direct victim of the damage may claim compensation from the tortfeasor. Third parties may not obtain compensation unless the victim's death deprives them of their means of support.

The plaintiff must prove the existence of the damage. If the amount of the damage cannot be established, the law allows the judge to assess it with due regard to the ordinary course of events and the measures taken by the injured party (Art. 42(2) CO).

As a general rule, all types of damage described above (¶512(1)) are compensated, provided the damage is reasonably certain and has been personally and actually suffered.

Damage resulting from personal injury includes the costs of medical treatment, compensation for the loss of earnings and – in the case of total or partial disability which affects the injured person's earning capacity – compensation for the loss of prospective earnings (Art. 46(1) CO).

Damage resulting from accidental death includes the costs of medical treatment (if any), funeral expenses, and the loss of prospective earnings in cases where the victim actually had, or, in all probability, would have had, dependants to support (Art. 45 CO).

Moral damage resulting from pain and suffering is compensated only in the limited cases provided by law. The beneficiaries of such a claim are the injured persons and close relatives of a deceased person (Art. 47 CO), and any person who suffers an unlawful injury of individual inherent rights such as honour and privacy (Art. 49 CO).

The amount of damages awarded may not exceed the amount of the loss that the victim has actually suffered. Unlike the American legal system, Swiss law does not allow punitive damages (¶1915(2)). As a general rule, Swiss courts adopt a conservative approach and are not willing to follow the trend in some other countries (e.g., the United States) towards very high awards. A Swiss award usually compensates for economic losses incurred but is rather modest in terms of compensation for pain and suffering.

Under certain circumstances, the court may reduce the amount of damages (Arts 43(1) and 44 CO). It may consider the following circumstances: the fact that the tortfeasor's negligence is slight, the victim's contributory negligence, a fortuitous event which caused or aggravated the damage, and specific economic and social conditions of the parties concerned.

¶517   Statute of Limitations

The general rules applying to contractual warranty (¶509) are also relevant in relation to extracontractual liability (Arts 127 to 142 CO).

Some specific rules deal with the length of the Statute of Limitations. Pursuant to Art. 60(1) CO, the ordinary Statute of Limitations is one year. This rather short period begins from the date the injured party receives knowledge of the damage and of the liable person. In any case, action must be brought within a period of ten years starting from the date on which the wrongful act took place.

These rules apply to liability for negligence as well as to strict liability.

UNJUST ENRICHMENT

¶518   General

Whoever has been unjustly enriched out of another person's property shall make restitution of such enrichment (Art. 62(1) CO).

Enrichment means increase of property (*lucrum emergens*) or non-diminution of property (*damnum cessans*). It consists of the difference between the actual state of the property and the state the property would have had if the unjust enrichment had not taken place.

¶519   Basis of unjust enrichment

An obligation originating from unjust enrichment arises if a person receives something without any valid reason (Art. 62(2) CO) (*condictio sine causa*), for instance, if he or she receives a double payment with respect to an invoice that has already been paid.

An obligation originating from unjust enrichment also arises if a person receives something for a reason which did not materialise (Art. 62(2) CO) (*condictio ob causam futuram* or *non secutam*), for instance, if he or she performs an obligation under a condition subsequent which does not occur.

An obligation originating from unjust enrichment further arises if someone receives something for a reason which subsequently ceases to exist (Art. 62(2) CO) (*condictio ob causam finitam*), for instance, if a performed donation is withdrawn.

An unjust enrichment can also have its basis in the behaviour of the enriched person (someone uses a thing which belongs to someone else), in the behaviour of a third person (a bank transfers a certain amount of money from the account of one customer to the account of another), or in a natural phenomenon (a herd of animals penetrates into a neighbour's property and eats all the grass).

¶520 Extent of restitution

In general, full restitution must be made for the unjust enrichment. However, restitution cannot be claimed to the extent that the recipient can establish that he was no longer enriched at the time of the claim, unless he dispossessed himself of the enrichment in bad faith, or in spite of the fact that he must have known of the restitution (Art. 64 CO).

A recipient of unjust enrichment has a claim for the reimbursement of necessary and useful expenditures. A claim for useful expenditures, however, is limited to the surplus value existing at the time of restitution if the recipient did not act in good faith when receiving the enrichment (Art. 65(1) CO).

¶521 Preclusion of recovery

Whoever voluntarily pays a non-existent debt cannot recover his payment unless he is able to establish that he paid the amount in error (Art. 63(1) CO).

Recovery is precluded if the payment was made in respect of a debt barred by the Statute of Limitations or in performance of a moral obligation (Art. 63(2) CO).

Recovery is also precluded if something is given with the intention of obtaining an unlawful or immoral result (Art. 66 CO).

¶522 Subsidiary remedy

A claim originating from unjust enrichment is generally subsidiary to other claims such as vindication (*in rem*) and contract (*in personam*) claims. A torts claim, however, does not exclude a claim originating from unjust enrichment but may be asserted alternatively if the enrichment is based on a tort committed by the enriched person.

¶523 Statute of Limitations

A claim of unjust enrichment is barred one year after the injured person knew of his or her claim, but, in any event, ten years after the claim arose (Art. 67(1) CO).

SELECTED BIBLIOGRAPHY

Eugen Bucher, *Schweizerisches Obligationenrecht, Besonderer Teil ohne Deliktsrecht* (Zürich, 1988)
Henri Deschenaux and Pierre Tercier, *La responsabilité civile*, 2nd edn (Bern, 1982)

Pierre Engel, *Traité des obligations en droit suisse, dispositions générales du CO* (Neuchâtel, 1973)

Theo Guhl, Hans Merz, Max Kummer, Alfred Koller and Jean Nicolas Druey, *Das Schweizerische Obligationenrecht mit Einschluss des Handels- und Wertpapierrechts*, 8th edn (Zürich, 1991)

Karl Oftinger and Emil W. Stark, *Schweizerisches Haftpflichtrecht*, 4th edn, 3 vols, (Zürich, 1975/1987/1989)

Pierre Tercier, *La partie spéciale du Code des obligations* (Zürich, 1988)

Andreas von Tuhr and Arnold Escher, *Allgemeiner Teil des schweizerischen Obligationenrechts*, vol. 2 (Zürich, 1974)

Andreas von Tuhr and Hans Peter, *Allgemeiner Teil des schweizerischen Obligationenrechts*, vol. 1 (Zürich, 1979)

6 Consumer Protection and Data Protection

PRINCIPAL LEGISLATION

Loi fédérale concernant la surveillance des prix/Preisüberwachungsgesetz/ Federal Price Supervision Statute, RS 942.20.

Loi fédérale sur le commerce des denrées alimentaires et de divers objets usuels/ Lebensmittelgesetz/ Federal Statute on Commerce in Foodstuffs and in Various Other Necessities, RS 817.0.

Loi fédérale contre la concurrence déloyale/Gesetz gegen den unlauteren Wettbewerb/ Federal Unfair Competition Statute, RS 241.

CONSUMER PROTECTION

¶601 Sources of law

The common basis of all statutory provisions aimed directly at consumer protection is Art. 31^{sexies} of the Federal Constitution, which states that the Confederation will take measures for the protection of the consumer, taking into consideration the general interests of the Swiss economy and respecting the freedom of trade and industry.

This is buttressed by Art. $31^{septies}$ of the Federal Constitution, which empowers the Confederation to issue regulations for the prevention of abuse in the setting of prices and to establish a system of price supervision and price recommendations for the goods and services of enterprises and organisations that dominate certain markets. This latter reference emphasises the close connection of consumer protection with antitrust (¶1201 et seq.) and unfair competition law (¶1207 et seq.).

The following federal statutes deal with consumer protection:

- the Federal Price Supervision Statute,

- the Federal Statute on Commerce in Foodstuffs and in Various Other Necessities of 8 December 1905 and 26 May 1936, as amended,

- in contract law, statutory provisions protect consumers from certain sales practices (Art. 6a CO, amended 1991), abusive rent (Art. 269 et seq. CO, amended 1990) abusive practices in connection with instalment purchases and prepayment plans (Art. 226a CO), and

- the Federal Unfair Competition Statute (Unfair Competition Statute) protects consumers from price-cutting merchants and certain advertising practices.

There are, of course, other statutory regulations which limit or control trade in certain types of consumer goods such as drugs. There are also consumer protection statutes in fields such as trade in toxic substances, electricity and explosives.

¶602   Consumer goods

The most important rules setting quality standards for consumer goods are found in the Federal Statute on Commerce in Foodstuffs and Other Necessities and its implementing ordinance. The cantonal authorities are responsible for applying these rules under the supervision of the Federal Public Health Office (*Office fédéral de la santé publique/Bundesamt für Gesundheitswesen*). At the border, the compliance of imported goods with the law is checked by the customs authorities. If the consumption or use of the foodstuffs or other necessities becomes hazardous to health or is life-threatening, non-compliance with the statutory rules may be sanctioned by imprisonment of up to two years and fines up to SFr 3,000.

The implementing ordinance likewise contains rules applicable to foodstuffs and other necessities. According to these rules, a newly introduced foodstuff that is not yet listed in the ordinance must be submitted to the Federal Public Health Office, which decides on its admission and determines its designation. Besides protecting the health and life of consumers, the law aims at preventing manufacturers from deceiving consumers by using confusing or unclear descriptions of goods.

The admission, registration and circulation of drugs is regulated and controlled, not by a federal statute, but by an intercantonal concordat dated 3 June 1971. Under this concordat, all cantons established a public association responsible for its implementation. The authorities may regulate prices of consumer goods under the Federal Price Supervision Statute (see ¶604).

Inaccurate or misleading statements of fact in connection with the sale of goods constitute unfair competition (Art. 3b Unfair Competition Statute). The use of abusive general conditions of sale is also considered unfair competition if they deviate considerably from the usual legal framework or lead to a highly unusual distribution of rights and obligations to the detriment of the purchaser of goods (Art. 8 Unfair Competition Statute) (¶208 and ¶1210(3)).

¶603   Consumer protection in other fields

There is no overall rent control, but a tenant may obtain relief under specific rules against abusive rent (Art. 269 et seq. CO). According to these rules, landlords are subject to certain restrictions when fixing automatic rent increases. The rules further define 'abusive rent' and give the tenant the right to challenge an increase. The Federal Supreme Court has determined that the landlord's rate of return should not be more than half of 1 per cent over the interest rate of a major bank for first mortgages; otherwise the rent will be regarded as abusive (ATF 112 II 152). A unilateral increase is prohibited (Art. 269d CO). In addition, in case of termination a tenant has the right to have his lease extended if the termination would lead to undue hardship for the tenant and if further conditions stated in the law are fulfilled (Art. 272 et seq. CO) (¶1722 and ¶1723).

For farming leases – for farms over a certain size – there are stringent rules under a specific federal statute in favour of the farm tenant (RS 221.213.2).

While the idea of a federal statute on consumer credit has not yet been realised, provisions of the Code of Obligations governing sales aim at preventing undesirable credit situations. The provisions on instalment payment transactions (Art. 226a et seq. CO) are applicable by analogy to the granting of loans for the acquisition of personal property under given circumstances (Art. 226m(2) CO). Among other things, the rules state the necessary contents of an instalment contract and the possibility for the buyer to rescind the contract within five days (Art. 226c CO). Comparable rules are established for sales with payment of the purchase price in advance (Art. 227a et seq. CO). Specifically, the purchaser may terminate the contract at any time if it is for more than one year (Art. 227f CO).

The application of the rules for sales and similar transactions is limited to certain specified categories (Arts 226m(3) and (4), 227b CO). Unfair practices in connection with consumer credit are prohibited under Art. 3(l) and 3(m) Unfair Competition Statute.

¶604   Price control

Beyond price control in specific areas such as rent or farm leases (¶1723), the Federal Price Supervision Statute, enacted 1 July 1986, contains the general regulatory scheme and thus carries out the constitutional mandate.

The Price Supervision Statute permits corrective measures, not only in connection with the sale of goods but also with the rendering of services. It does not apply, however, to remuneration for work and credits (Art. 1 Price

Supervision Statute). Corrective measures are permitted only if abusive prices are set for services as a result of the dominant position of the offeror.

The statute applies to cartels or similar organisations of private and public law which dominate a specific market as defined by the Federal Cartel Statute (¶1202(2)) (Art. 2 Price Supervision Statute). The Price Supervision Statute extends beyond the scope of the Cartel Statute because, in addition to private organisations, public organisations such as public utilities are subject to price supervision.

The Federal Government has appointed a commissioner for the supervision of prices (the Price Commissioner), who is integrated into the Federal Department of Public Economy. The Commissioner is popularly nicknamed '*Monsieur Prix*'. The Commissioner's job is to observe price developments and prevent or rescind abusive price increases or abusive maintenance of high prices. He regularly informs the public about his activity (Art. 4 Price Supervision Statute). The necessary close co-operation between the Commissioner and the Cartel Commission is based on statutory provisions which suggest co-operation with 'interested groups'. 'Interested groups' are not only consumer and industrial organisations but also the enterprises and businesses affected by an intended price control measure.

Cartels or similar organisations may submit intended price increases to the Price Commissioner for prior clearance (Art. 6 Price Supervision Statute). Anyone may inform the Commissioner of allegedly abusive prices. Upon a complaint, or on his own initiative, the Commissioner initiates an investigation. If abuse is established, the Commissioner first seeks an amicable settlement, which can be quite informal. If no settlement is reached, the Commissioner prohibits the increase or orders a price reduction. The amicable settlement or the order must be of limited duration. Whether a price is abusive is determined according to principles developed under the rules of the Cartel Statute. Prices may be held to be abusive only if prices in the specific market are not the result of effective competition (Art. 12 Price Supervision Statute). Specific rules determine whether prices charged by public organisations are abusive (Art. 14 Price Supervision Statute). Cartels, similar organisations, and third parties participating in the same market are obliged, upon request, to provide the Commissioner with information and documents.

The Commissioner's orders may be appealed to the Federal Department of Public Economy and, eventually, to the Federal Supreme Court. Both the enterprise or organisation affected by the order and consumer organisations have the right to appeal (Art. 21 Price Supervision Statute). Abusive prices and the refusal of information are subject to penal sanctions.

Thanks to the yearly reports of the Commissioner, which are published together with the report of the Cartel Commission, the Commissioner's accomplishments are reasonably well-known in spite of the relatively short period during which the Price Supervision Statute has been in force. A major part of the investigations conducted by the Commissioner since July 1986 concerned rates for electric power and other utilities supplied by public companies. In the field of private business organisations, the field most often concerned was repair and maintenance services for heating, computers and other office equipment, and cars.

Another means of price control, at least in the sense of consumer protection, is the ordinance on the disclosure of prices (RS 942.211), which requires consumer prices to be conspicuously indicated on the goods and in connection with certain services. The purpose of these rules is to allow the consumer to compare prices and to prevent misleading price information.

There is another kind of price protection, not so much in favour of consumers as in support of important and endangered professions or branches of the economy, or in favour of agriculture under a specific federal statute (RS 942.30). So far, the implementing regulations and decrees have mostly been concerned with agricultural products.

¶605 Federal Commission for Consumer Problems

A decree of the Federal Government of 26 February 1965 established the Federal Commission for Consumer Problems, which acts as an advisory body to the Federal Government and its departments in all matters of consumer policy. It may become active on its own initiative or upon request. This Commission issues reports from time to time on various subjects such as credit cards or the impact of the realisation of the European interior market on consumers. The Commission is also involved in the drafting of new statutes in the field of consumer protection and in the promotion of consumer information.

¶606 Advertising

In the field of advertising, consumer protection is effected through provisions of the Federal Unfair Competition Statute. The rules on price notification (¶1214) apply to the promotion of goods or services (Art. 17 Unfair Competition Statute). Misleading price information, especially misleading references to price reductions or other comparisons, is prohibited (Art. 18 Unfair Competition Statute).

The rules on unfair competition protect consumers against misleading price-cutting (Art. 3(f) Unfair Competition Statute), deception about the real value of an offer by the addition of giveaways (Art. 3(g) Unfair Competition Statute), and particularly aggressive methods of sales, e.g., exertion of psychological pressure in door-to-door sales or sales at parties.

The omission of certain elements in the advertising of instalment sales or consumer credits are acts of unfair competition (Arts 3(k) and 3(l) Unfair

Competition Statute). Similarly, the use of forms with incomplete or incorrect information about the object of an instalment sale or similar transaction is considered unlawful (Art. 3(m) Unfair Competition Statute).

In the field of advertising, self-control in favour of consumers is exercised through a private Commission for Fairness in Advertising (¶1207). This commission was established by a private foundation of the advertising industry. Anyone, including consumers or consumer organisations, may submit complaints against certain advertising practices to this Commission, which renders its decisions based on principles of advertising developed by itself or according to the International Code of Fair Practice in Advertising promulgated by the International Chamber of Commerce.

¶607   Procedural aspects of consumer protection

Remedies under the various consumer protection statutes may be sought by individuals or by consumer organisations.

Individual consumers may in their own name:

(1) inform the Price Commissioner of allegedly abusive prices;

(2) notify the Price Commissioner about a violation of the rules on foodstuffs and other necessities;

(3) submit a case of unfair advertising to the Commission for Fairness in Advertising;

(4) bring a case of abusive rent before the rent settlement board; or

(5) notify the Cartel Commission about an alleged restraint on competition (¶1205).

In addition, a consumer has, of course, recourse to all the remedies of tort law if affected directly by, e.g., an act of unfair competition, provided the conditions of extracontractual liability are met (proof of fault, damage and adequate causation) (¶512 and ¶513).

Consumer organisations of a certain national or regional importance are entitled to act in their own names under the Unfair Competition Statute in order:

(1) to prohibit an imminent violation of the rules on unfair competition, or to remove a prevailing violation or to request a declaratory judgment;

(2) to appeal an order of the Price Commissioner under the Price Supervision Statute regarding an abusive price increase or the maintenance of abusive prices; or

(3) to notify the Cartel Commission under the rules of the Cartel Statute (¶1205).

Under federal law, the cantons must provide a settlement procedure or a simple and quick court procedure for certain types of consumer actions and for claims under the Unfair Competition Statute (RS 944.8).

DATA PROTECTION

¶608 Sources of law

While non-personal data, e.g. financial information on a business or technical data regarding a production procedure, are protected under the rules governing protection of know-how and trade secrets (¶1322 and ¶1323), the concept of data protection is aimed at all information of an intimate nature about a person. Data protection as described hereinafter protects the individual against misuse of personal data by private persons or public authorities.

As between private parties, the rules for the protection of personality contained in the Civil Code (Art. 28 et seq. CC) provide for the protection of personal data against misuse, at least to some minimum extent.

In the relationship between citizens and the government, the following applies:

(1) At the *federal level*, there are currently mere guide-lines for the processing of personal data by the federal administration. A draft bill for a data protection statute (Draft) was published together with an accompanying report (Report) on 23 March 1988. As of summer 1991, the Draft is pending before the Federal Parliament. Within the federal administration, data protection is implemented by a service for data protection. This service is integrated into the Federal Justice Department. Other sources for data protection may be found in numerous federal statutes, especially in the fields of public administration (military, statistics) and criminal law (¶1323(3)).

(2) On an *international level*, Switzerland has adhered to the Convention for the Protection of Human Rights and Fundamental Freedoms concluded in Rome on 4 November 1950 (RS 0.101) (see ¶102(1) and ¶1801). The fundamental right of respect for a person's private and family life is stated in Art. 8 of this Convention. On the other hand, Switzerland has not yet ratified the Council of Europe's Convention No. 108 of 28 January 1981 for the protection of individuals with regard to automatic processing of personal data, pending the enactment of a federal statute based on the Draft mentioned above and the corresponding cantonal legislation.

(3) On a *cantonal level*, there are many provisions for the protection of personal data in the form of statutes, regulations, or at least guide-lines.

(4) On a *voluntary basis*, certain professional organisations (doctors, market researchers) have drafted regulations applicable to their members for the purpose of protecting personal data from misuse.

¶609   Storage, modification and transmission of data

All dealings with personal data, independent of means or procedure, particularly collection, storage, use, modification, publication, or destruction, will be subject to restriction and safeguards if the Draft is passed (see Art. 3(g)).

In private law (see ¶107 for the distinction between private and public law), the provisions of Art. 28 et seq. CC give no express indication as to the circumstances under which processing personal data is either a violation of personality or is justified. Case law is not very specific on this point. Processing data may infringe a person's right of personality if his or her sphere of privacy and confidentiality is affected (ATF 97 II 97, 109 II 353). The sphere of confidentiality covers facts of which only the person concerned or people who are very close to this person have knowledge, while the sphere of privacy is made up of the other parts of private life to which the broader public has no access. According to the rules established by the courts, data processing is illegal if it can impair an individual's sphere of confidentiality, sphere of privacy, or social reputation.

In the public field, individuals cannot invoke a specific constitutional right in the case of abusive processing of personal data but must base their claims on the general principle of personal freedom as it is expressed in Art. 8 of the Convention for the Protection of Human Rights and Fundamental Liberties. The Guide-lines of 16 March 1981 for the Processing of Personal Data in the Federal Administration provide certain rules to be observed by the federal administration in the processing of personal data. An accessory regulation on the registration and publication of data bases provides for the regular publication of a register of all data bases maintained by the federal administration.

Similar provisions for the processing of personal data are contained in a model cantonal data protection statute drawn up by a commission of experts. Various cantonal statutes have incorporated the principles of this model statute.

The Draft states the basic rules, particularly legality in the collection of personal data, correctness of data, and the proportionality of data processing (Art. 4 Draft). The federal authorities would have to register all data bases in a register which would be open to the public. Private persons would have to register if they regularly (a) processed data, and particularly protection-worthy personality profiles, or (b) supplied third persons with data, provided they did not do it in the performance of a legal obligation and without knowledge of the persons concerned (Art. 7(2) Draft).

The processing of personal data by private persons would not be allowed to infringe unlawfully upon their right of personality (Art. 9 Draft). A violation of a personality right could be justified by the consent of the person concerned, or if another private or a public interest outweighed the interest of the person concerned (Art. 10 Draft).

In the public field all processing of personal data by the federal administration would have to be based on a statute (Art. 14(1) Draft). Normally the collection of personal data would have to be apparent to the person concerned (Art. 15 Draft). The federal administration would be allowed to reveal personal data if there was a justification in the sense of the statute (Art. 16 Draft). Special rules would be established for data processing in the case of research, planning and statistics (Art. 19 Draft), and in the case of protection of state and military safety (Art. 21 Draft).

¶610   Right of access to, and correction of, data

Until a federal data protection statute is enacted, an individual's rights to inspect, and possibly correct, a personal data base maintained by another private person or entity remain very weak, as this claim would have to be based on the general provisions of personality right under Arts 28 et seq. CC. Apart from the difficulties involved in obtaining sufficient knowledge about a private data base, there are no established criteria on the admissibility of private data processing.

With regard to personal data registered by the authorities, the right to inspect and, if necessary, correct data is often expressly stated in statutes or regulations. With regard to the federal administration, these rights are granted to the person concerned under the guide-lines of 16 March 1981 (Arts 43 and 44 thereof). Cantonal statutes and regulations contain similar provisions. Failing such a provision, the right of access and, if necessary, correction must be based on general principles of law. The Federal Supreme Court has confirmed this right to inspect files based on Art. 4 of the Federal Constitution (ATF 113 Ia 10).

The Draft expressly states the right to information, not only with regard to a public authority but also with regard to private persons or entities (Art. 5 Draft). Exceptions to the right to information would be possible in a case of predominant public interest and in other specific situations, provided the exceptions were expressly stated in a statute. The right to correct false data would be granted in the case of both private and public data bases (Arts 12(1) and 22(2)(a) Draft), and would include destruction of false or inadmissible data.

¶611   Remedies against misuse of data

Under the current rules (Art. 28a CC), a person whose right of personality has been affected by misuse of personal data may request:

(1) the prohibition of an imminent infringement;

(2) the removal of an existing infringement; and

(3) a declaratory judgment confirming the illegality of an infringement.

In addition, the injured person may claim damages under the rules of tort law. The right of removal of infringement could be construed in the context of incorrect data as a claim to have the data removed from a file, or at least corrected.

In the field of public law, similar claims are available, at least where applicable statutes have been enacted. Pending enactment, relief must be sought under the rules governing the state's extracontractual liability.

The Draft would clearly improve the position of persons affected by misuse of their personal data. For the field of private law, the Draft refers to the remedies under Art. 28a CC. With regard to data bases kept and processed by the federal administration, the Draft provides the same claims as under private law, i.e., prohibition, removal or declaratory judgment (Art. 22(1) Draft), whereby the possibility to correct or destroy data is expressly stated. The person concerned would be able to request that the correction be notified to third parties, or even published (Art. 22(2)(b) Draft).

In addition, violations of provisions of the statute would be punished by penal sanctions (Arts 28 and 29 Draft). Individuals who established an interest worthy of protection would be able to ask the responsible federal administration to block the transmission of certain personal data (Art. 17(1) Draft).

¶612   Data flow across country borders

Under current law, no specific data protection provisions directly address data transmission across country borders. The rules outlined above also apply to data passed on to third parties across country borders.

Data transmission across country borders, of course, constitutes a criminal offence if it can be characterised as illegal intelligence activities in the political, economic or military field (Art. 272 et seq. Penal Code).

The Draft contains specific rules in connection with transmission of data abroad. According to Art. 4(5) of the Draft, data would not be disclosed abroad if the personality of the person concerned were put at grave risk following the disclosure because the country of destination lacks comparable data protection. The criteria for comparable data protection abroad are those expressed in the rules for data protection according to Art. 4 of the Draft; they include sufficient organisational and technical measures against unauthorised processing.

In addition, anyone who regularly transmitted, or who transmitted a considerable amount of personal data abroad, would have to notify the Federal Commissioner of Data Protection (Art. 23 et seq. Draft) unless he or she were discharging a legal obligation or the persons concerned had knowledge thereof (Art. 8(1) Draft).

'Abroad' in the sense of this provision means not only other states but also international organisations. The passing on of data within a multinational group of companies would be considered a transmission abroad. The omission of notification is a criminal offence under Art. 28 of the Draft.

¶613   Procedural issues of data protection

Claims in connection with misuse of personal data by private persons or entities would be brought before the ordinary civil courts. Under a specific jurisdictional rule, claimants would be able to sue either at the domicile of the defendant or at their own domicile (Art. 28(b) Draft). Persons who can establish that their rights of personality have been violated or are in danger of being violated by misuse of personal data, and that, in consequence, they are threatened with negative consequences which cannot easily be overcome, are entitled to preliminary injunctive relief (Art. 28c CC).

The Draft refers to the same rules of procedure for claims against private persons or entities (Art. 12 Draft).

With regard to claims against public authorities, the cantonal or federal rules of administrative procedure would apply. This is expressly stated in the Draft (Art. 22(4)), which provides for an appeal from decrees of a federal authority to the Federal Commission of Data Protection (Art. 22(5) Draft).

SELECTED BIBLIOGRAPHY

Andreas Bucher, *Natürliche Personen und Persönlichkeitsschutz* (Basel, 1986)
Lucas David, *Schweizerisches Werberecht* (Zürich, 1977)
Rainer Schweizer and Beat Lehmann, *Datenschutzrecht* (Zürich, 1988)

7 Share Corporations and other Business Organisations

PRINCIPAL LEGISLATION

*Code civil suisse/Zivilgesetzbuch/*Swiss Civil Code (CC), RS 210.

*Code des obligations/Obligationenrecht/*Swiss Code of Obligations (CO), RS 220.

*Ordonnance sur le registre du commerce/Handelsregisterverordnung/*Ordinance on the Register of Commerce, RS 221.411.

TYPES OF BUSINESS ENTITIES – REGISTER OF COMMERCE

¶701 Types of business entities

The share corporation (*Société anonyme*, SA/*Aktiengesellschaft*, AG; hereafter, SA) corresponds to the United States business corporation. It is by far the most widespread form of business organisation and corporate entity and the type best suited to meet the requirements of normal foreign business interests. Due to its special importance, it is discussed in detail below in ¶703 to ¶708. The other types of legal entities are briefly discussed below in ¶710 to ¶718.

¶702 Register of Commerce

Anyone trading, manufacturing or engaging in other business is obliged to register with the Register of Commerce (*registre du commerce/Handelsregister*) of the district in which the seat or place of business is located. Many legal entities, such as share corporations, limited liability corporations, co-operative corporations, etc., come into existence only when entered into the Register of Commerce.

¶701

Branch offices of Swiss business organisations are registered in the district of the branch office's place of business after the registration of the headquarters in its own district has been effected.

Branch offices of foreign business organisations are registered in the same way as branches of Swiss ones, unless foreign law requires a variation. For these branches, a representative residing in Switzerland and having power of representation must be appointed.

Registration of corporations is effected on the basis of a publicly authenticated deed. For registration of branch offices of foreign firms, certified copies and translations of the foreign Articles of Incorporation, an extract of the foreign Register of Commerce (or equivalent), and a board resolution establishing the creation of the branch office and appointing the resident representative must be submitted.

The Articles of Incorporation and the names of partners, board members and officers must be registered. Authenticated signatures of persons having signing power must be deposited.

Any alteration must also be registered (third parties cannot plead that they were ignorant of a registration).

Unless otherwise decreed, entries are published in the Official Journal of Commerce (*Feuille officielle suisse du commerce/Schweizerisches Handels-amtsblatt*).

The Registrar of the Register of Commerce may levy fines on persons and firms not complying with the law. Non-registered (Swiss) corporations have no legal existence. Non-registered branch offices may still do business.

When doing business, any individual or association of persons must use a corporate name (Arts 944 to 956 CO). Shelf registration of a corporate name, i.e. the reservation of a given name for future use, is not possible.

The Registrar supervises compliance with the applicable law. The meaning of a corporate name must be consistent with reality and may not be deceptive or against public policy (Art. 944(1) CO). National or territorial designations, e.g., 'International', 'Europe', 'Switzerland', may be used only with specific permission of the Federal Office of the Register of Commerce. The business designation of an individual must mention his or her family name, with or without the first name (Art. 945 CO).

To determine the availability and admissibility of a corporate name, inquiries should be addressed to the office of the Register of Commerce in advance. However, clearance and actual registration by the Registrar do not have a binding legal effect. Aggrieved third parties may still petition in court to have a branch office's name changed. They must use the corporate name of the head office, possibly with additions that are valid only for the branch office in question. The branch office of a foreign enterprise must include the place of business of both the headquarters and branch offices, as well as explicit designation as a branch office (Art. 952 CO).

¶702

If the names violate mandatory rules of law, they may not be used for Swiss branches of foreign enterprises.

Two firms in the same relevant area must not have the same firm name (Arts 946 and 951 CO).

For trade name protection, see ¶1313.

SHARE CORPORATIONS

¶703   Setting up a share corporation

(1)   Incorporation procedure

A share corporation (*Société anonyme/Aktiengesellschaft*; hereafter, SA) is a legal entity with its own corporate name. Its capital is fixed in advance and divided into shares. Only the capital of the corporation serves as security for the liabilities of the SA. The shareholders have no personal liability (Art. 620 CO). An SA is usually formed for a commercial purpose, but it may be formed for other purposes.

A share corporation needs no licence to do business, except for purposes for which a public concession is required, such as insurance, railways, etc.

Special provisions exist for share corporations engaged in the banking business.

The law provides for two different procedures to incorporate an SA, viz., incorporation by successive subscription and incorporation by simultaneous act (Arts 629 and 638 CO). Because incorporation by successive subscription is complicated and expensive, an SA is most commonly incorporated by simultaneous act. The following is a description of that procedure:

(a)   Meeting of the shareholders

An organisational meeting of the shareholders of the SA is held, with at least three founders attending in person or by proxy. At this meeting, the Articles of Incorporation are adopted, the first board of directors and the auditor are elected, and further items (e.g., the location of the principal place of business) are resolved. The resolutions of the organisational meeting must be embodied in a publicly authenticated deed. This should confirm:

(i) that the founders have subscribed to all shares;

(ii) that on each share the amount provided for by law or in the Articles of Incorporation is at the free disposal of the company and has been placed with the depository agency authorised by the canton of seat to receive these funds, or is covered by a contribution in kind mentioned in the Articles of Incorporation;

(iii) that the clauses of the Article of Incorporation concerning contributions in kind, acquisition of assets and founder benefits have been approved specifically; and

(iv) that the contracts relative to contributions in kind or acquisition of assets have been presented (Art. 638 CO).

There are no restrictions as to the nationality of shareholders or founders.

(b) Application to the Register of Commerce
The public deed must be filed with the Register of Commerce. The application to the Register of Commerce must contain a certificate confirming the appointment of the board of directors and the auditors as well as the nationality and domicile of the members of the board of directors. It must bear the duly certified signatures of the persons authorised to sign for the corporation.

The SA is incorporated only upon its entry in the appropriate Register of Commerce. Shares issued prior to registration are void. If the Register of Commerce accepts and approves the application, it is required to forward it to the Central Register in Berne for authorisation.

(c) Publication in the Official Journal of Commerce
After approval, the application may be entered in the appropriate cantonal register and published in the Official Journal of Commerce. The published information includes:

- the date on which the Articles were passed,
- the corporate name and location of the registered office,
- the purpose and duration of the SA,
- the amount of capital and the amount paid in,
- the par value and type of shares,
- the property received in payment of shares,
- privileges, if any, granted to certain classes of shares or to incorporators,
- names, residences and nationalities of directors and officers and the manner in which they may act and sign for the corporation, and
- the manner in which official corporate announcements will be made.

(d) Failure to comply with registration requirements
The legal entity comes into existence upon registration even if the prerequisites for valid registration were not fulfilled. If, however, the legal or statutory requirements have not been complied with in the course of establishment, and the interests of creditors or stockholders have been severely jeopardised or infringed as a result, the court may, upon request from a creditor or stockholder,

order the dissolution of the SA. After a petition is filed, the court may order interlocutory measures upon the request of any of the foregoing persons. The right of action at law expires if not brought within three months after publication in the Official Journal of Commerce (Art. 643 CO).

(e) Pre-registration acts
Acts committed in the name of the SA prior to its registration in the Register of Commerce are the personal joint and several responsibility of the persons performing them. If these obligations have been incurred explicitly in the name of the SA in establishment and are ratified by the SA within three months after registration in the Register of Commerce, the involved persons are released from their responsibility, and the SA is solely liable.

(2) Shareholders' rights
The shareholders cannot, without their consent, be deprived of those vested rights which they have acquired by virtue of their position as shareholders, viz., the right to participate in the shareholders' general meeting and rights based on provisions of law or the Articles of Incorporation. The rights include, in particular, the right of equal treatment, voting rights, the right to contest a decision of the shareholders' general meeting, the right to dividends and the right to a share of liquidation proceeds (Art. 646 CO).

(3) Articles of Incorporation
The Articles must state the corporate name, the seat of the registered office, the purpose of the enterprise, the amount of capital, the par value and type of shares issued, the manner of calling meetings, the voting rights of shareholders, the organisation of management and internal auditing, the manner in which directors and officers may act and sign for the corporation, the amount of the directors' qualifying shares and the form of the SA's announcements (Art. 626 CO). If a shareholder pays for his or her shares in kind, and if assets are to be acquired by the corporation from the shareholders or third parties, the details of the transaction must be defined in the Articles. The same applies to privileges granted to incorporators or other persons (Art. 628 CO).

The Articles may provide for regulations (by-laws) specifying the powers of different bodies in charge of management.

In general, any resolution of a shareholders' general meeting amending the Articles of Incorporation must be made in the form of a public deed. The board of directors must enter any resolution in the Register of Commerce, and the resolution becomes effective against third parties immediately upon registration. Changes of the corporate purpose, the removal of statutory provisions concerning restrictions of resolutions at the shareholders' general meeting, or issuance of shares with special voting rights require the consent of shareholders representing at least two-thirds of the entire capital. Holders of registered shares who have not consented to a resolution restricting the transferability of their shares are not bound by the resolution for a term of six months after publication of the resolution in the Official Journal of Commerce (Art. 648 CO).

Unless otherwise provided in the Articles of Incorporation, an extension or restriction of the scope of business within the original purpose, a merger, a change of the duration of the SA, a change of the corporate name, a change of the seat, and the dissolution of the SA before the fixed time require a resolution of the shareholders' general meeting in which the shareholders of two-thirds of all shares are present or represented. The same applies for the creation, amendment or repeal of preferred rights of certain shares. If the number of shares present or represented at such a meeting is insufficient for a quorum, a second meeting, at which one-third of all shares form the necessary quorum, may be called at least eight days later, unless the Articles of Incorporation provide otherwise (Arts 649 and 655 CO).

A share corporation can choose its corporate name freely; it must designate its legal nature only if names of living persons are used in the corporate name (Art. 950 CO).

The duration of the company may be perpetual or limited. A limited duration must be expressly stated in the Articles of Incorporation.

The Confederation levies a stamp tax of 3 per cent on the consideration received by the share corporation, but at least on the nominal value of the shares issued (¶1008). The notary drawing up the public instrument of the constituent meeting is entitled to a fee which is fixed by cantonal law.

¶704 Share capital

(1) Minimum amount, types of shares

The SA must have a minimum capital of SFr 50,000, of which at least 20 per cent or SFr 20,000 (whichever is higher) must be paid in cash or in kind. There is no authorised but unissued capital in the American or British sense, and the board of directors is not authorised to issue additional shares of stock. Furthermore, the SA is not allowed to buy its own stock. If it is felt that additional equity is necessary, a decision affecting that need can be made only by the shareholders. Any new equity must be paid in a mode similar to that at the time of incorporation.

Shares may be issued in registered or bearer form (Art. 622 CO). The SA must keep a register of owners of registered shares (Art. 685 CO). Both types of shares may be issued in any proportion fixed by the Articles. The Articles may provide for subsequent changes between the two types of shares and for the issuance of preferred shares. The par value of a share may not be less than SFr 100 except in case of financial restructuring. The stock certificates must be signed by at least one member of the board of directors. Bearer shares may be issued only if fully paid-in. Registered shares may be issued for a smaller amount than their nominal value, but the shareholder remains liable for the difference (Arts 621 to 622, 683 CO).

The Articles of Incorporation may provide for voting rights based on the number of shares held by each shareholder irrespective of the par value, so that each share has one vote. In such a case, the shares with a smaller par value, and therefore with privileged voting rights, must be issued as registered shares and be fully paid-in (Art. 693 CO).

The Articles may provide for shares with preferential rights as to dividends, shares in case of liquidation, subscription of newly issued shares (preferred shares), incorporator's certificates (*part de fondateur/Gründeranteilschein*) or profit-sharing certificates (*bon de jouissance/Genussschein*) (Arts 627(9), 654 to 658 CO). In theory, corporate law does not recognise the concept of non-voting stock, but in practice participation certificates (*bon de participation/ Partizipationsschein*) achieve the same purpose.

Although corporate law does not provide for the issuance of bonds that are convertible into shares, business practice has found ways to achieve the same result.

Stock certificates must state the corporate name, the SA's principal place of business, the nominal value of the share, the paid amounts, and the type of share (registered or bearer) if there are different types. The document must be signed by at least one member of the board of directors; if a large number of shares are issued, a facsimile signature may be used (Art. 622 CO).

If the board so allows, shareholders may, as a protective measure in the case of international conflicts, request that they be registered in a special register to be kept abroad, and that their stock certificates be annulled.

All shares have the legal character of securities (documents of title). Bearer shares can be transferred by the mere transfer of the instrument. Registered shares must be endorsed or assigned; with respect to the corporation, the transfer must be entered into the register of shareholders (Arts 4 and 685 CO). There are special rules for restrictions of transfer by the Articles. In particular, an SA may refuse to make an entry in the stock register, based on grounds stated in the Articles. The Articles may even provide that entry may be refused without disclosing the reasons therefor (Art. 686 CO). This may lead to a peculiar situation in which a purchaser may validly acquire restricted registered shares but will not be entitled to vote at the shareholders' meeting. In such a case, the financial rights pass on to the unapproved purchaser, while the voting rights remain with the person registered in the stock register.

¶704

(2) Financing of share corporation

The shareholders may make funds available to the SA in the form of loans. Under the tax authorities' rule of thumb, a debt-equity ratio of not more than 5 or 6 to 1 is required. The tax authorities argue that if the loan portion exceeds four-fifths of the total amount of capital and loans, the SA is undercapitalised, and the shareholders' loans may be treated in full or in part as equity for capital tax purposes. The interest on those loans may be treated as constructive dividends and disallowed as deductible expenses. In theory, excessive shareholder loans could also be treated as equity for stamp tax purposes, but in practice this risk is remote.

It has already been mentioned that the capital contribution of the founders and shareholders may be made in cash or in kind. The contribution of capital in kind may be made in two ways: either the contribution is made at the time of establishment, i.e., the founders contribute in kind to the capital and receive shares of stock in return, or the SA is founded with a cash contribution and, shortly afterwards, the cash is used to purchase assets or rights from shareholders or third parties.

There are no limitations as to what is allowed to be contributed in kind, and there are no provisions on the evaluation of the contributions. The interest of the public and, particularly, of the third-party creditors of the SA who rely on the existence of the registered and published capital at the time of establishment is safeguarded in two ways:

(a) both forms of contributions in kind must be clearly mentioned and designated as such in the Articles of the SA and will likewise be published in the Official Journal of Commerce;

(b) the founders are directly liable to the shareholders and the creditors for negligent acts carried out in conjunction with contributions in kind.

Corporate law, as a rule, does not prevent or limit the establishment of corporations by aliens or non-residents. In a few areas (e.g., vessels flying Swiss flag, banks, or real estate companies), special provisions require a specific majority of Swiss citizens as shareholders. There are no limitations and no extraordinary accounting procedures regarding non-resident alien shareholders of domestic subsidiaries of foreign corporations. Alien shareholding, however, may be relevant for obtaining double-taxation convention benefits. Without previous permission from the competent cantonal authority, aliens may not purchase shares in an SA whose actual purpose is the purchase and resale or the holding of Swiss immovable property (¶1709 et seq.). Likewise, without permission from the competent cantonal authority, aliens may not purchase shares in a corporation if more than one-third of its assets consists of Swiss immovable property and if the alien purchaser acquires or reinforces a dominant position within the SA by his or her purchase of the shares. A corporation whose statutory and actual seat is in Switzerland is still considered an alien if it is substantially controlled by aliens.

(3) Increase of share capital

A capital increase requires an amendment of the Articles of Incorporation; this amendment must be executed in the form of a public deed. The provisions regulating incorporation apply. Any offer for public subscription of the new shares must be made by means of a prospectus by which the public is invited to subscribe and which is signed by a duly authorised representative of the company in the name of the board of directors. The prospectus must contain:

- the date of registration in the Register of Commerce,
- the name and the registered office of the SA,
- the previous amounts and the composition of the capital stock, indicating the par value, kind and classes of the shares and preferential rights, if any,
- the profit-sharing certificates, if any, and their rights,
- the list of the board of directors and the auditors, the latest balance sheet, and profit and loss statement, together with the auditors' report,
- the dividends paid during the past five years or, if the company has existed for less than five years, since the establishment of the corporation,
- any debentures issued by the company,
- the resolution authorising the issuance of new shares, including the total amount, the par value and the issue price, as well as the number and type of new shares,
- the contributions in kind, the acquisitions of assets and preferential rights,
- the date from which the new shares rank for dividend purposes and the restrictions of the right to receive dividends and preferential rights, if any, and
- the date until which the subscription is binding.

This special prospectus may be dispensed with if the above information is contained on each subscription form (Art. 651 CO). Each shareholder has an option right to subscribe to the new shares in proportion to the number of shares held by him or her prior to the new issuance, unless otherwise provided in the Articles of Incorporation or in the respective resolution of the meeting of shareholders resolving the capital increase (Art. 652 CO).

(4) Reduction of share capital

A resolution of the general meeting that reduces the capital without simultaneously increasing the original capital by fully paid new capital requires an auditor's report stating that the claims of all creditors are covered notwithstanding the reduction in capital. The resolution of the general meeting must be published three times in the Official Journal of Commerce and in the manner of publication provided for in the Articles.

The resolution must notify the creditors that, within two months after the third publication, they may file their claims and demand satisfaction or security. A publicly authenticated document containing the auditor's report must show that the above provisions have been complied with.

Notification may be dispensed with if the reduction of the capital serves the exclusive purpose of eliminating a capital impairment caused by losses (Arts 732 to 735 CO).

(5) Acquisition of the corporation's own shares
The corporation may not ordinarily purchase its own shares or accept them as a pledge from its debtors. However, the company may, for instance, acquire its shares in order to reduce capital stock or, incidentally, obtain its own shares by purchasing other assets. These shares must not vote in the shareholders' general meeting and must be either cancelled or resold.

(6) Liability of share corporation
The corporation's liabilities may be covered only by the corporation's assets. Shareholders are liable only up to the amount of their subscriptions (Arts 620 and 680 CO).

¶705 Management and structure of share corporation

(1) Shareholders' meeting
The shareholders' meeting is the SA's highest authority. It may amend the Articles, elect and discharge the board of directors and the internal auditors, approve the balance sheet and the profit and loss statement, and declare dividends. The meeting is ordinarily called by the directors within six months after the close of each business year and, if necessary, by the auditors, the liquidators or the representatives of bondholders. By stating the purpose of the meeting in writing, shareholders representing at least one-tenth of all shares may demand that a shareholders' meeting be called. Notice of meetings must be given at least ten days in advance unless notice is waived by all shareholders (Arts 698 to 701 CO).

The law contains no provisions with respect to the place where general meetings are held. If the Articles do not provide otherwise, the meeting is held at the SA's principal place of business or at a place not too distant from the domiciles of the majority of shareholders. General meetings outside Switzerland are possible. If the general meeting has to make resolutions for which a publicly authenticated document is required outside Switzerland, the law of the foreign place governing public authentication must be observed. There must also be certification by the competent foreign authority.

Unless otherwise provided in the Articles, a registered shareholder may issue a written proxy to a third party; in the case of bearer shares, possession entails voting rights (Art. 689 CO).

(2) Board of directors

The board of directors consists of one or more members, all of whom must be shareholders (Art. 707 CO). The majority of the directors must be Swiss citizens residing in Switzerland. The Federal Government may grant exceptions for holding corporations if the majority of their holdings is in foreign countries (Art. 711 CO).

If there are several groups of shareholders with different legal status, the Articles must guarantee that each group will have at least one elected representative on the board of directors (Art. 708 CO).

The directors are elected and removed by the general meeting. The Articles provide for the directors' terms of office, three years being the maximum term for a director elected in the constituent meeting, and six years for a director elected in a later meeting (Arts 708 and 705 CO). Vacancies can be filled only by the general meeting.

Depending upon the size of the SA, there may be additional management levels, with the board acting in a supervisory capacity and the day-to-day business delegated to managers (*directeurs/Direktoren*, not to be confused with the English term 'directors'), lower echelons such as signatories, and others.

Unless otherwise provided by law, the power of the board of directors may be defined in the Articles of Incorporation or in a specific by-law provided for in the Articles of Incorporation. Even the framing of the by-law may be delegated, by the Articles of Incorporation, to the board of directors (Art. 712 CO).

Each member of the board of directors may, by written notification, require the chairman of the board to call a meeting. At the meeting, the members may require the managing officers and authorised representatives to provide all information concerning the conduct of business and any individual transaction. The board of directors may order the disclosure of all the books and records of the SA (Art. 713 CO). The board of directors appoints its chairman and secretary. It may further appoint, from among its members, one or more committees to supervise the conduct of business, prepare matters to be submitted to the board of directors, report to the board of directors on questions of importance (in particular, concerning the preparation of the balance sheet), and supervise the implementation of the board's resolution. The chairman and secretary must keep and sign minutes of the matters discussed and the resolutions passed. Minutes must be kept even when there is only one director (Arts 714 and 715 CO). The board of directors may adopt circular resolutions unless a director demands an actual meeting (Art. 716 CO). Unless otherwise provided in the Articles of Incorporation or relevant by-laws, the members of the board of directors are jointly and severally responsible for the management and the representation of the company (Art. 717 CO).

The board of directors is responsible for conducting the business of the company with due diligence. In particular, it:

(a) prepares the agenda of the shareholders' general meeting;

(b) implements its resolutions;

(c) draws up regulations for the proper conduct of the company's business;

(d) gives the necessary instructions to its management;

(e) supervises the persons who have been authorised to act for the company; and

(f) ensures that the activities of the company comply with the law, the Articles of Incorporation, and the by-laws.

The board of directors meets periodically, keeps minutes of its meetings and minutes of the shareholders' general meeting, keeps the necessary accounting records, and prepares the balance sheet and profit and loss statements in accordance with the provisions of the law (Art. 722 CO). The board of directors must submit a written annual report to the shareholders' general meeting on the company's financial position and the year-end result of its activities with any necessary explanations (Art. 724 CO).

If the last annual balance sheet shows that at least half of the nominal capital is no longer covered by net assets, the board of directors is obliged to call a shareholders' general meeting immediately and inform it of the situation. If there are reasonable grounds for assuming insolvency, an interim balance sheet must be prepared, based on liquidation values. If the liabilities exceed the assets, the board of directors must inform the court. The court thereupon may declare the company bankrupt. It may postpone the declaration if the board of directors or a creditor makes a request to this effect, and if there is a prospect of financial restructuring (Art. 725 CO).

(3) Statutory auditors

In order to control the board of directors, the general meeting of the shareholders elects one or more auditors (*organe de contrôle/Kontrollstelle*). In contrast to the members of the board of directors, they need not necessarily be shareholders. Even legal entities, such as trust companies or auditing associations, may be appointed as auditors (Art. 727 CO).

The auditors' duty is to check whether the balance sheet and the profit and loss account conform with the books of the company, and whether the books comply with the legal requirements for accounting and any special provisions of the Articles (Art. 728 CO).

The statutory auditors submit a written report to the general meeting recommending the acceptance or non-acceptance of the balance sheet and the accounts, with or without reservation. In addition, they give advice on the board of directors' proposals regarding the distribution of profits. This report is submitted before the general meeting can pass any resolutions concerning the accounts (Art. 729 CO).

The Articles or the general meeting may provide for other duties or extend the powers of the auditors. The statutory auditors may not, however, be entrusted with the statutory powers and duties of the board of directors (Art. 731 CO). See ¶801 et seq. regarding accounting in general and ¶826 et seq. on auditing in particular. Regarding the professional qualification of auditors, see ¶833.

(4) Employee participation

There is no required employee participation in the management of a corporation, and there is no government interference. A proposal to amend the Federal Constitution to introduce so-called co-determination, i.e., mandatory representation of employees on the boards of directors of share corporations, was rejected by public vote in 1976. A corporation's management is free, within the boundaries of the law, to run the corporation as it sees fit. Further, the management is free to hire and fire with notice ranging from periods of one to three months, or for cause without notice. There are no legal provisions requiring 'affirmative action'.

(5) Liability of founders, directors, auditors, liquidators

The liability of the board of directors is, in general, proportional to its relatively broad powers. The members of the board of directors, auditors, appointed directors, and managers of the company are responsible to the SA, as well as to the individual shareholders and the creditors of the SA, for damages caused intentionally or negligently by default of their duties (Art. 754 CO).

Similarly, if, on the occasion of the establishment of an SA or the issuance of shares or bonds, incorrect statements were made in a prospectus, circular, or similar notification, third parties involved (including lawyers and banks) may become liable to the SA, and to the individual stockholders and creditors for damage caused:

(a) by making incorrect or incomplete statements, or by concealing, in the Articles or in the founder's report, a capital contribution in kind, the acquisition of assets or special benefits in favour of stockholders or other persons, or by violating the law in any other manner by approving any of the above actions;

¶705

(b) by causing intentionally or negligently the official registration of the corporation based on inaccurate statements or documents;

(c) by knowingly contributing to the acceptance of subscriptions from insolvent persons.

The directors, managers, or auditors are responsible to the corporation for damage caused by an intentional or negligent default in their duties. Liquidators who intentionally or negligently default in their duties are similarly responsible to the dissolved SA, as well as to the stockholders and creditors. As long as the stockholders and creditors are damaged only indirectly, i.e., by damage caused to the SA, their claim is only for damages to be paid to the SA and not to them personally. This is to prevent the illegal repayment and reduction of corporate capital through damages. In addition, claims that any of the corporation's creditors may have for the above-mentioned reasons are further restricted in that they may be asserted only if the corporation has been declared bankrupt.

¶706 Distribution of profits of share corporation

All profits may be distributed to both foreign and domestic shareholders as dividends, except for 5 per cent of the net profit per year which must be allocated to the SA's general reserve fund until it reaches 20 per cent of the paid-in share capital.

The general reserve fund can be used freely to the extent that it exceeds half of the share capital. Otherwise, it may be used only to absorb losses or to cope with poor business conditions.

¶707 Dissolution and liquidation of share corporation

The SA is usually incorporated for an unlimited period of time, but may be dissolved and liquidated at any time if the shareholders so decide. Unless the Articles of the SA provide otherwise, such a decision can be taken at a general meeting of the shareholders where at least two-thirds of all the shares are present or represented. The shareholders also have the power to designate a liquidator. The decision to dissolve and liquidate, and the designation of the liquidator (whose task is to wind up the SA) must be filed with the Register of Commerce.

The liquidator, in turn, will have to announce the liquidation of the SA in the Official Journal of Commerce. In that announcement, the creditors of the SA are asked to file any claims they may have against the SA. This announcement must appear three times in the Official Journal of Commerce, and the SA cannot be cancelled in the Register of Commerce earlier than one year after the publication of the last of these announcements. Under special circumstances this one-year period may be shortened.

During the liquidation procedure, the SA maintains its corporate existence, which ends only with its cancellation in the Register of Commerce. This cancellation will be made by the Registrar after application and after it has received approval from the tax authorities.

Liquidation proceeds which exceed the share capital will be taxed in the same way as dividends; they are thus subject to the federal anticipatory tax of 35 per cent or as reduced by the various double taxation conventions that Switzerland has concluded with other countries (¶1007 and ¶1073).

An SA may be dissolved and liquidated for reasons other than the expiration of its fixed duration or the decision of the shareholders: namely, for good cause upon the application of shareholders holding at least one-fifth of the stock, and in the case of bankruptcy. The office of the Register of Commerce or a court may terminate an SA if it fails to meet some of the most important legal requirements, such as having a majority of Swiss citizens and residents on the board of directors, or if serious mistakes were made upon incorporation but later 'remedied' through the subsequent entry of the SA in the Register of Commerce.

¶708   Merger: dissolution without liquidation

Besides the outlined way of winding up with liquidation, there are several ways of dissolving a share corporation without liquidation, i.e., by merger, take-over and relocation to another country. If an SA is wound up in such way that its assets and liabilities are taken over by another share corporation, the following applies:

(1) The board of directors of the acquiring SA must issue a call for registration of claims by the creditors of the dissolved share corporation, according to the provisions which are applicable in the case of liquidation.

(2) The net assets of the dissolved company must be administered separately until its creditors are satisfied or secured. The administration is effected by the acquiring company.

(3) The members of the board of directors of the acquiring company are personally jointly and severally liable to the creditors for the separate administration.

(4) During the time of separate administration, the former place of *in personam* jurisdiction of the SA remains in effect.

(5) For the same period, the acquired net assets are deemed to be net assets of the dissolved SA, as far as the creditors of the dissolved SA are concerned. If the acquiring SA goes bankrupt, those net assets form a separate estate and are, as far as necessary, used exclusively for the satisfaction of the creditors of the dissolved SA.

(6) The merger of the net assets of the two companies is permitted only when net assets of a dissolved SA are distributed to its shareholders.

(7) The dissolution of the company must be registered in the Register of Commerce. The cancellation of the registration becomes effective after all creditors have been satisfied or secured.

(8) After the entry of the dissolution in the Register of Commerce, the shares of the acquiring SA designated for compensation are delivered to the shareholders of the dissolved company pursuant to the merger contract.

If an SA wishes to cancel its registration in the Register of Commerce because it has transferred its legal domicile to another country, it must submit proper evidence that it is in legal existence at its new legal domicile and, if there is a foreign register similar to the Register of Commerce, that it has been duly registered therein. The registration of the SA may be cancelled if the persons filing the application confirm that all creditors of the SA have been duly satisfied or agree with the deletion.

Several share corporations may be acquired by a newly formed SA in such a way that the net assets of the old share corporations become the net assets of the newly formed SA without liquidating the old ones. In this case, both the provisions for the incorporation of a company and those concerning the acquisition of one corporation by another are applicable. Furthermore, the following provisions apply:

(1) The corporations execute the merger contract in the form of a public deed. They set up the Articles of Incorporation of the new corporation, confirm the acquisition of the total stock and net assets of the old corporations, and appoint the necessary corporate bodies of the new corporation.

(2) The merger contract is approved by the general meeting of shareholders of each of the old share corporations.

(3) Based on the resolutions of approval, the new SA is declared incorporated in a public authenticated deed and entered in the Register of Commerce.

(4) The shares of the new SA are thereupon delivered in exchange for the old shares in accordance with the merger contract.

If an SA is dissolved in such a way that its assets and liabilities are acquired by a limited partnership with shares, the general partners are personally jointly and severally liable for the commitments of the dissolved SA. Further, the provisions regarding the acquisition of one share corporation by another share corporation are applicable.

¶708

If the net assets of a company are acquired by the Confederation, by a canton, or, under the guarantee of the canton, by a district or municipality, the shareholders can agree that a liquidation shall not take place. The resolution of the shareholders' general meeting is passed in accordance with the provisions applicable for the dissolution of an SA, and an application must be made for registration in the Register of Commerce. Upon the entry of this resolution, the transfer of the net assets of the SA, including its debts, is completed, and the SA's registration with the Register of Commerce is cancelled.

¶709   Branches of foreign corporations

A branch of a foreign corporation must be registered with the Register of Commerce at the place where the branch is located. The following information must be supplied:

- the names of the members of the board of directors,
- the country where it was organised,
- the trade name used in that country, and
- the name and nationality of the person in charge of the branch, who need not be a citizen of, but must be domiciled in, Switzerland and must have the power to represent the corporation in Switzerland.

The branch must have the same corporate name as its headquarters. In addition, the name of the branch must include the place of the branch and must indicate that it is a branch (e.g., 'XYZ Ltd, London, Geneva Branch').

The registration of the branch is published in the Official Journal of Commerce. The administrative burden involved in registering a branch office and keeping the registration current should not be underestimated.

The choice between the formal establishment of a share corporation (SA) and the opening of a branch of a foreign corporation in Switzerland is not always easy. Obviously, the costs of the staff and the premises of a given business enterprise in Switzerland are roughly the same, regardless of the legal structure. Since a corporation requires a board consisting of a majority of Swiss nationals residing in Switzerland, any foreign board member from the parent company must be offset by a Swiss. This may result in additional, but hardly decisive, expense.

Tax considerations may be more important for the decision but cannot be detailed here, since they depend primarily on the existence and contents of an applicable double taxation convention. Certainly, it will be of utmost importance that the earnings and profits, as well as the assets, of a Swiss permanent establishment maintained by a non-resident enterprise not be taxed twice. Usually the applicable double taxation convention contains specific allocation rules. In the absence of a treaty, the law of the domicile of the headquarters of the corporation may avoid double taxation, either by providing for a credit of Swiss income taxes paid or by excluding earnings, profits and assets of the Swiss permanent establishment from taxation in the headquarters' country. A Swiss branch of a non-Swiss company provides several tax planning advantages: one may use losses of the branch, deduct interest paid by the branch to the headquarters of the foreign corporation, etc. (see ¶1052(2)).

LIMITED LIABILITY COMPANIES AND CO-OPERATIVE CORPORATIONS

¶710   Limited liability companies

The limited liability company (*société à responsabilité limitée*, Sàrl/*Gesellschaft mit beschränkter Haftung*, GmbH; hereafter, 'Sàrl') is a separate legal entity formed by two or more individuals or companies under a corporate name and with fixed registered capital for commercial, industrial or other profit-making purposes. The owners or shareholders participate in the capital with fixed shares which do not correspond to corporate shares. In certain cases prescribed by law, the shareholders may be held liable for an amount in excess of their shares, but only up to the amount of the registered capital. The registered capital must amount to at least SFr 20,000 but may not exceed SFr 2,000,000. A minimum of 50 per cent must be paid in in cash or in kind by each of the registered capital shareholders at the formation of the company. A Sàrl is a cross between a share corporation (SA) and a partnership, but, unlike the widely used German GmbH, it does not offer any specific advantages over the corporation and is thus rarely used.

The firm name of a Sàrl may be freely chosen. It must, however, disclose that it is a limited liability company (Art. 949 CO).

The Articles of Incorporation must state the corporate name, the seat, the purpose, the amount of common capital, the capital contribution of each member and the form of notice given by the corporation. There are no restrictions as to the nationality of the members, but at least one of the business executives of the company must have his or her domicile in Switzerland.

The company is incorporated by the members by executing a publicly authenticated deed, including the Articles of Incorporation and a declaration of the shareholders stating that they have subscribed all capital contributions and that the amount required by law or by the Articles of Incorporation has been paid. The company is incorporated upon its entry into the Register of Commerce (¶702).

Any amendment to the Articles of Incorporation must be publicly authenticated and entered into the Register of Commerce (Art. 785 CO).

¶710

The documents issued to the members must not be negotiable instruments; rather, they are used only for documentary proof. All capital contributions and alterations thereof must be recorded and communicated yearly to the Register of Commerce. The assignment of a share requires a public deed and becomes effective with respect to the company only after the latter has received notice and has entered the transfer in the share register. Subject to contrary provisions in the Articles of Incorporation, the entry requires the consent of at least three-fourths of the members in number and common capital, except in the cases of transfer by death or marital property law (Arts 789 to 792 CO).

The members' meeting is the supreme body of the Sàrl. Every member has one vote for each SFr 1,000 of his or her contribution, unless the Articles of Incorporation provide otherwise. The total exclusion of a member from voting is prohibited. The members' meeting has exclusive competence for certain measures, e.g., revision of the Articles of Incorporation, appointment and removal of managers and internal auditors, adoption of the balance sheet and the profit and loss statement, distribution of profits and discharge of managers (Art. 810 CO).

In general, all members participate jointly in the management and the representation of the Sàrl, unless the Articles of Incorporation or a resolution of the members' meeting provides otherwise. By these two means, the company may confer management and representation upon non-members. The managers sign for the Sàrl by adding their names to the firm name (Arts 811 to 815 CO).

The rules of share corporations apply with certain modifications to the scope of representation of a Sàrl (Art. 814 CO).

The Articles of Incorporation may grant a right of withdrawal to the members. If applicable, members may petition the court to grant them the right to withdraw or to dissolve the Sàrl with cause. The Sàrl may, for the same reason, request the court to expel a member, but only with the consent of the majority of the members representing the majority of the common capital (Art. 822 CO).

The dissolution of a Sàrl is effected, according to the Articles of Incorporation, by a publicly authenticated resolution of at least three-quarters of the members, representing at least three-fourths of the common capital. It is also effected in the event of bankruptcy, by judgment or for other grounds provided by the law (Arts 820, 822 and 775 CO). The provisions for the share corporation apply to the liquidation procedure of a Sàrl.

Since a Sàrl is a separate legal entity, it is subject to federal and cantonal income and capital taxation.

¶711   Co-operative corporations

The co-operative corporation (*société cooperative/Genossenschaft*) has similarities with the United States co-operative. It is an entity organised along corporate lines, whose main purpose is the promotion or protection of specific economic interests of an unrestricted number of persons or commercially oriented companies. The capital is not fixed in advance, and the liability of the co-operative corporation is limited to its own assets unless the by-laws contain express stipulations to the contrary.

As to the corporate name of the co-operative corporation, the provisions for share corporations apply.

The co-operative corporation is incorporated by registration in the Register of Commerce. Its Articles of Incorporation, containing the corporate name, the seat, the purpose, the liabilities of members, if any, the organisation and the form of publication, must be in writing and be approved by a meeting of at least seven incorporators (Arts 830 to 838 CO).

The Articles of Incorporation may provide for certificates of membership. The certificates are made in the member's name. They do not constitute documents of title but are only documents of proof. The transfer of these certificates of membership confers membership rights to the transferee if a resolution of admittance is passed (Arts 852, 853 and 849 CO).

The supreme authority rests with the members' general meeting, which has the following powers: to pass or amend the Articles of Incorporation, elect directors and internal auditors, approve operating accounts and balance sheets, distribute profits and grant releases to directors, and exercise other powers provided for by law or by the Articles. The majority of directors must be members and Swiss citizens residing in Switzerland. The auditors must examine the conduct of business and the yearly accounts. The directors, the members of the executive committee, the auditors and the liquidators are liable for damages due to negligence or wilful violation of their duties (Arts 879 to 910, 916 to 920 CO).

New members may be admitted at any time upon written application. As long as the winding-up of the co-operative corporation has not been decided, the members may withdraw at any time, subject to restrictive conditions provided for in the Articles of Incorporation (Arts 839 and 842 CO).

The dissolution takes place as provided for in the Articles of Incorporation upon resolution of the general meeting of members, in the case of bankruptcy or in other cases provided by law (Art. 911 CO).

The co-operative corporation is a separate legal entity and, as an organisation, subject to federal and cantonal income and capital taxation.

¶711

PARTNERSHIPS

¶712   Ordinary partnerships

An ordinary partnership (*société simple/einfache Gesellschaft*) is a very loose organisation based on a contract without any particular formal requirements. It usually serves only a specific and temporary purpose (similar to a joint venture). It is not entered in the Register of Commerce (¶702) and carries no firm name of its own. Its main characteristic is the joint and several liability of the partners for the partnership's liabilities in regard to third persons.

An ordinary partnership is not a corporate body; it cannot acquire rights or assume obligations, and it has no standing to sue or to be sued; its rights and obligations pertain jointly and severally to all the partners (Art. 544 CO).

Unless otherwise agreed, each partner must contribute to the ordinary partnership an equal share of capital (goods, credits) or labour and have an equal share of the profits or losses. All partners participate jointly in the management unless they agree otherwise (Arts 531 and 535 CO). No partner may frustrate the purpose of the partnership (in particular, partners may not conduct a business in competition with the partnership).

If the management has been conferred upon a partner, third parties may assume that this partner can act for the partnership (or all the partners). If the partnership agreement does not provide otherwise, the personal creditors of one partner can execute only his or her share of liquidation of the partnership. But the partners are jointly and severally liable for the liabilities entered into (jointly) by the partnership or their representative (Art. 544 CO).

A partnership is terminated if its purpose is achieved, by agreement, death, incapacitation or bankruptcy of a partner, judicial dissolution for cause, and, in some circumstances, timely notice. The partners remain liable to third parties.

The ordinary partnership as an organisation is not subject to federal or cantonal income or capital taxation. Profits of the ordinary partnership are taxable as the personal income of the respective partners. Assets of the ordinary partnership are subject to the personal net-worth tax of the respective partners.

¶713   General partnerships

A general partnership (*société en nom collectif/Kollektivgesellschaft*) is an organisation of two or more individuals (corporations cannot be partners) with unlimited liability towards creditors, normally formed under a firm name for the purpose of operating a trading, industrial, or other enterprise based on commercial principles. A general partnership is formed under a partnership agreement and must be entered in the Register of Commerce. It corresponds roughly to the United States partnership.

The firm name must include the family name of at least one partner and indicate the existence of the partnership (Art. 947 CO).

The relationship between the partners is laid down by the partnership agreement or, in the absence of an agreement, by the rules for ordinary partnerships, with certain modifications relating to accounting and profit distribution (Arts 557 to 561 CO).

A general partnership is not a corporation. Nevertheless, it can acquire rights and assume liabilities, and it has standing to sue and to be sued. The partnership is liable for torts committed and legal transactions carried out by a partner when acting for the partnership (Arts 562 and 567 CO).

In order to be valid *vis-à-vis* third persons, restrictions on the representation of the partnership must be entered in the Register of Commerce. Otherwise, third parties may assume in good faith that each partner has the right to act for the partnership. Partners may be deprived of their right to represent the partnership with cause. Third parties may be appointed to act for the partnership only with the consent of all partners (Arts 563 to 565 CO).

The partners are jointly and severally liable with their entire assets for the liabilities of the partnership. A new partner is also liable for pre-existing liabilities of the partnership. Bankruptcy of the general partnership does not entail bankruptcy of the individual partners, nor vice versa. In order to receive satisfaction or security for their claims, the personal creditors of a partner are entitled only to his or her interest, remuneration and profits and share of liquidation. A partner can be rendered liable only for claims against the partnership and can be sued if the partnership is bankrupt, dissolved or executed and if the creditors have not been satisfied. This does not prejudice a partner's personal guarantee (Arts 568 to 573 CO).

Partners can be held liable even if they have left the partnership. Claims against individual partners for liabilities of the partnership are barred five years after the publication of their resignation or the dissolution of the partnership in the Official Journal of Commerce (Arts 591 to 593 CO).

With certain exceptions, the rules governing the dissolution of an ordinary partnership also apply to the dissolution of a general partnership. A general partnership can be dissolved if it declares bankruptcy. The partners who have the right to act for the partnership take care of the liquidation. If a partnership is dissolved, the partners, and in some cases the competent court, may appoint or remove special liquidators. These must be entered in the Register of Commerce. After the liquidation, the firm name must be cancelled in the Register of Commerce. The books and documents must be deposited for ten years in a place determined by the partners or, in the case of disagreement, at the office of the Register of Commerce (Arts 574 to 590 CO).

The general partnership as an organisation is not subject to any federal or cantonal taxation. Profits of the general partnership are taxable as the personal income of the respective partners. Assets of the general partnership are subject to the personal net-worth tax of the respective partners.

¶714   Limited partnerships

The limited partnership (*société en commandite/Kommanditgesellschaft*) differs from the general partnership in that at least one partner (the general partner) is fully liable for the debts and obligations of the firm, while the liability of the other partner or partners is limited up to a fixed amount of their contributions (limited partners). Natural persons may be both general and limited partners, while legal entities may only be limited partners (Art. 594 CO). This corresponds approximately to the United States limited partnership.

The establishment of a limited partnership is similar to that of general partnerships. The firm name must include the last name of at least one general partner and indicate the existence of the partnership (Art. 947 CO).

The relationship between the partners is laid down by the partnership agreement. In the absence of an agreement, the provisions for general partnership apply, with the following difference. The general partners are in charge of managing the partnership; limited partners have no right or obligation in this respect. They cannot object to ordinary business transactions. Limited partners are entitled to receive a copy of the balance sheet and the profit and loss statement, which may be audited by them or by an independent expert (Arts 598 to 601 CO).

A limited partnership may acquire rights and assume liabilities. It has standing to sue and to be sued in the same manner as a general partnership (Art. 602 CO).

Limited partners are responsible for the liabilities of the partnership up to the amount of their contributions, as entered into the Register of Commerce, unless they, or the partnership with their knowledge, have led others to believe that they would be liable for a higher amount. Limited partners are liable without limitation (Arts 603 to 609):

(1) for transactions concluded by them for the partnership without an express statement claiming that they acted as agents or under a power of attorney;

(2) for liabilities incurred before the registration of the partnership or of the limitation of their contributions, unless the creditor knew of their actual status; or

(3) if the last names of the limited partners form part of the partnership's firm name.

For general partners in a limited partnership, as a rule, the same provisions apply as for partners in a general partnership.

The provisions for dissolution and liquidation of a general partnership are applicable to a limited partnership, except that the death or incapacitation of, or establishment of guardianship for, a limited partner does not cause dissolution of the partnership (Arts 613 to 619 CO).

The limited partnership as a mere organisation is not subject to federal or cantonal income taxation. Profits of the limited partnership are taxable as personal income of the general or limited partners. Assets of the limited partnership are subject to the personal net worth tax of the general or limited partners.

¶715 Limited partnerships with shares

The limited partnership with shares, or partnership limited by shares (*société en commandite par actions/Kommanditaktiengesellschaft*) is a rather rare form of business organisation. It combines the characteristics of both the corporation and the limited partnership, and is utilised if one or more persons decide to assume the management of an enterprise as partners with full liability but need capital. The capital of the limited partnership with shares is divided into shares so that it can be raised by subscription. In addition to the corporate capital, one or more shareholders (the general partners) have joint unlimited personal liability in the same way as the partners of the general partnership (Arts 764 and 568 CO).

Unless specifically provided otherwise, the rules governing share corporations apply (see ¶703 et seq.).

The firm name must include the family name of at least one general partner and indicate the existence of the partnership and the corporate body (Art. 947 CO).

The general partners must be named in the Articles. They conduct the business, act and sign for the corporation and form the board of directors. The majority of the general partners must be resident Swiss citizens. The federal government may grant exceptions for holding corporations if the majority of their holdings are located in foreign countries. At least one general partner must be domiciled in Switzerland (Arts 765, 764 and 711 CO).

The consent of the general partners is required for the resolution of a general meeting whose subject is the extension or restriction of the scope of the business or the extension of the duration of the limited partnership with shares beyond a period fixed in the Articles (Art. 766 CO).

A statutory auditor must be appointed by the general meeting, in which the general partners have no right to vote. This auditor, as the supervisor, may, in cases of bad faith, sue the directors in court, even when he or she has been relieved from liability (Arts 768 and 769 CO).

The limited partnership with shares is dissolved by the retirement, death, incapacity or bankruptcy of all general partners. In all other respects the rules for the dissolution of the share corporation apply (Art. 770 CO).

The general partner may withdraw from the partnership by giving notice, just as in a general partnership. However, unless otherwise provided for in the Articles, the limited partnership with shares continues to exist if at least one general partner remains (Art. 771 CO).

The limited partnership with shares is an independent legal entity, separate from its general partners. As a result, the limited partnership is subject to federal and cantonal income and capital taxation.

ASSOCIATIONS, FOUNDATIONS AND TRUSTS

¶716 Associations

Originally, the typical association (*association/Verein*) was drawn up as an organisation to pursue non-profit objectives and engage in beneficial, scientific, cultural, political and social activities (Art. 60 CC). In fact, today many of the more important associations are established to pursue economic goals, for instance, professional organisations and trade unions. Non-profit associations may, for the better attainment of their goals, carry on an industrial or commercial activity (Art. 61 CC). But such additional activity must be of a subsidiary character; it may not be the principal object of the association.

The Federal Supreme Court has decided to allow atypical associations that were established for purely economic purposes as long as they do not carry on any industrial or commercial business as subsidiary activities to sustain the achievement of their economic purposes.

Associations acquire the status of a juridical person with a separate legal entity as soon as the Articles of Association are drawn up. The Articles must be drawn up in writing and state the intention to have a corporate existence and the object, means and organisation of the association.

Registration is compulsory for associations which carry on an industrial or commercial activity for the better attainment of their non-profit goal.

Even when registered, the association has no corporate name. Therefore, the legal provisions for the protection of corporate names (Art. 956 CO) do not apply. The name of the association is protected by the general provisions of Art. 29 et seq. CC.

The association's corporate bodies are:

(1) the general meeting of the members; and

(2) the officers.

The members' general meeting decides on the admission and expulsion of members, appoints and removes the officers, and decides on all matters not specifically assigned to any other body of the association. Any resolution affecting the association must be passed by the general meeting. The powers of the general meeting are limited by law; a change of the association's objective cannot be forced upon any of its members (Art. 65 et seq., 74 CC). The officers have the right and the duty to manage the affairs of the association and to represent it in accordance with the provisions of its Articles (Art. 69 CC).

At any time, new members can be admitted by simple resolution of the general meeting. All members have equal votes at the general meeting and are by law entitled to resign their membership, provided they observe the six-month period of notice before the end of a calendar or an administrative year (Art. 70 CC).

The contributions of the members to the association are fixed by the Articles of Association. If the Articles fail to fix contributions, members must contribute equally to the necessary expenses incurred in carrying out the object of the association and to the payment of its debts. If the members' contributions are fixed by the Articles, and they do not contain additional provisions to the contrary, the liability of the association is limited to its own assets.

An association may be dissolved by a resolution of the general meeting, in accordance with specific provisions of the Articles, by operation of law, or by court order (Art. 76 et seq. CC).

Associations with charitable or other non-profit objectives are usually exempt from taxation. Otherwise, associations are treated as individuals for federal income tax purposes. The cantonal treatment of non-exempted associations varies, but they are usually taxed as corporations.

¶717 Foundations

A foundation (*fondation/Stiftung*) is a separate legal entity constituted by the founder by dedicating funds for a specific object (Art. 80 CC). The intention of the founder, as evidenced by the stated purpose, is the essential and determining element of the foundation.

In contrast to all other forms of organisations provided by corporate law and mentioned above, the foundation is not a corporate entity constituted by members but an institution without members, provided with its own assets to attain a given specific object. In principle, the object, as defined by the founder, is fixed and cannot be modified after the establishment of the foundation. Fixed objectives and the absence of members make any provision for a specific decision-making process unnecessary. The officers of the foundation have, in principle, no decision-making power, only an executive function. The given objective of the foundation determines the use of its assets, which may only be used in furtherance of that objective.

A foundation is established in a publicly authenticated deed or in the form of a will (Art. 81 CC). After registration in the Register of Commerce, the foundation is established and has the status of a juridical person. For family and church foundations, registration is not required (Art. 87 CC). Foundations established by the founder with the intention to violate the rights of heirs or creditors can be challenged by the injured parties, just as in the case of a founder's gift to a third party (Art. 82 CC). Foundations with illegal or immoral objective cannot acquire the status of a legal entity.

The organisation of the foundation, especially its governing bodies, must be indicated in the deed of establishment (publicly authenticated instrument, last will). At least one body must be defined to manage and represent the foundation, according to the objectives that were specified by the founder. The function of this executive body may be discharged by an individual or a legal entity. In default of organisational provisions in the instrument of establishment, the supervisory authority must make all the necessary provisions. If the foundation cannot be organised in accordance with its object – for example, if the fund is clearly inadequate to carry out the object – the supervisory authority must devote the fund to another foundation that has a similar purpose, provided the founder does not oppose this and the instrument of establishment contains no contrary provision (Art. 83 CC).

Foundations are subject to the supervision of the Confederation or of the canton or municipality with which the object is connected (Art. 84 CC). The supervisory authority must ensure that the funds are used, in all cases, in accordance with the object of the foundation. The competent cantonal authority or federal supervising authority can bring about changes in its organisation if these changes are urgently required for the preservation of the funds and the maintenance of the object of the foundation (Art. 85 CC). The same procedure is provided by law to modify the object of the foundation where it has acquired a totally different significance or effect, so that the foundation has manifestly ceased to carry out the intention of the founder. The same procedure applies to the suppression or modification of the conditions imposed on the foundation, where they are prejudicial to the performance of its objective (Art. 86 CC).

The dissolution of a foundation takes place *ipso iure* where its object has become unattainable. It is dissolved by court order where its object has become illegal or immoral (Art. 88 CC). The governing bodies may not voluntarily dissolve a foundation.

It is most common to use the organisational form of a foundation to hold pension funds and other welfare schemes of corporations. For this specific type of foundations, additional provisions apply (Art. 89bis CC).

Foundations for pension and other welfare schemes are exempt from taxation. For the federal income tax, regular foundations are taxed as individuals. The cantonal treatment of non-exempt foundations varies: in some cantons, these foundations are taxed as individuals, and in others, as corporations.

¶717

¶718 Trusts

There is no law of trust. The function of trusts may be fulfilled by foundations, fiduciary contracts, mandate, and the concept of unjust enrichment. Foreign trusts may be recognised as legal entities unless the rules on piercing the corporate veil apply (¶719). For taxation of foreign trusts, see ¶1042.

PIERCING THE CORPORATE VEIL

¶719 Only where an entity is used against good faith

The corporate veil is pierced, and the separate existence of a corporate entity is disregarded altogether, only in exceptional cases. Where someone uses a legal entity in order to circumvent his or her legal obligations, such as to frustrate a non-competition clause or to escape taxation, the law looks at the economic realities rather than the legal form. If a legal entity is used to purchase Swiss immovable property in violation of the Federal Statute on the Acquisition of Immovables by Non-resident Aliens, the transaction is null and void, the entity is dissolved and its assets are confiscated.

SELECTED BIBLIOGRAPHY

Peter Forstmoser, *Schweizerisches Aktienrecht*, vol. 1 (Zürich, 1981)

Arthur Meier-Hayoz and Peter Forstmoser, *Grundriss des schweizerischen Gesellschaftsrechts*, 6th edn (Bern, 1989)

Robert Patry, *Précis de droit suisse des sociétés*, vol. 1 (Bern, 1976), vol. 2 (Bern, 1977)

Rudolf Tschäni, *Unternehmensübernahmen nach Schweizer Recht*, 2nd edn (Basel, 1991)

Nedim Peter Vogt and Rolf Watter, *'Switzerland'*, in *Mergers and Acquisitions in Europe*, 1990

Rolf Watter, *Unternehmensübernahmen* (Zürich, 1990)

8 Accounting and Auditing

PRINCIPAL LEGISLATION

Code des obligations/Obligationenrecht/Code of Obligations (CO), RS 220.

Ordonnance sur le registre du commerce/Handelsregisterverordnung/ Ordinance on the Register of Commerce, RS 222.411.

Ordonnance concernant l'enregistrement des documents à conserver/ Verordnung uber die Aufzeichnung vou aufzubewahrender Unterlagen/ Ordinance on the Registration and Preservation of Accounting Records, RS 221.431.

Loi fédérale sur les fonds de placement/Anlagefondsgesetz/Investment Funds Statute, RS 951.31.

Ordonnance sur les fonds de placement/Anlagefondsverordnung/Investment Funds Ordinance, RS 951.311.

Ordonnance sur les étrangers de placement fonds/Auslandfondsverordnung/ Ordinance on Foreign Investment Funds, RS 951.312.

Loi fédérale sur les banques et les caisses d'épargne/Bankengesetz/Banking Statute, RS 952.0.

Ordonnance sur les banques et les caisses d'épargne/Bankenverordnung/ Banking Ordinance, RS 952.02.

Ordonnance concernant les banques étrangères en Suisse/Auslandbanken-verordnung/Ordinance on Foreign Banks, RS 952.111.

Loi fédérale sur la surveillance des institutions d'assurance privées/ Versicherungsaufsichtsgesetz/Insurance Supervision Statute, RS 961.01.

Ordonnance sur la surveillance des institutions d'assurance privées/ Aufsichtsverordnung/Insurance Supervision Ordinance, RS 961.05.

Code pénal suisse/Strafgesetzbuch/Penal Code, RS 311.0.

ACCOUNTING IN GENERAL

¶801   The Swiss approach: conservatism and limited disclosure

The Swiss system of accounting and financial reporting is conservative. Article 663(2) CO allows management to undervalue assets in the balance sheet and to create other undisclosed reserves to the extent that the undervaluation appears necessary to ensure the continued prosperity of the company and an even dividend-distribution policy.

This practice of undisclosed ('hidden') reserves and limited disclosure, together with minimal protection and information of shareholders and creditors, especially where privately controlled companies are concerned, has been criticised.

Guide-lines and recommendations issued by the European Community are of increasing influence on both legislation and practice in the field of accounting and reporting.

¶802   Obligation to keep books of account

The general principles of commercial accounting that apply to all business entities recorded in the Register of Commerce are laid down in Arts 957 to 964 CO. They require that financial statements be complete, true and clear, and drawn up in accordance with generally accepted accounting principles. Business entities registered with the Register of Commerce must meet minimum accounting standards. They must keep such books of account as are necessary, according to the nature and extent of their business, to properly reflect the financial situation of the business and to determine liabilities and claims in connection therewith. Further, the books must accurately reflect the results of each business year.

The obligation of business entities to register their firm is governed by the Ordinance on the Register of Commerce. Under this ordinance, any entity carrying on a trade, manufacture or other business activity with a gross turnover in excess of SFr 100,000 must be registered and is required to keep books of account.

These entities are required to establish an inventory and a balance sheet at the start of their operations. Further, they must establish an inventory, a profit and loss account, and a balance sheet at the end of every business year. The inventory, the profit and loss account and the balance sheet must be drawn up within a reasonable period of time following the end of the business year.

Business entities that are required to keep books must keep those and their business correspondence on file for a period of ten years (Art. 962(1) CO). The profit and loss account and the balance sheet must be preserved in their original form; the other books and business correspondence can be kept on microfiches.

In case of litigation, the court can order that the books and correspondence be produced.

More detailed rules apply to share corporations and co-operative corporations. They define the rules and methods used for the determination of distributable profits and the protection of creditors. Other special provisions on financial accounting and reporting are contained in the Federal Banking Statute and in the statutes governing mutual funds, insurance companies and pension funds.

¶803   Rules applicable to share corporations and other entities

In addition to the general rules of accounting, the Code of Obligations regulates the preparation of financial accounts and reports, the distribution of dividends and contributions to legal and free reserves by share corporations.

These rules also apply to co-operative corporations and partnerships.

¶804   Criminal law

One who intentionally or negligently fails to keep proper books of account can be punished by fine or arrest (Art. 325 Penal Code). If bankruptcy is declared, the failure to keep books and to preserve the business records may result in a fine or imprisonment (Art. 166 Penal Code).

¶805   Special rules for banks, insurance companies, etc.

(1)   Banks

Banks must comply with more stringent accounting requirements than other share corporations.

The Banking Statute provides that a bank must draw up annual statements. The balance sheet must comply with the requirements of both the Code of Obligations and the Banking Statute. Banks with total assets of at least SFr 50 million must draw up an interim balance sheet every six months; those with assets of SFr 200 million or more must draw up an interim balance sheet every three months.

The structure of the annual statements and of the interim balance sheet is shown in the Banking Ordinance. Arts 23 to 27 of the Banking Ordinance contain an exhaustive list of the items to be included in the report. The balance sheet is published in the Official Journal of Commerce.

(2)   Companies listed on stock exchange

The operation of the stock exchanges and the listing of securities are governed by cantonal law (¶1104). In order to be listed on an exchange, share corporations must comply with a certain number of requirements stated in the applicable regulations. While listed corporations are required to keep books (as per Code of Obligations, Banking Statute, and the Investment Funds Statute if applicable), the regulations issued by the stock exchanges basically do not impose additional accounting requirements. The stock exchange regulations aim at ensuring sufficient disclosure of financial statements by the listed corporations.

(3) Investment funds

The Investment Funds Statute and Ordinance contain guide-lines on accounting and reporting (Art. 15 Investment Funds Statute and Arts 14 to 30 Investment Funds Ordinance). They contain, for example, detailed statements and an exhaustive catalogue of items to be entered on the books. Accounting systems are provided for investment funds investing in securities and immovable property (Arts 14, 25 and 26 Investment Funds Ordinance).

(4) Insurance companies

Insurance companies are subject to supervision by the Federal Insurance Office (¶1402). They must draw up their annual balance sheet on 31 December of each year. The balance sheet is published in the Official Journal of Commerce (Art. 21 et seq. Insurance Supervision Statute). Swiss insurance companies must file a succinct report covering the last business year with the Federal Insurance Office. Non-Swiss insurance companies are required to file each year with the Federal Insurance Office an exhaustive report, detailing almost every aspect of their financial situation and commercial activity (Art. 22 et seq. Insurance Supervision Statute). The Insurance Supervision Ordinance contains detailed guide-lines on the assets that the insurance companies are required to set aside as security (Art. 4 et seq.).

(5) Other requirements

In addition, various statutes, ordinances and decrees on both the federal and cantonal levels contain further guide-lines and requirements on accounting procedures. These provisions are of lesser importance. Mass transport systems, health insurance carriers and the state-controlled unemployment and old-age insurers must comply with specific requirements. Special provisions also apply to individuals or corporations in bankruptcy or analogous proceedings.

¶806 Tax accounting

Individuals and legal entities must comply with uniform, specific accounting and reporting requirements of the applicable tax statutes. As a rule, the annual statement established in accordance with the Code of Obligations and other statutes, such as the Banking and the Investment Funds Statutes, constitutes a sufficient basis for the tax assessment. However, the tax authorities are free to adjust the statements and balance sheets drawn up in compliance with these provisions in order to bring the statements into line with the provisions of the pertinent tax statute, provided mandatory accounting rules are not violated. Thus, unduly accelerated write-offs, excessive creations of reserves, inflated expenses and overstated pension plan contributions may be reduced (e.g., Art. 22(1)(b) Federal Income Tax Decree; Arts 25(b) and 45 Zurich Tax Statute; Art. 66(e) Geneva Tax Statute). The anticipation of future expenses, the deferred accrual of revenues and the failure to reduce liabilities as appropriate may also prompt the tax authorities to proceed to adjustments.

While the tax authorities are free to proceed to such adjustments, the taxpayers are bound *vis-à-vis* the tax authorities by their books of accounts. Statements established in accordance with the applicable principles cannot trigger the criminal responsibility of the taxpayer, even if they do not reflect the economic reality.

Since general accounting principles are more liberal than tax rules, corporations often establish different financial reports for the shareholders and the tax authorities.

ACCOUNTING PRINCIPLES

¶807   Sources of law

The Code of Obligations contains general rules of accounting that apply to all business entities. These rules are far from being exhaustive. In contrast, the part of the Code of Obligations dealing with share corporations contains rules that are more detailed. For practical reasons, the following overview is based mostly on the principles applicable to share corporations. If appropriate, reference is made to the principles governing other business organisations, such as partnerships or corporations with banking or investment activities.

¶808   Principles of valuation

Accountants must be prudent (principle of conservatism), limit themselves to simple inquiries (principle of economic feasibility), stick to the essentials (principle of materiality), consider that the entity is a going concern (principle of going concern), be truthful (principle of sincerity), be clear (principle of clarity) and be consistent (principle of continuity) (Arts 959 and 960 CO).

Fixed assets permanently used for the conduct of business (such as land, buildings, power installations, machinery, transportation equipment, tools and movable property) must be carried in the balance sheet at no higher than their purchase price, less the depreciation applicable under the circumstances. The same method of valuation applies to rights, concessions, patents, special manufacturing processes, licences, trade marks and similar intangible assets (Art. 665 CO). Inventory and other items for sale may not be carried at a higher value than their purchase price or manufacturing costs (Art. 666 CO). If the manufacturing costs exceed the market value on the date of the balance sheet, they must be considered. Quoted securities must not be valued at a price higher than their average stock exchange price during the month prior to the date of the balance sheet (Art. 667 CO). Unquoted securities may not be entered in the balance sheet at a value higher than cost, with appropriate consideration given to higher income (interest, dividends) and any possible increase in value.

¶809   Depreciation

In making adequate provisions for depreciation and obsolescence through write-offs, the straight-line, the declining-balance or the sum-of-the-years'-digits methods may be applied. Alternatively, depreciation may be provided for by creating a sinking or a replacement fund that appears on the liability side of the balance sheet (Art. 665(3) CO). The tax authorities may apply the method of writing off that they deem appropriate for the asset at issue (¶806).

¶810   Capital and reserves

Reserves to cover anticipated losses arising from contingent liabilities and transactions yet to be concluded must be reported (Art. 670 CO). They include set-asides for contingent liabilities, warranty works, other anticipated liabilities and reserves for unpaid taxes. The Banking Ordinance and various tax statutes contain similar provisions, allowing or obliging the accountant or taxpayer to set apart funds to compensate anticipated losses.

   The Code of Obligations requires share corporations to allocate one-twentieth of their net profits each year to a general reserve fund until this fund amounts to one-fifth of the paid-in capital (legal reserve fund). In addition, the following items must be paid into this fund, even if it exceeds one-fifth of the paid-in capital:

(1) proceeds from the issuance of shares in excess of par value (share premium, *agio*);

(2) the excess of the amount which was paid in on cancelled shares; and

(3) one-tenth of the amount distributed from net profits after deduction of ordinary allocations to reserves and the payment of a 5 per cent dividend to stockholders.

As long as the general reserve fund amounts to less than 50 per cent of the capital, it can be used only to absorb losses, to help the company to overcome periods of depressed business, or to relieve unemployment or mitigate its consequences (Art. 671 CO).

The Articles of Incorporation may provide that more than one-twentieth of the net profits shall be allocated to the general reserve fund in excess of one-fifth of the share capital. In addition, other types of reserve funds may be established (Art. 672 CO). The various reserve funds must be disclosed separately in the balance sheet.

The statutory rules on assessing assets constitute maximum amounts for determining the annual profit. However, since the rules do not provide for minimum amounts, the management is free to undervalue disclosed assets (and to overvalue disclosed liabilities).

¶811   Inventories

Raw materials, manufactured and semi-manufactured goods, inventories, and other items intended for sale must be listed in the books at the lower of cost value or market price (Art. 666 CO). The cost value may be determined according to the FIFO, LIFO or average method. For finished goods and goods for trade, the market value is defined as the sales price less costs of storage, administration, selling and distribution. Declining purchase prices for raw materials and other items that affect the value of finished or semi-finished goods have to be accounted for. In the case of work-in-progress, a foreseeable loss arising from low market prices must be anticipated and fully provided for.

¶812   Research, development and exploration

Research and development are usually not capitalised since tangible results are uncertain and probably remote in time. In addition, costs do not necessarily correspond to anticipated revenues. Costs of fundamental research are usually charged to the current profit and loss account. Costs of research and development directly related to a marketable product may, but need not, be capitalised up to the amount of reasonably anticipated future earnings; if capitalised, the costs are written off over five years at the latest as when corresponding revenue materialises.

Costs of establishing a share corporation or other business organisation may be capitalised as a separate item on the asset side of the balance, and must be written off on a straight-line basis over a period of five years or less.

Generally, the goodwill of a business does not constitute an asset. However, the acquirer of the assets and liabilities of an existing business may capitalise the goodwill paid for and properly identified. Depending on the nature of the goodwill, the acquirer then must write it off over a five-year period.

¶813 Long-term contracts

A contract to sell goods in the future, unlike unilateral contracts that do not involve mutual performances, need not be reported. If it is possible to anticipate the losses that will be suffered up to the closing date of the financial statement, they must be provided against. In contrast, expected profits may be taken into account only if they materialise. If performance of a long-term contract stretches over several business periods, the share corporation must list on its financial statements the costs stemming from its partial performance. Conversely, the share corporation may recognise an appropriate fraction of the anticipated overall profit.

¶814 Leasing

Generally, lessees need disclose neither their leased assets nor their leasing commitments, as a leasing agreement does not convey title to the leased item to the lessee.

Economically speaking, a lease can be tantamount to an outright purchase. As a result, there is a growing tendency to consider that the lessee, as economic proprietor, must report the leased item. This is particularly true in cases involving financial leasing. Lessees may decide to include leased assets and leasing commitments in their balance sheets, in which case they must clearly state that they have no formal title to these assets. In light of current case law and the view adopted by the majority of legal writers, leasing is still characterised as a mere rental agreement, i.e., payments made under the lease are fully booked as expenses.

The lessor is required to capitalise the assets leased and depreciate them over the period of the lease contract. A common alternative to a lease is a sale on a fixed instalment basis, where the seller retains title on the goods sold (¶904(4) and ¶1705(2)). In this case, the seller discloses the receivables not yet due at their net amount. In the business period when the instalments become due, the seller takes them into account as profit.

¶815 Foreign currency conversion

All items listed on the inventory, the profit and loss statement, and the balance sheet must be expressed in Swiss Francs. There is no requirement that the day-to-day accounting be done in Swiss currency.

As a general rule, exchange gains are recorded only when realised. Exceptions are made for cash and liabilities, precious metals and quoted securities. Losses are taken into account as soon as they are anticipated. Adequate provisions are made against risks arising from currency positions. These rules are not strictly followed by banks and financial institutions, however, which convert their foreign currency positions at the year-end rate.

¶816   Principle of imparity

As a rule, only revenue accrued and expenses incurred during a given accounting period are listed in the statements pertaining to this period. Revenue is reported upon delivery of goods or performance of services, unless the contract can be considered already performed at the time of its execution. In contrast, losses are reported as soon as they are anticipated (principle of imparity). If items stemming from a previous accounting period by way of exception are reported, they are disclosed separately on the statement.

¶817   Changes in price level

Inflation accounting is not practised, this accounting method being contrary to the Code of Obligations.

The management is well advised to disclose the impact of inflation in separate statements. By increasing the write-offs, adopting the LIFO method for the valuation of inventory, and creating reserves for the replacement of items, the management can account for inflation, at least partially.

¶818   Pensions

To secure payment of pension benefits, pension funds must be administered by legal entities separate from the employer (Art. 331 CO). Employer contributions to the fund are reported as expenses as soon as they become due or are approved. The liability to pay pensions must be reflected in the financial statements of these separate legal entities. This liability is treated like any other liability and must be disclosed to the extent that payments are anticipated.

¶819   Commitments and contingencies

Sureties, guarantees and security interests in favour of third parties are disclosed separately on the balance sheet or in a note to it. The balance sheet includes reserves to cover losses that can be foreseen to arise from commitments and contingencies. Other items such as guarantees securing one's own liabilities, warranties and capital commitments need not be disclosed.

¶820   Hidden or undisclosed reserves

Hidden reserves are part of the equity that does not appear as such on the balance sheet. Undisclosed reserves are created if assets are undervalued or liabilities overstated. As the statutory valuation principles set only the ceiling on the value of assets and the floor of the appraisal of liabilities, the management has wide latitude in undervaluing assets or overstating liabilities. The undervaluation of assets and overstatement of liabilities by the management is permitted, provided that it aims at securing the continued prosperity of the business or at maintaining a constant dividend-distribution policy (Art. 663 CO). However, assets such as machinery, goods or raw materials must not be valued at zero, nor must fictitious liabilities be listed. Disclosure of the valuation principles or variations in hidden reserves is not required by law. The auditors must be informed of the variations in hidden reserves, but they are not allowed to disclose them in their report to the shareholders. Corporate transactions, such as mergers and acquisitions, transfers of corporate domicile, financial restructurings and liquidations may lead to realisation of the hidden reserves for tax purposes. If they are deemed to be realised for tax purposes, the hidden reserves are included in the taxable income.

REPORTING

¶821   Sources of law

Articles 957 to 964 CO contain the general rules governing reporting. These general rules are complemented by the more specific rules that apply to share corporations (Art. 662 et seq. CO). Banks and investment funds are subject to additional regulations.

Article 27 of the Banking Ordinance requires for banks to publish annual accounts and other information in the Official Journal of Commerce. Similarly, companies subject to the Federal Investment Funds Statute must publish an annual report on their activities with the information required by law (Art. 15 Investment Funds Statute). Foreign investment funds must report additional items (Art. 6 Foreign Investment Funds Ordinance). Share corporations listed on a stock exchange are required to disclose additional information (Art. 6 Regulations Governing the Admission of Securities for Trading and Listing on the Zurich Stock Exchange; Art. 4 et seq. Regulations Governing the Admission of Securities for Trading and Listing on the Geneva Stock Exchange; Art. 8 Regulation of the Geneva Bourse). To be listed on a stock exchange, a foreign corporation must publish certain information (Art. 8 et seq. Regulations Governing the Admission of Foreign Securities to the Official Market of the Swiss Stock Exchanges).

¶822   Form and content of financial statements and business reports

Financial statements must contain a balance sheet (assets and liabilities) and an income statement (profit and loss account). Except for banks, investment funds and insurance companies to which special provisions apply, the statutory provisions do not define the items to be reported in the balance sheet and the income statement. The management is free to list the items it sees fit to disclose, except for a few items relating to the balance sheets of share corporations and co-operative corporations.

The presentation of the statements must be clear, complete and comprehensive so as to allow a reliable insight into the state of affairs (Art. 959 CO). This means that the presentation should not give rise to over-estimation of the company's financial position or be misleading in other respects. As a result of the mandatory lower-of-cost-or-market-price principle, management may be required to undervalue assets. Management is obliged to report the creation and dissolution of undisclosed reserves to the auditors (Art. 663(3) CO). The board of directors must prepare a business report for submission to the ordinary general meeting of shareholders. The financial statements of the corporation are submitted to the shareholder together with this business report. The report highlights the activities of the company and its financial position and comments on the financial statements. In view of the limited information disclosed in many financial statements, the business report is quite important in practice.

A generally accepted guide to the preparation of financial statements is the 'Uniform Charts of Accounts for Industrial and Commercial Enterprises' (Karl Käfer, *Kostenrahmen für Gewerbe-, Industrie- und Handelsbetriebe*, 10th edn), and the auditing manual of the Swiss Chamber of Auditing Firms and Certified Accountants (*manuel suisse de révision comptable/Revisionshandbuch der Schweiz*).

Banks must prepare detailed balance sheets to allow an extensive analysis of their liquidity and to give a fair insight into the structure of their loan portfolio. Insurance companies must list their income, expenses and reserves by the type of insurance and must give a detailed break-down of their assets.

Items listed on the financial statements must be reported in Swiss Francs (¶815). Only investment funds which invest a large majority of their assets in a specific foreign currency may choose that currency for financial reporting.

The following is a sample of the financial statements of a closely held trading company:

¶822

XYZ Ltd.

BALANCE SHEET – 31 December 1990

Assets

	SFr	SFr
Cash		100,000
Accounts receivable – trade		200,000
– other		2,000
Intercompany receivable		6,000
Goods in transit		120,000
Deposit		3,000
Fixed assets at cost	100,000	
Depreciation	−20,000	80,000
		511,000

Liabilities

	SFr
Bank overdraft	225,000
Accounts payable – trade	110,000
– other	3,000
Accrued liabilities	10,000
Intercompany loan	20,000
Share capital	100,000
Profit	43,000
	511,000

XYZ Ltd.

PROFIT AND LOSS STATEMENT
for the period of
1 January to 31 December 1990

	SFr	SFr
Sales		1,000,000
Cost of goods sold		750,000
Gross profit		250,000
Expenses		
Salaries	100,000	
Office rent	20,000	
Interest expenses	10,000	
Administration	30,000	
Professional fees	10,000	
Travel expenses	10,000	
Depreciation of fixed assets and cars	10,000	
Depreciation and start-up costs	20,000	(210,000)
Other income		
Interest income	2,000	
Exchange gain	1,000	3,000
Profit for the period		43,000

¶823   Consolidated financial statement

Groups of companies are not required to file consolidated financial statements. The following exceptions apply:

(1) Immovable property investment funds must include a consolidated balance sheet and income statement in their report.

(2) Foreign banks with branches in Switzerland must publish the branches' annual report together with the parent's report in order to permit a better appraisal of the branch's position within the parent organisation (Art. 8(1) Ordinance on Foreign Banks).

(3) To establish compliance with the equity and the credit risk, a bank that controls (either directly or indirectly) a business entity with activities in

the banking or financial field must draw up a consolidated balance sheet (Art. 12 Banking Ordinance). These consolidated balance sheets are not published.

The Swiss Chamber of Auditing Firms and Certified Accountants recommended in 1985 that corporations with international activities voluntarily publish consolidated financial statements.

¶824 Loss of share capital

If the balance sheet shows that net assets no longer cover at least half of the share capital, the board of directors must call an extraordinary general meeting of the shareholders and inform them of the situation. If there are reasonable grounds for assuming that the liabilities are in excess of the assets, an interim balance sheet must be prepared based upon liquidation values. If the company's assets no longer cover its liabilities, the board of directors must inform the court, which will declare the company bankrupt unless it decides, at the request of the board or a creditor, to postpone bankruptcy if there is a prospect of financial restructuring (Art. 725 CO).

It is common practice for companies belonging to a group of companies to avoid bankruptcy by having their main creditors (for instance, the parent company) sign a subordination agreement under which the credit extended to the company need not be repaid as long as less than half of the capital of the company is covered by net assets. The validity of such agreements is questionable. See ¶914.

¶825 Public filing requirements

Share corporations, partnerships, and co-operative corporations are not required to make their financial statements available to the public. However, these entities must disclose certain information to the Register of Commerce on incorporation: the minutes of the initial general meeting establishing the company and adopting the by-laws, a certificate evidencing that the share capital has been paid in, the names and addresses of directors and officers, and a declaration by the statutory auditors that they accept their assignment. This information, together with application files and supporting documents, is open to public inspection (Art. 930 CO).

Unlike the general public, the creditors of a share corporation have the right to inspect the latest financial statements of that corporation (Art. 704 CO; Art. 85 Ordinance on the Register of Commerce). Upon proof of their status, the creditors can file an application with the appropriate Registrar; the Registrar then requests the debtor company to submit the latest balance sheet and income statement as approved by the shareholders.

Business entities carrying on a regulated activity are required to file reports with the supervising authority. This is true for banks, which not only must publish their reports in a newspaper but are also required to submit these documents to the Swiss National Bank (Art. 7(1) Banking Statute; Art. 27 Banking Ordinance). Banks must publish an interim balance sheet in the Official Journal of Commerce or in a newspaper if the assets reported in the balance sheet are in excess of certain statutory fixed amounts (Art. 6(3) Banking Statute). Similar requirements apply to insurance companies, which are required to publish their statements in the Official Journal of Commerce (Arts 21 and 22 Insurance Supervision Statute). Investment funds are subject to certain filing requirements, and foreign funds must make copies of the fund prospectus and the latest statements available for investors at the domicile of the custodian bank (Art. 10 Ordinance on Foreign Investment Funds). Companies whose securities are listed on a stock exchange must publish their financial statements and issue a business report. In Zurich, the bank which filed the application to list a company on the stock exchange must hold annual reports at the disposal of stockholders and bondholders (Art. 6 Regulations Governing the Admission of Securities for Trading and Listing on the Zurich Stock Exchange). In Geneva, information must be disclosed in a Geneva newspaper; as to foreign securities, information must be published in a Geneva newspaper and filed with the secretary of the stock exchange (Art. 8 Regulations of the Geneva Bourse).

The law imposes certain filing requirements on a corporation *vis-à-vis* its shareholders:

(1) The ordinary general shareholders' meeting must be held within a period of six months after the end of the company's financial year.

(2) Ten days prior to the shareholders' meeting, the financial statements, business report, auditors' report and agenda for the meeting, together with the proposal for the distribution of the surplus, must be placed at the disposal of the shareholders at the head office and at all registered branches of the company.

(3) The date of the shareholders' meeting and the submission of the requested documentation must be announced to the registered shareholders by a special notice and to the holders of bearer shares through the Official Journal of Commerce.

The Articles of Incorporation may provide for filing requirements that are more favourable to shareholders than the statutory rules.

When publicly issuing equity or debt papers (e.g., shares or bonds), companies are obliged to publish a prospectus which must include, *inter alia*, the latest annual financial statements and the corresponding audit report (Arts 631, 632, 651, 752 and 1156 CO).

¶825

AUDITING

¶826   Ordinary partnerships

The Code of Obligations neither provides for an independent audit nor imposes any requirements as to the qualifications of the individuals auditing the books of an ordinary partnership (*société simple/Einfache Gesellschaft*, ¶712). Partners without management authority have the right to personally inform themselves of the state of the partnership's affairs. They also have the right to inspect the partnership books and records and to prepare a summary of the status of the common assets for their own use. This right is inalienable.

¶827   General partnerships and limited partnerships

In a general partnership (*société en nom collectif/Kollektivgesellschaft*, ¶713), all partners are involved in the business and have full access to all financial information. Each general partner shares in the responsibility for accounting and tax reporting. There is no legal obligation to have the accounts reviewed by an independent auditor.

The limited partnership (*société en commandite/Kommanditgesellschaft*, ¶714) is managed by the general partner(s). Limited partners have no right or obligation to participate in the management, but they are entitled to a copy of the balance sheet and profit and loss statement, and may personally inspect the books and documents or have them verified by an independent expert.

¶828   Share corporations

The general meeting of shareholders appoints one or more auditors. The auditors – individuals, trust companies or auditor associations – need not be shareholders; directors or employees of the corporation (*société anonyme/ Aktiengesellschaft*) must not be auditors. At the beginning of the life of the corporation, the auditors may be elected for only one year; thereafter, an appointment for not more than three years is possible. The auditors examine the accuracy of the books and financial statements; the directors are required to furnish any explanation desired by the auditors.

Without having seen the auditors' report, the general meeting of shareholders cannot pass any resolution on the balance sheet. Therefore, although the report provides only a limited review of the accounting, much less a review of the economic truthfulness of the statements, it is a prerequisite for the vote to release the board of directors from liability. While there is normally no requirement that auditors meet certain professional standards, under certain conditions only qualified auditors are permitted to audit the books of a share corporation (see ¶831(1)).

¶828

¶829   Limited liability companies

Managing partners of a limited liability company (*société à responsabilité limitée/Gesellschaft mit beschränkter Haftung*, ¶710) may audit the books themselves or retain the services of an outside auditor. Non-managing partners have the same auditing rights as the non-managing partners of an ordinary partnership, i.e., they have the right to personally inform themselves of the state of partnership affairs, to inspect the partnership books and records, and to prepare for their own use a summary of the status of the common assets. However, the partners can contractually provide for a special auditor who may examine whether the register of shares is duly kept.

¶830   Co-operative corporations

The co-operative corporation (*société coopérative/Genossenschaft*, ¶711) must arrange for auditors to review the conduct of its business and the balance sheet every business year. The auditors – individuals or corporations – are elected by the general meeting for a period of at least one year. The auditors need not be members of the co-operative corporation. The auditors examine in particular whether the accounts and the balance sheet tally with the books, whether the books are properly kept and whether the information on the co-operative corporation's business results and financial position complies with applicable law (Art. 907 CO). The auditors submit a written report with their proposal to the general meeting. The meeting cannot pass any resolution concerning the account and balance sheet unless it has received this report.

¶831   Special rules for banks, insurance companies, etc.

(1)   Qualified auditors
The Code of Obligations does not prescribe any standards for the audit.

In certain circumstances, the Code of Obligations and certain statutes require that auditors meet certain professional requirements. If the share capital of a corporation is five million francs or more, or if a corporation has issued bonds or intends to float a public issue, the balance sheet must be examined by independent professional auditors (Art. 723 CO). The Code of Obligations does not define what is meant by 'professional auditors', but the term is generally understood to refer to members of the professional accounting organisations.

(2)   Banks
Banks and similar financial institutions are supervised by the Federal Banking Commission (¶1108), which exercises its supervisory function mostly through private auditing firms independent of the bank (Art. 18 Banking Statute). Only an auditing company or a trust company that has been licensed by the Federal

Banking Commission as an auditing firm for banks can be retained for the audit. A bank-audit licence will be issued only to independent and qualified auditing companies that employ certified public accountants and deposit a security (Art. 35 Banking Ordinance).

Bank auditing firms that do not exercise the necessary care in auditing a bank may become liable. In addition to the specific rules laid down in the Banking Ordinance, various circulars and directives issued by the Federal Banking Commission regulate the duties of bank auditors.

The auditing report must reflect the financial situation of the bank accurately and express a definite opinion in regard to various points detailed in Art. 44 of the Banking Ordinance. The auditing firm checks whether the annual statement of condition complies with the requirements of the Code of Obligations, and the provisions of the Banking Statute and its Ordinance (Art. 19 Banking Statute). The auditors must determine whether the quota of own funds (equity and quasi-equity) and the liquidity requirements imposed by the Banking Statute and Ordinance are met. To this end, the auditors must personally verify the liquidity, the reported own funds, and the assessment and allocation of risks.

The auditors not only verify the financial situation of the bank, they also determine whether a bank is well organised, whether it has an adequate internal auditing and reporting system and whether the bank's management complics with the standards of sound banking practice as defined by statutory provisions, circular letters, case law and the practice of the Federal Banking Commission.

The auditing report must provide a definite opinion in regard to the various points of Art. 43 et seq. of the Banking Ordinance. The report is protected by banking secrecy and is made available only to bank management, members of the board of directors and the Federal Banking Commission. Only a summary report of a fairly standard nature (see ¶832) is made available to the shareholders and the general public.

(3) Investment funds

The activity of investment funds must be audited by a qualified auditing firm licensed by the Federal Banking Commission. If the fund is managed by a bank, the bank's auditors may audit the fund. Auditing companies of good reputation and individuals who preferably hold a federal diploma as certified public accountants are eligible as auditors (Art. 31 Investment Funds Ordinance). Pension funds and insurance companies must also be audited by qualified auditors.

The auditors are required to check whether the fund management and the custodian bank have complied with the law and the fund's regulations. The auditors report in detail on their examination and findings. Addressees of the report are the fund management, the custodian bank and the Federal Banking Commission. The auditors comment in particular on the internal organisation of the fund management and the custodian bank, the organisation of their parent corporation, and the accounting and reporting. Further, they report upon the fund's compliance with the law, the valuation at market value of the fund's assets, and the determination of the issue and redemption price of the share certificates. The auditors supply a special report on management of the fund, particularly regarding the amount of the statutorily required and actually available equity, the composition of the assets and the management's compliance with the legal principle that its business be limited to the management of investment funds (Art. 39 et seq. Investment Funds Ordinance).

(4) Insurance companies
Insurance companies are closely supervised by the Federal Insurance Office, with which they file annual reports on the company's compliance with the law, in particular in the field of the company's financial structure. The auditors' activity is limited to a review of the company's books, including verification of the company's compliance with the accounting methods contained in the Insurance Supervision Statute and Ordinance.

(5) Social security and pension funds
The insurance carriers providing coverage for old age, survivors and disability are either state-run or under intense government scrutiny. The auditors examine whether the insurance company is operating in compliance with the applicable law.

¶832   Auditing practice and auditors' report

The auditors' report states and explains (usually in the form of reservations) any material deviation from statutory requirements or good accounting practice, if any, and concludes with a recommendation to the general meeting of shareholders whether to approve or reject the financial statements submitted. It confirms that the proposal for the distribution of the surplus conforms to applicable law and the Articles of Incorporation.

A typical auditors' report may read as shown in the example set out below:

AUDITORS' REPORT

3 FEBRUARY 1990

To the General Meeting
of the Shareholders of
XYZ AG

As statutory auditors of your Company we have examined the financial
statements as of 31 December 1989 and for the year then ended as required
by the provisions of the law.

In our opinion:

- the balance sheet and the income statement are in agreement with the
  books of account;
- the books of account have been properly kept; and
- the information as to the financial position of the Company and the
  results of its operations complies with the requirements of the law as to
  valuation and the Company's statutes.

Based on the results of our examination we recommend that you accept the
annexed financial statements with a profit of SFr 43,000. The proposal for
the distribution of the surplus conforms to the law and the Articles of
Incorporation.

ACCOUNTING/AUDITING PROFESSION

¶833   CPAs and their Chamber

The accounting professionals (*expert comptable/Bücherexperte*) are comparable to
certified public accountants in the United States as far as their training and the scope
of the services offered are concerned. Apart from the requirement that certain
companies (e.g., banks, investment funds and insurance companies) be audited by
qualified or specially-licensed accountants, the tasks usually performed by
accountants may be carried out by members of other professions. The Swiss Chamber
of Auditing Firms and Certified Accountants (a private organisation) sets standards
for the accounting profession. The Chamber develops uniform principles to be
applied by the accounting profession and administers the examinations leading to
the federal diplomas of tax expert and accounting expert. The Chamber furthers the
continuing education of the members of the profession and develops the code of
ethics. Most accountants are members of the Chamber. Guide-lines issued by the
Chamber, such as the *Swiss Manual of Accounting*, have an almost binding

character and are followed by all members of the profession. Major corporations almost exclusively retain accountants and auditors who are members of the Chamber and hold a federal diploma.

Through the initiative of the Chamber, the Foundation for Accounting and Reporting Recommendations was created in 1984 with offices in Zurich. This independent private institution is the legal vehicle of the Board for Accounting and Reporting Recommendations. The Board reviews international developments, particularly developments in the European Community, and drafts guide-lines and recommendations. These are regularly released in German, French, Italian and English to enable members of the profession to apply recognised accounting principles. So far, the Foundation has issued the following recommendations:

- No. 0, Objectives, Subjects and Procedures of Accounting and Reporting Recommendations (1985).

- No. 1, Components of Financial Statements (1985).

- No. 2, Consolidated Financial Statements (1986).

- No. 3, Generally Accepted Accounting Principles.

- No. 4, The Translation of Financial Statements.

- No. 5, Valuation Directives for Consolidated Financial Statements.

The Foundation intends to issue recommendations on conversion of foreign currencies in consolidated financial statements, valuation of various positions and presentation of consolidated financial statements, cash flow computation, etc.

SELECTED BIBLIOGRAPHY

Karl Blumer and Adolphe Graf, *Die kaufmännische Bilanz*, 9th edn (Zürich, 1986)
Ernst Bosshard, *Die kaufmännische Buchführung, Teilband VI/3b, Zürcher Kommentar* (Zürich, 1984)
Gérald-Charles Bourquin, *Le principe de la sincérité du bilan* (Genève, 1976)
Carl Helbling, *Bilanz- und Erfolgsanalyse*, 7th edn (Bern, 1989)
Karl Käfer, *Die kaufmännische Buchführung, Band VIII, Berner Kommentar* (Bern, 1980)
Karl Käfer, *Kontenrahmen für Gewerbe-, Industrie- und Handelsbetriebe*, 10th edn (Zürich, 1987)
Jean-Pierre Leu, *Bilan et états financiers des S.A.* (Genève, 1976)
Swiss Chamber of Auditing Firms and Certified Accountants, *Manuel suisse de révision comptable/Revisionshandbuch der Schweiz*, loose-leaf service, 1987
André Zünd, *Revisionslehre* (Zürich, 1982)

¶833

9 Insolvency, Debt Collection, Attachments and Bankruptcy

PRINCIPAL LEGISLATION

Loi fédérale sur la poursuite pour dettes et la faillite/*Bundesgesetz über Schuldbetreibung und Konkurs*/Federal Statute on Debt Collection and Bankruptcy, RS 281.1.

Loi fédérale sur le droit international privé/*Bundesgesetz über das internationale Privatrecht*/Federal Private International Law Statute, RS 291 (translated by Pierre A. Karrer and Karl W. Arnold, *Switzerland's Private International law Statute 1987*, Deventer, 1989).

PROTECTION OF CREDITORS' RIGHTS PRIOR TO INSOLVENCY

¶901 Gathering information about the debtor

The best way for a potential creditor seeking to protect himself against losses as a result of a debtor's insolvency is to obtain information about the potential debtor, such as the debtor's reputation in the community and his or her business record. Gathering information concerning a guarantor who may have secured the debtor's payments is also recommended.

A creditor may request information directly from the debtor. If the debtor publishes annual financial statements, the creditor may obtain a copy. Many Swiss companies, however, do not publish annual reports and financial statements (¶821 et seq.) and are likely to refuse to show unpublished statements to a creditor. A creditor will not obtain as much information from the annual statements of a Swiss company as he or she would be likely to obtain, for instance, from an American company. Under Swiss accounting law, a company is not allowed to present its financial status in a better light than it actually is.

However, undisclosed reserves are permitted to a large extent, and their creation is considered good business practice.

Certain information may be available from banks, especially the bank of the debtor. To be sure, a bank would not disclose any information pertaining to a customer without the customer's consent.

Useful information is available from the Registrar of the Register of Commerce, where information on file is open to public inspection. A creditor may request an extract from the Register which shows the statutory purpose of the company, its date of establishment, its share capital, the members of the board of directors, and the names of those officers and managers who have signing authority for the company. An extract will further show whether the prospective debtor is a company of substance or a letterbox firm. Pursuant to Art. 704 CO, a creditor that proves his or her claim against a share corporation may petition the Register of Commerce to order the share corporation to supply its last financial statements to that creditor (ATF 111 II 282).

In some cantons, the creditor has access to certain tax data, such as the amount of taxable capital and the annual taxable net profits of a company. In other cantons, no information on taxes is given to the creditor, or access to this information is limited.

If creditors can show prima facie that a payment from the debtor is overdue, or that any other legitimate interest exists, they may request an extract from the Debt Collection Office at the seat or domicile of the debtor, showing information on orders to pay issued by the office during the past two or three years. If the extracts show that several orders to pay were issued, or that one was issued for a substantial amount of money, this may indicate that the debtor is in financial difficulty.

The creditor may commission an information agency to collect financial information on a debtor. However, these agencies have access only to information available to the general public and to information made available to them voluntarily by the debtor. Some Chambers of Commerce, e.g., the Swiss-German Chamber of Commerce in Switzerland, may be able to provide information on a debtor.

There are, of course, many other private sources of information which may be quite useful for obtaining reliable information about the debtor's financial situation and standard of business. For example, there are cases where all companies operating in the municipality of a defaulting debtor stopped selling goods, while foreign vendors were happily increasing their sales to the same customer.

¶902   Guarantees from third parties

The creditor may wish to seek some undertaking from a third party that the debtor will pay or, under certain circumstances, that a third party will pay in lieu of the debtor. The third party either:

(a) issues a suretyship (*cautionnement/Bürgschaft*);

(b) signs a guarantee (*garantie/Garantie*); or

· (c) assumes the obligation of the purchaser as a joint obligor (*obligation solidaire/Solidarverpflichtung*).

See also ¶216.

Under a suretyship, the surety guarantees the ability of the debtor to pay; with a guarantee, the guarantor guarantees the payment as such.

A suretyship must be in writing. The maximum amount of liability must be explicitly stated in the deed. There are two types of suretyships:

(a) the simple suretyship, under which the seller must generally put the purchaser into bankruptcy before enforcing the claim against the person who signed the suretyship; and

(b) the joint suretyship, under which the creditor has a claim against the surety once the payment is overdue and the debtor has been given notice.

The guarantee is a promise to pay, regardless of whether the debtor owes money to the creditor or not. Guarantees are quite often issued by banks.

Under certain circumstances, it may be difficult to distinguish between a suretyship and a guarantee. As a result, it is advisable to mention the maximum liability incurred in all guarantee or suretyship documents which are governed by Swiss law or are likely to be enforced in Switzerland.

The following draft for a guarantee signed by a bank in Zurich may serve as an illustration:

Dear Sir or Madam:

You are concluding a contract ('the contract') with X.Y. on 1 May 1992, for the supply of .... at the price of one million Swiss Francs. As security for the payment of this merchandise, an indemnity by a bank will be furnished. At the request of X.Y., we herewith irrevocably undertake to pay you upon first demand any amount up to SFr 1,000,000 (one million Swiss Francs), waiving all rights of objection and defence arising from the contract, upon your written confirmation that:

(a) you have delivered the merchandise in accordance with the contract, and that

(b) you have not received payment at maturity for the sum claimed under this letter of indemnity.

The total amount of this indemnity will be reduced by any payment effected by us thereunder.

¶902

For the purpose of identification, any claims hereunder must be presented through a first-class bank as an intermediary, confirming that the signatures on such claims are binding on your firm.

Our undertaking is valid until 1 May 1993 (May first, nineteen hundred and ninety-three) and expires in full automatically if your written confirmation is not in our possession on or before that date.

This undertaking is governed by Swiss law, and the place of jurisdiction is Zurich.

Zurich, 1 May 1992

....

It may be advisable for the creditor to ask the purchaser to arrange for a contract under which a company or a relative will assume the debt. Then the debtor remains liable for the payment of the purchase price while an additional person or company becomes jointly liable for the payment. Again, it may be difficult to distinguish between joint assumption of a debt and a surety.

¶903　Contractual penalties and assignment of claims

A contractual penalty is a provision in the contract which states that the debtor must pay a certain sum of money (or perform another obligation) in the event that the creditor is not satisfied. This instrument does not adequately protect the creditor: when debtors are unwilling to pay the purchase price, they tend to be even less willing to pay a penalty.

Unlike the law in many other countries, Swiss law does not prohibit the use of contract penalties (¶202(3)). Penalty clauses are valid and enforceable even if no actual loss was suffered. Only in particular instances where the penalties agreed upon are excessively high can the judge reduce them at his or her discretion. The courts in Switzerland, however, are reluctant to hold that penalties agreed to by the parties are excessive.

The assignment of a claim involves a change in creditor (and not a change of debtor as occurs in the assumption of a debt). The assignment of claim must be in writing (Art. 165 CO; see ¶209).

A purchaser may assign a claim against a third party debtor to the seller on a fiduciary basis in order to secure the purchase price. This is often done if purchased goods are resold by the purchaser shortly after being received. The first purchaser then assigns his or her claim to the first seller for the sales price. This can be an effective instrument for protection if the first creditor or debtor notifies the third-party debtor of the assignment of the claim and instructs him or her to pay the new creditor directly.

The assignment of future claims is valid. One may assign an undetermined number of future claims arising in a specific business relationship with a particular debtor. This method is frequently used by banks extending a loan to a business entity.

¶904   Pledges, mortgages and retention of title

(1) Pledges

For the purpose of securing a present or future claim, movable goods can be given in pledge (*gage/Pfand*) by delivering possession of the movables to the creditor or to a third person holding the pledge for the creditor (pledgeholder) (Art. 884 CC). If bona fide creditors take possession of the pledged movables, they acquire the rights of the pledgee over them, even when the pledgor has no right to dispose of them. No pledge can be established as long as the pledgor retains exclusive control over the movables.

A pledge can be made upon another pledge by written advice to the pledgee of the new pledge, and instructing him or her to deliver the goods to the second pledgee once the first pledgee's own rights to them have been satisfied. Where the same goods are pledged to several creditors in succession, the creditors will be satisfied from them in the order of their priority, determined by the dates of the pledges.

Claims and other rights can be pledged if they are assignable. Bearer shares can be pledged by mere delivery to the pledgee. In the case of registered shares, their delivery must be supplemented by an endorsement or written assignment (Art. 901 CC).

(2) Mortgages

Security interests in immovable property include mortgages (*hypothèque/ Grundpfandverschreibung*) and mortgage notes (*cédule hypothécaire/ Schuldbrief*). A mortgage is a security for a claim for which the pledgor remains personally liable. It is not incorporated in a negotiable document. By contrast, a mortgage note is incorporated in a negotiable document, and the document certifies the validity of the claim.

(3) Debentures

In a debenture (*hypothèque mobilière enregistrée/Fahrnisverschreibung*), possession of the pledged property need not be transferred; instead, an entry is made in the appropriate official register. Debentures exist only where official registers are kept, i.e. for cattle, ships, and aircraft.

When an intangible property right is incorporated in a document, it can be pledged by transferring possession. Otherwise, a written agreement is required.

Unless specified, bulk property such as inventories or enterprises may not be pledged. Non-payment of the underlying debt does not cause forfeiture; rather, the property is sold and the pledgor is entitled to the excess amount received, if any.

Generally, there are no special rules applicable to foreign creditors. Still, to acquire immovable property or control a real estate company, non-Swiss residents need the permission of the appropriate authorities (¶1709 et seq.). Similarly, a mortgage giving the foreign mortgagee rights similar to ownership (e.g., through economic dependence on the mortgagor) is not permitted without prior approval.

Where creditors are in possession of movables (e.g., securities) with the debtor's consent, they may retain possession until their claim is satisfied, if the claim is enforceable and, by its nature, closely connected with the movables retained. This connection is deemed to exist where the parties are trading or business partners and both possession and claim arise from their business relations (Art. 895 CC). A lien extends even to goods which are not the property of the debtor, provided that the creditor took possession thereof in good faith. The lien is always subject to the rights of third parties derived from prior possession.

(4)   Retention of title
Retention of title, also called reservation of property (*pacte de réserve de propriété/Eigentumsvorbehalt*), for movables transferred by a creditor (seller) to a debtor (purchaser), may be provided for by agreement but must be entered in a special register at the debtor's domicile. Retention of title in favour of a seller who has not been fully compensated is valid only after registration, and affects only the creditor and the debtor. Third parties who are bona fide purchasers are protected, notwithstanding the registration of the retention of title. In case of seizure or bankruptcy of the debtor, the retention of title is considered a pledge, and its liberation may be requested by a registered creditor. See also ¶1705(2).

(5)   Enforcement of mortgage or pledge
The security interest is enforced, and the enforcement of a debt that is secured by a pledge is initiated, by a request for execution (*réquisition de poursuite en réalisation du gage/Pfandverwertungsbegehren*) filed with the Debt Collection Office at the debtor's domicile or where the property is located. The debtor may deny the existence of the debt and declare opposition within ten days. If no opposition is declared, or if the debt is supported by a valid judicial or administrative decree or publicly certified document, the asset is sold by the Office. Any forfeiture clauses

are void. The debtor and the creditor may agree that the security interest in the pledged goods can be executed without going to court.

DEBT COLLECTION

¶905 Debt collection proceedings

Debt collection proceedings mark the beginning of the enforcement of money claims, including foreign currency claims. The enforcement of money claims, including the provision of money as security, is regulated by the Federal Statute on Debt Collection and Bankruptcy.

(1) Order to pay

The execution begins with an order to pay (*commandement de payer/ Zahlungsbefehl*), which is transmitted to the debtor by the competent Debt Collection Office upon the mere application of the creditor (*réquisition de poursuite/Betreibungsbegehren*). The application must be filed with the Debt Collection Office at the seat or domicile of the debtor, and must include the names and addresses of the creditor and the debtor, the amount and interest requested, and a reference to the document upon which the claim is based. The document must at least indicate the ground for the claim. The order to pay directs the debtor to pay in 20 days or to file an 'opposition' within ten days.

(2) Opposition

The debtor then usually pays or denies that he or she owes the money to the creditor. If the debtor refuses to admit the debt, he or she must declare 'opposition' (*opposition/Rechtsvorschlag*) within ten days. This can be done orally to the person serving the order to pay, or in writing to the Debt Collection Office issuing the order.

(3) Removal of opposition

If the debtor declares opposition and the creditor still wishes to collect the amount due, the creditor must institute ordinary court action. However, he or she may be able to obtain a court decree to lift the opposition in summary proceedings upon presentation of an enforceable judgment. This usually means a judgment rendered by a domestic or a foreign court, the award of an arbitral tribunal, or a similar order by a competent authority. Alternatively, the creditor may present evidence of a publicly notarised deed or an acknowledgement of debt signed by the debtor. If a written acknowledgement of debt is supplied, the removal is provisional (*mainlevée provisoire/provisorische Rechtsöffnung*); if a judgment is presented, opposition is definitively removed (*mainlevée définitive/definitive Rechtsöffnung*). Any provisional removal of opposition becomes final if the debtor fails to bring an ordinary court action for a declaratory judgment that the debt does not exist.

If the debtor failed to declare 'opposition', or if the opposition has been removed by ordinary judgment or an 'elimination decree', the creditor may request that the execution continue. Three procedures are available:

(a) either by the seizure of specific assets of the debtor (*saisie/Pfändung*); or

(b) against companies or merchants, institution of bankruptcy proceedings (*faillite/Konkurs*);

(c) for debts secured by pledge or mortgage, realisation of this security (*réalisation du gage/Pfandverwertung*).

(4) Seizure

Assets estimated to be sufficient to cover the debt, interest and associated costs can be seized (*saisie/Pfändung*) if opposition has not been declared or has been removed. It is not possible to seize property or income (wages) necessary for the livelihood or job of the debtor and his or her family.

Other creditors who request seizure within a period of 30 days can participate in the seizure; additional property will eventually be seized to cover these additional debts. In this case, all the creditors form a 'group of creditors'. One or more groups may subsequently be formed to pursue claims for other property seized on their behalf.

The claim of third parties who request the liberation of assets from seizure due to their ownership thereof gets the asset adjudicated, unless their claims are contested.

(5) Execution

Upon request by a creditor (*réquisition de vente/Verwertungsbegehren*), and after a certain period of time has elapsed, property that has been seized can be sold and the proceeds distributed among the creditors. Certain claims, such as those made for salaries or family support payments, are privileged. If there are privileged creditors and the proceeds do not cover all the liabilities, a schedule of creditors is established before the proceeds are distributed among them. This schedule can be challenged in court. If unpaid claims remain, each unpaid creditor receives a 'certificate of loss' (*acte de défaut de biens/Verlustschein*).

The procedure to realise a pledge or mortgage is similar to that employed in cases of seizure. For unpaid claims, every unpaid creditor receives a certificate of loss which attests to his or her outstanding debt.

¶905

BANKRUPTCY

¶906 Initiation of bankruptcy proceedings

Only those debtors who are entered in the Register of Commerce are subject to bankruptcy proceedings. Persons whose whereabouts are unknown or who have defrauded their creditors are also subject to bankruptcy proceedings. Individuals who are otherwise not subject to bankruptcy proceedings may voluntarily declare themselves insolvent (*déclaration d'insolvabilité/Insolvenzerklärung*); this subjects them to bankruptcy proceedings.

If a debt is evidenced by a bill of exchange or a cheque, the creditor may request a special 'bill of exchange execution' (*poursuite pour effets de change/ Wechselbetreibung*). The time periods are then shortened, and 'opposition' must be granted by a court order. There is no additional initial procedure for a debtor's bankruptcy proceedings.

At the creditor's request, which is filed with the competent Debt Collection Office, the debtor is notified and threatened with bankruptcy. The bankruptcy court declares that bankruptcy proceedings should begin if no opposition is declared, or if the opposition is definitively removed, unless certain permissible objections are sustained by the court.

¶907 Debtor's assets subject to bankruptcy

All assets owned by the bankrupt debtor are subject to bankruptcy, with the exception of certain property necessary for the livelihood and continuation of professional activities of the debtor and his or her family. All claims against the debtor become due, except claims which are secured by immovable property. Non-financial obligations of the bankrupt are converted into financial obligations denominated in Swiss Francs. The bankrupt debtor may no longer dispose of his or her assets. Third parties may request transmissible property which is in the possession of the bankrupt debtor (for reasons of ownership) to be separated from the bankruptcy assets. A seller may request the return of unpaid goods which have been forwarded to the bankrupt debtor but which are not yet in his possession when bankruptcy is declared ('right of stoppage in transit').

¶908 Bankruptcy proceedings

The bankruptcy office draws up an inventory of the debtor's assets and publishes a notice of the bankruptcy. It orders all creditors and debtors to file their claims and to announce their debts. The debtor's estate is administered by the bankruptcy office, which may be replaced by one or more persons elected by the creditors.

The creditors may elect a committee of creditors to supervise the administrators and to authorise them to take certain important measures. The creditors meet for the elections and discussion of any other urgent matters. The administration establishes a schedule of claims (*état de collocation/Kollokationsplan*). Thereafter, the creditors meet again to decide on all important matters, including the realisation of assets by public auction or private sale. Subsequent meetings may be held.

If the creditors should decide not to pursue a possible claim of the bankrupt debtor, each creditor may ask for an assignment of the waived claims. The proceeds from the assigned claims serve, first, to cover the assignees' costs of execution and, second, to cover their claims. Any surplus funds go into the bankrupt's assets.

After the proceeds have been distributed, the bankruptcy court receives a final accounting and declares the bankruptcy closed. All of the creditors receive a 'certificate of loss' for the unpaid balance of their claims.

When the assets found do not warrant the expenses of ordinary proceedings, the bankruptcy court may order summary proceedings instead. The bankruptcy office then proceeds with the liquidation without the participation of the creditors. Any creditor may demand ordinary bankruptcy proceedings by advancing the required costs.

If no assets are found, the bankruptcy court orders the bankruptcy closed, and no certificates of loss are issued. Within a certain period of time, any creditor may institute an execution of seizure against the debtor in order to obtain a certificate.

In 1989, 5,494 bankruptcies were declared in Switzerland.

REORGANISATION

¶909   In general

Basically, there are three types of composition (*concordat/Nachlassvertrag*):

  (1) stay of payment during a certain time period;

  (2) the payment of a percentage on all non-privileged debts; and

  (3) the abandonment of all or some of the debtor's assets to his creditors.

One of these forms of composition may be elected by any debtor, even after execution proceedings have begun. The debtor must apply for a stay of payment with the 'composition authority', submitting a statement of his or her assets and liabilities and a draft composition plan. If the authority grants the composition, a commissioner is appointed. The debtor may, under the supervision of the commissioner, continue his or her business, but may not sell nor pledge any assets.

If the composition liquidation is confirmed, the creditors hold a meeting to elect liquidators and a committee of creditors to supervise the liquidators. Assets are realised and the proceeds are distributed to the creditors in a procedure similar to bankruptcy. Special regulations apply to banks, hotels, farms, and some other businesses.

ATTACHMENT

¶910   In general

In order to secure creditors' financial claims, assets belonging to the debtor may be seized by 'attachment' (*séquestre/Arrest*). An application for attachment is submitted to the competent authority, usually a court at the location of the debtor's assets. Pursuant to Art. 271 of the Debt Collection and Bankruptcy Statute, the attachment is granted in summary and ex parte proceedings, based on prima facie evidence, if the applicant can substantiate that:

(1) the debtor has no fixed domicile in Switzerland or elsewhere; or

(2) the debtor intends to evade his or her obligations or is about to escape; or

(3) the debtor's presence is only transient; or

(4) the debtor has no domicile in Switzerland; or

(5) the creditor has a definite or a provisional certificate of loss against the debtor.

In the first two cases, an attachment may be applied for even when the creditor's financial claims have not yet matured. If an attachment is granted, these claims mature by operation of law.

In an international transaction, whenever a mature financial claim is not satisfied, it is common practice to attach a bank account or other assets of the foreign debtor that can be located in Switzerland. Careful specification and accurate location of the debtor's assets are necessary for the attachment application to be successful. The search for a debtor's assets by way of 'fishing expeditions' (for example, all accounts, deposits or other assets kept by the debtor in banks A, B and C in Zurich) is not permitted.

Once an attachment is granted, the creditor must initiate legal proceedings within ten days after obtaining the attachment, by filing an order to pay at the place of the attachment. If the debtor declares opposition to the payment order, the creditor must – to maintain the attachment – have the opposition eliminated by presenting a valid judicial or administrative decree or a publicly certified document proving the existence of the debt or must initiate action against the debtor within ten days. This action may be brought at the place of the attachment (*forum arresti*), but it can also be initiated at the debtor's domicile or before an arbitral tribunal, if any has been agreed upon. The final judgment obtained against the debtor will enable the creditor to satisfy the claims from the attached assets. See ¶1910 and ¶2014.

UNDUE PREFERENCE AND FRAUDULENT TRANSACTIONS

¶911   Undue preference in insolvency

Debtors confronted with the possibility that their assets are about to be seized to satisfy the claims of their creditors are likely to consider giving them away to friends or relatives for little or no consideration. Under Swiss law, these attempts to defraud creditors can be challenged in two ways:

(1) Creditors may be permitted to recover property which has been fraudulently given away. The legal basis for recovering the property is found in the Debt Collection and Bankruptcy Statute.

(2) Debtors who engage in such transactions may face criminal charges under the Penal Code.

The Debt Collection and Bankruptcy Statute and the Penal Code are both federal statutes. In contrast, the applicable procedural law is cantonal law. For example, a Zurich court might determine in a procedure under the Zurich Rules of Civil Procedure (*Zivilprozessordnung*) that a creditor has a valid claim against a third party who received the proceeds of a transaction ruled as fraudulent under federal debt collection and bankruptcy law, while a Geneva court might determine whether a bankruptcy crime was committed under the Penal Code according to the Geneva Code of Criminal Procedure (*code de procédure pénale*).

Experience shows that bankruptcy trustees are often reluctant to initiate court proceedings. Actions to set aside a fraudulent transaction are time-consuming, and the outcome is often uncertain. Furthermore, it may take two or more years before the creditors can meet to assign rights to a chosen creditor to challenge the transaction. Experience shows that district attorneys are reluctant to prosecute bankruptcy crimes, since prosecution may necessitate a meticulous review of thousands of documents written in several languages and require a good understanding of complex financial transactions.

In Switzerland, a person who commits a fraudulent transaction is not subject to punitive damages. However, attorneys' fees can be awarded to successful creditors. When the defendant is a person of some financial means, a large number of cases are settled before a final judgment is reached.

The following discussion is limited to fraudulent transactions related to bankruptcy. Similar provisions apply to seizure and reorganisation.

¶912 Fraudulent transactions in bankruptcy

(1) In general

Fraudulent transactions can be set aside by a court judgment. The bankruptcy trustee may initiate an action (Art. 285 Debt Collection and Bankruptcy Statute). If the creditors at their meeting decide not to challenge the allegedly fraudulent transaction, each individual creditor may request the assignment of the bankrupt estate's right to challenge the transaction in court (Art. 260 Debt Collection and Bankruptcy Statute). If one or more creditors are successful in challenging the transaction in court, the proceeds so obtained from the defendant will be distributed among them until their claims have been fully satisfied. If the proceeds exceed the total amount claimed by the plaintiffs, the balance will be given to the other creditors who previously asserted claims during the bankruptcy proceedings (Art. 260 Debt Collection and Bankruptcy Statute).

An action may be brought against individuals or legal entities that have conspired with the debtor in the allegedly fraudulent transaction, or their heirs and successors in law, or any third party who has acted in bad faith and has come to possess the assets of the fraudulent transaction (*actio pauliana* of Roman law; (*action révocatoire/Anfechtungsklage*).

The following transactions are considered fraudulent:

(a) Gift or donation

Gifts and donations are fraudulent if made within six months prior to bankruptcy (Art. 286 Debt Collection and Bankruptcy Statute). Donations include those in which the debtor bought an annuity contract (Art. 516 CO) or usufruct (Art. 746 CC).

(b) Insolvency

The following transactions are fraudulent if made within six months prior to bankruptcy by a debtor who was insolvent at the time of the transaction (Art. 287 Debt Collection and Bankruptcy Statute):

(i) giving security without legal obligation for an already existing liability;

(ii) discharge of a financial claim by means other than the payment of cash or other customary methods;

(iii) payment of a debt which was not yet due.

the beneficiary of the transaction did not know that the debtor was insolvent, the transaction is not fraudulent. However, the burden of proof is on the beneficiary. In a court procedure, the defendant must prove that he or she was unaware of the debtor's insolvency.

(c) Intentional undue preference

Any transaction which is made by the debtor with the intention of discriminating against one or more of the creditors is fraudulent if the fraudulent intention was known, or could have been known, by the person who transacted business with the debtor (Art. 288 Debt Collection and Bankruptcy Statute). Insolvency at the time that the fraudulent transaction was made is not required. This provision applies even to transactions made more than six months before bankruptcy.

(2) Remedies

Transactions held to be fraudulent by the court are not void generally, but only in respect to the plaintiff (Art. 291 Debt Collection and Bankruptcy Statute).

The plaintiff, if successful, may sell the assets involved in the fraudulent transaction for his own benefit. If the transaction consisted in waiving a claim, the claim can be reinstated if the transaction is successfully challenged.

(3) Statute of Limitations

The fraudulent transaction may be challenged only within five years of its occurrence (Art. 292 Debt Collection and Bankruptcy Statute).

CRIMINAL AND CIVIL LIABILITY

¶913 Bankruptcy crimes

Article 163 of the Penal Code makes fraudulent bankruptcy or undue preference a criminal offence. Fraudulent bankruptcy is committed by a debtor who intentionally endangers the rights of the creditors and is later declared bankrupt. The rights of creditors are endangered by an actual or fictitious reduction of the debtor's assets, e.g., by destroying, damaging or hiding assets, or by creating fictitious debts, or by falsifying accounting books or balance sheets. The sanction is imprisonment for up to five years. A third party who commits the offence can be punished with imprisonment for up to three years.

Further, under Art. 165 of the Penal Code, reckless bankruptcy is a criminal offence. Reckless bankruptcy is committed by debtors who, through gross recklessness, excessive extravagance, risky speculation or gross negligence in the exercise of their profession, cause their insolvency or aggravate their financial situation while already insolvent. They may be punished with imprisonment if bankruptcy proceedings are initiated against them.

Other bankruptcy crimes include:

- failure to keep books as required by law (Art. 166 Penal Code),
- giving preference to one creditor to the detriment of others (Art. 167 Penal Code),
- purchasing votes at a creditors' meeting (Art. 168 Penal Code), and
- disposal of attached assets or assets recorded in bankruptcy proceedings (Art. 169 Penal Code).

In addition, debtors commit a criminal offence if they do not assist a bankruptcy trustee in the performance of the latter's duties (Art. 323 Penal Code). The sanction is imprisonment for up to two weeks.

Likewise, a third party who does not co-operate with the bankruptcy trustee may become criminally liable (Art. 324 Penal Code).

¶914   Civil liability of corporate executives and auditors

If the annual balance sheet of a corporation shows that at least half of the share capital is no longer covered by net assets, the board of directors must call an extraordinary general meeting of the shareholders and inform them of the situation. If there are reasonable grounds for assuming insolvency, an internal balance sheet based on liquidation values must be prepared. If the company's assets no longer cover its liabilities, the board of directors must inform the court. The court will declare the corporation bankrupt unless it decides, at the request of the board of directors or of a creditor, to postpone bankruptcy because there is a good prospect for financial restructuring. In that case, the court must take all appropriate steps to preserve the assets of the corporation, for example by requesting an inventory or appointing an administrator.

In practice, many corporations attempt to avoid bankruptcy by having their main creditors sign a subordination agreement, under which the credit extended to the corporation need not be repaid as long as less than half of the capital of the corporation is covered by its net assets. Groups of corporations often subordinate credits in this manner in order to avoid the bankruptcy of affiliated corporations. The validity of subordination agreements has been disputed.

As a rule, a subordination agreement is held to be valid if:

(1) the corporation's assets calculated at their liquidation value cover the corporation's liabilities; and

(2) the corporation granting the subordination of its claim does not fall into bankruptcy by subordinating its claim.

Managers and directors of the board are liable to the shareholders and creditors of the corporation if they omit to call an extraordinary general meeting of the shareholders to inform them of the situation, and if the omission results in losses. They are likewise liable if they have omitted to inform the court that the assets of the corporation no longer cover its liabilities.

If the external auditors of the corporation notice that half of the share capital of the company is lost or that the liabilities of the corporation are no longer covered by its net assets, they must inform the board of directors about the situation, and have a duty to call an extraordinary general meeting of the shareholders. Otherwise, the auditors may be liable for any losses suffered by the shareholders and the creditors of the corporation as a result of the omission (see *Blätter für zürcherische Rechtsprechung* 89, 1991, Nr. 94; BGE 116 II 533).

TRANSNATIONAL ASPECTS OF INSOLVENCY

¶915   In general

(1)   Previous law
Until recently, the international bankruptcy law of Switzerland adhered to the strict principle of territoriality of bankruptcy. As a consequence, a bankruptcy declared outside Switzerland had, in principle, no effect in Switzerland. A few exceptions were provided for in bilateral treaties, e.g., the one between Switzerland and France. A foreign debtor who has a branch office in Switzerland may be declared bankrupt in Switzerland with respect to the liabilities of the Swiss branch office.

The Swiss assets of a foreign company which declared bankruptcy outside Switzerland were not necessarily handed over to the foreign bankruptcy receiver. As a result, creditors who had knowledge of Swiss assets belonging to a foreign company which had declared bankruptcy abroad could attach the Swiss assets. Their claims were satisfied out of the goods attached, which often resulted in their receiving preferential treatment over other creditors.

(2)   Federal Private International Law Statute
The Federal Private International Law Statute of 1987 covers not only conflicts of laws (private international law), but also conflicts of jurisdictions, enforcement of foreign judgments in Switzerland, international arbitration and international insolvency. Chapter 11 of the statute covers the international law aspects of bankruptcy and composition.

¶915

Under Chapter 11 of the Statute, a foreign bankruptcy decree issued in the country of the debtor's domicile may now be recognised in Switzerland upon application by the foreign bankruptcy receiver or one of the creditors, provided that:

(a) the decree is enforceable in the country where it was issued;

(b) its recognition is not against public policy; and

(c) the country which issued the decree grants reciprocity to Switzerland.

(3) Recognition of foreign bankruptcy

An application for recognition of a foreign bankruptcy decree is filed with the court where the assets are located. When the assets are located in several places, jurisdiction lies with the asset that is designated first. Claims of the debtor in bankruptcy are deemed to be located at the domicile of the debtor.

Once a motion to recognise a foreign bankruptcy decree has been made, the court may, upon petition, order conservatory measures. Actions in attachment which are pending or have become pending during the recognition proceedings are suspended until the proceedings are concluded.

The judgment on the recognition of the foreign bankruptcy decree is published in Switzerland. A recognition is officially communicated to the office of execution, the bankruptcy office, the office of the land register, the office of the Register of Commerce at the location of the assets and, depending on the case, the Federal Office of Intellectual Property. The same applies for closing, suspending and cancelling the proceedings.

Unless otherwise provided, the recognition of a foreign bankruptcy decree has the same consequences for the debtor's assets in Switzerland as a bankruptcy declared under Swiss law. Actions for avoidance of preferences are determined by Swiss law. They can be brought by a foreign receiver in bankruptcy or by one of the creditors in bankruptcy.

In the schedule of claims, the only claims entered are those secured by a pledge located in Switzerland and non-secured priority claims, provided the creditors are domiciled in Switzerland. When a creditor has been partly satisfied in foreign bankruptcy proceedings, the amount received must be credited towards the dividends in the Swiss bankruptcy proceedings.

After the creditors have been satisfied, the balance is made available to the foreign receiver in bankruptcy or to the creditors. The balance may be disposed of only after the Swiss court has recognised the foreign bankruptcy decree. The court examines, in particular, whether the claims of creditors domiciled in Switzerland have been adequately taken into account in the foreign schedule of claims. If the foreign schedule of claims is not recognised, the balance must be distributed among those creditors domiciled in Switzerland who are unsecured and have no priority under bankruptcy law. The same applies if no foreign schedule of claims is submitted for recognition during the time fixed by the Swiss court.

(4) Recognition of foreign composition
Similar rules apply to foreign financial reorganisation and composition proceedings.

SELECTED BIBLIOGRAPHY

Kurt Amonn, *Grundriss des Schuldbetreibungs- und Konkursrechtes*, 4th edn (Bern, 1988)

J. Alfred Büchi, Isaak Meier and Urs Bosshard, *Grundzüge des schweizerischen Schuldbetreibungsrechts*, vol. 1, 2nd edn (Zürich, 1982 and 1983)

Antoine Favre, *Droit des poursuites* 3rd edn (Fribourg, 1974)

Hans Fritzsche, *Schuldbetreibung und Konkurs nach schweizerischem Recht*, vol. 2 (Zürich, 1968)

Hans Fritzsche and Hans Ulrich Walder, *Schuldbetreibung und Konkurs nach schweizerischem Recht*, vol. 1, 3rd edn (Zürich, 1984)

Pierre-Robert Gilléron, *Poursuite pour dettes, Faillite et Concordat*, 2nd edn (Lausanne, 1988)

10 Taxation

PRINCIPAL LEGISLATION

Federal

Arrêté du Conseil fédéral sur la perception d'un impôt fédéral direct/ Bundesratsbeschluss über die direkte Bundessteuer/Federal Income Tax Decree (FITD), RS 642.11.

Loi fédérale sur les droits de timbre/Stempelabgabengesetz/Federal Stamp Tax Statute (FSTS), RS 641.10; translated by Marcus Desax, *Swiss Stamp Tax Legislation*, translation of statute, main circulars and directives pertaining to the federal stamp tax, published by Swiss-American Chamber of Commerce, Zürich, 1986.

Arrêté du Conseil fédéral instituant un impôt sur le chiffre d'affaires/ Warenumsatzsteuerbeschluss/Federal Wholesale Tax Decree, RS 641.20.

Loi fédérale sur l'impôt anticipé/Verrechnungssteuergesetz/Federal Anticipatory Tax Statute (FATS), RS 642.21.

Arrêté du Conseil fédéral instituant des mesures contre l'utilisation sans cause légitime des conventions conclues par la Confédération en vue d'éviter les doubles impositions, 'arrêté relatif aux abus'/Bundesratsbeschluss betreffend Massnahmen gegen die ungerechtfertigte Inanspruchnahme von Doppel-besteurungsabkommen des Bundes, 'Missbrauchsbeschluss'/Federal Decree on Measures Regarding Abuse of Double-Taxation Conventions ('Abuse Decree'), RS 672.202.

Pestalozzi Gmuer & Heiz, *Rechtsbuch der Schweizerischen Bundessteuern*, Swiss federal tax statutes, decrees, ordinances, circulars, directives, etc., Basel (since 1937).

Cantonal (selected)
Geneva

Loi générale sur les contributions publiques/Income Tax Statute.
Loi sur les droits d'enregistrement/Registration Tax Statute.
Loi sur les droits de succession/Inheritance Tax Statute.

Zurich

Gesetz über die direkten Steuern/Income Tax Statute.

Gesetz über die Erbschafts- und Schenkungssteuer/Inheritance and Gift Tax
  Statute.

CASE LAW

Besides the official reporter of the judgments of the Swiss Federal Supreme
Court (ATF, see ¶109(2)), tax cases of this court are reported in *Archives de
droit fiscal suisse*/*Archiv für Schweizerisches Abgaberecht* (the French
abbreviation '*Archives*' is used in this chapter).

TAX SYSTEM IN GENERAL

¶1001   Political background – economic aspects

(1) Political background

The present Swiss tax system is based on a tradition of long standing and reflects
the political structure of the Confederation. Its 26 cantons (states) have their own
constitutions and broad legislative and administrative powers in tax and fiscal
matters, as they have autonomy and sovereignty in their own territory in all
matters not expressly reserved to the Confederation by the Federal Constitution.
The cantons, in turn, confer taxing powers upon the municipalities in different
degrees. Consequently, there are 27 separate tax jurisdictions and three different
levels of taxation (federal, cantonal, and municipal). Due to the fact that the tax
laws and tax rates vary from canton to canton and from municipality to
municipality, the choice of domicile or seat is an important element of tax
planning.

   Most Swiss tax laws provide only a general framework. This often requires
difficult tax problems to be submitted to the authorities for advance rulings on
the application of the tax law to a certain set of facts. The discussions are
conducted informally in a climate of mutual trust; they often lead to a result
satisfactory to both the taxpayer and the tax administration. Many cantons offer
special tax concessions to certain types of companies if specific conditions are
met (domiciliary, holding, service, mixed company tax status, etc.). Treatment
under a privileged tax status is regularly discussed in advance. Several cantons
offer incentives to encourage new foreign investment.

(2) Economic aspect

After a long period of deficits, public sector finances (federal, cantonal and municipal) showed the results set out in Table 10.1 for 1986, 1987 and 1988 (source: *Swiss Statistical Yearbook*, 1991).

Table 10.1: Public sector finances

in million SFr	1986	1987	1988
Confederation:			
revenue	25,144	24,902	27,881
expenditures	23,176	23,861	26,633
Cantons:			
revenue	31,797	33,000	35,274
expenditures	31,409	32,494	34,828
Municipalities:			
revenue	23,707	24,767	25,958
expenditures	23,394	24,209	26,031
Total:			
revenue	68,033	69,752	74,888
expenditures	65,364	67,647	73,267
balance	2,669	2,105	1,621

The aggregated revenues of the Confederation, cantons and municipalities had the structure shown in Table 10.2 overleaf in the years 1986, 1987 and 1988 (source: *Swiss Statistical Yearbook*, 1991).

While the income taxes paid by individuals and corporations yield more than 50 per cent of total public revenue, the income taxes paid by individuals produced the bulk of the public revenue in 1987:

	SFr
federal income tax of individuals	3,808 million
cantonal income taxes of individuals	11,289 million
municipal income taxes of individuals	9,769 million
total individual income tax receipts	24,866 million

¶1001

Table 10.2: Aggregated Swiss Revenues

in million SFr	1986	1987	1988
total revenue of Confederation, cantons and municipalities	68,033	69,752	74,886
income/net worth/capital taxes	38,751	39,144	42,237
federal wholesale tax	7,353	7,912	8,523
special consumer taxes	1,568	1,664	1,627
import duties	3,759	3,774	3,961
other taxes	1,385	1,423	1,501
other revenues	15,217	15,835	17,037
revenue per resident in SFr	10,350	10,538	11,226

Tax revenue is divided between taxation of consumption, i.e., wholesale tax, consumer taxes, import duties (approximately 27 per cent of total revenue), corporate income and capital tax (approximately 9 per cent), federal withholding tax (approximately 3.5 per cent), stamp taxes (approximately 4 per cent), and property tax of individuals (approximately 3.5 per cent).

¶1002   Sources of law

(1)   Federal law

The Federal Government is empowered to enter into international tax conventions which, after approval by the Federal Parliament and due ratification, become sources of law equal to federal statutes. Tax conventions become automatically applicable domestic law; they override any previously or subsequently enacted law.

The division of fiscal powers between the Confederation and the cantons follows the principle that the Confederation may collect only those taxes specially allocated to it by the Federal Constitution, while the cantons may raise all the taxes which are not reserved to the Confederation by the Federal Constitution. The basic principle governing the entire system of Swiss tax law is that a tax may be levied only if there is a legal basis (principle of legality of the tax): a tax may be imposed and collected only by virtue of a legislative act duly passed and promulgated by Parliament and approved by public referendum.

The following are the major taxes and duties levied at the federal level:

- *Customs duties* (Arts 28 and 30 Federal Constitution).
- *Federal wholesale tax* (Art. 41ter(1)(a) and (2) Federal Constitution; implemented by Federal Wholesale Tax Decree). See ¶1066.

- *Stamp taxes* (Art. 41bis(1)(a) Federal Constitution; implemented by Federal Stamp Tax Statute and corresponding Ordinance). See ¶1008 to ¶1010.

- *Federal income tax of individuals and corporations* (Art. 41ter(1)(c) and (5) Federal Constitution and Art. 8 Transitory Provisions of Federal Constitution; implemented by Federal Income Tax Decree).

- *Federal anticipatory tax* (Art. 41bis(1)(b) Federal Constitution; implemented by Federal Anticipatory Tax Statute and corresponding Ordinance). See ¶1007.

- *Military exemption tax* (Art. 18(4) Federal Constitution; implemented by Federal Military Exemption Tax Statute and corresponding Ordinance). See ¶1017.

Various administrative regulations and instructions interpreting federal statutes and ordinances and directing their application, such as circular letters (*circulaires/Kreisschreiben*), instructions (*instructions/Wegleitungen*) or notes (*notices/Merkblätter*), are issued by the Federal Tax Administration. They are addressed to the cantonal tax administrations or directly to taxpayers. These instructions and regulations do not constitute sources of law, rather they are interpretations of law by the highest tax authorities and reflect their practice. These instructions have considerable practical importance.

For certain levies (e.g., for customs duties and certain stamp taxes), the Confederation has exclusive fiscal sovereignty. As far as it is not forbidden by the Federal Constitution, the cantons – as sovereign states – have the power to collect all taxes other than those falling within the exclusive competence of the Confederation. Since the exclusive competence of the Confederation extends only to a relatively limited number of taxes, the cantons have a great deal of liberty in shaping their fiscal system. Their main fiscal resources lie in income, net-worth, inheritance and property taxes.

(2) Cantonal law

The cantons' power to tax is restricted by several provisions of the Federal Constitution, such as the prohibition of:

(a) taxes which would be contrary to the principle of equality before the law;

(b) confiscatory taxes;

(c) prohibitive taxes on trades and professions; and

(d) intercantonal double taxation.

In addition, federal legislation prohibits the cantons and municipalities from taxing the funds administered by the Confederation. The same applies to immovable property, institutions and other assets belonging to the Confederation.

¶1002

Moreover, international law, mainly tax conventions, also restricts the fiscal sovereignty of the cantons.

Most cantonal constitutions contain certain principles for the taxation of income, net-worth and property. In all cantons, the levying of taxes is governed by statute. Beside the formal tax statutes, important sources of law include the implementing ordinances issued by the cantonal parliaments or by the cantonal executives. Like the Federal Tax Administration, the cantonal tax authorities issue regulations and instructions containing their interpretation of the law and their practice.

(3) Municipal regulations
In all cantons, the municipalities are authorised to collect property and income taxes, which they usually do by applying a multiplier to the cantonal tax.

(4) Case law
Important sources of law include the decisions handed down by the boards of tax appeals (*commission de recours/Rekurskommission*), by cantonal courts, and by the Federal Supreme Court when it reviews the assessments of the cantonal and federal tax authorities.

(5) New federal legislation for 'tax harmonisation' and for federal income tax
A statute titled 'Tax Harmonisation Statute' was adopted by the Federal Parliament on 14 December 1990 and will become effective on 1 January 1993 (*Loi fédérale sur l'harmonisation des impôts directs des cantons et des communes/Bundesgesetz über die Harmonisierung der direkten Steuern der Kantone und Gemeinden*). The new legislation aims at harmonising the various cantonal tax systems and will significantly affect the cantonal rules pertaining to the determination and assessment of taxable income. According to the transitory provisions of the Tax Harmonisation Statute, the cantons have until the end of the year 2000 to revise their income tax laws.

On 14 December 1990 a Federal Income Tax Statute (*Loi fédérale sur l'impôt fédéral direct/Bundesgesetz über die direkte Bundessteuer*) was adopted. The new statute should become effective on 1 January 1995 and replace the Federal Income Tax Decree of 9 December 1940. However, as the Federal Government may collect only the taxes specially allocated to it by the Federal Constitution, and since a first public vote of 2 June 1991 refused to adopt a provision in the Federal Constitution enabling the Federal Government permanently to raise an income tax on individuals and legal entities (beyond the expiration of the current tax regime in 1994), the constitutional basis still remains to be created.

¶1002

(6) 1991 amendment of Federal Stamp Tax Statute

On 4 October 1991, the Federal Parliament passed an amendment to the Federal Stamp Tax Statute. A referendum (see ¶102(3)) against this law has been announced. If the requisite 50,000 signatures are collected by 13 January 1992, the amendment will have to be submitted to public vote. Otherwise, it will become effective by mid-1992.

The amendment contains the following changes of the FSTS:

(a) *Repeal of certain issuance stamp taxes*
The issuance of shares in Swiss investment funds would no longer be taxed. The issuance tax would not be levied on the capital of a foreign share corporation moving its seat to Switzerland and on shares issued in a financial restructure of a share corporation after capital impairment.

(b) *Repeal of certain transfer stamp taxes*
The transfer stamp tax would no longer be levied on purchases and resale of securities constituting the commercial stock of professional securities dealers. Bonds and shares of foreign debtors denominated in foreign currencies, as well as money market instruments could be issued free of transfer stamp tax. The brokerage of foreign bonds between foreign parties would also be exempt.

(c) *Introduction of issuance stamp tax on Swiss bonds*
Bonds issued by Swiss residents would be subject to a prorated tax from 0.06 to 0.12 per cent per year.

(d) *New definition of securities dealers*
Share corporation, limited liability companies and co-operations which list in their balance sheets taxable securities of more than SFr 10 million are deemed 'securities dealers' and are therefore taxpayers for securities transfer stamp tax purposes.

¶1003 Prohibition of intercantonal double taxation

The sovereignty of the cantons to levy taxes is restricted by Art. 46(2) of the Federal Constitution, which reads as follows: 'Federal legislation will contain the necessary provisions against double taxation.' Up to now, no federal statute on the avoidance of intercantonal double taxation has been enacted. The Federal Supreme Court, however, has construed this Article to grant a constitutional right which can be asserted in a constitutional complaint to the Federal Supreme Court (*recours de droit public/staatsrechtliche Beschwerde*). In deciding these complaints, the Federal Supreme Court has created a whole body of legal principles with the purpose of avoiding intercantonal double taxation. These principles are binding on the cantons and have priority over cantonal law. There are also intercantonal conventions, mostly dealing with tax benefits or tax exemptions of charitable institutions. All intercantonal conventions, however, must conform to the principles of the constitutional right against intercantonal double taxation. Most cantonal tax laws contain rules against double taxation.

Double taxation is defined as the levy of an identical or similar tax by two political subdivisions or local authorities of the same level on the same person with respect to the same tax base and for the same period of time. Double taxation therefore requires that an identical or similar tax be imposed by two political subdivisions of the same level, such as two cantons, there is no double taxation if the same or similar type of tax is imposed by the Confederation and a canton.

Intercantonal double taxation is avoided through exemption. The capital and income allocated to the head office or to a branch in one given canton will be exempt from taxation by all other cantons. The allocation of capital and income is done under the 'indirect method': it is not the books kept by the head office or the branches which are decisive; rather, all the income and capital of the company is aggregated and then re-allocated to the head office and to the branches based on certain allocation factors.

With respect to the allocation of income, these rules work as follows:

(1) An advance allocation of income (*praecipuum/préciput/Vorabzug*) of 10 per cent to 20 per cent of the total corporate income is allocated to the head office.

(2) The remainder is then allocated based on certain factors:
   (a) *manufacturing companies* – production factors, i.e., capital (assets plus capitalised rent) plus labour (capitalised labour expense);
   (b) *trading companies* – the respective turnovers.

(3) In certain special cases, such as banks, if the remainder of income could not be allocated based on the above criteria, the allocation follows the 'direct method', i.e., is based on the books kept by the head office and the branches.

PRINCIPAL TAXES

¶1004   Income taxes of individuals and corporations

The Federal, cantonal and municipal governments levy income taxes on individuals and corporations.

Income taxation of individuals is described in detail in ¶1027 et seq.

Income taxation of partnerships and other entities that are not legal entities is described in ¶1046.

Income taxation of legal entities in general and of share corporations in particular is detailed in ¶1047 et seq.

¶1005   Net-worth tax of individuals

The cantonal and municipal governments, but not the Federal Government, levy taxes on the net worth of individuals. The tax is described in more detail in ¶1043.

¶1006   Capital tax of corporations

A tax on the capital of corporations is levied at all three levels. For details see ¶1055 et seq.

¶1007   Federal anticipatory tax (withholding tax)

(1)   Source of the law – taxpayers

(a)   Source of the law
Pursuant to the Federal Anticipatory Tax Statute (FATS) (*Loi fédérale sur l'impôt anticipé/Verrechnungssteuergesetz*) of 13 October 1965, as amended, the Federal Government levies an anticipatory (sometimes translated as 'withholding') tax (*impôt anticipé/Verrechnungssteuer*) on income from movable capital, lottery gains and insurance benefits (Art. 1(1)). The primary aim of the anticipatory tax with respect to resident taxpayers is to ensure that all income derived from capital property is duly reported to the tax authorities.

(b)   The taxpayer
The anticipatory tax is not a real burden for Swiss resident individual or corporate taxpayers who discharge their tax obligation, as the tax is credited (for individuals; the excess anticipatory tax over the individual's tax liability is refunded) or fully refundable (for corporations and other legal entities) in the following year. The only 'burden' consists of loss of interest on the tax withheld.

Non-resident individuals and corporations are not entitled to a refund of the anticipatory tax, unless specifically provided for by an applicable international double-taxation convention. Exceptions to this rule are discussed below.

The anticipatory tax must be paid by the payer of the taxable benefit, e.g., the dividend-paying company or interest-paying bank (Art. 10(1) FATS), not the recipient. Members of the board of directors and liquidators of corporations are jointly and severally liable for the payment of the anticipatory tax due on dividends, other benefits of a financial nature or liquidation proceeds (Art. 15 FATS). The payer must pass the tax on to the recipient by withholding it from the payment which is subject to the tax. If the tax is not withheld, the effective payment is regarded as a net payment after tax, and the taxable amount is 'grossed up', with the effect that a tax of 53.85 per cent of the net payment is due. This duty may not be waived by agreement (Art. 14 FATS; ATF 108 Ib 475).

Non-payment of the tax entails a fine of up to SFr 10,000. In particular cases defined and narrowly limited by the law, it is possible to report the occurrence of taxable payments in writing to the Federal Tax Administration instead of withholding (Art. 20 FATS and Art. 24(1) of the Implementing Ordinance; ATF 94 I 472). For payments by insurance companies, reporting instead of withholding is the usual procedure.

(2)   Object of taxation

(a)   Income from movable capital
The most important object of the anticipatory tax is income from movable capital (Art. 4(1) FATS). It comprises interest, rent, profit distributions (dividends), and similar income derived from:

(i) bonds, serial promissory notes, serial mortgage notes and registered notes issued by a Swiss resident;

(ii) shares of companies and co-operative corporations, and participation certificates of Swiss resident entities;

(iii) shares of investment trusts or similar funds issued by a Swiss resident or by a foreigner in connection with a resident; or

(iv) deposits with Swiss banks and savings banks.

The Implementing Ordinance of 19 December 1966 to the Federal Anticipatory Tax Statute defines income from securities as any benefit of a financial nature to the creditor or shareholder other than repayment of capital. In particular, liquidation proceeds in excess of the paid-in capital, gratuitously issued shares (stock dividends), and undisclosed distributions of profits (constructive dividends) are subject to the tax.

Article 4(2) of the Federal Anticipatory Tax Statute provides that the transfer abroad of the seat (domicile) of a share corporation, limited liability company, co-operative corporation or investment trust is treated as a liquidation for the purposes of the anticipatory tax.

The statute provides the following express exemptions from the anticipatory tax (Art. 5(1) FATS):

(i) retained earnings and profits of a corporation, limited liability company, or co-operative corporation which are transferred to the reserves of another entity of same kind upon merger, transformation, or corporate division;

¶1007

(ii) interest on savings accounts and deposits if the amount of interest is less than SFr 50 per year;

(iii) capital gains in, and capital repayments from, investment trusts paid through a separate coupon;

(iv) interest on deposits in insurance funds, welfare funds, and similar institutions which provide for old-age, survivors and disability benefits.

(b) Lottery gains
Gains in excess of SFr 50 from lotteries, sweepstakes, bets, pools and the like organised in Switzerland are taxable (Art. 6 FATS).

(c) Insurance benefits
Payments of capital under life insurance policies and annuities and pensions are taxable if the insurance is part of a Swiss portfolio, and if the beneficiary is a Swiss resident when the insured event occurs (Art. 7(1) FATS).

(3) Tax rates
The anticipatory tax rates are 35 per cent on income from movable capital and lottery gains, 15 per cent on annuities and pensions, and 8 per cent on other insurance payments.

(4) Payment of tax
The tax liability arises when the taxable benefit becomes due or when the payment of the insurance benefit is made. Except for insurance companies, the tax must be withheld by the payer of the taxable benefit and be remitted to the Federal Tax Administration within a short time limit (usually 30 days) (Art. 16 FATS). The anticipatory tax due from co-operative corporations is assessed on the basis of annual tax returns.

The collection of anticipatory taxes is subject to a five-year Statute of Limitations, which starts to run in the year following the one in which the tax claim arose (Art. 17(1) FATS).

(5) Refund/credit of anticipatory tax
The anticipatory taxes are reimbursable by way of cash refunds (for corporate taxpayers) or credits to income taxes (for individuals), subject to the following conditions:

(a) The asset and the income derived therefrom on which the anticipatory tax was withheld must be duly reported.

(b) Individuals are entitled to a full refund of anticipatory taxes if they are subject to an unlimited tax obligation when the taxable payment becomes

¶1007

due (Art. 22 FATS and Art. 51(1) of the Implementing Ordinance). Individuals who are subject to a limited tax obligation and who pay cantonal and municipal taxes on the income on which an anticipatory tax is levied may claim a refund thereof up to the amount of the regular cantonal and municipal income and net-worth taxes paid, provided that the anticipatory tax arises during the period when they are subject to a limited tax obligation.

(c) Legal entities and trading companies that are not legal entities may claim a refund if their corporate seat or headquarters is in Switzerland when the taxable payment becomes due (Art. 24(2) FATS). The same applies to associations of persons or conglomerations of assets without legal personality if they have an organisation in Switzerland and are active or are managed here (Art. 24(5) FATS). Investment funds may claim a refund if they are subject to taxes (Art. 10(2) FATS).

(d) Non-resident recipients of income on which the anticipatory tax has been levied cannot claim a refund unless this is specifically provided for by an applicable double taxation convention. Foreign enterprises with a permanent establishment in Switzerland may claim a refund if the assets from which the taxable income is derived are attributable to the Swiss permanent establishment (Art. 24(3) FATS). Foreign legal entities and foreign non-profit organisations are entitled to refunds of anticipatory taxes that are withheld on income derived from those assets that are exclusively used for religious, educational, or similar purposes in the interests of non-resident Swiss citizens (Art. 24(4) FATS).

Claims for refunds must be submitted on official forms after the expiration of the calender year in which the taxable payment becomes due (Art. 29(1) and (2) FATS). Under certain circumstances, earlier refunds are possible. The right to a refund is subject to a Statute of Limitations of three years (Art. 32(1) FATS). Shorter time-limits apply under several double taxation conventions.

(6)   Procedural aspects
The collection of the anticipatory tax is generally based on the principle of self-assessment (exception: tax on benefits from co-operative corporations). Whenever an anticipatory tax liability arises, the taxpayer must file a return with the necessary documentation and pay the tax. The Federal Tax Administration is entitled to inspect and audit the taxpayer's books and other relevant documents.

The decisions of the Federal Tax Administration concerning assessment, collection or refund of anticipatory taxes may be challenged with a 'motion to reconsider' (*opposition/Einsprache*) filed in writing within 30 days with the Federal Tax Administration. Decisions by the Federal Tax Administration upon

¶1007

a motion to reconsider may be brought before the Federal Supreme Court within 30 days by means of an administrative-law appeal.

Requests for credit filed by resident individuals are handled by the cantonal income tax authorities; all other refunds are dealt with by the Federal Tax Administration. The tax administration may require additional information relevant for the credit or refund. Decisions of cantonal authorities are subject to a motion to reconsider to be filed within 30 days. The decision on the motion to reconsider may be appealed within 30 days before the cantonal board of tax appeals; its decision may be challenged within 30 days by means of an administrative-law appeal before the Federal Supreme Court.

Article 47(1) of the Federal Anticipatory Tax Statute provides that the Federal Tax Administration may require a bond to be posted for taxes, interest and costs, even if they are not yet finally assessed or due for payment, if:

(a) the tax collection appears to be jeopardised; or

(b) the taxpayer is domiciled abroad, is about to relocate his or her domicile outside Switzerland, or is about to have its registration cancelled in the Register of Commerce; or

(c) the taxpayer is or has repeatedly been in arrears in paying the tax.

Decisions requiring such security must indicate the amount to be secured, the place where security is accepted, and the reasons. A decision requiring a bond to be posted has the effect of an attachment order in the sense of Art. 274 of the Federal Statute on Debt Collection and Bankruptcy (¶910). The decision may be challenged within 30 days by means of an administrative-law appeal to the Federal Supreme Court. The appeal does not suspend the execution of the decision.

Evasion of anticipatory tax entails fines of up to SFr 30,000 or three times the amount of the tax evaded. The same applies to obtaining unjustified tax credits or refunds, or other advantages. Stiffer penalties are reserved under federal administrative criminal law (notably in cases of fiscal fraud).

¶1008   Federal stamp tax on issuance of securities

(1)   Taxable transactions

Based on the Federal Stamp Tax Statute ('FSTS') (*Loi fédérale sur les droits de timbre/Stempelabgabengesetz* of 27 June 1973, as amended), the Federal Government levies a stamp tax on the issuance of certain securities (Arts 1(1) and 5 FSTS) (*droits de timbre/Stempelsteuer*). The word 'stamp' is a relic of the time when payment of the tax was acknowledged by stamping the document. The stamp has disappeared, but the tax and its name have remained! The issuance tax is levied in the following situations:

(a) the creation or increase, for consideration or gratuitously, of the par value of participation rights in the form of:

    (i) shares in Swiss share corporations or limited partnerships with shares;

    (ii) shares in Swiss limited liability companies;

    (iii) shares in Swiss co-operative corporations; or

    (iv) profit-sharing certificates of Swiss corporations, limited liability companies or co-operative corporations. Documents evidencing claims on the net profit or the liquidation proceeds are deemed profit-sharing certificates.

(b) The creation of shares in an investment fund by a Swiss resident or by a foreign resident jointly with a Swiss resident, including the transfer of the net profits of the assets of the fund to the capital account of the investor (but see ¶1002(6)).

The term 'creation of participation rights' includes the following transactions:

(a) contributions to the capital of the share corporation, limited liability company or co-operative corporation by the shareholders without corresponding consideration, and without increase in the capital of the company as registered with the Register of Commerce or the paid-in amount of the shares of the co-operative corporation;

(b) the transfer of ownership of the majority of the participation rights in a Swiss share corporation, limited partnership with shares, limited liability company or co-operative corporation whose business is wound up or whose assets have been brought into liquid form; and

(c) the transfer of the seat of a foreign share corporation to Switzerland without reincorporation (but see ¶1002(6)).

(2) Exemptions

Transactions with respect to certain types of companies, such as non-profit organisations, those dedicated to public interest goals and small co-operative corporations, are exempt from the issuance stamp tax. Participation rights created or increased by using previously paid premiums on shares (*agio*) or contributions by the shareholders are also exempt, provided that the entity demonstrates that the issuance stamp tax on the premiums or contributions was paid (Art. 6 FSTS).

(3) Liability for tax – rates, assessment and payment

The tax claim arises when participation rights are created or increased, when they are registered in the Register of Commerce, when capital is contributed, or when the ownership of the majority of participation rights is transferred (Art. 7 FSTS).

¶1008

The issuance stamp tax on participation rights is 3 per cent. The tax is calculated on the consideration received by the company or other entity for the creation or increase of participation rights; it must be calculated at least:

(a) on the par value;

(b) on the amount of contribution to capital; or

(c) on the net assets or the par value of all existing participation rights of the economically liquidated entity when ownership of the majority of participation rights is transferred.

The tax on shares in investment funds amounts to 0.9 per cent and is calculated on the amount received by the investment fund in consideration for the shares, or on the net profits transferred to the capital account. Assets and claims are valued at their fair market value at the time of their contribution (Art. 8 FSTS).

Privileged tax rates apply in the case of mergers and similar transactions, reorganisation and spin-offs (1 per cent; see ¶1061(2), ¶1062(3), and ¶1063(2)) and relocation of foreign corporations to Switzerland without re-incorporation (1.5 per cent; see ¶1064(2)).

The company or other entity issuing participation rights or receiving a capital contribution is liable for the tax. The tax usually falls due 30 days after the tax claim arises. In the event of an open or tacit corporate financial restructuring, the due date may be extended, or the tax may even be waived if the levy of the issuance tax entails serious hardship (Art. 12 FSTS).

(4) Statute of Limitations

The tax claim is barred by the Statute of Limitations and can no longer be collected after five years from the end of the calendar year during which it arose.

(5) Remedies

All necessary decisions are rendered by the Federal Tax Administration and may be challenged within 30 days after their notification by means of a motion to reconsider filed in writing with the Federal Tax Administration. The Federal Tax Administration's decisions on the motion to reconsider may be appealed within 30 days after their notification by means of an administrative-law appeal filed with the Federal Supreme Court.

¶1009   Federal stamp tax on transfer of securities

(1) Taxable transactions

Pursuant to the Federal Stamp Tax Statute ('FSTS'; for French and German designations see ¶1008(1)), the Federal Government levies a transfer stamp tax on the transfer of certain securities and similar documents if at least one of the parties to the transaction or an intermediary qualifies as a domestic securities dealer (Art. 13(1) FSTS). 'Transfer' means any transfer of ownership in securities against a consideration.

(2)   Taxable securities
The following are taxable securities (Art. 13(2) FSTS):

(a) The following instruments issued by a Swiss resident:

(i) bonds, including bonds guaranteed by a mortgage pursuant to Art. 875 CC, annuity bonds, mortgage notes, bank-issued medium-term notes, certificates of deposit;

(ii) corporate shares, shares in limited liability companies and co-operative corporations, profit-sharing certificates;

(iii) shares in investment funds; or

(iv) bills of exchange and similar instruments, as well as other payment orders and promissory notes made to order or payable to bearer.

(b) Instruments issued by a foreign resident that serve the same economic purpose as those listed in paragraph (a).

(c) Certificates evidencing subparticipations in the instruments listed in paragraphs (a) and (b), and in claims arising from loans.

If no physical security (document) is transferred, the books of accounts and other documents evidencing the transfer are deemed securities (Art. 1(2) FSTS).
See ¶1002(6) for 1991 amendment of the FSTS.

(3)   Securities dealer defined
Anyone who qualifies as a Swiss securities dealer (*commerçant suisse de titres/inländischer Effektenhändler*) under the Stamp Tax Statute owes the tax, is liable for its collection and must register on his own initiative with the Federal Tax Administration. For the purposes of the Stamp Tax Statute, the following are considered securities dealers (Art. 13(3) FSTS):

(a) individuals, legal entities and partnerships that are engaged, professionally and with the intention of deriving a profit, in the business of purchasing and selling taxable securities for their own or for a third party's account;

(b) the managements and custodian banks of investment funds;

(c) share corporations, limited liability companies and co-operative corporations not falling within paragraph (a):

(i) the principal goal of which, as stated in the Articles of Incorporation, consists of holding investments in other companies, provided that the capital of the

¶1009

share corporation, company or co-operative corporation, as stated in the Articles of Incorporation, amounts at least to SFr 500,000, or

(ii) of which, according to the most recent balance sheet, more than half of the assets consist of taxable securities and claims, provided that this half amounts at least to SFr 1,000,000.

See ¶1002(6) for 1991 amendment of the FSTS.

(4) Exemptions

The Swiss National Bank is exempt from its portion of the tax on transactions concluded by it in furtherance of its monetary and credit policy. Further, the following transactions are exempt from the transfer tax (Art. 14 FSTS):

(a) The issuance of Swiss corporate shares, shares in limited liability companies and co-operative corporations, profit-sharing certificates and shares in investment funds, including firm underwriting by a bank or holding company and allocation in a subsequent issue.

(b) The contribution in kind of securities as payment for Swiss corporate shares, shares in limited liability companies and co-operative corporations, profit-sharing certificates and shares in investment funds.

(c) The acquisition of bills of exchange and similar instruments, other payment orders and promissory notes made to order or payable to the bearer, and subparticipations in claims arising from loans by a bank within the meaning of the Federal Banking Statute, by the Swiss National Bank or by a central mortgage-bond institution, for its own account.

(d) The transfer of subscription rights.

(e) The return of securities for cancellation.

(5) Tax liability – rates – assessment basis

The tax claim arises when the transaction is concluded or, in the case of conditional transactions or grants of option rights, when the transaction is executed.

The transfer tax is calculated on the consideration; it amounts to 0.15 per cent for securities issued by a Swiss, and to 0.3 per cent for securities issued by a non-Swiss resident. A reduced rate of 0.1 (Swiss issuer) or 0.2 per cent (non-resident issuer) applies to bonds, bills of exchange and similar instruments, other payment orders and promissory notes made to order or payable to the bearer with a maturity of no more than three months, and for certificates of subparticipation in all of the above securities (Arts 16 and 16(a) FSTS).

The transfer tax is owed by the registered securities dealer (Art. 17 FSTS). If both parties are securities dealers, each of them owes half of the tax. If securities dealers act as intermediaries, they owe half of the tax for the parties to the

¶1009

transaction who do not identify themselves as registered securities dealers. The securities dealers are deemed intermediaries:

(a) if they establish the statement of account to their principals at the original conditions agreed upon with the other party;

(b) if they merely indicate opportunities for transactions to the contracting parties; or

(c) if they transfer the securities on the day of acquisition.

If securities dealers firmly underwrite securities at their issue, they are deemed parties to the transaction. If they, as subparticipants, acquire securities from other registered securities dealers and pass them on during the issue, they are exempt from their portion of the tax (Art. 18 FSTS).

If a transaction is concluded abroad, and if one of the parties to the transaction is a foreign bank or a foreign broker, that party's portion of the tax obligation is not due; however, half the tax is owed if a securities dealer acts as an intermediary between two foreign banks or foreign brokers. A transaction is deemed to be concluded abroad:

(a) if both parties are located abroad when the declarations leading to the conclusion of the transaction are issued; or

(b) if the transaction is concluded by letter or by telecommunication between a Swiss location and a foreign location, and if the statements of account are to be established by the foreign bank or the foreign exchange agent.

See ¶1002(6) for 1991 amendment of the FSTS.

(6) Procedure and payment of tax

Anyone who bears a stamp tax obligation pursuant to the Stamp Tax Statute must register with the Federal Tax Administration *sua sponte*. The transfer tax falls due 30 days after the end of the quarter during which the tax claim arose (Art. 20 FSTS). On the due date of the tax, the taxpayers must, on their own initiative, file the required statements and the verifying documentation with the Federal Tax Administration and, at the same time, pay the tax (Art. 34 FSTS).

The securities dealers owe the tax. They must organise and keep books so as to allow for reliable ascertainment and proof, without special effort, of the facts that have importance for determining the tax obligation and for calculating the amount of the tax. If the taxpayers use an electronic data-processing system, it may be used for the levy of the taxes only on the condition that it does an exact and complete processing of all transactions and amounts essential for tax purposes, and on the further condition that the documents necessary for the calculation of the tax are adequately classified and legible from the original verifying documentation to the annual profit and loss statement and the statement of account. Taxpayers have the duty to furnish comprehensive information to the Federal Tax Administration (Art. 35 FSTS). The Federal Tax Administration is entitled to audit the taxpayers' books of account, the verifying documentation and other documents at their premises.

(7) Statute of Limitations
See ¶1008(4).

(8) Remedies
See ¶1008(5).

¶1010   Federal stamp tax on insurance premiums

(1) Taxable transactions
According to Art. 21 of the Federal Stamp Tax Statute ('FSTS'; for French and German designation see ¶1008(1)), a stamp tax is levied on the payment of insurance premiums on policies that are:

(a) part of the Swiss portfolio of an insurer subject to the supervision of the Federal Insurance Office or of a Swiss insurer enjoying public law status; or

(b) taken out by a resident from a foreign insurer not subject to federal supervision.

(2) Exemptions
The payment of premiums for the following types of insurance is exempt from the stamp tax:

- life insurance (capital and annuities insurance),
- health and disability insurance,
- accident insurance,
- insurance for transportation of goods,
- insurance against damage caused by natural forces to farmland and plants,
- unemployment insurance,
- hailstorm insurance,
- cattle insurance,
- reinsurance,
- comprehensive insurance of aircraft and ships that are primarily used abroad for the professional transportation of persons and goods, and

- insurance against fire, theft, glass breakage and water damage, and insurance of credit, machinery and jewellery, provided the taxpayer demonstrates that the property insured is located abroad.

(3) Tax liability – rates – assessment and payment

The tax claim arises upon payment of the premium. The tax is calculated on the net cash premium and amounts to 5 per cent; for third-party liability and comprehensive car insurance it amounts to 1.25 per cent (Art. 24 FSTS).

The tax is owed by the insurer. If the insurance is taken out from a foreign insurer, the resident insured is liable for the tax (Art. 25 FSTS). The tax falls due 30 days after the end of the quarter during which the tax claim arose (Art. 26 FSTS).

(4) Statute of Limitations

See ¶1008(4).

(5) Remedies

See ¶1008(5).

¶1011   Federal wholesale tax

The Federal Government levies a wholesale tax on delivery of goods from the wholesaler to the retailer. This one-phase tax is levied instead of a sales or value added tax. For details of this tax, see ¶1066 et seq.

¶1012   Immovable property transfer tax

The Federal Government does not tax transfers of immovable property. In some cantons transfers of immovable property are not subject to a tax but are subject to land register fees; in all other cantons, transfer taxes are levied either by the cantonal government or by the municipalities.

Taxable transfers are *inter vivos* transfers of title to immovable property and transactions that are economically equivalent to these transfers. Thus, the transfer of all or a majority of the shares of a real estate company is, as a rule, deemed to be a taxable transfer. The tax is computed on the purchase price or, if the price cannot be determined or appears to be arbitrary or unusually low, by appraisal of the fair market value of the property. In some cantons, the value of accessories is included.

The cantonal laws provide for exemptions for various types of transfers, e.g., transfers through inheritance or gift, transfers in the course of privileged transformations, mergers or split-offs of enterprises, and many others.

In most of the cantons, the person who must pay the tax is the person to whom the property is transferred, but the transferor is jointly and severally liable for payment. Some cantons provide that both parties to the transaction must pay the tax.

The tax rates range roughly between 0.1 and 4 per cent. Where the transfer must be entered in the land register, the tax is provisionally assessed and collected by the office of the land register. In other cases, the taxpayer must file a return with the municipal tax office or land register office within a certain period.

¶1013   Tax treatment of capital gains

(1)   Capital gains defined
In tax law, the term 'capital gains' describes any increase in the value of an asset resulting from special economic conditions or events rather than from the personal efforts of the taxpayer. As a general rule, capital gains are taxable only upon realisation. The most important example of realisation is the disposition of the asset in exchange for a valuable consideration, which is usually accomplished through a sale, an exchange, or expropriation.

Depending on the level of taxation (federal, cantonal, municipal), the category of the taxpayer (individual or corporate), and the kind of assets involved (movable or immovable, private or business), capital gains may be:

(a) included in the taxable income;

(b) subject to special gains taxes; or

(c) entirely tax-free.

(2)   Capital gains on movable private assets
In regard to movable assets, gains realised by individuals on the disposition of private (i.e., non-business) assets must be distinguished from gains realised by individuals on the disposition of business assets and by corporate taxpayers on the disposition of assets.

For the purpose of the federal income tax and most cantonal income taxes, capital gains realised on movable assets are taxable only if the assets belonged to the business property of the taxpayer and if the taxpayer is legally required to keep ordinary books. Capital gains on private movable assets are tax-exempt under federal, and almost all cantonal, tax laws.

(3)   Capital gains on movable business assets
In the majority of cantons, capital gains on movable business assets qualify as income subject to tax, even if the taxpayer is not obliged to keep ordinary books. In some cantons these capital gains are taxed only if the taxpayer must keep books or manages a business in a commercial manner.

As capital gains realised in a business context are taxable, the distinction between business property and private property is important in determining the taxable income of individual entrepreneurs and members of a partnership. The Federal Supreme Court has developed rules for the allocation of assets and liabilities. Assets are considered business property if they were acquired for business purposes or serve the business, or if they otherwise qualify as business property by their nature (ATF 110 Ib 121, 94 I 464). The subjective intention of the taxpayers and the source for the financing of the acquisition of the asset are regarded as a mere indication for classification. The actual use in business is decisive either directly (through the nature of the asset) or indirectly, e.g., if put up as a pledge for business debts. The classification as business or private property is particularly difficult if the asset is used simultaneously for business and private purposes. The federal, and most cantonal, tax authorities allow allocation of value according to actual use; some cantons classify the asset according to its preponderant use.

(4) Capital gains on immovable property
Gains realised on the sale or other disposition of immovable property are taxed. The method of taxation varies from canton to canton and depends on whether the gain is realised on private or business immovable property.

(a) Immovable private assets
Private gains on the sale of immovable property are not taxed on the federal level unless the gains result from the taxpayer's professional activity, in which case gains are taxable as ordinary income. Private gains on immovable property are taxable in all cantons, but the method of taxation varies. While some cantons provide for a special immovable property capital gains tax (*impôt sur les gains immobiliers/Grundstückgewinnsteuer*), other cantons subject these gains to ordinary income taxation.

(b) Immovable business assets
In the majority of cantons, gains on immovable business assets are included in the income subject to the normal income tax; however, in some cantons (including Zurich and Bern), they are subject to a special immovable property capital gains tax (¶1014). In the canton of Zurich, the increase in value is subject to the special tax, while any recaptured tax-effective depreciations of prior years are included in the income subject to the normal income tax.

In most cantons (except Zurich and Bern) capital gains realised by immovable property brokers on the sale of land belonging to their businesses are regarded as income from independent gainful activity. They are, therefore, subject to ordinary income tax.

Capital losses are deductible for income tax purposes to the extent that corresponding capital gains are included in the taxable income. If immovable

¶1013

property capital gains are subject to the special tax, corresponding losses cannot be set off (¶1014).

(c) Assessment of the capital gain
Only those immovable property capital gains that have been realised are taxable. The legal rules regarding realisation vary, but basically provide two categories of taxable transactions:

   (i) sales, exchanges and other transactions in which the transferor parts with the legal power of disposition of the asset;

   (ii) transactions by which the actual ability to dispose of immovable property or the beneficial ownership in immovable property is transferred without a civil law transfer of title (ATF 104 Ia 251, 102 Ia 342; *Archives* 52, 305).

Transactions of the second category (where beneficial ownership changes without civil law disposition) include:

● the transfer of all or the majority of the capital stock in a real estate company,

● the establishment of public or private easements and servitudes (e.g., the right to build on another person's land), as far as these encumbrances permanently and substantially limit ownership rights, and

● the grant of rights of pre-emption or of first refusal.

Like taxable transactions, tax-exempt transactions vary from canton to canton. Typical tax-exempt transactions are transfers:

● in connection with a compulsory sale or execution,

● for purposes of zoning, rectifying boundaries, or consolidating agricultural plots,

● in connection with reorganisations of enterprises which do not result in any significant modification in ownership,

● in connection with mergers or split-offs of enterprises if certain conditions are met (see ¶1061 and ¶1063),

● in connection with the setting up, continuation or dissolution of a marital community of property or with a divorce, and

● at the partition of an estate.

Subject to various conditions, many cantons exempt gains realised on the disposition of immovable property if the proceeds are reinvested in other immovable property in the same canton.
As a general rule, the amount of the taxable capital gain is the difference between the net amount realised and the investment value. The investment value consists of the acquisition price, the expenses connected with the acquisition,

and any subsequent expenditures that increased the value of the property. The acquisition price is usually defined as the price entered in the land register, including all further payments by the purchaser. Different regulations apply if the property was acquired in a tax-free transaction: some cantons deem the fair market value at the time of the tax-free acquisition to be the acquisition price, while other cantons take the value at the time of the last taxable transfer.

The tax rates are generally progressive, based on the amount of gain (usually certain deductions and tax-free amounts apply) and the holding period (higher tax rates for short holding periods). The rate structure varies widely from canton to canton. After a holding period of five years the tax rate in most cantons is between 25 and 40 per cent.

¶1014   Special tax on immovable property

Some cantons impose special annual taxes on immovable property, which is usually defined according to the rules of Art. 655 CC, namely land, buildings, independent and permanent rights entered into the land register, and mines.

These taxes are levied in addition to the net-worth and capital taxes and are structured as a tax on an object (*in rem*) – rather than a tax on the person of the taxpayer (*in personam*) – without allowing the deduction of debts.

The taxation of immovable property is at the cantonal level in some cantons and at the municipal level in others. Usually, the taxes are assessed and collected by the tax office in the municipality in which the property is located; the assessment decision may be challenged by the taxpayer in a motion to reconsider and appeal procedure which follows the rules applicable to income taxation. The immovable property tax is levied only on land situated in the tax-levying community (the canton or the municipality). In the case of immovable property situated in different communities, the tax payable to each community is determined according to the relative value of the portion situated within its borders.

The rates applied to immovable property are proportional in most cantons, and usually range from 0.05 to 0.2 per cent. Often, the municipalities may determine the tax rate themselves within the range provided for in the law.

¶1015   Cantonal taxes on documents and securities

(1)   Cantonal stamp taxes on certain documents

Ten cantons (including Geneva and Basel, but not Zurich) levy stamp taxes on the preparation or use of certain documents such as public deeds, documents used in legal proceedings, business contracts, and similar instruments. The stamp taxes vary from canton to canton. They may be based either on the size of the paper used ('format stamp') or on the amount involved in the document ('graduated stamp'), or they may be 'fixed stamps' on certain documents such as certificates, diplomas, patents, licences, passports, savings bank books, and many others.

All documents subject to the federal stamp tax and all documents issued in proceedings under the federal procedure for debt collection and bankruptcy are exempt from cantonal stamp taxes. Further exemptions under cantonal law may apply.

(2) Stamp tax on the transfer of securities
In addition to the federal securities transfer stamp tax, the cantons of Zurich, Geneva and Basel levy a transfer tax of 0.01 per cent. The stock exchanges of Zurich and Basel add a charge of 0.005 per cent on stock exchange transactions.

¶1016 Other indirect taxes

Other indirect taxes levied by the Confederation are:

- the federal beer tax,
- the federal taxes on distilled liquors,
- the federal tobacco tax,
- the federal duty on heavy trucks,
- the federal tax for the use of national highways ('highway sticker').

¶1017 Federal military service exemption tax

Article 18 of the Federal Constitution imposes the duty on each male Swiss citizen to serve in the armed forces. Strictly speaking, this federal military service exemption tax (*taxe d'exemption du service militaire/ Militärpflichtersatz*) is not a tax but a payment in lieu of discharging the service obligation. The exemption tax is determined on the basis of the taxpayer's total net income from all sources (world-wide income, even if not taxable in Switzerland). The exemption tax consists of a fixed 'personal tax' (minimum SFr 120) and an income tax of up to 3 per cent. The exemption tax base is reduced by certain personal deductions, and the amount of the exemption tax payable is reduced according to the taxpayer's age and the time already served.

TAX ADMINISTRATION AND PROCEDURES

¶1018 Authorities

(1) Federal tax authorities
In matters of federal taxation the Federal Government is the supreme executive authority. The Government has delegated the administration of taxes to the

Federal Department of Finance (*Département fédéral des finances/ Eidgenössisches Finanzdepartement*), which includes the Federal Tax Administration (*Administration fédérale des contributions/Eidgenössische Steuerverwaltung*) and the Federal Customs Administration (*Administration fédérale des douanes/Eidgenössische Zollverwaltung*). The Federal Tax Administration is divided into three principal divisions:

(a) Principal Division of Stamp and Anticipatory Taxes (*Division principale des droits de timbre et de l'impôt anticipé/Hauptabteilung Stempelabgaben und Verrechnungssteuer*), charged with the collection of the federal stamp and anticipatory taxes, refund of the anticipatory tax to legal entities and partnerships and supervision of anticipatory tax credits (and refunds) to individuals by the cantonal tax authorities.

(b) Principal Division of Federal Income Tax (*Division principale de l'impôt fédéral direct/Hauptabteilung direkte Bundessteuer*), charged with supervising the assessment and collection of the federal income tax by the competent cantonal tax authorities.

(c) Principal Division of Wholesale Tax (*Division principale de l'impôt sur le chiffre d'affaires/Hauptabteilung Warenumsatzsteuer*), charged with the collection of the wholesale tax.

Two subdivisions provide services of a more general nature: the Division of International Tax Law and Double Taxation (*Division des affaires de droit fiscal international et de double imposition/Abteilung für internationales Steuerrecht und Doppelbesteuerungssachen*) and the Division of Financial Statistics and Documentation (*Division statistique et documentation/Abteilung Statistik und Dokumentation*). There is also the Section of Military Service Exemption Tax (*Section de la taxe d'exemption du service militaire/Sektion Militärpflichtersatz*), which is responsible for the military service exemption tax (collected by the cantonal tax administrations). This section maintains contact with the Swiss consulates regarding this taxation of Swiss nationals abroad.

(2) Cantonal tax authorities
The administration of cantonal taxes is handled by the competent cantonal finance departments, in particular by their tax administrations. Larger municipalities also have separate tax offices. In most cantons, income taxes – including the federal income tax – are assessed by special tax commissions, functioning at the municipal, district or cantonal level. Other taxes are assessed either by the cantonal tax office, which, in many cantons, assesses the income taxes of legal entities, or by the special cantonal or municipal administrations responsible for particular taxes (taxes on transfers of immovable property,

inheritance and gift taxes, motor vehicle taxes, dog taxes, etc.). Assessment is regularly supervised by the cantonal tax administration.

¶1019   Calculation, tax and payment periods

(1)   Different cantonal systems

Although taxes on income, net worth and capital are generally levied and paid annually, the rhythm of filing tax returns and the method of assessment varies among cantons. While most cantonal taxes are computed and assessed in periods of two successive calendar years, beginning with an odd numbered year, e.g., 1989/90 or 1991/92, other cantons, including Geneva and Zurich, use an accounting period of one calendar year. In either case, if a company uses a fiscal year other than a calendar year, the financial results of the calendar year are deemed, for tax purposes, to be those of the fiscal year ending within the given calendar year. For instance, if a company's fiscal year ends on 30 June, its financial results for the year ending 30 June 1989 are deemed to be the results of the calendar year 1989.

(2)   Calculation, tax and payment periods

For the purposes of computing, assessing and paying income taxes, three different periods are important; the calculation period, the tax period and the payment period.

(a)   Calculation period

The calculation period (*période de calcul/Berechnungsperiode*) is the period during which income is (or was) realised; it serves as the basis for computing the tax. It may consist of one or two years. Exceptionally, the calculation period can be less than a one-year period, e.g., for newly established companies or companies changing their fiscal year, or for individuals becoming subject to taxes for the first time.

(b)   Tax period

The tax period (*période de taxation/Veranlagungsperiode*) is the calendar year or years for which the tax is levied (the period in which the tax claim arises). The tax is generally, but not always, levied on the basis of the calculation period which immediately precedes the tax period. For federal income tax purposes, the assessment of the tax arising in 1989 and 1990 (tax period) is based on the average yearly income of the years 1987 and 1988 (calculation period). For a tax period consisting of two years, the tax for each year is computed on the basis of the average taxable income per year of the two-year calculation period. If a canton provides for a one-year tax period, the tax is levied on the basis of the taxable income realised in the one-year calculation period.

(c)   Payment period
The payment period (*période de paiement/Zahlungsperiode*) is the calendar year during which the tax must be paid, which can be the year in which the tax claim arises (tax period) or the year immediately following it.

(3)   'Praenumerando' and 'postnumerando' assessments
The federal and most cantonal income taxes apply the *praenumerando* (pre-payment) system, where the tax is assessed and collected before the end of the tax period on the basis of two-year calculation period. In this case, the tax for each year of the two-year tax period is levied on the basis of the average yearly taxable income of the two-year calculation period. Some cantons apply a *praenumerando* system with annual assessment (e.g., Zurich for corporations) or with biannual assessment based on a one-year computation period (e.g., Zurich for individuals). A *postnumerando* (post-payment) assessment system, where the taxpayer is assessed annually on the basis of the current tax year's income (e.g., for the tax year 1990 on the income realised in 1990), is applied by some cantons, primarily to corporations (e.g., cantons of Zug and City of Basel), but in the canton of the City of Basel also to individuals. Under this system, tax returns must be filed annually during the year following the tax year.

Under the *praenumerando* assessment system, substantial fluctuations in income due to extraordinary events may result either in a hardship or a windfall to the taxpayer. In such cases, the tax laws allow the taxpayer to adjust taxable income by means of an intermediary assessment (*taxation intermédiaire/ Zwischenveranlagung*). The events justifying an intermediary assessment are specified in the tax laws. Typical events are the commencement or termination of gainful activity, a fundamental change of profession, and an increase in net worth due to inheritance or gift. An intermediary assessment is applied only to the income or net worth affected by the special event. That part of income is assessed on the basis of the current year for the current and for the following tax year. No intermediary assessment is necessary where the *postnumerando* assessment system is applied.

¶1020   Filing of income tax returns – assessment of the tax

(1)   Filing a tax return

(a)   In general
Both federal and cantonal income taxes are handled by the cantonal tax authorities. These tax authorities keep a register of all individuals and corporations subject to tax or presumed to be so.

At the beginning of each tax period, the tax authorities send tax return forms to all taxpayers on their list of presumed taxpayers. In parallel, the taxpayers are directed by public notice to file tax declarations. Taxpayers who do not receive tax return forms are not relieved of the duty to file; rather, they must obtain the necessary forms at the office of the municipal or cantonal tax authority. Usually, this form, together with instructions, contains all information necessary for the levy of both the federal and cantonal income taxes.

The return is due within 30 days of receipt or by the date indicated on the tax return, usually 31 March of the first year of the tax period. Corporate taxpayers may usually file their returns by the end of April or June. The first extension of the time limit is granted upon request; further extensions are granted only under certain circumstances. Failure to file a return results in serious consequences, such as losing the right to file a motion to reconsider; penalties for failure to pay taxes and for withholding information necessary to the tax authorities may be imposed.

(b)   New taxpayers
When they first become subject to Swiss taxes (e.g., by becoming a resident), individuals must file a tax return estimating their income for the remainder of the calendar year in which they have become a taxpayer. A tax return form is sent to these individuals shortly after registration with the municipal authorities. A company is usually required to file its first tax return in the calendar year following the year of incorporation.

(2)   Documents attached to tax return
The completed tax return is signed by the taxpayer and the taxpayer's spouse and filed with all necessary supplementary documentation, such as salary certificates, a balance sheet and a profit and loss statement (to be filed by those taxpayers required under the Code of Obligations to keep books), lists of securities and other capital investments, lists of liabilities with the names of creditors and amount of interest charged, and any other information that may be required by the tax authorities.

(3)   Tax audit
The duty of the taxpayer to co-operate in the assessment of taxes is not limited to the filing of returns. The taxpayer may be ordered to appear personally and to submit any additional information and documentary evidence that may be required to proceed to a correct and lawful assessment. Self-employed individuals are required to keep and present records on their business income and property, even if they are not under an obligation to keep books under applicable commercial law. The tax authorities can audit the taxpayer's or partnership's books as they see fit. As far as specified in the applicable tax laws, the tax

¶1020

authorities may demand information from third parties, including administrative and judicial authorities, but not banks or attorneys-at-law and other privileged persons.

On the other hand, taxpayers have the right to be heard and to produce additional evidence in their favour that is relevant for the assessment; within certain limits, they have access to their file at the tax authority.

(4) Discretionary assessment

Whenever the tax authority finds that the data furnished by the taxpayer are inadequate or that conclusive proof of their accuracy has not been produced, it may proceed to a 'discretionary assessment'. Article 92(1) FITD provides that taxpayers who have been so assessed forfeit their right to file motions to reconsider and appeals if, by the discretionary assessment, their taxable income or net worth was not increased by more than 20 per cent over the last assessment. Similar provisions are found in some cantonal tax laws. Other cantons (e.g., Zurich) provide that the taxpayers who file motions to reconsider against a discretionary assessment bear the burden of proof that the assessment is inadequate.

If the discretionary assessment subsequently turns out to have been insufficient, it may be adjusted and the taxpayer will be subject to penalties for tax evasion (Art. 92(2) FITD).

After the assessment authority has completed its review, it sends the taxpayer an assessment decision indicating the amounts of taxable income and net worth or capital, and often of the tax payable. In some cantons (e.g., Zurich) the notification takes place only if the assessment deviates from the taxpayer's own declaration. The taxpayer is able to verify from the computation of the tax attached to the tax bill that the return has been accepted.

(5) Time limitation of assessment

The right to assess a taxpayer for a given tax year is time-barred after periods of usually three to six years after the end of the tax period. If taxes are not assessed because of tax evasion, a special Statute of Limitations of, in general, five years (in Zurich: ten years) applies.

¶1021 Motion to reconsider – judicial review

(1) Motion to reconsider

A taxpayer who is dissatisfied with the final assessment decision may file a motion to reconsider (*réclamation/Einsprache*) with the authority that has rendered the decision, usually within 30 days from the day the assessment notice was served or when the assessment was otherwise brought to the attention of the taxpayer. The motion to reconsider may also be filed if the assessment is based on information contained in the tax return. When filing a motion, a statement must be submitted with express reasons and a request for reconsideration and correction of the assessment decision. The taxpayer must submit all the documents relating to the motion. After the assessment is reconsidered, a date may be set for a hearing before the tax commission. The motion to reconsider is a precondition for appeal. In some cantons (e.g., Zurich) the cantonal government has the right to challenge the assessment by a motion to reconsider.

The authority reviewing the case upon motion to reconsider has full investigative powers. It is not limited to an examination of the particular item protested but may change the assessment in an area that was not challenged by the taxpayer. This may result in a reversal of the assessment decision that is detrimental to the taxpayer (*reformatio in peius*). The withdrawal of a motion to reconsider by the taxpayer does not prevent an investigation if it appears that the original assessment was deficient, even if the taxpayer pays all taxes assessed when the motion to reconsider is withdrawn (Art. 104 FITD).

The taxpayer has a specific right to be heard, i.e., to appear before the authority, present his or her case, and submit documents relating to the motion to reconsider.

The decision on the taxpayer's motion, as a rule, is rendered within three months and served upon the taxpayer by registered mail. It indicates the elements of the taxpayer's liability, includes a brief statement of reasons and informs of the taxpayer's right to appeal, the time limit and the authority with which the appeal must be filed. The decision on the motion to reconsider becomes effective unless a timely appeal is taken.

(2) Judicial review

(a) Appellate authorities in general
With regard to the federal income tax, the cantonal assessment authorities' decisions on motions to reconsider may be appealed to the cantonal board of tax appeals (*commission de recours/Rekurskommission*). With the appeal, the taxpayer must resubmit all the supporting evidence. The cantonal board of tax appeals may take any action deemed necessary, including a complete reassessment of the tax obligation. The decisions may be challenged before the Federal Supreme Court by means of an administrative-law appeal.

In cantonal and municipal tax matters, decisions on motions to reconsider are subject to appeal to a cantonal body, which is often identical to the board of tax appeals for the federal income tax. Some cantons have a second-level instance of appeal whose structure and composition varies.

Under the Federal Constitution, a taxpayer who alleges a violation of constitutional rights may challenge a decision in cantonal and/or municipal tax matters before the Federal Supreme Court by means of a constitutional complaint (*recours de droit public/staatsrechtliche Beschwerde*). The main constitutional rights which may be the object of a complaint are the right of equality before the law (Art. 4 Federal Constitution, see ¶106), the principle of legality of the tax and the prohibition of intercantonal double taxation (Art. 46(2) Federal Constitution, see ¶1003).

(b)   Appeal to the cantonal boards of tax appeals
A taxpayer may challenge the decision on the motion to reconsider by means of an appeal (*recours/Beschwerde* or *Rekurs*) to the cantonal board of tax appeals. The time limit to do so is usually 30 days. The federal, cantonal and municipal tax administrations involved are generally also entitled to bring an appeal, even where they have no right to bring a motion to reconsider.

The grounds for an appeal may be manifold: inadequate finding of the relevant facts, inaccurate application of the law or abuse of discretion by the assessment authority. The written appeal must contain a clear request, detailed reasons and a list of the documentary evidence, which should be attached if possible. The tax laws usually state that the other party may file an answer within a time limit set by the board of tax appeals. Generally, there are no further pleadings. The board of tax appeals examines all factual and legal aspects of the case. It may consider new facts and newly submitted evidence. It has the same investigative powers as the assessment authority and is not bound by the requests of the parties. The decision of the board of tax appeals may, in consequence, be to the taxpayer's detriment or go beyond the taxpayer's requests. It must include the holdings, provide detailed reasons and list the legal remedies.

(c)   Second-level appeals
In federal income tax matters, a decision of a cantonal board of tax appeals may be challenged by an administrative-law appeal to the Federal Supreme Court within 30 days after communication. The taxpayer and the cantonal and federal administrations for the federal income tax have standing to file an appeal. Grounds for the appeal may be:

(i) violation of federal law, including international treaties;

(ii) incorrect or incomplete findings of the legally relevant facts; or

(iii) gross inadequacy of the decision.

Upon receipt of an appeal, the Federal Supreme Court allows the other party and the cantonal board of tax appeals to file answers. The parties may be ordered to appear at a hearing. The Federal Supreme Court may go beyond the request of the parties, either to their advantage or to their detriment.

In cantonal income tax matters, the legal remedies against an appellate decision in cantonal or municipal tax matters are subject to cantonal law. In many cantons, second-instance appeals may be filed against violations or arbitrary application of the law, but not against the ascertainment of facts.

¶1021

(d) Constitutional complaint to the Federal Supreme Court
A constitutional complaint to the Federal Supreme Court is possible only if no other remedy against cantonal decisions is available and if a violation of the Federal Constitution is alleged. However, if a violation of the prohibition on intercantonal double taxation is claimed (¶1003), the complaint may be filed as soon as the taxpayer learns that the canton whose jurisdiction is denied has attempted to tax him or her. A constitutional complaint must be filed within 30 days after communication of the challenged assessment.

¶1022   Collection and payment of tax

(1)   Time tax is due
Federal, cantonal and municipal income taxes are collected annually by the canton which assessed the taxes. The authority in charge of tax collection varies from canton to canton. Cantonal income taxes are often collected by municipal tax offices.

The cantonal tax laws usually provide for the cantonal government to set a specific date each year on which the tax of the tax year becomes due, and the discount rate to be allowed in the case of pre-payment. The federal income tax is usually due on 1 March. The period within which the tax must be paid is usually 30 days from the due date. Taxpayers who miss that payment period must pay late-payment interest as of the first day following the expiration of the payment period. They receive a notice to that effect and are subject to debt collection proceedings if they do not pay. Relief, such as extensions, or even waivers, of tax may be granted in hardship cases.

The fact that an assessment is not yet ready, or has been protested by means of motion to reconsider or appealed against, does not suspend the obligation to pay the tax on time. In such cases the taxpayer receives a provisional tax statement based on the figures declared in the tax return or, if no return has been filed, on a discretionary assessment or the return of the preceding tax period.

Taxpayers with no domicile in Switzerland, or whose attitude appears to put the enforcement of the tax claim in jeopardy, may be ordered by the tax administrations to put up adequate security. Such an order is immediately enforceable and is equivalent to an executory judgment; it does not require final assessment of the taxpayer. The order may be appealed, but the appeal does not suspend the execution of the order.

(2)   Statute of Limitations for collection
The collection of tax is subject to a time limitation, usually five years from the due date or from the final assessment decision. The running of the Statute of Limitations is interrupted by the recognition of a tax claim or by any action by

the authorities designed to recover the tax. In certain cases (e.g., as long as the taxpayer has no domicile in Switzerland, or if the time limit to pay taxes is extended), the running of the Statute of Limitations is suspended. Computation errors can be corrected within a period of three years from the date of the assessment.

¶1023   Withholding taxes on income of individuals

The income tax of individuals is usually assessed based upon their tax returns. In some cases individual income taxes may be withheld at source instead:

(1) All income subject to the federal anticipatory tax (see ¶1007).

(2) In many cantons, foreigners with only a temporary residence permit are subject to a withholding tax on gross salaries and wages paid by an employer who is a resident of the respective canton. The withholding tax rates are designed to cover all federal, cantonal and municipal income taxes on salary income. The employer who must withhold the tax and pay it to the local tax authorities usually gets a certain percentage of the tax as reimbursement for the costs of collecting the tax. Qualifying individuals who earn high salaries are subject to the ordinary assessment, either subsequently or in lieu of withholding tax on the salary. This withholding tax is controversial under the non-discrimination clauses of double-taxation conventions.

(3) In some cantons, taxes on directors' fees, profit sharing and other compensation of non-resident executives of Swiss corporations and other legal entities are withheld at source, i.e., at the place where the paying entity is domiciled. The double taxation conventions generally do not prohibit this levy. The tax usually covers federal, cantonal and municipal taxes. It is calculated on the gross amount of compensation; no deductions are permitted. The tax rates range between 15 and 25 per cent (in Zurich: 22 per cent).

(4) Several cantons provide for withholding at source for income that non-resident public entertainers, such as actors, musicians and athletes, derive from their independent activity in Switzerland. The tax usually covers federal, cantonal and municipal taxes. It is calculated on the gross remuneration, but lump-sum deductions (25 to 33 per cent) are allowed. The tax rates range roughly between 5 and 15 per cent.

(5) In some cantons, in the absence of provisions to the contrary in double taxation conventions, interest income of non-residents on debts secured by mortgages and other securities on Swiss immovable property is subject to a flat withholding tax at the place where the immovable property is

located. In the canton of Zurich the tax rate is 15 per cent. The withholding tax is fully credited against the federal income tax.

(6) Some cantons withhold taxes on retirement salaries, pensions, annuities and lump-sum payments made to non-residents from cantonal public funds.

¶1024   Tax-loss carry-forward

(1)   Persons entitled

Generally, losses from one source of income (business, employment, capital) can be set off against income from another source within the same calculation period. Where the calculation period is two years, the net loss of one year of the period may be set off against the net income of the other year. In addition, the tax laws tend to allow the carry-over of net losses beyond one calculation period, provided the taxpayer is a legal entity conducting a business or an individual entrepreneur with the obligation to maintain regular books of account.

(2)   Periods of tax-loss carry-forward

For the federal income tax a net operating loss in one calculation period may be carried forward to three subsequent calculation periods.

Example: The results of the years 1989 and 1990 show an average net operating loss of 100. This loss may be carried forward to the first calculation period if there is sufficient income against which it can be set off. It may be carried forward as a deductible loss up to and including the calculation period 1995/96, which is the basis for the tax period 1997/98.

The cantonal loss carry-forward periods vary widely. The canton of Zurich, which has a one-year calculation period, allows the carry-over of losses for four years.

(3)   No tax-loss carry-back

Swiss federal and cantonal tax law does not allow the carry-back of a loss to prior calculation periods.

¶1025   Supplementary taxes and penalties

(1)   Supplementary taxes

Under most cantonal tax laws, a supplementary tax may be assessed if it appears from previously unknown facts or on the basis of new evidence that a tax had been underassessed or had not been assessed at all. The underassessment need not be due to unlawful behaviour of the taxpayer (tax evasion, etc.). In contrast, under federal and some cantonal income tax laws, a supplementary tax may be assessed only in conjunction with tax evasion proceedings. As a general rule, a supplementary tax may be levied only if the tax authority, applying all due diligence in the assessment proceedings, could not have discovered the relevant facts. If the taxpayer reported income completely and correctly, no supplementary tax may be levied. Usually, a Statute of Limitations of five years applies to each underassessed year.

(2) Penalties

Taxpayers providing misleading or false information regarding their tax liabilities are subject to a penalty tax. In addition, they may be punished by fine and/or imprisonment.

Penalty taxes are imposed in cases of tax evasion or tax fraud as a multiple of the underpaid or jeopardised tax. The actual amount of penalty tax is fixed by the tax authority in its discretion within the statutory limits.

Fines are primarily imposed for minor violations and for offences committed by persons other than the taxpayers themselves. The maximum amounts are set in the tax laws.

Imprisonment is provided for by the tax laws for serious cases of tax fraud. A court may impose this penalty only in criminal proceedings.

The categories of violation of tax laws are discussed in ¶1069.

¶1026   Claims for refund – revision – rectification of arithmetical errors

(1) Claims for refund

Refunds of taxes paid are possible only if expressly provided for in the law. A tax that has become executory and enforceable is rarely refundable.

A refund is granted on the tax authority's own initiative or upon the taxpayer's petition. Overpaid taxes are refunded by the tax authorities at their own initiative if a final or intermediary assessment, a decision upon motion to reconsider, an appeal or a revision results in a lower tax, or if tax liability is terminated earlier by reasons of death or departure abroad. A claim for a refund may be filed only if it shows that the tax was paid in error or that a tax not legally due was collected in execution proceedings.

Claims for a refund are subject to a time limit of three (e.g., for the federal income tax) to five years following the payment of tax or the date on which the tax had become enforceable.

(2) Revision of assessment in favour of the taxpayer

Revision is an extraordinary remedy against final and executory assessment decisions. Although not specifically mentioned in the Federal Income Tax

Decree, under the case law of the Federal Supreme Court the remedy of revision is available against these decisions if:

(a) the assessing or the deciding authority violated essential procedural principles;

(b) the authority disregarded essential and material facts that could have been ascertained from the records;

(c) the taxpayer presents material new facts or evidence that could not have been produced at the time of the original proceedings; or

(d) a decision of a 'Competent Authority' is rendered in a matter governed by a double taxation convention.

The grounds for revision in cantonal tax matters are basically similar to those in federal tax matters.

The petition for revision must be filed with the authority that last dealt with the challenged decision. The time limit is 90 days from the discovery of the grounds for revision, but usually not later than five years after the relevant assessment year has expired (or after notification of assessment). Ordinary legal remedies are available if the petition is rejected.

(3) Rectification of arithmetical errors
Purely arithmetical errors in the calculation of the amount of tax can be corrected by the tax authorities even if the decision has otherwise become incontestable and executory. Rectification is made either on the tax authority's own initiative or at the taxpayer's request.

INCOME TAXATION OF INDIVIDUALS

¶1027 Taxable income in general

Individuals are subject to federal, cantonal and municipal taxes on income from all sources. Although the federal and the various cantonal tax laws vary in their treatment of exemptions, allowances and personal deductions, most of them adhere to the same general principles in determining gross income. The laws usually do not define the term 'gross income' but, rather, declare that the total of all receipts from the following sources are subject to taxation (Art. 21 et seq. FITD; Art. 19 et seq. Zurich tax statute):

(1) income derived from gainful activity (employment income, income from operating a business as a single proprietor, income realised as a member of a general or limited partnership, etc.);

¶1027

(2) compensatory income (received as a substitute for income that ceased as a result of the voluntary or involuntary termination of an individual's gainful activity, e.g., pensions and other retirement income, disability payments, health and accident insurance payments, and severance pay);

(3) income derived from immovable property;

(4) income from movable property (e.g., interest, dividends, and royalties); and

(5) income from capital gains and revaluation gains if the taxpayer is under an obligation to keep books.

Income from all categories is usually combined and taxed at one rate, with the exception that annuities, pensions and other retirement income usually qualifies for more favourable tax treatment.

The expenses incurred in realising income and the allowances fixed by law can be deducted from gross income.

The taxpayer and the taxpayer's spouse are taxed on their aggregated income. They must file a joint tax return; a separate return is not possible.

¶1028   Unlimited and limited tax obligations: residence

(1)   Distinction

The income and net worth tax liabilities of individuals are a consequence of a person's connection to the taxing jurisdiction. The tax obligation may be unlimited or limited.

Taxpayers who have their residence or legal domicile in the tax-levying community (Confederation, canton, municipality), or who stay there for an extended period of time, are under an unlimited tax obligation and are assessed on income from all sources, domestic or foreign, and on all net worth. There are two exceptions to this general rule: immovable property located abroad (and related income) and income from a permanent establishment abroad are, in general, not subject to Swiss taxes. A limited tax obligation is based on an economic rather than on a personal connection to the tax-levying community. Non-residents usually have such a limited tax obligation with regard to income derived from Swiss immovable property or from a Swiss permanent establishment.

Domicile is the principal form of personal attachment that results in residence for tax purposes. In the absence of any treaty provision governing domicile, the statutory rules are fully applicable. The basic element in determining domicile is the individual's intent to stay permanently at a given place (Art. 23(1) CC). Formal indications such as the lease of an apartment or a work permit from the foreigners' police are irrelevant. The decisive factor is that the individual in question has established the centre of his or her personal and economic interests in Switzerland. Domicile is retained until a new one is actually acquired (Art. 24(1) CC). Consequently, an individual temporarily leaving the country does not lose Swiss residence for tax purposes as long as domicile is not acquired elsewhere. Residence for tax purposes terminates only if the circumstances show that the centre of the taxpayer's personal and economic interest has been transferred abroad. An individual staying in Switzerland and unable to prove a domicile elsewhere becomes subject to income taxation on the basis of the stay.

Treaties to avoid double taxation of income may define residence differently.

(2) Unlimited tax obligation: taxation of residents
Individuals have an unlimited tax obligation at the federal, cantonal and municipal levels:

(a) if their residence is in Switzerland, in a specific canton or a specific municipality;

(b) if they are staying within the tax jurisdiction and exercise a gainful activity there (in some cantons, only after a minimum stay); or

(c) if they are staying in the tax jurisdiction without exercising a gainful activity for a specific minimum period of time (six months for the federal income tax; in the cantons, as a rule, three months).

Persons with unlimited tax liability are taxed on their world-wide income. Unlimited income tax liability begins with the formal taking of residency or the actual stay in the jurisdiction, and ends with the formal termination of the residence or the actual departure from the jurisdiction.

(3) Limited tax obligation: taxation of non-residents
Persons domiciled or resident outside Switzerland but having an economic connection of some intensity to Switzerland have a limited tax obligation.

The most important economic connections which give rise to a limited tax obligation are:

(a) ownership of, or a life interest (usufruct) in, immovable property located in the respective jurisdiction;

(b) ownership of a business, partnership, or other entity lacking juridical personality in the relevant jurisdiction;

(c) maintenance of a permanent establishment in the respective jurisdiction; or

(d) activity as a member of the board of a Swiss share corporation.

Individuals who are subject to a limited tax obligation pay income tax only on the income derived from the sources giving rise to the limited tax obligation. The rate of tax depends upon the total world-wide taxable income. As a result, persons under a limited tax obligation must list their world-wide income and net

¶1028

worth in their Swiss tax return or accept the application of the top income tax rate.

¶1029   Nature of income – definition of taxable income

(1) 'Income' defined

The term 'income' is not definitively defined in the tax laws; instead, forms of income are summarily included or are described by way of example (Art. 21 et seq. FITD; Art. 19 et seq., Zurich tax statute). All descriptions conform to the formula of the Federal Supreme Court, which defines income as the sum of all economic values realised by a person within a specific time period and which can be disposed of by that person without reducing the person's assets for the livelihood of that person or for other purposes. However, not the total income but only the net amount after the gross income has been reduced by admissible deductions and allowances is subject to income taxation.

Table 10.3: Example of Computation of Taxable Income

Income	SFr	SFr	SFr
Income items:			
• gross employment income received by the taxpayer and the taxpayer's spouse			80,000
• gross income from professional business services			20,000
• gross income from occasional activity (directors' fees)			10,000
• payments from social security funds, unemployment and accident insurance, etc.			–
• income from the use of immovable property			6,000
• dividends on securities, yield on loan			12,000
• income from undivided estates and partnerships			2,000
• pension (SFr 6,000) at 60% taxable			3,600
• lottery gain			1,000
Gross income			134,600

Income	SFr	SFr	SFr
Gross income (carried over)			134,600
Deduction of expenses connected			
with the earning of income			
(income-connected expenses):			
● expenses incurred in earning income	7,000		
● maintenance of real estate	13,000	20,000	
Deductions for particular expenses			
(other expenses):			
● interest paid	24,000		
● insurance premiums	2,000	26,000	(46,000)
Net Income			88,600
Deductions:			
● deduction for persons supported	900		
● deduction for children	8,000		(8,900)
Taxable Income			79,500

(2) Different types of income

In principle, four different categories of income may be distinguished:

    (a) income from gainful activity (employed or self-employed);

    (b) income from movable or immovable property;

    (c) income from other sources; and

    (d) extraordinary income.

¶1030 Income from gainful activity

Individuals' income from employment or self-employment is always taxable income, inclusive of all secondary income, e.g. seniority bonuses (some cantons grant complete or partial relief under certain conditions), commissions, employee shares, gratuities, bonuses, shares in profit, tips and income-in-kind. Profits realised by a self-employed individual on the sale of business assets also constitute taxable income.

Whether a gainful activity is exercised full- or part-time, or whether it is exercised with or without the intent to generate income is immaterial.

¶1031   Insurance proceeds and annuities

Substituted income is defined as benefits which are granted in lieu of regular income from gainful activity (wage and salary substitution, unemployment compensation, daily compensation from health and accident insurance, pensions, social security, etc.). Different forms of substituted income are taxed differently.

(1)   One-time insurance benefits and capital payments received

(a)   Redeemable life insurance
Capital payments from redeemable life insurance are tax exempt at the federal and cantonal levels; in the cantons of Aargau and Graubünden they are tax exempt only in so far as the entitlement to the benefit does not arise out of an employment relationship.

(b)   Compulsory occupational pension plans
The Federal Statute on Occupational Pension Plans allows all contributions to qualifying compulsory pension plans to be deducted. On the other hand, it provides for full taxation of the benefits.

For federal income tax purposes, capital payments are taxed separately at the rate which would be applicable if a corresponding annuity were paid in lieu of the capital benefit (taxation at the annuity rate).

In contrast, the cantons apply different procedures for the taxation of capital payments from retirement plans.

(c)   Capital benefits from self-financed retirement funds
The Federal Statute on Occupational Pension Plans provides for special tax benefits for individual savings in the context of a self-financed retirement plan. For federal income tax purposes, capital benefits are taxed differently at the more favourable rate applicable to annuities. Some cantons (including Zurich, Berne and Zug) have adopted this form of taxation; others have different regulations.

(d)   Other insurance payments
Other payments from non-redeemable insurance (pure risk life insurance, one-time bonuses arising out of the employment relationship, and accident insurance) are taxed for federal income tax purposes either separately at the rate applicable to annuities or together with other income.

(2)   Periodic insurance payments received
Periodic insurance payments (from life insurance, pension plans, social security and disability, annuities and others) are taxed at different rates.

¶1031

(a) Social security benefits
For federal income tax purposes and in most cantons, old-age pension payments
and annuities for disability (compulsory federal social security and disability
insurance, the 'first pillar'; see ¶1501) are taxed only on 80 per cent of their
total amount.

(b) Compulsory occupational pension plan benefits
Benefits from compulsory retirement plans (the 'second pillar'; see ¶1507 et
seq.) are, in principle, fully taxed. Special rules apply for a transition period until
the year 2002.

(c) Others
Other periodic insurance benefits are subject to federal tax and to tax in most
cantons, according to the degree of third-party financing. In some cantons (e.g.,
Geneva) they are always fully taxed.

(3) Supplementary benefits received
Supplementary benefits are exempt from taxation both at the federal level and
in the majority of cantons. Geneva and some other cantons tax them at the same
rate as old-age, survivors and disability benefits.

(4) Benefits received from military insurance
Benefits from military insurance are exempt from taxation both at the federal
and at all cantonal levels.

¶1032   Income from use of immovable property

Income derived from Swiss immovable property in the sense of Art. 655 CC, is
fully taxable under federal and cantonal income taxation. This income includes
rental or lease fees, the rental or lease value of immovable property used
personally by the taxpayer, the value of a life estate and fees for a right to build
or other servitudes. Rental lease values and the life estate are assessed at the
federal level and in most cantons on the basis of their fair market value.

¶1033   Income from movable property

Income from movable property covers all receipts from property, life interests
(usufruct) in movable objects, or assets which cannot be the object of immovable
property. This category of income includes interest and dividend payments or
other benefits derived from claims and investments (loans, savings accounts,
bonds, capital stock and other securities) and receipts from the lease or rental

of movable objects and from use of rights (licence or trade mark fees, royalties, etc.). This income is fully taxable at all levels.

¶1034   Capital gains and capital losses

Income tax treatment of capital gains is different on the federal and on the cantonal and municipal levels (see ¶1013).

Only capital gains realised on movable or immovable assets in the course of business by a taxpayer who is obliged to keep books under corporate law or who qualifies as a professional real estate or securities dealer are subject to the federal income tax.

For the purposes of cantonal and municipal income taxes, one must distinguish between capital gains realised on movable or immovable assets and between assets belonging to the private or business property of the taxpayer. (For the taxation of immovable property capital gains see ¶1013(4).) Capital gains from the disposition of personal property that is used in a business are generally not taxable if the assets are sold under duress and the proceeds are reinvested in similar property.

Recent case law tends to restrict the concept of a tax-free private capital gain for federal income tax purposes. Gains from transactions that would appear to generate private capital gains have been characterised as ordinary income in the following circumstances:

(a) an exchange of shares in an operating company for other shares in the transferor's own holding company which have a higher nominal value;

(b) possibly in a leveraged buyout;

(c) a sale of shares as part of a transaction in which the sale is financed by the assets of the acquired company (see ¶1065(4));

(d) a sale of shares in a company followed immediately by the liquidation of that company; and

(e) a gain in large-scale financial futures transactions (*Archives*, 59, 709).

¶1035   Employee shares and share options

(1)   Federal income tax

In a circular of 17 May 1990, the Principal Division for the Federal Income Tax of the Federal Tax Administration laid down the rules applicable to taxation of employee shares and options. The costs of employee shares and options constitute deductible business expenses for the employer to the extent that these expenses are actually incurred (Art. 49(1)(d) FITD). At the employee's level, the receipt of shares at a price below fair market value constitutes an allowance of a financial value in the difference between cost and market value. To the extent that this allowance is granted on account of the employment relationship, it constitutes taxable income to the employee under Art. 21(1)(a) FITD. Shares and option rights granted by the employer must be listed in the salary certificate that each employer has to provide to the employee to be filed with the employee's tax return.

Different categories of employee shares are treated under the rules laid down in the circular as described in (a) to (d) below.

(a) Unrestricted shares
These shares can be freely disposed of by the employee immediately after their acquisition. Taxable income is realised immediately in the difference between the fair market value of the shares and the purchase price paid by the employee.

(b) Restricted shares

(i) Period of restrictions with or without limited obligation to resell. The employee immediately obtains title to the shares but cannot dispose of them until a certain period of time has expired. The restriction may go beyond a mere time restriction on resale, in that the employer may reserve the right to repurchase at a price below market value in specified situations, e.g. if the employee leaves the employment within the period of restriction. The shares remain deposited with the employer, but the employee obtains dividends and can vote the shares.

The employee obtains unrestricted possession only when the period of restriction on resale and the employer's right to repurchase the shares expire. Notwithstanding the restriction, employees are deemed to have realised taxable income when they obtain title to the shares. Because of the restriction on resale, the net present value of the shares is discounted at the rate of 10 per cent for every year of restriction up to a maximum of ten years. Possible gains or losses when the restriction expires are not taken into consideration.

Table 10.4 on p. 228 applies in calculating the net present value.

Example: The employee can dispose of the shares after a period of six or 12 years.

fair market value	SFr 3,000
less price of acquisition	SFr 500
difference	SFr 2,500

Taxable income from employment services in the case of six-year restriction: SFr 2,500 x 0.56447 = SFr 1,411 (12-year restriction: SFr 2,500 x 0.38554 = SFr 964).

¶1035

Table 10.4: Calculating net present value

Period of restriction in years	allowance of financial value in per cent (discount rate: 10% p.a.)
1	90.909%
2	82.645%
3	75.131%
4	68.301%
5	62.092%
6	56.447%
7	51.316%
8	46.651%
9	42.410%
10	38.554%

(ii)   Blocking period with unlimited obligation to resell.   If the employer retains an unlimited repurchase right (not merely a resale restriction on the shares), the mere granting of the shares does not entail realisation of taxable income by the employee. The potential difference between the price of acquisition and the repurchase price will be taxed as income from employment at the time when the shares are resold to the employer or, at the latest, when the employment is terminated.

(c)   Employee shares to be remitted only upon reaching retirement age
In this case the employees obtain title to the shares when they are granted, but the shares are remitted to the employees only later. The granting of the shares does not constitute a payment of a pension right which would enjoy favourable tax treatment; rather, it constitutes taxable income realised immediately. The value is discounted according to the number of years between the moment of granting and retirement age (up to a maximum of ten years). Possible gains or losses realised at the time the shares are remitted are not taken into consideration.

(d)   Taxation of options
The tax treatment of options depends upon whether the employee can sell them. If the options cannot be sold, taxable income is realised only upon the exercise of the option; the income is equal to the difference between the then fair market value and the option price. If the option can be sold, the fair market value of the option at the time of its granting constitutes taxable income. If the option is subsequently sold at a higher price, or if the employee exercises the option and purchases the shares, the gain realised constitutes a non-taxable capital gain.

¶1035

(2) Cantonal income taxes
The cantons generally follow the rules applicable to the federal income tax.

¶1036   Other types of income

(1) Lottery gains
Gains from lotteries are included in regular income for federal tax purposes and in about half of the cantons. In some cantons they are taxed separately and the normal income tax rate applies; in others they are subject to a special tax with its own rate, beginning at a predetermined level. In the canton of Jura they are income-tax free.

(2) Appreciation of business assets
Appreciation of business assets must be included in taxable income if certain conditions are met. As a general rule, appreciation is taxable only if it is shown on the taxpayer's books. For federal and some cantonal income tax purposes, a further condition is that the taxpayer be obliged to keep books. Other cantons require that the taxpayer effectively keep books, or that the taxpayer's business be commercially managed.

Income from property subject to a life interest (usufruct) is included in the taxable income of the usufructuary.

(3) Alimony and child support payments
Alimony paid to a divorced or separated spouse is included in the ordinary taxable income of the recipient in all cantons, but not at the federal level. At the federal level and in most cantons, child support payments are not taxable to the recipient. In some cantons, such as Fribourg, Schaffhausen, Ticino, Geneva, Vaud and Neuchâtel, child support payments are included in the ordinary taxable income of the recipient.

¶1037   Deductions

(1) Types of deductions
Swiss tax laws allow for a variety of deductions, which may be divided into the following categories:

  (a) deductions for disbursements necessary for the earning of income (income-connected expenses, sometimes referred to as 'organic' deductions);

  (b) other actual disbursements not directly connected with the earning of income (other expenses); and

¶1037

(c) personal deductions granted by law for social and socio-political reasons. While expenses must actually be incurred and deductions are admitted only against documented evidence, personal deductions are granted in flat amounts without any further justification.

The system does not require any causal connection between a personal deduction and the source of the income. The taxpayer may, for example, deduct maintenance expenses connected with immovable property from employment income, even if there is no income from the particular piece of property against which those expenses can be set off. Similarly, losses suffered in a partnership may be set off against income from capital.

Expenses that are not connected with the production of income or the maintenance of the sources of income are non-deductible. Normal personal expenses are non-deductible even if necessitated by the taxpayer's social position. However, additional expenses incurred by the taxpayer in earning income, such as costs of work clothing and travel, are deductible. Entertainment expenses are deductible only if incurred solely in connection with earning income. The taxpayer must show that the expenses claimed were necessary for the performance of the trade or profession.

As a general rule, medical expenses are not deductible; certain cantons allow limited medical deductions.

(2)   Income-connected expenses
Expenses directly connected with the earning of income or the maintenance of the sources of income are deductible.

The following income-connected expenses are recognised:

(a) All expenses incurred to earn income or to maintain the sources of income. They are calculated differently for employed and self-employed individuals. Employment costs of employed individuals are usually given as lump-sum deductions. In many cantons the taxpayer can deduct those effective employment costs that exceed the standard or lump-sum deduction if they can be proved.

(b) Expenses for the taxpayer's professional or vocational education and training are not income-connected; they are usually regarded as non-deductible personal expenses. Unlike ordinary educational expenses, expenses incurred in maintaining or improving professional skills are deductible income-connected expenses. Among these expenses are the costs of participation in conventions, membership in professional societies or associations, and similar expenses incurred by the taxpayer in order to meet the increasing demands of a profession.

¶1037

(c) Commuting expenses – usually the cost of public transportation – are deductible. If a taxpayer uses a car for business purposes, the costs of operating the car are deductible.

(d) Self-employed individuals may deduct depreciation and write-offs on business assets, provided they are commercially justified and recorded in the taxpayer's books. For the federal and most cantonal taxes there are guide-lines which fix maximum depreciation rates for different categories of assets. Certain cantons (e.g., Zurich and Aargau) have a liberal system of 'immediate depreciation': the taxpayer is largely free in the valuation of depreciable business assets. For certain assets, a residual value (e.g., 20 per cent of cost) must be kept. Private assets cannot be depreciated tax-effectively. Therefore, employed individuals cannot deduct any depreciations.

(e) Provisions charged to the profit-and-loss account by self-employed individuals are tax-effective to the extent that they are commercially justified. They are deductible if made for liabilities of uncertain amount existing in the fiscal year, or for direct risks of losses on current assets.

(f) Interest paid on loans may be deducted from gross income by all individual taxpayers.

(g) Taxes and other public levies not connected with the earning of income, and costs of private litigation, fines and criminal proceedings, are not deductible by individuals.

(3) Other deductible expenses

The tax laws expressly allow other actual expenses to be deducted even though they are not income connected. The reason for these deductions is that they are considered to be of a socio-political nature or important to the taxpayer's economic base.

(a) As a rule, debt interest paid is deductible whether or not it is income-connected (Art. 22(1)(d) FITD).

(b) Contributions to the compulsory social security system (the 'first pillar'; ¶1501) are fully deductible for federal, cantonal and municipal tax purposes. Premiums paid for life, accident and other types of insurance are deductible up to a maximum of SFr 1,100 per adult and SFr 400 per child for the federal income tax (Art. 22(1)(h) FITD).

(c) Contributions to compulsory occupational pension plans (the 'second pillar'; ¶1507 et seq.) are fully deductible both at the federal and at all cantonal levels. Contributions to self-financed individual retirement accounts (the 'third pillar') can be deducted at the federal and all cantonal levels, but only to a limited degree. The maximum deduction is increased from year to year but is limited to 20 per cent of the employment income of individuals who do not contribute to a compulsory occupational pension institution ('second pillar'), and in any case to a maximum deductible amount (as of 1991) of SFr 23,040. For those employees contributing to an occupational pension plan the applicable ceiling is SFr 4,608 (as of 1991).

(d) Contributions for charitable and public interest purposes can be deducted up to a certain amount and under certain conditions both at the federal level and in most cantons (except Lucerne, Uri, Nidwalden and Ticino). Under federal income tax law, the deductibility of charitable contributions is limited to taxpayers with a statutory obligation to keep books.

(e) Deductions for the employment income of the taxpayer's spouse are allowed both at the federal level and in most cantons. Deductions are allowed in the form of fixed amounts or percentages of the spouse's employment income, with a maximum limit (e.g., for the federal income tax, 20 per cent, with a minimum of SFr 2,000 and a maximum of SFr 5,000); some cantons do not provide for a special deduction, and others apply a two-income-earner partial splitting system.

¶1038   Personal deductions

'Personal deductions' reflect personal and economic conditions of life (civil status, support of children and other relatives, age, ability to work, etc.) rather than identified expenditures. The federal and cantonal income tax laws contain a great variety of regulations:

(1) The federal and all cantonal income tax laws either allow personal deductions or deductions for married couples (e.g., under Zurich income tax SFr 8,600) and/or set separate rates for unmarried taxpayers and married couples. Some cantons (Fribourg, Neuchâtel, Graubünden, and Aargau to a limited extent) have a 'splitting' system to reduce the progression of tax rates. Under this system, the total family income is taxed at a rate which would apply to a lower income.

(2) Federal and cantonal income tax laws (except Vaud) grant several deductions for children (e.g., under federal income tax SFr 4,300, and under Zurich income tax SFr 4,500 per child). In some cantons the deduction increases for every additional child. Certain cantons grant extra studying allowances for children.

(3) Deductions for the support of other individuals are available under federal and all cantonal income tax laws (e.g., under federal income tax SFr 4,300, and under Zurich income tax SFr 2,000 per person).

(4) Retired or disabled individuals may claim a special deduction in most of the cantons, but not, e.g., in the cantons of Uri, Obwalden, Zug, Baselland, Valais, Neuchâtel and Geneva, nor under federal income tax law.

(5) Taxpayers paying alimony to a (former) spouse may deduct the full amount in all cantons. This deduction is not granted under federal income tax law. Payments effected to support children who do not live together with the taxpayer are deductible only in some cantons and not for the federal income tax.

¶1039   Lump-sum taxation

(1)   Entitlement
Foreign residents with unlimited Swiss tax liability who do not engage in any gainful activity in Switzerland and have never done so, and Swiss nationals who, after an absence of at least ten years, take up residence in Switzerland without engaging in any gainful activity, may opt to be subject to a special lump-sum tax.

Lump-sum taxation (*taxation forfaitaire/Pauschalbesteuerung*) is a special method of computing tax (as opposed to ordinary income taxation), and is available at the federal level and for cantonal and municipal tax purposes in some cantons, including Zurich, Geneva and Zug. While qualifying foreigners may continue indefinitely to be subject to lump sum taxation, Swiss nationals are assessed in the ordinary fashion as from the end of the calendar year following the year of their return to Switzerland.

(2)   Calculation
The federal lump-sum tax is assessed on the basis of either the aggregate of estimated living expenses or the sum of certain income items, whichever is greater. The expenditures that are taken into account are those made annually by the taxpayer world-wide for the Swiss-resident dependants of the taxpayer (such as lodging, clothing, food, servants and other personnel, education, sport, hobbies, entertainment, holidays and travel, maintenance of house, cars, yachts, airplanes, animals, and any other living expenses). The minimum amount of taxable expenses is deemed to be equal to one and a half times the annual cost of room and board, or five times the annual rent of the dwelling (or rental value of the owned dwelling) in Switzerland.

The lump-sum tax must amount at least to the tax that would be due on the sum of:

(a) income from immovable property in Switzerland;

(b) income from Swiss capital investments, including claims secured by mortgage in Switzerland;

(c) income from other movable property located in Switzerland;

(d) income from copyrights, patents, and similar rights used in Switzerland (royalties);

(e) retirement salaries, annuities and pensions from Swiss sources; and

(f) foreign-source income for which the taxpayer, under the provision of a double taxation convention entered into by Switzerland, claims total or partial relief or refund of foreign taxes withheld at source.

The following deductions are allowed:

(i) expenses for the maintenance and administration of Swiss immovable property; and

(ii) administration costs for Swiss capital investments.

Other expenses, in particular debt interest and annuities, are not deductible. If an applicable double taxation convention so provides, further income items, reduced by related expenses, may be included in the income calculation.

The applicable tax rate is determined by the aggregate of expenses or income items as above. Income items need be declared only to the above-mentioned extent. Taxpayers who choose not to claim treaty benefits for income items subject to foreign withholding taxes need not declare the items. As long as the assessment proceedings are not terminated, the taxpayer may always elect to be assessed in the ordinary manner.

The cantonal lump-sum taxation systems are similar to that on the federal level. They usually cover the cantonal net-worth tax as well.

¶1040   Tax rates and computation of tax

(1)   Federal income tax

The income and net worth of individuals are usually taxed at progressive rates. The rates at which federal, cantonal and municipal governments levy taxes vary widely. For the purpose of determining the applicable income tax rate, Swiss-source income and all foreign-source income (e.g., income from immovable property located outside Switzerland or from a permanent establishment abroad), although not taxable, are aggregated.

The federal income tax levied on individuals is determined from a scale of graduated rates. No tax is levied on taxable income lower than SFr 9,700; the effective maximum rate is 11.5 per cent and applies to income of SFr 595,200 or higher. Table 10.5 shows the actual amount of federal income tax payable at various taxable income levels for married and unmarried individuals (tax year 1991):

Table 10.5: Federal income tax at certain income levels (tax year 1991)

taxable income	amount of federal tax for unmarried taxpayers		amount of federal tax for married taxpayers	
(in SFr)	(in SFr)	(in %)	(in SFr)	(in %)
20,000	80	0.400	12	0.060
50,000	836	1.672	586	1.172
80,000	3,050	3.812	2,137	2.671
100,000	5,043	5.043	4,072	4.072
120,000	7,311	6.092	6,672	5.560
140,000	9,951	7.108	9,272	6.622
160,000	12,591	7.869	11,872	7.420
180,000	15,231	8.461	14,472	8.040
200,000	17,871	8.935	17,072	8.536
300,000	31,071	10.357	30,072	10.084

(2) Cantonal taxes

In addition to the federal income tax, each canton levies a tax on the income of individuals. In most cantons, the tax consists of:

(a) the progressive base tax rate (*barème de l'impôt/einfache Staatssteuer*) for the canton;

(b) the cantonal multiplier (*taux* or *centimes additionnels/Steuerfuss*), which is applied to the cantonal base tax rate to yield the effective progressive cantonal tax rate for the year; and

(c) the municipal multiplier, which is applied to the cantonal base tax rate to provide the effective progressive municipal tax rate for the year.

Depending on the financial situation of the canton or the municipality, the multiplier is periodically adjusted by the competent legislative body and is subject to compulsory or optional public referendum. Some cantons do not use the multiplier system of setting their effective tax rates for the year. Instead they use tax rate schedules which they revise in accordance with financial needs. In these cantons the municipal tax is expressed as a multiple of the cantonal tax.

The effective tax rates differ greatly from canton to canton and even from municipality to municipality within the same canton. Federal, cantonal and municipal taxes have to be added in order to determine the total tax burden on an individual's income. The following schedule gives examples on the total

¶1040

effective tax rate in per cent (federal, cantonal and municipal taxes) paid by an unmarried individual (A) and a family with two children (B) in 1990:

Gross Income	City of Zurich A	City of Zurich B	City of Zug A	City of Zug B	City of Geneva A	City of Geneva B
	%		%		%	
SFr 50,000	9.95	4.79	6.96	2.36	15.37	4.53
SFr 80,000	13.08	8.11	8.71	4.68	18.46	11.60
SFr 100,000	14.71	9.87	9.56	5.90	20.04	14.52
SFr 150,000	17.72	13.14	11.06	7.80	22.61	18.53
SFr 200,000	19.82	15.44	11.37	9.11	24.49	21.04

¶1041   Correction of inflationary shift into higher tax brackets

Article 41(5) of the Federal Constitution sets the principle (for the federal income tax) of periodic relief for the progressive effect of inflation (*progression à froid balte progression*). The applicable federal law for the avoidance of this progressive effect was enacted on 1 January 1985 and provides for a compulsory and complete adjustment of the tax rates and allowances if the consumer price index has risen by more than 7 per cent since its last adjustment.

There are no similar constitutional provisions for cantonal or municipal taxes. However, 21 cantonal tax laws contain provisions for avoiding the progressive effect of inflation.

¶1042   Taxation of fiduciary relationships

A fiduciary relationship exists if one person (principal: *fiduciant/Treugeber*) transfers title to certain assets or property to another person (fiduciary/trustee: *fiduciaire/Treuhänder*) who undertakes to hold and administer the transferred property in the trustee's own name, but for and on account, as well as according to the instructions, of the principal, and to return the property to the principal when the fiduciary agreement expires.

As a rule, fiduciary property and the related income is taxable to the beneficial (economic) owner, i.e., the principal. Fiduciary relationships are recognised for tax purposes only if certain conditions are met. In particular, the taxpayer who claims to be a fiduciary must submit a written fiduciary agreement dating from the time that the fiduciary relationship was established. The agreement must indicate the name and address of the principal, the transferred property, and the fiduciary fee to be paid (0.1 to 0.2 per cent). The agreement must clearly show that all risks and expenses connected with the administration of the transferred property are borne by the principal. The fiduciary property must be shown separately in the taxpayer's accounts. In its guide-lines of October 1967, the Federal Tax Administration laid down the rules under which fiduciary relationships will be recognised for tax purposes.

NET-WORTH TAXATION OF INDIVIDUALS

¶1043   Cantonal net-worth tax

At the federal level, no tax is levied on the net worth of individuals. The net-worth tax is levied by the cantons and municipalities on the fair market value of total taxable assets, less liabilities and standard deductions according to personal circumstances. The net-worth tax base includes almost every type of asset held by individuals, including immovable property, intangible personal property, securities, cash, redemption value of life insurance policies, investments in proprietorships or partnerships, and other beneficial interests.

Beneficial – not legal – ownership is decisive for the allocation of assets for tax purposes. Consequently, for the purposes of net-worth taxation, property under usufruct and in trust is included in the tax base of the usufructuary or beneficiary.

Certain assets (personal and household effects and the like) are exempt from taxation. Some cantons fully or partially exempt investments in companies which do business and are fully subject to taxation in the same canton as the taxpayer. In computing the value for net-worth taxation purposes, taxpayers may deduct from the total market valuation of their taxable assets: (i) any mortgages and other liabilities, and (ii) a generally allowed tax-exempt amount (e.g., in Zurich: SFr 57,000 for an individual taxpayer and SFr 114,000 for married couples or separated, divorced or widowed individuals with children).

The net-worth tax rates are progressive in most cantons. They range from about 0.04 to 0.9 per cent. The following schedule gives examples for four major cities (in 1990):

| Net worth | *Effective tax rate in % in the city of* | | | |
	Zurich	*Zug*	*Berne*	*Geneva*
SFr 200,000	0.059	0.194	0.320	0.169
SFr 500,000	0.154	0.281	0.398	0.387
SFr 1,000,000	0.267	0.346	0.493	0.549
SFr 5,000,000	0.584	0.407	0.663	0.889

Resident taxpayers who have an unlimited tax obligation pay the cantonal net-worth tax on all assets, except extracantonal and foreign immovable property and assets attributable to an extracantonal or foreign permanent establishment. If an individual owns assets in several cantons, the assets located in a particular canton – less a proportional part of the taxpayer's liabilities – will be subject to the taxes of the canton. Generally, intangible property is considered to be located at the residence of the taxpayer. Taxpayers who have a limited tax obligation pay the tax on immovable property within the canton and on assets belonging to a permanent establishment within the canton.

Immovable assets are, in many cantons, subject to an additional object tax (see ¶1014).

ESTATE AND GIFT TAXES

¶1044   Cantonal inheritance and estate taxes

(1)   Power to tax – inheritance and estate taxes distinguished
The Federal Government has no competence to levy inheritance or estate taxes. All cantons, with the exception of the canton of Schwyz, levy inheritance and/or estate taxes. In most cantons, the municipalities receive a share of the cantonal inheritance or estate tax. In the canton of Graubünden, the municipalities have taxing authority of their own; in the cantons of Vaud and Fribourg, they may collect inheritance taxes as a percentage of the cantonal tax (*centimes additionnels*). In the canton of Lucerne, the acquisition of the decedent's property by a descendant is exempt from the cantonal inheritance tax but may be subject to a municipal inheritance tax.

Whereas the inheritance tax (the predominant form of death tax) is levied on the share of inheritance or legacy passing to the individual heir or legatee, the estate tax is imposed on the net value of the decedent's entire estate. Estate taxes still exist in the cantons of Graubünden, Solothurn, and Neuchâtel.

Inheritance and estate taxes are subject to the constitutional protection against intercantonal double taxation (¶1003). The Federal Supreme Court has upheld the principle that movable property may be taxed by the canton of the decedent's last domicile and immovable property by the canton of its site.

Inheritance or estate taxes are imposed upon the heirs, legatees and other beneficiaries of property or other rights acquired by reason of death or declaration of absence of the former owner of such property or rights. The preconditions of the tax liability vary according to the cantonal laws. As a rule, the domicile of the beneficiary is irrelevant. The tax liability generally arises if the decedent had

¶1044

his or her last domicile within the canton or if (regardless of the decedent's last domicile) immovable property located in the canton's territory is transferred by reason of death. A few cantons subject certain categories of movable property located in their territory to tax, even if the decedent's last domicile was in another canton or abroad. For example, the canton of Geneva taxes household furnishings and objects of art situated in its territory, regardless of the decedent's last domicile, unless such taxation conflicts with the rules on intercantonal taxation or with international treaties.

(2) Taxable transfers

As a general rule, transfers of property or other rights by reason of death are subject to inheritance and estate taxes.

(a) Transfer to statutory heirs

All persons who take title to the property of an intestate decedent by operation of law are statutory heirs:

(i) *Transfers to direct descendants and ascendants* – Transfers to direct descendants are often taxable. In some cantons, transfers to children or parents of the decedent are exempt.

(ii) *Transfers to the surviving spouse* – The surviving spouse may take title to the property of the decedent under inheritance law or through the dissolution of the matrimonial (statutory or contractual) property regime at death. Property acquired under inheritance law is generally taxable; however, the surviving spouse is, in the majority of the cantons (e.g., in the canton of Zurich, but not Geneva, exempt from inheritance taxes).

(iii) *Transfers to the canton and municipality* – In the absence of heirs, the inheritance may devolve to the canton or municipality of the decedent's last domicile. Such transfers are generally tax-exempt.

(b) Transfer to instituted heirs or legatees

By last will, the testator may institute one or several heirs, or leave a legacy of part of his property to a beneficiary (legatee). Unlike an heir, a legatee does not take title to the entire property of the decedent but rather to specific assets that are part of the estate, or a debt that the legatee owed to the testator may be forgiven.

The transfer of property to an instituted heir or a legatee is taxable in all cantons.

Where the legacy consists of a life-interest (*usufruct*; *usufruit/Nutzniessung*) or a similar right, generally the beneficiary is taxed on the capitalised value of the life-interest, while the owner is taxed on the fair market value of the property less the capitalised value of the life-interest. In some cantons, however, the owner is taxed for the full value of the property regardless of the usufruct, whereas the beneficiary is not subject to tax at all.

The testator may by will require an instituted heir to bequeath the inheritance (or what is left of it at the time of the heir's death) to another person, the reversionary heir (*appelé/Nacherbe*). In such a case, the inheritance is acquired first by the instituted heir and then by the reversionary heir. In the majority of cantons, the inheritance tax is imposed twice, namely upon the transfer of the property to the instituted heir and upon the transfer to the reversionary heir. The applicable tax rate depends on the relationship of each heir to the decedent, as well as on the value of the assets transferred.

If a decedent establishes a foundation and contributes part or all of his or her property to it by last will, the foundation pays inheritance tax provided it is recognised as an independent taxpayer for income and net-worth tax purposes. Foundations established for purposes of tax avoidance, such as family foundations where the founder, the beneficiaries, or the foundation's executive body continue to exercise control over the foundation's assets and income, are disregarded for tax purposes. The inheritance tax on a transfer to a family foundation whose beneficiaries are members of the testator's family is usually levied at the highest rate applicable.

(c)   Other transfers by reason of death

According to cantonal legislation, certain further transfers are subject to the inheritance or estate tax:

- All cantons subject gifts in contemplation of death to inheritance and/or estate tax.

- In some cantons, transfers *inter vivos* in consideration of future inheritance are subject to inheritance or estate taxes; in other cantons, they are subject to gift tax.

- In the majority of cantons, transfers of insurance proceeds that mature at death are subject to inheritance tax, regardless of whether the insurance policy named a beneficiary.

(3)   Determination of the tax basis

The tax laws contain specific provisions on the valuation of the taxable inheritance, estate or legacy. As a rule, the net value of the property transferred as of the day of the decedent's death is relevant. Some cantonal tax statutes provide exeptions for special cases. If a transfer of property at death is subject to a condition, the value of the property is determined as of the day the condition materialises. With respect to a reversionary heir, the value of the property transferred is determined (in the canton of Zurich and nine other cantons) as of the day the first heir dies.

¶1044

As a general rule, the fair market value of the acquired property or rights and the relationship between the decedent and the recipient of the property determine the inheritance or estate tax liability. Special valuation rules apply to securities, real estate and insurance payments:

(a) Securities listed on a stock exchange are valued at their stock exchange price as of the day the decedent dies. Some cantonal tax statutes provide for a reduction of that value for inheritance tax purposes if the average yield of these securities is below a certain minimum. Stock which is not publicly traded, and whose fair market value is therefore not readily ascertainable, is valued according to the guide-lines that the Federal Tax Administration issues yearly.

(b) Agricultural immovable property is, in most cantons, assessed at a value that reflects only its current yield, not its inherent value.

(c) The valuation of other real property varies greatly from canton to canton. Some cantons (such as Zurich and Geneva) take the fair market value into account. Other cantons, however, apply lower valuations.

(d) Life-interests (usufructs), rents, pensions, and similar rights to fixed or determinable annual or periodical income are generally taken into account at their capitalised value, although the capitalisation rules may vary from canton to canton.

(e) Insurance proceeds are taxed at the value that is actually received by the beneficiary (as in Zurich), or at their full or reduced redemption value. In the canton of Geneva, the redemption value applies to those insurance proceeds that mature at a time after the decedent's death; proceeds maturing at death are taxed at the value actually received by the beneficiary.

As a rule, inheritance or estate taxes are levied on the net value of the property transferred by reason of death. Therefore, the estate's liabilities, as well as certain debts that the estate incurs after the death of the decedent (such as funeral expenses and litigation costs), are deductible for these purposes. Heirs who lived in the decedent's household are entitled to maintenance from the estate for a period of 30 days following the decedent's death (Arts 474 and 606 CC). Nine cantons expressly provide for a deduction of such claims as a liability of the estate. A few cantonal inheritance tax statutes, such as Zurich's, provide that beneficiaries are allowed to deduct payments that they made to the decedent *inter vivos* in consideration of the promise of a future share in the decedent's estate.

(4) Exemptions and allowances
Exemptions and allowances for inheritance and estate tax purposes vary widely from canton to canton. Many cantons exempt transfers to descendants, ascendants

¶1044

and/or the surviving spouse. The Zurich Inheritance and Gift Tax Statute, for example, provides for an unlimited marital deduction; allowances amount to SFr 100,000 for transfers to the decedent's descendants and parents, and SFr 10,000 for transfers to siblings, grandparents, fiancé(e)s, godchildren, foster-children, and household employees who have been employed for at least ten years. In addition, the Zurich law provides for an additional allowance of SFr 20,000 for any descendant who is under 20 years of age or in need of support. Exemptions or allowances may also apply to certain categories of property, such as household furnishings (e.g., canton of Zurich: SFr 70,000 if acquired by descendants) and customary gifts at death.

Transfers to federal, cantonal and municipal governmental bodies, as well as charitable organisations and certain other institutions such as pension plans under the Federal Occupational Pension Plan Statute, are tax exempt. Extracantonal or foreign governments and entities may be exempt on the basis of reciprocity agreements.

(5)   Tax rates

Inheritance and estate tax rates are generally progressive. Estate tax rates (cantons of Solothurn, Graubünden and Neuchâtel) depend on the value of the estate. Inheritance tax rates are generally determined with regard to the value of property transferred, as well as the relationship between the decedent and the beneficiary.

> **Example**: In the canton of Zurich, (i) a base tax rate is determined with respect to the value of property transferred; (ii) a multiplier, which depends on the relationship between the decedent and the beneficiary, is then applied to the basic tax rate; (iii) the tax rate so determined is then applied to the value of the property transferred.

In the canton of Zurich, the maximum inheritance tax rate is 36 per cent. It applies to taxable transfers with a value in excess of SFr 1 million to certain distant relatives or non-relatives of the decedent. In certain other cantons the maximum inheritance tax rate may be as high as 60 per cent in the case of transfers to non-relatives. Generally, however, the rate applicable to transfers to direct descendants is below 10 per cent.

(6)   Assessment, collection and remedies

The assessment rules for inheritance and estate taxes vary from canton to canton. In most cantons (e.g., Zurich, Geneva), taxes are assessed on the basis of an estate inventory made by a cantonal and/or municipal authority at the decedent's last domicile. In some cantons, the inventory may also be drawn up by the heirs or by a notary public. The assessment proceedings are usually initiated by the assessment authority after it has received notice of a taxable transfer at death. In a few cantons, however, the assessment proceedings are initiated by the

¶1044

beneficiaries, who are required to file a tax return or a private estate inventory within certain deadlines. The cantonal laws generally require the beneficiaries to co-operate and provide information during the assessment procedure. The beneficiaries may inspect the files. They are entitled to a properly notified assessment which includes the establishment of the tax base and the computation of the tax. Such assessments may be challenged by a motion to reconsider and/or an appeal to the cantonal executive or judicial authorities. The final cantonal decision may be challenged by means of a constitutional complaint to the Federal Supreme Court.

As a rule, inheritance and estate taxes become due upon notification of the assessment to the taxpayer. The deadlines for payment of the tax are relatively short (e.g., 30 days in the canton of Zurich). They start running on the day on which the taxpayer is notified, regardless of any motion to reconsider or appeal filed against the assessment. Many cantons, however, provide for payment reliefs or tax waivers in special cases.

(7) Personal tax liability
Different systems of liability apply to the payment of inheritance or estate taxes. Zurich and 15 other cantons make each heir (statutory or instituted) jointly liable for the inheritance tax, but the liability is limited to the amount of the heir's share in the inheritance. In the canton of Geneva and four other cantons, the heirs are jointly liable for the tax with their entire net worth. As a rule, the heirs' joint tax liability includes the taxes due on legacies; they are entitled to recover such taxes from the legatees. Eight cantons make the legatees jointly liable for the inheritance tax up to the net amount of legacy received. In the canton of Zurich, the legatees are liable for the tax due on the legacy but not for the taxes on the shares of inheritance. The cantons of Aargau and Ticino make even the executor of the will and the administrator of the estate jointly liable for taxes.

(8) Penalties
Penalties with respect to inheritance and estate taxes are generally analogous to those that apply to income and net-worth taxes. Violations of the duty to co-operate or inform are subject to fines. Fines are also imposed on beneficiaries who commit tax evasion. Tax fraud may be punished with fines or imprisonment. See ¶1069.

(9) Statute of Limitations
In most cantons, the right to commence assessment proceedings for inheritance or estate taxes expires ten years after the end of the year of the decedent's death. Some cantons provide for shorter Statutes of Limitations. In the case of tax fraud, the right to commence criminal proceedings and to claim subsequent taxes expires after ten years in 16 cantons.

¶1044

The right to collect properly assessed taxes usually expires five years after the day the tax became due.

¶1045   Cantonal gift taxes

Gift taxes may be levied by the cantons and municipalities but not by the Confederation. The cantons of Lucerne and Schwyz do not impose any gift taxes; in the case of Lucerne, however, *inter vivos* transfers that occur during the five-year period immediately preceding the death of the decedent are included in the estate. Most of the other cantons levy gift taxes. In the canton of Graubünden, the municipalities impose gift taxes of their own, whereas in the cantons of Vaud and Fribourg they levy municipal taxes (*centimes additionnels*) as a percentage of the cantonal gift tax.

Again, the levying of gift taxes is limited by the constitutional exclusion of double taxation (¶1003). Gift taxes on movable property may be imposed by the canton in which the donor resides at the time of the *inter vivos* transfer. In the case of immovable property, however, the canton where the property is situated is entitled to levy gift taxes.

A taxable transfer is defined as any gift within the meaning of Art. 239 CO, i.e., any *inter vivos* transfer of property by one person to another person without adequate consideration. If a transfer is made for less than adequate consideration, the gift tax is levied on the difference between the fair market value of the property transferred and the consideration actually paid. The rejection of an inheritance, the waiver of a right before it has vested or the transfer of property in fulfilment of a moral duty (such as support payments to needy siblings) are not considered gifts. Under a number of cantonal tax statutes, *inter vivos* transfers in anticipation of future inheritance, an *inter vivos* transfer of property to a foundation, a transfer of insurance claims that endure during the donor's lifetime and forgiveness of indebtedness to a solvent debtor are taxable events.

The valuation of the property transferred follows the rules applicable to the valuation of property for estate and inheritance tax purposes. Therefore, the value as of the day of the transfer or the day the donee took title to the property is decisive.

Exemptions from the gift tax vary from canton to canton. Generally, certain contributions to governmental bodies, charitable and other non-profit organisations, and pension plans are exempt. The so-called customary gifts to the spouse and descendants, as well as payments for education purposes, are exempt. The extent to which such transfers are tax-free generally depends on the relationship between the donor and the donee.

The gift tax liability arises with the execution of the gift. As a rule, the donee is liable for payment of the gift tax, which is assessed and collected on the basis of a self-declaration (tax return or notification) to be filed within a certain period (e.g., in Zurich: three months) after the execution of the gift. Several cantons provide that the donor is jointly (e.g., Zurich) or subsidiarily (e.g., Geneva) liable for the gift tax.

The gift tax rates are generally the same as for inheritance tax purposes. Therefore, progression of the rates is determined by two factors: the value of the property transferred, and the relationship between the donor and the donee. In some cantons, however, the value of previously executed gifts is taken into consideration for the purpose of determining the appropriate tax rate.

The deadlines for payment of the tax, the rules for the appeals procedure, and the penalties are the same as those for inheritance tax purposes.

TAXATION OF ORDINARY PARTNERSHIPS AND OTHER BUSINESS ORGANISATIONS THAT ARE NOT LEGAL ENTITIES

¶1046   Taxation of partners

Organisations that are not legal entities, such as general partnerships (*société en nom collectif/Kollektivgesellschaft*, Art. 552 et seq. CO, see ¶713), limited partnerships (*société en commandite/Kommanditgesellschaft*, Art. 594 et seq. CO, see ¶714) and ordinary partnerships (*société simple/einfache Gesellschaft*, Art. 530 et seq. CO, see ¶712), are not taxable. Instead, each partner or member is liable for federal, cantonal and municipal income taxes on his share of the partnership's profits. Partnerships are, however, required to disclose specific information to the tax authorities in connection with the assessment of their partners.

Non-resident partners of a Swiss-domiciled general, limited or ordinary partnership are generally deemed to have a permanent establishment in Switzerland. They are under a limited tax obligation (¶1028) and are taxed on their share of the net profits and net assets, the applicable tax rate being determined on the basis of the non-residents' worldwide income and net worth.

Non-resident partnerships with a permanent establishment in Switzerland are, for the purpose of federal and some cantonal income tax laws, treated as independent taxpayers. At the federal level, they pay income taxes according to the rules applicable to individuals. If a partner in a non-resident partnership is a Swiss resident, the amount of tax paid by the partnership on that partner's share is credited to his personal income tax levied on that share (Art. 20(2) FITD). In the cantons of Zurich and Geneva, however, non-resident partnerships are non-taxable organisations; their income is exclusively attributed to their partners.

PRINCIPLES OF CORPORATE INCOME TAXATION

¶1047   Power and jurisdiction to tax

(1)   Power to tax legal entities

The Confederation, the cantons and most municipalities may tax legal entities.

Those entities whose juridical personality is recognised under applicable federal civil or cantonal public law (for the distinction between civil and public law, see ¶107) are subject to taxation in Switzerland. The same holds true, as a rule, for foreign legal entities. Foreign tax subjects are treated analogously to those legal entities of Swiss law which have the most similar legal structure (Art. 52(1) FITD). The tax obligation of legal entities also means that any lawfully established legal entity is recognised and treated as an independent taxpayer, even if it is controlled by a single shareholder.

However, for tax purposes, the principle of recognition of Swiss or foreign legal entities may be limited by the doctrine of tax avoidance (see ¶1070): the existence of a legal entity may be disregarded for tax purposes if the legal entity was established or used for the mere or primary purpose of tax avoidance. In such a case, its income and net assets are attributed to the taxpayer who tried to use the legal entity as a shield.

(2)   Jurisdiction to tax legal entities

(a)   Personal connection

As a rule, a legal entity is taxed at the place of its statutory seat (place of incorporation). However, if the seat has a mere formal meaning and if no activity is conducted there, the jurisdiction to tax the legal entity is vested in the place where it is effectively managed and controlled.

(b)   Economic connection

Immovable property and permanent establishments of a legal entity with its seat or place of effective management and control outside the canton (for cantonal income tax purposes) or abroad (for federal income tax purposes) vest the power to tax in the places of their location and subject the legal entity to a limited tax obligation.

(3)   Duration of tax liability of legal entities

The tax obligation of a legal entity in a canton starts with its incorporation, its registration with the Register of Commerce, the establishment of its domicile, or its acquisition of taxable assets. The tax obligation is terminated when the registration in the Register of Commerce is cancelled, the seat is transferred outside the canton or abroad, or the taxable assets are disposed of.

(4) Tax exempt entities

Some entities of private and public law are exempt from taxation. The Confederation, with all its public institutions and operations, is exempt from cantonal and municipal income taxes. Usually, the cantons and municipalities and their public institutions are fully or partly exempt from taxation. Further exemptions are extended by federal and cantonal tax laws to institutions of social security, occupational pension plans, and other institutions of public or private law (¶1501 et seq.) to the extent that they are dedicated to purposes deemed to be in the public interest (especially public, charitable, educational and religious goals).

¶1048   Tax treatment of various legal entities

Depending on their structure and function, legal entities are either subject to the income and net-worth taxes applicable to individuals, or to special corporate income and capital (net equity) taxes.

(1) Share corporations and other commercial legal entities

At the federal level and in all cantons, share corporations (¶703 et seq.) and companies (including limited partnerships with shares, ¶715, and limited liability companies, ¶710) are subject to special corporate income taxes and supplementary taxes on capital (net equity).

(2) Co-operative corporations

At the federal level and in the majority of cantons (including Zurich and Geneva), co-operative corporations (¶711) pay the regular corporate income and capital taxes. Two cantons (Zug and Fribourg) tax only profit-orientated co-operative corporations, while non-profit co-operative corporations are taxed in the same way as individuals. Special progressive tax rates apply in the canton of Geneva.

(3) Associations and foundations

Associations (¶716) and foundations (¶717) are, at the federal level and in the majority of cantons, subject to taxes on income and net worth according to the rules governing individuals. Contributions of their members that are provided for in the Articles of Incorporation are not included in the association's and foundation's taxable income; expenses are deductible in so far as they exceed the tax-free allowances.

At the federal level, associations' and foundations' income is taxed at progressive rates, and their net worth is taxed at a linear rate of 0.0825 per cent. The canton of Zurich applies special linear tax rates to the taxable income and net worth of associations and foundations; associations whose taxable income is less than SFr 7,000 and whose taxable net worth does not exceed SFr 70,000 are not taxed. Some cantons tax associations with commercial activities in the same way as companies. In the canton of Geneva, associations and foundations are generally taxed in the same way as companies, but at special progressive rates.

Foundations and associations that act in the public interest may be exempt from taxation. In the cantons of Zug and Uri, all foundations are exempt from cantonal taxation.

(4)   Other legal entities

Special treatment is afforded to corporate entities and institutions of public law (¶107), church communities, political subdivisions, school communities, and the corporate entities of cantonal public law. Such entities usually pay income and net-worth taxes in the same way as individuals; however, under certain conditions they may be exempt from taxation.

¶1049   Resident legal entities

A legal entity is considered resident, domiciled and subject to an unlimited tax obligation (¶1028) if it has its 'seat' in Switzerland, or in the canton concerned. A company has its seat where it is incorporated and registered with the Register of Commerce. However, if a legal entity has its seat abroad, or in one canton, but is effectively managed and controlled in Switzerland, or in another canton, it is deemed to be resident in Switzerland, or in that other canton, respectively (¶1053).

Resident companies pay taxes on their world-wide net income and capital (net equity), except income from, and assets consisting of, extracantonal or foreign immovable property and income attributable to, and assets consisting of, an extracantonal or foreign permanent establishment. The applicable income tax rates are determined on the basis of the total world-wide net income (including exempt income).

Distributions of resident companies are subject to the federal anticipatory tax at the rate of 35 per cent, or as reduced by an applicable double-taxation convention (see ¶1073(2)).

¶1050   Non-resident legal entities

Non-resident legal entities are subject to a limited tax obligation (¶1028) in Switzerland, or in the canton involved, if they have an economic connection to a Swiss canton (immovable property or a permanent establishment). Foreign legal entities pay federal, cantonal and municipal taxes on income from Swiss immovable property, on interest income from loans secured by mortgage on Swiss immovable property, and on income attributable to a permanent establishment (in particular a branch) in Switzerland, and on the respective capital invested.

Other income derived by a non-resident legal entity from Swiss sources is not taxable. However, the federal anticipatory tax is withheld from dividends from Swiss companies and interest paid by Swiss banks to both resident and non-resident recipients (¶1007(2)).

A non-resident legal entity is treated in the same manner as the resident entity to whose legal structure it is most similar.

¶1051   Concept of permanent establishment

For the purposes of intercantonal and international taxation, a permanent establishment is generally defined as a fixed place of business where an enterprise carries on a qualitatively and quantitatively essential part of its business. More particularly, the term includes a branch, a place of management, a factory, a workshop, or a purchase or sales office. A foreign legal entity having a permanent establishment in Switzerland becomes subject to a limited tax obligation (¶1028) at the federal level and in the canton concerned. The limited tax obligation pertains to income from Swiss or foreign sources which is attributable to the permanent establishment and to the capital invested in the permanent establishment.

A legal entity that resides in one Swiss canton and has a permanent establishment in another canton is subject to an unlimited tax obligation in the canton where it is resident, and subject to a limited tax obligation in the canton where it has its permanent establishment. In order to avoid intercantonal double taxation, the entity is generally treated as a whole; the canton where the permanent establishment is located is not entitled to tax directly the income earned through the permanent establishment, but only a certain quota of the total taxable income of the entire enterprise.

¶1052   Taxation of branches of Swiss and non-Swiss corporations

(1)   Foreign branch of Swiss corporation
Domestic law provides for tax exemptions for profits and capital attributable to a foreign permanent establishment, even in the absence of an international double taxation convention. A branch generally constitutes a permanent establishment.

The federal taxes on income and capital of a Swiss legal entity which maintains a permanent establishment abroad are reduced by a share attributable to the permanent establishment in the proportion that the production factors of the foreign operation bear to those of the entire operation (Art. 55(1) FITD). This provision (as well as analogous provisions of the cantonal tax statutes) uses the concepts of total profits and total tax. As a result, the corporation can never be taxed on more than its aggregate net profits earned in Switzerland and abroad. No Swiss income tax may be levied if the corporation suffers an aggregate loss, irrespective of whether this loss is derived from the operation of the Swiss headquarters or of the foreign branch (see examples below).

There are several ways to calculate the share of 'foreign' income that determines the tax reduction. If separate accounts are kept at the Swiss headquarters and at the foreign permanent establishment, the 'foreign' share of income may be determined on the basis of the permanent establishment's accounts. Otherwise, the 'foreign' share of income may be determined on the basis of auxiliary factors, such as the branch's invested capital, payroll, and turnover.

Example 1: Corporation X SA has its seat and headquarters in Zurich and a branch in a foreign country. The foreign branch keeps separate accounts. The financial statements of X SA, which reflect the entire operation, show a net profit of 70 in 1989 and a net profit of 30 in 1990. The accounts of the foreign branch show a net profit of 30 in 1989 and a loss of (10) in 1990.

(a) Federal income tax, 1991–92

	total result	*Switzerland*	*abroad*
1989	70	40	30
1990	30	40	(10)
1989–90	100	80	20
Average	50 (100%)	40 (80%)	10 (20%)

The Swiss tax authorities may attribute an advance share (*praecipuum*; *préciput/Vorausabzug*) of income to the Swiss headquarters in order to take into account the predominant influence of the central management. Assuming that the federal tax authorities claim an advance share of 20 per cent, the 'foreign reduction' is calculated as follows:

	total result	*Switzerland*	*abroad*
Advance share 20%	10	10	0
Remaining net profit	40 (100%)	32 (80%)	8 (20%)
Taxable income	50 (100%)	42 (84%)	8 (16%)

'Foreign reduction' = 16%

¶1052

(b) Zurich Cantonal and Municipal Income Taxes, 1990 and 1991

  (i) *1990*:

	total result	Switzerland	abroad
Profit 1989	70 (100%)	40 (57%)	30 (43%)
Advance share 20%	14	14	0
Remaining net profit	56 (100%)	32 (57%)	24 (43%)
Taxable income	70 (100%)	46 (66%)	24 (34%)

'Foreign reduction' = 34%

  (ii) *1991*:

	total result	Switzerland	abroad
Profit 1990	30 (100%)	40 (100%)	(10) (0%)
Taxable income	30	30	0

No 'foreign reduction' is available

The Federal Supreme Court confirmed in a recent decision (*Archives*, 58, 351) that under certain circumstances Art. 55(1) FITD obliges Switzerland to take losses that result from the operation of a foreign permanent establishment into account. In particular, the Court held that Art. 55(1) FITD does not allow a limitation of the 'foreign reduction' of tax *in casu*, by setting off the foreign permanent establishment's profit against its earlier losses.

Example 2: The accounts of X SA and its foreign branch show the following results:

	total	Switzerland	abroad
Calculation period 1	(90)	10	(100)
Calculation period 2	20	100	(80)
Calculation period 3	120	20	100

The federal income tax situation looks as follows:

Calculation period 1: The profit of 10 realised at the Swiss headquarters is not taxed; the total loss of (90) is relevant.

Calculation period 2: The net profit of 20 (Swiss profit of 100 less foreign loss of (80)) is taxable. However, the taxable income of 20 may be set off against the loss carry-over from calculation period 1 of (90).

Calculation period 3:	total	Switzerland	abroad
	120 (100%)	20 (16.66%)	100 (83.33%)
Advance share 20%	24	24	0
Remaining net profit	96 (100%)	16 (16.66%)	80 (83.33%)
Taxable income	120 (100%)	40 (33.33%)	80 (66.66%)

The full 'foreign reduction' of 66.66 per cent must be granted under the above-cited decision of the Federal Supreme Court; a set-off of the 'foreign' income share against earlier 'foreign' losses is prohibited.

The remaining loss from calculation period 1 of (70) (i.e., (90) less 20 which could be set off in calculation period 2) may be deducted from the total net profit of 120. Therefore, the taxable income is 50. The tax calculated on the income of 50 is reduced by 66.66 per cent.

(2) Swiss branch of foreign corporation

Non-resident corporations are subject to the federal and to cantonal and municipal taxes on income from Swiss and foreign sources and on capital that is attributable to a permanent establishment in Switzerland. The term 'permanent establishment' must be interpreted according to the provisions of the applicable double taxation convention, if any, and of federal and cantonal internal law.

A non-resident corporation doing business in Switzerland through a branch generally maintains a permanent establishment.

A non-resident corporation which maintains a permanent establishment in Switzerland pays that part of the tax, computed on the basis of the total factors, which corresponds to the ratio of the factors of the Swiss operation to those of the total operation (Art. 52(2) FITD). This 'indirect' apportionment method is also applied in intercantonal taxation. It limits Switzerland's taxing authority to a portion (maximum 100 per cent) of the total net income and capital of the foreign corporation. The apportionment may be carried out on the basis of the permanent establishment's separate accounts ('direct' method) or various production factors such as turnover, pay-roll, and assets ('indirect' method).

The double taxation conventions entered into by Switzerland, however, allow the application of the 'direct' method (internationally also known as the 'separate entity approach') for the income apportionment: the net income or loss of the permanent establishment is determined on the basis of its separate accounts or other auxiliary factors, without taking the total results of the enterprise into account.

Example 3: Y Inc., a foreign corporation, has a branch in Switzerland which keeps separate accounts. The aggregate of the foreign and Swiss operations results in a net profit of 100 in calculation period 1, and a net loss of (100) in calculation period 2. The accounts of the Swiss branch show a net profit of 40 in calculation period 1, and a net profit of 20 in calculation period 2. The federal tax situation is as follows:

¶1052

	total	Switzerland	abroad
Calculation period 1	100	40	60

The taxable income of the Swiss branch is 40.

	total	Switzerland	abroad
Calculation period 2	(100)	20	(120)

The taxable income of the Swiss branch is 20, regardless of the aggregate loss.

The provisions on the determination of a permanent establishment's taxable income and capital vary from canton to canton. The practice of the cantonal tax authorities in international cases, however, tends to apply the 'direct' (or 'separate entity') method, even if the 'indirect' method is expressly mentioned in the cantonal tax statutes.

A Swiss branch of a foreign corporation that exclusively renders services to its foreign headquarters may be treated as a service company: it will be taxed at least on a deemed net profit that corresponds to a certain percentage (at least 10 per cent) of its total operating expenses ('cost plus' taxation).

Certain types of income from Swiss sources (e.g., income from immovable property located in Switzerland, including gains realised on the disposition thereof, income from claims secured by Swiss real estate or mortgages thereon, and Swiss-source dividends and bank interest) are always subject to Swiss taxes, even if not realised through a permanent establishment in Switzerland.

From a tax planning point of view, the use of a Swiss branch rather than a Swiss subsidiary of a foreign corporation may, under certain circumstances, be an interesting option. The advantages depend, however, on the tax situation in the home country of the foreign enterprise and on the existence of an international double taxation convention. In particular, the use of a branch may be advantageous if the domestic tax law of the foreign enterprise or the applicable treaty provides for a tax exemption rather than a tax credit with respect to profits of branches (permanent establishment). The level of Swiss income tax on branch profits is often relatively low: as a rule, at least the same deductions that apply to resident corporations are granted to a permanent establishment of a foreign corporation. For example, the Swiss tax authorities usually accept that an arm's length interest is charged on that portion of funds received from the foreign headquarters which is not treated as equity (*capital de dotation/ Dotationskapital*) of the branch. See also ¶1059(2).

Example 4:   *Swiss branch*
                                        balance sheet

Assets	100	Loan	80
		Equity	20
	100		100

Swiss branch
profit and loss account

Turnover	100	Operating expenses	70
		Interest (8% of 80)	6.4
		Net profit	23.6
	100		100

Cantonal tax privileges are usually also available to permanent establishments of foreign corporations if they meet the applicable requirements.

As a rule, the transfer of profits from a Swiss branch to the foreign headquarters is not subject to Swiss withholding taxes (unlike the distribution of profits of a Swiss subsidiary to its foreign parent company, which is subject to the federal anticipatory tax of 35 per cent or as reduced by treaty).

¶1053   Effective management and control

A legal entity is normally considered a resident of the place where it was incorporated (where it now has its seat). However, an entity incorporated abroad, or of another canton, may nevertheless be considered a resident of Switzerland, or of the other canton, if it is effectively managed and controlled there. Conflicts of residence between the seat and the place of effective management and control may be resolved in an international setting on the basis of an applicable double taxation convention, and in an intercantonal situation by the Federal Supreme Court upon a constitutional complaint by the taxpayer. The canton claiming authority to tax based on effective management and control from its territory must prove such facts.

From a mere domestic tax point of view, an entity incorporated in Switzerland is deemed to be a Swiss resident, notwithstanding the fact that it is actually managed and controlled from abroad. The foreign place of management and control may be recognised as a foreign permanent establishment if sufficient evidence is shown. All income attributable to the foreign place of management would be exempt from Swiss income taxes.

The applicable double taxation convention usually resolves the conflict of 'dual' residence in favour of the place of effective management and control. The seat in Switzerland may still qualify as a permanent establishment, unless it is nothing more than a letterbox.

¶1054 Intercompany pricing – transfer of earnings – debt v equity

(1) Adjustments to taxable income

Corporate taxable income is generally determined on the basis of the balance of the profit and loss account(s) of the business year(s) closed in the calculation period. The net profit (or loss) may, however, be adjusted by certain items, particularly by expenditures or missing income which is the result of the granting of favourable treatment to a related party. The benefiting party is typically the shareholder or parent company, or another company which is directly or indirectly controlled by the same shareholders. Such transactions conflict with the principle of 'dealing at arm's length' which is generally applied where business transactions between related parties are involved. A corporation which either does not receive adequate consideration for its performance to a related party, or pays an excessive price for the performance of its related counterpart is deemed to grant a benefit of a financial value (constructive dividend). Such benefits are added to the taxable income of the corporation which grants them.

> **Example 1**: Corporation X and corporation Y are subsidiaries of corporation Z. X sells a machine to Y at a price of 50. The fair market value of the machine is 100; the book value is 40. Although the books of X show a gain of only 10, the taxable income of X will be increased by 60.

> **Example 2**: Corporation Y (as above) renders management services to corporation X, which pays a management fee of 100. The tax inspector finds that an arm's length fee would have been only 60. The difference of 40 is disregarded as a business expense for income tax purposes.

> **Example 3**: Corporation X buys a patent from its parent company Z, at a price of 100. The patent turns out to be worth only 40. X depreciates the patent by 60. This depreciation will be disallowed for income tax purposes.

(2) Levy of the federal anticipatory tax

In addition to the adjustment of taxable income, the federal anticipatory tax is levied on the distribution of a benefit of a financial value (constructive dividend). Under the practice of the Federal Tax Administration, the anticipatory tax must be charged to the *direct* beneficiary, i.e., the recipient of the benefit of financial value. Thus, in Examples 1 and 2 above the anticipatory tax must be passed on to the directly benefiting sister companies rather than to the (indirectly benefiting) parent company.

(3) Determination of arm's length price

When called to judge whether a particular transfer price conforms to the arm's length principle, the tax authorities frequently refer to the 'comparable uncontrolled price' method, i.e., they make a direct reference to prices in comparable transactions between enterprises independent of each other, or between the group and unrelated parties. There are, however, many cases where no useful evidence of uncontrolled transactions is available for a number of reasons. In these instances, the tax authorities may apply the 'cost plus' method, which, starting from the cost of providing the goods or services, allows the addition of whatever cost and profit mark up is deemed appropriate. The 'resale price' method may also be applied, this method, starting from the final selling price, subtracts the cost and an appropriate profit mark-up. These methods are basically in line with the OECD Report (1979) on 'Transfer Pricing and Multinational Enterprises'. It is important to note that, for purposes of determining a proper arm's length price with respect to intangibles, the 'commensurate with the income standard' is generally not applied.

The guide-lines on interest rates payable among related parties are amended from time to time. The latest version of 10 July 1990 provides that advances to shareholders or affiliated companies in Swiss currency must bear interest of at least 7 per cent if they are financed with equity and if the company has no interest-bearing debt. If the advance is financed with borrowed funds, the interest rate on the advance must exceed the financing costs by at least 0.25 per cent to 0.5 per cent; in any event the interest rate must be at least 7 per cent. If a Swiss corporation takes a loan from its shareholder or an affiliated party, it should not pay interest of more than 8 per cent if the loan is in Swiss Francs; lower rates apply for loans to finance immovable property (7 per cent to 7.75 per cent). The application of these maximum interest rates generally requires that the borrowing company not be 'thinly-capitalised' (¶1058(2)).

In the international field the Swiss tax authorities apply the guide-lines of the above-mentioned OECD Report of 1979.

TAXATION OF SHARE CORPORATIONS

¶1055   Corporate income defined

(1) Income determination by net-worth comparison

Share corporations and other entities treated the same way are taxed on their taxable income or 'net profit' earned during the calculation period.

¶1055

The corporate 'net profit' is generally defined as the difference between the net worth at the beginning and the end of the calculation period, increased by the value of withdrawals from capital and reduced by the value of contributions to capital (method of income determination by net-worth comparison).

Companies are required by law to prepare annual balance sheets and profit and loss statements according to the general accounting provisions of the Code of Obligations, or the special accounting and valuation provisions of corporate law.

The balance of the profit and loss statement is recognised as the basis for the determination of the taxable 'net profit' if the legal accounting rules are observed. Once the accounts are approved by the general meeting of the shareholders, they are final and binding upon the corporate taxpayer. They may be rectified only if mandatory accounting rules have been violated.

(2) Balance sheet for tax purposes – adjustment to income – non-deductible items

The 'net profit' determined under the net-worth comparison method may require certain adjustments for specific tax purposes, even when the balance sheet and profit and loss statement have been properly prepared (resulting in a so-called 'balance sheet for tax purposes').

All payments made and charged to the profit and loss account which were used to cover expenses that are not 'commercially justified' (i.e. reasonable business expenses), as well as excess depreciations and provisions, are added to the balance of the profit and loss account. In some cantons income taxes paid are not deductible, while they are deductible for federal income tax purposes.

On the other hand, in many cantons, certain items of income which are exempt from income taxation (such as capital gains on immovable property) are deducted from the balance of the profit and loss account. Net losses carried over from prior tax periods are also deductible within certain limits (¶1024).

(a) Commercially unjustified expenses

The tax authorities may disallow the deduction of certain expenses charged to the profit and loss account, even if such accounting is in line with generally accepted accounting principles. Examples of such 'unjustified' expenses are payments made in connection with the purchase or improvement of capital assets, voluntary payments to third persons, open and hidden (constructive) dividends and distributions of profits.

(b) Commercially unjustified depreciations and reserves

In order to be deductible, depreciation must be in line with normal business practice. Only income-producing business assets may be depreciated. All expenditures that are capitalised can be depreciated. Assets that are not subject to normal wear and tear are not depreciable. As a rule, buildings – but not land – may be depreciated. Intangible assets (patents, trade marks, copyrights, concessions, secret formulae, purchased goodwill) are depreciable.

According to the case law of the Federal Supreme Court, a depreciation is 'commercially justified' and deductible only if it is based on an actual decline in value of an income-producing asset during the calculation period. Since this so-called principle of reality of depreciation is often difficult to apply, the tax authorities have issued guide-lines indicating standard methods and rates of depreciation for several kinds of assets. As a rule, both the straight-line method and the declining-balance method of depreciation are accepted for tax purposes. The taxpayer may also change the depreciation method once chosen, unless the change primarily aims at avoiding tax. Extraordinary depreciation may be justified under specific circumstances (abnormal declines in value, unforseeable losses, etc.). The canton of Zurich is known for its quite liberal practice with respect to admissible depreciation. In some cases the system of 'immediate depreciation' is allowed, according to which certain assets may be entirely written down during the year the asset is acquired.

By analogy, reserves are deductible in so far as they are consistent with normal business practice. Under the case law of the Federal Supreme Court, reserves are admissible to secure assets that have become uncertain (e.g., bad debt reserves), or to cover probable risks of losses (e.g., reserves for surety obligations).

(c) Taxes
Taxes paid or due during the tax period may be deducted for federal corporate income tax purposes, and in the majority of cantons.

(d) Contributions to occupational pension plans
Statutory contributions to such pension plans for the taxpayer's own personnel are deductible in so far as such contributions exclusively serve the purpose of providing for benefits in the event of death, old age and disability.

(e) Contributions to public-interest institutions
For federal income tax purposes, contributions are deductible if they are made for purposes that are exclusively of public interest and if any inappropriate use of such contributions is excluded. In the canton of Zurich, contributions to the canton, its municipalities and their institutions, as well as to other legal entities which are exempt from cantonal taxation because they serve public interest goals, may be deducted; the amount of the deduction, however, is limited to 20 per cent of the taxable income before such contributions. The provisions of the canton of Geneva foresee an unlimited deduction of contributions to charitable and other public interest institutions.

¶1055

(f) Recession (job creation) reserves
To some extent, a reserve for future creation of jobs may be constituted, and is recognised for federal income tax purposes, by private enterprises with at least 20 employees; the cantons may reduce the minimum staff requirement to ten employees.

Eligible enterprises may contribute a maximum of 15 per cent, but at least SFr 10,000, of their annual net income after deduction of any losses carried forward, to an interest-bearing job creation reserve fund with the Federal Treasury or to an escrow account with a Swiss bank. The total reserve fund is limited to 20 per cent of the annual sum of salaries paid as defined under the federal social security legislation; the Federal Government may increase the limit to 30 per cent for special capital-intensive industries.

The annual contributions to such funds are deductible for federal income tax purposes to the extent that the cantons and municipalities allow tax-free formation of such reserves. Under this condition, the recession reserves are treated as open reserves constituted from previously taxed income. The job creation reserves are taxed when the enterprise is eventually liquidated. Transferring the share corporation's seat abroad or opening a foreign permanent establishment is treated as liquidation or partial liquidation.

The federal authorities may release the job creation reserve funds upon the enterprise's request if impending or actual economic difficulties are shown. They may generally release the reserve funds for the entire territory of Switzerland or several cantons, or for certain or all economic branches in the case of impending or actual recessions.

(3) Deduction of net operating losses
A corporate taxpayer who suffers a net operating loss in a given tax period is treated as follows:

(a) Cantons with one-year calculation periods
In those cantons where the calculation period for corporate income taxation is one year (e.g., Zurich and Geneva), a corporate taxpayer suffering a net operating loss in a given year will not pay any income tax in the tax year (period) for which the loss year serves as the calculation period. In addition, that loss may be carried forward (but never back) to a limited number of tax years (e.g., four years in Zurich), to be set off against net operating profits from the respective calculation periods.

Example 1: X SA is a corporation with its seat in Zurich. The profit and loss accounts show the following results:

tax period (year)	calculation period (year)	net profit (loss)	taxable income	loss carry-forward
1986	1985	(100)	0	100
1987	1986	15	−1 0	85
1988	1987	10	—2 0	75
1989	1988	20	—3 0	55
1990	1989	25	—4 0	30
1991	1990	20	—5 20	none

The net loss of 100 suffered in 1985 is the tax calculation base for the tax year 1986, and may be carried forward and set off against taxable net profits for four further tax years (1987 to 1990). The remaining loss carry-over of 30 can no longer be set off against taxable net profits for the tax years 1991 and thereafter.

(b)   Confederation and cantons following federal two-year system
The federal income tax and 11 cantonal tax laws are based on the *praenumerando* tax system (¶1019(3)), with calculation periods of two years and a possibility of tax loss carry-forwards for three periods, i.e. six years. Net profits and losses within the same base period are set off against each other so that the actual carry-forward may amount to seven years.

Example 2:

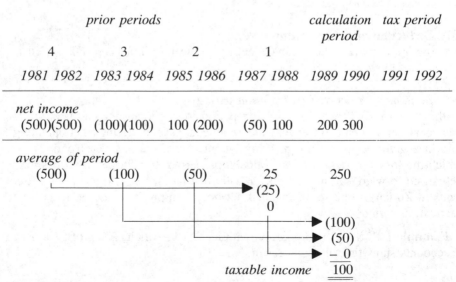

	prior periods				calculation period	tax period
4	3	2	1			
1981 1982	1983 1984	1985 1986	1987 1988	1989 1990	1991 1992	

net income
(500)(500)   (100)(100)   100 (200)   (50) 100   200 300

average of period
   (500)   (100)   (50)   25   250
                                                  (25)
                                                   0
                                                            (100)
                                                             (50)
                                                            – 0
                              taxable income   100

The average loss incurred in the period 1981–82 of 500 can be set off against subsequent profits as follows: a portion of 25 can be set off against the average profit of 25 earned in the 1987–88 period. The remaining loss portion of 475 cannot be deducted after the 1987–88 period.

Where a corporation which has accrued losses is financially restructured by forgiving its debts, the above limitations of tax loss carry-forwards are usually suspended: any prior losses may be set off against the 'restructuring gain' resulting from the forgiveness of debt (¶1062).

¶1056   Computation of tax – tax rates

The amount of corporate income tax is generally computed on the basis of the corporation's taxable income, which is determined as described above.

(1)   Tax periods and calculation periods

At the federal level, the *praenumerando* system with tax periods and calculation periods of two years applies (¶1019(3)): corporate income taxes of a given tax period (e.g., 1991–92) are calculated on the basis of the average taxable net income of the two-year period preceding the tax period (calculation period: average net income of 1989–90, adjusted and reduced by prior net operating losses, if any).

Many cantons apply different tax computation systems. For example, Zurich and Geneva use the *praenumerando* system with one-year tax and calculation periods, while Zug and the City of Basel use the *postnumerando* system where the tax year and the calculation year are the same.

(2)   Tax rates

The rates for corporate income taxes are generally set progressively; the progression usually depends on the profitability, i.e., the ratio between taxable income and net equity (yield).

(a)   Rates of the federal income tax

In federal corporate income taxation, a 'three-level-tariff' is applied. The entire taxable income is first subject to a proportional basic tax of 3.63 per cent. Then, supplemental proportional taxes are levied: at first 3.63 per cent on the portion of taxable income that exceeds 4 per cent of the 'proportional capital', and then 4.83 per cent on the portion that exceeds 8 per cent of the 'proportional capital'; the aggregate tax rate is limited to 9.8 per cent.

'Proportional capital' is the average equity (i.e., paid-in capital, previously taxed retained earnings, other open reserves and dissimulated equity) of the calculation period, considering any capital increases during such period.

Whenever the taxable income exceeds 23.15 per cent of the 'proportional capital', the maximum tax rate of 9.8 per cent applies.

(b)   Rates of the cantonal taxes
In most of the cantons, the tax rate is a combination of two elements: a (progressive) statutory tax rate which is set in the cantonal tax statute, and cantonal and municipal multipliers that are usually fixed by the cantonal and municipal legislative bodies for a period of one or several years. Therefore, the amounts of cantonal and municipal corporate income taxes are usually determined in two steps:

  (i) the statutory rate is applied to the taxable income, resulting in the so-called 'simple state tax'; and

  (ii) cantonal and municipal multipliers are applied to the 'simple state tax', resulting in the actual amount of the tax.

In Zurich, the statutory ('simple') corporate tax rate is determined by a 'three-level-tariff' very similar to the federal corporate income tax tariff (4 per cent basic tax, plus 5 per cent on the portion of income between 4 per cent and 8 per cent of taxable capital, plus 5 per cent of income in excess of 8 per cent of taxable capital). The maximum 'simple' state tax rate for corporations is 12 per cent. For 1991, the aggregate cantonal and municipal multiplier for a company located in the city of Zurich is 2.38, including church taxes. Hence, the actual income tax rate for a company located in the city of Zurich varies between 9.52 per cent (i.e., 4 per cent x 2.38) and 28.56 per cent (i.e., 12 per cent x 2.38).

In about half of the cantons (including Geneva), the statutory rates of corporate income tax depend directly on the ratio between taxable income and net equity at the beginning or end of the calculation period, or the average equity during the calculation period.

¶1057   Taxation of corporate distributions

(1)   Regular distributions
Regular profit distributions of a share corporation with respect to stock ('dividends') require a decision of the general meeting of the shareholders. Dividends may be declared only if certain conditions of corporate law are met. For tax purposes, distributions to the shareholders that do not represent a repayment of capital, including payment of undisclosed (constructive) dividends or liquidation proceeds, are treated as dividends.

Dividends are paid out of the share corporation's net income. They may not be charged to the profit and loss account. Accordingly, dividend distributions are *not* recognised as deductible expenses.

The regular distribution of a dividend is, at the level of the share corporation, subject to the federal anticipatory tax at the rate of 35 per cent. The tax is calculated on the gross amount of the dividend (¶1007(2)).

The share corporation itself is liable for the anticipatory tax. It must declare the dividend on a special tax form, indicating the date of the general shareholders' meeting that decided the distribution and the day when the dividend becomes due. The corporation is required by law to pass the anticipatory tax on to the shareholder. In the case of a cash distribution, the corporation must withhold the tax from the gross dividend and remit it to the Federal Tax Administration within 30 days from the due date of the dividend.

If the share corporation fails to charge the anticipatory tax to the shareholders, the actual amount paid to the shareholders is regarded as a 'net' dividend after the deduction of the 35 per cent tax. The tax is then calculated on the basis of a ficticious 'grossed-up' dividend.

Example: A company distributes a dividend of 100 and fails to pass the anticipatory tax on to the recipients. The payment is regarded as a net dividend after the deduction of the 35 per cent anticipatory tax, i.e., 65 per cent of the 'gross' dividend. Therefore, the 'grossed-up' dividend amounts to 153.85 (100 per cent), resulting in a tax of 53.85 (35 per cent of 153.85), for which the company is liable.

Individual or corporate shareholders residing in Switzerland may recover the full amount of anticipatory tax withheld, provided they duly report as income the gross amount of the dividend.

Shareholders residing abroad cannot recover the anticipatory tax, unless expressly provided for by an applicable double taxation convention (¶1073(2)).

(2) Extraordinary distribution

Tax treatment of extraordinary corporate profit distributions in connection with merger, split-off and liquidation is discussed in ¶1061, ¶1063 and ¶1065.

(3) Constructive dividends (undisclosed profit distributions)

Constructive dividends or undisclosed profit distributions (granting of a benefit of a financial nature – *prestation appreciable en argent/geldwerte Leistung*) may be described as disbursements by a company or similar entity to its shareholders, members or other affiliated parties that appear on the company's records as business expenses charged to the profit and loss account, as payments charged to asset accounts, as a transfer of corporate property, or as a waiver of a valid claim, but which are actually made by reason of the company-shareholder relationship rather than in an ordinary business transaction. The Federal Supreme Court characterises the constructive dividend as follows (ATF 107 Ib 325):

¶1057

(a) The company grants a benefit of a financial value to a shareholder, member or other affiliated party without receiving adequate consideration in return.

(b) The benefit would not have been made available to a third party under arm's length dealing, or would not have been made in the same manner or amount.

(c) The lack of proportion between the benefit granted by the company and the consideration received in return could be, or should have been, apparent to the officers of the company.

The concept of the constructive dividend must be distinguished from the concept of tax avoidance, in that the intention to avoid tax or to obtain a fiscal advantage is not a prerequisite for a constructive dividend (¶1070).

Typical examples of re-characterisation as constructive dividends would be 'business expenses', such as excessive salaries paid to officer-shareholders, excessive interest paid on shareholders' loans, excessive rent paid on property belonging to a shareholder, excessive royalties paid to related persons, etc. Other examples of constructive dividends are the acquisition of property from a shareholder at a price in excess of fair market value, or loans extended to a shareholder without serious expectation of repayment. Depreciation on such fictitious assets is not deductible. A corporation selling property to a shareholder at a price below market value makes an undisclosed dividend distribution. Constructive dividends often result from intercorporate 'profit-shifting', e.g., inadequate transfer prices for deliveries between affiliated companies. Further examples are the waiver of (adequate) interest on loans extended to shareholders, affiliated companies or other related parties, rent-free leases of corporate property to a related party, and the rendering of gratuitous services to related parties.

The tax consequences of constructive dividends are adjustment of the taxable income of the company (non-recognition of business expenses, depreciations, write-offs; or the addition of the missing fair consideration to income), and the levy of the 35 per cent federal anticipatory tax, which must be charged by the corporation to the beneficiary. If the beneficiary is entitled to recover the anticipatory tax, and if certain additional restrictive conditions are met, the company may, upon special request, meet its tax obligation by a simple declaration of the taxable benefit in lieu of paying the anticipatory tax.

¶1058   Tax on capital

(1)   Taxable capital defined

At the federal level and in all cantons, corporations pay an annual tax on capital and reserves (equity). Capital tax rates are proportional at the federal level and in most cantons. The federal capital tax rate is 0.0825 per cent. Cantonal capital tax rates are usually the combination of a statutory rate and an annual cantonal and/or municipal multiplier. The combined cantonal and municipal capital tax rates range between approximately 0.26 and 1 per cent per annum.

Taxable capital is defined under federal and many cantonal tax laws as the sum of paid-in share capital, open reserves, and previously-taxed undisclosed reserves. The taxable capital cannot be less than the paid-in share capital, even if the latter is no longer fully covered by net assets; hence, there is no tax loss carry-forward for capital tax purposes.

Open reserves represent the difference between the net equity (difference between assets and liabilities) and the nominal share capital of the company. Elements of the open reserves are, in particular, the legal reserve fund as required by Art. 671 CO, any reserve funds provided for by the Articles of Association, and any other previously-taxed retained earnings shown on the liability side of the balance sheet. Open reserves may also stem from contributions of the shareholders to capital and premiums on shares which are not taxable income.

Undisclosed reserves are constituted by undervaluation of assets or overvaluation of liabilities. If such constitution of undisclosed reserves is disallowed by the tax authorities, e.g., if depreciations on assets and the constitution of reserves are added back to corporate taxable income because they are not considered to be commercially justified (¶1055(2)), such undisclosed reserves will be taxed as income and are then included in the taxable capital. However, some cantonal tax laws (e.g., Geneva) provide that the paid-in share capital and all open and undisclosed reserves (whether taxed as income or not) are subject to the capital tax. In practice, this is limited to undisclosed reserves on real estate (difference between book value and official appraisal) and on securities quoted on the stock exchange (difference between book value and tax value according to a list issued annually by the Federal Tax Administration). As the burden of proof for the existence of undisclosed reserves lies with the tax authorities, undisclosed reserves on other assets or liabilities are usually not taken into account.

(2) Undisclosed equity – thin capitalisation rules

As a rule, only equity is subject to the capital tax. However, debt stemming from a shareholder or another affiliated party may, under certain circumstances, be treated as equity and be subject to the capital tax ('undisclosed equity').

Federal income tax law contains no provisions on the requisite proportion between the debt and equity of a corporation. However, the Federal Tax Administration has issued guide-lines regarding the financing of Swiss real estate companies; these guide-lines contain instructions as to how the taxable capital of such companies must be determined. They state that, in the absence of statutory provisions, 'undisclosed equity' may be taxed if the recognition of debt-financing would, in the given case, allow the company to evade the tax. This is the case, in particular, if the company could not carry out its business without the borrowed funds and could not obtain such financing from an unrelated party, and if the borrowed funds are exposed to unusual risk. In practice, the tax authorities usually require that real estate assets be financed at least 20 per cent by equity. Thus, the taxable capital of a real estate company corresponds at least to 20 per cent of its real estate assets at market value. The Federal Supreme Court has approved these ratios.

Foreign-controlled Swiss holding or finance companies cannot obtain relief from foreign withholding taxes under double taxation conventions if their interest-bearing debts exceed six times their equity.

There are no official federal tax guide-lines on minimum equity for other types of corporations. However, the Federal Tax Administration usually requires that the following portions of assets evaluated at market value be covered by equity:

- 20 per cent of immovable property,
- 50 per cent of other fixed assets (machinery, equipment, etc.),
- 15 per cent of inventory and other current assets,
- 10 per cent of bonds in Swiss currency,
- 20 per cent of bonds in foreign currencies,
- 40 per cent of shares quoted on the stock exchange,
- 50 per cent of other shares and investments in companies.

A number of cantonal tax statutes contain express provisions on the taxation of undisclosed equity that, depending on the cantons, apply to all or only to specific types of companies (e.g., holding or real estate companies). The cantons sometimes subject at least a certain portion of the balance sheet assets (e.g., one-sixth) to the capital tax.

Where no statutory or administrative 'thin capitalisation' rules exist, the tax authorities may recharacterise the debt shown on the balance sheet as equity only if its recognition as debt would result in tax avoidance (¶1070). The Federal Supreme Court has held (ATF 99 Ib 375) that the debt-financing of a corporation by its shareholders constitutes tax avoidance if:

(a) the corporation would be unable to function without the borrowed means;

(b) borrowings in an amount similar to that obtained from the shareholders would, under normal business conditions, not be available from an unrelated third party;

(c) the shareholder debts are exposed to full business risks as equity;

(d) the chosen financing structure can be explained only by the shareholders' intention to obtain interest rather than a dividend from their corporation.

¶1058

In so far as a corporation's debts are re-characterised as 'hidden equity' for capital tax purposes, interest paid thereon is not deductible as a business expense for income tax purposes. If such interest is paid to a related party, it is subject to the anticipatory tax (¶1007(2)).

¶1059 Corporate tax privileges

(1) Holding companies

For income tax purposes, holding companies may be divided into two different types:

  (a) the 'mixed holding company' or 'investment company'; and

  (b) the 'pure' holding company.

(a) The 'mixed holding company' or 'investment company'
'Mixed holding companies' and 'participation/investment companies', organised as share corporations or similar legal entities, perform normal industrial or commercial activities but, in addition, hold substantial investments in one or several Swiss or foreign companies or similar entities. A tax privilege for dividend income from such investments in other companies is available at the federal cantonal and municipal levels in order to eliminate or reduce the effect of a multiple tax burden on profits generated by lower-tier members of groups of companies. The tax privilege usually consists of a reduction of income tax in the proportion that the 'investment income' bears to the total income of the investment company. 'Investment income' includes all receipts that are treated as profit distributions with respect to stock, such as open or constructive dividends, liquidation proceeds and stock dividends, bonuses and interest on corporate shares, but not repayments of share capital or capital or revaluation gains on investments in companies. In addition, to qualify for the tax privilege, the investment in another company must generally be substantial: it must be directly held and represent at least 20 per cent of the other company's capital, or have a minimum value of usually SFr 2 million.

At the federal level, the tax is reduced in the proportion that the gross income from investments in other companies bears to the 'overall gross income'. 'Overall gross income' includes all profits from regular industrial or commercial activities, capital or revaluation gains, and dividends, as well as other passive income (interest, royalties, rents, commissions, etc.), after deduction of business expenses that are exclusively related to regular activities.

For cantonal tax purposes, the ratio between the 'net' income from investments in other companies and the taxable net income generally determines the tax reduction. 'Net income from investments in other companies' is usually deemed to be the amount of gross dividends received after subtracting a proportional share of financing costs and administrative expenses.

The actual income tax of an investment company is computed as follows:

(i) the tax is calculated as if no privilege applied;

(ii) then, the percentage that the income from investments in other companies represents of the total income is multiplied by the ordinary tax;

(iii) finally, the resulting amount is subtracted from the ordinary tax.

Example: Company X has an 'overall gross' income of 150 and a net income of 100. The gross income from investments in other companies is 40; 'net' income from investments in other companies (after deduction of proportional financing costs and lump-sum administrative expenses of 5%) is 35.

(i) *Federal income tax*

net income = 100

ordinary income tax: 9.8% of 100 = 9.8

tax reduction factor:

$$\frac{\text{gross income from investments in other companies}}{\text{overall gross income}} = \frac{40}{150} = 26.66\%$$

tax reduction = 9.8 x 0.2666 = 2.613

reduced tax = 9.8 – 2.613 = 7.187

(ii) *Cantonal/municipal income tax*

net income = 100

ordinary income tax: assessed 20% = 20

tax reduction factor:

$$\frac{\text{net income from investments in other companies}}{\text{overall net income}} = \frac{35}{100} = 35\%$$

tax reduction = 20 ×0.35 = 7

reduced tax = 20 – 7 = 13

In the canton of Geneva, all revenues derived from investments in other companies that have the character of a profit distribution are exempt from corporate income taxation.

¶1059

(b)   The 'pure' holding company

(i)   Federal income tax.   The Federal Income Tax Decree does not provide for any special 'pure holding' tax status, but all ('mixed' and 'pure') holding companies are granted the proportional tax reduction for income from investments in other companies.

(ii)   Cantonal income taxes in general.   Companies and comparable entities (in some cantons, even foundations) whose exclusive, or at least primary, purpose is the holding or administration of investments in other companies (corporations and other 'capital companies') are treated as holding companies. A few cantonal tax statutes do not permit any activities other than holding and administering such investments. Most of the cantons, however, allow the holding company to pursue ancillary activities to a limited extent. The nature and extent of such ancillary activities is usually determined by the administrative practice of the respective canton. Generally, the holding activity must clearly prevail over the other activities; any industrial, trading or other commercial activities, at least within Switzerland, are excluded. Within these limits, holding companies in many cantons may hold and exploit other investments and intangible property (patents, trade marks, copyrights, industrial know-how, etc.).

Many cantons require the investments held in other companies to be substantial, e.g., to consist of capital interests of at least 20 per cent or of a certain minimum value (SFr 1 or 2 million). A number of cantons require a certain minimum share of the holding company's assets to consist of (qualifying) investments and/or a minimum amount of its revenue to be derived from investments.

All cantonal income tax statutes provide for a special privileged tax status for 'pure' holding companies. In almost all cantons, pure holding companies are generally exempt from ordinary income taxes and pay only a substantially reduced capital tax. If a pure holding company owns immovable property within the canton concerned, the holding status may not be available or, if available, the pure holding company may be subject to ordinary taxation on such property and income derived therefrom.

(iii)   Geneva.   In the canton of Geneva, the cantonal income tax exemption for holding companies is not general but limited to 'income from investments in other companies', which term, however, has been defined in a broader sense than usual by the cantonal tax administration (circular letter of 21 November 1988). For Geneva cantonal tax purposes, the term 'income from investments in other companies' is not limited to profit distributions (dividends) but extends to interest revenue from any affiliated company, realised capital gains on investments and revenues from the sale or waiver of subscription rights to stock of affiliated companies. 'Affiliated' companies are generally all entities that

belong to the same group of companies of which the Geneva holding company (*société de participation financière*, SPF) is a member, especially companies in which the SPF holds a capital interest of at least 20 per cent or otherwise exerts a determining influence, or companies which hold an investment in the SPF of at least 20 per cent.

Under Geneva law, there are basically two different types of holding companies, namely the SPF (see above) and the 'portfolio management company' (*société de portefeuille*). The latter has the exclusive purpose of managing its own portfolio of securities (shares, investment certificates, bonds, etc.). The *SPF* is a company whose purpose and permanent activity is holding and administering financial investments in other Swiss or foreign companies. For the *SPF* to qualify for the special status, each annual balance sheet of the *SPF* must show that at least 70 per cent of its assets consist of investments in 'affiliated' companies (defined above), and that the investments are of a certain duration. Both types of companies are exempt from cantonal and municipal income tax on 'income from investments in affiliated companies' in the broader sense as described above, and on any revenue from the portfolio securities; they pay a flat tax of 5 per cent on interest revenues that do not qualify for the tax exemption, and ordinary income tax on any other revenues.

(2)   Zurich administrative company
The canton of Zurich offers a privileged tax status to an 'administrative company' (*Verwaltungsgesellschaft*, Art. 50bis Zurich Tax Statute).

A share corporation (but also a Zurich branch of a non-Swiss corporation) qualifies as an 'administrative company' if it does not conduct any trade or business in Switzerland and restricts itself to administering its assets. It may carry out ancillary functions such as collecting claims, accounting, and factoring for affiliated companies or for its own commercial activities outside Switzerland. Financing activities are also permitted: this possibility makes a Zurich branch of a foreign corporation very attractive if the applicable double taxation convention between the foreign country and Switzerland exempts the branch income from taxation in the country where the headquarters are located. The 'administrative company' is allowed to have limited facilities and personnel in the canton, and to derive nominal income from Swiss sources.

The 'administrative company' enjoys the following tax advantages:

(a) Income derived from qualifying investments (20 per cent or more of the share capital, or investments in excess of SFr 2 million), including capital gains on such investments, is tax free.

(b) Other income from Swiss sources is taxed at the ordinary rates.

¶1059

(c) The remaining foreign-source income is reduced for tax assessment purposes at a rate commensurate with the company's activity in Switzerland; this rate is determined by the tax authorities.

The reduction of the remaining foreign-source income for assessment purposes is between 60 and 90 per cent. If the 'administrative company' realises only nominal income (less than 10 per cent of the total income) from Swiss sources, and if the facilities and personnel in Switzerland are minimal, the rate will be 90 per cent or close to it. If the Swiss facilities and personnel are substantial, then the reduction will be 60 per cent.

The status of an 'administrative company' is granted only upon request.

Figure 10.1 shows a simplified calculation of the taxable income of an 'administrative company' which has been granted the maximum reduction of 90 per cent.

Figure 10.1: Taxable income of a Zurich administrative company

	Total	Foreign source	Investments	Swiss source
Sales	7,200	7,000		200
Costs of sales	6,500	6,400		100
Gross margin	700	600		100
Other income				
Dividends	1,000		1,000	
Licence fees	1,000	1,000		
Capital gains on investments	1,200		1,200	
Immovable property	200			200
Total income	4,100	1,600	2,200	300
Expenses	800	600	100	200
Net profit (before tax)	3,300	1,000	2,100	200

reduction: 90% ⟶   100

Taxable income   300
Net income from Swiss sources
+ foreign-source income
reduced by 90%

TAXATION OF SELECTED CORPORATE TRANSACTIONS

¶1060   Establishment of share corporation

A share corporation pays tax on income and capital from the day it is registered with the Register of Commerce. The establishment of a corporation gives rise to the levy of the federal stamp tax on the issuance of corporate shares (¶1008). This tax amounts to 3 per cent of the value received by the corporation in exchange for the shares but at least 3 per cent of the nominal (face) value of the shares.

The corporation is initially funded with equity, and possibly also with debt. The initial equity is either equal to the nominal share capital or, if the issuance price of the shares exceeds their nominal value, is composed of the share capital and a capital premium (*agio* reserve).

Where the share capital is not paid in cash but in kind through contribution of non-liquid assets, valuation problems arise, primarily for issuance stamp tax purposes but also for income tax purposes. The Federal Tax Administration generally examines whether the contribution in kind to the capital is adequately valued.

Example 1: Corporation X SA is established with a nominal share capital of SFr 100,000 (100 shares of SFr 1,000 par value each). The issuance price per share is fixed at SFr 2,000 (i.e., SFr 1,000 par value and SFr 1,000 share premium, *agio*). X SA and the founding shareholders agree that the shares will be paid by transferring a complex of assets (machinery, tools, patents, etc.) at a transfer value of SFr 500,000 to the company; a shareholders' loan is extended for the difference of SFr 300,000. The original balance sheet of X SA is as follows:

X SA
(*in SFr 1,000*)

Assets	500	Debt	300
		Share capital	100
		Agio reserve	100
	500		500

The following situations can be distinguished:

(1)   Undervaluation of assets contributed
In the view of the Federal Tax Administration, the fair market value of the contributed assets in Example 1 is SFr 700,000 instead of SFr 500,000 (the

¶1060

figure agreed upon by the shareholders). Thus, the shareholders receive less equity in X SA than the net value that they contribute to the capital. The difference of SFr 200,000 is regarded as an undisclosed (but perfectly legal!) contribution to capital. This contribution is included in the base for calculating the issuance stamp tax.

The question arises whether X SA is bound by the lower transfer value of the assets. This value is binding for commercial accounting purposes (Art. 665 CO). However, for income tax purposes, in certain cases the value of the assets may be adjusted to the fair market value. This is the case where the shareholder is not subject to any income tax on the capital gain (market value less book value) realised upon the transfer of the assets to X SA, and where not only the difference (if any) between the transfer value (SFr 500,000) and the book value, but the entire capital gain is taken into consideration for the shareholder's income tax purposes. In any other cases, X SA cannot adjust the transfer value for the purpose of its income tax calculation, i.e., any future gain realised upon a sale or adjustment of value on the balance sheet will be included in its taxable income.

(2) Overvaluation of assets contributed

The actual market value of the contributed assets in Example 1 appears to be only SFr 400,000 instead of SFr 500,000. In other words, X SA enters fictitious assets of SFr 100,000 on its balance sheet, thus violating Arts 624(1) and 650(1) CO, while the shareholder receives a corresponding over-compensation. The over-compensation is classified as a benefit of a financial nature (constructive dividend) subject to the federal anticipatory tax at the rate of 35 per cent, and a subsequent depreciation to the market value or a book loss suffered upon a sale will be disregarded for income tax purposes.

(3) Calculation period if first year is short

A particular method for the assessment of income tax applies to newly established corporations under tax systems where corporations are assessed according to the *praenumerando* method, such as under the federal income tax law (¶1019(3)). For the tax period during which the corporation is established, the net (average) income of that tax period constitutes the basis (calculation period) for calculation of the tax. The same calculation period is used for the next tax period.

Example 2: X SA is incorporated on 1 July 1991, i.e., in the federal income tax period 1991–92. The first balance sheet is established by 31 December 1991. The first 'half' business year shows a net income of 50. The net income amounts to 200 in 1992, 300 in 1993, and 400 in 1994.

The *federal income tax* for 1991–92 is calculated on the following basis:

¶1060

Net income 1991	(180 days)	=	50
1992	(360 days)	=	200
Total income 1991-92	(540 days)	=	250

One year average $(360 \text{ days}) = \dfrac{250 \times 360}{540} = \underline{\underline{166.66}}$

Tax at maximum rate of 9.8%	=	16.33
Tax for 1991 (180 days)	=	8.16
Tax for 1992 (360 days)	=	16.33

The tax for the next federal income tax period (1993–94) is again based on the average income of 1991–92 (166.66). The tax amounts to 16.33 for each year (if maximum rates apply). The average income during 1993 and 1994 (350) forms the basis for the tax period 1995–96. The tax at maximum rates amounts to 34.3 for each year.

Where income taxes are assessed according to the *postnumerando* system (tax period = calculation period; ¶1019), the tax of the first year of existence of the corporation is levied *pro rata temporis*.

¶1061   Merger of share corporations

(1)   Merger defined
A merger under Swiss corporate law is an amalgamation of at least two legal entities into one. A merger may be through absorption (assets and liabilities of one or several entities are assumed by another existing entity) or combination (consolidation; assets and liabilities of merged entities are assumed by a newly formed entity). 'Genuine' mergers (merger of share corporations, partnerships limited by shares, and co-operatives) do not involve the liquidation of any entity concerned: the assets and liabilities of the absorbed entities pass over to the successor entity through 'universal succession'. All other mergers of corporate entities involve a liquidation of the dissolved entities: assets and liabilities pass over to the successor through singular succession (so-called 'merger-like concentrations').

(2)   Issuance stamp taxes
The issuance of participation rights in connection with a merger or merger-like concentration is subject to a reduced issuance stamp tax of 1 per cent of the amount received by the successor entity in exchange for the participation rights, or at least 1 per cent of the face value of such rights (¶1008(3)).

(3)   Income taxes
Corporate mergers and merger-like concentrations involve income tax consequences at the levels of:

(a) the surviving entity;

(b) the dissolved entity; and

(c) the shareholders of the dissolved entity.

(a)   Income tax consequences for the surviving entity
As a consequence of the (universal or singular) succession in all assets and liabilities of the dissolved entities, the surviving entity assumes all fiscal duties of the dissolved entities. Thus, it must pay all income taxes of the dissolved entities due until the end of the current tax period. This rule of 'extended tax succession' applies to the federal and most cantonal income taxes.

> **Example 3**: X SA is merged into Y SA, effective 1 July 1990. X SA earned net profits of 100 in 1987, 1988, and 1989, and a net profit of 50 until the merger on 1 July 1990. Y SA's net profits amounted to 200 in 1987, 1988, and 1989; 100 in the first semester of 1990 and 150 in the second semester of 1990 (after the merger).
>
> *Taxable income of X SA* (federal income tax):
> Tax period 1989–90:
>   average profits of 1987–88   100
>   tax is due thereon for the entire tax period
>   ('extended tax succession')
>
> *Taxable income of Y SA*:
> Tax period 1989–90:
>   average profits of 1987–88   200
>
> Tax period 1991–92:
>   own profits of 1989–90:
>   200 + 100 + 150   450
>   plus profits of X SA from 1 Jan. 1989 to 30 June 1990:
>   100 + 50   150
>   600
>   average profits 1989–90   300

The example shows that the surviving entity must include in its taxable income all profits and losses of the dissolved entity that never become a basis for calculation due to the *praenumerando* system. It is disputed whether this practice of the Federal Tax Administration is supported by the Federal Income Tax Decree.

(b)   Income tax consequences for the dissolved entity

As a genuine merger does not involve a liquidation of the dissolved entity, the 'undisclosed reserves' of such entity are normally not subject to a liquidation tax. However, the tax authorities allow a tax-free merger only under the following conditions:

  (i) the surviving entity must be subject to an unlimited Swiss tax obligation (¶1028);

 (ii) the business operation of the dissolved entity must be continued and remain basically unchanged;

(iii) the shareholders of the dissolved entity must become shareholders of the surviving entity; and

(iv) the surviving entity must assume all assets and liabilities of the dissolved entity at their book value. The surviving entity must pay all outstanding taxes of the dissolved entity for the entire current tax period (extended tax succession) and include all non-taxed profits of the dissolved entity in its own taxable income determination for the next tax period (see Example 3 above).

Further conditions may be required in special cases. A tax-free 'merger-like concentration' is basically subject to the same conditions.

(c)   Income tax consequences for the shareholders

The shareholders who receive shares of the surviving entity in exchange for shares of the dissolved entity are not taxed unless they receive dividends in cash or in kind, stock dividends or any other payments. A shareholder which is required to maintain account books (c.g., a share corporation) realises a taxable gain if it enters the new shares received in exchange for the shares in the dissolved entity at a value that exceeds the original base in the shares of the dissolved company.

> **Example 4:** A SA is a wholly-owned subsidiary of X SA; B SA is a wholly-owned subsidiary of Y SA. B SA is merged into A SA. Y SA receives new A shares at a nominal value of 200 in exchange for B shares. Y's basis in the B shares was 100 (nominal value of the B shares). Y SA enters in its books the nominal value of the A shares (200) received in exchange. Y SA has realised 'undisclosed reserves' on the B shares to the extent of 100 and will be taxed on this book gain. It would not be taxed, however, if the new A shares were shown at 100 only.

(4)   Merger of subsidiary company into its parent company

Special rules apply to mergers and equivalent concentrations between a parent company and its subsidiary. Where a subsidiary is merged into its parent company (absorption), the parent company may realise a so-called 'merger gain' or 'merger loss' resulting from differences between the basis of the parent in the subsidiary's shares and the net book value of the assets and liabilities of the subsidiary that are taken over by the parent.

(a) Merger gain

Example 5:

Balance sheet parent before merger

shares		debt	50
subsidiary	100	equity	50
	100		100

Balance sheet subsidiary

assets	500	debt	300
		equity	200
	500		500

Balance sheet parent after merger

assets	500	debt	350
		equity	150
	500		500

The parent has realised a merger gain of 100 (150 minus 50).

(b) Merger loss

Example 6:

Balance sheet parent before merger

shares		debt	200
subsidiary	500	equity	300
	500		500

Balance sheet subsidiary

assets	700	debt	400
		equity	300
	700		700

Balance sheet parent after merger

assets	700	debt	600
		equity	100
	700		700

Merger loss = 300 minus 100 = 200

Under some circumstances, the merger gain may be characterised as income from investments in other companies, for which a special tax reduction ('participation relief', ¶1059) is available. The merger loss is deductible for income tax purposes only as long as such merger loss is 'genuine': the merger loss is disregarded to the extent that the dissolved subsidiary has sufficient

¶1061

'undisclosed reserves' on its assets and liabilities, which are transferred to the parent company and continue to exist as such.

> **Example 7**: The fair market value of the assets of the dissolved subsidiary in Example 6 above is 800. The parent enters these assets on its balance sheet at the unchanged book value of 700. Thus 'undisclosed reserves' of 100 are transferred to the parent company. The merger loss is genuine and recognised to the extent of 100 (200 minus 100).

¶1062   Financial restructuring of share corporation

(1) Point of departure: capital impairment

Losses of a corporation may lead to a capital impairment (the assets no longer cover the liabilities).

> **Example 1**:

X SA balance sheet

assets	400	debts	
accumulated loss	600	unrelated parties	400
		shareholders	400
		share capital	200
	1,000		1,000

(2) Measures of financial restructuring

In such a situation, the members of the board and the statutory auditors must inform the court, which will declare the company bankrupt unless it is shown that a financial restructuring may be expected (Art. 725(3) and (4) CO). Financial restructuring within the meaning of Swiss tax law comprises all measures to reconstruct a 'healthy' capital structure on the balance sheet. Such measures may consist of a write-down of the share capital (without repayment, often followed by a paid capital re-increase), contributions of the shareholders without consideration (*à fonds perdu*), and forgiveness of debts by the creditors and/or shareholders. The book gains ('restructuring gains') resulting from such measures should be applied to offset accumulated and actual losses and be available for subsequent depreciations and constitutions of provisions as far as necessary.

> **Example 2**: The shareholders of X SA (as above) resolve the following restructuring measures:

¶1062

- write-down of the share capital by 100   100
- forgiving of all shareholder debts   400
- additional contribution of 200 by the shareholders   200

total restructuring gain   700

- application of the restructuring gain to account for
  subsequent depreciations and liability provisions   100
  and to set off the accumulated loss   600
                                                                                   700

- application of the additional shareholder contribution
  to reduce the third-party debts by 50% (200)

Restructuring account

write-down of share capital	100	subsequent depreciations	
forgiveness of shareholder		and liability provisions	100
debts	400	loss elimination	600
cash contribution	200		
	700		700

X SA balance sheet after restructuring

assets	300	debts	
		unrelated parties	200
		shareholders	–
		share capital	100
	300		300

(3) Tax consequences of financial restructuring

Book gains resulting from benefits received from *unrelated* parties (debt forgiveness, government contributions, etc.) are qualified as 'genuine restructuring gains'. However, such gains are not taxed as far as they are applied to offset accumulated losses (regardless of the statutory limitations of tax-loss carry-forwards) and to account for the necessary subsequent depreciations and liability provisions. These losses and expenses can no longer be carried forward for income tax purposes.

'Restructuring gains' resulting from the reduction of the share capital without repayment or contributions *à fonds perdu* of the shareholders are *not* treated as 'genuine' gains but characterised as capital contributions which do not affect the profit and loss account. In consequence, any elimination of losses or subsequent asset depreciation or liability provision so financed is disregarded for income tax purposes: such losses and expenses may be deducted from future profits within the statutory tax-loss carry-forward periods (¶1024).

The predominant doctrine takes the view that 'restructuring gains' resulting from forgiveness of debts by the shareholders should generally not be considered 'genuine' gains, but capital contributions. However, the Federal Tax Administration and the Federal Supreme Court take a more restrictive position, which was summarised in the Administration's circular letter No. 14 of 1 July 1981 (*Archives*, 50, 63) and confirmed in the Federal Supreme Court's decision of 28 September 1989 (ATF 115 Ib 269): under this view, 'restructuring gains' resulting from forgiveness of debts by the shareholders are usually 'genuine' and must be recognised as income. Exceptions are allowed if the forgiven debt was a shareholder loan which:

(a) had been treated as undisclosed equity (¶1058(2)) prior to the financial restructuring; or

(b) was granted because of losses incurred due to unfavourable business conditions, and would not have been granted by an unrelated party under comparable circumstances.

Example 3: The financial restructuring measures for X SA (as in Example 2 above) have resulted in a total 'restructuring gain' of 700. The forgiven shareholder debts of 400 derive to the extent of 200 from unpaid purchases of goods. The subsequent business years show average net profits of 200. The prior losses and restructuring expenses can be deducted from such profits to the extent of 500 (700–200). The deduction is, however, subject to the further condition that the loss in question has been suffered within the statutory limitation period for tax-loss carry-forwards.

Restructuring measures of the shareholders that qualify as capital contributions are, in principle, subject to the issuance stamp tax at the rate of 3 per cent. However, in hardship cases this tax may be waived upon request. The Federal Tax Administration regularly assumes hardship in situations where a capital impairment must be corrected; however, the stamp tax is not waived if the corporation had been undercapitalised, e.g., where forgiven shareholder loans should have been regarded as undisclosed equity (¶1058(2)).

¶1063   Division of share corporation: split-up, spin-off

(1)   Corporate divisions defined
The division of a share corporation into two or more corporations is taxwise possible in the form of a 'split-up' or a 'spin-off'.

(a) Split-up

Split-up means the transfer of *all* assets and liabilities of economically independent operational units of one company to at least two new corporations in exchange for their shares, which are then distributed to the shareholders.

Example 1:

X SA before 'split-up'

assets operation A	500	debt A	200
assets operation B	500	debt B	300
		share capital	300
		reserves/retained	
		earnings	200
	1,000		1,000

X SA establishes subsidiary A SA by transferring the assets and debt allocated to operation A, and subsidiary B SA by transferring the assets and the debt allocated to operation B, both in exchange for A or B shares, respectively, which are subsequently distributed to the shareholders of X SA. X SA is dissolved.

Situation after 'split-up'

A SA

assets operation A	500	debt A	200
		share capital	150
		reserves/retained	
		earnings	150
	500		500

B SA

assets operation B	500	debt B	300
		share capital	150
		reserves/retained	
		earnings	50
	500		500

(b) Spin-off

A 'spin-off' is a transfer of *certain* assets and liabilities of an operational unit of the corporation to a new subsidiary in exchange for shares of the subsidiary,

¶1063

or to a sister company which issues shares to the shareholders of the transferring corporation.

Example 2: X SA (as above) establishes subsidiary B SA by transferring its operation B with debt B in exchange for B shares.

Situation after 'spin-off'

X SA

assets operation A	500	debt A	200
loan B SA	300	debt B	300
shares B SA	200	share capital	300
		reserves/retained	
		earnings	200
	1,000		1,000

Example 3: The shareholders of X SA (as in Example 1) establish a new corporation, Y SA. X SA distributes its operation B including the debt B to the shareholders, charging the difference to its retained earnings and reserves. The shareholders contribute the assets and debt of operation B to Y SA in exchange for Y shares of 200.

Situation after 'spin-off'

X SA

assets operation A	500	debt A	200
		share capital	300
		reserves/retained	
		earnings	–
	500		500

Y SA

assets operation B	500	debt B	300
		share capital	200
	500		500

Example 4: Same procedure as in Example 3, but the net value of operation B (500 minus 300 = 200) is charged to the share capital account of X SA.

¶1063

Situation after 'spin-off'

X SA

assets operation A	500	debt A	200
		share capital	100
		reserves/retained	
		earnings	200
	500		500

Y SA

assets operation B	500	debt B	300
		share capital	200
	500		500

Here, the total nominal value of share capital held by the shareholders remains unchanged (300), while in Example 3 they receive 200 additional nominal share capital.

(2) Tax issues to be considered in corporate division

The most important tax issue in connection with all forms of corporate division is the question whether realisation of 'undisclosed reserves' of the dividing corporation is subject to taxation, or whether such taxation can be deferred. The answer depends on the tax characterisation of the transaction as a (partial) liquidation (with the tax consequence of immediate taxation of undisclosed reserves) or as a mere reorganisation of continuing business activities. This question must be answered separately for the purposes of the federal income tax and the cantonal and municipal income taxes for each form of corporate division.

The following tax problems should also be considered:

● Are special immovable property gains and transfer taxes due, or can such taxes be deferred?

● What are the effects on the tax attributes (basis, tax-loss carry-forward) of the companies involved?

● Is the privileged 1 per cent federal issuance stamp tax rate applicable to the issue of new shares instead of the ordinary 3 per cent rate (Art. 9(1)(a) FSTS; but see ¶1002(6))?

● Is a securities transfer stamp tax due?

¶1063

- Will the federal anticipatory tax on corporate profit distributions be levied, or can such tax be deferred, or may the tax obligation be discharged by notice of the taxable benefit?

- What are the tax consequences at the level of the shareholders of the dividing corporation? Do they realise income, and what kind of income (dividends, taxable or tax-free capital gains)?

Given these uncertainties, it is advisable to discuss the tax consequences of a corporate division in advance with the competent federal and cantonal tax authorities (see ¶1002(1)).

(3)   Conditions for deferral of income taxation
In the case of a 'spin-off' of part of the assets and liabilities to a subsidiary (see Example 2), the conditions for a deferral of income taxes on undisclosed reserves of the dividing corporation may be summarised as follows:

(a) The base in the shares of the new subsidiary in the books of the dividing corporation must not exceed the net book value of the excess amount of transferred assets over the transferred liabilities. The new subsidiary may not increase the net book value of the assets and liabilities taken over from its parent company.

(b) The 'spin-off' must not be made for the purpose of a liquidation or sale of part of the corporation's business or single assets, but only for a reorganisation of an ongoing business.

(c) Often, the assets and liabilities transferred to the new subsidiary form an independent operational business unit. However, this is not a general requirement for a tax-free 'spin-off' to a subsidiary. It is, however, questionable whether a 'spin-off' of immovable property to create a real estate subsidiary may be effected tax-free if the 'spin-off' assets do not qualify as an independent operational business unit. In a recent decision (ATF 115 Ib 263) the Federal Supreme Court did not allow a tax-free spin-off of non-operational immovable property to a separate real estate company, which was established in addition to an operating company in connection with the legal transformation of an individual's business. At the cantonal level, however, the special real estate capital gains and transfer taxes may be levied. In the canton of Zurich, for example, the immovable property capital gains and transfer taxes are deferred where such property is transferred in connection with a corporate division, provided, however, that the transferred immovable property is a part of an independent business operation that is continued after the reorganisation (Arts 161(f) and 180(f) Zurich Income Tax Statute).

¶1063

(4)   Tax consequence for the parent company

The 'spin-off' may have the effect of making either the future parent company or the subsidiary a holding company.

(a)   Creation of a holding company

If all assets and liabilities are transferred to one or more new subsidiaries, the transferring corporation will become a holding company. At the level of the new subsidiaries, the undisclosed reserves will be taxed when they are actually realised through sale, liquidation, etc. The parent company will, for the purposes of cantonal and municipal taxes, enjoy a general income tax exemption (holding privilege). In order to secure the condition of ongoing business and to prevent the parent company from indirectly realising the undisclosed reserves by a sale of the shares of the new subsidiary (the gain from which could not be taxed due to the holding privilege), the cantonal tax authorities usually require that the shares of the subsidiaries not be sold within a certain period (five to seven years). The new Art. 50ter of the Zurich Tax Statute (in force since 1 January 1991) provides that a full year's tax of 6 per cent (plus cantonal and municipal multipliers) will be levied on any capital or book gain if investments in other companies that are brought into a holding or administrative company (¶1059) are sold or appreciated in value within ten years; no deductions are allowed. Regarding other assets left in the parent company, the undisclosed reserves thereon are usually deemed to have been realised for the purpose of cantonal income taxes: because of the holding privilege, they can no longer be taxed. In practice, the cantonal tax authorities sometimes waive the immediate taxation of such undisclosed reserves on the condition that the respective assets not be sold during the same blocking period. In some cantons, it is possible to establish the amount of undisclosed reserves as basis for income taxation for the event the holding company is liquidated or transfers its seat outside the canton.

(b)   Creation of sub-holding company

The 'spin-off' of a subsidiary may also be effected for the purpose of creating a sub-holding company: while the operating business is left in the original company, investments in other companies are brought into a new subsidiary. See Figure 10.2 (page 286).

While the cantonal tax status of the dividing corporation does not change, the new sub-holding company will again qualify for the cantonal income tax exemption (holding privilege). In consequence, the undisclosed reserves on all investments and other property transferred to the sub-holding company can no longer be taxed. The cantonal tax treatment of such undisclosed reserves is the same as in the case discussed in (a) above: certain cantons levy the liquidation tax immediately, while others grant a tax deferral under the condition of a

¶1063

Figure 10.2: Creation of a sub-holding company

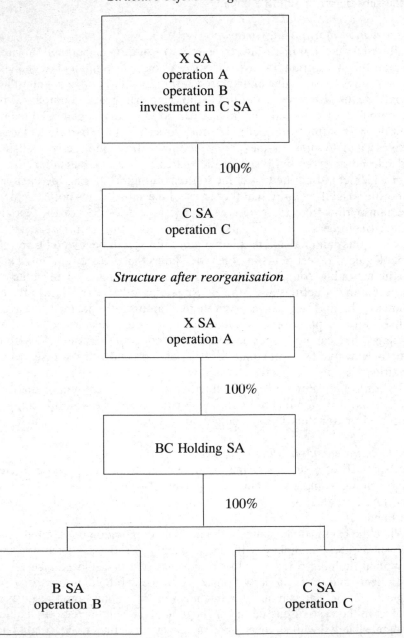

Structure before reorganisation

X SA
operation A
operation B
investment in C SA

100%

C SA
operation C

Structure after reorganisation

X SA
operation A

100%

BC Holding SA

100%

B SA
operation B

C SA
operation C

¶1063

blocking period. In the canton of Zurich, the new Art. 50ter Income Tax Statute (see (a) above) applies to investments transferred to a sub-holding company.

(c) Creation of parallel or sister companies
Some additional conditions are set for the deferral of the taxation of undisclosed reserves in the case of the creation of parallel or sister companies.

The assets and liabilities transferred to the parallel or sister company must always form an independent operational unit. In the past the tax authorities had required the shareholding relations to remain entirely unchanged.

Example 5: A and B each own 50% of the shares of X SA. X SA transfers one of its operations to Y SA. The tax authorities required A and B to hold the shares of Y SA in the same proportion.

The recent practice is more flexible: all that is required is that all of the original shareholders continue their business engagement. The question of whether and to what extent an involvement of new shareholders in the transferee corporation is possible without taxation of the undisclosed reserves is disputed, and has not yet been decided. The most recent practice tends to allow a tax-free split-up or spin-off under certain conditions, by creating sister or parallel companies whereby the shareholdings are also split-up. See Figure 10.3 on page 288.

Example 6: A and B each own 50% of the shares of X SA. X SA has two operations, A and B. Operation B is transferred to a new corporation, B SA; the share capital of X SA is reduced by 50%. B receives all shares of B SA in exchange for its X shares. X SA and B SA agree to co-operate for ten years. See Figure 10.3 (page 288).

A corporate division always implies the creation of at least one new entity, with new participation rights whose issue is subject to the issuance stamp tax. Where the division may be qualified as a mere reorganisation of a continuing business, the federal issuance stamp tax is levied at the reduced rate of 1 per cent.

The federal anticipatory tax and income taxes at the level of the shareholders of the dividing corporation may become due where such shareholders receive benefits of a financial value, especially if they receive more nominal share value than they held before (e.g., if the dividing corporation does not reduce its own share capital but its reserves for the payment of the new shares), or if the division must be classified as a (partial) liquidation of the dividing corporation leading to the immediate taxation of undisclosed reserves.

In Figure 10.4 (page 289), reserves and retained earnings of 250 have been distributed to B and have been transformed into nominal share capital, whose subsequent distribution or payment would not be subject to the anticipatory tax. A SA must charge the anticipatory tax of 87.5 (35 per cent of 250) to B; if he is a Swiss resident B pays income tax on 250 and may recover the anticipatory

Figure 10.3: Recent practice regarding shareholdings (Examples 5 and 6)

Situation before division

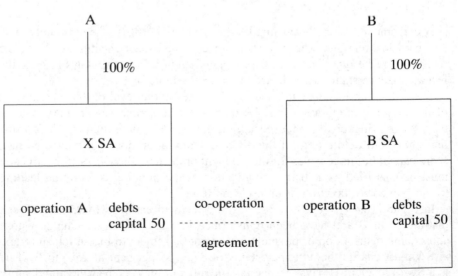

Situation after division

Figure 10.4: Transposition of retained earnings into nominal share capital (Example 6)

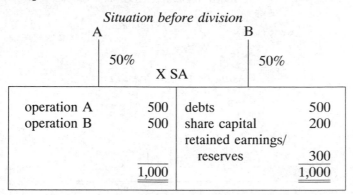

Situation before division

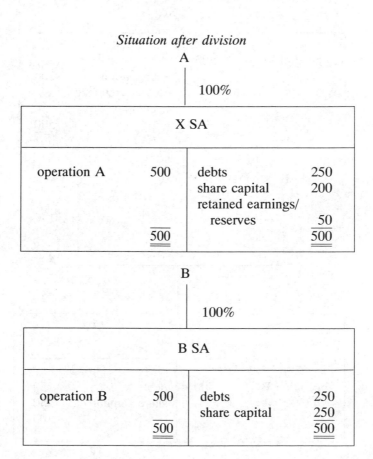

Situation after division

Figure 10.5: No tax-free spin-off (Example 6, in fine)

Situation before division

(as in Figure 10.4)

Situation after division

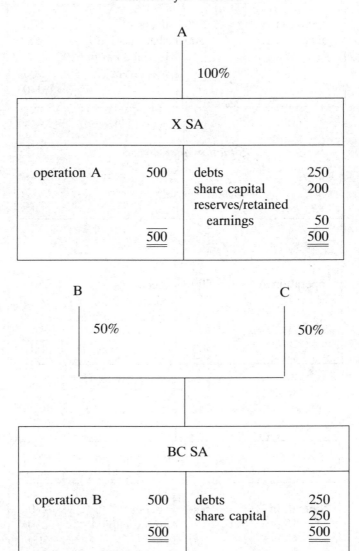

¶1063

tax. A pays income tax on 100: his share in X SA's equity is 250 before and after the division; however, the nominal value held by A is increased by 100 (100 before, 200 after the division).

In Figure 10.5 (page 290), A and B are taxed as in Figure 10.4. The undisclosed reserves on operations A and B are taxed at the level of X SA since B gives up half of his investment in favour of the new shareholder C (no tax-free spin-off).

¶1064   Corporate migration

(1) Emigration
The transfer of a corporation's seat abroad is treated as a liquidation for federal and cantonal income tax purposes, as well as for federal anticipatory tax purposes.

If a corporation's seat is just transferred from one canton to another, the tax codes of some cantons provide for the assessment of a cantonal 'liquidation gains tax'. Certain other cantons tend to assess such a tax even without an explicit basis in their tax statutes.

(2) Immigration
The issuance stamp tax is levied at the rate of 1.5 per cent on the fair market value of the net assets of the corporation at the time of the transfer of the seat to Switzerland, but calculated at least at the par value of the currently existing share capital (Art. 9(1)(c) FSTS). But see ¶1002(6) for the 1991 revision of the FSTS.

¶1065   Liquidation

(1) Liquidation defined
Liquidation is the ordinary way of legally dissolving a corporation. It consists of the alienation of the assets, the repayment of the debts, the restitution of the share capital, and the distribution of the surplus (if any) to the shareholders. The liquidation ends with the cancellation of the registration of the corporation in the Register of Commerce. A share corporation can be dissolved without liquidation in the case of merger (Arts 748 to 750 CO; ¶708).

In addition, a corporation may be economically dissolved without a formal liquidation through a takeover of its assets and liabilities by another person or legal entity. Mere economic dissolution does not lead to the legal 'death' of the corporation; however, it may have the tax consequences of a liquidation as discussed below. On the other hand, the tax consequences of a liquidation may be avoided or deferred if a corporation is formally liquidated in connection with a 'merger-like concentration' (¶1061) or a corporate division which qualifies as a reorganisation of a continuing business (¶1063).

(2) Tax consequences at the corporation's level
In tax law, liquidation means the alienation or realisation of the assets of an enterprise. Typically, liquidation taxes are not connected with a formal liquidation of a corporation. A (full or partial) liquidation in the tax sense usually implies the realisation and taxation of the undisclosed reserves (difference between market and book values) on the liquidated assets and liabilities.

(a) Termination of corporate tax liability
As a rule, the general tax liability of a corporation ends after the termination of the liquidation procedure, i.e., when the business activities have been terminated, all liabilities discharged, all assets liquidated, and any surplus has been distributed. Special rules apply where a corporation is dissolved without a formal liquidation, in particular by merger.

(b) Current taxation during the liquidation period
During the liquidation period, the corporation continues to be taxed on its income and capital. Federal, and some cantonal, tax laws provide that these taxes may be calculated according to the rules applying to individuals if this results in lower tax assessments. Under the *praenumerando* tax assessment system (which applies to the federal, and most cantonal, corporate income taxes), the corporation pays income tax on the basis of its ordinary profits during the calculation period (the preceding one or two business years), calculated *pro rata temporis*.

> **Example 1**: X SA made net profits of 100 in 1989 and 50 in 1990. On 1 March 1991 the general meeting of the shareholders resolves the liquidation of X SA. The liquidation procedure is terminated on 31 August 1992.
>
> The current direct federal tax (tax period 1991–92) during the liquidation procedure is calculated on the basis of the average income (ordinary profits) of the two preceding years (1989–90), i.e., 75. Assuming a tax rate of 8%, the tax for one year amounts to 6. The tax due for 1991 equals 6, for 1992 (eight months) the tax amounts to 4.

Extraordinary profits realised during the calculation period or during the current tax period are, for federal income tax purposes and in many cantons, subject to a special full year's tax. All capital gains realised and appreciations of value recorded in the books are considered extraordinary profits. Hence, all undisclosed reserves realised through the liquidation of the assets and discharge of liabilities are subject to the full year's tax ('liquidation gains tax'). If, upon the liquidation, assets are transferred in kind to the shareholders, the liquidation gain is considered to be the difference between the fair market value and the book (income tax) value.

¶1065

Example 2: The net profits of X SA (as in Example 1) included a book gain of 20 on sold inventory in 1989, and a gain of 10 from the dissolution of a bad debt reserve in 1990. During the liquidation period X SA realises further book gains on assets of 30; in addition, X SA transfers a car at its book value of 30 to a shareholder; the market value of the car is 50.

The extraordinary profits of 20 (1989) and 10 (1990) must be excluded when calculating the taxable income for the current tax period 1991–92. Therefore, the taxable income (average of ordinary profits in 1989–90) amounts to 60. The tax on 60 is due for 1991 (full year) and 1992 (eight months).

The extraordinary profits of 20 (1989), 10 (1990), 30 (1991–92), and the assumed capital gain on the car of 20 are subject to the full year's liquidation gains tax. The liquidation expenses and business losses that could not be set off against ordinary profits may be deducted.

In those cantons where corporate income taxes are assessed according to the *postnumerando* system (tax period = calculation period), the extraordinary profits realised upon liquidation are taxed together with the ordinary profits.

(c) Federal anticipatory tax on liquidation proceeds
The difference between the net amount of liquidation proceeds and the nominal share capital constitutes the final liquidation dividend, which is subject to the 35 per cent federal anticipatory tax to be withheld from the final distribution. The directors and liquidators are personally liable for the withholding tax. The same holds true for '*de facto*' liquidators. Assets distributed in kind are taxed at market value.

(3) Tax consequences at shareholder's level
The tax consequences at the level of the shareholders of a liquidated corporation depend on whether the shares are included in the private portfolio of an individual shareholder, or whether they belong to the business assets of an individual shareholder or are owned by a corporate entity.

Individuals realise taxable income to the extent that their net return from the shares of the liquidated corporation (regardless of the anticipatory tax withheld) exceeds the nominal value of the shares. The purchase price of the shares is not taken into consideration when determining whether the shareholder has realised taxable income.

Example 3: X SA has a nominal share capital of 100. In 1988, A acquired 20% of the outstanding X shares (i.e. nominally 20) at a price of 60. During 1991 X SA is liquidated. The net liquidation proceeds amount to 200. Accordingly, X gets 40 (20%) for his shares. Although he has realised an economic loss of 20, he must include 20 (40 net return less 20 nominal value) in his taxable income. This calculation does not yet consider that the return of 40 has been reduced by the anticipatory tax of 7 (35% of 20), which, however, is recoverable when A duly reports the 20 as income.

This so-called 'nominal value principle' has been criticised by commentators; it is, however, constantly applied in Swiss tax practice and by the courts.

If the shares of the liquidated corporation belong to the business assets of an individual (or a partnership), the difference between the liquidation proceeds and the book (income tax) value of the shares is considered taxable business (employment) income.

> **Example 4**: A is self-employed. He holds all shares of X SA (nominal share capital: 100) in his business assets. On the balance sheet of his business he has a base in the X shares of 200. A liquidates X SA. The liquidation results in a net return (anticipatory tax not considered) of 300. A realised 100 (300 – 200) as business income.

The same tax treatment applies where the shares of the liquidated corporation belong to a corporate entity (as, by definition, such an entity can only own business assets). Where the shares constitute an investment in other companies, the federal and cantonal tax reductions for holding income apply (¶1059). Companies with a cantonal holding or domiciliary tax privilege do not pay any cantonal income tax on the liquidation return from the shares.

(4) The theories of 'transposition' and 'partial liquidation'

The 'partial liquidation' and 'transposition' tax theories have been developed as a logical consequence of the 'nominal value principle' (see (3) above) and against the background that capital gains on private movable property are tax-free under federal tax law and the law of almost all cantons.

(a) Transposition theory

The transposition theory (Federal Tax Administration's, circular letter No. 6 of 3 February 1987) is applied where individual taxpayers, though apparently realising a (tax-free) capital gain on corporate shares held in their private portfolios, economically transpose (in the view of the tax authorities) reserves and retained earnings of their corporation (taxable to them if and when distributed) into nominal share capital or into an account receivable of the corporation, which can be paid back free of tax.

> **Example 5**: (typical): A holds the share capital of X SA (nominal value: 100) in her private portfolio. X SA has substantial retained earnings. A wants to restructure her investments. She creates a holding company, A-Holding SA, with nominal share capital of 100. A transfers her shares of X SA to A-Holding SA at a (fair) price of 700. The transfer price is paid as follows: A receives A-Holding shares of 100 and a loan receivable from A-Holding SA of 600.

¶1065

Subsequently, the repayment of this loan is financed with dividends distributed by X SA to its new shareholder A-Holding SA. These dividends will in practice remain tax-free at the level of A-Holding SA (holding privilege). The Federal Supreme Court has repeatedly held that at the level of the individual shareholder such a transaction may be taxed as if the operating corporation (X SA) had been liquidated. Therefore, the amount of 600 would be taxed as income derived from movable capital property (dividend).

Alternatively, A might receive nominal share capital in A-Holding SA of 200; the remaining 500 are recorded as a premium on shares (an *agio* reserve) in the books of A-Holding SA. In this case, A would be taxed only on 100 (additional nominal capital); the premium on shares would be taxed when actually distributed to A.

(b) Theory of partial liquidation

(i) Genesis of this theory. The tax theories of direct or indirect partial liquidation are based on an extensive application of the theory of substance over form.

In 1963 the Federal Supreme Court decided that a shareholder whose stock is redeemed by the corporation at a price that exceeds the face value realises a portion (in economic terms) in the liquidation proceeds of the corporation. Accordingly, the shareholder was taxed on the excess of the redemption price over the nominal value (*Archives*, 30, 180).

A further decision of the Federal Supreme Court of 1971 (*Archives*, 40, 517) on the anticipatory tax was based on the following facts: A Swiss corporation purchased the shares of another Swiss corporation from its (foreign) individual shareholder at a fair price which was substantially higher than the nominal value of the shares. The acquiring entity, however, did not have sufficient funds to pay the purchase price in cash. Hence, it took out a substantial loan from its shareholder. The repayment of the loan was financed out of the future cash flow derived from the dividends of the acquired entity. The acquiring entity was unable to show sufficient business (non-tax) reasons for such a procedure. The refund of the anticipatory taxes withheld from the dividend of the acquired entity was refused by the Court, arguing that, in economic terms, the shareholder had actually partially liquidated the company when he had sold its shares.

While these holdings may be justifiable on the basis of the specific facts of the cases, more recent developments in the theory of partial liquidation are much more controversial.

(ii) Indirect partial liquidation. The following case is deemed an 'indirect partial liquidation':

Example 6: A 'poor' corporation, X SA, acquires the shares of a 'rich' corporation, Y SA, from its individual shareholder. A substantial part of the purchase price is, directly or indirectly, financed with assets of Y SA. For example, the 'poor' corporation takes a loan from, or has a substantial dividend declared by, its new 'rich' subsidiary to pay off the seller, or the seller has his 'rich' corporation pledge its assets to provide the purchasing 'poor' corporation with a bank loan which is applied to pay the purchase price.

A decisive element for the theory of indirect partial liquidation to be applied, is that the seller knew or had reason to know (such as where there is lots of excess liquidity in the target and the acquiring corporation has few funds of its own) that the acquirer would finance the purchase price, at least in part, with funds that were ultimately coming from the acquired corporation. In the above-described scenario, the tax authorities will argue that there is an indirect partial liquidation. Accordingly, to the extent that the purchase price has been so financed, the seller will be treated as if he had received a dividend in such amount, which gives rise to taxable income in his hands, instead of having realised a capital gain upon the disposition of stock which is generally tax-free (*Archives*, 59, 717).

(iii)   Direct partial liquidation. The following case is deemed a 'direct partial liquidation':

Example 7: An individual shareholder, A, owns a 'rich' company. A gets an offer for her shares from a corporate acquirer, which is, however, not interested in all the assets (in particular liquid funds) of the target. A therefore causes the target to extend a loan in a considerable amount to herself, thereby reducing the target's value. Subsequently she sells the target's stock to the corporate acquirer. The latter pays the purchase price, in part, by assuming A's debt *vis-à-vis* the target. Now the acquiring corporation causes the target to declare a substantial dividend distribution. This dividend is, however, set off against the acquiring corporation's debt, which formerly was the seller's debt. The Federal Supreme Court considered such a transaction as a constructive dividend of the acquired corporation to the seller (*Archives*, 54, 211, *Coffee Holding* case).

The crucial point for the court to conclude that there was a constructive dividend was that the seller had constituted an indebtedness *vis-à-vis* her corporation (the target), which she never intended to pay back and for which there was no business reason. In other words, the seller had received a benefit from her corporation without any true and adequate consideration.

(iv)   Criticisms by legal writers. In particular the 'indirect partial liquidation' theory has been heavily criticised by the overwhelming majority of the Swiss doctrinal writers. At least for federal income tax purposes, however, it has been confirmed several times by the Federal Supreme Court. In two recent decisions

¶1065

(ATF 115 Ib 249 and 256; ASA 59, 717) the Court made it clear that the taxation of a 'liquidation gain' at the level of the seller of corporate shares is always dependent upon the condition that the shares be transferred from the private property of the seller to the business property of the purchaser who is obliged to keep ordinary books of account, and that the seller actively co-operates in the 'hollowing out' of the sold corporation, and that he or she is, or should be, aware that the withdrawn means will not be returned to the corporation.

FEDERAL WHOLESALE TAX

¶1066 The system of the federal wholesale tax

(1) Power to tax – principle of the wholesale tax
The federal wholesale tax (*impôt sur le chiffre d'affaires*, ICHA/ *Warenumsatzsteuer*, WUST) was introduced in 1941. The Federal Government's constitutional authority to levy the wholesale tax expires in 1994. The wholesale tax contributes roughly one-fourth to the total federal revenue and about one-eighth to all federal, cantonal and municipal revenues.

The Federal Wholesale Tax Decree (*Arrêté du conseil fédéral instituant un impôt sur le chiffre d'affaires/Bundesratsbeschluss über die Warenumsatzsteuer*) provides for a single-transaction tax: only the transfer of goods from the wholesaler to the retailer is taxable. The tax is neither levied on services (with some exceptions), nor on export sales and domestic sales with subsequent direct exportation.

The wholesale tax is levied from and collected through manufacturers, importers and dealers who are registered with the Federal Tax Administration as 'wholesalers' (*grossiste/Grossist*). They may import and purchase goods tax free. The prices of their sales to non-wholesalers include the wholesale tax.

All domestic sales and other transfers and importation of goods from a wholesaler to the retailer and/or consumer, if not expressly exempt, are subject to the wholesale tax. In addition, wholesalers pay the tax for goods destined for their own consumption.

(2) Taxpayers: Wholesalers and registered wholesalers
Even if the economic effect of the wholesale tax is that of a consumption tax, legally the wholesalers are liable to the tax. All enterprises trading in goods or manufacturing goods or buildings (including processing, repairing, etc.) with an annual domestic turnover exceeding SFr 35,000 are 'wholesalers' for wholesale tax purposes if more than 50 per cent of the turnover is derived from wholesale transfers, or more than SFr 35,000 of the turnover is derived from transfers of used goods. Persons selling goods purchased for resale and producing goods or

buildings are deemed wholesalers if more than 25 per cent, or more than SFr 35,000 of the annual turnover, including internal use and tax-free transactions, is derived from self-produced goods or buildings. Professional book publishers are wholesalers independently of their turnover. Persons who purchase domestic agricultural products from non-wholesalers for more than SFr 1,000 per calendar quarter are taxed even if they are not wholesalers. Farmers, gardeners, foresters, and winegrowers, restaurants and hotels, certain private and public institutions, art painters and sculptors are exempt as wholesalers under certain conditions.

Traders or manufacturers not otherwise qualifying as wholesalers under the applicable provisions may petition the Federal Tax Administration to be registered as voluntary wholesalers if they show valid reasons, and if the granting of the wholesaler status does not result in unjustified tax advantages.

All persons, except wholesalers, are liable to the wholesale tax on all imports of goods into Switzerland. The tax is levied from the importer together with the import customs duty.

(3) Object of wholesale tax

Domestic transfers of goods and importations of goods are the object of the wholesale tax.

Transfers may be:

- the disposition of goods (sales, exchanges, etc.);
- the delivery of goods produced, processed, assembled, repaired or otherwise transformed in accordance with a construction contract or a mandate; or
- the construction of buildings for a third person's account.

The following transactions are deemed taxable transfers of goods:

- the internal use of own goods by a wholesaler (if a wholesaler consumes goods purchased tax free or of own production); or
- the purchase of domestic agricultural products from their producers, if both the producer and the purchaser are not wholesalers subject to the tax.

Services are not subject to the wholesale tax. Several goods are exempt from the wholesale tax. These include in particular, those goods mentioned in the tax-free list:

- food,
- non-alcoholic beverages,
- gas,
- water,
- electricity,

¶1066

- heating fuels,
- certain soaps and detergents,
- cattle,
- poultry,
- fish,
- cereals,
- seeds,
- flowers,
- fodder,
- fertilisers,
- plant protection sprays,
- medicines,
- newspapers,
- periodicals, and
- books.

Finally, the following transactions are tax-free:

- the exportation of goods, including all works on goods for export, and foreign wholesales;
- transfers of goods to, and importations of goods by, a wholesaler if the wholesaler supplies a special 'wholesaler declaration', or if the goods are contained in the special tax-free list of wholesale goods.

(4) Tax rates

Two different tax rates apply:

(a) 9.3 per cent on domestic wholesale deliveries (deliveries of goods for resale or as raw material for the manufacture of goods or buildings), on the importation of goods for the same purposes, and on purchases of domestic agricultural products by non-wholesalers; and

(b) 6.2 per cent on 'retail' deliveries (deliveries of goods to consumers for consumption), and on the importation of goods for the consumption and the internal use of wholesalers.

Wholesale and retail transfers are distinguished according to how the purchaser deals with the delivered merchandise. The price and amount of delivered goods are irrelevant in this respect. All deliveries not qualifying as wholesale deliveries (i.e., for resale or as raw material for the manufacture of goods or buildings) are deemed retail deliveries.

¶1066

Applying two tax rates is meant to achieve an equal tax charge of the consumer prices, which should be 6.2 per cent on the price paid by the ultimate purchaser, i.e., the consumer. This rate applies to sales from wholesalers directly to consumers, on construction for consumers, on internal consumption, and on direct importations of goods by consumers. However, if there is a retailer (non-taxpayer) between the wholesaler (taxpayer) and the consumer, the retailer purchases the goods at the wholesale price and sells them at the retail price. The legislature has assumed that the retail price is 150 per cent of the wholesale price. This is the economic reason for the tax rate being increased by 50 per cent on wholesale deliveries.

In practice, however, the margin of the retailer is often less than 50 per cent. In such cases, the 9.3 per cent tax on the wholesale price results in a higher tax than the 6.2 per cent tax which would apply to the retail sales price. Therefore, retailers whose margin on retail sales is less than 50 per cent may apply for registration as voluntary wholesalers. This enables them to purchase goods free of wholesale tax and to pay the 6.2 per cent tax on transfers to consumers at the retail price.

(5) Tax computation basis

In the case of sales or the processing of goods, the tax is computed on the price received. For buildings, this amount is often reduced by 25 per cent.

The wholesale tax due on the delivery, the transportation and insurance costs, and any refunded consideration may be deducted from the price.

The tax on importation of goods is calculated on the value of goods 'delivered Swiss border', including import customs duties and other charges payable, but excluding the wholesale tax itself.

The tax on goods for internal consumption is calculated on the customary consumer price.

The wholesaler may, in certain cases, obtain a tax credit for the wholesale tax previously paid on the goods. This may be the case, for example, if the wholesaler purchases goods from a non-wholesaler who, in turn, had bought them from a wholesaler or had to pay the import wholesale tax. The credit of prior tax is available if the wholesaler uses the goods for resale or as material for the professional manufacture of goods or buildings. The wholesaler may also obtain a tax credit for the import tax paid by himself.

(6) Avoidance of multiple tax charge

The overall tax charge on the price of goods paid by the ultimate consumer amounts to 6.2 per cent. The law provides for a number of measures to avoid multiple tax charges on goods on their way from the Swiss border or from the domestic producer to the ultimate consumer:

¶1066

(a) Wholesale transfers and importations by wholesalers are exempt from the tax if the wholesaler makes a 'wholesaler's declaration' (*déclaration de grossiste/Grossistenerklärung*) to the supplier or to the customs authorities. The wholesaler's declaration states that the purchased goods are destined for resale or as material for the professional manufacture of goods or buildings. Goods acquired for resale and material for professional manufacture are taxed only when they leave the wholesalers. A hidden multiple tax charge (*taxe occulte/Schattensteuer*) results from the fact that the wholesalers are unable to purchase free of wholesale tax their fixed and operating assets, such as production plants, machinery, tools, cars, office equipment, etc.

(b) No wholesaler's declaration may be used where a wholesaler purchases goods from a non-wholesaler. However, the wholesaler may credit the previously paid tax on such goods.

(c) The construction of buildings for a third person's account is always a retail delivery. The tax must be paid by the wholesaler carrying out the construction. Subcontractors working for another contractor must pay the tax on their own constructions. In contrast, the contractor does not owe any tax on the constructions made by his subcontractors, even if the invoicing is done by the contractor.

¶1067 Assessment and collection of the wholesale tax

Qualifying wholesalers must register with the Federal Tax Administration. The same applies to voluntary wholesalers and purchasers of domestic natural products. Wholesalers must file a wholesale tax return within one month following the end of each calendar quarter, reporting all their (taxable and tax-free) transactions and internal consumption. Wholesalers may use the cash method of accounting or, with special permission, the accrual method of accounting. The resulting tax is the same, whichever method is used, as the tax base is always the consideration received. Wholesale taxes are assessed on the basis of the tax returns if filed by the taxpayers. The taxpayer's assessment is reviewed by the Federal Tax Administration, whose decision may be challenged first by a motion to reconsider and, subsequently, by an administrative law appeal filed with the Federal Supreme Court.

The collection and review of the self-assessments of the wholesale tax on domestic wholesale transaction is within the competence of the Wholesale Tax Division of the Federal Tax Administration. The tax on importation of goods is collected by the Federal Customs Administration together with the customs duties, if any. The procedural provisions of the Customs Statute govern the assessment and collection procedure of the importation tax.

¶1068   Imports to and exports from Switzerland

Imports of goods to Switzerland are subject to the import tax at the rate of 6.2 per cent if the goods are imported by or for the account of a non-wholesaler, and if they do not appear on a tax-free list. Imports of taxable goods by a wholesaler are tax-exempt if the wholesaler makes a 'wholesaler's declaration' (see ¶1066(6)).

Direct export deliveries of goods are not subject to the wholesale tax. In addition, 'domestic deliveries for export' are exempt. A domestic delivery (which would be subject to the domestic wholesale tax if made by a wholesaler to a non-wholesaler) is 'for export' if it is followed by direct exportation of the goods by the recipient, which fact must be proved by the wholesaler. The domestic customer of the wholesaler must directly export the goods without any prior use or transformation within Switzerland.

ENFORCEMENT OF TAX LAWS

¶1069   Fiscal criminal law

(1)   Power to legislate

The purpose of fiscal criminal law is enforcement of the provisions of the tax laws, which refer not only to the payment of tax, but also to various procedural duties of the taxpayers and other persons, such as co-operation, information and disclosure requirements. As the due fulfilment of such duties is an essential precondition for the true and complete ascertainment of the facts which determine the tax burden, fiscal criminal law, unlike general criminal law, is dominated by the principle of result rather than by the principle of guilt. However, guilt (at least negligence) is normally a precondition for any tax penalty (*nulla poena sine culpa*).

The federal legislature is competent to legislate in the entire field of criminal law (Art. 64bis Federal Constitution). General criminal law is governed by the Federal Penal Code (PC). Further criminal provisions are enacted in other federal legislation (special criminal law), in particular in the Federal Stamp Tax Statute (Art. 45 et seq.), the Anticipatory Tax Statute (Art. 61 et seq.), the Federal Income Tax Decree (Art. 129 et seq.), the Wholesale Tax Decree (Art. 36 et seq. and Arts 52 and 53), and in the Federal Statute on Administrative Criminal Law (RS 313.0).

The cantons are authorised by Art. 353(2) PC to establish criminal provisions for the protection of their cantonal tax laws. With respect to the application of their fiscal criminal law, most cantonal tax laws refer to the respective provisions of the Penal Code (Arts 1 to 110).

(2) Tax contraventions

Offences of this mildest category are committed by taxpayers or third persons bound to furnish information, who fail to file a return, produce books of account, produce or file certificates or similar documents, appear for a hearing, or post securities, or who otherwise fail to discharge procedural duties that may lawfully be imposed by the competent tax authority. Tax contraventions (*contravention fiscale/Steuerwiderhandlung*) are generally subject to fines which may amount to SFr 10,000 (maximum SFr 25,000 in the canton of Vaud).

(3) Tax evasion

A taxpayer who deliberately or negligently causes a non- or under-assessment of tax by failure to inform, disclose or discharge other duties commits tax evasion (*soustraction fiscale/Steuerhinterziehung*). Obtaining an unjustified tax refund or tax waiver is treated in the same manner. As a rule, tax evasion is conditioned upon the non- or under-assessment to be final. A mere attempt to evade tax is usually treated as a special tax offence subject to fines. The attempt to evade tax can be punished only if committed deliberately.

Tax evasion is generally punished with a penalty tax, which may be a percentage or, in serious cases, a multiple of the tax evaded (e.g., in Geneva: maximum ten times the evaded tax!). In addition, of course, the tax so evaded must also be paid.

(4) Tax fraud

Tax fraud (*fraude fiscale/Steuerbetrug*) is a qualified form of tax evasion. It may be described as a deception of the tax authorities in order to evade tax through an under-assessment or no assessment at all, by using false, forged, or otherwise incorrect documents or other fraudulent means in proving the alleged correctness of the tax return. The mere use of incorrect figures in the tax return itself never constitutes tax fraud. Tax fraud always implies deliberate action; *dolus eventualis* (akin to reckless disregard) is sufficient.

Tax fraud can be punished with jail sentences (usually up to three years) and/or fines in addition to the penalty tax for tax evasion. The tax evaded is due as well. The penalties for attempted tax fraud vary from canton to canton. Attempted tax fraud is usually treated as a separate tax offence subject to fines.

A special form of tax fraud is inventory fraud, which is committed by heirs (or other persons indicated by the laws) who intentionally mislead the tax authorities during the inventory proceedings following the death of a person, with the intention to evade estate or inheritance taxes.

(5) Embezzlement of withholding taxes on salaries

All cantons, except Zug, Basel, and Neuchâtel, provide for a withholding tax on salary payments to foreign employees who do not possess permanent resident

¶1069

permits (¶1609 and ¶1610). An employer who is required to withhold the income taxes from these employees' salaries commits embezzlement if he uses the tax withheld for his own or somebody else's benefit instead of remitting it to the tax office. Under the cantonal tax statutes, embezzlement of withholding taxes is punishable with jail sentences of up to three years and/or fines.

(6) Self-incrimination
The tax laws usually provide that offenders may file a notice of a self-incrimination as long as they are not aware that an audit has been initiated. Self-incrimination generally leads to a reduction, or in some instances to a waiver of the penalty.

(7) The offenders
If the taxpayer is a legal entity, the directors, officers, representatives, agents, or employees of a corporate taxpayer with respect to which taxes have been evaded can be punished under a number of tax laws if they personally carry out deceptive acts.

As a rule, legal entities are not punishable (principle of guilt), but those individuals who have committed, or participated in, the tax offence as representatives or officers of the legal entity are liable. However, under federal income tax law, legal entities can be punished for tax evasion (Art. 130(4) FITD). In addition, the directors or officers of the legal entity can be punished if they are personally guilty (i.e., if they have acted deliberately or negligently).

Aiders, abettors, and accomplices to the tax offences can be punished, usually with fines. For the federal income tax, aiders, abettors, and accessories are liable only if the offence has actually been committed, not only attempted.

(8) Procedure
As a rule, tax offences are investigated and punished by the tax authorities themselves. However, in the case of tax fraud or embezzlement of withholding taxes, where jail sentences may apply, the ordinary criminal courts are competent. In such a case, the investigation is usually led by the administrative authorities, which pass the records of the case on to the cantonal attorney-general for the attention of the criminal court. Two parallel proceedings (before the administrative authorities and in the criminal courts) are possible in certain cases concerning income taxes offences.

¶1070   Tax avoidance – substance over form

Tax avoidance is not a criminal offence and is therefore not subject to penalty.

The concept of tax avoidance has been developed by the Federal Supreme Court under the substance-over-form doctrine (*imposition selon la réalité économique/wirtschaftliche Betrachtungsweise*). Taxpayers are free to use any of the methods of operation and forms of organisation available under the law. Their choice of legal form is recognised for tax purposes, even if it results in tax savings. However, the tax authorities may disregard a legally acceptable transaction if its recognition would allow the taxpayers to avoid the tax (*éluder l'impôt/die Steuer umgehen*) which would become due if they had structured the transaction properly.

The Supreme Court has repeatedly held that taxpayers may structure their dealings any way they please within the law, even if tax savings are achieved. A transaction may, however, be disregarded if its main purpose is tax avoidance. The Supreme Court has developed the following elements of tax avoidance:

(1) The legal form chosen by the taxpayer is 'unusual' (*insolite/ungewöhnlich*) or inadequate to achieve the purported goal and contrary to ordinary business practice.

(2) The taxpayer's primary motive for chosing such legal form is to achieve substantial tax savings.

(3) The taxpayer would, in fact, realise considerable tax savings if the legal form chosen were accepted by the tax authorities.

In practice, if the legal form chosen by the taxpayer is unusual or inadequate and leads, in fact, to considerable tax savings, it is presumed that the primary purpose is saving taxes. The taxpayer may overcome this presumption by showing that he or she had valid business reasons for choosing the particular legal form which prevail over the tax considerations. The concept of tax avoidance may also result in an application of the step-transaction doctrine.

If there is tax avoidance, the legal form chosen by the taxpayer is disregarded and he is treated as if he had chosen a legal form appropriate to achieving his goal.

Examples of tax avoidance inlude:

● Article 332(2) of the Geneva Income Tax Statute and Art. 44 of the Zurich Income Tax Statute provide that legal entities whose establishment or existence serves the sole purpose of tax avoidance or tax shifting are disregarded for tax purposes. Their income and net worth (or their capital) can be attributed to the beneficial owner.

● Financing a lump-sum one-time premium for a life insurance policy by means of a loan taken out from the insurance company, in order to pay deductible debt interest instead of non-deductible periodic insurance premiums, may constitute tax avoidance (*Archives*, 50, 624).

● The tax-free transformation of the business of a self-employed individual or a partnership into a corporation, with the subsequent sale of the corporate shares in order to realise a tax-free capital gain on private movable assets instead of a taxable 'liquidation gain' on business assets, which would arise if these were sold directly, is considered tax evasion (*Archives*, 47, 325).

¶1071 Legal assistance – exchange of information in tax matters

(1) Domestic legal assistance

As a rule, all federal, cantonal and municipal administrative and judicial authorities are obliged to transmit any information necessary for the adequate and complete assessment of the taxpayers to the tax authorities. This principle is not limited by the confidentiality obligation of civil servants. However, the constitutionally guaranteed secrecy of mail and telegraph communications (Art. 36 Federal Constitution) is reserved.

All cantons are party to an intercantonal concordat of 1948, which prevents them from concluding any special arrangements with taxpayers concerning their tax liability. It also provides for the exchange of information where taxpayers transfer their domicile to another canton, or where property is transferred to a newly established foundation or to a domiciliary company. In practice, the cantonal tax authorities exchange tax information on a voluntary basis. The exchange should be limited to the information that must be provided by the taxpayers themselves.

(2) International legal assistance

Swiss doctrine and practice generally distinguishes between administrative assistance (*entraide administrative/Amtshilfe*), i.e., exchange of information between tax administrations and judicial assistance (*entraide judiciaire/Rechtshilfe*), i.e., mutual assistance of judicial bodies.

(a) Administrative assistance

Switzerland grants administrative assistance in tax matters to foreign tax authorities on the basis of international double taxation conventions. As a general rule, Swiss administrative assistance is limited to exchanging information which is necessary for the correct application of the convention and for the prevention of its abuse. Most treaties contain explicit wording to that effect. However, unlike the rules of the OECD Model Double Taxation Convention on Income and on Capital of 1977, an exchange of information with respect to the taxes covered by the applicable convention is not granted unless the taxpayer requests that the convention be applied. In other words, Switzerland is prepared to exchange information if the application of the convention is at stake, but will refrain from providing any information if the information requested is to be used only for the domestic purposes of the other state.

The United States of America is the only country in relation to which Switzerland has agreed to exchange not only the information necessary to carry out the provisions of the convention, but also the information necessary to prevent fraud or the like in relation to the taxes that are the subject of the convention (Art. XVI I(1) United States/Swiss Double Taxation Convention of 1951). The Swiss authorities consider this provision to be applicable only in cases of tax fraud, as defined under Swiss law.

(b) Judicial assistance
The law of judicial assistance in criminal matters is explained in ¶1819 to ¶1824. As a general rule, Switzerland does not grant judicial assistance in fiscal matters (taxation, customs, currency exchange regulations) to foreign states. Judicial assistance can be granted by way of exception if the alleged offence qualifies as fiscal fraud (*escroquerie en matière de prestations et de contributions/ Abgabebetrug*), including its attempt. Fiscal fraud need not necessarily involve the use of false or forged documents; any fraudulent behaviour (*astuce/Arglist*) that is analogous to fraud (*escroquerie/Betrug*) under Art. 148 of the Penal Code suffices, even if the sole purpose of such conduct was to reduce foreign tax charges.

Judicial assistance granted by Switzerland in cases of fiscal fraud is limited to the taking of statements from witnesses and the gathering of documents. Extradition, prosecution and punishment on behalf of a foreign country, or the enforcement of a foreign criminal sentence are not available.

Under the Treaty between Switzerland and the United States on Mutual Assistance in Criminal Matters of 1973, Switzerland grants judicial assistance in cases of alleged violations of United States laws on lotteries, professional games of chance and the like, and in cases of commerce in narcotics and toxic substances, firearms, explosives, etc., including attempts or conspiracy to commit such offences. Furthermore, Switzerland may, in special cases, grant judicial assistance with respect to income tax offences of individuals who are suspected of having ties to organised crime.

(3) Secrecy provisions
Switzerland's ability to render administrative or judicial assistance may conflict with Swiss public policy (*ordre public*) or economic interests, in particular with the provisions on tax secrecy, banking secrecy, the prohibition of acts on behalf of a foreign state in Switzerland, and the prohibition of industrial espionage. This may partly explain Switzerland's cautious attitude with respect to the rendering of legal assistance. For example, Article XVI of the United States/Swiss Double-Taxation Convention of 1951 provides that any information exchanged pursuant to the Convention shall be treated as a secret, and shall not be disclosed to any person other than those concerned with the assessment and collection of

the taxes which are the subject of the Convention. No information shall be exchanged which would disclose any trade, business, industrial or professional secret. In particular, Swiss banks are prevented, under penalty of law, from disclosing information relating to bank accounts and bank transactions to persons other than the client, except in relation to criminal or bankruptcy proceedings. According to the case law of the Federal Supreme Court, bank secrecy does not prevent the exchange of information under Article XVI of the United States/Swiss Double Taxation Convention in cases of tax fraud.

AVOIDANCE OF INTERNATIONAL DOUBLE TAXATION

¶1072   Domestic law

Residents of Switzerland are taxed on their world-wide income and net worth (unlimited tax liability; ¶1028). However, the Federal Income Tax Decree and cantonal tax statutes exempt foreign immovable property and income derived therefrom, as well as permanent establishments situated abroad.

Non-residents are subject to tax in Switzerland with respect to immovable property located in Switzerland, income and capital of a Swiss permanent establishment, income from a Swiss business enterprise, fees earned as a member of the board of a Swiss share corporation and pensions paid by a Swiss public institution (limited tax liability; ¶1028). Cantonal tax statutes may subject other types of income to cantonal taxation as well.

Whether a person is residing or sojourning in Switzerland, and therefore subject to unlimited tax liability, is decided under the cantonal tax statute, the Federal Income Tax Decree, and the applicable case law. Persons who take up residence in Switzerland in order to engage in a gainful activity are subject to tax in Switzerland from the first day. However, persons who stay in Switzerland solely for the purpose of medical treatment or education are not considered to be residents of Switzerland, irrespective of the length of their stay. In any other case, unlimited tax liability is triggered after a certain period of physical presence in Switzerland. The length of the period that causes a person to be subject to an unlimited tax liability depends on whether that person owns or rents a home.

¶1073   Double taxation conventions

(1)   Treaty-making power of the Confederation and the cantons

(a)   The Confederation
The Confederation has the power to enter into treaties with other countries. Switzerland has concluded double taxation conventions with respect to taxes on

income with over 30 countries. Some of them deal only with income taxes, not with net-worth taxes. All conventions, however, cover municipal and cantonal income taxes, as well as the federal income tax. Except for a few old double taxation conventions (most notably the one with the United States dating from 1951), the conventions generally follow the Model Convention of the OECD.

The conventions with France, Austria and Germany provide special rules with respect to border workers, i.e., persons who reside in these countries and commute daily to their workplaces in Switzerland. Border workers are taxed only in their country of residence. With regard to Germany, the protocol of June 1971 gives details on the taxation of border workers. As to Italy, a separate agreement exists (dated 3 October 1974), stating that the salary of border workers is subject to tax at the place of work.

Switzerland has concluded ten conventions on estate and inheritance taxes. It is not expected that the number of such treaties will grow in the near future. None of the above-mentioned estate and inheritance tax treaties deals with gift taxes.

(b)   Cantons
In some areas the cantons are allowed to enter into agreements with foreign countries. Most of them deal with the exemption from estate and gift taxes, or contributions to charitable organisations. Geneva concluded a special agreement with France on the income taxation of border workers. Such agreements must not contain provisions conflicting with the sovereignty and the treaties of the Confederation.

(2)   Double taxation conventions and other international agreements regarding taxation currently in effect
The following international treaties are in effect as of summer 1991.

With Algeria
Income Tax: *Accord du 17 mars 1972 entre le Conseil fédéral suisse et le Gouvernement de la Republique algérienne démocratique et populaire pour éviter la double imposition des revenus provenant de l'exercice de la navigation aérienne* – RS 0.672.912.71.

With Argentina
Income Tax: *Echange de notes du 13 janvier 1950 entre la Suisse et l'Argentine concernant l'imposition des entreprises de navigation maritime ou aérienne* – RS 0.672.915.45.

With Australia
Income Tax: *Convention du 28 février 1980 entre la Suisse et l'Australie en vue d'éviter les doubles impositions en matière d'impôts sur le revenu (avec protocole)* – RS 0.672.915.81.

¶1073

With Austria
Income and Net-Worth Taxes: *Convention du 30 janvier 1974 entre la Confédération suisse et la République d'Autriche en vue d'éviter les doubles impositions en matière d'impôts sur le revenu et sur la fortune (avec protocol des négociations)* – RS 0.672.916.31.

Income Tax: *Arrangement des 5/6 décembre 1974 entre la Suisse et l'Autriche sur les modalités du dégrèvement concernant les dividendes, intérêts et redevances de licences* – RS 0.672.916.311.

Estate Tax: *Convention du 30 janvier 1974 entre la Confédération suisse et la République d'Autriche en vue d'éviter les doubles impositions en matière d'impôts sur les successions* – RS 0.672.916.32.

With Belgium
Income and Net-Worth Taxes: *Convention du 28 août 1978 entre la Confédération suisse et le Royaume de Belgique en vue d'éviter les doubles impositions en matière d'impôts sur le revenu et sur la fortune* – RS 0.672.917.21.

Income Tax: *Echange de notes du 29 juin 1959 entre le Conseil fédéral suisse et le Gouvernement belge concernant l'imposition des entreprises de navigation maritime ou aérienne en Suisse et au Congo belge* – RS 0.672.982.15.

With Brazil
Income Tax: *Echange de notes du 22 juin 1956 entre le Gouvernement suisse et le Gouvernement brésilien concernant l'imposition des entreprises de navigation maritime et aérienne* – RS 0.672.919.85.

With Bulgaria
Income Tax: *Echange de notes du 20 janvier 1969 entre la Suisse et la Bulgarie concernant l'imposition des entreprises de navigation maritime ou aérienne* – RS 0.672.921.45.

With Canada
Income and Net-Worth Taxes: *Convention du 20 août 1976 entre la Suisse et le Canada tendant à éviter les doubles impositions en matière d'impôts sur le revenu et sur la fortune* – RS 0.672.923.21.

With China
Income and Net-Worth Taxes: *Convention du 6 juillet 1990 entre la Confédération suisse et la République populaire de Chine en vue d'éviter les doubles impositions en matière d'impôts sur le revenu et la fortune* – RS 0.672.924.91.

¶1073

With Czechoslovakia

Income Tax: *Echange de notes du 26 avril 1960 entre la Suisse et la Tchécoslovaquie concernant l'imposition des entreprises de navigation aérienne* – RS 0.672.974.15.

With Denmark

Income and Net-Worth Taxes: *Convention du 23 novembre 1973 entre la Confédération suisse et le Royaume du Danemark en vue d'éviter les doubles impositions en matière d'impôts sur le revenu et sur la fortune (avec protocole des négociations)* – RS 0.672.931.41.

Income and Net-Worth Taxes: *Echange de lettres du 20 mars 1978 entre le Conseil fédéral suisse et le Gouvernement danois concernant l'extension aux îles Féroé de la convention du 23 novembre 1973 entre la Suisse et le Danemark en vue d'éviter les doubles impositions en matière d'impôts sur le revenu et la fortune* – RS 0.672.931.411.

Estate Tax: *Convention du 23 novembre 1973 entre la Confédération suisse et le Royaume du Danemark en vue d'éviter les doubles impositions en matière d'impôts sur les successions* – RS 0.672.931.42.

Estate Tax: *Echange de lettres du 20 mars 1978 entre le Conseil fédéral suisse et le Gouvernement danois concernant l'extension aux îles Féroé de la convention du 23 novembre 1973 entre la Suisse et le Danemark en vue d'éviter les doubles impositions en matière d'impôts sur les successions* – RS 0.672.931.421.

With Egypt

Income Tax: *Convention du 20 mai 1987 entre la Confédération suisse et la République arabe d'Egypte en vue d'éviter les doubles impositions en matière d'impôts sur le revenu (avec annexe)* – RS 0.672.932.15.

With Finland

Income and Net-Worth Taxes: *Convention du 27 décembre 1956 entre la Confédération suisse et la République de Finlande en vue d'éviter les doubles impositions dans le domaine des impôts sur le revenu et sur la fortune (avec protocole final)* – RS 0.672.934.51; *Echange de lettres du 27 mai 1970* – RS 0.672.934.510.

Income Tax: *Arrangement du 1er mars 1974 entre la Suisse et la Finlande au sujet de la procédure de dégrèvement concernant les dividendes et les intérêts* – RS 0.672.934.511.

Estate Tax: *Convention du 27 décembre 1956 entre la Confédération suisse et la République de Finlande en vue d'éviter les doubles impositions dans le domaine des impôts sur les successions (avec protocole final)* – RS 0.672.934.52.

¶1073

With France
Income and Net-Worth Taxes: *Convention du 9 septembre 1966 entre la Confédération suisse et la République française en vue d'éviter les doubles impositions en matière d'impôts sur le revenu et sur la fortune (avec protocole additionnel)* – RS 0.672.934.91.

Estate Tax: *Convention du 31 décembre 1953 entre la Confédération suisse et la République française en vue d'éviter les doubles impositions en matière d'impôts sur les successions (avec protocole final)* – RS 0.672.934.92.

With Germany
Estate Tax: *Convention du 30 novembre 1978 entre la Confédération suisse et la République fédérale d'Allemagne en vue d'éviter les doubles impositions en matière d'impôts sur les successions* – RS 0.672.913.61.

Income and Net-Worth Taxes: *Convention du 11 août 1971 entre la Confédération suisse et la République fédérale d'Allemagne en vue d'éviter les doubles impositions en matière d'impôts sur le revenu et sur la fortune (avec échange de lettres)* – RS 0.672.913.62.

Income Tax: *Protocole du 17 octobre 1989 (avec échange de notes)* – RS 0.672.913.621.

With Ghana
Income Tax: *Echange de notes du 6 décembre 1963 entre la Suisse et le Ghana concernant l'imposition des entreprises de navigation maritime ou aérienne* – RS 0.672.936.35.

With Greece
Income Tax: *Convention du 16 juin 1983 entre la Confédération suisse et la République hellénique en vue d'éviter les doubles impositions en matière d'impôts sur le revenu (avec protocole)* – RS 0.672.937.21.

With Hungary
Income and Net-Worth Taxes: *Convention du 9 avril 1981 entre la Confédération suisse et la République populaire hongroise en vue d'éviter les doubles impositions en matière d'impôts sur le revenu et la fortune (avec protocole)* – RS 0.672.941.81.

With Iceland
Income and Net-Worth Taxes: *Convention du 3 juin 1988 entre la Confédération suisse et la République d'Islande en vue d'éviter les doubles impositions en matière d'impôts sur le revenu et sur la fortune* – RS 0.672.944.51.

With India
Income Tax: *Accord du 28 août 1958 entre le Conseil fédéral suisse et le Gouvernement de l'Inde concernant la double imposition des entreprises de navigation aérienne* – RS 0.672.942.35.

¶1073

With Indonesia
Income Tax: *Convention du 29 août 1988 entre la Confédération suisse et la République d'Indonésie en vue d'éviter les doubles impositions en matière d'impôts sur le revenu (avec protocole)* – RS 0.672.942.71.

With Iran
Income Tax: *Echange de notes des 9 septembre 1956/7 février 1957 entre la Suisse et l'Iran concernant l'imposition d'entreprises aériennes* – RS 0.672.943.65.

With Ireland
Income and Net-Worth Taxes: *Convention du 8 novembre 1966 entre la Confédération suisse et l'Irlande en vue d'éviter les doubles impositions en matière d'impôts sur le revenu et sur la fortune (avec échange de lettres)* – RS 0.672.944.11.

Income and Net-Worth Taxes: *Protocole du 24 octobre 1980 entre la Confédération suisse et l'Irlande à l'effet de modifier la convention en vue d'éviter les doubles impositions en matière d'impôt sur le revenu et sur la fortune signée à Dublin le 8 novembre 1966* – RS 0.672.944.111.

With Italy
Income and Net-Worth Taxes: *Convention du 9 mars 1976 entre la Confédération suisse et la République italienne en vue d'éviter les doubles impositions et de régler certaines autres questions en matière d'impôts sur le revenu et sur la fortune (avec protocole additionnel)* – RS 0.672.945.41; *Echange de lettres du 28 avril 1978* – RS 0.672.945.411.

Income Tax of Border Workers: *Accord du 3 octobre 1974 entre la Suisse et l'Italie relatif à l'imposition des travailleurs frontaliers et à la compensation financière en faveur des communes italiennes limitrophes* – RS 0.642.045.43.

With the Ivory Coast
Income Tax: *Convention du 23 novembre 1987 entre la Confédération suisse et la République de Côte d'Yvoire en vue d'éviter les doubles impositions en matière d'impôts sur le revenu* – RS 0.672.928.91.

With Japan
Income Tax: *Convention du 19 janvier 1971 entre la Suisse et le Japon en vue d'éviter les doubles impositions en matière d'impôts sur le revenue (avec échange de notes)* – RS 0.672.946.31.

With Kenya
Income Tax: *Echange de lettres des 26 février/30 octobre 1973 entre la Suisse et le Kenya concernant l'imposition des entreprises de navigation aérienne* – RS 0.672.947.25.

¶1073

With Lebanon
Income Tax: *Echange de notes des 26 juin/11 septembre 1957 entre la Suisse et le Liban concernant l'imposition des entreprises de navigation aérienne* – RS 0.672.948.95.

With Malaysia
Income Tax: *Convention du 30 décembre 1974 entre le Conseil fédéral suisse et le Gouvernement de Malaisie en vue d'éviter les doubles impositions en matière d'impôts sur le revenu* – RS 0.672.952.71.

With Malta
Income Tax: *Echange de lettres du 30 mars 1987 entre la Suisse et Malte concernant l'imposition des entreprises de navigation maritime et aérienne* – RS 0.672.954.55.

With Morocco
Income Tax: *Accord du 17 mars 1970 entre la Confédération suisse et le Royaume du Maroc concernant l'imposition des entreprises de navigation maritime ou aérienne* – RS 0.672.954.95.

With the Netherlands
Income Tax: *Convention du 12 novembre 1951 entre la Confédération suisse et le Royaume des Pays-Bas en vue d'éviter les doubles impositions dans le domaine des impôts sur le revenu et sur la fortune (avec annexes, protocole final et protocol additionnel)* – RS 0.672.963.61.

Estate Tax: *Convention du 12 novembre 1951 entre la Confédération suisse et le Royaume des Pays-Bas en vue d'éviter les doubles impositions dans le domaine des impôts sur les successions (avec protocole final)* – RS 0.672.963.62.

With New Zealand
Income Tax: *Convention du 6 juin 1980 entre la Confédération suisse et la Nouvelle-Zélande en vue d'éviter les doubles impositions en matière d'impôts sur le revenue (avec protocole)* – RS 0.672.961.41.

With Norway
Income and Net-Worth Taxes: *Convention du 7 septembre 1987 entre la Confédération suisse et le Royaume de Norvège en vue d'éviter les doubles impositions dans le domaine des impôts sur le revenu et sur la fortune (avec protocole)* – RS 0.672.959.81.

Estate Tax: *Convention du 7 décembre 1956 entre la Confédération suisse et le Royaume de Norvège en vue d'éviter les doubles impositions dans le domaine des impôts sur les successions (avec protocole final)* – RS 0.672.959.82.

¶1073

With Pakistan
Income Tax: *Convention du 30 décembre 1959 entre la Confédération suisse et la République du Pakistan en vue d'éviter les doubles impositions en matière d'impôts sur le revenu* – RS 0.672.962.31.

With Poland
Income Tax: *Echange de notes du 13 juin 1961 entre la Suisse et la Pologne concernant l'imposition des entreprises de navigation maritime et aérienne* – RS 0.672.964.95.

With Portugal
Income and Net-Worth Taxes: *Convention du 26 septembre 1974 entre la Suisse et le Portugal en vue d'éviter les doubles impositions en matière d'impôts sur le revenu et sur la fortune (avec protocole additionnel)* – RS 0.672.965.41.

With Romania
Income Tax: *Echange de notes du 28 mai 1968 entre la Suisse et la Roumanie concernant l'imposition des entreprises de navigation maritime ou aérienne* – RS 0.672.966.35.

With Singapore
Income and Net-Worth Taxes: *Convention du 25 novembre 1975 entre la Confédération suisse et la République de Singapour en vue d'éviter les doubles impositions en matière d'impôts sur le revenu et sur la fortune (avec protocole)* – RS 0.672.968.91.

With South Africa
Income Tax: *Convention du 3 juillet 1967 entre la Confédération suisse et la République d'Afrique du Sud en vue d'éviter les doubles impositions en matière d'impôts sur le revenu* – RS 0.672.911.81.

With South Korea
Income Tax: *Convention du 12 février 1980 entre la Suisse et la République de Corée en vue d'éviter les doubles impositions en matière d'impôts sur le revenu (avec protocole)* – RS 0.672.928.11.

With the Soviet Union
Income Tax: *Convention du 5 septembre 1986 entre la Confédération suisse et l'Union des République socialistes soviétiques relative à des questions fiscales* – RS 0.672.977.21.

Income Tax: *Echange de notes du 18 janvier 1968 entre la Suisse et l'Union des Républiques socialistes soviétiques concernant l'imposition des entreprises de navigation maritime ou aérienne* – RS 0.672.977.25.

¶1073

With Spain
Income and Net-Worth Taxes: *Convention du 26 avril 1966 entre la Confédération suisse et l'Espagne en vue d'éviter les doubles impositions en matière d'impôts sur le revenu et sur la fortune (avec échange de lettres)* – RS 0.672.933.21.

With Sri Lanka
Income and Net-Worth Taxes: *Convention du 11 janvier 1983 entre la Confédération suisse et la République démocratique socialiste de Sri Lanka en vue d'éviter les doubles impositions en matière d'impôts sur le revenu et sur la fortune (avec protocole)* – RS 0.672.971.21.

With Sweden
Income and Net-Worth Taxes: *Convention du 7 mai 1965 entre la Confédération suisse et le Royaume de Suède en vue d'éviter les doubles impositions en matière d'impôts sur le revenu et sur la fortune* – RS 0.672.971.41.

Income and Net-Worth Tax: *Arrangement du 29 novembre 1985 entre la Suisse et la Suède concernant l'exécution des art. 10 et 11 de la convention du 7 mai 1965 entre la Suisse et la Suède en vue d'éviter les doubles impositions en matière d'impôts sur le revenu et la fortune* – RS 0.672.971.411.

Estate Tax: *Convention du 7 février 1979 entre la Confédération suisse et le Royaume de Suède en vue d'éviter les doubles impositions en matière d'impôts sur les successions* – RS 0.672.971.42.

With Trinidad and Tobago
Income Tax: *Convention du 1er février 1973 entre la Suisse et la Trinité-et-Tobago en vue d'éviter les doubles impositions en matière d'impôts sur le revenu* – RS 0.672.975.41.

With Tunisia
Income Tax: *Accord du 3 avril 1970 entre la Suisse et la Tunisie pour éviter la double impositions des revenus provenant de l'exploitation des navires et aéronefs* – RS 0.672.975.85.

With Turkey
Income Tax: *Echange de lettres du 29 juin 1990 entre la Suisse et la Turquie concernant l'imposition des entreprises de navigation aérienne* – RS 0.672.976.35.

With the United Kingdom
Income Tax: *Convention du 30 septembre 1954 entre la Confédération suisse et le Royaume-Uni de Grande-Bretagne et d'Irlande du Nord en vue d'éviter les doubles impositions en matière d'impôts sur le revenu* – RS 0.672.936.711.

¶1073

Income Tax: *Convention du 8 décembre 1977 entre la Confédération suisse et le Royaume-Uni de Grande-Bretagne et d'Irlande du Nord en vue d'éviter les doubles impositions en matière d'impôts sur le revenu* – RS 0.672.936.712.

Estate Tax: *Convention du 12 juin 1956 entre la Confédération suisse et le Royaume-Uni de Grande-Bretagne et d'Irlande du Nord en vue d'atténuer les doubles impositions en matière d'impôts sur les successions* – RS 0.672.936.72.

With the United States
Income Tax: *Convention du 24 mai 1951 entre la Confédération suisse et les Etats-Unis d'Amérique en vue d'éviter les doubles impositions en matière d'impôts sur le revenu* – RS 0.672.933.61.

Income and Net-Worth Taxes: *Convention du 9 juillet 1951 entre la Confédération suisse et les Etats-Unis d'Amérique en vue d'éviter les doubles impositions dans le domaine des impôts sur la masse successorale et sur les parts héréditaires* – RS 0.672.933.62.

With Uruguay
Income Tax: *Echange de notes du 30 décembre 1965 entre la Suisse et la République d'Uruguay concernant l'imposition des entreprises de navigation maritime ou aérienne* – RS 0.672.977.65.

With Venezuela
Income Tax: *Accord du 7 novembre 1985 entre le Conseil fédéral suisse et le Gouvernement de la République du Venezuela en vue d'éviter la double imposition en matière de transports aériens* – RS 0.672.978.55.

With Yugoslavia
Income Tax: *Echange de notes des 4 novembre/29 décembre 1964 entre la Suisse et la Yougoslavie concernant l'imposition des entreprises de navigation maritime ou aérienne* – RS 0.672.981.85.

With Zambia
Income Tax: *Application à la Zambie de la convention avec la Grande-Bretagne et l'Irlande du Nord en vue d'éviter les doubles impositions en matière d'impôts sur le revenu* – RS 0.672.982.31.

With Zimbabwe
Income Tax: *Application au Zimbabwe de la convention avec la Grande-Bretagne et l'Irlande du Nord en vue d'éviter les doubles impositions en matière d'impôts sur le revenu* – RS 0.672.982.71.

(3)   Method of avoiding double taxation – tax credits
Switzerland has always favoured the method of 'exemption with progression', both intercantonally and internationally. This method is applied irrespective of

whether the contracting state taxes the income allocated to it. Even in cases where the contracting state applies another method to avoid double taxation, Switzerland does not depart from its exemption system, except with respect to the taxation of dividends, interest and royalties.

Under some old treaties, Switzerland agreed to include in the tax basis only the net amount of dividends and interest, after deduction of the non-refundable withholding tax. Switzerland grants a tax credit only where a double taxation convention provides for it. Based on the Federal Decree of 1951 on the Implementation of the Confederation's Double Taxation Conventions (*Arrêté fédéral concernant l'exécution des conventions internationales conclues par la Confédération en vue d'éviter les doubles impositions/Bundesbeschluss über die Durchführung von zwischenstaatlichen Abkommen des Bundes zur Vermeidung der Doppelbesteuerung*, RS 672.2), the Federal Parliament granted the Federal Government the power to institute a procedure to secure a tax credit where a double taxation convention provides for such credit. Based on this law, the Ordinance on Tax Credits (*Ordonnance relative à l'imputation forfaitaire d'impôt/Verordnung über die pauschale Steueranrechnung*, RS 672.201) was issued. This ordinance grants a credit against Swiss taxes for the non-refundable foreign withholding tax on dividends, interest and royalties. Because of the complexity of the Swiss tax system, usually a lump-sum tax credit is granted. The credit may be claimed only if the item of income at issue is subject to Swiss taxes. If such income is subject only to the federal income tax but exempt from cantonal and municipal tax, the credit is granted only partially. The lower of the remaining withholding tax and the Swiss taxes on such income constitutes the maximum creditable amount.

Under certain circumstances, if the amount of the foreign non-refundable withholding tax exceeds SFr 1,000, either the taxpayer or the tax administration can ask for an exact calculation of the tax credit. The tax credit may be claimed within three years after the end of the calender year in which the respective item of income accrued or was paid. The tax credit is granted against federal, cantonal and municipal income taxes.

PROVISIONS AGAINST ABUSE OF DOUBLE TAXATION CONVENTIONS

¶1074   Domestic law

(1)   'Abuse Decree'

Tax treaties basically apply only to persons (individuals or corporations) who reside in one or both of the contracting states and who are the beneficial owners of the income to which the treaty applies. In order to prevent non-residents of Switzerland from benefiting from double taxation conventions entered into by the Confederation, Switzerland has enacted certain unilateral measures against treaty abuse. They are set forth in the Decree of the Federal Government on Measures Against Improper Use of Tax Conventions Concluded by the Swiss Confederation (the so-called 'Abuse Decree'; *'arrêté relatif aux abus'/* *'Missbrauchsbeschluss')* (*Arrêté du Conseil fédéral instituant des mesures contre l'utilisation sans cause légitime des conventions conclues par la Confédération en vue d'éviter les doubles impositions/Bundesratesbeschluss betreffend Massnahmen gegen die ungerechtfertigte Inanspruchnahme von Doppelbesteuerungsabkommen des Bundes*). The Decree is based on the Federal Decree on the Implementation of the Confederation's Double Taxation Conventions (¶1073(2)), which gives the Federal Government the authority (among other things) to enact measures against abusive relief from taxes levied at source. The 'Abuse Decree' therefore applies only to taxes levied at source. It lists the conditions that must be met by the taxpayer in order to obtain tax relief from withholding taxes by virtue of a Swiss double taxation convention. Its rules have been clarified by a circular letter of the Federal Tax Administration.

(2) Application of 'Abuse Decree'
The 'Abuse Decree' applies only to treaty-protected income, i.e., income that is derived from sources within the other contracting state and for which a partial or a full relief from taxes withheld at source has been granted by virtue of the applicable double taxation convention. Primarily, this income comprises dividends, interest and royalties, but it may also include other types of income, provided that there has been a relief from tax withheld at the source. The computation of the relevant treaty-protected income is always based on the gross amount of the income from which the non-refundable tax levied by the other contracting state is deducted.

The tests of 'residence' and 'beneficial ownership' are standard requirements applicable to all double taxation conventions that Switzerland has entered into. Residence requires a person to be a bona fide resident. Beneficial ownership requires the claimant to be entitled to the full use and enjoyment of the property giving rise to the relevant income and the income itself. For these purposes, interposed persons such as agents or nominees are disregarded for tax purposes, and are themselves not entitled to treaty relief.

(3) Abuse of double taxation conventions
A tax treaty relief claimed by a resident individual, legal entity or partnership is considered abusive if the relief substantially benefits, directly or indirectly, persons not entitled to such treaty relief. The Abuse Decree and the corresponding circular letter of the Federal Tax Administration state four specific abuse criteria:

¶1074

(a) Conduit

Not more than 50 per cent of the treaty-protected income may be transferred, directly or indirectly, to unentitled persons. This limitation is intended to avoid the transfer of an excessive and untaxed portion of treaty-protected income to persons who are not entitled to it. The Federal Tax Administration has developed a sophisticated practice in applying the conduit clause. All payments that reduce the net income of a Swiss resident taxpayer are subject to this clause. Any transfer of treaty-protected income, such as payment of interest, royalties, development costs, advertising and travel expenses, and depreciation of any kind of asset, including incorporeal goods and processes, is applied towards the conduit percentage if the transfer was made to the benefit of a person not entitled to treaty relief. Of course, it is irrelevant whether the ultimate recipient of the treaty-protected income is fully taxed or not in his country of residence. For the purposes of this test, the interposing of another Swiss entity is disregarded.

(b) Accumulation

The circular letter of the Federal Tax Administration furthermore requires a corporation in which persons not entitled to treaty benefits hold, directly or indirectly, a substantial interest to make annual profit distributions. A substantial interest, for these purposes, primarily means direct or indirect investment, by vote or value, in 50 per cent of the company's outstanding capital stock. However, under the practice of the Federal Tax Administration, other controlling interests of any kind are considered equivalent to a substantial interest, so that all persons who are either legally or factually in a position to benefit in some way from treaty-protected income, such as by contractual arrangement or by virtue of their factual ability to influence or control the profit distribution policy, are covered.

A profit distribution is considered appropriate for these purposes if at least 25 per cent of the gross amount of the treaty-protected income is distributed by way of dividend. Constructive dividends are taken into account when computing this minimum profit distribution. If a Swiss entity has been interposed between the distributing Swiss company and the person not entitled to treaty benefits, such interposed entity is again required to make the 25 per cent minimum profit distribution (after reduction of Swiss taxes, if any). Such compulsory dividend distribution may be waived only where the company has incurred 'commercially justified' losses. Therefore, it is not waived if the losses result from excessive interest payments or expenses for depreciation. However, losses due to currency fluctuations or adverse stock market conditions are, in general, recognised as 'commercially justified'. The amount left after the minimum dividend and the maximum transfer may be accumulated as undistributed profit to the extent that no Swiss expenses such as taxes and directors' and legal fees are deducted.

¶1074

(c)   Financing
With respect to corporations, the interest-bearing debt *vis-à-vis* persons not entitled to treaty benefits may not exceed six times the amount of equity (stated capital plus legal reserve plus retained earnings). The rate of interest paid on such debt may not exceed the appropriate rate of interest which is periodically fixed by the Federal Tax Administration. This clause is again designed to prevent companies from passing on treaty-protected income to persons not entitled.

(d)   Partnerships and family foundations
Partnerships that are not actively engaged in business in Switzerland, and foreign-controlled family foundations are not entitled to treaty relief if more than 50 per cent of the treaty-protected income is for the benefit of unentitled persons.

If the Federal Tax Administration determines that relief from foreign withholding tax by virtue of a Swiss double taxation convention has been abusively obtained, it will refuse to grant the official confirmation solicited on the form which is to be sent to the foreign tax authority in order to obtain a refund of tax, or, if necessary, will revoke such confirmation. If the tax relief has already been granted abusively, the Federal Tax Administration will ask the taxpayers to reimburse the amount at issue, and will then transmit it to the tax authorities of the appropriate contracting state. If, despite these measures, the improper use of a double taxation convention cannot effectively be prevented, the Federal Tax Administration may inform the tax authorities of the other contracting state about the case. The penalties applicable in case of non-compliance with the 'Abuse Decree' are the same as those contained in the Swiss Anticipatory Tax Statute.

¶1075   Convention provisions preventing treaty-shopping

A number of tax treaties entered into by Switzerland explicitly refer to the 'Abuse Decree' (see ¶1074(1)).

With respect to the tax treaties with Belgium, France, Germany and Italy, the 'Abuse Decree' has, in slightly modified form, been embodied in the double taxation convention itself. The most important modifications are that royalties and interest (and, in the case of Germany, capital gains realised upon the disposition of movable property as well) must be subject to ordinary taxation for cantonal and municipal tax purposes. This requirement is, of course, aimed at Swiss-based companies that have been granted a privileged tax status. Furthermore, these abuse provisions in these conventions cover all taxes which are reduced or waived by virtue of the convention, whether levied at source or by way of assessment.

Finally, the conventions with the Netherlands, the United States of America and the United Kingdom state that relief with respect to withholding tax on dividends is granted only if the relationship between the company paying the dividend and the company recipient of the dividend has not been established, or is not maintained primarily in order to benefit from such reduction of withholding tax.

With respect to the lump-sum taxation which can be granted to individuals under certain circumstances, the double taxation conventions with Belgium, France, Germany and Italy state that the persons who are not subject to ordinary taxes in Switzerland at the federal, cantonal and municipal level are not considered residents of Switzerland for purposes of the respective double taxation convention.

SELECTED BIBLIOGRAPHY

Adam Boleslaw Boczek, *Taxation in Switzerland*, Harvard Law School, World Tax Series (Chicago, 1976)

Francis Cagianut and Ernst Höhn, *Unternehmungssteuerrecht*, (Bern/Stuttgart, 1986)

Ernst Höhn, *Steuerrecht*, 6th edn (Bern/Stuttgart, 1984)

——, *Handbuch des internationalen Steuerrechts der Schweiz* (Bern/Stuttgart, 1984)

Ernst Känzig, *Die Eidgenössische Wehrsteuer* (direkte Bundessteuer), Part 1, 2nd edn (Basel, 1982)

Heinz Masshardt, *Kommentar zur direkten Bundessteuer*, 2nd edn (Zürich, 1985); with supplement, 1989, by Beat Jung and Peter Agner

Dieter Metzger, *Handbuch der Warenumsatzsteuer* (Bern, 1983)

Robert Pfund, *Die Eidgenössische Verrechnungssteuer*, vol. 1 (Basel, 1971); vol. 2 by Robert Pfund and Bernhard Zwahlen (Basel, 1985)

August Reimann, Ferdinand Zuppinger and Erwin Schärrer, *Kommentar zum Zürcher Steuergesetz*, 4 vols. (Bern, 1961–69), with supplement by Ferdinand Zuppinger, Erwin Schärrer, Ferdinand Fessler and Markus Reich (Bern, 1978)

Jean-Marc Rivier, *Droit fiscal suisse – L'imposition du revenu et de la fortune* (Neuchâtel, 1980)

——, *Droit fiscal suisse – Le droit fiscal international* (Neuchâtel, 1983)

——, *Introduction à la fiscalité de l'entreprise*, 2nd edn (Lausanne, 1990)

Walter Ryser, *Introduction au droit fiscal international de la Suisse* (Bern, 1980)

¶1075

11 Banking and Finance

PRINCIPAL LEGISLATION

*Loi fédérale sur la Banque nationale/Nationalbankgesetz/*National Bank Statute, RS 951.11.

*Loi fédérale sur les fonds de placement/Anlagefondsgesetz/*Investment Funds Statute, RS 951.31.

*Ordonnance sur les fonds de placement/Anlagefondsverordnung/*Investment Funds Ordinance, RS 951.311.

*Ordonnance sur les fonds de placement étrangers/Auslandanlagefondsverordnung/*Ordinance on Foreign Investment Funds, RS 951.312.

*Loi fédérale sur les banques et les caisses d'épargne/Bankengesetz/*Banking Statute, RS 952.0.

*Ordonnance sur les banques et les caisses d'épargne/Bankenverordnung/*Banking Ordinance, RS 952.02.

*Ordonnance de la Commission fédérale des banques concernant les banques étrangères en Suisse/Auslandbankenverordnung/*Ordinance on Foreign Banks, RS 952.111.

INTRODUCTION

¶1101 Importance of banking and finance in Switzerland

Switzerland is one of the world's leading financial centres. The main factors which helped Switzerland to achieve this position are a stable political situation, the country's capacity for saving, a stable currency with minimum transfer restrictions, traditionally low interest rates, and highly sophisticated and secure financial institutions. Domestic and international investors find a favourable financing climate and can rely upon the quality and efficiency of the banking system nationwide.

Switzerland has a universal banking system. Banks can engage in all financial services, including securities transactions. Foreign-controlled banks and branches of foreign banks enjoy the same treatment as domestic institutions. The major Swiss banks maintain a nationwide network of branches and are – through subsidiaries and branches – also represented on the large international markets.

SOURCES OF THE LAW

¶1102   Public and private, federal and cantonal

The legal sources, both public and private, governing banking and finance in Switzerland are manifold and widespread (for the distinction between public and private law, see ¶107). Federal public law is the source for the regulation of the currency and the money market, banking institutions and investment funds. The regulation of securities trading and stock exchanges lies within the legislative power of the cantons. The provisions of domestic public law and of international conventions in the area of criminal law, tax law and legal assistance are of particular importance for banking and finance. Contract and corporate law (the private law areas which affect banking and finance most) are federal and are codified in the Civil Code (CC) and the Code of Obligations (CO).

¶1103   Federal public law

(1)   Federal Constitution

Several provisions of the Federal Constitution provide the basis for federal legislation on the regulation and supervision of the financial markets and banking:

- Article 31 gives the federal legislature the power to regulate banking.
- Article 31^{quinquies} and Art. 39 authorise the Swiss National Bank to exercise monetary and currency control.
- Articles 38 and 39 provide for the federal coins and banknotes privilege.

Other general provisions of the Federal Constitution that are important for banking and finance are Art. 31 (freedom of trade and industry) and Arts 64 and 64bis (power of the Confederation to legislate in the areas of civil and criminal law).

(2)   Banking statute and ordinances

The Banking Statute and its related ordinances are the instruments through which the Federal Banking Commission supervises banks. The Banking Statute includes, among other things, provisions on the following regulatory issues:

- definition of banks and other financial institutions and conditions for the granting of banking licences (Art. 1 et seq.),

- equity, liquidity and other operational requirements for banks, financial statements (Art. 4 et seq.),
- control and audit (Art. 18 et seq.),
- supervision by the Federal Banking Commission (Art. 23 et seq.),
- postponement of maturity, moratorium, and provisions for bankruptcy and arrangements with creditors (Art. 25 et seq.),
- civil liability of banks and individuals who act for banks (Art. 38 et seq.),
- bank secrecy (Art. 47), and
- penalty provisions (Arts 46 and 48 et seq.).

The Banking Statute is complemented by the Banking Ordinance, which specifies in detail the provisions of the Banking Statute, and by the Ordinance on Foreign Banks, which governs branches, agencies, and representative offices of, and the acceptance of deposits by, foreign banks in Switzerland.

(3) National Bank Statute

The National Bank Statute governs the organisational structure and the operations of the Swiss National Bank, as well as the functions to be exercised by it. Those include, in particular, the traditional central bank functions. In addition, the National Bank Statute contains provisions regarding the relationship between the National Bank and the Federal Government, as well as the Federal Banking Commission.

(4) Investment Funds Statute and ordinances

The Investment Funds Statute and the Investment Funds Ordinance regulate investment funds whose managements have their legal domicile in Switzerland. Investment funds need an authorisation from the Federal Banking Commission. If the fund management is not vested in a bank, it must use the services of a custodian bank, which, in turn, needs an authorisation from the Federal Banking Commission. The Investment Funds Statute and the Investment Funds Ordinance further provide detailed rules with respect to capitalisation, investment guide-lines and diversification. Under the Ordinance on Foreign Investment Funds, the public solicitation in or from Switzerland of certificates in a foreign investment fund (i.e., a fund whose management is domiciled abroad and which is incorporated or organised under foreign law) requires an authorisation from the Federal Banking Commission. The authorisation is granted to a representative bank, which must have its legal domicile in Switzerland or be a Swiss branch of a foreign bank.

(5) Other federal public law

In the Federal Penal Code (*Code pénal suisse/Schweizerisches Strafgesetzbuch* – RS 311.0), the provisions on insider trading (Art. 161 Penal Code) and the provisions on money laundering (Art. 305bis and Art. 305ter Penal Code) are of particular importance for the financial sector (see ¶1140 and ¶1141).

Another important statutory source is the Statute on International Legal Assistance in Criminal Matters (*Loi fédérale sur l'entraide internationale en matière pénale/Bundesgesetz über internationale Rechtshilfe in Strafsachen* – RS 351.1). This statute specifies the conditions which must be met by requests of foreign countries to obtain information that is covered by bank secrecy for use in criminal investigations abroad. In addition to the statute, there are a number of treaties on international legal assistance in criminal matters entered into by Switzerland, the most important of which from a practical point of view is the Treaty between the Swiss Confederation and the United States of America on Mutual Assistance in Criminal Matters of 25 May 1973 (*Traité entre la Confédération Suisse et les Etats Unis d'Amérique sur l'entraide judiciaire en matière penale/ Staatsvertrag zwischen der Schweizerischen Eidgenossenschaft und den Vereinigten Staaten von Amerika über gegenseitige Rechtshilfe in Strafsachen* – RS 0.351.933.6), supplemented by an exchange of letters of 10 November 1987 (*Echange de lettres entre la Suisse et les Etats Unis d'Amérique relatif à l'entraide judiciaire dans des procédures administratives complémentaires concernant les requêtes ayant trait à des opérations d'initiés/Briefwechsel zwischen der Schweiz und den Vereinigten Staaten von Amerika betreffend Rechtshilfe in ergänzenden Verwaltungsverfahren bei Insideruntersuchungen* – RS 0.351.933.65) (see ¶1140 and ¶1819 et seq.).

Federal tax laws directly affect foreign investors. The Federal Anticipatory Tax Statute (*Loi fédérale sur l'impôt anticipé/Bundesgesetz über die Verrechnungssteuer* – RS 642.21) subjects all income from bank deposits, as well as from equity and debt instruments of Swiss issuers, to a withholding tax of 35 per cent (relief to foreign investors depends on the applicable double taxation conventions – see ¶1073(2)). The Federal Stamp Tax Statute (*Loi fédérale sur les droits de timbre/Bundesgesetz über die Stempelabgaben* – RS 641.10) provides, *inter alia*, for stamp taxes on the issuance and transfer of securities (see ¶1008 and ¶1009).

¶1104   Cantonal public law

(1)   Stock exchanges; dealing in securities

(a)   Cantonal law, federal law in the making
Since no federal regulation on trading in securities and stock exchanges has been enacted, this remains a domain of cantonal legislation. In consequence, no federal supervisory agency comparable to foreign securities commissions exists in Switzerland. However, federal legislation is being considered; in June 1991, an

expert commission submitted a draft for a federal securities law to the Federal Government.

Zurich, Geneva and Basel host the Swiss stock exchanges and are the only cantons which have enacted legislation governing stock exchanges and dealings in securities. In Zurich and Basel, dealers in securities, whether admitted to the floor or engaging in over-the-counter transactions, need a cantonal licence. In Geneva, on-the-floor dealers must register with the cantonal government.

(b) Zurich

Zurich is the major stock exchange and the most important market for dealing in securities. The Statute on Professional Dealings in Securities (*Gesetz betreffend den gewerbsmässigen Verkehr mit Wertpapieren*) regulates all professional dealings in securities in the canton. It authorises the cantonal government (*Regierungsrat*) to enact banking ordinances and to grant licences for professional dealers in securities on and off the stock exchange (see ¶1123). It also stipulates that the dealers admitted to the stock exchange constitute, and must hold membership in, the Zurich Stock Exchange Association.

The Stock Exchange Association operates the exchange on the basis of its own Articles of Association, trading rules and customary practices, which are all subject to approval by the cantonal government. The stock exchange is supervised by the Stock Exchange Commissioner, who is appointed by the cantonal government. All provisions relating to the Zurich Stock Exchange are compiled in the Zurich Stock Exchange Manual (*Handbuch der Zürcher Effektenbörse*); they consist of a mixture of cantonal statutory provisions and semi-private rules and customs of the banks that run the stock exchange.

(c) Geneva

In contrast to Zurich, the cantonal government (*Conseil d'Etat*) of Geneva has much less influence, and leaves the operation of the stock exchange on a self-regulatory basis to the members of the stock exchange. The cantonal and private provisions regulating the Geneva stock exchange are collected in a special manual (*Manuel de la Bourse de Genève*).

(2) Cantonal banks

Article $31^{quater}(2)$ of the Federal Constitution directs the federal legislature to take into consideration the special position of cantonal banks. Each canton has a cantonal bank; very few have two. As a rule, they are public institutions whose equity has been supplied by the canton. Cantonal banks can be distinguished from other banks by the fact that each canton guarantees its bank's liabilities. Cantonal banks are exempt from various provisions of the Banking Statute. Their organisation and scope of business are defined by cantonal legislation (see ¶1113).

¶1105   Federal private law

Federal private law governs banking contracts and the relations of banks and financial institutions with customers (for the distinction between public and private law, see ¶107). In particular, the Code of Obligations is of the utmost importance to financial services. Its contract law provisions apply to the relations between banks and customers, and its commercial law part encompasses the rules to be followed by corporations when issuing shares and debt instruments.

REGULATION AND SUPERVISION OF FINANCIAL MARKETS

¶1106   Sharing of responsibilities

The power to regulate and supervise the financial market is vested in the National Bank and the Federal Banking Commission. The traditional role of the National Bank is that of a central bank; the main objective to be pursued by the Federal Banking Commission under the Banking Statute is creditor protection. The National Bank and the Federal Banking Commission are together trying to expand their traditional functions into an overall supervision of the financial market. They take the position that pure policing functions are insufficient to ensure the integrity and smooth functioning of the Swiss financial market.

The high level of self-regulation maintained by the banking and financial industry is a Swiss tradition. The dominant role of the Swiss Bankers Association, however, came under scrutiny by the Swiss Cartel Commission in 1989. The Swiss Cartel Commission recommended abolishing or changing many conventions of the Swiss Bankers Association, which it considered more anti-competitive than self-regulatory.

¶1107   Swiss National Bank

The National Bank (*Banque nationale suisse, BNS/Schweizerische Nationalbank, SNB*) is a semi-public share corporation. Around 40 per cent of its shares are held by private shareholders; the remaining 60 per cent are held by the cantons, the cantonal banks and other public institutions. While not a shareholder, the Federal Government has broad powers under the National Bank Statute to influence and supervise the National Bank's activities. Twenty-five members of the Board of Directors (*conseil de banque/Bankrat*) of the National Bank, including the chairman and the vice-chairman, are appointed by the Federal

Government, and only 15 are elected by the shareholders. The regulations of the Board of Directors, its business report and its annual financial statements are subject to approval by the Federal Government, the last two prior to submission to the shareholders' meeting. The National Bank is managed by a Directorate (*direction générale/Direktorium*) consisting of three members elected by the Federal Government. Together with the Federal Banking Commission, the Directorate is the most influential governmental agency in the banking and finance sector. The registered office of the National Bank is in Berne, but the Directorate is domiciled in Zurich. In addition, several branches are spread around Switzerland.

The main duties of the National Bank are to regulate the country's money supply, facilitate payment, and implement a credit and currency policy in the best interest of the country (Art. 39(3) Federal Constitution and Art. 2 National Bank Statute). In addition, it closely co-operates with the Federal Government in order to protect the public interest and acts as a lender of last resort. Profitability is not an objective of the National Bank.

The National Bank's traditional means of regulating the money supply is its banknotes and coins privilege. To facilitate payments and money transfers, the National Bank renders various services to domestic banks, industry and commerce, foreign banks, central banks and international institutions. For example, it offers giro accounts, co-operates with and facilitates bank clearing, and exercises the traditional banking functions for the Federal Government.

The objective of the National Bank's credit and currency policy is to maintain the purchasing power of the Swiss Franc. The regulation of the Swiss Franc exchange rate has been a major means of reaching this goal since the institution of flexible currency exchange rates. The National Bank influences interest and currency exchange rates through:

(1) facilitation of credit, in particular to banks, traditionally in the form of discounting bills of exchange (*crédit d'escompte/Diskontkredit*) and granting margin advances (*crédit lombard/Lombardkredit*), and regulation of the interest rates;

(2) purchase and sale of securities, money market instruments, gold and foreign currencies, by direct intervention as well as in forward and swap transactions;

(3) broad powers to influence inflow of foreign capital and export of domestic capital, including the power to direct banks to maintain interest-free minimum reserves on deposit with the National Bank (for monetary controls presently in place, see ¶1152).

The National Bank also represents Switzerland in international monetary organisations such as the Bank for International Settlements, the Club of Ten and the International Monetary Fund (in which Switzerland is considering a change from observer status to membership).

¶1108   Federal Banking Commission

The Federal Banking Commission (*Commission fédérale des banques*, CFB/ *Eidgenössische Bankenkommission*, EBK) is the supervisory authority over banks and investment funds. It was created in 1935 following the enactment of the Banking Statute. In 1967, the Investment Funds Statute entrusted the Federal Banking Commission with the supervision of investment funds as well.

The Federal Banking Commission is regulated by Art. 23 et seq. of the Banking Statute. It consists of seven to nine members elected by the Federal Government. The statutory provisions ensure that the Federal Banking Commission is independent from the Federal Government, the National Bank and the banking industry. The members of the Federal Banking Commission must meet high professional and personal qualifications. The Federal Banking Commission is assisted by a permanent Secretariat (*Secrétariat/Sekretariat*) whose head is also elected by the Federal Government. The Secretariat deals with the day-to-day work, prepares and executes the decisions of the Federal Banking Commission, communicates with banks and bank auditors, and conducts administrative enforcement investigations.

The Federal Banking Commission issues the decisions necessary to enforce, and supervises compliance with the provisions of, the Banking Statute (Art. 23bis(1) Banking Statute). It may demand information necessary to fulfil its task from the banks and auditors (Art. 23bis(2) Banking Statute). If the Federal Banking Commission learns of a violation of the Banking Statute or other irregularities, it is authorised to take all necessary remedial actions (Art. 23ter(1) Banking Statute). The instruments available to the Federal Banking Commission to perform its responsibilities include the power to grant and withdraw banking licences and to supervise, and if necessary to intervene in, the financial structure, management and operations of banks and bank-like finance companies. It has the power to request all information necessary to perform its functions from banks and bank auditors. In addition to individual decisions directed at individual banks or bank-like finance companies (which are subject to direct review by the Federal Supreme Court), the Federal Banking Commission has the power to enact ordinances (the most prominent example being the Ordinance on Foreign Banks) and issue general instructions and guide-lines to banks, bank-like finance companies and external bank auditors through circulars. The way in which the Federal Banking Commission has interpreted the bank licence requirement of continuous assurance of irreproachable business conduct (Art. 3(2)(c) Banking Statute, see ¶1119) is particularly important.

The Federal Banking Commission has the general power to regulate and supervise investment funds. Under the Investment Funds Statute, it has the power to authorise the establishment of domestic investment funds and to supervise their activities. It also grants authorisations to foreign investment funds for public solicitation of purchase of their certificates in Switzerland in accordance with the Ordinance on Foreign Investment Funds.

A semi-annual bulletin (*Bulletin/Bulletin*) and the yearly report (*Rapport de gestion/Jahresbericht*) published by the Federal Banking Commission are the sources from which current policies and proposed future legislation can be determined. More and more, the Federal Banking Commission considers itself not just a supervisory authority over banks to secure creditors' interests but also, together with the National Bank, a guardian of Swiss national economic interests and a proper and functioning financial market.

¶1109 Cantonal authorities – self-regulatory organisations

Cantonal authorities exercise regulatory and supervisory functions over stock exchanges, dealings in securities and cantonal banks.

In addition, self-regulation is a long-standing tradition in Switzerland's banking and finance industry. The leading self-regulatory organisation is the Swiss Bankers Association (see ¶1110 and ¶1111). Furthermore, the Association of Swiss Exchanges (*Association des Bourses Suisses/Vereinigung der Schweizer Börsen*), whose members are all Swiss stock exchanges, has adopted two self-regulatory instruments with considerable impact on the banking and securities industry.

The first is the Swiss Admission Board (*Instance Suisse d'Admission/ Schweizerische Zulassungsstelle*), presently operating under the Regulation (*Règlement/Reglement*) regarding the Swiss Admission Board, effective since 17 September 1990. The Swiss Admission Board has the power to decide on the admission of Swiss and foreign securities for listing; the decision has binding effect upon the individual stock exchanges (see also ¶1149). The second is the Swiss Take-Over Code of 1 September 1989 (see ¶1150).

Following a recommendation of the Federal Cartel Commission, the Association of Swiss Exchanges terminated the Agreement on Commission Rates (*convention de courtage/Courtage Konvention*) as of the end of 1990. This convention provided for a very strict and, in the Federal Cartel Commission's view, anti-competitive system of fixed commissions and rebate allowances in securities transactions. The consequences of this Swiss 'big bang' for the Swiss securities markets and its participants remain to be seen.

SWISS BANKERS ASSOCIATION AND OTHER ORGANISATIONS

¶1110   Swiss Bankers Association

The Swiss Bankers Association (*Association Suisse des Banquiers/ Schweizerische Bankiervereinigung*) is the leading organisation of the Swiss banking and finance industry. Its purpose is to safeguard and represent the interests and rights of the Swiss banking business, to defend its members against unfair competition and to protect Swiss savings. Its members are banks and similar institutions, such as bank-like finance companies, securities firms, investment fund managements, other finance and holding companies, and auditing firms. In addition, individuals holding leading positions in these institutions are admitted as members. The membership list encompasses virtually all institutions in the banking and financial sector, except for some foreign, namely United States, institutions which have not become members because of home market antitrust concerns.

The Swiss Bankers Association concentrates on representing the interests of the Swiss banking and financial community before federal and cantonal lawmakers, regulatory and supervisory agencies, and in various Swiss and foreign organisations. For instance, it was instrumental in the creation of bank industry organisations such as Telekurs AG and SEGA. It further engages in public relations work for the banking sector.

In addition, it influences banking and finance directly through self-regulatory measures. These include guide-lines and recommendations on banking procedure in order to reach generally accepted industry standards, and conventions.

¶1111   Conventions of Swiss Bankers Association

The most important self-regulatory instruments of the Swiss Bankers Association are its conventions. The conventions are agreements with binding effect on their signatories. Although the Swiss Bankers Association strongly recommends adhesion, its members are free to decide whether or not to submit to the conventions. However, institutions are under pressure to adhere to the conventions in order to avoid a disadvantageous position in the market. The conventions cover various aspects of the banking business; most of them include agreements on binding schedules and fees for banking services. Agreements on interest rates are less common; they are traditionally covered by local or regional conventions.

In 1989, the conventions were the subject of an investigation by the Federal Cartel Commission. The Federal Cartel Commission concluded that many conventions are wholly or partly anti-competitive to an extent which is not permissible under federal antitrust legislation (see Publications of the Federal

Cartel Commission 3/1989). As a result of consultations between the Federal Cartel Commission and the Swiss Bankers Association and of an order of the Federal Government, various conventions have been or will be either eliminated or changed. Out of 19 conventions in force in 1989, about 15 will survive.

¶1112   Other organisations and associations

Swiss banks have formed various service organisations in order to facilitate banking transactions and procedures. The two most important are Telekurs AG and SEGA Swiss Securities Clearing Corporation (*SEGA Société suisse pour le virement de titres SA/SEGA Schweizerische Effekten-Giro AG*). Both are corporations controlled by Swiss banks which make use of their services.

Telekurs AG provides interbank services and domestic and international financial information of all kinds. It runs Swiss Interbank Clearing (SIC) and the Electronic Funds Transfer/Point of Sale (EFT/POS) system, and is responsible for the Eurocheque system, 'Bancomat' and Eurocard (Switzerland) SA, the Swiss banks' credit card organisation. SEGA is the Swiss securities clearing house (see ¶1148). Swiss banks are major users of the electronic banking communications system maintained by the Society for Worldwide Interbank Financial Telecommunication (SWIFT).

In addition to the Swiss Bankers Association, banks have entered into various further associations, such as associations of cantonal banks, Swiss regional banks, Swiss private banks, foreign banks in Switzerland, Swiss commercial and investment banks, and Swiss holding and finance companies.

The stock exchanges have formed the Association of Swiss Exchanges (see ¶1109).

BANKS AND OTHER MARKET PARTICIPANTS

¶1113   Universal banking

Switzerland has a universal banking system. Banks engage in all types of banking activities, such as acceptance of deposits, extension of loans, payment transactions, dealing in securities, precious metals and foreign exchange, portfolio management, custody and deposit services, and underwriting. The criteria commonly used to categorise banks are size, geographical scope of activities, Swiss or foreign control, tradition and special legal status. The structure of the Swiss banking community as of 1989 may be summarised as shown in Table 11.1.

Table 11.1: Structure of the Swiss banking community 1989

Type of bank	Number of banks	Total assets in million SFr	Number of employees
Cantonal banks	29	195,173	17,995
Big banks	5	509,713	62,875
Regional and savings banks	210	88,607	8,369
Loan associations	2	31,225	3,027
Consumer credit banks	11	5,560	1,449
Other banks:			
Swiss-controlled	80	50,312	10,392
foreign-controlled	118	97,756	15,174
Bank-like finance companies:			
Swiss-controlled	27	2,553	177
foreign-controlled	110	22,527	1,777
Branches of foreign banks	17	27,432	2,135
Private banks	22	5,624	2,658
Total	631	1,036,482	126,028

(1) Cantonal banks
Each canton has at least one cantonal bank (*banque cantonale/ Kantonalbank*) which is usually a public institution created by cantonal law whose liabilities are guaranteed by the respective canton. Cantonal banks traditionally serve the needs and demands of the canton and its population. Their main activities are the acceptance of savings, the granting of secured commercial or mortgage loans, and banking services for the canton. Only recently, cantonal banks have begun to expand their activities into areas such as foreign transactions, investment advice and portfolio management. Since they are supervised by the cantons, they are, to a large extent, exempt from the provisions of the Banking Statute. With the extension of their activities, the Federal Banking Commission has lately been trying to gain more regulatory and supervisory powers over the cantonal banks. See also ¶1104(2).

(2) Big banks
The big banks are, in order of total amount of assets:

- Union Bank of Switzerland (*Union de Banques Suisses*, UBS/ *Schweizerische Bankgesellschaft*, SBG),

- Swiss Bank Corporation (*Société de Banque Suisse*, SBS/*Schweizerischer Bankverein*, SBV),
- Credit Suisse (*Crédit Suisse*, CS/*Schweizerische Kreditanstalt*, SKA),
- Swiss Volksbank (*Banque Populaire Suisse*, BPS/*Schweizerische Volksbank*, SVB), and
- Bank Leu (*Banque Leu/Bank Leu*).

Since 1990, Credit Suisse and Bank Leu have been controlled by CS Holding.

The big banks are true universal banks and are the main players in domestic and international banking. In 1989, their foreign assets amounted to SFr 242,273,000, or the equivalent of approximately two-thirds of the aggregate foreign assets of all Swiss banks of SFr 382,177,000.

(3) Regional and savings banks
This group traditionally consisted of mortgage, local and regional banks, as well as savings associations. Like the cantonal banks, they show to various degrees a trend towards more universal banking activities. Unlike some of the larger cantonal banks, regional and saving banks are stricter in the observance of traditional geographic boundaries.

(4) Loan associations
The loan associations, which are in principle legally independent entities, are organised in two major federations, namely the *Union suisse des Banques Raiffeisen/Schweizer Verband der Raiffeisenbanken* and the *Fédération vaudoise des caisses de crédit mutuel*. The loan associations are usually organised in the form of co-operatives and are spread in small communities all over Switzerland. They accept deposits from non-members, but loans and credits are available only to members of the co-operative and only against security. Measured not by business volume but by the social importance of the services rendered, loan associations are the main pillars of the Swiss banking system. In 1989, 1,229 loan associations were members of either of the two above-mentioned federations.

(5) Other banks
This category includes all banks which do not fall into another category. Other banks can be banks whose shares are listed on stock exchanges or whose equity is privately held. They can be universal banks or banks specialising in particular banking services, the most important of which are commercial banking services, stock exchange transactions, investment advice and portfolio management. This category includes all Swiss subsidiaries of foreign banks to which a Swiss banking licence has been granted.

¶1113

The consumer credit banks form a sub-category.

(6) Bank-like finance companies
This category consists mainly of foreign bank-like finance companies. Bank-like finance companies are subject only to Arts 7 and 8 of the Banking Statute (reporting and notification obligations to the National Bank) and are not allowed to accept, or even recommend themselves publicly for the acceptance of, deposits. They finance themselves entirely from shareholders' funds and bank loans. The vast majority of bank-like finance companies are subsidiaries of foreign banks and brokers; they primarily engage in the underwriting business and act as securities dealers. Further, they have started to enter other traditional banking fields, such as acting as intermediaries in corporate financing and offering asset management services.

As of 1 January 1990, the Banking Ordinance was amended in order fully to submit certain types of bank-like finance companies, in particular all underwriters, to the Banking Statute (see also ¶1114). The bank-like finance companies affected by the amendment have until the end of 1992 to obtain a banking licence.

(7) Branches of foreign banks
A number of foreign banks maintain a branch in Switzerland instead of a subsidiary. Some foreign banks have both a Swiss subsidiary and a branch.

(8) Private banks
The private banks represent the roots of banking in Switzerland. Their establishment goes back to the eighteenth century. Despite their small business volume, private banks still have a major potential for influence in the Swiss banking community. Private banks are organised as partnerships, with personal liability extending to all private assets of the partners. Their main activities are asset management and underwriting, and their client base predominantly consists of private individuals. If they do not publicly recommend themselves for the acceptance of deposits, they are exempt from some of the provisions of the Banking Statute.

¶1114   Banks in general

Article 1 of the Banking Statute subjects banks, including private banks and savings banks, to the statute. It further provides that credit banks with waiting periods (*caisses de crédit à terme différé/Kreditkassen mit Wartezeit*), as well as finance companies and individual proprietorships which publicly solicit customer deposits, are considered banks. Securities dealers and portfolio managers who do not engage in regular banking business are expressly exempted from the Banking Statute. Since the Banking Statute does not positively define what a bank is, the concrete details have been left to the Federal Banking Commission and the Federal Supreme Court, which reviews ordinances and individual decisions of the Federal Banking Commission. In practice, institutions which are engaged in traditional banking business are considered banks. In line with the main purpose of the Banking Statute, namely the protection of bank creditors, much emphasis was put in the past on the activities reflected on the asset side of the balance sheet. The characteristic of a bank was that its profits had to stem from the difference in interest rates for loans and deposits. Accordingly, until the end of 1989, institutions were considered banks only if they accepted deposits and granted loans and credits.

Since interest-indifferent banking activities such as underwriting, dealing in securities, investment advice, portfolio management and investment banking have recently become a more and more important part of the banking business, and since these activities are increasingly performed by institutions other than banks, the Swiss banking regulators reconsidered the traditional definition of a bank. At the suggestion of the Federal Banking Commission, the Federal Government amended the Banking Ordinance as of 1 January 1990, and extended the Banking Statute's scope of application. Its new Art. 2a defines banks as institutions whose main area of activity is financing business. More particularly, banks are institutions which:

(1) for their own account, publicly solicit customer deposits or substantially refinance themselves with banks which are not major shareholders in order to provide financing to an undefined number of persons or enterprises (Art. 2a(a) and (b)); or

(2) underwrite securities or other unsecured rights with the same function (*droits-valeurs/Wertrechte*) on a firm commitment or commission basis, and publicly offer them on the primary market (issuing houses) (Art. 2a(c)).

In addition, the amendment of the Banking Ordinance clarified the definition of public solicitation for the acceptance of deposits. According to its Art. 3, public solicitation exists if deposits are regularly accepted from 20 creditors who are neither banks nor closely related to the accepting institutions. The practical consequence of this change is to subject to the Banking Statute large financial intermediaries and those bank-like finance companies which act as underwriters. The institutions affected must obtain a full banking licence by the end of 1992.

Certain categories of banks are exempt to various degrees from the provisions of the Banking Statute. Exemptions apply to the National Bank, central mortgage bond institutions (*centrales d'émission de lettres de gage/Pfandbriefzentrale*), cantonal banks and private banks. The Bank for International Settlements, whose registered office is in Basel, is fully exempt.

¶1114

¶1115   Licence, incorporation and organisation of a bank

Before a bank can start operating in Switzerland, it must obtain a banking licence from the Federal Banking Commission. Before a licence is granted, a bank cannot be entered in the Register of Commerce. The licence is granted if (Art. 3(2) Banking Statute):

(1) the bank precisely defines the scope of its business in the Articles of Incorporation, by-laws and regulations and provides for an internal organisation that is adequate for its business, including the creation and definition of duties of separate bodies for supervision, management and control;

(2) the bank maintains the fully paid-in minimum capital required by law (presently SFr 2 million); and

(3) the individual members of the board of directors and the managers (a majority of whom must be Swiss residents) enjoy a good reputation and assure proper business conduct.

A bank has a constant obligation to notify the Federal Banking Commission of all amendments to its Articles of Incorporation, by-laws and internal regulations in so far as they change its business purpose, scope of operations (including the opening of branch offices in Switzerland and abroad), capital, or internal organisation (Art. 3(3) Banking Statute). The auditors of a bank are charged with safeguarding the continuous observance of the conditions for obtaining a bank licence. The Federal Banking Commission has the power to revoke the licence if the conditions are no longer met or if the bank is in gross breach of its legal obligations (Art. $23^{quinquies}$ Banking Statute).

Although a bank theoretically has a choice as to the legal form of its business organisation, the usual form is that of a share corporation. The minimum capital of SFr 2 million has become a theoretical number because it will make the regulators and the public suspicious and will deeply cut into the bank's lending limits. The bank is subject to the legal provisions applicable to share corporations in general. Furthermore, it must observe the binding organisational guide-lines of the Banking Statute (Art. 3(2)(a)) and the Banking Ordinance (Arts 7 to 10). In its Articles of Incorporation, by-laws, or internal regulations, the bank must define its business, showing the nature of its principal activities in clear detail. The regular activities and the geographical scope of the bank's business must be expressly listed. The scope of business in terms of operations and geographical reach must correspond to the bank's financial resources and internal organisation. The bank must adopt an internal business regulation which clearly states the decision-making procedure and the powers and duties of the management and the board of directors. For high risk business activities such as lending, foreign currency and stock exchange transactions, separate internal regulations must be drafted. Larger institutions must provide for a strict separation between the board of directors, whose duties are supervision, control and making the principal decisions, and management, which is in charge of the day-to-day operations and decisions. The practice of the Federal Banking Commission also requires larger institutions to maintain an internal control organisation.

Only banks which have obtained a banking licence are allowed to use the term 'bank' or 'banker' in the corporate name, in advertising, etc. In addition, Art. 4^{quater} of the Banking Statute states that banks must abstain throughout the world from misleading publicity, or from taking undue advantage of their Swiss domicile or of Swiss traditional practices or institutions.

¶1116   Equity and liquidity requirements – lending limits

(1)   Equity and liquidity requirements

In order to ensure permanent solvency, banks must maintain an adequate relationship between (a) their equity and their total liabilities, and (b) their liquid and marketable assets on the one hand and their short-term liabilities on the other (Art. 4(1) Banking Statute).

These principles are spelled out – taking into account the scope of business and type of bank – in the Banking Ordinance, which defines 'equity', 'liquid and marketable assets' and 'short-term liabilities' in detail and sets exact equity/liabilities and liquidity ratios (Arts 11 to 19 Banking Ordinance). The banks must constantly fulfil the equity and liquidity requirements. Liquidity statements must be regularly filed with the Federal Banking Commission.

The present provisions are the result of a revision of the Banking Ordinance as of 1 January 1990. The purpose of the revision was to adapt the Swiss rules to the recommendations of the Bank for International Settlements' Basel Committee on Banking Supervision and the corresponding Council Directive of the European Community No. 89/647 on the solvency ratio for credit institutions. On the one hand, the revisions relaxed the extremely strict Swiss provisions in order to strengthen Swiss banks' international competitiveness; on the other hand, the revisions submitted certain new financial instruments, which do not affect the banks' balance sheets, to the equity requirements. The new rules remain considerably stricter than the common international standard and the minimum standard as defined by the Basel Committee and the European Community's directive. The Swiss banks' actual equity/liabilities and liquidity ratios considerably exceed those required by law and make them the world's leaders in this respect.

Regarding holding companies, see ¶1118.

(2) Lending limits

To ensure diversification of risk, Art. 4 of the Banking Statute states that loans granted to any single customer and an investment in any single undertaking must bear an appropriate relationship to the bank's equity. Again, the principle is laid down in the Banking Ordinance (Art. 21), which gives special consideration to loans to public authorities and the nature of the existing security. It further provides that a bank must report to the Federal Banking Commission if the total liability of a single customer or an investment in a single undertaking exceeds a certain percentage (which depends on the type of customer and liability or investment) of its equity.

Article 4ter of the Banking Statute states that loans to related parties, including members of the board of directors, managers and controlling shareholders, may be granted only in line with generally accepted principles of banking.

(3) Reserve allocation

Article 5 of the Banking Statute provides for an allocation of profits to legal reserves which generally conforms to the reserve provisions applicable to share corporations under the Code of Obligations, but differs in some details.

¶1117 Accounting and auditing – reporting and publication

(1) Accounting and auditing

First, the provisions of Art. 620 et seq. CO are applicable to banks if they are organised as share corporations. Secondly, the Banking Statute provides additional accounting and auditing rules. With respect to accounting, the Banking Statute and the Banking Ordinance prescribe in detail the format to be followed for banks' annual financial statements and interim balance sheets.

Traditionally, banks took advantage of a system that allowed undisclosed reserves to be created or reduced liberally (for undisclosed reserves in general, see ¶801). In 1990, however, the Federal Banking Commission introduced new rules which substantially limit the possibility of creating undisclosed reserves. In particular, they forbid the creation of undisclosed reserves by reducing income positions or increasing expenses. Furthermore, the new rules require banks to disclose any material reduction of undisclosed reserves in their financial statements.

Article 8 of the Banking Statute provides that banks must appoint a special independent, external bank auditor in addition to the statutory auditor required by corporate law. Auditing firms that perform bank audits must be recognised by the Federal Banking Commission. The conditions for recognition are independence, high professional standing of the individuals conducting the audit and an adequate business organisation.

In 1990, 21 auditing firms were recognised by the Federal Banking Commission; all of them are well-established and highly recognised Swiss and international auditing firms. Bank auditors can act as the bank's statutory auditors.

The responsibilities and duties of the bank auditors reach far beyond those of the statutory auditors. Apart from auditing and reporting on the banks' annual and interim financial statements, bank auditors must ensure that the banks comply with all relevant legal provisions. Article 43 et seq. of the Banking Ordinance list several dozen items on which the auditors must express an opinion in their report. Bank auditors may carry out on-the-spot examinations. In order to enable their auditors to perform their duties, banks are obliged to give them access to all relevant information. The bank auditors also have the right to request adequate corrective measures from the bank if they discover irregularities. In the case of non-compliance by a bank, the bank auditors must report to the Federal Banking Commission. Events which jeopardise the security of the bank or constitute serious legal violations must be reported immediately to the Federal Banking Commission.

(2) Reporting and publication requirements

The main reporting requirements of banks and bank auditors are:

(a) submission of the statutory auditors' report to the shareholders;

(b) submission of the bank auditors' report to the board of directors, statutory auditors and the Federal Banking Commission;

(c) upon the request of the Federal Banking Commission, submission by banks and bank auditors of any information that the Commission deems necessary;

(d) submission of annual and interim financial statements and any other necessary information to the National Bank.

Banks are required to publish financial statements and additional information within four months of the end of their business year in the Official Journal of Commerce. Interim balance sheets must be published semi-annually by banks with total assets of SFr 50 million or more, and quarterly by those with assets which exceed SFr 200 million.

¶1118 Holding structure, permanent investments

There are no restrictions on banks acquiring investments in companies in or outside the banking and finance sector. The accounts of directly or indirectly controlled subsidiaries (Swiss or foreign) engaged in the banking, finance or real estate business must be consolidated. A bank must meet the equity requirements on the basis of both the unconsolidated and consolidated financial statements

(Art. 12(2) Banking Ordinance). The book value of permanent investments in companies subject to the consolidation requirement must be financed by equity at the rate of 100 per cent; non-consolidated permanent investments in companies are subject to 40 per cent equity financing (Arts 13(1)(a)(9) and (11)).

If a bank is a subsidiary of a group of companies, the bank must submit to the Federal Banking Commission consolidated accounts which prove that the ultimate holding company (which is not subject to the Banking Statute) complies with the equity requirements of the Banking Statute (*Crédit Suisse and CS Holding* v *Federal Banking Commission*, ATF 116 Ib 331).

In order to obtain a banking licence, subsidiaries of foreign banking groups must confirm to the Federal Banking Commission that the parent bank is supervised by its home authorities on a consolidated basis that includes the Swiss subsidiary. Further conditions are imposed on a case-by-case basis by the Federal Banking Commission if the Swiss bank is a subsidiary of an investment banking group (e.g., a subsidiary of a United States broker-dealer subject to Securities and Exchange Commission supervision) which is not subject to supervision equivalent to that of the Federal Banking Commission.

¶1119   Irreproachable business conduct

Article 3(2)(c) of the Banking Statute requires (as a condition of retaining a banking licence) that the persons charged with the administration and management of a bank assure the proper conduct of business operations (*présente toute garantie d'une activité irréprochable/Gewähr für eine einwandfreie Geschäftstätigkeit bieten*). The application of this provision is a major means by which the Federal Banking Commission supervises banks.

Irreproachable business conduct must be assured both by the bank and by each person who exercises functions in a managerial position and whose conduct might jeopardise the security of the bank. Irreproachable business conduct must be assured continuously; it also extends to the administration and management of banking subsidiaries.

Under the practice of the Federal Banking Commission, banks must be run by capable professionals with reliable characters. Among other things, criminal acts and breaches of external supervisory or internal regulations are irreconcilable with irreproachable business conduct.

The main obligations imposed on banks under Art. 3(2)(c) of the Banking Statute are:

(1) the duty to inquire into the economic background of a transaction if there are indications that the transaction may be part of an illegal or improper scheme, or if it is an extremely complicated, unusual or important transaction;

(2) the duty to abide by the law;

(3) the duty to ascertain the identity of customers and beneficial owners of assets on deposit; and

(4) the duty to abstain from participating in money laundering transactions.

The usual sanction against individuals who do not guarantee irreproachable business conduct is an order by the Federal Banking Commission requiring the bank to dismiss the individuals. In addition, these individuals will be prohibited from taking up management positions in another bank. Against the bank as an institution, the Federal Banking Commission may impose the sanctions available to it under the Banking Statute, including withdrawal of the banking licence.

¶1120   Civil and criminal liability

Article 38 et seq. of the Banking Statute contain a detailed set of provisions on the civil liability of banks and individuals who act for banks, and on the criminal penalties for breaches of the provisions of the Banking Statute.

¶1121   Foreign-controlled banks – branches of foreign banks

Foreign-controlled banks, whether subsidiaries of foreign banks or not, are fully subject to and must fully comply with the Banking Statute. Banks are deemed foreign-controlled if foreigners, directly or indirectly, own more than 50 per cent of the share capital or the voting rights, or if they otherwise have a dominant influence. Legal entities controlled by foreign individuals, and individuals who are neither Swiss citizens nor have a permit for permanent residence in Switzerland, are deemed foreigners.

Articles 3bis and 3ter of the Banking Statute impose additional conditions on foreign-controlled entities that wish to obtain a banking licence. The most important requirement for the permit is reciprocity. A licence will be granted only if the home country of the controlling persons or entities allows the establishment and the operation of a Swiss-controlled bank under conditions comparable to those under which foreign banks in Switzerland are allowed to operate. In 1990, the Federal Banking Commission recognised reciprocity, sometimes with limitations, for the following countries:

- Austria,
- Belgium,
- Canada,
- Denmark,
- Finland,

- France,
- Germany,
- Greece,
- Hong Kong,
- Ireland,
- Israel,
- Italy,
- Japan,
- Luxembourg,
- the Netherlands,
- New Zealand,
- Norway,
- Portugal,
- Spain,
- Sweden,
- the United Kingdom, and
- the states of California, Colorado, Connecticut, Florida, Illinois, Indiana, Massachusetts, New York, Ohio, Pennsylvania, Texas and Wisconsin.

In addition, the name of the foreign-controlled bank must in no way indicate or suggest that it is Swiss-controlled, and the bank must represent to the National Bank that it will conform to Switzerland's credit and monetary policies. Foreign-controlled banks also have a duty to inform the National Bank of the nature of their business activities and relations with other countries.

A special licence for foreign-controlled banks is required if a bank is newly incorporated or if an existing bank becomes foreign-controlled. In addition, each change of control through acquisition by foreigners from foreigners is subject to approval by the Federal Banking Commission.

The Federal Banking Commission has defined the conditions for the opening of Swiss branches by foreign banks in the Ordinance on Foreign Banks. Foreign banks that open a branch or a representative office in Switzerland need a licence from the Federal Banking Commission; the reciprocity requirement also applies to branches. In addition, unless otherwise stated in the Ordinance on Foreign Banks, the Banking Statute applies to foreign branches by analogy, except for the equity and liquidity requirements. The Ordinance on Foreign Banks contains special provisions for foreign branches on such topics as reports to the Federal Banking Commission, assets to be held in Switzerland, deposit of security, and annual financial statements and their publication and auditing. Instead of equity, branches of foreign banks must hold at least 10 per cent of the branch's assets in Switzerland.

¶1122   Finance companies

With the subjection of most bank-like finance companies to the Banking Statute, finance companies, whether bank-like or not, have lost their practical importance (see ¶1113(6) and ¶1114). Finance companies that recommend themselves for the acceptance of deposits have always been deemed banks under the Banking Statute. In 1989, only four such companies were operating in Switzerland. Industrial and commercial finance companies without bank-like operations remain outside of the scope of the Banking Statute. This group mainly consists of companies which engage in group financing.

¶1123   Securities dealers

Securities dealers who only trade in securities and engage in transactions directly related thereto, are not banks in the sense of the Banking Statute as long as they do not engage in regular banking business. Since most Swiss securities dealers are banks, the community of professional securities dealers mainly consists of subsidiaries and branches of foreign brokerage houses. Securities dealers as such are unregulated, except for the cantons of Zurich, Basel and Geneva, where they need a cantonal licence for floor and over-the-counter trading.

Under the Statute on Professional Dealings in Securities of the Canton of Zurich, a licence is granted only to individuals or corporations of good standing and reputation who possess the necessary specialist knowledge. If the licence is granted to a company, it must appoint a representative who will be subject to the law in addition to the company itself. Licences are granted only to individuals or companies resident in the canton or having a business domicile there. Licences are issued to dealers admitted to the floor (A-licence) or to over-the-counter dealers (B-licence). A person who deals in securities without a licence is subject to criminal sanctions.

Professional securities dealers must register with the Federal Tax Administration as taxpayers for the securities transfer stamp tax; branches of foreign brokers which merely act as forwarding agents for their foreign home offices are exempt (see ¶1009(3)).

It is expected that the proposed federal securities legislation will provide for federal regulation and supervision of securities dealers.

¶1124   Portfolio managers

Portfolio managers as such are unregulated, and do not fall under the Banking Statute as long as they merely administer their clients' funds and do not conduct a banking business. Portfolio or asset management has been traditionally a very important part of Switzerland's financial services business. This is due to high expertise, stable economic conditions and the bank secrecy. The variety of institutions and individuals who compete in the portfolio management business include banks, professional securities dealers, trust companies, corporate and individual portfolio managers and lawyers. However, in recent years the portfolio management business has also attracted market participants and moneys of sometimes dubious quality and reputation. To prevent a misuse of the very liberal market framework to the detriment of the international standing of the financial market, provisions to regulate certain aspects of portfolio management have been enacted or are under consideration. One is the Due Diligence Convention among the Swiss banks, under which Swiss banks must identify the beneficial owner of assets held (see ¶1142). Further, criminal provisions against money laundering have been enacted (see ¶1141). In addition, the Federal Government has appointed an expert commission to propose federal regulation for all as yet unregulated financial services areas.

The Swiss Bankers Association (¶1110) has adopted guide-lines for the exercise of asset management mandates by banks. They provide, *inter alia*, that a portfolio management mandate may be entrusted to a bank only in writing, that the bank must have a sufficient organisation to exercise the mandate and that the mandate is limited to the usual banking transactions, such as the sale and purchase of securities and precious metals and fixed-term deposits in savings and current accounts. Other transactions may be entered into only on the basis of a written order by the customer. Investments must be chosen by the bank only on sufficiently reliable information, and the bank must avoid concentrating on only a few investments. Although the guide-lines are binding neither on the members of the Swiss Bankers Association nor on non-banks active in portfolio management, they represent the generally accepted standard which a portfolio manager in Switzerland must live up to. If a customer brings suit against a portfolio manager for breach of contract, a court will take the guide-lines as a measure for the care and diligence to be observed by portfolio managers in general.

BANKING CONTRACTS AND RELATIONS WITH CUSTOMERS

¶1125   Freedom of contract – standard contracts

The relations between banks and customers are a matter of private law (for the distinction between private and public law, see ¶107). Within the boundaries of the law, banks and customers are free to agree on the terms of their contractual relationship. Except for express mandatory provisions, the Civil Code and the Code of Obligations apply only subsidiarily. In practice, there is not much room for contract negotiations by a customer with a bank. Banking contracts are highly standardised in standard contract forms and general conditions. In addition, banks are sometimes bound by non-negotiable terms and conditions fixed in the conventions of the Swiss Bankers Association.

Three banking policy issues have a practical impact on banking contracts. The banks have a contractual obligation to preserve bank secrecy (see ¶1135 to ¶1138). The criminal provisions on money laundering and the Due Diligence Convention impose upon the banks a duty to ascertain the beneficial owner of the deposited funds (see ¶1141 and ¶1142).

¶1126   Opening an account – general conditions

For the most common banking contracts, such as account opening contracts, safe deposit contracts or pledges, the banks use standard forms which regulate the rights and obligations of the parties in detail. Their main objective is to establish a clear contractual basis between the parties; protection of the banks against losses and exclusion of liability are the second most important feature.

The account opening forms state who is contracting with the bank, who is empowered to sign (i.e., to dispose of the account), and whether powers of attorney (if any) remain valid after the death of the account holder. For commercial accounts, they specify the power of individuals to sign on behalf of the corporate account-holder.

When entering into a contractual relationship with a bank, customers are regularly asked to acknowledge in writing that they accept the bank's general conditions. The general conditions specify the principal rules which apply to all contractual relations between the customer and the bank. The most important topics covered by the general conditions are signing powers and their verification, set-off, pledge, waiver of liability, handling of customer complaints, termination of the contractual relationship, change of general conditions, applicable law and jurisdiction. All standard forms provide that Swiss law shall be applicable and subject the customer to the non-exclusive jurisdiction of the courts at the bank's registered office (for the legal issues arising from general conditions, see ¶208).

Article 100(1) CO provides that a party to a contract cannot waive claims arising from the intentional conduct or gross negligence of the other party. Whether banks can contractually exclude liability for simple negligence is in dispute. The exclusion was traditionally upheld by the Federal Supreme Court. However, the recent practice of the Federal Supreme Court is to submit banks to Art. 100(2) CO, which provides that waivers of claims for simple negligence are null and void if the liability arises out of a licensed business (ATF 112 II 454).

¶1126

¶1127   Deposits

(1)   Savings accounts

Banks offer a variety of savings accounts. They differ mainly with respect to the time limits and maximum amounts for withdrawals. Some accounts are available only to certain groups (e.g., junior and retired savings accounts) or serve a special purpose (salary accounts, savings for a house, old-age provision). Although savings are short-term moneys, they have high economic stability and are mostly used by banks for long-term financing. Interest rates vary according to market conditions. Savings are not ensured. In the case of bankruptcy, claims arising from savings accounts are privileged over other claims in the amount of SFr 10,000 per customer (Art. 15 Banking Statute). In addition, the banks have agreed in Convention XXIII of the Swiss Bankers Association to pay out up to SFr 30,000 per customer if a bank goes bankrupt, subject to final accounting on the basis of the liquidation proceeds. Savings on deposit with cantonal banks are guaranteed by the respective cantons.

(2)   Current accounts

Current accounts are mainly used for business purposes, in order to make and receive payments and deposit cash surpluses *in conto corrente*. They are often coupled with the extension of an overdraft facility by the bank to the customer. Periodically, the balance is drawn and, if acknowledged by the parties, results in a novation of the individual entries, i.e., only the existing balance remains due between the parties (Art. 117(2) CO).

(3) Fixed-term deposits

Fixed-term deposits (*dépots à terme/Festgeldanlagen*) have a term between a few days and a year. The banks have set the minimum limit for the acceptance of fixed-term deposits at SFr 100,000 (with a recent tendency to go down to SFr 50,000) for terms between three months and one year, and at SFr 500,000 to 1 million for shorter terms. Interest is higher than on savings accounts, and a growing consciousness of interest rates by customers, and the availability of high cash surpluses on the part of customers, has created a strong trend to shift deposits from savings accounts to fixed-term deposits. Fixed-term deposits are used by banks in interbank transactions and the commercial loan business.

Like all interest on customer deposits with Swiss banks, interest on fixed-term deposits is subject to the 35 per cent federal anticipatory tax (see ¶1007). The tax is not levied if fixed-term deposits are placed in the Euromarket; this is done by banks on a fiduciary basis in their own name but for the account and risk of the customer. In contrast to domestic fixed-term deposits, banks charge a commission for fiduciary deposits on the Euromarket.

(4)   Medium-term notes

Medium-term notes (*certificats de dépôt/Kassaobligationen*) are bank securities issued over the counter on demand of customers on a day-to-day basis. Their term is between three and eight years with typical denominations of SFr 1,000, 5,000, 10,000, 50,000 and 100,000. Interest is paid yearly. The interest rate for newly issued medium-term notes is periodically adjusted according to market conditions. They bear a higher yield than savings accounts, and it is customary to transfer savings which are not needed on a short-term basis into medium-term notes. The proceeds from medium-term notes are the main source from which banks grant mortgages.

(5)   Money market

There is a domestic interbank money market in which selected non-banking institutions can participate. The available instruments include demand funds, day-to-day and call money, and time deposits. In addition, the major banks are active participants in the Euromoney market.

Money market papers are subject to the federal securities transfer stamp tax (see ¶1009), which prevents the evolution of a regular market. It is proposed to abolish this tax (see ¶1002(6)). As a substitute, the banks initiated a market for money market book claims (*créances comptables à court terme/Geldmarktbuchforderungen*). Initially, money market book claims were issued only by the Confederation, and no secondary market existed. Now, however, the instrument is more widely used by domestic and foreign issuers, offered to the public and traded in a secondary market. For private investors, money market book claims are an alternative to fixed-term deposits.

(6)   Interest on deposits

As of July 1991, a major bank paid the following rates of interest:

- Savings accounts: 5.25%
- Current accounts: 0.25%
- Fixed-term deposits: 7.375%
- Medium-term notes: 6.5%

¶1128   Business loans and consumer credit

(1)   Types of loans

Various types of loans are available from banks. Loans can be distinguished as short- or long-term, secured or unsecured, commercial or private, or by the use of loan proceeds (e.g., export financing, consumer credit). The following description is not exhaustive. For mortgage loans see ¶1129.

(a) Overdraft facilities on current accounts

Overdraft facilities are usually granted without security if the volume of the customer's business enables the bank to monitor his or her financial situation. They are convenient for customers, who can borrow only what they need at the moment. Interest is calculated only on the used overdraft portion. Overdraft facilities are demand loans. The banks' standard form contracts state that they can be called at any time.

(b) Fixed-term loans

Fixed-term loans are typically evidenced by a loan agreement in which the borrower acknowledges receipt of the loan proceeds and undertakes to repay the loan plus interest in accordance with the terms agreed upon with the bank. The range of fixed-term loans encompasses everything from small advances to individuals for private purposes to multimillion syndicated loan facilities. Fixed-term loans are extended unsecured or secured, depending on the individual circumstances.

(c) Discount credits

Discount credits are an important type of commercial loan. The bank grants advances against transfers of bills of exchange or similar securities after subtracting an interest discount for the remaining term. Banks can rediscount papers of first-rate quality with the National Bank. This possibility, plus the fact that discount credits are short-term and have a high degree of security, accounts for the importance of this instrument.

(d) Export loans

Loans for the financing of the export of goods are granted either to the exporter or the foreign importer. If the foreign importer is the borrower, the exporter is usually required to guarantee repayment of the loan as a joint and several debtor. Export loans can be covered by the Federal Government's export risk guarantee (*garantie de risque à l'exportation/Exportrisikogarantie*), which insures the political and transfer risk (commercial risk only for public institutions that act as importers or guarantors), and, upon motion of the exporter, the fabrication risk. The foreign exchange risk is not insurable.

The remaining uninsured risks are split between the bank and the exporter. The exporter takes the commercial risks and the uninsured political and transfer risks for the principal; the bank bears the uninsured political and transfer risk on the interest, and the commercial risks only if the importer is a first-rate debtor or if a first-rate foreign bank guarantee is available. Foreign exchange risks must be hedged by the exporter.

¶1128

(e) Consumer credits

Consumer credits are relatively small loans granted to private persons for the purchase of consumer goods. They are repayable in regular monthly instalments. Consumer credits have a fixed interest rate and a fixed term between six and 48 months. They are usually granted against insufficient security; this is reflected in high interest rates. None the less, losses have in the past been very low, and accordingly, consumer credits are a very profitable retail banking business.

(2) Security

Except for mortgages on real estate, the following types of security are most commonly used by banks to secure loans:

- pledge of realisable securities (the condition for perfection is delivery of possession to the bank),
- pledge of life insurance policies,
- pledge of trade goods if represented by bills of lading and other documents of title (otherwise uncommon because of the practical difficulty of transferring possession of the goods to the bank),
- assignment of receivables, and
- personal suretyships (*cautionnement/Bürgschaft*) and guarantees (*garantie/Garantie*). See ¶216 and ¶902.

(3) Interest charged

As of July 1991, a major Swiss bank charged the following rates of interest, depending on the security furnished:

- Overdraft facilities: 8.5 to 9.5%
- Fixed-term loans: 9 to 9.5%
- Discount credits: 9.25%
- Export loans: 8.5 to 9.75%
- Consumer credits:14 to 16%

¶1129 Mortgage loans

Loans may be secured by real estate in the form of mortgages (*hypothèque/ Grundpfandverschreibung*) or mortgage notes (*cédule hypothécaire/Schuldbrief*) (see ¶904(2)and ¶704(5)). Mortgage loans are granted independently of the purpose of the loan. The loan may be used to acquire real estate, to finance construction or to mobilise the value of real property. Mortgages are claims *in rem* and can therefore be enforced against whoever owns the real estate, regardless of any personal obligation of the owner. Mortgage notes are negotiable instruments issued to name or bearer and may be transferred and pledged.

With certain exceptions, mortgages and mortgage notes become effective only upon entry in the land register (see ¶1706). They rank in priority according to the designation in the land register. While mortgages were traditionally granted with fixed interest rates, flexible interest rates have recently become more common. The interest rates are influenced by rank of priority.

Switzerland has the highest mortgage indebtedness level in the world. Accordingly, mortgages and mortgage interest rates are of extraordinary importance to Swiss banks and the Swiss economy. Because of the social consequences which high mortgage interest rates can have, they are a major political issue.

As of July 1991, a major Swiss bank charged 8.25 per cent for granting a mortgage with first-rank priority.

¶1130   Payment transactions

The predominant method of making payments is by money transfer order (*ordre de paiement/Zahlungsauftrag*). The customer instructs the bank to pay to the credit of a third person's bank account, with the same or another bank, or to a third person's postal account, a certain amount to the debit of the customer's own account. Payments are settled between banks either through giro accounts with the National Bank or through the Swiss Interbank Clearing System. A further important method of payment is the postal account system, which works in interaction with bank clearing systems.

Cheque accounts as such are not known in Switzerland, although payment by Eurocheques (guaranteed up to SFr 300 per cheque) is becoming more and more important, especially because Eurocheques may be denominated in any major currency. The popularity of credit cards has increased recently. None the less, payment in cash remains much more common than in other countries. EFT/POS and EC-direct (where the eurocheque card is used for a direct debit on the cardholder's account) are still in the development phase.

In commercial transactions, bank cheques (cheques issued by and drawn against a bank) and letters of credit are important means of payment.

¶1131   Commitments on order of customers

Banks regularly furnish suretyships or guarantees to third parties on the order of customers. Suretyships are accessory obligations which secure the customer's main obligation. Towards the recipient of a suretyship, the bank can invoke all the defences which are available to the main debtor. As a rule, a creditor can call on the surety only if the main debtor has failed to fulfil his or her obligations. Suretyships are used only in purely domestic transactions and are subject to strict formal requirements.

In international transactions, the provision of bank guarantees is the rule. Bank guarantees are independent obligations of the bank. Payment can be demanded irrespective of whether the obligation of the customer is due or enforceable. Bank guarantees are not codified in the Code of Obligations, and legal problems arise if the obligation entered into cannot clearly be classified as a suretyship or a guarantee. This is of practical consequence since the validity of suretyships depends on the observance of strict mandatory formal requirements (see ¶216 and ¶902). If the instrument is classified as a guarantee, it is considered under Swiss law in line with the internationally accepted practice on bank guarantees. For an example of a guarantee, see ¶902.

Banks also provide services in international sales transactions by granting documentary credits to, and making documentary collections for, customers. The banks' standard forms make documentary credits and collections expressly subject to the 'Uniform Customs and Practice for Documentary Credits' and the 'Uniform Rules for Collections' of the International Chamber of Commerce. In addition, the Federal Supreme Court has developed an extensive case law on documentary credits.

¶1132   Securities and precious metals – safekeeping

Dealing in securities includes the purchase and sale of securities and similar instruments for customers, underwriting, investment advice, and portfolio management services. Gold, silver, platinum and palladium are the precious metals traded in Switzerland. Zurich maintains one of the most important world gold markets. Although gold dealings have been dematerialised by collective safekeeping and gold certificates, half of the world's physical gold trading still goes through Zurich.

For safekeeping, collective or individual safekeeping accounts are available. The services of a bank under the safekeeping contract include the usual administrative transactions, such as the collection of dividends and interest coupons, repayments of principal, and the monitoring of calls for redemption, conversion and pre-emptive rights. Swiss securities are usually held in collective safekeeping, either in the bank's own vault or with SEGA. Foreign securities are usually deposited in the Swiss bank's name with foreign correspondent banks. For individual safekeeping accounts, the customer's securities or other valuables are physically separated from the collective safekeeping deposits.

Swiss banks also let safekeeping deposit boxes to which only the customer has access.

¶1133   Foreign exchange – swaps

The banks maintain a telephone market for foreign exchange among themselves and with customers. Transactions entered into include cash or spot transactions, fixed forward transactions, swaps and (to a limited extent) foreign exchange options.

Borrowings by foreign debtors in the capital market are regularly used for foreign currency or interest rate swaps.

¶1134 Other banking services

Other important banking services are investment banking and trust or fiduciary services.

Typically through subsidiaries or affiliates, the major banks engage in special financing techniques such as factoring, forfaiting, leasing and venture capital financing.

BANK SECRECY

¶1135 Scope of bank secrecy

Bank secrecy is protected by Art. 47 of the Banking Statute, which reads as follows:

'(1) Anyone who discloses a secret entrusted to him or her in his or her capacity as an officer, employee, mandatory, liquidator or commissioner of a bank, as a representative of the Federal Banking Commission, or as an officer or employee of a recognised auditing firm, or anyone who has become aware of a secret in this capacity, or anyone who tries to induce others to violate professional secrecy, shall be punished by a prison term not to exceed six months or by a fine not exceeding SFr 50,000.

(2) If the act has been committed by negligence, the penalty shall be a fine not exceeding SFr 30,000.

(3) The violation of professional secrecy remains punishable even after termination of the official or employment relationship or the exercise of the profession.

(4) Federal and cantonal regulations concerning the obligation to testify and to furnish information to a government authority shall apply.'

The provision was enacted in 1934 to protect the safety of the bank deposits of political refugees against the attack of the Nazi regime. It is the Swiss view that bank secrecy is necessary to ensure and protect customers' trust in the Swiss banking system.

Breach of bank secrecy is a criminal offence. A violation of Art. 47 of the Banking Statute must be prosecuted by the court *sua sponte*, independently of a complaint by the injured party.

Breach of bank secrecy constitutes a breach of contract or a tort. The contract between a bank and its customer, irrespective of its qualification or nature, includes the bank's obligation to keep confidential information which is entrusted to it during the contractual relationship. In addition, violation of bank secrecy may be a violation of personal privacy, which is protected by Art. 28 CC. Even before Art. 47 of the Banking Statute was enacted, the Federal Supreme Court consistently held that the private sphere of a person includes information relating to the person's financial affairs and personal assets. Interference with the personal sphere is a tort in the sense of Art. 41 et seq. CO. Both breach of contract and tort make a bank liable for any damage suffered by the injured party. Taxes and penalties which become payable as a result of the breach of bank secrecy do not constitute a compensatable damage (ATF 115 II 72).

Violation of bank secrecy may lead to administrative sanctions by the Federal Banking Commission (Arts 23ter and 23^{quinquies} Banking Statute). The Federal Banking Commission considers violations of bank secrecy to be improper business conduct. Possible sanctions include a warning, a request to dismiss the individual who committed the breach, and, ultimately, withdrawal of the banking licence.

¶1136 Extent of bank secrecy

All entities fully subject to the Banking Statute are bound by bank secrecy. This includes all foreign banks and all Swiss branches of foreign banks. Foreign subsidiaries or foreign branches of Swiss banks are not subject to Art. 47 of the Banking Statute. Criminal sanctions can be imposed only upon the individuals listed in Art. 47(1) of the Banking Statute (see ¶1135); the bank is liable for civil damages and is subject to administrative sanctions. Individuals remain bound by bank secrecy even after the termination of their employment.

All facts entrusted to or discovered by individuals in the exercise of their profession are protected by bank secrecy. This includes all business and contractual relations between the bank and its customers. It includes all information relating to the financial situation of the customer and the customer's relationships with other banks and third persons. Furthermore, legal writers have taken the position that information on transactions between non-customers and other banks, of which a bank learns, is protected.

The criminal nature of Art. 47 of the Banking Statute makes sense only if any breach, whether occurring in or outside Switzerland, is punishable. The question arises, however, whether it is possible as a practical matter for the Swiss authorities to prosecute breaches of bank secrecy which have been committed outside Switzerland.

¶1137   Consent of customers

Customers (which term includes all persons whose confidential information must be kept secret), as the 'masters of their secrets', can waive protection of bank secrecy. No special form is required for a waiver. It may be given explicitly (in writing or orally) or implicitly, or by agents or proxies. Waivers under compulsion, e.g., under pressure or sanctions of a foreign court or a foreign law enforcement agency, may be considered invalid.

Apart from the customer's consent, the confidentiality obligation continues only as long as the customer has a reasonable interest in the information being kept secret.

¶1138   Bank secrecy in civil and criminal proceedings

(1)   Civil litigation

(a)   Bank as a party
If a customer sues a bank, the bank cannot be expected to remain bound by bank secrecy while defending the lawsuit. A customer who insists on the bank secrecy obligation would act against the principle of dealing in good faith (*venire contra factum proprium*: Art. 2 CC).

If a bank sues a customer, it is entitled to disclose confidential information to the extent necessary to pursue the claim. However, the bank's interest in pursuing the action must outweigh the customer's confidentiality interest. This is not the case for frivolous actions or actions for insignificant amounts.

(b)   Bank officers as witnesses
Whether a bank officer must testify and produce documents as a witness in a lawsuit pending before a court depends on the respective federal or cantonal rules of procedure (Art. 47(4) Banking Statute):

- In eight cantons (including Geneva and Berne), bank officers have the right to refuse to testify.

- In 11 cantons (including Basel), bank officers have, in principle, an obligation to testify.

- The procedural rules of eight cantons (including Zurich and Ticino) and the Federal Code of Civil Procedure provide for a balancing test: the court must decide whether or not to direct the bank officer to testify after balancing the interests involved on a case-by-case basis.

However, in all cantons in which a bank oficer is or may be compelled to testify, protective measures are available in order to limit disclosure to the extent necessary to allow the court to render a just and fair decision.

(c) Foreign litigation

The exception of Art. 47(4) of the Banking Statute (see ¶1135) applies only to Swiss litigation. In litigation abroad, the bank's duty to preserve bank secrecy is absolute. In an increasingly international business environment, the conflicts of the disclosure rules of foreign jurisdictions and bank secrecy may put Swiss banks under considerable pressure. This is particularly true if a bank is a party and is required to disclose the names of customers who are not parties to the litigation. In such cases, bank secrecy may hinder banks from effectively defending their interests. United States courts have introduced a practical test in order to balance third parties' interests in disclosure and the bank's confidentiality obligation (see, e.g., *Minpeco, S.A.* v *Conticommodity Services, Inc.*, 116 FRD 517 (SDNY 1987)).

The issue is less acute if the information that a Swiss bank is called upon to disclose in foreign litigation in which it is a party or a witness can be obtained by judicial assistance in civil proceedings. Switzerland grants judicial assistance in civil proceedings on the basis of either international treaties or the principle of comity of international law (see ¶2016). If judicial assistance is granted under a treaty obligation, bank officers may, with limitations, be compelled to testify. The extent to which bank officers must testify if judicial assistance is granted as a matter of comity, is not entirely settled.

(2) Criminal proceedings

(a) In Switzerland

All codes of criminal procedure require banks to testify and produce documents in criminal prosecutions and before criminal courts. Protective measures are available if the information to be disclosed by the bank concerns third parties who are not the subject of the criminal prosecution. Bank officers have an obligation to inform the examining judge if their testimony concerns the secrets of third persons.

(b) International judicial assistance in criminal matters

In principle, when Switzerland grants judicial assistance to a foreign state in a criminal matter, banks are obliged to supply an officer as witness and produce all relevant documents. The principle is subject to various limitations which especially aim at protecting the interests of uninvolved third parties. Further, judicial assistance is granted only for acts which are considered criminal offences under Swiss law (principle of speciality). Foreign administrative and tax proceedings are, as a rule, considered non-criminal under Swiss law. Therefore, the express condition that the requesting foreign state must not make use of the information received beyond the proceeding for which judicial assistance was expressly granted, is of particular importance for information provided by Swiss banks (for further details on international judicial assistance in criminal matters, see ¶1071 and ¶1822).

(3) Foreign parent companies and foreign supervisory authorities

As a rule, confidential information protected by bank secrecy may be electronically processed abroad or disclosed to foreign parent companies or home offices, but not to foreign regulatory or supervisory banking authorities. However, the concrete application of this principle remains largely unsettled.

¶1139   Other confidentiality obligations

The disclosure of business or manufacturing secrets is punishable under Arts 162 and 273 of the Penal Code. Secrets protected under these provisions may, but need not, constitute banking secrets. However, such cases are rare.

Article 162 of the Penal Code is designed to protect private interests. It prohibits the disclosure of information which has been entrusted by one party to a contract to the other with the obligation to keep it secret.

Article 273 of the Penal Code, which outlaws economic espionage, is designed to protect Swiss economic interests at large. This provision prohibits disclosure of business or manufacturing secrets to, among others, foreign states, foreign courts, foreign administrative agencies and foreign officials. Even if the master of the secret has agreed to the release, disclosure may be punishable if the Swiss economic interest in confidentiality prevails over the interest of the disclosing party or the 'master of the secret'. This would be the case if the information would affect Swiss national security, or if its disclosure would dramatically damage the economy. Information protected by Art. 273 of the Penal Code must always have a Swiss nexus. This provision often creates difficult situations if Swiss citizens are required to disclose information to foreign authorities. As far as Swiss interests are concerned, there is no procedure by which the disclosing party could obtain a ruling from Swiss authorities that Art. 273 of the Penal Code does not apply to a given conduct.

'Chinese walls', i.e., the separation of information obtained by one banking division from the other, have only recently become a topic of discussion in Switzerland. As yet, there are no settled legal rules that apply to conflicts of interest arising from the fact that banks hold confidential information from one customer which might be of importance in rendering services to another customer. The concept of Chinese walls appears to be incompatible with the corporate law principle that the knowledge of the component bodies of a company is deemed to be the knowledge of the company as a whole. On the one hand, a bank is bound to keep information from one customer confidential towards all other customers. On the other hand, it is uncertain whether a bank would be able to convince a court that investments made for customers by the portfolio management division were proper although it did not have access to material information which was available to the investment banking division.

OTHER BANKING POLICY ISSUES

¶1140   Insider trading

Since 1 July 1988, insider trading has been a criminal offence in Switzerland. Article 161 of the Penal Code was enacted not least as Switzerland's contribution to the battle against international insider trading. It enables Switzerland to grant legal assistance to foreign states in criminal investigations against insider trading. Whether the provision will gain practical importance domestically remains to be seen.

Article 161 of the Penal Code punishes the misuse of privileged confidential information (i.e., information that is not available to the public) in stock exchange transactions in order to realise a profit or prevent a loss. The criminal offence can be committed by insiders or tippees. Insiders are members of the board of directors, managers, auditors or agents of a company or its subsidiary or parent company, members of a government agency or public servants, or auxiliaries of the defined circle of persons. A tippee is a person to whom confidential information has been directly or indirectly communicated and who is aware that the information has been disclosed unlawfully by an insider.

The insider information must be such that it will substantially influence the price of securities listed or pre-listed on a Swiss stock exchange. This is presumed if the information relates to a new issue of securities, a merger or an acquisition, or to facts of comparable effect. Case law will have to define what 'facts of similar importance likely to substantially affect the price of listed securities' are. If all the other conditions are met, Art. 161 of the Penal Code applies by analogy to confidential information relating to a co-operative or a foreign company. Insider trading is punishable only if committed intentionally. The penalty is imprisonment of up to three years for insiders and up to one year for tippees, or, alternatively, a fine.

Insider trading relating to securities which are exclusively traded over the counter is not punishable; however, insider trading transactions occurring over the counter but relating to listed securities are punishable. The rule of the Penal Code which allows courts to order the confiscation of illegal profits for the benefit of the Government or for transfer to the injured party (Arts 58 and 60 Penal Code) also applies to profits arising from illegal insider trading. In addition, the general civil remedies of contract and tort law are available.

In an exchange of letters of 10 November 1987, Switzerland agreed with the United States to grant assistance in civil or administrative proceedings of a quasi-criminal nature conducted by the Securities and Exchange Commission and related to insider trading. The new criminal provision now allows Switzerland to grant broad international legal assistance in criminal matters in insider cases.

¶1141 Money laundering

Effective 1 August 1990, two new provisions directed against money laundering were added to the Penal Code. Article 305bis of the Penal Code (money laundering) punishes any person who intentionally takes an action which is aimed at frustrating the ascertainment of the origin, the discovery, or the freezing of assets which he or she knows, or should know, were obtained in a criminal manner. The standard sanction of Art. 305bis of the Penal Code is imprisonment for up to three years or a fine up to SFr 40,000; in serious cases, the sanction is imprisonment for up to five years, together with a fine of up to SFr 1 million. A serious case occurs when the offender acts as a member of a criminal organisation or laundering group, or accumulates a large turnover or substantial profits. Under Art. 305ter of the Penal Code (insufficient care in financial transactions), any person who professionally accepts, takes on deposit, invests, or helps to transfer foreign assets, and who fails to observe the care required under the circumstances to ascertain the identity of the beneficial owner, can be punished. The provision applies irrespective of whether money laundering was committed or attempted. The sanction of Art. 305ter of the Penal Code is imprisonment for up to one year or a fine of up to SFr 40,000.

The offence of money laundering can be committed by anyone; the offence of insufficient care in financial transactions is limited to individuals engaged in rendering professional financial services. Accordingly, the provision applies not only to bank employees but also to individuals acting for bank-like finance companies, brokers, portfolio managers, trust companies and law firms. Although only individuals can commit crimes under the Penal Code, the legal entity for whom the offender is acting may still be subject to administrative sanctions. A bank whose employee has failed to observe due care in financial transactions may be punished by the Federal Banking Commission for failing to ensure continuous irreproachable business conduct (Art. 3(2)(c) Banking Statute) (see ¶1119).

Some crucial issues under Art. 305ter of the Penal Code are yet to be settled by case law. First, it is unclear whether an individual who receives assets from another individual who is subject to Art. 305ter can rely upon the transferor's observance of care, or whether the recipient must make an independent determination. Secondly, the legal term 'beneficial owner' was previously unknown to Swiss law. Contract law is based on the principle that a contractual relationship exists only between the parties who enter into a contract, and that a party to a contract may disregard any contractual obligations of the other party to third parties. The introduction of the concept of the 'beneficial owner' in criminal law may have as yet unforeseeable consequences with respect to the opportunity for third parties to bring contractual claims or for foreign governments to request legal assistance. Thirdly, the relation between the new provisions and the Due Diligence Convention (see ¶1142) is unsettled.

On an international level, the new provisions set a very high standard. They also give the authorities a basis on which to grant legal assistance in foreign money laundering investigations.

¶1142   Due Diligence Convention

In the 1970s, Swiss banks came under pressure from abroad and in Switzerland due to cases in which they were accused of assisting bank customers in the abuse of bank secrecy. In 1977, pressure from the regulatory authorities led to the conclusion of an agreement on the observance of care by banks in accepting funds and on the practice of banking secrecy (Due Diligence Convention, *Convention de diligence/Sorgfaltspflichtvereinbarung*), among the Swiss National Bank, the Swiss Bankers Association and the member banks. The present form of the Convention dates to 1 July 1987, and was entered into by the Swiss Bankers Association and its member banks without the participation of the Swiss National Bank.

The purpose of the Due Diligence Convention is to safeguard the reputation of Swiss banking and to establish rules which guarantee irreproachable business conduct with respect to the acceptance of deposits and in relation to bank secrecy.

Furthermore, it prohibits banks from actively assisting customers in capital flight in countries with currency control, or avoiding taxes by issuing incomplete or misleading statements. However, the Convention is intended neither to enforce foreign public law in Switzerland nor to change the contractual relationship between banks and customers.

The main principle stated in the Due Diligence Convention is that banks must clearly identify the parties with whom they are contracting, as well as the beneficial owners of funds (if not identical to the contracting party), when:

(1) opening an account;

(2) opening a securities deposit;

(3) entering into a fiduciary transaction;

(4) renting safe-deposit boxes; or

(5) accepting cash amounts exceeding SFr 100,000.

Exemptions exist for individuals residing in Switzerland and for Swiss and foreign banks. If there is reasonable doubt whether the party with whom the bank is contracting is the beneficial owner of the assets, or if a customer opens an account as a fiduciary, the bank must obtain a declaration in which the contracting party either acknowledges that it is the beneficial owner or, if not, identifies the beneficial owner. If the contracting party is a domiciled company (i.e., a company with no business premises and no personnel), the bank must obtain a declaration from the board of directors as to the identity of the controlling shareholder(s), irrespective of whether the company is domiciliary in Switzerland or abroad. Exemptions exist if the domiciliary company is a subsidiary of a group of companies or if the identity of the controlling shareholder(s) is known to the bank. In some very narrowly defined cases, lawyers or notaries who open an account on a fiduciary basis do not have to disclose the beneficial owner(s).

The Due Diligence Convention also applies to the opening of numbered accounts. Contrary to popular belief, it has never been possible to open a bank account in Switzerland without identifying oneself. Numbered accounts are accounts which are carried under a number or a code word rather than the name of the customer. The only purpose of numbered accounts is to increase confidentiality within the bank. The name of the customer is known only to a very limited circle of employees. The bank always knows who the customer is.

Banks are not allowed to open accounts if they do not comply with the provisions of the Due Diligence Convention. If, in the course of the contractual relationship, the bank becomes aware that a customer's conduct is not in line with the principles laid down in the Due Diligence Convention, the bank must terminate the contractual relationship.

The Due Diligence Convention is a self-regulatory instrument. Violations by banks may lead to sanctions in the form of fines, which are subject to review in arbitration. It is the Federal Banking Commission's view that the Convention sets a minimum standard to be observed by all banks, whether they have formally adhered to the Convention or not. Non-compliance with the Convention is regarded by Federal Banking Commission as improper conduct to be remedied by regulatory sanctions in accordance with Art. 23ter et seq. of the Banking Statute.

Since 1 July 1991, the Federal Banking Commission no longer accepts the use by banks of forms B1 and B2 which, in the Federal Banking Commission's

¶1142

view, are incompatible with Art. 305*ter* of the Penal Code (insufficient care in financial transactions, see ¶1141). Lawyers or notaries or members of the Swiss Trust and Auditing Association who opened an account on a fiduciary basis did not have to disclose the identity of the beneficial owner if they signed forms B1 or B2, which stated that the person opening the account knew the beneficial owner. The ruling of the Federal Banking Commission directs banks to replace existing forms B1 and B2 by 30 September 1992 with a written declaration of the contracting party identifying the beneficial owner.

Case law will have to determine whether, by complying with the Due Diligence Convention, banks exercise sufficient care in financial transactions, as defined in Art. 305*ter* of the Penal Code. If the answer is in the affirmative, the Due Diligence Convention might serve as a model for self-regulation for non-banking industry segments to which Art. 305*ter* of the Penal Code applies.

DEALING IN SECURITIES AND STOCK EXCHANGES

¶1143 Securities in general

Many types of securities are traded in Switzerland. They can be issued by companies having their domicile in Switzerland (domestic securities) or having their domicile abroad (foreign securities). The following types of securities which are commonly traded in Switzerland can be distinguished:

(1) Equity securities.

(2) Debt instruments.

(3) Warrants and other instruments.

(1) Equity securities

The most important domestic equity securities are shares (*action/Aktie*). The main rights carried by shares are the rights to vote, to receive dividends and to receive capital repayment out of liquidation proceeds. Shares are issued in either bearer or registered form. Bearer shares can be transferred by simple delivery of the share certificate. Registered shares are issued in the name of the holder and can be transferred only by endorsement on the share certificate or by delivery of the share certificate with a separate assignment. In addition, the new owner must be registered in the company's register of shareholders. The Articles of Incorporation of the share corporation provide for, and all major companies have adopted, restrictions on the transfer of registered shares. Typically, share corporations issue general rules in which they set percentage limits above which a single owner of registered shares will not be entered in the register. These restrictions are aimed in particular against foreign individuals and corporations. In addition, the board of directors usually has the right to refuse registration at its entire discretion without disclosure of a reason. Registered shares are usually voting shares, with a par value which may be up to five or even ten times smaller than that of bearer shares.

Further types of domestic equity securities are participation and dividend-right certificates (*bon de participation/Partizipationsschein*; *bon de jouissance/ Genussschein*). They are both non-voting equity securities. Participation certificates entitle the holder to a share in the profits and liquidation proceeds; under certain conditions, dividend-right certificates entitle the holder to a preferential dividend as well.

All domestic equity securities can be acquired by foreign investors. Limitations placed by share corporations on the entry of acquirers in the shareholders' register withhold the right to vote from foreign investors but do not affect the financial rights, in particular the dividend right, attached to the acquired share.

Special requirements exist for the listing of foreign equity instruments on Swiss stock exchanges (see ¶1149). Outside the stock exchanges, foreign equity securities are freely tradable.

(2) Debt instruments

Debt instruments are issued in Switzerland in public issues as bonds (*emprunt par obligations/Anleihensobligation*) and in private placements as notes. They always give the holder the right to receive interest as well as repayment of the principal. In addition to straight bonds or notes, there are convertibles (*obligation convertible/Wandelobligation*), which give the holder the right to convert the principal into equity. Bonds or notes with warrants attached give the holder the right to acquire additional equity (*emprunt à option/Optionsanleihe*). The terms for conversion or exercise of the warrants are fixed at issuance. The warrants are usually detachable and tradable separately.

(3) Warrants and other instruments

An increasingly popular instrument is the covered warrant (*option couverte/ gedeckte Option*, also *Stillhalteroption*). Covered warrants are commonly issued by a bank or a subsidiary of a banking group, and give the holder the right to acquire a predetermined number of equity securities (of a company related to the issuer) during a given period at a set price. They are called covered warrants because the issuer usually (but not necessarily) covers its exposure with warrants or shares of the target company. Recently, index, interest, currency and commodities warrants have appeared on the market. They give the holder the right (against payment of the issue price) to receive certain cash payments that are linked to the changes in the underlying index, interest or exchange rate, or commodities price. Under certain conditions, covered warrants can obtain a stock exchange listing. A telephone market is maintained by the bank that has issued or underwritten the warrants.

The exotic instruments, which have recently gained some importance in the European market, are of no practical importance in Switzerland.

Investment fund certificates, traded options and financial futures will be dealt with separately (see ¶1147 and ¶1151).

¶1144 Syndication

Until the investigation of banking practices by the Swiss Cartel Commission in 1989, the underwriting business was characterised by anti-competitive conventions. As a result of the Cartel Commission's report and recommendations, the permanent syndicate of Swiss banks for Swiss debtors from the public sector was abandoned. The permanent syndicate of the big banks for foreign bond issues has been formally abandoned: the big banks now allow foreign-controlled banks to participate in their syndicates. The mostly foreign-controlled banks and bank-like finance companies which were excluded in the past from the syndicate of the big banks now act in a permanent syndicate (*Vereinigtes Syndikat*) and are very active in *ad hoc* syndication, in particular in the field of notes and covered warrants. Entities other than banks or bank-like finance companies have a negligible role in the underwriting business.

Swiss banks, especially the big three (see ¶1113(2)), remain very strong in the underwriting business for Swiss equity and debt securities. This is due to their very high placing power and the strong ties that companies maintain with their banks.

The syndication of foreign debt instruments is strongly dominated by the Swiss big banks, and a few foreign-controlled banks and bank-like finance companies. Under the National Bank's current capital export regulations, only banks and bank-like companies in the sense of Arts 7 and 8 of the Banking Statute may participate in the underwriting of foreign debtors' Swiss Franc bond or note issues. In addition, under the change of the Banking Ordinance which became effective on 1 January 1990, all bank-like finance companies which regularly engage in underwriting will have to obtain a full banking licence by the end of 1992. In the future, the underwriting business will accordingly remain the exclusive domain of banks which have obtained a licence from the Federal Banking Commission.

Eurobond issues, i.e., the issue of bonds denominated in currencies other than Swiss Francs, are presently (except for dual currency issues) of no importance. This is due to the fact that a stamp duty on the transfer of securities is payable on the firm underwriting as well as on the placement. The abolition of this stamp duty has been voted on by the Federal Parliament and may bring back part of the Euromarket to Switzerland (see ¶1002(6)).

Since the Swiss National Bank has been able (through informal agreements) to secure the assistance of foreign central banks in enforcing the rule that only Swiss banks and bank-like finance companies may underwrite issues in Swiss Francs, there is no Euromarket for bonds or notes in Swiss Francs. The National Bank has announced that it will reconsider the syndication rule if, as a result of the contemplated stamp duty statute revision, Switzerland would again become an attractive place for Euromarket issues.

In Switzerland, firm underwriting is the main placement technique for equity capital increases of corporations and for debt securities in general. Placement on a commission basis is confined to the issuance of shares of corporations which go public. The Federal Government sells bonds by tender; this procedure is also occasionally used for other securities issues. Direct placement is used by Swiss banks for their own share and debt securities issues.

Syndicates operate either under fixed syndicate agreements in the case of permanent syndicates, or under separate syndicate agreements for each issue in the case of *ad hoc* syndicates. The syndicate agreement defines the obligations and the rights of the syndicate members, particularly the participation percentages and the distribution of commission revenue.

The lead manager has the overall responsibility towards the syndicate and the issuer for the issue. The lead manager puts together the syndicate, negotiates the issue with the issuer, drafts the necessary documentation, including the issue agreement and prospectus, distributes the securities among, and pays the commission revenue to, the syndicate members, ascertains receipt of the proceeds by the issuer and is in charge of the listing of the securities. The rights and obligations of the issuer on the one hand and the syndicate on the other are defined in the issue agreement. The more important provisions of the issue agreement relate to issue of securities by issuer and placement undertaking by syndicate members, issue price, commissions and expenses, and (for debt securities) terms, representations and warranties, events of default, security, and the governing law and jurisdiction.

¶1145   Public issues

(1)   Definition of public offering
There is no statutory definition of 'public offering'. It is the current view that the term should be construed in accordance with international standards. Characteristically, securities are offered in a public offering to an unlimited number of investors who are unrelated and unknown to the issuer. The offer is usually widely distributed by direct mailings to potential investors and by newspaper advertisements.

According to current views, whether the offering of firmly underwritten securities by a syndicate constitutes a public offering depends on the nature of the securities. While the sale of firmly underwritten shares by a syndicate is considered a private placement which does not require the distribution of a prospectus, the distribution of debt securities in a firm underwriting is considered a public offering. The dispute is largely academic since firmly underwritten shares are regularly listed on the stock exchanges, which require the issuance of a listing prospectus or advertisement.

(2) Shares

If the shares of a corporation are publicly offered at incorporation (see ¶703), a prospectus in accordance with Art. 631 CO must be published. The prospectus must be signed by all the founders and must include the following information:

- the fundamental provisions of the Articles of Incorporation (as required by Art. 626 et seq. CO),
- contributions in kind, assets to be acquired immediately after incorporation and benefits to founders, if any, as well as the essence of the founders' report, if any,
- the date until which a subscription is binding,
- the places where subscriptions are accepted,
- the issue price,
- the amount to be paid in on the shares, and
- the places where payment is accepted.

If the subscription bulletins include the names of all the founders as well as the above-listed information, a special prospectus is not needed.

If an existing company publicly offers new shares, a prospectus in accordance with Art. 651 CO must be published in the name of the board of directors. The following information must be included:

- the date of registration of the share corporation in the Register of Commerce,
- the name and registered office of the share corporation,
- the existing amount and composition of share capital, including par value of shares, classes of shares and preferential rights, if any,
- dividend-right certificates,
- the composition of the board of directors and auditors,
- the last financial statements with the auditors' report,
- the dividends paid in the last five years or since incorporation,
- debt securities issued by the share corporation,

- the shareholders' resolution on the issuance of the new shares, in particular the total amount, par value and issue price, as well as the number and classes of new shares,

- contributions in kind, assets to be immediately acquired after the issuance, and preferential rights,

- the date when the right to receive dividends and enjoy preferential rights for the new shares will begin, as well as restrictions, if any, and

- the date until which the subscription is binding.

If the above-mentioned information is included in the subscription bulletins, a special prospectus is not needed.

If the shares of a foreign corporation are publicly offered in Switzerland, no prospectus is required. Customarily, if not yet listed, shares of Swiss or foreign corporations are publicly offered in Switzerland in connection with the listing of the securities on the stock exchanges. The listing requirements provide for the issuance of a listing prospectus (see ¶1149).

(3) Bonds

Article 1156 CO provides that bonds may be publicly offered or listed on a stock exchange only on the basis of a prospectus. The prospectus requirement applies to bonds of both Swiss and foreign debtors. The prospectus must comply with the requirements for a prospectus for the issuance of new shares (Art. 651 CO). In addition, the prospectus must include detailed information on the loan, in particular the terms for interest payments and principal repayments, special security for the loan, and representation of the bondholders.

(4) Prospectus liability

Article 752 CO provides that, in case of a public offering of shares, any person who participated in the publication of a prospectus which does not comply with the legal requirements or which contains false information is liable for the ensuing damage suffered by the shareholders. Art. 1156(3) CO contains the same provision with respect to liability in the case of a public offering of bonds.

Prospectus liability applies in every case where a prospectus is issued, irrespective of whether the prospectus was required by law or published voluntarily.

¶1146 Private placements

(1) Definition of private placement

Private placements are defined as the placement of securities by a bank with its existing clientele without public solicitation. Anything that goes beyond this is considered a public offering (see ¶1145).

(2) Notes

Notes are an important instrument that is primarily used by foreign debtors to raise capital on the Swiss market. In 1989, the private placement of notes by foreign debtors far exceeded the public offering of bonds in the number of issues as well as the total amount of capital raised.

Notes are commonly defined as debt instruments with a term of two to eight years and denominations of SFr 50,000 or more, which are privately placed with sophisticated investors and are not traded on the stock exchanges. In all other respects, notes are practically identical with bonds. In particular, they are often issued as convertible notes or notes with warrants attached. Banks that engage in the issue of notes maintain a secondary market over the telephone.

In order to guarantee a minimum amount of protection to investors, the Swiss Bankers Association adopted the Agreement on Notes of Foreign Debtors (Convention XIX) in 1987 under pressure from the regulatory authorities. The agreement applies to privately placed note issues of foreign debtors with a minimum denomination of SFr 50,000. It requires the lead underwriter to draft a prospectus. The prospectus must comply with Art. 1156 CO and disclose additional information with respect to the conditions of the particular note issue. The prospectus is not distributed or published by the underwriters but must be held at the disposal of potential investors who request a copy. The Convention further provides for some minimum continuous disclosure obligations on the part of the underwriting banks and the issuer.

¶1147   Investment funds

(1)   Types of investment funds

In 1989, there were 205 domestic investment funds with total assets of SFr 39,521 million. Thirty-two of these funds were real estate funds with total assets of SFr 9,411 million. In addition, 143 foreign investment funds had licences for public solicitation in Switzerland. These figures underline the importance of investment funds in Switzerland. Domestic, as well as foreign, investment fund certificates distributed in Switzerland offer investors a variety of choices to satisfy individual investment needs. Investors may choose among share funds, bond funds, money-market funds, mixed securities funds, real estate funds or mixed funds investing in both real estate and securities. They may choose funds denominated in various currencies, funds which primarily aim at equity growth through capital gains, or funds which restrict themselves to interest and dividend income. Other investment funds concentrate on investments in restricted geographical areas or special industries.

Domestic and foreign investment funds are regulated by the Investment Funds Statute, the Investment Funds Ordinance and the Ordinance on Foreign Investment Funds (see ¶1103).

(2) Domestic investment funds

Domestic investment funds are defined in Art. 2 of the Investment Funds Statute as pools of assets collected from investors through public solicitation, to be commonly invested and managed by the fund management for the account of the investors in accordance with the principle of diversification of risk. Accordingly, contrary to foreign funds organised as corporations, domestic investment funds are open-end funds on the basis of individual collective investment contracts entered into by the fund management with the investors.

The fund's assets are the property of the investment fund management. Investors acquire a contractual claim against the investment fund management for an amount equal to their share in the net asset value of the fund. The investors' claims are represented by securities in the form of investment fund certificates. The investment fund certificates may be resold to the investment fund management at any time.

Only banks, as defined by the Banking Statute, or share corporations or co-operatives whose exclusive purpose is the management of investment funds can act as fund managers. They need an authorisation from the Federal Banking Commission. In addition, fund managers who are not banks must comply with certain minimum capital requirements and must deposit the fund's assets with a custodian bank, which also needs an authorisation from the Federal Banking Commission. The fund management and the custodian bank must submit the fund regulations for approval to the Banking Commission. The fund regulations contain the rights and obligations of the fund management and the custodian bank on the one hand, and of the investors on the other. They must be printed in their entirety on the fund certificate and include, among other things, the name of the fund, the name, registered office and remuneration of the fund management and custodian bank (if any), calculation of issue and repurchase price, and guide-lines for the investment policy (Art. 11 Investment Funds Statute and Art. 10 et seq. Investment Funds Ordinance). Both the investment fund and the activities of the fund management and the custodian bank must be audited yearly by an auditing firm recognised by the Federal Banking Commission.

The fund management is subject to various duties and restrictions. It must invest the fund assets in the exclusive interest of the investors. In this regard, the Investment Funds Statute and the Investment Funds Ordinance provide detailed investment guide-lines and minimum equity requirements to be observed by fund managers. Furthermore, the fund management has an extensive yearly reporting duty to investors and the Federal Banking Commission.

The fund management and the custodian bank are liable for any damage arising from a breach of statutory or contractual obligations. They are also subject to administrative sanctions by the Federal Banking Commission, which may revoke the authorisation granted to the fund management and custodian bank, appoint a curator, direct the transfer of the collective investment contracts to a new fund management or custodian bank and, as a last resort, decide that the investment fund must be liquidated. The Investment Funds Statute also provides for criminal sanctions.

(3) Foreign investment funds

Foreign investment funds are funds whose fund management is domiciled abroad. They may publicly solicit the sale of their fund certificates in Switzerland only after an authorisation by the Federal Banking Commission has been granted. An authorisation is issued only to banks and Swiss branches of foreign banks as defined in the Banking Statute.

The Ordinance on Foreign Investment Funds contains detailed requirements for foreign investment funds. These requirements are similar to those of the Investment Funds Statute for domestic funds. The requirements relate to management, investment policies, open-end character, auditing and reporting, and disclosure to investors.

The bank which represents the foreign investment fund in Switzerland is charged with various responsibilities towards the investors, the National Bank and the Federal Banking Commission. The Federal Banking Commission has broad supervisory powers, including the right to revoke the foreign investment fund's authorisation.

¶1148 Stock exchanges and secondary market

(1) Stock exchange transactions

The stock exchanges are the major markets for trading equity securities of Swiss and foreign corporations. A considerable amount of trading of bonds, warrants and investment fund certificates also occurs on the stock exchanges (for the organisation of the stock exchanges, see ¶1104). Trading occurs in a bid-and-ask system, *à la criée*. Members exchange their offers orally at the ring, and the conclusion of transactions is recorded by stock exchange officials. The types of transactions which can be carried out on the stock exchanges include cash transactions, fixed forward transactions (which are executed on a fixed future date at fixed terms) and premium transactions (in which a future date and terms of execution are agreed upon but with the buyer's right to withdraw from the contract against payment of a premium).

Transparency with respect to pricing and volume is limited. During trading, an electronic ring information system gives access to trading prices at other stock exchanges. Stock exchange closing prices of listed securities are published daily; prices paid over the counter are not published. The members of the stock exchanges are obliged to report the volume of their on-the-floor and off-the-floor transactions in Swiss equity securities, warrants and investment fund certificates only. No reporting requirement exists for securities dealers who have not been admitted to the floor.

Special trading markets are maintained by the stock exchanges for securities which do not (yet) meet the requirements for official listing (*Nebenbörse* in Zurich, *marché annexe* in Geneva and *ausserbörslicher Handel* in Basel). Trading occurs at the ring before or after normal trading hours and conforms in principle to the official trading. In Zurich, the *Nebenbörse* is supervised by the stock exchange commission, and trading is official. In Geneva and Basel, the market is supervised by the association running the exchange rather than by the official stock exchange commissioner; accordingly, trading, although regulated, is unofficial.

In 1990, the members of the stock exchanges of Zurich, Geneva and Basel approved a plan for a nationwide electronic trading system. Its main feature will be the electronic matching of orders. It is planned to start in 1992 with the trading of straight bonds, with the trading of other debt securities to follow. In addition, the desirability of including shares and equity derivatives in the electronic trading system is being discussed.

(2) Over-the-counter trading

In Switzerland, there is no obligation to conclude securities transactions through the stock exchanges. Banks and securities houses maintain a regular semi-electronic market outside the stock exchanges, in particular for bonds, notes and other securities which are not traded (either officially or unofficially) on the stock exchanges. However, listed securities can be, and are regularly, traded off the floor. Customarily, the lead manager is expected to act as a market maker for firmly underwritten securities which have been privately placed.

(3) Relationship between bank and customer in securities transactions

As a rule, banks conclude securities transactions as self-contracting parties, i.e., they act towards the customer as buyer or seller even if the customer's order is executed over the stock exchange or matched with another customer's order. This system is considered to be in the interests of the bank as well as the customers. Customers do not have to deal with unknown third parties; rather, they have a reliable counterpart whose standing ensures payment of the sold, or delivery of the bought, securities. Confidentiality is increased since the bank has no obligation to disclose the third party to its customer and vice versa.

It is common practice in Switzerland for banks or securities dealers to offset customers' buy orders against other customers' sell orders, or to satisfy customer orders by delivering securities from, or taking securities into, their own trading accounts. The transactions are concluded off the floor but at current official trading prices. Since the transactions are confirmed to the clients as having been executed on the stock exchanges, the price-making is not always entirely

¶1148

transparent. Civil liability and administrative sanctions may result if a bank executes an order at a price which gives it an improper profit.

Since 1 January 1991, commissions in securities transactions have been freely negotiable between buyer and seller.

(4) Settlement of securities transactions

Switzerland has its own clearing system for settling securities transactions. It is maintained by SEGA (see ¶1112). More than 500 Swiss banks participate in the SEGA system. Like Euro-clear or Cedel, SEGA acts as a security deposit and clearing centre for collective securities safekeeping and ownership transfers on a book entry basis. Transactions between banks are settled on the basis of delivery against payment, by crediting or debiting the securities or clearing account of the banks involved. Since 1988, SEGA has also provided, under certain conditions, for the settlement of transactions in Swiss registered shares.

A sister company of SEGA, the Swiss Nominee Company (SNOC) acts as a nominee for all registered shares of foreign companies listed in Switzerland.

A second sister company is Intersettle, the Swiss Corporation for International Securities Settlements. Intersettle is developing a securities clearing system that operates internationally to settle securities transactions in all current foreign curencies.

¶1149 Listing requirements

(1) Initial listing

Issuers must obtain admission to list their securities for official trading on a Swiss stock exchange.

An application to list securities requires previous clearance from the Swiss Admission Board (see ¶1109). The decision on applications is made on the basis of various quality criteria. These include country risks, transferability of payments, borrowing power in the home country, security for investments, marketability and fair disclosure. Rating is a further criterion, although no minimum rating is required.

Although each stock exchange has its own listing requirements, they do not differ materially. A uniform listing regulation is in preparation. The following description is based on the regulations governing the listing of securities (shares and bonds) on the Zurich Stock Exchange. Certain securities, such as warrants or investment fund certificates, are subject to additional or other requirements.

The application for admission to list a security must be filed by a member of the stock exchange. Securities of domestic and foreign issuers whose wide distribution allows normal trading and on which the information required for listing is provided, are accepted for listing. The information relates to the issuer as well as the securities for which listing is applied. The issuer must provide access to its audited financial statements and have a paid-in capital of SFr 5 million in the case of Swiss issuers and SFr 10 million in the case of foreign issuers. The securities to be listed must have a minimum par value or market capitalisation. In addition, the securities must comply with formal requirements in order to be tradable and to enable the investors to exercise the rights arising from the securities. The application for listing must be supported by detailed documentation. The stock exchange member filing the application must undertake certain obligations with respect to the listing procedure itself, and continuous disclosure thereafter (see (2) below).

Either the publication of a listing prospectus or the making available of a prospectus, combined with the publication of a listing advertisement, is required for admission. Both the prospectus and the advertisement must fairly disclose the information included and should enable investors to assess the quality of the security. The data and information which the prospectus must contain on the issuer and the guarantor, if any, include details on corporate data, composition of equity, voting rights, composition of the corporate bodies, dividend history, details on existing debt issues, financial statements and the accounting principles applied, major subsidiaries and group companies, and the most recent unaudited financial statements. The following information must be provided on the security for which listing is requested: the legal basis of the security, a detailed description of the security, a description of the voting rights (for shares), and (for bonds) the terms and conditions and information on security provided, if any. The prospectus may be in German, French, Italian or English.

Instead of a prospectus, a listing advertisement can appear in German in a newspaper published regularly in Zurich. The purpose of the advertisement is to draw public attention to the proposed listing. The advertisement is an abbreviated version of the information contained in the prospectus. It must clearly indicate where the listing prospectus is available to investors and in which language it is written. It must further state that only the listing prospectus will govern the listing application, and that the advertisement does not represent a prospectus in accordance with Arts 651 and 1156 CO.

(2) Continuous disclosure

Corporate law does not provide for any continuous public disclosure obligations on the part of corporations. Some minimum continuous disclosure obligations are contained in the listing regulations of the stock exchanges. In addition, Convention XVIII of the Swiss Bankers Association provides for continuous disclosure obligations by lead underwriters of foreign debtors' notes.

Various corporations have begun to release more information to the public than is required by statutory or self-regulatory rules. In particular, corporations which are trying to gain access to foreign capital markets, or which have their main operations in foreign jurisdictions, are faced with extensive foreign disclosure rules. Further, larger and medium-sized corporations are discovering that an open information policy furthers the liquidity of the securities which they list on domestic stock exchanges and helps to obtain better conditions for capital market operations.

¶1150   Take-overs

There are no legal provisions regulating take-overs in Switzerland. As of 1 September 1989, the Association of Swiss Exchanges adopted a self-regulating instrument, the Take-Over Code ('the Code') (*Code suisse des offres publiques d'achat/Schweizerischer Uebernahme-Kodex*). The federal securities legislation which is presently (1991) being considered by the Federal Government is likely to include statutory provisions on take-overs.

The Code, influenced by the London City Code on Take-overs and Mergers and the EC's proposed 13th Directive on take-overs and other general bids, is designed to regulate public offers for equity interests in corporations whose shares are traded on Swiss stock exchanges. The purpose of the Code is to enable shareholders and the target company to make decisions on the basis of clear information, to help avoid market manipulation and to ensure the observance of good faith by the participants. The Code is a contractual agreement among the Swiss stock exchanges and is binding only on their members. Offerors, targets and other participants, such as banks which are not members of a stock exchange, are not obliged, and cannot be compelled, to follow the Code. In spite of its private character, the Code has been widely accepted. All major acquisitions since its adoption have complied with the Code (e.g., Philip Morris's acquisition of Jacobs Suchard, and Credit Suisse's acquisition of Bank Leu).

The Code requires that shareholders in comparable situations be treated equally, and that the offer be subject only to conditions which cannot be influenced by the offeror. The Code further contains provisions regarding the publication of the offer, the period during which the offer is open for acceptance, the extension, withdrawal and revision of the offer, and the procedure in case of a counter-offer. In the case of a partial offer, acceptances must be treated on a pro rata basis. As soon as the offeror holds more than 50 per cent of the voting rights, it must satisfy all acceptances in full. The publication of the offer must contain the identity of the offeror and those acting in concert with it, and disclose agreements with shareholders or the corporate bodies of the target company, the number of shares for which the offer is made, and information regarding shareholder interests already held. The offer must further give particulars of the financing and specify the offer price in detail. The target company and the Commission for Regulation of the Association of Swiss Exchanges must be informed of the offer as soon as it is published. In addition, an accounting firm must certify to the Commission for Regulation on behalf of the offeror that the offer complies with the Code. During the offer, the offeror is prohibited from manipulating the price and, in particular, may not sell any securities. Within the boundaries of Swiss law and its Articles of Association, the target company has full discretion in the choice of defensive measures. These may include, in particular, the refusal to register the offeror as shareholder for the registered securities that it has acquired. The Commission for Regulation monitors compliance with the Code. In case of breach, the Commission for Regulation takes appropriate measures, including the publication of its observations, recommendations and decisions.

The Code does not oblige shareholders to disclose holdings in excess of a certain percentage. It is applicable only to public offers; creeping take-overs by way of undisclosed purchases remain unregulated. In general, the Code subjects the offeror to stricter rules than the target company. The target company is under no obligation to disclose relevant financial information which could help the shareholders in their decision. The Code is also of no help when it comes to defensive measures. Swiss share corporations' right under corporate law to refuse or restrict the registration of acquirers of registered shares and to deprive them of voting rights remains untouched.

¶1151 Traded options and financial futures – commodities

(1) Derivative instruments
Switzerland has an exchange for traded options and financial futures, the Swiss Options and Financial Futures Exchange (SOFFEX: see (2) below). Banks also maintain an over-the-counter market for financial futures; except for a limited market for gold options maintained by the Swiss banking community, banks do not engage in commodities trading. Access to foreign commodities markets is secured by the presence of Swiss subsidiaries or branches of foreign commodities brokers. Options represented by securities are regularly traded on the Swiss stock exchanges and over the counter as bonds or notes with warrants attached, or as independent (covered) warrants.

The Federal Banking Commission and the Swiss Bankers Association have issued guide-lines to be observed by banks in trading options and financial futures for customers or for their own account.

(2) Swiss Option and Financial Futures Exchange (SOFFEX)
SOFFEX is operated by Swiss Options and Financial Futures Exchange AG, a share corporation with registered offices in Zurich, whose shareholders are the stock exchanges of Zurich, Geneva and Basel and the five largest Swiss banks. Its objective is to operate a fully automated trading and clearing system for Swiss traded options and financial futures. SOFFEX is a self-regulating exchange and is not subject to governmental supervision by federal and cantonal authorities.

Stock exchange members, banks, and professional dealers in securities, options or futures with premises and personnel in Switzerland or Liechtenstein can become members (licencees) of SOFFEX. Members must submit to strict trading and clearing rules and regulations.

SOFFEX works as a fully automated electronic trading system in which members interact throughout Switzerland via computer terminals. Orders or quotes entered into SOFFEX by members are automatically executed by the central computer, which matches buy and sell orders. Members are obliged to conduct all transactions through the SOFFEX system, and for each option and financial future, market makers are appointed who have a duty permanently to maintain buy and sell quotes. Brokers act either as agents for customers or as principals on their own account. Contracts are entered into between SOFFEX and its members.

SOFFEX maintains a sophisticated clearing system. SOFFEX members are either general clearing members, direct clearing members or non-clearing members. Non-clearing members have to secure the services of a general clearing member, which is the financially responsible party to SOFFEX. Direct clearing members can clear their own transactions but cannot clear transactions for other members. Since the SOFFEX system is highly dependent on the reliability and credibility of its clearing members, SOFFEX has set very strict financial, legal and organisational conditions which a clearing member must fulfil. Only banks, as defined by the Banking Statute, can become clearing members. In addition to the clearing system, SOFFEX's functioning is further ensured by a sophisticated automatic margin system.

In standard form contracts, SOFFEX prescribes the contractual basis on which members may accept customers' orders. In addition, members are obliged to inform customers of the special risks of traded options and financial futures.

Presently, SOFFEX offers trading in standardised traded options on the stock of 11 large Swiss corporations and on two stock market indices. SOFFEX also offers trading in two stock markets, index futures and an interest rate future.

MONETARY CONTROLS

¶1152 Liberal international currency policy

Although monetary control provisions were always in force, Switzerland has traditionally followed a very liberal international currency policy. The only monetary control provisions presently in place are maintained by the National Bank under the powers given to it by Art. 8 of the Banking Statute. It provides that banks and bank-like finance companies must inform the National Bank before they conclude or participate in certain capital export transactions. The National Bank may object to the transactions or subject them to special conditions, if it is in the interests of the national currency, development of interest rates, or economic welfare. The following transactions must be reported to the National Bank if they involve SFr 10 million or more:

- loans in favour of foreign borrowers, including firm underwriting of bond or note issues,
- the purchase and issuance of shares of foreign corporations,
- credits and investments abroad with a term of one year or more,
- participation in the first placement of debt certificates issued by foreign debtors with a maturity of one year or more.

The National Bank regularly issues instructions under Art. 8 of the Banking Statute regarding current capital export regulations. The latest capital export regulations are dated 1 March 1990, and provide for a general permit for most transactions covered by Art. 8 of the Banking Statute, with the exception of transactions with debtors in certain countries and share, bond and note issues. The only major restriction that remains in place relates to the possibility of participating as a syndicate member in issue transactions of foreign issuers. Only banks and bank-like finance companies, as defined by the Banking Statute, may become members of syndicates for the conclusion of issue transactions denominated in Swiss Francs or for dual-currency issues linked to the Swiss Franc. Foreign banks may participate only in privately placed issue transactions that are useful in the execution of an international debt rescheduling agreement (see also ¶1144).

SELECTED BIBLIOGRAPHY

Emilio Albisetti, Max Boemle, Paul Ehrsam, Max Gsell, Paul Nyffeler and Ernst Rutschi, *Handbuch des Geld-, Bank- und Börsenwesens der Schweiz*, 4th edn (Thun, 1987)

Emilio Albisetti, Max Gsell and Paul Nyffeler, *Bankgeschäfte*, 4th edn (Zürich, 1990)

Maurice Aubert, Jean-Philippe Kernen and Herbert Schönle, *Le secret bancaire suisse*, 2nd edn (Bern, 1982)

Daniel Bodmer, Beat Kleiner and Benno Lutz, *Kommentar zum Schweizerischen Bankengesetz* (Zürich, 1990)

Urs Emch and Hugo Renz, *Das Schweizerische Bankgeschäft*, 3rd edn (Thun, 1983)

Daniel Guggenheim, *Les contrats de la pratique bancaire suisse*, 2nd edn (Genève, 1982)

Henri B. Meier, *Swiss Capital Markets*, 2nd edn (London, 1985)

Peter Nobel, *Praxis zum öffentlichen und privaten Bankenrecht der Schweiz* (Bern, 1979), Supplement, 1984

Christian J. Meier-Schatz and Kim D. Larson, 'Switzerland', in: Harold S. Blumenthal (ed.), *International Capital Markets and Securities Regulating* Chapter 8D (New York, 1990)

12 Antitrust and Unfair Competition

PRINCIPAL LEGISLATION

*Loi fédérale sur les cartels et organisations analogues/Kartellgesetz/*Federal Cartel Statute, RS 251.

Loi fédérale contre la concurrence déloyale/Gesetz gegen den unlauteren Wettbewerb, Federal Unfair Competition Statute, RS 241.

*Ordonnance sur les liquidations et les opérations analogues/Ausverkaufsverordnung/*Liquidation Sales Ordinance, RS 241.1.

ANTITRUST

¶1201 Sources of law

(1) History and importance of law

A national competition policy and a specific antitrust law are both relatively new phenomena. Before the first antitrust statute was enacted, courts had dealt for a long time with cartels on the basis of general or private-law principles, especially the protection of individual rights (Arts 27 and 28 CC). In 1964, the Federal Cartel Statute came into force. It is based on Art. $31^{bis}(3)$ of the Federal Constitution, which provides for legislative rules 'against economically or socially harmful effects of cartels and similar organisations'. The Cartel Statute was substantively revised and amended in 1986.

Switzerland is a country with a long-standing tradition of cartels. Even today, many anti-competitive agreements exist within many important business sectors. It is, therefore, somewhat surprising that, in practical terms and compared to other countries, antitrust law has not played a major role in business law so far. Civil lawsuits were brought relatively infrequently and were almost never successful. The Cartel Commission intervened only in extreme cases and, by and large, followed a policy of compromise. This situation will probably change in the near future. Following the enactment of the revised Cartel Statute, the Cartel Commission has already shown a substantially more aggressive attitude towards cartels. As a decision of the Federal Supreme Court of 1986 (ATF 112 II 268) shows, it is quite likely that the new rules will be applied by the courts in a stricter, more pro-competitive way. On the whole, antitrust law will probably become a much more important factor in doing business in Switzerland. The scene may even change dramatically if the country has to adapt to the EC competition rules after the Treaty negotiations between the EFTA and the EC concerning a new European Economic Area (EAA) becomes effective. See ¶112(3).

(2) Legislative policies
In its basic approach to competition policy, the Cartel Statute may be classified as a statute of abuse prevention. This regulatory approach is dictated by Art. 31bis(3) of the Federal Constitution, which does not provide for any (subjective or objective) *per se* prohibitions of cartels.

All types of restraints on competition and all anti-competitive practices are examined according to individual circumstances under a broadly defined rule of reason. With respect to its fundamental policy goals, the Cartel Statute has a dualistic conception: it aims at protecting the economic freedom of individual competitors, and at preserving competition as an economic and social institution.

The main source of law is the Cartel Statute itself, with its provisions of private, public and criminal law. Of minor importance are the By-Laws of the Cartel Commission (RS 251.1) and the Ordinance on the Fees of the Cartel Commission (RS 251.2). In addition to domestic law, international antitrust rules apply, namely Art. 15 of the EFTA Agreement and Art. 23 of the Free Trade Agreement between Switzerland and the EC. Finally, Switzerland has a specific regulatory regime on governmental supervision of prices (¶604).

¶1202 Scope of antitrust legislation

(1) In general
The Cartel Statute applies to anti-competitive practices of private enterprises and of partly or totally state-owned entities. Although consumer organisations may have an impact on competition, they remain beyond the reach of the antitrust laws.

Territorially, the Cartel Statute covers restraints of competition which have effects in Switzerland, regardless of their origin. This principle is not expressly stated in the Cartel Statute but is nowadays universally recognised.

All agreements, decisions and measures of collective labour matters are beyond the scope of the Cartel Statute. This distinction between the 'labour market' and the 'market for goods and services', although hotly disputed, is well-founded, as collective bargaining is the subject of collective labour legislation. Only agreements which deal *exclusively* with labour relations are exempt; cartel law becomes applicable when labour-related measures are used to restrain competition in the market for goods and services.

The most important jurisdictional rules relate to the essential topic of cartel law, namely to cartels and similar organisations.

(2) Cartels and market-dominating enterprises

(a) Cartels

Cartels are agreements, decisions and legally unenforceable arrangements which influence, or are likely to influence, the market for certain goods and services by collectively restricting competition, particularly by regulating the production, sale or purchase of goods, or by regulating prices or business conditions (Art. 2(1) Cartel Statute).

This provision catches only horizontal restraints, i.e., anti-competitive practices between producers or dealers at the same distribution level, not individual vertical restraints. Moreover, the provisions on cartels do not apply to merger agreements or any other form of contractual acquisitions.

The Cartel Statute mentions several means of restricting competition, e.g., through formal agreements or through informal decisions. Even legally unenforceable arrangements do not escape its reach.

The term 'restriction of competition' is defined broadly. The purpose of guaranteeing free market entry is to encourage potential and actual competition. The list of examples of anti-competitive behaviour is not exhaustive. The Cartel Statute covers all forms of behaviour which influence or are likely to influence the market. The statute applies when the impairment of competition was subjectively intended but failed, and when no restraint of competition was intended but none the less ensued.

However, only restraints that actually have an impact on the relevant market are subject to the Cartel Statute. In defining the relevant market, Switzerland follows the concept of functional interchangeability. Whether products and services are exchangeable is determined by referring to the average consumer and by taking the circumstances of particular markets into account.

Restraints are unlawful if they have an impact upon the relevant market by reducing the alternatives available to competitors, suppliers or purchasers to a significant extent.

Since its amendment in 1986, the Cartel Statute has applied to anti-competitive recommendations. They are treated on an equal footing with cartels, but only when they obviously bring about a collective restriction of competition.

(b) Vertical restraints

(i) Price fixing agreements.   Vertical price fixing agreements are treated like cartels when they are imposed or enforced by a cartel or a similar organisation (Art. 3(1) Cartel Statute). This provision covers all forms of resale price maintenance, i.e., minimum and maximum prices as well as fixed rebates or other conditions. However, it is not applicable to individual settings of prices without the participation of a cartel or a similar organisation (see ¶1202(2)). This is inconsistent from the viewpoint of competition policy, since Art. 5 of the Cartel Statute does not set this condition for exclusivity and distribution agreements (see (ii) below). Article 3(2) of the Cartel Statute includes price recommendations if they have the effect of a vertical resale price maintenance.

(ii) Exclusivity and distribution agreements.   Cartel law covers vertical exclusivity and distribution agreements which have a significant impact on the relevant market (Art. 5 Cartel Statute). This provision catches only certain types of vertical restraints. Exclusivity agreements force sellers to sell to, and purchasers to purchase from, the exclusive contractual partner. Distribution clauses restrict the resale of a product by forbidding a supplier to sell to certain other dealers (customer restrictions) or to sell into a certain territory (territorial restrictions). Article 5 of the Cartel Statute applies only to formal agreements: vertical recommendations or vertical concerted practices are not affected. It does not require the participation of a cartel or a similar organisation (¶1202(2)), rather it comes into play only when the vertical restraint has a significant influence on the market. A qualified market impact is most probable when parallel vertical restraints are widely used in a certain economic sector, or when newcomers face considerable barriers to market entry, for instance because of oligopolistic market structures.

(c) Market-dominating enterprises

The Cartel Statute defines market-dominating enterprises ('similar organisations' in its terminology) as follows (Art. 4(1) Cartel Statute): participants which dominate or significantly influence the market for certain products or services, be they:

  (i) single enterprises,

  (ii) enterprises which tacitly and mutually co-ordinate their business
       practices, or

  (iii) enterprises linked by financial participation or other means.

As elsewhere, the central question is determining the relevant market power. The courts, the Cartel Commission and the commentators all agree that there is no single relevant criterion. They call for a broader view that would consider all of the three traditional elements: market structure, market behaviour and market performance. In practice, structural elements play the most influential role. This is reflected in the wording of the Cartel Statute itself (Art. 4(2)), which requires that all relevant facts on the supply and demand side be considered, such as:

(i) the number of competitors and their market shares;

(ii) forms of buying and selling;

(iii) the financial power and interdependence of enterprises; and

(iv) the dependence of companies on their suppliers or customers.

The last-mentioned element in particular reveals that the Cartel Statute covers market power relationships on the demand side.

Article 4 of the Cartel Statute mentions three types of market-dominating enterprises:

The first type consists of single enterprises, i.e., individuals or companies with the necessary market power.

The second type, namely enterprises engaging in concerted practices, is, of course, more problematic. It is sometimes difficult to draw the line between market-dictated parallel conduct and concerted practices. A simple voluntary imitation or adjustment of behaviour may make good business sense and is not covered by Art. 4 of the Cartel Statute. This is especially true for the well-known phenomenon of parallel behaviour in oligopolistic structures. Rather, the law aims at conscious and wilful co-ordination of business practices by partners at the same functional level, i.e., among producers, among wholesalers or among retailers. A majority of the commentators say that recommendations and price leaderships do not fall under Art. 4 of the Cartel Statute.

The third type of market-dominating firms consists of enterprises that are linked together financially or otherwise (Art. 4(1)(c)). The most prominent example is a group of companies controlled by a holding company.

¶1203   Private antitrust law

(1)   Relationship of the cartel to third parties

Articles 6 and 7 of the Cartel Statute, the major substantive rules governing the relationship of the cartel to third parties, represent the core of private cartel law (for the distinction between private and public law, see ¶107). Article 6 of the Cartel Statute defines unlawful restraints on competition, and Art. 7 states the justification for an otherwise prohibited restraint.

(a)   *Unlawful restraints of competition*

Article 6 of the Cartel Statute declares all measures of a cartel or a similar organisation unlawful when they exclude or significantly hinder third parties from competing, or hinder them in a significant way from taking up or exercising competition in a given particular market. Examples of anti-competitive measures are the following:

- refusal to sell or discrimination against buyers with respect to prices or conditions,
- refusal to buy, discrimination against sellers with respect to prices or conditions, or the requirement of unreasonable prices or conditions,
- predatory pricing, or
- boycott of employees.

Activities which affect third parties equally in their efforts to compete are also covered; examples are tying contracts and abusive general conditions of purchase or of sale.

Quite reasonably, minor (*de minimis*) anti-competitive effects are ignored; only significant anti-competitive effects are prohibited.

The complete elimination of competitors occurs quite rarely in the real world. More frequent, but also more difficult to define, is the significant restraint of actual or potential competition for third parties. An older Federal Supreme Court theory predominantly applied quantitative criteria, for example the significance of the anti-competitive effects expressed in lost turnover or lost profit. This approach was severely criticised in the literature. Recent decisions (e.g., ATF 112 II 268) reflect a more nuanced approach by requiring a certain intensity which, directly or indirectly, influences the third parties' freedom of action. The Federal Supreme Court particularly stressed the need to switch to other products or to use counter-measures. This last criterion appears to be helpful, since it is more reliable for drawing the line between unlawful antitrust measures and ordinary business practices. The test is whether counter-measures become prohibitively expensive to a reasonable competitor. As the text of the Cartel Statute itself emphasises, the most significant indication of a restraint is whether unreasonable barriers to market entry are set up.

The list of anti-competitive measures given by Art. 6 is again not exhaustive. First, measures by the seller, particularly boycotts and discrimination against buyers as to prices and conditions, are mentioned. Economically reasonable price policies like quantity discounts or rebates for certain dealer services do not fall under the law. Article 6 further mentions discrimination against suppliers through unreasonable prices or conditions by buyers. Predatory pricing can be relevant under the antitrust laws. (For price cutting as an unfair trade practice, see ¶1209(5)). Finally, the Cartel Statute covers the not very important case of a boycott of employees. Much more significant is Art. 6(3), which maintains that the provisions apply not only in cases of discrimination among competitors but also when the other market side is exploited. Business activities which affect all other competitors equally can be abusive. This is true for tying contracts and clearly abusive general business conditions.

(b)   Justification
Restraints of competition are lawful:

  (i) if they can be justified by overriding legitimate private interests; and

  (ii) if their effects are not contrary to the interest of the public at large (Art. 7(1) Cartel Statute).

Article 7 of the Cartel Statute makes it clear that antitrust law does not contain any *per se* rules. In the form of a blanket clause, it states that the prohibition of Art. 6 does not apply when the conditions of the exemption are met.

The most important justification of restraint of competition is 'overriding legitimate interests'. The crucial question of whether predominant private interests are sufficient, or whether the general (public) interest has to come into play, had already arisen under the old Cartel Statute. During the legislative reform leading to the Cartel Statute of 1986, an early consensus emerged that the public interest has to play some role. But, conceptually, it was not clear whether the restraints should make a (positive) contribution to the general interest, or whether they should (negatively) not interfere with the public interest. The text which was finally adopted clearly shows that the former approach prevailed.

Restraints on competition are justified only when they respect the principle of proportionality. This prerequisite is met if:

  (i) the restraint is apt to attain the desirable goal;

  (ii) it does not go further than required by the goal; and

  (iii) less restrictive alternatives are unavailable.

A reasonable balance must be struck between the effects on freedom of competition and the advantages of the private market system. In addition, commentators and the Federal Supreme Court require equal treatment of the excluded outsiders amongst themselves.

Overriding legitimate interests are defined as follows (Art. 7(2) Cartel Statute):

● safeguarding fair and undistorted competition,

● creating adequate professional and entrepreneurial conditions,

● promoting a desirable structure in a certain branch of an industry or a profession, or

● implementing resale price maintenance to the extent necessary to guarantee the quality of products or customer services.

¶1203

All exemptions are limited in so far as the restraint on competition may not have the exclusive purpose of preventing market entry by new competitors (Art. 7(3) Cartel Statute).

The examples of legitimate interests given in Art. 7(2) of the Cartel Statute are by no means exhaustive. They all clearly relate to some aspects of the public interest.

It is legitimate to adopt private measures to protect fair and undistorted competition even if the outsider does not violate the Unfair Competition Statute. Cartels and market-dominating enterprises are allowed to implement and maintain sufficiently high standards in their branch of industry or profession, provided these standards are reasonable and not merely prompted by financial interests. Anti-competitive measures may be necessary to implement optimal structures in terms of regional equilibrium, economic sectors and enterprise sizes. This justification is of particular importance in the cases of co-operation agreements and concentration processes. But it is undisputed that those measures may not be used just to preserve the status quo; they must promote the optimal structure in view of a broader general interest. Finally, resale price maintenance may be necessary to ensure the quality of products or of customer services.

(2) Internal matters of the cartel

Articles 14 to 19 of the Cartel Statute deal with the legal relationship among the members of a cartel themselves. They determine the permissible degree of self-imposed anti-competitive obligations. Since they play a minor role in practice, they are described only briefly.

To be valid, a cartel agreement must be in writing. The same is true for vertical price maintenance contracts and exclusivity and distribution contracts (Art. 14 Cartel Statute). If a cartel commitment becomes an excessive burden on a particular member, the latter may be released from its contractual obligation if the member's position has appreciably deteriorated or if there is another significant reason (Art. 15 Cartel Statute). In addition, exit may not be impeded by requiring a compensation payment or by setting excessive periods of advance notice (Art. 16 Cartel Statute). Finally, members of a cartel, or partners in a vertical price maintenance or exclusivity or distribution agreement, are protected against disproportionately heavy sanctions (Art. 17 Cartel Statute).

¶1204 Public antitrust law

(1) Antitrust authorities and their functions

(a) Cartel Commission

The Cartel Commission (*Commission des cartels/Kartellkommission*) is the most important regulatory agency established under public cartel law. It is independent of the federal administration and consists of selected academics, business people and consumers (Art. 20 Cartel Statute). It works with a small staff (Secretary's Office: *secrétariat/Sekretariat*), which is headed by a director (Art. 24 Cartel Statute).

The Commission has a series of advising, investigating and recommending functions. It constantly observes the competition scene and makes recommendations to the Federal Government on competition policy matters (Art. 25 Cartel Statute). It also advises the Federal Government on legislative measures which may influence competition. Moreover, the Commission provides courts and administrative bodies with opinions regarding competition problems, and regularly publishes decisions in the antitrust field.

The Commission's investigative powers are practically and politically more important. It can start a preliminary investigation on its own initiative or when it is informed by third parties of an alleged restraint of competition (Art. 28 Cartel Statute). This relatively informal and quick procedure, which had developed without a specific legal basis under the old Cartel Statute, was formally introduced in Art. 28 of the new Cartel Statute. Preliminary investigations are very frequent. The president of the Cartel Commission and the director of the Secretary's Office try to make the parties reach a settlement and are often successful.

The most important policy instrument of the Commission is an investigation (*enquête/Untersuchung*) under Art. 29 of the Cartel Statute. Investigations are in-depth inquiries and imply a formal administrative procedure. The Commission also has certain administrative procedural powers. The subject of an investigation under Art. 29 of the Cartel Statute is whether a cartel or a market-dominating enterprise has economically or socially harmful effects.

The Cartel Statute contains no substantive provisions related to merger control. In an earlier legislative draft an attempt had been made to introduce mandatory advance notification to the Commission for mergers and other acquisitions above a certain size. Parliament, however, did not pass this measure. In the new Cartel Statute, only a left-over provision survived, which authorises the Commission to start an investigation if a merger or another acquisition results in or considerably increases a dominant position, and if economically and socially harmful effects appear to be likely (Art. 30 Cartel Statute). This provision does not create any new powers for the Commission, but it makes it clear that the Commission may investigate mergers and acquisitions.

The Commission can not only investigate anti-competitive behaviour, but it can also issue recommendations (*recommendation/Empfehlung*) to cartels and market-dominating enterprises. If it detects economically and socially harmful effects, it advises the participants to modify or abandon their cartel agreements or business practices (Art. 32 Cartel Statute).

(b)   The Federal Department of Public Economy
The Federal Department of Public Economy (*Département fédéral de l'économie publique/Eidgenössisches Volkswirtschaftsdepartement*) is one of the seven

¶1204

departments of the Federal Government. It works together with the Cartel Commission (Art. 20(2) Cartel Statute). It can direct or suggest that an investigation under Art. 29 be conducted, and is the body to whom all reports (*rapport/Bericht*) of the Commission are addressed (Art. 33 Cartel Statute).

Undoubtedly, the most important function of the Department is to issue binding orders to cartels and similar organisations to modify or abandon anti-competitive measures (Art. 37 Cartel Statute). Formal orders may replace informal recommendations which have been formally rejected or disregarded by the addressee. The contents of the order often follow the Commission's recommendations. However, the Department may order tougher or milder measures. In each case, the recipients of the order have the right to be heard. The Federal Department of Public Economy has recently re-emphasised its firm intention to issue orders if recommendations are not accepted or not followed.

(2) Economically and socially harmful effects

Article 29 of the Cartel Statute is the core provision of public cartel law. It defines more precisely the central concept of economically and socially harmful effects, and provides guide-lines to the Cartel Commission for its evaluation of cartels and similar organisations.

Article 29 of the Cartel Statute details the steps in the Commission's investigation. First, the beneficial and detrimental results of cartels and similar organisations are ascertained. If the Commission finds significant restraint or distortion of competition, it weighs the positive and negative effects ('*saldo* method'). In this complex procedure, the Commission's central concern is to keep competition alive. But the Commission also looks at other important effects, e.g., at production and distribution costs, prices, quality, supply of national sources, the structure of an economic sector, the interests of regions, the competitiveness of firms domestically and abroad, and the interests of workers and consumers (Art. 29(2) Cartel Statute). It is important to note that all these relevant criteria clearly relate only to aspects of the broader public interest. Merely private interests do not come into play in this whole procedure.

The last step in this evaluation process consists of a judgment: cartels and market-dominating enterprises are harmful economically and socially if effective competition is eliminated in the relevant market, unless this elimination is absolutely indispensable in the light of the overall general interest (Art. 29(3) Cartel Statute).

The interpretation of this provision of the Cartel Statute is disputed. A correct reading of the statute seems to be as follows: the elimination of effective competition, as such, is harmful. The restraint of competition is justified only if warranted by the public interest and if the public interest can be accomplished by restraint. These are cases in which the Cartel Commission would normally intervene, yet in which cartels or market-dominating enterprises are exceptionally allowed to carry out this restraint of trade.

¶1205   Enforcement and remedies

(1)   Private actions

A competitor who is restricted in his freedom of competition has standing to bring a claim. A civil action may also be filed by professional and trade associations whose purpose is to promote the interests of their members and whose members themselves have standing to sue (Art. 8(2) Cartel Statute).

Private cartel law actions are brought in the first instance before a cantonal court (Art. 10 Cartel Statute). They may be formulated as:

(a) a declaratory action to establish the unlawfulness of the restraint;

(b) an action to restrain interference;

(c) an action for damages; or

(d) an action for (non-monetary) satisfaction (Art. 8(1) Cartel Statute).

Plaintiffs may request conservatory measures if they are able to make a prima facie case that competition is hampered (Art. 13 Cartel Statute). In all these civil proceedings, business secrets of the parties must be preserved (Art. 12 Cartel Statute).

Cantonal decisions may be appealed to the Federal Supreme Court (Art. 11 Cartel Statute).

(2)   Governmental enforcement

As stated above (¶1204(1)(a)), the Cartel Commission can initiate various investigations into cartels and market-dominating enterprises. For formal investigations under Arts. 29 and 30 of the Cartel Statute, the Commission has wide-reaching investigatory powers (cf. Art. 31 Cartel Statute). In the first round, the Commission asks questions. If the material facts cannot sufficiently be ascertained, the Commission may order the cartel members and third parties to testify and formally require them to produce all relevant documents. All these instructions must be given in the form of an order to produce evidence. The parties are given the opportunity to comment upon the factual findings of the Commission's investigation.

An administrative order to produce evidence may be appealed to the Federal Supreme Court (Art. 38(1)(c) Cartel Statute).

The Commission can only make inquiries and recommendations. If they are not followed by the recipients, the Federal Department of Public Economy may issue binding orders (cf. ¶1204(1)(b)). These orders can be appealed to the Federal Supreme Court (Art. 38(1)(a) Cartel Statute).

The cartel law provides for penal sanctions. Those who do not abide by accepted recommendations of the Commission, binding orders of the Federal Department of Public Economy, or decisions of the Federal Supreme Court may be fined up to SFr 100,000 (Art. 39 Cartel Statute). A fine of SFr 20,000 is provided for participants or third parties who violate procedural rules, such as the obligation to testify or produce documents (Art. 40 Cartel Statute).

¶1206 International antitrust law

(1) Substantive provisions

(a) European Free Trade Association (EFTA)
The EFTA, of which Switzerland is a full member, established in its basic Convention the following rule with respect to restrictive business practices (Art. 15):

> 'Member States recognise that the following practices are incompatible with this Convention in so far as they frustrate the benefits expected from the removal or absence of duties and quantitative restrictions on trade between Member States:
>
> > (a) agreements between enterprises, decisions by associations of enterprises and concerted practices between enterprises which have as their object or result the prevention, restriction or distortion of competition within the Area of the Association;
> >
> > (b) actions by which one or more enterprises take unfair advantage of a dominant position within the Area of the Association or a substantial part of it;
> >
> > ...'

This provision is obviously modelled after Arts 85 and 86 of the EC Treaty. Partly because the EFTA lacks an autonomous enforcement procedure, these antitrust rules have in practice so far played only a very minor role.

(b) Treaty between the EC and Switzerland
Article 23 of the Free Trade Agreement between the EC and Switzerland reads as follows:

> 'The following are incompatible with the proper functioning of the Agreement in so far as they may affect the trade between the Community and Switzerland:

(i) All agreements between undertakings, decisions by associations of undertakings and concerted practices between undertakings which have as their object or effect the prevention, restriction, or distortion of competition as regards the production of or trade in goods;

(ii) Abuse by one or more undertakings of a dominant position in the territories of the contracting parties as a whole or in a substantial part thereof;

....,'

This provision almost literally reproduces Arts 85 and 86 of the EC Treaty. The antitrust rules of the Free Trade Agreement have never played any significant role in business practice. Until now, no formal decisions or procedures have been initiated under Art. 23 of the Free Trade Agreement.

(2) Enforcement

(a) EFTA Treaty provisions

The lack of adequate enforcement mechanisms was, from the outset, the major weakness of the EFTA rules on competition. The EFTA Agreement itself does not provide for any special procedures. In the Copenhagen Declaration of 1965, the Council of Ministers introduced a simplified and informal bilateral procedure against violations of the competition provisions (Copenhagen Protocol). Once a partner state is informed by an enterprise that it has been affected by anti-competitive behaviour in the sense of Art. 15 of the EFTA Convention, the government must investigate the restraint on competition and offer a remedy according to its own cartel law.

Article 23 of the Free Trade Agreement with the EC faces similar enforcement problems. There is no central organ with powers of investigation and decision. Moreover, the provision itself is, according to both the Cartel Commission and the Federal Supreme Court, non-self-executing. The only sanctions available in the event of an infringement are countervailing safeguarding measures. The Agreement contains a special procedure for this purpose in Art. 27(3). This procedure is initiated by the complaint of one of the parties. The Joint Committee investigates the case on the basis of information provided by the parties. If the Joint Committee comes to the conclusion that Art. 23 has indeed been violated, the offending party is asked to redress the violation. If no settlement is reached at the consultations, preliminary measures may be ordered.

(b) Internal provisions of the Cartel Statute

The new Cartel Statute of 1986 introduced in Arts 42 and 43 two provisions which have the explicit function of executing the antitrust rules of the EFTA

¶1206

Convention and the Free Trade Agreement with the EC. The legislative intent behind the two rules was to establish an internal national procedure in which the objections of an international treaty partner can be investigated and, when necessary and desirable, brought to a decision by Swiss authorities.

If a party to an international agreement alleges anti-competitive agreements or practices that violate the respective treaty, the Federal Department of Public Economy may ask the Commission to evaluate the facts. On the basis of this investigation, and after holding a hearing with the parties concerned, the Department decides, upon recommendation of the Commission, on further proceedings. Complaints in the EFTA Council or in the Joint Switzerland-EC Committee that enterprises organised restrictions on competition that violate the respective treaty rules will trigger an investigation. Because they must respect the sovereignty of the individual states, the Council and the Committee are not able to order coercive procedures for the taking of evidence. It is, therefore, up to the national legislation to provide for means of investigation. The Swiss representative in the EFTA Council or on the Joint Committee does not certify that a violation has occurred before the procedure under Art. 42 of the Cartel Statute has taken place.

For political reasons, the Department of Public Economy has broad discretion with respect to the introduction of procedures related to international cartel law. The Department may require the Commission to investigate or immediately to introduce a specific procedure. Moreover, after seeing the Commission's results, it is entirely up to the Department to define what further steps ought to be taken.

If certain agreements or practices violate an international treaty, the Federal Department of Public Economy, after consulting the Federal Department for Foreign Affairs, may ask the Commission to recommend to the participating parties to abandon or modify these agreements, or to stop these business practices. The finding of whether a certain business practice violates international treaties is made exclusively by Swiss authorities. Moreover, the Department of Public Economy again has considerable discretion in structuring its procedure. It may require the Cartel Commission to make the necessary recommendations to the initiators of the restraints on competition. Whether the recommendations are finally issued lies entirely in the hands of the Department, which considers conformity with *ordre public* and other public policy aspects.

The affected parties have the right to be heard before the Commission (Art. 43(2) Cartel Statute). The procedure follows Arts 37 to 39 of the Cartel Statute. The Department may issue strict orders against the participants with criminal consequences (cf. Art. 39 Cartel Statute). The parties can appeal these orders (Art. 38 Cartel Statute). In this appeal it can only be claimed that the order failed to comply with the principle of proportionality (Art. 43(3)).

¶1206

UNFAIR COMPETITION

¶1207   Sources of the law

Unfair competition is concerned with fairness in the market place. It aims at the quality of competition. By contrast, the antitrust rules of the Cartel Statute seek to guarantee the freedom and functioning of the competitive process.

On a federal level, the cornerstone is the Federal Unfair Competition Statute of 19 December 1986, in force since 1 March 1988. It contains the basic principles of fair competition and a series of examples of unfair practices, as well as various consumer protection rules (see ¶601 et seq.). The purpose of the Unfair Competition Statute is to guarantee fair and correct competition in the interest of all participants (Art. 1 Unfair Competition Statute); in this respect, it clearly differs in its object from the Cartel Statute. Prior to the enactment of an earlier federal statute against unfair competition in 1943, protection against unfair practices had to be sought under personality rights, in particular under Art. 48 CO. This provision, which was part of tort law, was replaced by the federal statute of 1943, which was based essentially on free competition as one of the most important pillars of the economy.

The 1943 statute aimed at the abuse of economic competition. Although the old statute provided reasonable measures against unfair practices, it had a series of shortcomings that the current Unfair Competition Statute has remedied, such as protection against exploitation of a third-party performance, protection against misleading price undercutting, and improvement of consumer protection and the position of consumer organisations. An important improvement is that the requirement of an actual competitive relation between a claimant and an alleged unfair practitioner has been abolished. Although the courts had already done away with this requirement to a certain extent under the old law (ATF 108 II 327), the situation of the individual consumer has been improved substantially by the abolition of this requirement (Art. 9 Unfair Competition Statute; see ¶1213).

In a less general way, the rules for the protection of personality of Art. 28 et seq. CC guard against unfair competition; so do the provisions protecting the names of individuals (Art. 29 CC) and of corporations (Arts 951 and 956 CO).

On the international level, Switzerland is a member of the Paris Convention for the Protection of Industrial Property in its Stockholm version of 1967 (RS 0.232.04). Under Arts 10bis and 10ter of the Convention, Switzerland is bound to provide effective protection against unfair competition (as defined by the Convention) to nationals of the other member countries. Protection must be provided against confusing or false allegations about a competitor and misleading information about one's own goods.

Beyond the statutory rules, private organisations undertake to guarantee certain standards of fair competition. The most important organisation is the Commission for Fairness in Advertising (*Commission suisse pour la loyauté en publicité/Schweizerische Kommission für die Lauterkeit in der Werbung*), established by a private foundation of the advertising industry. This Commission acts as a court of arbitration and decides on advertising practices brought before it by applying the principles of advertising developed by the Commission itself, or contained in the International Code of Fair Practice in Advertising of the International Chamber of Commerce.

¶1208   Unfair trade practices in general

According to Art. 2 of the Unfair Competition Statute, every behaviour or business activity which is misleading or violates the principle of good faith in other ways, and which influences the relation between competitors or between merchants and consumers, is unfair and illegal. The legislature deemed a general provision to be better adapted to the rapid changes prevailing in competition than an exhaustive list of specific practices. The general clause of Art. 2 provides the statutory basis for judging cases which are not specifically allowed by the subsequent provisions of the Unfair Competition Statute. The general principle has to be interpreted in connection with the purpose of the Unfair Competition Statute as defined in Art. 1, i.e., to guarantee fair and unhindered competition in the interest of all participants. The circle of potential unfair trade practices is drawn widely by the general clause. Since the scope of the law has been extended to acts or behaviour affecting the relationship between merchants and consumers, the former requirement of the existence of a direct competitive relationship has been waived.

Court decisions based on the general clause, even that of the old statute, are scarce. Nevertheless, the clause has its practical importance, particularly with regard to new trade practices which may not be caught by one of the specific provisions of the statute. While deception is the only element mentioned as an example of an unfair practice, any interpretation of the general clause should take the following basic principles into account:

(1) Competition must be enhanced by proper positive performance; hindering and disparaging competitors is unlawful.

(2) Goods and services must be correctly and clearly described.

(3) The personality of the consumer must be respected.

(4) The public interest, e.g., in a widespread system of supply, must be preserved.

Most of these principles not only serve as guide-lines for the interpretation of the general clause, but also constitute the underlying rationale of the specific provisions of the Unfair Competition Statute.

¶1209　Unfair advertising and sales methods

(1)　Previous case law still relevant

Among the practices specifically defined in the Unfair Competition Statute as unfair, advertising and sales methods occupy a central position. Most of the practices described had already been prohibited under the previous law; in consequence, a long line of cases illustrates what is considered unfair and illegal in connection with advertising and sales.

(2)　Presentation of one's own goods and services

Deception is possible first of all in connection with the presentation of the competitor's own goods and services. Any deception with regard to quality, quantity, price, origin or sales conditions of one's own goods or services is prohibited. Consequently, any information about the business, name, goods, work performance, price, stock or business relations which is incorrect or misleading, or which unduly favours third parties is regarded as unfair (Art. 3(b) Unfair Competition Statute). The same holds true for incorrect titles or professional qualifications which could create the impression of special expertise (Art. 3(c) Unfair Competition Statute). This concept of correct information about one's own business includes the obligation to use the company name as it has been registered in the Register of Commerce (ATF 103 IV 202). The use of a company name in advertising should allow other competitors or consumers to identify the source of the advertising.

　　With regard to prices and their indication in general beyond advertising, additional statutory rules can be found in Arts 16 et seq. of the Unfair Competition Statute (requiring the merchant to indicate effective prices and prohibiting misleading prices) and in the Federal Ordinance on the Notification of Prices (requiring prices of consumer goods and of certain services to be clearly stated) (see ¶604).

(3)　Deceptive information about the goods and services of others

Deception is prohibited in connection with information about the goods and services of others. Like information about one's own goods and services, references to others must be correct and not misleading and, in addition, statements about others must not be unnecessarily disparaging (Art. 3(a) Unfair Competition Statute). This provision aims at protecting the personality and the reputation of a competitor against disparagement (*dénigrement/Herabsetzung*) (ATF 92 IV 95). Likewise, practices leading to confusion with the goods, work, performance or business of a third party are unlawful (Art. 3(d) Unfair Competition Statute). This provision aims at preventing the practice of passing-off or counterfeiting. Rules similar to those of trade mark law apply with regard to limits on the monopolisation of certain terms, designs or figures (such as generic terms or numbers) which must remain open for general use (see ¶1309). Therefore, the use of a competitor's design or advertising may be deceptive only if the design or advertising is original or imaginative and, in consequence, is viewed by the consumer as an element of the identity of a given merchant's goods. Whether an act of counterfeiting or passing-off is deceptive is decided according to the ability of the average consumer to distinguish the goods or services in question. The concept of the distinctiveness of goods and services or elements thereof is decisive in this connection.

(4) Comparative advertising
This is yet another variety of information about the goods and services of others. Such practices are examined not so much under the aspect of deception, as with regard to possible disparagement. Comparative advertising which is misleading is prohibited because it is unclear, incomplete or irrelevant and causes incorrect or false impressions (ATF 104 II 124). The comparison may further be deceptive if essential facts have been omitted (ATF 55 II 178). Only the comparable may be compared (ATF 104 II 133). A fair comparison in advertising or otherwise must further be objectively true (ATF 104 II 127, 102 II 291, 94 IV 38, 87 II 116).

Finally, even if it is correct and not misleading, a comparison is regarded as unfair if it is unnecessarily disparaging, e.g., if the comparison:

(a) is made without due regard to material facts;

(b) is disproportionate; or

(c) unnecessarily refers to the goods and services of a competitor. This would in particular be the case if a comparison is made merely in order to benefit from the good reputation of a competitor or of a competitor's products. 'Unnecessarily' in this context means without a justifying reason (ATF 102 II 292).

In spite of all these limiting aspects, the law still follows the rule that comparative advertising is admissible if within the limits of fair competition.

(5) Unfair sales methods
Certain marketing practices which contain elements of deception or unreasonably influence consumers are deemed unfair practices. Although premiums are admissible in principle, they are regarded as unfair if they deceive the consumer about the effective value of the goods offered (Art. 3(g) Unfair Competition Statute). Aggressive sales methods which affect a consumer's liberty of decision are also regarded as unfair (Art. 3(h) Unfair Competition Statute). This provision does not prohibit all kinds of aggressive sales methods, merely practices where

¶1209

the consumer comes under psychological coercion. Typical examples of improper methods are bus tours for sales, sales at private parties or, under certain circumstances, door-to-door sales. Since 1 July 1991, the consumer has been protected against these kinds of aggressive sales: Article 40a et seq. CO grants a right of rescission which must be exercised within seven days.

Lotteries in which participation depends on the conclusion of a contract, in particular the purchase of goods, are prohibited under a special Federal Statute on Lotteries and Commercial Betting. Whether there is coercion for a purchase is determined not with regard to the effective system of the sales lottery, but rather on the basis of the impact of the advertising of the sales lottery on the average consumer (ATF 99 IV 30).

When goods, works or performances are offered, their quality, quantity, purpose, benefit or danger must not be concealed (Art. 3(i) Unfair Competition Statute). A consumer may be deceived in this regard through a lack of information about the product itself, or by methods of packaging which imply greater quantities than are effectively contained. This provision should in particular help to improve product information.

Price undercutting, in the sense of repeated selling below cost, is regarded as an unfair practice if it is used in advertising and the consumer is deceived about the capacities of the seller or those of competitors (Art. 3(f) Unfair Competition Statute), e.g., if price undercutting is limited to a few goods only (loss-leader), while the consumer is led to believe that it applies to all or a major part of the goods offered. This provision is a new one, enacted only with the current statute. Deception is the element that renders price undercutting illegal. Price undercutting is assumed if the sales price is below the prime cost of similar goods, works or performances. This reversal of the burden of proof is a clear advantage for the claimant affected by unfair advertising of price undercutting. If a defendant competitor can establish his effective cost price, this will be relevant for judging his sales method (Art. 3(f) Unfair Competition Statute, last sentence). In view of the different objects of protection, sales below cost may be unlawful under the rules of the Cartel Statute (see ¶1203(1)(a)).

The prohibition of certain deceptive methods in connection with advertising for instalment sales or consumer credits has a clear consumer protection character (Art. 3(k), (l) and (m) Unfair Competition Statute).

¶1210   Interference with contractual relations – abuse of standards

(1)   Effects of contract upon third parties
Contracts normally affect only the contracting parties, and only a contracting party can bring suit for breach of contract. As a result, there is no remedy under

contract law (as opposed to tort law) against a third party who induces one of the contracting parties to breach the contract. Third parties may induce a contracting party to breach a contract either in order to enter into a similar contract themselves, or to obtain the results of the breach of contract (e.g., trade secrets); in any case, their acts contravene the basic principle that contracts must be performed (*pacta sunt servanda*) and are deemed unfair if they are undertaken in order to benefit from the breach of contract (Art. 4(a) and (b) Unfair Competition Statute). A specific example of the general prohibition on inducing a breach of contract is an effort to convince a purchaser under an instalment purchase agreement plan or a debtor under a consumer credit to revoke or terminate the contract so that a new contract can be concluded with the inducing party (Art. 4(d) Unfair Competition Statute).

(2) Breach of trust
A specific variation is the inducement of employees or other agents to breach or spy out the trade secrets of their employers or principals (Art. 4(c) Unfair Competition Statute; see ¶1323).

(3) Breach of law or contract
Fairness in competition implies that all competitors will abide equally by applicable statutory rules or regulations, and that they will reap no benefit from illegal practices such as non-observance of these legal or regulatory rules. While, for example, a patent holder has a direct claim for patent infringement against the infringer, a licensee of an invention has no claim under patent law against a competitor who infringes the patent in question. The rules against unfair competition may grant him relief.

The Unfair Competition Statute considers unfair the non-observance of regular working conditions, e.g., maximum working hours, whether they are imposed by statutory rules or collective labour agreements or prevail otherwise in a given trade or place (Art. 7 Unfair Competition Statute). While this provision clearly aims at fairness between competitors, the use of abusive business conditions is prohibited in order to protect consumers as well.

The provision of Art. 8 of the Unfair Competition Statute focuses on preventing the abuse of business conditions which are normally prepared and used by the stronger of the two parties in a purchase of consumer goods. Such provisions are outlawed if they deviate considerably from the statutory framework, or provide for an uneven distribution of rights and obligations irreconcilable with the nature of the transaction. Not every deviation from the legal framework is unfair, only those that are made to the detriment of the consumer. In addition, there is abuse of business conditions if a consumer confronted with fine print is not made aware of but, rather, is deceived about, deviations from normal standards.

¶1210

¶1211   Exploitation of third-party performance

(1)   Unfair competition law's reach beyond industrial property

In principle, one may use another person's industrial or intellectual achievements unless a patent, copyright, or other intellectual property law prohibits it. The use becomes unlawful if it shows parasitic aspects. Although parasitic exploitation has always been regarded as unfair, the Unfair Competition Statute introduced a specific provision (Art. 5 Unfair Competition Statute) that made it easier to prevent it.

(2)   Types of violations

Article 5 of the Unfair Competition Statute distinguishes three different ways by which someone can get hold of a third party's intellectual or industrial achievements:

First, Art. 5(a) of the Unfair Competition Statute covers the situation in which the work product has come into possession by mutual consent. The term 'work product' used in this provision has a narrow meaning. It implies a certain intellectual or other material effort which leads to a result. A mere thought does not enjoy protection under the Unfair Competition Statute. Unlawful exploitation means industrial or commercial application of the work product. Merely copying a plan is not prohibited unless the copy is used to achieve a concrete result. The Unfair Competition Statute mentions tender offers, calculations and plans.

Secondly, exploitation of a work product is unfair if possession was obtained indirectly through a third person to whom it was entrusted by the author of the work. To be unfair, the exploitation must be made in bad faith, i.e., with the knowledge that the person passing on the work product was not authorised to do so. This would be the case, for example, if a principal passed a would-be contractor's offer and corresponding plans on to another contractor for execution. The principal would have acted unfairly under Art. 3(a) of the Unfair Competition Statute, and the second contractor would be found guilty of unfair competition under Art. 5(b).

Finally, Art. 5(c) of the Unfair Competition Statute prohibits the appropriation and exploitation of the marketable work product of another person by copying through technical procedures without corresponding efforts of one's own. This provision is not aimed at creating a new category of monopoly in addition to patents, utility models, trade marks or copyrights, and does not prohibit the imitation of third-party performance; rather, it requires any imitation of a not otherwise protected work product to involve appropriate efforts by the imitator. By referring to technical procedures of reproduction, the law presupposes that sufficient efforts are not undertaken in connection with copying, pressing, dubbing and similar duplication techniques. Only the appropriation of a 'marketable' result is unfair. This makes it clear, once more, that mere ideas or methods are not protected. It further means that any adaptation or variation of a third party's work product which requires intellectual or material efforts on the part of the adaptor is permitted. This provision against improper exploitation of third-party performance can be applied to the unauthorised copying of sound and video recordings. Protection is granted not only to the copyright holders who enjoy a monopoly under the applicable statute anyway, but also to record producers (ATF 85 II 439, 87 II 335). Another field of application is the reprinting of books for which the copyright has expired, or the use of catalogue photographs.

¶1212   Industrial and trade secrets

There is no absolute protection of trade secrets under the Unfair Competition Statute, but certain patterns of behaviour or practices are deemed unfair acts. In particular, the exploitation or referral to others of trade secrets which have been ferreted out or obtained in another illegal way is unfair (Art. 6 Unfair Competition Statute). An example of an illegal act is inducing employees or agents to disclose or ferret out the trade secrets of their employers or principals, even if the particular trade secret is not exploited thereafter (Art. 4(c); see ¶1210). Trade secrets enjoy protection beyond the law of unfair competition under private or criminal law (¶1322 et seq.).

¶1213   Remedies

(1)   In general

All persons who are threatened or impaired in their economic interests may assert the remedies provided for by law (Art. 9(1) Unfair Competition Statute). Both the merchant who is affected by a competitor's unfair practices and the consumer may challenge the practices. In addition, consumer organisations of a certain national or regional importance have standing to sue; so do professional or trade unions which according to their by-laws are authorised to further the economic interests of their members (Art. 10(2) Unfair Competition Statute). The right of consumer organisations or unions does not extend to claims for compensatory or punitive damages (Art. 9(3) Unfair Competition Statute).

(2)   Actions available

Persons affected or threatened by unfair competition may request under Art. 9 of the Unfair Competition Statute:

(a)   an injunction against an imminent infringement;

(b)   the removal of an effective infringement, a cease and desist order; or

(c) a declaratory judgment as to the illegality of the infringement if it continues to have damaging effects.

In addition, the publication of the court order may be requested (Art. 9(2) Unfair Competition Statute). This should allow the claimant to remedy false, misleading or unnecessarily disparaging statements.

Under tort law, damages and compensation for pain and suffering are obtainable. Because of the need to establish fault and the problem of showing the amount of damage suffered, an action for damages is, in practice, not a very effective means of compensating the victim. In addition, awards of damages are usually rather modest (see, e.g., ATF 96 II 245).

(3) Jurisdiction

The ordinary courts at the domicile of the alleged unfair competitor have jurisdiction. Subsidiarily, if the alleged unfair competitors have their domicile or seat outside Switzerland, claims may be brought before the courts of the place where the unfair acts were committed or where they had their effects (Art. 129 Private International Law Statute).

(4) Injunctions

An injunction granted in summary proceedings is available to a claimant who can show the existence of a violation of the rules against unfair competition and an obvious damage. The provisional and conservatory measures can be taken under the provisions protecting privacy (Arts 28c to 28f CC). Injunctions requested under summary proceedings normally take three to five weeks.

(5) Commission for Fairness in Advertising

The Commission for Fairness in Advertising (¶1207) offers arbitration services. If it finds that unfair competition has occurred, the Commission issues a cease and desist order, which, if not accepted, is followed by publication of the cease and desist order with full identification of the unfair competitor.

(6) Criminal law

Unfair practices constitute misdemeanours if undertaken intentionally, and are punishable with imprisonment or fines up to SFr 100,000. A punishment requires criminal charges to be filed by the aggrieved competitor, a consumer or a consumer organisation.

¶1214   Administrative rules

The Unfair Competition Statute contains public law rules (for the distinction between public and private law, see ¶107) in so far as it obliges merchants to indicate prices when selling and advertising goods (Arts 16 and 17 Unfair

Competition Statute). It further prohibits misleading prices, especially deceptive price reductions (Art. 18 Unfair Competition Statute; see Art. 3(a) Unfair Competition Statute).

The rules for clear and correct price notifications to consumers are enforced not only through claims brought by deceived consumers or aggrieved competitors under the private-law rules of the Unfair Competition Statute, but also directly by the competent cantonal authorities (Art. 20 Unfair Competition Statute) under the supervision of the federal authorities. In consequence, consumers or competitors having knowledge of deceptive practices may simply notify the competent cantonal authority instead of filing a lawsuit in their own name.

¶1215 Sales

Sales, in the narrow terminology of the Unfair Competition Statute, are liquidation sales and similar actions whereby the seller, through public advertisements, offers special discounts or other benefits but only for a limited period of time. The sales require a permit from the competent cantonal authority (Art. 21(1) Unfair Competition Statute). Based on the authorisation in the Unfair Competition Statute, the Federal Government issued an Ordinance on Liquidation Sales and Similar Actions, which has been in force since 1 March 1988 (the Liquidation Sales Ordinance).

Certain categories of goods (such as food, soaps and detergents, and body care products) are exempted from the permit requirement (Art. 1(2)(a) Liquidation Sales Ordinance). Further, the rules of the Liquidation Sales Ordinance do not apply to liquidations which are ordered or supervised by a governmental authority, such as the liquidation of a company in a bankruptcy proceeding (Art. 1(2)(b)).

The limits on advertising a permitted sale are regulated in Art. 9 et seq. Sales are permitted for a limited time only, up to a maximum of six months, and are subject to a series of other requirements. After a permitted liquidation sale, the applicant must not re-open a similar business within a period of one to five years; the time period is determined by the cantonal authority.

Non-compliance with the rules of the Liquidation Sales Ordinance constitutes a criminal offence if committed intentionally (Art. 25 Unfair Competition Statute).

SELECTED BIBLIOGRAPHY

François Brunner, *Document: Le projet de révision de la loi fédérale sur les cartels, Revue suisse du droit international de la concurrence* (1982), pp. 55 et seq.

Lucas David, *Schweizerisches Werberecht* (Zürich, 1977)

——, *Schweizerisches Wettbewerbsrecht*, 2nd edn (Bern, 1988)

Eric Homburger, *Kommentar zum Schweizerischen Kartellgesetz* (Zürich, 1990)

Eric Homburger and Jens Drolshammer, *Schweizerisches Kartell- und Monopolrecht, Bibliographie/Gerichtsentscheide/Arbeiten der Kartellkommission/Materialien* (Bern, 1981) (supplementary volume, 1987)

Edmond Martin-Achard, *La loi fédérale contre la concurrence déloyale du 19 décembre 1986* (Lausanne, 1988)

Isabelle Romy, Eve W. Gautier and Martin Wernli, *Concurrence déloyale: textes legislatifs et répertoire des arrêts fédéraux* (Lausanne, 1989)

Walter R. Schluep, '*Switzerland*', in J.O. Kalinovski (ed.), *World Law of Competition*, Unit B, Part 11 (Vol. 6) (New York, 1981)

——, '*Wirksamer Wettbewerb*', *Schlüsselbegriff des neuen schweizerischen Wettbewerbsrechts* (Bern, 1987)

Leo Schürmann and Walter R. Schluep, *Kommentar zum Kartellgesetz und Preisüberwachungsgesetz* (Zürich, 1988)

Roger Zäch (ed.), *Kartellrecht auf neuer Grundlage* (St Gallen, 1989)

All reports of the Federal Cartel Commission and an overview of its activities are published in: *Publications de la Commission suisse des cartels et du préposé à la surveillance des prix/Veröffentlichungen der Schweizerischen Kartellkommission und des Preisüberwachers*

13 Industrial and Intellectual Property

PRINCIPAL LEGISLATION

Loi fédérale sur les brevets d'invention/Patentgesetz/Federal Patent Statute, RS 232.14.

Ordonnance relative aux brevets d'invention/Patentverordnung/Patent Ordinance, RS 232.141.

Loi fédérale sur les dessins et modèles industriels/Muster- und Modellgesetz/ Federal Statute on Industrial Designs and Models, RS 232.12.

Loi fédérale concernant la protection des marques de fabrique et de commerce, des indications de provenance et des mentions de récompenses industrielles/ Markenschutzgesetz/Federal Trade Mark Statute, RS 232.11.

Ordonnance sur la protection des marques de fabrique et de commerce/ Markenschutzverordnung/Trade Mark Ordinance, RS 232.111.

Loi fédérale concernant le droit d'auteur sur les oeuvres littéraires et artistiques/ Urheberrechtsgesetz/Federal Copyright Statute, RS 231.1..

Loi fédérale contre la concurrence déloyale/Gesetz gegen den unlauteren Wettbewerb/Federal Unfair Competition Statute, RS 241.

Loi fédérale sur la protection des obtentions végétales/Sortenschutzgesetz/ Federal Statute for the Protection of Plant Varieties, RS 232.16.

PATENTS

¶1301 Sources of law

In view of the general globalisation of markets, particularly for technology, supranational rules for the protection of inventions will become increasingly important. However, since patent law is still governed by the principle of territoriality (i.e., protection of an invention against infringement has to be sought with the ordinary courts in the country where the infringement occurred), national law still applies to most basic aspects of patent protection. To a certain degree, these national rules have been harmonised through international conventions.

The primary sources of patent law are the Federal Patent Statute of 25 June 1954 (Patent Statute, RS 232.14) as amended in 1976, and its implementing Ordinance of 19 October 1977 (Patent Ordinance, RS 232.141) as amended in 1986.

A Bill to further amend the Patent Statute, dated 16 August 1989, is under parliamentary discussion. This Bill aims at improved protection of inventions in the field of biotechnology (see ¶1324), the abolition of official prior examination, the admission of product-by-process claims, more severe criminal sanctions against patent infringement and other changes.

On the international level, Switzerland is not only party to the Paris Convention in its Stockholm version of 14 July 1967 (RS 0.232.04), but also to the European Patent Convention of 5 October 1973 (RS 0.232.142.2). In addition, Switzerland has ratified the Patent Co-operation Treaty of 19 June 1970 (RS 0.232.141.1), the Strasbourg Convention for the unification of certain patent elements (RS 0.232.142.1), the Strasbourg Convention on the International Classification of Patents of 24 March 1971 (RS 0.232.143.1), and the Budapest Treaty on international recognition of deposit of micro-organisms for patent procedures of 28 April 1977 (RS 0.232.145.1). Of the bilateral treaties in the field of patents, the most important is the treaty with Liechtenstein of 22 December 1978, effective since 1 April 1980 (RS 0.232.149.514). Switzerland and Liechtenstein became a combined territory for patent purposes in the sense of Art. 45 of the Patent Co-operation Treaty.

¶1302   Domestic patents

(1) Patentability
Not every invention is patentable. In order to obtain patent protection, an invention must meet the criteria in the rules of the Patent Statute, as interpreted and refined by the courts.

Under these rules, a patent may be obtained if an invention is new and technically advanced, in the sense of representing an 'inventive step' on the one hand and being industrially applicable and useful on the other.

(2) Novelty
Novelty is determined by comparing the invention as defined by the patent claim with the 'state of the art' (Arts 1(2) and 7 Patent Statute). Everything that has been made accessible to the public by written or oral description, by use or in another way before the patent application is filed must be considered as part of the 'state of the art' (Art. 7(2) Patent Statute). 'Accessible to the public' does

not necessarily mean that an invention has been published in the strict sense but that access is possible (ATF 95 II 363). The relevant date for accessibility is the application date or the priority date by which the inventor has applied for patent protection for the same invention in another country of the Paris Convention, which must not be more than 12 months prior to the filing of the application in Switzerland. Novelty is missing only if all elements of the invention are reflected in one source of the 'state of the art'. Each source must be compared individually with the invention: a combination of sources is not permitted (ATF 94 II 319). In connection with novelty, the law provides for a few specific rules (Art. 7a et seq. Patent Statute) on prior identical patent applications, misuse of information relating to the invention, international exhibitions and new use of known substances.

(3) Inventive activity
Anything that manifestly follows from the 'state of the art' shall not be patented as an invention (Art. 1(2) Patent Statute). Therefore, besides being new, an invention must be the result of an inventive activity, and may not just be derived from the 'state of the art'. Whether an invention represents an 'inventive step' is often the main issue in nullity proceedings, where the court normally has recourse to the opinion of an expert in the relevant field. The basis for the determination of the 'inventive steps' is, again, the 'state of the art' (see preceding paragraph). There are various and different criteria for the 'inventive step', such as a long-existing unsatisfied need in the industry, considerable technical progress (ATF 102 II 373), and complicated and costly research which led to the invention in question (ATF 93 II 504). The fact that the experts in the field of the invention are surprised is not necessarily an indication that something is an 'inventive step' (ATF 114 II 82).

(4) Industrial applicability
Industrial applicability (Art. 1(1) Patent Statute) is not easily definable. The invention must be apt to be produced industrially or as a working tool. A procedure which can only be used privately does not fulfil these requirements. Nevertheless, a device which by electronic means helped to determine a person's critical days from the point of view of his or her biorhythm, was regarded as industrially applicable. On the other hand, a scheme for protection against cosmic radiation was denied industrial applicability.

(5) Usefulness
The requirement of usefulness is normally the least important obstacle to obtaining a patent. Usefulness is defined as the social value of an invention for the satisfaction of a human need.

¶1302

(6)   Non-patentable invention

Certain types of inventions are expressly excluded from patent protection by the Patent Statute or do not qualify as inventions in the sense of this statute, e.g. inventions which would be immoral or contrary to public order (Art. 2(a) Patent Statute), methods of surgical or therapeutic treatment and of diagnosis applied to the human or animal body, new varieties of plants or breeds of animals, and essentially biological processes for the production of plants or animals. On the other hand, inventions regarding microbiological processes and the relating products are patentable (Art. 1a Patent Statute). In addition, a federal statute (RS 232.16) protects plant varieties, and the improvement of patent protection in the field of biotechnology is one of the objects of a currently pending Bill for the amendment of the Patent Statute (¶1301 and ¶1324 et seq.). Computer software is excluded from patent protection; protection for software must be sought under the rules of copyright instead (¶1321 et seq.).

(7)   Filing patent applications

For the filing of a patent application, the following documents have to be submitted to the Federal Intellectual Property Office (*Office fédérale de la propriété intellectuelle/Bundesamt für geistiges Eigentum*, in 3003 Bern):

(a) application form (available from the Office);

(b) technical drawings referred to in the description or in the claims; and

(c) description of the invention, together with one or more patent claims.

The description must carry a title that gives the invention a clear and concise technical designation. This designation must not be misleading. The description must contain the 'state of the art' as it is known to the applicant, followed by a description of the invention in such a way that the average expert in the field understands the technical problem and its solution.

Together with the application, or within a time limit set by the Office, the following items must be submitted or paid:

(a) application fee and claim fees;

(b) abstract on the technical aspects of the invention;

(c) two more copies of the technical documentation;

(d) power of attorney for the agent, if any;

(e) fee for search and examination, if any.

Within 16 months from the date of application or the priority date, the inventor must be named and the certificate of priority has to be submitted (Art. 21 Patent Ordinance).

¶1302

(8)   Examination

All inventions are subject to an examination by the Office as to the industrial applicability of the invention and its possible exclusion from patentability under the Patent Statute (¶1302(4) and (6) above). In addition, the Office examines the fulfilment of the formalities, and sometimes, if necessary, grants a period of time for the correction of defects. Decisions of the Office may be appealed to the Federal Supreme Court.

The Office examines the following inventions for novelty and 'inventive steps': inventions relating to not purely mechanical processes for the improvement of raw or manufactured textile fibres for use in the textile industry and respective processes, and inventions relating to chronometric technology. If an application is subject to an additional examination, the applicant has to pay both a fee for determination of the 'state of the art' and a fee for the examination of novelty and 'inventive steps' carried out by the Office. If the result is positive and the applicant has paid the printing fee, the application will be published. During three months from the date of the publication, anybody may oppose the granting of the patent for lack of novelty or 'inventive steps', for being excluded from patent protection or for lack of title to the invention.

(9)   Duration

Patents are granted for a period of 20 years counting from the filing date of the application, provided the annual fees are paid (see (10) below).

Apart from expiration, non-payment of annual fees or successful opposition if the invention is subject to additional examination, a patent can only be defeated based on a declaratory judgment by a competent court stating the nullity of the patent. To justify their activity, infringers of patents routinely invoke the nullity of the patent.

(10)   Fees

The application fee amounts to SFr 100, plus supplementary fees for printing and for filing an application for more than ten claims.

The special fees for applications subject to additional examination are SFr 1,200 for the search of the 'state of the art' and SFr 600 for the examination for novelty and 'inventive steps'.

The annual fee for a patent gradually increases from SFr 100 for the third year from the filing to SFr 800 for the twentieth year.

(11)   Scope of patent protection

The effect of the patent is the exclusive right to the industrial (as opposed to private, non-professional) use of the invention. The use of the invention reserved to the patent owner includes manufacturing, offering or selling the patented product and the use of the patented process. If the invention concerns a process, the exclusive rights of the patent owner extend to the immediate products of this process (Art. 8(3) Patent Statute).

Legal actions may be taken under civil or criminal law against persons who unlawfully use the patented invention or assist others in doing so. A patent is infringed only if there is a territorial connection between Switzerland and the unlawful use of the invention. For an action to be successful, either the use itself (e.g. manufacture, use, sale or offering) must take place in Switzerland or the activities committed abroad must show effects within Switzerland (ATF 100 II 237). Not only the use of the patented invention but also its imitation is considered an infringement. The area of protection of a patent is broader than just the patent claims themselves.

A patent owner may seek a remedy against patent infringement with the cantonal courts designated for patent matters (Zurich: *Handelsgericht*; Geneva: *Cour de justice civile*); appeal to the Federal Supreme Court is possible. The plaintiff may ask for declaratory or injunctive relief, or damages. Upon the plaintiff's motion, the court may order the sale or destruction of unlawfully manufactured products or the facilities used to produce them. The publication of a court decision may be ordered. The wilful infringement of a patent is a criminal offence punishable by imprisonment or a fine of up to SFr 20,000.

(12) Patent, licences, assignment

The applicant or owner of a patent may permit third parties to use the invention under a licence. The licence may be entered in the patent register, thus becoming effective against third parties. Otherwise there are no formalities for the granting of a licence. A right to be granted a licence is provided for by law in the case of dependent inventions, i.e., when a patented invention cannot be used without violating a prior patent (Art. 36 Patent Statute). Compulsory licences may further be obtained if a patented invention is not exploited for a period of more than three years from the date the patent is granted, or in the case of inventions in the public interest (Art. 40 Patent Statute).

A patent or an application may be assigned by a written instrument; no further formalities are necessary. If the assignment should be recorded in the patent register, it requires the certified signature of the assignor.

A patent may be the object of execution or attachment proceedings and may be pledged.

¶1303 European patents

Switzerland is a member of the European Patent Convention (RS 0.232.142.2). In consequence, patent protection may be obtained not only through an application with the Federal Intellectual Property Office (¶1302), but also through an application for a European patent with the European Patent Office.

Domestic patent law in general, and the Patent Statute in particular, governs European applications and patents, as well as international applications pursuant to the Patent Co-operation Treaty (PCT, RS 0.232.141.1) if the application covers Switzerland. These patents are primarily governed by the provisions of Art. 110 et seq. of the Patent Statute (for European patents) and Art. 132 et seq. (for PCT applications). The general rules of the Patent Statute are subsidiarily applied as long as they are in conformity with the applicable convention.

The application procedure for a European patent is governed by the rules of the European Patent Convention (Art. 75 et seq.). The owner of a European patent covering Switzerland has the same rights as the owner of a domestic patent. Unlike domestic patent applications, applications for a European patent are subject not only to a formal examination but also to an examination as to novelty and 'inventive steps', irrespective of the subject matter of the invention. In consequence, applications for a European patent are always published and are subject to opposition by third parties.

Patent protection may also be obtained through a PCT application filed with a foreign patent office and referred to the Federal Intellectual Property Office. An application for Switzerland under the rules of the PCT is governed by the provisions of the Patent Statute.

Although Switzerland is not a member of the European Community, the 1975 Convention on Patents for the Common Market and the patent rights granted thereunder will become available for owners of European patents, even if the owner is not domiciled within a country of the European Community. The convention for a community patent has not yet become effective.

INDUSTRIAL DESIGNS AND MODELS

¶1304 Sources of law

Industrial designs, in the sense of a physical shape or form (possibly in combination with colours) to be used in the industrial production of an object, may be protected if the relevant statutory rules are followed. Unlike a patented invention, which defines a technical rule, an industrial design covers the aesthetic aspects of an object and, therefore, is closer to copyright. An industrial design does not require creative activity but only a relative originality.

The sources of law are the Federal Statute on Industrial Designs and Models of 30 March 1900, as amended (RS 232.12), the Federal Ordinance of 27 July 1900 (RS 232.121), and the Federal Statute on Priority Rights for Patents and Industrial Designs and Models of 3 April 1914 (RS 232.13).

Switzerland is a member of the Hague Convention for the International Depositing of Industrial Designs and Models of 28 November 1960 (RS 0.232.121.2), and of the Locarno Convention for the International Classification of Industrial Designs of 8 October 1968 (RS 0.232.121.3).

¶1305   Registration of industrial designs or models

Applications for the registration of an industrial design or model are filed with the Federal Intellectual Property Office. The application must indicate the applicant, its agent, the creator of the design or the model if not identical with the applicant, and, in general terms, the object of the design or model. An application may cover more than one design or model and may be submitted openly or under seal. The applicant may request that the design or model be kept secret for the first five years of protection. The designs or models must be submitted in drawings, photographs or specimens.

The deposit of an industrial design or model is invalid and may be cancelled if a court finds that the industrial design or model was not new at the time it was deposited, that the applicant had no title, that the contents of a sealed design or model were misleadingly described, or that the contents of the deposition are in conflict with federal laws or international treaties or are immoral in nature.

Under the Hague Convention, protection of a design or model may also be obtained by filing an application with the International Office of the World Intellectual Property Organisation in Geneva. This application has the same effect as a national application; applicants are not required to base an international application on a national registration.

¶1306   Legal protection of industrial designs and models

Protection is granted against the unlawful use of an industrial design or model (e.g., its use for promotion or commercial exploitation), provided it has been deposited according to the rules of the federal statute or the Hague Convention. The protection is available for a maximum of 15 years from the date of deposit, provided the necessary fees have been paid.

The owner of an industrial design or model is protected not only against the unlawful use of the design or model itself, but also of imitations thereof. Imitation occurs if the original design may be distinguished from the imitation only under close scrutiny and similarity prevails with regard to the protected elements of a design or model.

Infringement of an industrial design or model permits the owner to seek injunctive relief and damages from the infringer. A court may further order the sale or destruction of unlawfully manufactured products or equipment used for their manufacture. Wilful infringement is a criminal offence, punishable with imprisonment or a fine.

The owner of an industrial design or model may grant licences for commercial use or assign his or her rights. In order to be effective with regard to third parties, the assignment or the licence must be entered in the register of designs and models. Industrial designs or models may be the object of execution or attachment proceedings, or of a pledge.

TRADE MARKS AND TRADE NAMES

¶1307 Sources of law

Trade marks and trade names play an important part in the promotion and marketing of goods and services. They provide a practical means by which the consumer can attribute goods and services to a specific manufacturer or distributor. They form part of the good-will and the corporate identity that a business has built up. While trade marks are among the most typical industrial property rights, trade names contain an additional element of personality right. By definition, trade marks are devices that are used only for the distinction or determination of the origin of goods. Trade names, on the other hand, are primarily used to identify business entities.

Trade marks are governed first of all by the Federal Trade Mark Statute of 26 September 1890, as amended (Trade Mark Statute), and its implementing ordinance of 24 April 1929 (Trade Mark Ordinance). A draft for a new trade mark statute of 21 November 1990 (the Draft) is currently being discussed and has been widely accepted. The enactment of the Draft is expected.

Unlike trade marks, trade names are not governed by one statute but are dealt with in various federal statutes. Provisions on trade names are primarily found in the Code of Obligations (Art. 944 et seq. on corporate names), the Ordinance on the Register of Commerce (RS 221.411, Arts 39, 44 to 46 and 70), the Trade Mark Statute (Art. 2), and the Civil Code (Arts 29 and 30 on name rights).

Both trade marks and trade names find additional protection under the provisions of the Unfair Competition Statute (RS 241, ¶1207 above).

The registration and protection of trade marks and trade names of holders not domiciled in Switzerland are governed by the rules of the Paris Convention for the Protection of Industrial Property (RS 0.232.04, Stockholm Revision), the Madrid Convention for the Registration of Trade Marks (RS 0.232.112.3, Stockholm Revision), and the Treaty of Nice on International Classification of Goods and Services (RS 0.232.112.9, Geneva Revision).

¶1308   Creation of trade marks: first use

Trade mark law currently holds that the trade mark right is not created by registration but by the first use of the trade mark in Switzerland, i.e., on the goods or the packaging of the goods. Therefore, registration is not decisive for the trade mark right but is only a prerequisite for being granted the protection provided by the Trade Mark Statute against infringements. In consequence, the first user has priority (even if he or she has not registered) over the owner of a subsequent registration who has not yet used the trade mark. This concept of first use might be overturned once the Draft is enacted; in that case, the trade mark right would be created by the entry of the trade mark in the register (Art. 5 Draft).

¶1309   Registration of trade marks

In spite of the first user concept discussed above, registration is recommended under the current rules as well, since a valid registration is prima facie evidence of first use (Art. 5 Trade Mark Statute), and grants the owner three years within which to start using a trade mark without losing his or her trade mark right because of non-use (Art. 9(1) Trade Mark Statute).

Currently, only industrial companies, other producers or distributors of goods, or unions or associations thereof may obtain a trade mark registration (Arts 7 and 7bis Trade Mark Statute). The Draft will allow for registration by non-commercial owners as well.

A registered trade mark may only be two-dimensional. The shape of a mascot or a bottle cannot be registered as a trade mark; only a two-dimensional version can be registered (see industrial models, ¶1304).

Since a trade mark must be used to identify and distinguish the goods of a specific producer or distributor, it must have distinctive characteristics. The name of the goods themselves may not serve as a trade mark, even if it is new. The need for distinctiveness further rules out words that merely describe the goods (e.g., 'Top Set' for cigarettes) or simple geometric forms, letter combinations or numbers. These trade marks may be registered once their use is established and they have gained distinctiveness in spite of their generic character. With regard to descriptive terms not admitted as trade marks, the Federal Supreme Court has adopted a rather broad interpretation, e.g., by ruling out *'alta tensione'* for knitted women's wear (ATF 114 II 371). According to the general rule that certain words and terms must be reserved for the public domain and may not be monopolised, public coats of arms, national emblems or emblems of Swiss communities may not be used in trade marks. Specific federal statutes set general rules for the use of public coats of arms, other public emblems, and names of international organisations (RS 232.21 et seq.).

The application must specify the goods for which the trade mark is to be used. This list of goods will be crucial for the range of protection of a trade mark. It must be precise: inexact lists of goods are invalid, with the consequence that the trade mark lacks protection. Currently, service marks are not registered in Switzerland. This disadvantage for the service industry will be corrected by the Draft.

Finally, in order to be registered, a trade mark must be distinguishable from prior registered trade marks with regard to essential elements. Whether this requirement is fulfilled is decided based on the overall impression that the trade mark leaves on the average consumer.

The Federal Intellectual Property Office admits a trade mark in cases of doubt, and leaves it to the owner of the prior trade mark to raise opposition. The question of whether trade marks are similar is, of course, the major issue in connection with infringements (see ¶1310 below). Similar criteria, such as the similarity of the goods for which the trade mark is used, apply.

¶1310   Scope of trade mark protection

A trade mark grants its holder the exclusive right to use it for the goods for which the trade mark is registered and for substitutes of the goods. Protection is granted under the Trade Mark Statute against unauthorised use of the same or a confusingly similar trade mark for the same or similar goods (Art. 24(a) Trade Mark Statute). According to the principle of territoriality governing trade mark law, trade mark infringement occurs only if the infringing trade mark has been used in Switzerland on the goods or the packaging. In addition, the goods must be put into circulation within Switzerland. Free ports are regarded as Swiss territory for that purpose. The repackaging of goods with an infringing trade mark in a free port, even if destined not for Switzerland but for re-export, has been considered a trade mark infringement (ATF 110 IV 108). The use of an infringing trade mark other than on the goods themselves (e.g., only in promotion or in correspondence) is not considered a trade mark infringement, but may be an act of unfair competition (¶1207 et seq.).

Whether one trade mark is confusingly similar to another is decided based on the ability of the average consumer in the market of the goods in question to distinguish between them. The average consumer would normally not see or hear the two conflicting trade marks at the same time. The overall impression, as it can be recalled by the consumer, not the individual elements of a trade mark, is decisive. On the other hand, the main elements of a trade mark are more easily memorised and normally determine the overall impression. Trade marks that differ only in minor elements of design and colour are, therefore, not sufficiently distinct. In view of the main purpose of a trade mark, namely to identify the origin of goods, the similarity of the goods for which similar trade marks are used is an important consideration. The more similar the goods are, the more the trade marks must differ from each other. The risk of confusion between two trade marks can be decided not only visually, but also acoustically.

As the purpose of a trade mark is the identification and prevention of confusion with regard to the origin of goods, the owner of a famous trade mark needs more than usual protection against confusion of consumers, because its name and reputation may be damaged if goods of a poor quality are circulated under its famous trade mark, even if the goods differ substantially from its customary goods. Currently, the holder of a famous trade mark can find relief only under the rules of unfair competition (¶1207). In contrast, the Draft will give the holder of a famous trade mark the right to exclude and prevent the use by a third person for any kind of goods, if this use blurs the distinctiveness of the famous trade mark or takes advantage of the trade mark (Art. 15(1) Draft).

The following actions are deemed acts of infringement:

(1) the use of an infringing trade mark on one's own goods;

(2) the sale, offering, or bringing into circulation of goods with an infringing trade mark;

(3) conscious participation in such acts; and

(4) refusal to indicate the origin of products or goods that bear an infringing trade mark (Art. 24 Trade Mark Statute).

Legal action may be taken under civil or penal law against trade mark infringement. The plaintiff may request injunctive or declaratory relief, or damages. Upon the plaintiff's motion, the court may order the attachment and destruction of goods with an infringing trade mark or the equipment used for the infringement. In view of the possible confusion created by an infringing trade mark, the publication of the court decision is also important. Wilful trade mark infringement is a criminal offence, punishable by imprisonment or a fine. Actions may be brought by the owner of a trade mark and, under certain circumstances, by consumers of goods with an infringing trade mark, but not by the licensee of a trade mark holder or by consumer organisations. Actions must be brought before the court designated by the cantons for trade mark matters (Zurich: *Handelsgericht*; Geneva: *Cour de justice civile*) (Art. 29 Trade Mark Statute), either at the domicile of the infringer or, if the infringer has its domicile outside Switzerland, at the place where the trade mark infringement occurred or had its effects.

The Draft will strengthen civil and criminal remedies against trade mark infringement (Art. 53 et seq. Draft).

¶1310

¶1311 Transfer of trade mark rights: licence and assignment

The licensing and assignment of a trade mark are possible, provided the consumer will not be misled by the assignee's or licensee's use of the trade mark. Licences and assignments are valid only if there are either close economic ties between the parties (representing a certain guarantee that the quality of the goods for which the new user will use the trade mark will remain the same as with the original holder), or if the part of the business of the original trade mark holder where the goods were produced is taken over by an assignee or licensee. Trade mark licences may not be registered, and it is, therefore, a good idea to make consumers aware of the licence relationship by affixing a label on the goods themselves.

¶1312 Duration of trade mark protection

There is no statutory term for a trade mark right. A trade mark registration is valid for 20 years and may be renewed for further periods indefinitely. The existence of a valid trade mark right is dependent on the use of the trade mark in Switzerland. If the trade mark has not been used for three consecutive years on goods circulated in Switzerland or on the wrappings or containers, a court may order the cancellation of the trade mark if an interested party requests the cancellation. The Draft extends the period of permitted non-use to five years (Art. 12 Draft). Use of the trade mark in a form that differs only in non-essential elements is considered sufficient.

Once a trade mark is registered, the registration will terminate by expiration in the case of non-renewal, withdrawal by the registered holder, an order from the Federal Intellectual Property Office if a trade mark has been registered in error, or a court order.

¶1313 Trade names: registration and protection

(1) Selection of trade names

Although businesses may select their names freely, they have to observe certain rules established in the interest of the public if they seek registration and protection. While sole proprietorships and partnerships have to include the name of the proprietor or at least one partner in their names, companies (particularly corporations) are bound only by general rules. Corporations that use names of persons in their trade names have to indicate their incorporation by adding *SA* or *AG*, 'Corporation', or the like to their names. See ¶702.

Apart from this, the content of the trade name must be true, not misleading and not contrary to the public interest (Art. 944(1) CO). Elements which merely serve advertising purposes are not allowed in a company name (Ordinance on the Register of Commerce – RS 221.411, Art. 44(1)). National, territorial or regional designations are allowed in trade names only if the Federal Office of the Register of Commerce grants permission. Branches must use the same trade name as the company to which they belong; in the case of branches of companies domiciled outside Switzerland, the Swiss branch must include the location of the main office, its own location and a specific designation as a branch in its name, e.g., XYZ Corporation, New York, Zurich Branch.

(2)   Registration of trade names
Registration in the Register of Commerce is mandatory for anyone conducting a trading, manufacturing or other commercial business. The trade name has to be registered at the place of the company's main office (Art. 934(1) CO). Businesses may register even if they are not required to do so. Swiss branch offices of firms who have their main office abroad must register. A duly authorised person residing in Switzerland with authority to represent the branch must be appointed (Art. 934(2) CO). The Register of Commerce admits not only corporations and co-operative corporations, but also sole proprietorships, partnerships, associations and foundations. In addition, it is possible to register emblems as a special name for one's premises. Such emblems are subject to the same rules as trade names, i.e., they must be true, not misleading, not purely promotional, etc. (See ¶1209.)

(3)   Scope of trade name protection
Trade names registered in the Register of Commerce and published in the Official Journal of Commerce grant the holder an exclusive right of use (Art. 956 CO). The holder of a registered trade name enjoys protection against the unauthorised use of its name by anyone else. Since company names must be clearly distinguishable from any company name registered earlier, a claim against unauthorised use may be made not only against identical but also against confusingly similar trade names. Whether there is a risk of confusion between two trade names is decided based on a comparison of the two trade names overall, and not by comparing individual elements only. The main element which sticks in the memory of the public, and especially the persons dealing with the companies in question, is decisive. A risk of confusion was, therefore, assumed between 'Interstop AG' and 'Intershop Holding AG' (ATF 97 II 236). The owner of a registered trade name does not even have to tolerate the false impression created by a similar trade name that two companies are economically or legally related (ATF 98 II 70).

   If there is a trade name infringement, claims for injunctive relief and, in case of fault, for damages are available (Art. 956(2) CO).

   If trade names are registered in the Register of Commerce and are used as trade marks, i.e., on goods, packaging material or containers, the trade names are given the benefit of protection under trade mark rules (¶1308).

¶1313

Trade names which are not registered in the Register of Commerce – a situation faced by companies which just do business in Switzerland without having a subsidiary or branch there – are protected under the more general rules of name-protection in the Civil Code (Art. 29(2) CC), or under the rules against unfair competition (¶1207 et seq.).

¶1314   International aspects of trade mark protection

Because Switzerland is a member of the Madrid Convention for the registration of trade marks (RS 0.232.112.3, Stockholm Revision), the holder of a trade mark in another member country can obtain trade mark protection by including Switzerland in the list of countries applied for in connection with an international registration. The application is processed through the national trade mark office of the applicant and through the International Office in Geneva. A company with a branch registered in Switzerland may benefit from the Madrid Convention and apply for an international registration in the name of its Swiss branch, even if it is not domiciled within a member country of the Convention.

Foreign industrial companies and other producers or distributors of goods are allowed to register their trade marks if their country of domicile grants the same right to trade mark holders (Art. 7(1)(2) Trade Mark Statute). In such a case, foreign applicants from another member country of the Paris Convention for the Protection of Industrial Property may benefit from a rule of this Convention if they file an application in Switzerland not later than six months after applying in their home country.

The problem of parallel imports and their admissibility under trade mark rules has been solved by the argument that a trade mark infringement occurs only if the public is deceived. The holder of a trade mark may, therefore, not prevent the importation of the same quality of goods produced by the same trade mark holder or a related company abroad, because the public is not deceived about the quality of the product and does not associate the product with a specific local producer but only with the group as such. The case is different if local companies of the same group produce different qualities of the same goods but still use the same trade mark. In such a case, consumers are deceived if they are confronted with goods originating from a foreign member of the group but bearing the same trade mark as the one used by the Swiss producer of the same group. Hence, the Swiss company and holder of the trade mark in Switzerland may prevent the importation of the goods produced abroad (ATF 105 II 55). The treaty between Switzerland and the EC does not compel Switzerland to apply the provisions of the EC Treaty governing the trade of goods between member countries if preventing parallel imports based on trade marks is no longer possible.

Trade names of companies that are domiciled outside Switzerland and are not registered in Switzerland are treated the same way as non-registered trade names of Swiss companies. The fact that they may be registered in their home countries does not improve their situation. This is in line with the requirement of equal treatment for foreigners from other member countries, as provided in Art. 8 of the Paris Convention for the Protection of Industrial Property.

COPYRIGHT

¶1315   Sources of law

Copyright rules govern such different things as computer software, the Saturday night appearance of a local rock band, and the latest *haute couture* fashion design from Paris. The main source of law is the Federal Copyright Statute of 7 December 1922 (Copyright Statute, RS 231.1). Considerable efforts have been made in the past to revise this statute. A draft for a new copyright statute, dated 19 June 1989 (the Draft), is under parliamentary discussion. In addition, there are federal rules for the exploitation of copyrights.

On the international level, Switzerland is a member of the Universal Copyright Convention of 6 September 1952 (RS 0.231.0), and has ratified the Berne Convention for the Protection of Works of Literature and Art in its Stockholm version of 14 July 1967 (RS 0.213.14). In addition, Switzerland plans to adhere to the Rome Convention on Protection of Performers, Producers of Phonograms and Broadcasting Organisations, and to ratify the 1971 Convention against Phonogram Piracy and the 1974 Satellite Convention.

¶1316   Objects and owners of copyright

(1)   Objects of copyright protection
Although the Copyright Statute refers to works of literature and art, it is obvious that this definition must be interpreted in a very broad sense in order to include objects such as computer software. The interpretation given by the statute itself (Art. 1(2) Copyright Statute) includes scientific and geographic works and representation even if of a technical nature, choreographic works and pantomimes, recordable acts of all sorts, musical works, and works of art like drawings, paintings and sculptures.

An object or work has to be an 'original intellectual creation with individual features'. The aspects of originality and individuality are decisive in qualifying a work, object or act capable of copyright (ATF 113 II 196, 110 IV 105). Considerations of usefulness or aesthetics are irrelevant. A work must be new in the sense that it must be an original creation by its author. This excludes all works based on a work the author has known. On the other hand, translations, adaptations or variations of a work are treated as new works (Art. 4(1) Copyright Statute), with the rights of the copyright holder of the adapted original remaining reserved.

The requirements for copyright protection have raised questions in connection with software protection. The Draft expressly lists computer programs as protected works (Art. 2(2)(i) Draft).

There is a limit for copyrights, particularly in connection with objects such as furniture. If the shape of a chair, for example, is determined solely by its use as a chair, there is no room for individuality and, by extension, no copyright. On the other hand, even functional designs may contain elements of individuality and originality and may be copyrighted (ATF 113 II 196). The degree of originality required is not very high, but it must reach a certain level, which is clearly above the originality required in connection with industrial designs and models (¶1304 et seq.).

(2) Owner of copyright
The original owner of a copyright is always the individual author. Companies may never be authors, because they create works only through their employees or agents. Employers or principals become owners of copyrights in works created by their employees or agents only subsidiarily, based on an assignment provided for in a specific contract or in the statutory rules governing their relationship (ATF 100 II 169). The same rule applies to situations where a work is created by a multitude of persons, as in the production of a movie.

Producers of phonograms have no original copyright in the works reproduced by them; they must rely on the rules of unfair competition in the case of piracy (¶1211). Similarly, performing artists like singers or the members of an orchestra currently have a copyright of their own in their performance only if it may be regarded as an interpretation or adaptation of the original work of music or literature (ATF 110 II 411). Copyrights of performing artists are included in the revised copyright statute and are granted a minimum level of protection (Art. 34 et seq. Draft).

¶1317 Rights and protection

(1) Obtainment and scope of copyright
The object of copyright is formed in the mind of its author, but becomes a protectable object only after its communication. The communication may use various means, such as spoken or recorded language (including computer language), sound and pictures (whether recorded or not), and physical embodiment. The communicated form of an object may indicate whether it fulfils the requirements of individuality and originality.

¶1317

Unlike patents, trade marks and similar industrial property rights, objects of copyright need not be registered: there is no copyright register. Therefore, no formalities are necessary to create and maintain a copyright, although it is a good idea to apply copyright reservation notices to all copies of a work (where feasible) in accordance with international practice. The notice improves the author's chances in a copyright infringement suit.

The author's copyright is extensive. It includes the exploitation of the work in every possible way, including reproduction, circulation, public performance and transmission by telecommunications. These rights of exploitation may be licensed or assigned partially or completely, but the personal copyright always remains vested in the author. In consequence, the author may prevent an alteration of the work that impairs the integrity thereof, even if he or she has sold the work; in addition, he or she retains the right to be always identified as the author of the work.

A work is protected under copyright rules for the life of the author plus 50 years (Art. 36 Copyright Statute). Works published anonymously or under a pseudonym are protected for 50 years from the date of publication (Art. 37 Copyright Statute). According to the Draft, the same period of protection would apply to computer software and copyrights of performing artists and producers of phonograms (Art. 39 Draft).

(2) Copyright infringements and remedies
During the period of protection, the author and his or her successors have an exclusive right in the object of copyright and its use and exploitation. There are, however, a few exceptions to this monopoly. The most important is the exception for private use, which in turn, and in view of today's reproduction facilities, has its limits. Profit-orientated reproduction is not permitted in this connection. The Federal Supreme Court has ruled that the reproduction of newspaper articles in a company's internal circular letter with a volume of 530 copies does not qualify as private use. The copying of records and videos for private use is not a copyright infringement. The Draft tries to define private use in the personal field more narrowly, by limiting it to persons who are closely connected, such as relatives or friends (Art. 19(1)(a) Draft). Other exceptions to the exclusive right of the copyright holder are the right of quotation, the right to use melodies but not whole compositions, the right to use factual newspaper articles as opposed to essays, and the right to reproduce speeches in connection with the reporting thereof (Art. 24 Copyright Statute). Other important exceptions are schoolbooks and works of art which are permanently placed in areas open to the public.

Apart from these exceptions made in the public interest, all other use of a copyrighted object is considered an infringement, particularly the reproduction of a work by any means, the selling, offering or circulation of copies of the work, and public performance and transmission by telecommunications or by

¶1317

other means. Legal action may be taken under the civil or criminal law against copyright infringers. The owner of the copyright may seek injunctive or declaratory relief, or damages. Upon motion, a court may order the attachment, sale or destruction of unauthorised copies of the work or facilities used for their production. A temporary restraining order may be obtained, but it must be followed by a formal claim. Wilful copyright infringement is a criminal offence which will be prosecuted upon motion by the copyright holder, and which is punishable by a fine of up to SFr 5,000 (Art. 50 Copyright Statute). These sanctions will be increased considerably by the Draft, to imprisonment and fines of up to SFr 100,000 (Art. 63(2) Draft).

One court is designated by each canton to handle all copyright cases (Zurich: *Obergericht*; Geneva: *Cour de justice civile*). This court has jurisdiction if the infringer has its domicile there, or if the infringing activities were committed or had their effect within the canton.

SEMICONDUCTOR CHIP PROTECTION

¶1318 Scope of legal protection

Apart from computer software (¶1321 et seq.), microchips (integrated circuits made from semiconducting material) are a major element of today's technology. Copying is relatively easy. Legal protection against copying is available under the rules of unfair competition (¶1211) as an act of unfair exploitation of third-party performance. Copyright protection is usually unavailable because the chips, unlike certain computer software, lack originality and are usually not the result of intellectual activity.

In order to provide protection on international level, a convention for the protection of microelectronic semiconductor circuits was agreed upon in May 1989 in Washington. The EC has issued a guide-line in the same field. In order to obtain equal treatment for its own industry, Switzerland is taking the necessary steps to ratify the Washington Convention, e.g., the introduction of a federal statute for structure protection.

Although semiconductor chips are protected against copying under the rules against unfair competition, a draft statute for the protection of structures of integrated circuits was submitted to Parliament on 19 June 1989, together with the Draft for a revised copyright statute (¶1315) (Structure Statute; *Loi fédérale sur la protection des topographies de circuits intégrés/Topographiengesetz*). This statute would grant protection to uncommon three-dimensional structures of integrated circuits. Not originality, as with copyrightable software, but rarity would be the element required for protection of a structure. Registration with

¶1318

the Federal Intellectual Property Office would be a prerequisite for protection, which would last for a period of ten years from the application. However, there would be a limited period of protection of two years for structures which are not registered but simply circulated (Art. 9). The producer of a structure would have the exclusive right to reproduce the structure in any form, and to circulate and exploit it by any possible means.

The owner of a structure would benefit from the same civil and criminal remedies against infringement as those granted by the revised copyright statute against copyright infringement (¶1317). This protection would be granted to all structures of Swiss producers or Swiss branches of foreign producers and, irrespective of the producer, to structures having their first circulation in Switzerland. The same protection would further be granted to producers under the rules of the Washington Convention.

TRADE SECRETS AND KNOW-HOW

¶1319   Sources of law

There is no specific statute governing the rights in trade secrets and know-how and their protection, although at least industrial and commercial secrecy is a well-established legal concept. Know-how, on the other hand, is a term used by the contracting parties in connection with the definition of proprietary information and data which is not covered by patent or similar statutory rights for intellectual or industrial property.

While know-how is a general term, trade secrets are information which is neither public knowledge nor generally accessible. Trade secrets in that sense are not only all facts related to a manufacturing process or method, but also facts of a commercial nature which are neither in the public domain nor generally available, in the secrecy of which the holder has a justified interest and which the holder actually wishes to be kept secret (ATF 103 IV 284).

In the absence of a specific statute, protection of trade secrets and know-how depends mainly on the holder's own protective measures, whether factual (by non-divulgence) or contractual (through confidentiality or obligations not to compete). In specific circumstances, the holder may find additional support in statutory rules provided for other fields, particularly in connection with rules against unfair competition, rules of criminal law or rules for employment contracts. Where former trade secrets are embodied in patents or works capable of copyright, protection under the patent or copyright statute is the most effective way to protect the trade secret.

¶1320 Statutory protection of trade secrets

(1) Unfair competition and trade secrecy

The Unfair Competition Statute grants protection for trade secrets and know-how in two different connections. According to Art. 4(c) of the Unfair Competition Statute, inducing employees, agents or other assistants to divulge or spy out their employer's or principal's industrial or commercial secrets is considered an act of unfair competition. While this provision aims at the act of influencing others to infringe a trade secret, Art. 6 of the Unfair Competition Statute makes exploiting or communicating a trade secret which has been discovered in an illegal way an act of unfair competition. In connection with the protection of performance, trade secrets might further be protected from unauthorised use under Art. 5(a) and (b) of the Unfair Competition Statute, which makes the unauthorised exploitation of the results of someone else's work (like drafts, calculations or plans) an act of unfair competition. In such cases the remedies offered by the Unfair Competition Statute are available to the holder of the trade secrets (¶1207).

(2) Criminal law protecting trade secrets

Trade secrets may also be protected under certain criminal law provisions. This is most directly the case for Art. 162 of the Penal Code, which threatens with imprisonment or a fine any person who betrays an industrial or commercial secret which, pursuant to a statutory or contractual obligation, he or she should preserve. Persons taking advantage of the betrayal are subject to the same punishment. Under given circumstances, the infringement of trade secrets may constitute an abuse of confidence in the sense of Art. 140 of the Penal Code, e.g., if trade secrets are embodied in calculations or construction designs (ATF 81 IV 281).

(3) Contractual secrecy obligation

Some contractual relationships, such as employer-employee or principal-agent, contain a fiduciary duty to keep secret and not personally exploit the employer's or principal's trade secrets, even in the absence of an express contractual provision to this effect. The rules of the Code of Obligations on employment contracts expressly confirm this obligation in Art. 321a(4). Accordingly, during their employment, employees must neither make use of nor inform others of any fact to be kept secret, such as, in particular, manufacturing or business secrets that come to their knowledge while in the employer's service. This secrecy obligation continues even after the employment ends, but only to the extent required to safeguard the employer's legitimate interests. A similar obligation is stated for the agent in Art. 418d CO. The employer has the power to commit the employee to an obligation not to compete even after termination of the employment relationship, but this prohibition must be reasonably limited in terms of place, time and subject (Art. 340a(1) CO).

(4) Other laws

If the specific conditions are fulfilled in a given case, trade secrets and know-how might enjoy the protection of still other provisions of law, e.g., Art. 273 Penal Code (on economic espionage), Arts 179 et seq. (on violation of secrecy or privacy), and Art. 161 (on use of insider information). Other grounds of protection are the statutory secrecy obligations of certain groups of professionals such as lawyers and doctors (Art. 321 Penal Code), and the bank secrecy rules in Art. 47 of the Federal Banking Statute (¶1135 et seq.). Private law rules for the protection of personality (Art. 28 et seq. CC) and rules in connection with the right to inspect the books of a company (Arts 697(2) and 857(2) CO) also support the protection of trade secrets. Lastly, many rules of civil or administrative procedure safeguard trade secrets in connection with investigations and the taking of evidence.

SOFTWARE PROTECTION

¶1321 Statutory protection – programs

Software or computer programs are neither patentable nor the object of a specific statute.

A first draft Bill for the revision of the Copyright Statute of 18 December 1987 allocated a whole chapter to special protection of data processing programs (draft Bill of 18 December 1987, Art. 81 et seq.). The rules of this draft Bill proposed protection against unauthorised use, copying, sale or other means of exploitation for a period of 25 years from the development of the program. This idea was abolished due to the reaction of the computer industry. Another draft for a copyright statute, dated 19 June 1989, lists computer programs among the works capable of being copyrighted (draft Bill of 19 June 1989, Art. 2(2)(i)).

Whether and when this draft will pass Parliament and be enacted is quite uncertain, as it has drawn criticism from various sides.

¶1322 Software copyright

Software protection must be sought under the rules of the Copyright Statute in its current version, which dates from 7 December 1922. In consequence, software must qualify as a work under rules that were originally designed for works of literature and art. These rules are inadequate for software, particularly when it comes to requirements of originality and statistical uniqueness. As a result, copyright protection is not available for programs that are not original. Under certain circumstances, this gap may be closed by using the rules against unfair competition (¶1207 above). According to Art. 5(c) of the Unfair Competition Statute, it is considered an act of unfair competition to take over and exploit the marketable result of somebody else's work by technical reproduction without adequate effort of one's own.

Another consequence of the fact that software is protected by copyright is that only the embodiment of a program, not its 'idea', is protected.

Copyright rules permit private use of a work, so the copying of software for private use cannot be prohibited. However, the courts have adopted a restrictive interpretation of the term 'private use', at least where the copying of software in large business entities is concerned.

¶1323   Software contracts

There are no specific rules on software contracts (e.g., sale, purchase, licence or maintenance contracts); rather, the general rules of contract law apply. These rules also govern the concept of shrink-wrap licences, with the result that the seller of the software has to establish that a purchaser has noticed the licensing conditions. Otherwise, these conditions have not become part of the purchase agreement, and there is no valid licence agreement.

BIOTECHNOLOGY

¶1324   Sources of law

The term 'biotechnology' is used for such different things as the breeding of plant varieties, the breeding of animals and the invention of living organisms. Statutory protection is available in two partially overlapping areas which are dealt with by two different international organisations: by WIPO (World Intellectual Property Organisation) for certain biotechnological inventions and by UPOV (*Union internationale pour la protection des obtentions végétales*) for plant varieties.

Switzerland is a member of both the UPOV Convention of 1961, as amended in 1972 and 1978 (RS 0.232.161 and RS 0.232.162, respectively), and the European Patent Convention, in effect for Switzerland since 7 October 1977 (RS 0.232.142.2). Nationally, this dualism is reflected on the one hand by the Federal Statute for the Protection of Plant Varieties of 20 March 1975, in effect since 1 June 1977 (RS 232.16), with its implementing order (RS 232.161), and on the other hand by the Federal Patent Statute of 25 June 1954, as amended (RS 232.14).

In the case of plant varieties, the inventor or breeder who wants protection has no choice of statute because plant varieties are not patentable under Art. 1a of the Patent Statute. This is a consequence of Art. 2(1) of the UPOV Convention, which excludes double protection under both patent and plant variety rules.

¶1325   Plant varieties

The purpose of the Federal Statute on the Protection of Plant Varieties is the protection of the breeding of novel plant varieties. Varieties are admitted for protection and examined with regard to novelty, sufficient homogeneity, resistance and distinctiveness. The variety must belong to one of the species that are listed in the appendix to the implementing order (RS 232.161). A federal research institute is responsible for carrying out the examination.

If a variety is granted protection under the statute, it is registered in the register of varieties (Art. 32 et seq. Plant Varieties Protection Statute). Variety protection lasts 20 years from the date protection is granted. The protection period may be extended by the Federal Government to 25 years under specific conditions. The owner of a protected plant variety has the exclusive right to produce, offer for sale or sell for profit propagation material of the protected variety. However, protection of a variety prevents neither the use of the propagation material to breed a new variety nor the sale thereof.

If his or her exclusive rights are infringed, the owner can demand cease and desist orders, removal of the infringement and damages. Preliminary relief is usually available. In addition, certain infringements of variety protection are criminal offences which are punishable by imprisonment or a fine.

¶1326   Biotechnology patents

Patent protection is available for microbiological procedures and the products or materials obtained as a result of the procedure (Art. 1a Patent Statute). In addition, all plants or their propagation material are patentable, while inventions of essentially biological procedures for the breeding of plants or animals are excluded from patent protection (Art. 1a Patent Statute). With regard to novelty, the Federal Supreme Court has ruled that the presence of a substance in nature is not detrimental to the novelty of the substance as long as it has not become public knowledge. It has further been decided that new ways to carry out a generic procedure may be new although the generic procedure is already known. In connection with biotechnological inventions, agricultural applicability is equivalent to industrial applicability. Of course, microbiological inventions have to fulfil the same criteria of novelty, inventive step and industrial applicability as other inventions (¶1302).

If the micro-organism is not sufficiently described in the application for a patent for a microbiological procedure, it has to be deposited with a special office authorised by the Federal Intellectual Property Office. It is possible to deposit such organisms as viruses, plasmids, hybridome cells, and cell lines in connection with a patent application.

The remedies against infringement of biotechnological patents are defined in the Federal Patent Statute (¶1302). Infringement of a biotechnological patent is presumed if a biotechnological product containing a substance, e.g., a patented cell line, that is an essential element of an existing biotechnological patent, is manufactured or sold. According to the principle of 'exhaustion of patent right', the patent holder may not prevent the use or resale of a patented product. However, this rule does not apply to the manufacture of a patented product. In connection with biotechnological inventions, it may be assumed that the exhaustion does not apply to biomaterial obtained by propagation of the biomaterial supplied by the patent holder. Reproduction and commercialisation of propagation material would be considered a patent infringement.

¶1327 Animals

There are no specific statutory rules for the protection of processes for breeding animals. Patent protection would be available for new animals but is excluded for species of animals (Art. 1a Patent Statute). Procedures for breeding animals are patentable as long as they are not essentially biological. Microbiological procedures are patentable, even if they are essentially biological (Art. 1a, second sentence, Patent Statute).

Patents for animals or for procedures for breeding animals are subject to the ordinary rules of patent law, particularly with regard to patentability and remedies against infringement (¶1302).

SELECTED BIBLIOGRAPHY

Rudolf Blum and Mario Pedrazzini, *Das Schweizerische Patentrecht*, 2nd edn (Bern, 1975)

Heinrich David, *Kommentar zum Schweizerischen Markenschutzgesetz*, 3rd edn (Basel, 1974) (with supplement by Lucas David)

François Dessemontet, *'La protection des programmes d'ordinateur'*, in *EDV-Software: Rechtsschutz* (Lausanne, 1986)

Max Kummer, *Das urheberrechtlich geschützte Werk* (Bern, 1968)

Mario Pedrazzini, *Patent- und Lizenzvertragsrecht*, 2nd edn (Bern, 1987)

Georg Rauber, *Der urheberrechtliche Schutz von Computerprogrammen* (Zürich, 1988)

Manfred   Rehbinder   and   Roland   Grossenbacher,   *Schweizerisches Urhebervertragsrecht* (Bern, 1979)
Michael Ritscher, *Der Schutz des Design* (Bern, 1986)
Alois Troller, *Immaterialgüterrecht*, 3rd edn (Basel, 1983/1985)
Alois Troller and Patrick Troller, *Kurzlehrbuch des Immaterialgüterrechts*, 3rd edn (Basel, 1989)
Patrick Troller, *Kollisionen zwischen Firmen, Handelsnamen und Marken* (Basel, 1980)

14　Private Insurance Law

PRINCIPAL LEGISLATION

Loi fédérale sur la surveillance des institutions d'assurance privées/
Versicherungsaufsichtsgesetz/Federal Insurance Supervision Statute, RS 961.01.

Loi fédérale sur le contrat d'assurance/*Versicherungsvertragsgesetz*/Federal
Insurance Contract Statute, RS 221.229.1.

PRIVATE INSURANCE AND SOCIAL SECURITY

¶1401　Private insurers providing social security benefits

Insurance by private insurers tends to be voluntary, whereas government
insurance schemes are compulsory. The bodies of law governing the two types
of insurance are distinct, and their administration by the insurance carriers is
quite different.

Private insurers are organised as share corporations or, in some cases, as
co-operative corporations. They are particularly active in the fields of insurance
against loss and damage and third-party liability and life insurance.

Private insurers also provide social security benefits within the framework of
the applicable statutes. Occupational pension plans, government Old-Age and
Survivors Insurance, disability insurance, occupational accident insurance and
military compensation plans are considered part of social security (see ¶1501).

Private insurers are free to write policies whose benefits exceed the minima
provided in social security laws. In carrying out these activities, the insurers
must comply with special regulations that apply to this specific activity.
Third-party liability insurance is heavily regulated as far as car accident liability
insurance is concerned.

Some aspects of these types of activities are traditionally in the province of
state bodies. It is a Swiss particularity that in all cantons fire insurance is a
government scheme, which operates according to insurance principles but is
administered by a special government authority. Often the public expense for

maintaining fire fighting units is also covered under this system. The amount of the insurance premiums is commensurate with the value of the buildings. The insurance covers fire and disasters such as storms, avalanches, landslides and earthquakes. In a few cantons building insurance includes furniture and fixtures kept inside buildings. The insurance benefits usually cover the costs of the immediate reconstruction of the same building. Anyone who constructs a different building or refrains from rebuilding receives only a substantially reduced flat compensation. Private insurers may not offer insurance coverage for risks that are covered by a government building insurance scheme.

SUPERVISION OF INSURANCE COMPANIES

¶1402   Government supervision of insurers

(1)   Licence requirement
Article 43(2) of the Federal Constitution assigns the task of supervising private insurers to the Federal Government. The Federal Insurance Supervision Statute (RS 961.01) has been in effect since January 1979. The law is enforced by the Federal Insurance Office (*Office fédéral des assurances privées/Bundesamt für Privatversicherungswesen*).

In order to do insurance business in Switzerland or in another country from Swiss headquarters, an insurer needs a licence. As a rule, only share corporations and co-operative corporations qualify for a licence. Since a subsidiary of a foreign insurer is treated on the same footing as a Swiss insurer, this requirement also applies to these subsidiaries.

The Articles of Incorporation and the General Conditions of Insurance must be submitted for approval to the Federal Insurance Office.

An insurance business licence is granted only to companies with a minimum share capital (life insurers: SFr 10 million; risk of loss or damage insurers: SFr 5 to 10 million; legal risk insurers: SFr 0.5 million) and a security fund consisting of a free surplus. In order to obtain a licence, insurers must make a deposit of SFr 20,000 to SFr 500,000, depending on the type of insurance involved. Once the operations have started, the insurer is required to make additional deposits to secure future benefits.

(2)   Foreign insurers
Foreign insurers that have branches in Switzerland need not necessarily be organised as share corporations or co-operative corporations. They may apply to the Federal Insurance Office for permission to be organised according to the laws of their home country.

Foreign insurers are not required to meet the statutory minimum share capital. Instead, they must make a showing that they provide security comparable to that required by Swiss law. Similarly, branches or agencies of foreign insurers are not required to keep a surplus fund. The insurers must have been licensed or permitted to write insurance policies in their home country for three years in order to qualify for a licence (Art. 14 Insurance Supervision Statute). Life insurers must make a minimum deposit of SFr 0.5 million. The minimum deposit for accident, third-party liability, fire, transport, credit and health insurance is SFr 100,000 each, and for other types of insurance, SFr 20,000 each. Once operations have started, the required deposits increase for all types of insurance, and may be as high as 50 per cent of the premiums collected in Switzerland in the last business year. A Swiss citizen must be appointed country manager (*mandataire général/Generalbevollmächtigter*) of the branch or agency of a foreign insurance carrier. The main Swiss branch is domiciled at the place of residence of the country manager; this place is consequently the place where the Swiss courts have jurisdiction over the foreign insurers.

(3) Scrutiny of premiums

An insurer must conduct its business so as to be always able to meet its financial obligations. Solvency is jeopardised if, for instance, risky investments are made, or if premiums are set at an unreasonably low level with a view to undercutting competition. The insurance premium schedules are closely scrutinised. They must meet the economically required minimum but they may not be substantially above the market level, even if the insurer company has a monopoly position. Within these wide limits, competition and the freedom of trade contained in the Federal Constitution are guaranteed.

Some areas of insurance have more stringent premium controls (Art. 20 Insurance Supervision Statute). This is particularly true for automobile third-party liability insurance. Here, a premium schedule commensurate with the risks and costs involved is established after consulting all insurers; this premium schedule is then declared binding on all. In connection with this type of insurance, it is possible to provide for premium increases and discounts depending on risk development (*bonus* and *malus*). Competition between insurers, therefore, is limited to the way claims are processed and the way clients are treated.

(4) General Conditions of Insurance

The General Conditions of Insurance are subject to approval by the Federal Insurance Office. Most private insurance policies are standardised. In the interests of the insured, it is important that the standardised policies be complete and easy to understand, and that they allocate rights and obligations fairly. In addition to

¶1402

government supervision, the insured or the beneficiary in a particular case can challenge in court specific provisions contained in the General Conditions.

(5) Non-insurance business
A private insurer must not engage in non-insurance business and must keep the various insurance areas separate. Consequently, the same insurer may not write both personal insurance and insurance against loss and damage (Art. 13 Insurance Supervision Statute). Legal defence insurance must be separate from all other forms of insurance. Large insurers which wish to offer their customers comprehensive insurance services set up subsidiaries or are organised as holding companies.

(6) Other aspects of supervision
Some types of insurers are not subject to supervision or are subject only in part. For example, employee pension foundations are subject to special supervision, and insurance carriers writing policies as an accessory activity are subject to a simplified type of supervision. Besides government supervision, there are requirements that auditing be done by qualified auditors (see ¶833).

Insurance supervision is exercised from the time business is started and, to ensure solvency of the carrier and proper business dealings, during business operations (Art. 17 et seq. Insurance Supervision Statute). Supervision is also exercised when the insurance carrier goes out of business or goes into liquidation (Art. 40 Insurance Supervision Statute).

All business activities of Swiss insurers, both in Switzerland and abroad, are subject to scrutiny by the Swiss Federal Insurance Office. The rationale is that even a sound business activity in Switzerland cannot safeguard the interests of the insured if the insurer engages in risky activities abroad (Art. 17 Insurance Supervision Statute). In contrast, the supervisory authorities, for practical and legal reasons, refrain from supervising the business activities of a foreign insurer outside Switzerland; they limit themselves to reviewing the Swiss portfolio of the foreign insurer (Art. 18 Insurance Supervision Statute).

INSURANCE CONTRACTS

¶1403 Federal Insurance Contract Statute
The Federal Insurance Contract Statute (RS 221.229.1) is divided into three parts. The first part contains provisions that are applicable to all types of insurance contracts (Arts 1 to 47). A further category of provisions applies exclusively to property insurance. Historically, these provisions were meant to govern insurance

against loss of or damage to property. Increasingly, case law applies them, if appropriate, to insurance covering economic loss (Arts 48 to 72). The last set of provisions governs life, health, and accident insurance (Arts 73 to 96). Certain statutory provisions are mandatory.

¶1404   Types of insurance

(1)   Insurance against loss of, or damage to, property
This type of insurance includes fire, hail, transport, theft and other property insurance. It provides coverage for loss of, or damage to, any physical or incorporeal item (for instance, buildings, furniture, machinery, or credit risk). The insured events may be the destruction of, damage to, loss of value of, or loss of the item.

The consequential damages caused by the triggering event can also be insured. However, there must be an express agreement between the parties to this effect. This agreement, strictly speaking, is not insurance against loss or damage; rather, it is insurance against economic loss. If, for example, machinery is put out of order due to a fire, the actual value of the machinery is paid under a policy providing for coverage for property damage. If the manufacturer does not want to be left with the lost profits sustained as a result of the interruption of business, he or she must purchase insurance covering the corresponding risk.

Usually, benefits paid out under an insurance policy against loss or damage fall short of the replacement value of the insured item, because only the actual value of the item is paid out. As a result of depreciation and inflation, payment of the replacement value can be secured only by taking out additional coverage.

Swiss insurers usually offer insurance against loss or damage in the following areas: fire, water, glass, transport, theft, car damage, business interruption insurance, and credit insurance.

(2)   Insurance against economic loss
This type of insurance provides assets insurance. If the assets of the beneficiary were damaged as a result of a triggering event, the insurance company pays regardless of whether the beneficiary, in fact, forfeited profits or suffered losses.

Accordingly, individuals may insure their liability to a third party (for instance, professional liability insurance for a lawyer, accountant or physician). Legal defence insurance is also a form of liability insurance. Insurance against the damage resulting from an unforeseen cancellation of a performance (e.g., an open air performance must be cancelled because of bad weather) also falls into this category.

Swiss insurers usually offer insurance against economic loss in the following areas: business interruption, weather, legal cost, third-party liability insurance (e.g., driving risks, professional liability).

(3) Life, health and accident insurance

In this type of insurance the insured events are death, disability, injury, illness or old age. The insurance benefit, usually a lump sum of money, may be claimed regardless of whether damages were suffered. Benefits paid pursuant to private insurance contracts supplement benefits paid under compulsory insurance plans such as government Old-Age and Survivors Insurance, Disability Insurance, occupational pension plans, and occupational accident insurance (see ¶1501). If an insured event occurs, the insured sum is paid, regardless of whether this amount covers the insured's financial needs in full or only partially. Life and accident insurance can be taken out several times for the same insured event.

The risk of death may be insured by the beneficiary or, with the latter's approval in writing, by a third party (Art. 74 Insurance Contract Statute). It is quite common for employers to take out, for instance, travel insurance for their employees, entitling the survivors to a particular insured sum if the employee dies while travelling on business.

¶1405 Insurance contracts

Unlike most contract types, the insurance contract is not regulated in the Code of Obligations. Rather, it is regulated in the Insurance Contract Statute. If a specific provision cannot be found in this Statute, the general provisions of the Code of Obligations govern the contract.

The Insurance Contract Statute applies neither to reinsurance contracts nor to contracts entered into by insurance carriers that are not fully under government supervision. These contracts are governed exclusively by the provisions of the Code of Obligations.

An insurance policy comes into being in the way that any other contract does, i.e., by mutual consent between the parties following an offer and acceptance. An application for an insurance policy is binding on the offeror as soon as it is dispatched. Moreover, the application necessarily remains open for 14 days (Arts 1 and 3 Insurance Contract Statute).

Coverage usually starts as provided in the General Conditions of Insurance, that is, with payment of the first premium. A written policy is an important document for practical reasons, but an insurance contract need not be in writing (Art. 11 Insurance Contract Statute). The document simply evidences the benefits; it does not embody them.

In all types of insurance contracts, the parties must specifically agree on the risk and the insured object (individual, property or assets). The amount of the benefits is an essential point only in the field of life, health and accident insurance. Since in the area of property and assets insurance the amount of damage sustained can be ascertained after the occurrence of the event, the amount of the insurance benefits in these types of insurance need not be stated in advance.

Further essential elements of an insurance contract include the premiums and the term of the contract. Insurance contracts that are entered into for an undetermined period without possibility of termination are void.

¶1406   Obligation to pay premiums

If the ownership of the insured object changes, another individual may become liable for the payment of the premiums (Art. 54 Insurance Contract Statute). Such a change occurs in particular when immovable property is sold. In such a case, all insurance contracts pertaining to the immovable property pass to the new owner unless the insurer terminates the policy within 14 days after having become aware of the change of ownership. Conversely, within the same period the new owner may decline to continue to be covered under the policies.

There are special rules on the consequences of late payment of premiums. These rules differ substantially from the general principles in the Code of Obligations governing the consequences of late performance (Arts 20 and 21 Insurance Contract Statute). The initial premium is due at the time the contact is made; subsequent premiums are due at the beginning of each new insurance period. If the premium is due and payment is not made on time, the insurer may notify the policy-holder in writing of the open account and set a time limit of 14 days for the policy-holder to pay the premium. If payment is not made within this period, the insurance coverage lapses automatically. If the coverage involves life insurance, the contract may subsequently be terminated by the insurer against payment of the redemption value (Arts 90 and 93 Insurance Contract Statute). If the insurer does not collect the premium within two months after the maturity date, it is presumed to have waived its claim to the premium and to have cancelled the policy.

¶1407   Discharge of ancillary duties

As the main obligation flowing from an insurance contract, the insurer is obliged to pay out benefits at the occur rence of the insured event, while the policy-holder must pay premiums. In addition to these obligations, there are numerous ancillary duties that the beneficiary must discharge in order to qualify for benefits. The duties are geared towards limiting the risk borne by the insurer and providing it as quickly as possible with information that allows it to determine and mitigate damages.

As a rule, the policy-holder must discharge these duties. However, if the policy benefits a third person, most duties must be performed by the beneficiary. If the duties are not discharged properly, benefits may be reduced or are forfeited altogether, depending upon the amount of negligence involved.

The policy-holder or the beneficiary, as appropriate, is required to notify the insurer immediately after the occurrence of the insured event. Regardless of the circumstances, the insurer may ask the policy-holder or beneficiary to provide additional and more specific information about the insured event (Arts 38 to 40 Insurance Contract Statute).

The insurer may not be hindered or prevented from determining the damage and the cause of the triggering event. Unless safety measures require otherwise, damaged property may not be altered without the consent of the insurer. Similarly, all parties involved have a duty to mitigate damages.

¶1408 Changes of risk

If, through no fault of the policy-holder, the risk increases during the insurance period, the policy-holder must notify the insurer lest coverage for the increased risk stop. If the notification is duly made, the insurer remains bound unless a contractual provision grants it the option to terminate the policy (Arts 28 to 30 Insurance Contract Statute). In collective insurance contracts, these rules apply only to those particular groups of insured persons or things that are affected by the increased risk (Art. 31 Insurance Contract Statute).

Conversely, the right to have the premium reduced following a reduction of the risk exists only if the lapsed additional risk was covered by an additional premium (Art. 23 Insurance Contract Statute).

¶1409 Occurrence of the insured event

Special statutory provisions limit benefits if the insured event was brought about intentionally or with gross negligence by the policy-holder (Art. 14 Insurance Contract Statute).

If the insured event is caused by gross negligence, the insurer may reduce the benefits according to the degree of fault. Slight negligence, by contrast, leaves the benefits untouched, and any contractual provision to the contrary is void (Arts 14 and 98 Insurance Contract Statute).

The occurrence of the insured event may lead to a total or partial loss of the insured object. If new things replace destroyed property, a new policy must be written (Art. 24 Insurance Contract Statute; Art. 119 CO).

In contrast, partial destruction of an insured object does not end an existing insurance contract. In cases involving insurance against risk of loss, the insurer may terminate the policy following the occurrence of the insured event. Termination must be notified at the latest when the insurance benefits are paid out. The premium paid for the remainder of the current insurance period must be refunded.

¶1410 Car liability insurance

Road traffic law contains special provisions on compulsory car liability insurance. Any registered motor car operator is strictly liable for damages sustained by persons and objects as a result of the operation of the motor vehicle (including motorcycles and lorries) (¶1514(2)). This liability insurance is an asset insurance in the sense that any reduction of assets resulting from liability to third parties is compensated. No motor vehicle may be operated unless its registered operator has taken out liability insurance benefits of at least SFr 500,000 per accident for personal damage. Minimum benefits depend on the size and type of the motor vehicle.

The party who sustained damages has a direct claim against the insurer. The insurer may not raise defences that are based on the insurance policy (e.g., unpaid premiums) against the injured party. Neither may it retain benefits or reduce them. If a special provision in the policy or in the Insurance Contract Statute gives the insurer a defence (e.g., intentional acts and gross negligence), it may take measures against the person who took out the insurance.

If several persons are involved in an accident, their claims for damages may exceed the maximum sum provided in the liability insurance policy. In such a case, the court allocates the insured sum amongst them. A liability insurance policy passes by operation of law to the new registered operator of a car unless the new operator already has liability insurance. The old insurer may terminate the policy within 14 days after being notified of the change of registered operator.

Special rules apply to cars operated by federal and cantonal government officials. Foreign-registered cars operated in Switzerland are covered by special third-party liability insurance taken out by the Swiss Confederation if the insurance of their country of registration provides no or only insufficient liability coverage. The insurance benefits may be denied to claimants from countries which do not grant reciprocity to Switzerland in this respect.

SELECTED BIBLIOGRAPHY

Roland Brehm, *Le contrat d'assurance RC* (Genève, 1983)
Willy Koenig, *Schweizerisches Privatversicherungsrecht*, 3rd edn (Bern, 1967)
——, 'Der Versicherungsvertrag', in *Schweizerisches Privatrecht*, vol. VII/2 (Basel/Stuttgart, 1979)
Alfred Maurer, *Schweizerisches Privatversicherungsrecht*, 2nd edn (Bern, 1986)
Hans Roelli and Max Keller, *Kommentar zum Schweizerischen Bundesgesetz über den Versicherungsvertrag, Die allgemeinen Bestimmungen, Art. 1 bis 47* (Bern, 1962)

15 Social Insurance and Occupational Pension Plans

PRINCIPAL LEGISLATION

*Loi fédérale sur l'assurance-vieillesse et survivants/AHV-Gesetz/*Old-Age and Survivors Insurance Statute, RS 831.10.

*Loi fédérale sur l'assurance-invalidité/IV-Gesetz/*Disability Insurance Statute, RS 831.20.

*Loi fédérale sur la prévoyance professionnelle vieillesse, survivants et invalidité/ Berufsvorsorgegesetz/*Occupational Pension Plan Statute, RS 831.40.

*Loi fédérale sur l'assurance-maladie/Krankenversicherungsgesetz/*Health Insurance Statute, RS 832.10.

*Loi fédérale sur l'assurance-chômage obligatoire et l'indemnité en cas d'insolvabilité/Arbeitslosenversicherungsgesetz/*Unemployment Insurance Statute, RS 837.0.

*Loi fédérale sur l'assurance-accident/Unfallversicherungsgesetz/*Accident Insurance Statute, RS 832.20.

INTRODUCTION

¶1501   'First pillar' and 'second pillar' of social security

Switzerland is not quite a welfare state. The benefits awarded under the different statutory insurance plans are sometimes quite limited, and make exclusive reliance on government insurance inadvisable. Under the compulsory plans, a retired person, in the best of cases as of 1 January 1991, receives up to approximately SFr 20,500 annually from an occupational pension plan and up to approximately SFr 19,000 from Old-Age insurance (statutory maxima). These amounts are meant to cover 80 per cent of the pre-retirement wages of employees on the lower third of the income scale. While, under these circumstances, it is advisable for low-income employees to supplement the statutory schemes with their own savings or the purchase of insurance that goes beyond the statutory minima, for high-income earners additional coverage is truly a necessity.

The safety net comprises first and foremost the government Old-Age, Survivors and Disability Insurance. This insurance constitutes the 'first pillar' of social security (¶1502) and is meant to cover basic necessities following retirement. This insurance is supplemented by the compulsory occupational pension plan. Under this second type of insurance, the 'second pillar', employees fund a personal account from which a pension is paid out after retirement. The core social network is supplemented by personal savings, the third pillar.

Employers are required to buy insurance against occupational accidents and diseases (workmen's compensation insurance), and to take out, on behalf of their employees, insurance against non-occupational accidents. Moreover, in many parts of the country, health insurance has been declared mandatory by cantonal legislation, in particular for individuals on the lower end of the income scale.

The system is further complemented by military compensation plans and unemployment insurance.

As of 1 January 1991, contributions to Old-Age and Survivors Insurance, Disability Insurance, Military Compensation Plans and Unemployment Insurance amounted to 10.5 per cent of the payroll (without cap). The employer and the employee share this burden equally.

COMPULSORY GOVERNMENT INSURANCE

¶1502   Old-Age and Survivors Insurance

(1)   Organisation of Old-Age and Survivors Insurance
The most important type of social security in Switzerland is Old-Age and Survivors Insurance (*Assurance-vieillesse et survivants*, AVS/*Alters- und Hinterlassenenersicherung*, AHV). This insurance is administered by compensation funds (*caisse de compensation/Ausgleichskasse*) that are run either by the state or by employers' associations. In practice, the private funds are of greater importance than the state-run bodies. In fact, each canton is required to establish only one compensation fund. The Federal Government maintains, *inter alia*, a compensation fund for Swiss who, although living abroad, wish to adhere to Old-Age and Survivors Insurance on a voluntary basis.

The main purpose of these compensation funds is to process and equalise contributions and benefits. The Old-Age and Survivors Insurance is based on the principle of redistribution: the collected premiums are instantly applied to pay benefits to retired persons and disabled individuals. Hitherto, the insurance has worked well on this system, since, as a result of its mandatory character, the pool of contributing individuals basically comprises the entire active population.

Over the years, an individual may work for several employers. It is possible that not all of these employers are affiliated with the same compensation fund. Each time an employee comes to deal with another compensation fund, the latter opens a new individual account for the employee. When the insured employee retires or dies, these accounts are consolidated and the final entitlement to benefits is ascertained. Benefits consist of a full or only a partial pension.

(2) Premiums of Old-Age and Survivors Insurance

Contributions to the Old-Age and Survivors Insurance are made through a 4.2 per cent payroll deduction. The employer matches the amount and assesses a small administration fee. The employer is personally responsible for proper payroll deductions and timely payment of the sums involved to the appropriate compensation fund. Self-employed persons pay their premiums based on the tax returns filed with the federal tax authorities. The applicable rate is 7.8 per cent (Arts 5 and 8 Old-Age and Survivors Insurance Statute). If premiums are paid late or not at all, Old-Age Insurance authorities do not hesitate to collect the overdue premiums. In fact, they are known to be merciless in collecting outstanding payments. They proceed under favourable public-law provisions and use coercive measures under administrative law.

Under certain circumstances, directors of corporations may become personally liable for the payment of premiums. They are well advised to make sure that premiums are paid without delay as soon as the corporation shows the slightest sign of financial difficulties or slowness in making payments. Moreover, as a precautionary measure, the directors should take care to set aside the funds necessary to pay upcoming premiums.

While there is a cap on the amount of benefits, premiums must be paid on all earned income without limitation. Old-Age and Survivors Insurance is social insurance properly speaking: it redistributes income from high-income earners to individuals on the lower end of the income scale. This mechanism results in essence in a substantial payroll tax for high-income earners.

(3) Benefits of Old-Age and Survivors Insurance

After retirement age (65 for men and 62 for women), every individual, whether Swiss or foreign, receives a pension under the insurance plan. A full pension is awarded if the individual had regularly been paying contributions.

An individual who regularly pays premiums is assured of at least the minimum full pension upon retirement. This is not the case if an individual fails to pay premiums regularly. In this case, the benefits may fall well short of the minimum full pension. Depending upon their income and net worth, Swiss citizens may qualify for an extraordinary pension. Non-Swiss nationals may qualify for an extraordinary pension pursuant to an applicable treaty. Otherwise, the individual receives only a partial pension.

The exact sum of the full pension depends upon the amount of the overall earnings and, accordingly, contributions. As of 1 January, 1991, the amount of the monthly pension for a single person ranged between SFr 800 and SFr 1,600. Spouses are jointly entitled to a monthly pension between SFr 1,200 and SFr 2,400 (Arts 34 and 35 Old-Age and Survivors Insurance Statute). If an insured individual dies prior to retirement age, leaving dependants, the latter are entitled to survivors pensions. Payments of lump sums are restricted to young spouses.

(4) Social security for foreigners

Premiums are levied on all income earned in Switzerland. However, only beneficiaries retiring in Switzerland qualify for benefits under this scheme. Foreigners may have to pay premiums for years without receiving benefits after departure from Switzerland. Fortunately, exceptions to this rule are becoming more and more frequent. They flow from social security treaties between Switzerland and the foreigner's state of citizenship. Non-Swiss insured may claim a partial refund of their contributions, provided payments have been made for at least a year but not more than ten years and no benefits have been claimed. Further, their country of origin must grant reciprocity.

The Federal Social Security Office regularly updates a loose-leaf binder that lists, country by country, the applicable treaties and statutes in the field of Old-Age, Survivors and Disability Insurance. Pursuant to most treaties that Switzerland has entered into with other countries, payments by a foreigner to Swiss Old-Age and Survivors Insurance are deemed to have been made to the social security system in the foreigner's country of citizenship.

There is a treaty between Switzerland and the United States (RS 0.831.109.336.1; 32 U.S.T. 2165 and TIAS 9830). A salient feature of this treaty is that the United States, under certain circumstances, takes into account premiums paid to Swiss social security in order to compute the benefits of a United States citizen under the United States social security system. Further, eligible United States retired persons receive pensions even if they reside outside Switzerland. Since the United States does not grant reciprocal rights, the premiums that a United States citizen paid to Swiss Old-Age and Survivors Insurance are not refundable.

United States individuals who are assigned to a job in Switzerland for a period not exceeding five years are exempt from the requirement to pay premiums to Old-Age, Survivors and Disability Insurances if they provide the appropriate compensation fund or their employer in Switzerland with a certificate from the

¶1502

Social Security Administration in Baltimore, Md., attesting that they are insured under the United States social security system (Form USA/CH 10; the form can be obtained under the No. 318.000.1 from the Federal Central Office of Printed Matters and Materials in 3003 Berne). The period of five years can be extended.

¶1503   Disability Insurance

(1)   Benefits of Disability Insurance
Disability Insurance (*assurance-invalidité*, AI/*Invalidenversicherung*, IV) works on principles similar to those of Old-Age and Survivors Insurance. Private and state-run compensation funds usually administer both systems.

Benefits are triggered by disability. The latter is defined as any permanent or long-lasting reduction of the ability to earn income as a result of an impairment of physical or mental health caused by a birth defect, disease or accident.

Disability Insurance provides rehabilitation measures and compensatory payments. Individuals suffering a disability must first try to be compensated by their private accident or health insurance carriers. Social disability insurance is paid only after private insurance payments run out. Usually, the relevant period of time is two years. During this waiting period, comprehensive medical checks are performed at the behest of the disability insurance authorities in order to assess the prospects of rehabilitation and the degree of disability.

If rehabilitation measures fail or prove impossible, Disability Insurance pensions are granted. The amount of the pension is determined in accordance with the principles used to calculate an Old-Age and Survivors Insurance pension. The amount of disability pensions also depends upon the degree of disability. When the beneficiary reaches retirement age, Old-Age Insurance benefits are paid and Disability Insurance benefits cease.

(2)   Premiums for Disability Insurance
Like Old-Age and Survivors Insurance, Disability Insurance covers the entire population and is financed through payroll deductions. For Disability Insurance, employers are required to deduct 0.6 per cent from the payroll, and to match this amount. Self-employed persons pay the full percentage.

¶1504   Military Compensation Plans

The government Military Compensation Plan (*allocation pour perte de gain/ Erwerbsausfallsentschädigung*) functions according to the principles that govern the Old-Age and Survivors Insurance. The plan is administered by the same compensation funds and is financed through a payroll deduction of 0.25 per cent, matched by the employer. Foreigners, women and men alike, are required to make contributions.

¶1503

Under the plan, individuals are reimbursed for income they lose as a result of their military reserve or civil defence duties. These reimbursements are of particular importance for employers and self-employed individuals. Employees derive only indirect benefits from this type of insurance.

Employers are required to pay their employees regular wages during military reserve duty. Men up to the age of 32 are called up for a three-week tour of duty each year; beyond this age they are called somewhat more rarely. At the end of his yearly reserve duty, the reservist is issued a certificate entitling him to benefits under the Military Compensation Plan. If he received his regular wages during his tour of duty, the employee must hand this certificate over to the employer to cash it with the appropriate compensation fund. Although the available compensation falls far short of reimbursing the employer for all of the wages paid, employers are well advised to make sure that they receive this certificate.

¶1505 Unemployment Insurance

(1) Benefits of Unemployment Insurance

Under the Swiss concept of Unemployment Insurance, benefits are awarded to a laid-off employee who does not succeed in finding a new job. Further, an allowance is provided if an employer fails to pay wages due to insolvency. Since wage claims are privileged in bankruptcy proceedings, in most cases the insurance fund will eventually be able to recover wage payments so these payments are tantamount to mere advances.

Benefits are limited in time: in a period of two years, payments are basically restricted to one year (Art. 35 Unemployment Insurance Statute). The daily allowance amounts to between 70 and 80 per cent of the insured wages. As is the case with compulsory accident insurance, only wages of up to SFr 97,200 can be insured (Art. 3(1) Unemployment Insurance Statute).

(2) Premiums for Unemployment Insurance

Unemployment Insurance is operated along the same lines as Old-Age and Survivors Insurance. Employers make a 0.2 per cent payroll deduction and match this amount with their own funds. There is a cap: premiums are due only up to the insured amount of SFr 97,200.

¶1506 Family allowance schemes

On a nationwide basis, family allowance schemes exist only for an insignificant number of workers. However, most cantons have adopted regulations requiring employers to pay a monthly allowance per child. Usually, these allowances are financed exclusively by employers or some kind of contribution system administered by a compensation fund. These allowances are limited and rarely exceed SFr 100 per month per child.

COMPULSORY OCCUPATIONAL PENSION PLANS

¶1507   Sources of the law

This type of insurance was regulated by statute only recently. Like health and accident insurance, it is compulsory for employees as a matter of federal law. The extent of the coverage and the latter's financing are largely left to private initiative and individual choice.

The roots of today's occupational insurance go back to the end of the nineteenth century. At that time, farsighted employers established special funds destined to assist needy employees. Some of these funds grew into pension schemes funded by contributions of both employer and employees and still exist today. As a result, persons retiring from large companies and public administration bodies routinely benefit from substantial pension plans. However, not all employees were insured. In order to secure at least minimum benefits for all employees, the Swiss legislature established an extensive occupational insurance plan in 1982. The statutory provisions set minimum standards for pensions plans but leave it to employers to establish them. Further, employers are encouraged to provide benefits in excess of the statutory minima (Art. 76 Occupational Pension Plan Statute – RS 831.40).

¶1508   Organisation of pension plans: Private funds

Employers are required to have their pension funds administered by a separate legal body. Employers have the choice of establishing their own employee benefit foundation (see ¶717) or adhering to a foundation together with other employers. Alternatively, employers can entrust an insurance company with the administration of their pension plan.

Employee-benefit foundations can be established easily and are not difficult to administer. They are subject to official supervision comparable to the regular supervision of foundations. The chief purpose of this supervision is to make sure that minimum organisational standards are met. Regardless of their legal structure, pension benefit-plans must be administered by an equal representation committee composed of employers and employees (the foundation council) (Arts 51 and 76 Occupational Pension Plan Statute). The members of the foundation council are answerable to the supervisory authorities and, in case of financial problems, to the beneficiaries.

This liability is similar to the liability of the directors of a corporation and, therefore, can be covered by insurance. Any substantial modification in the composition of the assets that is not provided for in the by-laws needs approval from the supervising authorities. The formation of free reserves or funds in excess of the capital required to cover benefits must be approved by the supervising authorities.

In investing their assets, pension funds must duly spread the risks. Further, they are required to submit their annual statements to the supervisory authorities for approval. Since dealings between the employer and the pension funds are permitted only to a very limited extent, they are looked into very carefully.

Often, small pension funds and employers with a small number of employees take out a collective insurance policy from an insurer. If the staff exceeds approximately 100, it tends to be advantageous for technical reasons for the pension funds to make direct investments. Even though a pension fund that makes a direct investment exercises an activity similar to that of an insurer, it remains subject to supervision by the employee-benefit authorities. All but the largest pension funds take out a policy from an insurer to cover the risks involved with disability benefits under professional insurance.

A pension fund which has not taken out a collective insurance policy invests the assets itself or has an investment fund invest them. Since such a fund makes collective investments on behalf of employee-benefit pension funds, it is also subject to supervision by the authorities. Most investment funds are managed by banks. Recently, the concept of collective funds was developed. Pursuant to this concept, a single employee-benefit foundation makes investments on behalf of several affiliated corporations. Within this fund, the employees of each of the corporations constitute a separate group of beneficiaries with tailor-made plans.

¶1509 Premiums and benefits

In order to meet mandatory statutory requirements, the pension plan must provide at least old-age and disability benefits (disability pensions depending on the degree of disability), death benefits (pensions to surviving dependants), and a waiver of premiums in case of disability.

Starting at age 17, all employees are compulsorily insured under an occupational pension plan. However, until the age of 24, they are insured only against disability and risk of death. Full occupational pension plan coverage starts at the age of 24. The amount of these benefits depends on the premiums that the insured paid prior to retirement (retirement age is 65 for men and 62 for women).

If an employee's annual wages are less than SFr 19,200, his or her income is not subject to premiums for occupational insurance. Conversely, income in excess of SFr 57,600 is not insured pursuant to the statutory provisions (Art. 7

Occupational Pension Plan Statute). Therefore, for the purpose of assessing the premiums, wages exceeding the maximum wages that are statutorily insurable are not taken into account. The statutory premiums levied on the qualifying income vary according to age and gender. On average, contributions amount to 12 per cent of income. Of this amount, the employer bears roughly 60 per cent, while a payroll deduction is made for the remaining 40 per cent. The contributions made over a period of 40 years roughly add up to an amount five times as high as the insured's annual salary.

The premiums that an employee pays over time are credited to the employee's individual account. This account bears interest at a (moderate) rate defined in the statute. Since the insurable wages and, by extension, the premiums fluctuate, it is not possible to determine the amount of the end capital in advance. When a beneficiary reaches retirement age, the accumulated capital is translated into a monthly pension according to rules laid down in the statute. As a rule of thumb, the annual allowances correspond to 7.2 per cent of the accumulated capital. Payments are made until death. Benefits are regularly adjusted for inflation.

Mandatory employee benefits are paid out to the beneficiary on a monthly basis; a lump sum refund of the accumulated capital is not allowed. A refund is possible only under stringent circumstances. For instance, a foreigner who definitively leaves Switzerland is entitled to a refund if he or she paid premiums for more than nine months (Art. 30 Occupational Pension Plan Statute).

While the statute exhaustively regulates how premiums and benefits are processed and calculated, it does not require pension funds to adhere strictly to these regulations. Provided that the supervisory authorities are satisfied that the employees receive at least the benefits stated in the statute, pension funds are relatively free to apply their own plans. Many corporate employers offer pension plans that set uniform premiums regardless of gender and age, or provide insurance coverage far beyond the statutory maximum.

¶1510   Free movement between pension funds

The current statutory provisions prove unsatisfactory in so far as they discourage employees from changing jobs. If employees take up a new job, under the statute they become affiliated with the pension fund of the new employer. In the process, the payments that the employee made over the years are transferred to the new pension fund. As a result of the transfer, the employee forfeits the matching payments made by the previous employer in part or in full, depending on the length of the terminated employment contract. This forfeiture penalises employees who move to new jobs and has given rise to extensive criticism. As of summer 1991, a Bill aimed at securing the transfer of the totality of the accumulated capital is being discussed in the Federal Parliament. It is likely to be adopted.

Pension funds are not subsidised by the Government. The latter limits itself to supervisory activities and to the provision of an alternative pension fund for employees whose employers, such as foreign embassies and the like, are not required to provide pension benefits. The number of employers within this category is very limited.

Pension funds are required to transfer a small percentage of the premiums collected to a security fund, which accumulates capital for the purpose of reinsuring all pension funds in Switzerland.

¶1511   Taxation of premiums and benefits of pension plans

Employers can, for tax purposes, deduct premiums and expenses incurred in administering pension funds from their gross income as business expenses. Similarly, employees can deduct premiums from their gross income. As far as pension funds themselves are concerned, they are exempt from taxes.

Conversely, all benefits paid to beneficiaries under occupational insurance plans are taxable income. Because of this, the deductions result in a mere tax deferral.

¶1512   Economic impact of occupational pension funds

The largest pension funds administer the accounts of almost 50,000 employees and boast several thousands of millions of francs in assets. Most of these large funds had existed well before occupational pensions became compulsory. They tend to provide benefits that are far in excess of the statutory minima. The need for these funds to invest their enormous assets in a secure way has led to extensive investments in immovable property. Since prices for immovable property have become unreasonably high, in part as a result of such investments, temporary restrictions on investments in immovable property by pension funds have been adopted.

HEALTH AND ACCIDENT INSURANCE

¶1513   Private health insurance

(1)   Broad coverage of population
Today, over 99 per cent of the resident population is covered by some health insurance plan. Proposals to make basic health insurance compulsory will essentially result in more uniform coverage. Presently, insurance coverage is highly individualised due to the existence of numerous different insurance plans.

Since 1960, the number of insurance carriers has decreased by 50 per cent, due to high administrative costs and unfavourable risk development. The general cost explosion in health care leads to conflicting views between patients, physicians, and hospitals on one side and insurance carriers on the other. The desire of the former to obtain or offer optimal health care based on the latest technological developments conflicts with the carriers' endeavour to reduce costs.

(2) Organisation: private insurance

Health insurance, at least as far as basic coverage is concerned, is largely regulated in the Health Insurance Statute. The statute sets forth the requirements (concerning benefits and organisation) that an insurance carrier must meet in order to qualify for state subsidies. For the time being, health insurance is not compulsory nationwide. The cantons, and in part even the municipalities, may make health insurance compulsory. Some cantons and a number of the larger cities have done so. Usually, only individuals and families on the lower end of the income scale are required to buy insurance.

Health insurance means individual insurance. However, insurance carriers may write collective policies in order to insure the staff of a company according to uniform principles. Health insurance is financed by premiums paid by the policy-holder and subsidies from the Confederation and, in part, from the cantons.

There are many insurance carriers. Under the statute, both public and private bodies may qualify as carriers. Once qualified, they are under an obligation to treat all members equally and to operate on a non-profit basis. Carriers that are not run by the state must be organised as associations, foundations or co-operative corporations and are subject to supervision by the Federal Social Security Office.

(3) Extent of coverage of health insurance

To obtain coverage under an insurance carrier's health insurance plan, an individual does not merely take out a policy; rather, he or she becomes a member of the carrier. Carriers have only limited leeway in setting the requirements that an applicant must meet in order to become a member. Any applicant who is less than 60 years old is entitled to membership. Because children are good risks, even unborn babies are often eligible for coverage. Pursuant to a specific statutory provision, the carriers may not impose waiting periods in excess of five years for any specific health risk.

Health insurance covers the costs of outpatient treatment by a physician of one's choice. Statutory provisions detail the recognised treatments. Hospital care is also covered. Physicians and hospitals charge patients staying in public wards only moderate fees. These fees are covered by basic health insurance. In contrast, a patient who wants to stay in a private room, which offers richer food and to

¶1513

some extent better care, must pay a surcharge unless he provides additional insurance.

The cantons may release physicians and hospitals from the obligation to adhere to maximum fee schedules where the treatment of particularly well-off patients is concerned. As a result, these treatments are only partially covered by basic health insurance. In order to be entirely covered, well-off patients must buy additional insurance. Additional insurance can be bought from private life insurance companies; it may also be obtained from health insurance carriers in exchange for increased premiums.

(4) Free movement between health insurance carriers

Since some insurance carriers limit their activity to certain areas or certain segments of the population, policy-holders frequently switch from one carrier to another. In such cases, the switching individual benefits from the statutory possibility of joining another carrier within three months on the same conditions (Arts 7 to 11 Health Insurance Statute). In particular, the new carrier is not allowed to impose waiting periods during which certain diseases are not covered.

(5) Benefits and sick pay from health insurance

Depending upon the length of the employment contract, employees have a statutory right to sick pay for several weeks. In order to prevent employees from going without any pay after sick pay runs out, employers usually take out collective policies under which sick employees obtain benefits for an extended period of time. Carriers routinely limit payment of substitute wages (usually 80 per cent) to 720 days in a period of 900 days.

¶1514 Compulsory accident insurance

(1) Insured individuals

Since 1984, accident insurance has been compulsory for practically all individuals employed in Switzerland. It is also compulsory for employees who temporarily work abroad for a Swiss corporation. Conversely, employees who are temporarily assigned to a job in Switzerland by a foreign company do not fall within the scope of accident insurance (Art. 2 Accident Insurance Statute). Accident insurance is not compulsory for employees working part-time (less than 12 hours a week) or for retired persons. An employee is defined as anybody who is required to pay premiums to the government Old-Age and Survivors Insurance. Self-employed individuals may elect to be insured. Individuals who do not have a job do not qualify for coverage.

(2) Risk covered by compulsory accident insurance

Compulsory insurance includes insurance for occupational accidents and diseases (workmen's compensation) and for non-occupational accidents.

The definition of an accident is constantly being refined in order to draw a clear line between accidents on the one hand and illness which is covered under other insurance plans on the other. The delimitation is of practical importance, because benefits paid under the accident insurance plan tend to be more extensive than those paid under health insurance. This is particularly true for the payment of compensation for lost earnings.

An accident is a sudden, unintended impact of an unusual external factor on the human body (Art. 9 Accident Insurance Statute). For instance, straining a muscle when getting into an upright position after staying for an extended period of time in a squatting position is not an accident. In contrast, straining a muscle by bumping into another player while playing soccer constitutes an accident. Similarly, if someone drowns while swimming, he or she suffers an accident.

An occupational disease is covered by compulsory accident insurance if it is a result of exposure to harmful substances or hazardous work (Art. 9 Accident Insurance Statute). In practice, insurance carriers refer to a frequently updated list containing the names of diseases that trigger the insurance.

(3) Premiums for compulsory accident insurance

The employer is required to take out the necessary policies and pay the premiums for occupational accident and health insurance (Art. 91 Accident Insurance Statute). However, the employer is free to deduct the premium for the non-occupational accident insurance from the payroll. The amount of the premium is determined as a fraction of the insured's wages and depends upon the line of business involved. Hazardous activities result in higher premiums than, for example, clerical work.

(4) Benefits of compulsory accident insurance

Mandatory insurance provides only basic benefits. As of 1 January 1991, the maximum wages that can be insured amount to SFr 97,200 (Art. 22 Accident Insurance Statute). Additional insurance must be bought for the insurance of wages in excess of the statutory maximum. Similarly, additional insurance is required to insure risks that are normally excluded from basic insurance.

Benefits include reimbursement for medical care and rehabilitation measures provided on an outpatient or inpatient basis. Moreover, they include allowances for lost earnings and, in the case of disability, pensions. The allowances and pensions are awarded on the basis of the insured wages, i.e., the wages earned by the victim of the accident immediately prior to the accident. Payments cannot

¶1514

be in excess of the statutory maximum income or, if applicable, the additional amount insured.

Benefits are reduced if the insured caused an accident by gross negligence (for instance, mountain climbing without appropriate equipment or parachuting from a high-rise building). The reductions of benefits may be prevented by taking out additional insurance.

Starting on the third day following the accident, a daily allowance of 80 per cent of the relevant wages is paid. As a result, unless otherwise provided, the employer's obligation to pay wages pursuant to the employment contract is suspended with the payment of the daily allowances. If the employer chooses to continue paying wages, he or she is entitled to the allowances.

The victim of an accident is reimbursed for proper medical care and, if necessary, training to take up the former job or any other suitable professional activity. If a victim of an accident is prevented from taking up a professional activity due to a permanent disability, he or she has a lifelong claim to a disability allowance. The amount of this allowance depends on the degree to which future earning capacity is impaired. Further, the victim of the accident is entitled to compensation for pain and suffering. The amount of this type of benefit is determined according to detailed scientific schedules and defined as a percentage of maximum yearly earnings.

If, as a result of his or her disability, an individual requires assistance even for the simplest daily activities, he or she is entitled to a helplessness allowance. The allowance is granted in the form of a pension and, depending upon the degree of helplessness, may substantially exceed the insured income. The allowance is not granted during hospitalisation.

If an insured individual dies as a consequence of an accident, the surviving dependants are entitled to a survivors pension. Under certain circumstances, the surviving spouse can trade his or her pension (40 per cent of the relevant salary) for a lump-sum payment.

Various statutory provisions ensure that the monetary benefits are used for the intended purpose. By way of example, it is not possible to assign or pledge a claim to benefits. Pensions are regularly adjusted for inflation. This also applies to the maximum insurable earnings under the compulsory insurance scheme.

(5) Organisation: government agency
Accident insurance policies are routinely issued by insurance companies that are subject to insurance supervision. In parallel, policies are issued by the state-run Swiss Accident Insurance (*Caisse nationale suisse d'assurance en cas d'accidents*, CNA/*Schweizerische Unfallversicherungsanstalt*, SUVA). This federal agency sets the important standards of health and safety at the workplace. Employers are free to choose the insurer that suits their needs best.

¶1514

PROCEDURE

¶1515   Multiple insurance benefits – sequence of benefits

The same event can trigger benefits from different insurance carriers. However, in the area of health insurance, over-insurance is not permitted. Insurance carriers may withhold benefits if an insured person obtains benefits from another carrier. As a result, individuals are advised not to buy more insurance than necessary. As a rule, a health insurer must pay first, before the Military Compensation Plan or accident and disability insurance. In contrast to health insurance, daily sickness allowances may be cumulated. Since this type of insurance is a form of property insurance, benefits from different carriers can be claimed, provided the actual loss of earnings is not overcompensated.

In the area of compulsory accident insurance, detailed statutory provisions govern which type of insurance must pay first. Accident insurance benefits and benefits from other carriers taken together may not exceed the actual loss of earnings or the actual costs of rehabilitation; if necessary, accident insurance benefits are reduced.

¶1516   Legal remedies of social insurance law

Pursuant to federal statutes, claims for insurance benefits are not heard by regular courts. For the purpose of hearing these claims, the cantons have set up special courts that in most instances are either separate bodies or divisions of existing administrative courts. Decisions of insurance carriers or compensation funds can be appealed to these special courts. Some minimum procedural requirements are set by federal law (standing to lodge an appeal, time-limits, award of costs, disclosure and discovery, etc.). These special courts operate speedily and inexpensively.

In the last instance, a decision can be appealed to the Federal Insurance Court under certain circumstances. See ¶2003.

SELECTED BIBLIOGRAPHY

Federal Social Security Office, *Directives sur le statut des étrangers et des apatrides AVS/AI (Wegleitung über die Stellung der Ausländer und Staatenlosen in der AHV/IV)*, loose-leaf service.
Pierre Yves Greber, *Droit suisse de la sécurité sociale* (Lausanne, 1982)

Stefan W. Hepp, *The Swiss Pension Funds* (Bern, 1990)

Alfred Maurer, *Schweizerisches Sozialversicherungsrecht*, vols. 1 and 2 (Bern, 1979)

——, *Schweizerisches Unfallversicherungsrecht* (Bern, 1985)

16 Labour Law, Residence and Work Permits

PRINCIPAL LEGISLATION

*Code des obligations/Obligationenrecht/*Code of Obligations, RS 220.

Loi fédérale sur le travail dans l'industrie, l'artisanat et le commerce/Arbeitsgesetz/ Federal Labour Statute, RS 822.11.

*Loi fédérale sur le séjour et l'établissement des étrangers/Bundesgesetz über die Ausländer und Niedergelassenen/*Federal Statute on the Temporary and Permanent Residence of Foreigners, RS 142.20.

*Ordonnance limitant le nombre des étrangers/Verordnung über die Begrenzung der Zahl der Ausländer/*Ordinance on the Limitation of Gainfully Employed Foreigners, RS 823.21.

FRAMEWORK

¶1601 Freedom of contract

Switzerland regulates relatively few areas of the contractual relationship between employers and employees and, as a result, has a system of labour law which is readily comprehensible and generally more favourable to the employer than the labour law of many other jurisdictions. A slow change in the employee's favour is taking place. In 1988, for example, the rules regarding employees' protection against unlawful dismissal were made more stringent.

There are three sources of law:

(1) The Code of Obligations (Arts 319 to 362) regulates individual employment contracts, collective bargaining contracts, standard-provision contracts for certain types of employees and, in part, social security. This is the most important legislation on employment contracts.

¶1601

(2) The Federal Labour Statute sets maximum weekly working hours, minimum breaks and holidays, security at the workplace and the protection of female employees and minors.

(3) The Federal Statute Governing the General Applicability of Collective Labour Agreements provides that in specific circumstances collective labour contracts may be declared applicable to all employers and employees in designated industries or divisions of industries. In practice, the collective labour contracts determine the contractual relationship between employers and employees in important sections of trade and industry. The most important federal collective labour contracts are the Collective Labour Contract for the Building Trade, the Collective Labour Contract for the Hotel and Restaurant Trade and the Collective Labour Contract for the Metal Industry.

Together with the collective labour agreements, the Code of Obligations mentions the standard-provision employment contract. This is a contract that establishes similar key provisions (concerning conclusion, content and termination) for specific kinds of employment relationships like those contained in collective labour agreements. While collective labour agreements are actually entered into by employers or employer organisations and employee organisations, the standard-provision employment contract is an official decree, usually of the cantonal authority. Within the framework of the Code of Obligations, it stipulates subsidiary employment provisions from which, however, individual employers and employees may freely deviate by mutual consent. In practice it is used in economic sectors in which employees do not have the necessary bargaining power (such as households, agriculture).

EMPLOYMENT CONTRACTS

¶1602 Form

Generally, no specific form is required for a contract of employment (Art. 320 CO). The contract of employment must be in writing only where it relates to certain categories of employees, e.g. apprentices (Art. 344a CO), travelling sales representatives (Art. 347a CO) and workers employed at home (Art. 351a CO), or where other special circumstances exist, e.g., the contract provides for overtime, other than as determined by law (Art. 321c(3) CO), or an employee subject to a standard-provision employment contract consents to non-standard provisions (Art. 360 CO). Non-competition agreements must also be in writing (Art. 340 CO).

¶1603   Employee's and employer's rights and obligations

(1)   Working hours

With certain exceptions, the maximum working hours for industrial and technical workers, office as well as other white-collar employees (including retail personnel) are 45 hours a week. For other workers, the maximum hours are 50 hours a week (Art. 9 Labour Statute). The maximum weekly working hours may be exceeded under certain exceptional circumstances in accordance with prescribed limitations on hours and pay for overtime. In practice, working hours are shorter because of special provisions in collective labour agreements.

Regular day-time work must not begin before 5 a.m. in the summer or 6 a.m. in the winter, and must not continue beyond 8 p.m. Minimum breaks are required as follows: for a working day of more than five and a half hours but not more than seven hours, 15 minutes; for a working day of more than seven hours but not more than nine hours, 30 minutes; for a working day of more than nine hours, one hour (Art. 10 Labour Statute). If employees are not allowed to be away from their working place during the required break, the break period is included in determining the length of the working day (Art. 15 Labour Statute). Except in special circumstances, work at night and on Sundays is not permitted (Arts 16 and 18 Labour Statute). However, Arts 17 and 18 Labour Statute provide for several exceptions which may be granted by the cantonal authority.

Even stricter rules apply solely to women (Arts 33 to 36 Labour Statute).

Persons not subject to the foregoing restrictions include, among others, clergy, managerial employees, and employees active in science or in independent artistic pursuits (Art. 3 Labour Statute).

For public holidays, see ¶120.

(2)   Minimum vacations

Employers must give employees one day off every week, usually Sunday. Other arrangements for days off may be made with the employee's consent (Art. 329 CO). Further, employers must give employees at least four weeks' annual vacation (Arts 329a, 429c and 429d CO). For employees under the age of 20, the minimum is five weeks' annual vacation. The employee must take a minimum of two weeks' annual vacation at one time. While the employment relation lasts, mandatory vacation time must not be replaced by monetary compensation.

(3)   Maternity/paternity rights

Swiss law grants no paternity rights in relation to employment. Swiss law does, however, recognise the special cases of pregnant women and nursing mothers (Arts 324a and 336c CO; Art. 35 Labour Statute).

For example, a pregnant woman or nursing mother may not be required to do work which would constitute hardship for her. Except with her consent, a pregnant woman may not work beyond normal working hours. She may take time off or discontinue work on giving notice of her wish to do so and without having to observe the minimum periods of notice. In addition, an employer is prohibited from giving notice of termination to a pregnant female employee and for 16 weeks after the birth of her child. Any notice given within this period is void (Art. 336c CO).

A woman is not permitted to work during the eight weeks after the birth of her child. If she wishes, this period may be reduced to six weeks, provided that her doctor confirms that she is able to return to work. A nursing mother may only begin work, with her consent, eight weeks after the birth of her child. An employer must give a nursing mother the necessary free time to nurse her child while at work.

In order to ensure proper rest before and after childbirth, the law requires that the time allocated for a female employee's vacation must not be shortened if she was absent from work for less than two months due to pregnancy and childbirth.

A woman unable to work because of pregnancy and childbirth is entitled to compensation for a limited period, provided she has been or was contracted to be employed for more than three months. This limited period is generally three weeks of full pay for the first year of service. After that, it increases in accordance with the length of employment and other special circumstances. Additional compensation may be stipulated by the parties, or may be determined by a standard provision contract or a collective bargaining agreement.

Apart from labour law, social security laws provide protection for the pregnant woman. Regulations on the medical cost of maternity is found in the Federal Health Insurance Statute.

(4)   Confidentiality of employer's secrets

The confidentiality of an employer's secrets is protected by both civil and criminal law. Under civil law (Art. 321a CO) employees have a duty to keep their employers' trade secrets confidential, both during and, to a lesser extent, after the term of their employment. Trade secrets include secrets regarding technical knowledge and those regarding the commercial aspects of the employer's business.

Under criminal law (Arts 162 and 273 Penal Code; Arts 6 and 23 Unfair Competition Statute), employees who breach their duty of confidentiality by betraying or selling a trade secret to a third party can be punished by a fine, or possibly imprisonment. Other more general violations are also within the reach of the criminal law. For example, a person breaching a contractual or other legal duty to keep a trade secret, or any person making use of the breach, can be punished by a fine or imprisonment. Similarly, a person who makes a trade secret available to foreign authorities may be subject to a fine or even imprisonment. Certain special types of employees, such as government or bank

¶1603

employees, are subject to special laws regarding the violation of their employers' secrets. See ¶1322 et seq. and ¶1210(2).

(5) Non-competition clauses

Employees who have full legal capacity may bind themselves in writing to the employer to refrain from engaging in any competitive activity after termination of the employment relationship. In particular, they may undertake neither to operate a business for their own account which competes with the employer's business, nor to work for nor participate in such a business. The prohibition against competition is binding only if the employment relationship provides the employee with knowledge of customers or to manufacturing or business secrets, and if the use of the knowledge could significantly damage the employer (Art. 340 CO). The prohibition must be reasonably limited in terms of place, time and subject in order to preclude an unreasonable impairment of the employee's economic prospects. It may exceed three years only under special circumstances. The court may in its discretion limit an excessive prohibition against competition, taking into account all circumstances, and it shall give due consideration to the employer's contribution (Art. 340a CO). If employees breach the prohibition against competition, they are liable to the employer for damages.

If a penalty for non-performance in the event of breach has been agreed upon, employees may free themselves from the prohibition by payment of this penalty unless the contract provides otherwise. Such penalties are common and valid (¶202(3)). However, the breaching employees remain liable for any further damage (Art. 340b(2) CO). If specifically agreed upon in writing, the employer may, in addition to the penalty for breach and the compensation for further damage, obtain an injunction against a situation which violates the contract (i.e., obtain specific performance of the non-competition clause, in so far as this is justified by the violated or threatened interests of the employer and by the behaviour of the employee: Art. 340b CO).

A prohibition against competition lapses if it can be proved that the employer no longer has a significant interest in its maintenance. Furthermore, the prohibition expires if the employer terminates the employment relationship without a valid reason, or if the employee terminates the employment relationship for a valid reason for which the employer is responsible (Art. 340c CO). Non-competition clauses can be reinforced by penalties for non-performance in the event of a breach of covenant.

¶1604   Termination of employment contract

The provisions concerning the termination of employment contracts were amended in 1988. The main purpose of this amendment was to improve employees' protection from abusive termination.

¶1604

(1) Ordinary termination

If an employment contract has been entered into for a specific term, it terminates at the end of that term without notice unless the employment contract is continued after the end of the specific term. In that case, the employment contract becomes a contract for an indefinite term. If the contract has a term of more than ten years, the employee may give notice of termination at any time after the tenth year, and the termination becomes effective at the end of the sixth calendar month following the notice (Art. 334 CO).

If an employment contract has no specific term, either the employee or the employer may give notice of termination. Notice must be received by the other party. Subject to what follows below, notice becomes effective (Arts 335, 335a and 335c CO):

(a) with a one-month notice period at the end of the month, if the contract has been in force for less than one year;

(b) with a two-month notice period at the end of the month, if the contract has been in force for one year or more but for less than ten years;

(c) with a three-month notice period at the end of the month, if the contract has been in force for ten years or more.

These rules may be modified by specific agreement between the employer and the employee. The notice requirement may be altered by legal provisions, e.g., those found in collective labour contracts and standard-provision employment contracts, but the notice period must ordinarily not be reduced to less than one calendar month (Art. 335c CO).

At any time during a probation period, either the employee or the employer may give notice of termination with a notice period of seven days (Art. 335b CO).

The termination is considered abusive (see Art. 336 CO) if declared:

(a) because of a personal characteristic of the other party (e.g., sex, race, age), unless that trait is severely impairing the labour relationship;

(b) because the other party practises a right guaranteed by the constitution (e.g., religion or membership in a political party);

(c) to prevent the other party from filing claims arising out of the labour relationship (e.g., a claim for a bonus payment);

(d) because the other party asserts, in good faith, claims arising out of the labour relationship;

(e) because the other party is discharging compulsory military service, civil defence service, women's military service, Red Cross service or a compulsory statutory duty;

¶1604

(f) because of the employee's affiliation, or non-affiliation, with a union, or lack thereof, or because he or she performs work for a union; or

(g) while the employee is an elected representative of an employee or a labour organisation, unless the employer proves grounds for notice.

The party who serves an abusive notice must pay the other party compensation; the amount will be determined by the court but will not exceed six months' wages of the employee. The party who files a compensation claim for abusive termination must give written notice to the opposing party before the end of the notice period. If the parties do not agree to continue their labour relationship, the claimant must file a claim no later than 180 days after the end of the labour relationship.

The employer may not serve notice of termination in any of the following four situations (Art. 336c CO):

(a) during compulsory military or civil defence service or Red Cross service lasting more than 12 days, and during a period of four weeks before the beginning and after the end of service;

(b) in the case of full- or part-time absence from work due to illness or accident, as long as the employee is not at fault for the illness or accident (in the first year of employment during 30 days; from the second to the fifth year of employment during 90 days; and from the sixth year of employment during 180 days);

(c) during pregnancy and 16 weeks after the employee has given birth to a child;

(d) during foreign-aid service in which the employee participates with the consent of the employer, and where the competent federal authorities have ordered the service.

Any notice of termination given by an employer during the periods mentioned above is void. Any notice given prior to the period is effective, but the notice period does not run during the period when the giving of notice would be ineffective.

(2) Termination of employment contract with immediate effect for cause
Both employer and employee may terminate the employment contract without notice (i.e., with immediate effect) if they have 'cause'. There is cause if the parties can no longer be reasonably expected to continue the employment relationship with loyalty and trust. Whether or not cause exists is a decision made largely at the court's discretion.

The immediate dismissal of an employee for cause is an extraordinary measure, and may therefore be resorted to only under very serious circumstances, namely if the offending act actually destroys the trust between the parties. The Code of Obligations does not specify the types of offences by an employee which would justify immediate dismissal for cause. The courts may find cause in the following situations:

(a) gross dishonesty, i.e., deception, embezzlement or theft within the business;

(b) consistent refusal to perform requested work (including overtime, which may be expected in accordance with the legal principles of loyalty and trust);

(c) entering into competition with the employer;

(d) gross insults against the employer; and

(e) repeated failure to appear at work in spite of several warnings.

An employee has the same right as the employer to terminate the employment contract without notice. The Code of Obligations does not give specific examples of circumstances in which an employee can no longer reasonably be expected to continue the employment contract. But the Code of Obligations does provide that an employee may terminate the employment without notice when the employer is insolvent, unless the employee receives sufficient security from the employer within a reasonable time after making a request to leave work.

(3 Obligations upon termination

Upon the termination of an employment contract, all claims arising from it become due (Art. 339 CO). Each party must make restitution for everything received during the period of the employment relationship from the other party, or from third parties for the other party's account (Art. 339a CO).

Employees who have served 20 or more years and are at least 50 years of age are entitled to receive special compensation from the employer when they stop working (Art. 339b CO). The amount of the special compensation may be determined by written agreement, by the terms of a standard provision contract, or by a collective labour agreement, but it may not be less than the compensation which the employee would receive for two months' work (Art. 339c CO). If the amount of the special compensation is not so determined, the court will set it with due regard to the circumstances, but the amount must not exceed the compensation which the employee would receive for eight months' work. With the advent of pension plans, the scope of this provision of the Code of Obligations has been reduced substantially: no special compensation is due to the extent that the employee receives payment from a pension plan financed by the employer's contributions. Similarly, employers who guarantee the employee's compulsory future pension plan payments or arrange to have a third party provide a guarantee, are not required to pay any special contribution (Art. 339d CO). In addition, the special compensation need not be paid if:

(a) the employee serves notice of termination other than for cause; or

(b) the employer serves notice of immediate termination for cause; or

(c) it would constitute hardship for the employer to pay the special compensation.

The special compensation provided for in Art. 339b CO falls due upon termination of employment but may be paid at a later time if it is so determined by written agreement, by the terms of a standard-provision contract or collective labour agreement, or by order of a court (Art. 339c CO).

Apart from the above-mentioned special compensation, no severance pay may be claimed by a terminated employee.

COLLECTIVE LABOUR AGREEMENTS

¶1605   Nature

Rather than seeking a resolution of labour problems through intricate legislation, the Swiss have made broad use of the collective labour agreement (*Convention collective du travail/Gesamtarbeitsvertrag*). Such agreements are usually made by workers' organisations (trade unions covering an entire industrial sector or smaller groups covering only a specific vocation) on the one side and by a single employer or an organisation of employers on the other. As to their content, the collective labour agreements mainly regulate questions of salary, working hours, vacation, notice of termination of the employment relationship, occupational safety and social insurance. By means of collective labour agreements, employers and employees together are able to regulate most aspects of the working relationship, including whether the workers have a right to strike, and, if so, in what circumstances.

Switzerland is one of those industrialised nations in which labour unrest is very rare. Other countries envy Switzerland for its so-called 'work-peace'. Collective labour agreements have worked very well. In 1937 a 'peace agreement' was concluded by workers' and employers' organisations in the metal industry. It was a milestone, and initiated the development of collective labour agreements obliging employers and employees to maintain absolute work-peace and providing for compulsory arbitration instead of strikes. Since those days, strikes have remained extremely rare.

The most important federal collective labour contracts are the following (with the date of latest renewal or amendment):

¶1605

- Collective Labour Contract for the Hairdresser's Trade, 3 March 1989/7 March 1990,

- Collective Labour Contract for the Hotel and Restaurant Trade, 15 May 1989/12 December 1989,

- Collective Labour Contract for the Furniture Trade, 31 July 1987/22 February 1990,

- Collective Labour Contract for the Metal Industry, 30 November 1988,

- Collective Labour Contract for the Joiner's Trade, 27 October 1988/19 January 1989,

- Collective Labour Contract for the Plasterer's and Painter's Trade, 26 March 1990,

- Collective Labour Contract for the Building Trade, 10 February 1989/4 May 1990.

¶1606 Application

No individual worker can be forced to adhere to a collective labour agreement. Moreover, collective labour agreements usually require that an employee who chooses not to adhere to the agreement must be permitted to work under the same conditions as an employee who does sign the agreement. However, these agreements are intended to benefit the workers' organisations; accordingly, an employee who is not a party to the collective labour agreement is outside the scope of protection. Collective labour agreements can be made universally applicable to all workers and employers of a given segment by the competent authorities (cantonal or federal).

PARTICIPATION IN MANAGEMENT AND WORK COUNCILS

¶1607 Not required by law

Worker participation in the management of a corporation is not required by law. In 1976 two draft laws providing for workers' participation were rejected in a public referendum.

¶1607

RESIDENCE AND WORK PERMIT REGULATIONS

¶1608   Sources of law

The Federal Statute on the Temporary and Permanent Residence of Foreigners and its implementing ordinance are the basic regulations regarding aliens who reside in Switzerland. The Federal Ordinance on the Limitation of Gainfully Employed Foreigners contains the requirements for aliens working in Switzerland. These federal laws partly delegate powers to the cantons. Therefore, there are also cantonal ordinances and regulations governing the status of foreigners.

All of these provisions, whether federal or cantonal, have to be seen against the background of a population which is more than 15 per cent foreign.

A foreigner who wishes to stay in Switzerland needs a permit. With the exception of the permanent residence permit, the necessary permit is limited in time and can be subject to conditions. The permit authorises the foreigner to stay in Switzerland and to engage in certain types of gainful activity. Unlike the majority of other countries, Switzerland does not require a special work permit in addition to the temporary residence permit.

Within the scope of applicable law and the international treaties concluded by Switzerland, the authorities may grant and extend permits at their discretion. Generally speaking, the competent authorities have wide discretion. A vested right to a permit exists only when the law so provides. In their decisions, the authorities take into account the requirements of national policy, the capacity of the country to absorb immigrants, the labour market, the requirements of education, science and research, and the human and social aspects, as well as the relationship of the foreigner with Switzerland.

To avoid excessive immigration of foreigners, the number of first-time temporary residence and seasonal permits is limited. There is no limit, however, on the granting of permanent residence permits or the conversion of seasonal permits into temporary residence permits. Most types of permits are restricted by annual quotas, allotted to each of the cantons as cantonal quotas. For particular cases, there is a special federal quota (the OFIAMT quota; so-called because it is set by the Federal Office of Industry, Trade and Labour) as a kind of reserve. Within the framework of these annual allocations or quotas, the competent authorities grant the permits. In the aggregate, they cannot grant more permits than are allocated for the year.

The regulations governing the limitation of admission and the quota restrictions do not apply to the following:

(1) a foreigner who is married to a Swiss woman, and the foreign children of a foreigner and a Swiss woman;

(2) Liechtenstein citizens;

(3) refugees and stateless persons recognised by the Federal Office of Police;

(4) foreigners who became disabled in Switzerland (provided they are unable to continue their previous activity or cannot reasonably be expected to do so);

(5) officials of foreign governments assigned to Switzerland; and

(6) correspondents of newspapers, magazines, etc., with their main office abroad.

¶1609   Temporary residence permits

The standard temporary residence permit is actually called a 'one-year work permit' because it must be extended every year. The extension, however, is normally a matter of routine. The one-year residence permit is subject to cantonal and federal quotas, as mentioned above.

The permit describes the purpose for which it is issued (job description of the permit holder), and the foreigner must leave if the purpose of his or her stay has been accomplished or can no longer be accomplished.

If the one-year work permit holder wants to change employers or the canton of residence, he or she needs approval from the competent authorities. After one year of residence, approval is not difficult to obtain.

Foreigners who come to Switzerland because they are managers or qualified specialists, or because they are continuing their education may receive a work permit of a limited duration (six to 12 months) for this purpose.

The so-called 120-day permit has the advantage of not falling under the quota system because it does not lead to residence in Switzerland. The foreigner with a permit has to retain his or her residence abroad and will not be granted a new 120-day permit right after expiration of the first one. Likewise, it is forbidden to use 120-day permits for foreigners who rotate in the same job. Nevertheless, the 120-day permit is convenient where work in Switzerland is necessary only for a short time and for a specific task.

Non-working foreigners, such as students and pensioners over 60 years of age, may receive a residence permit if they comply with the conditions of the permit. Non-working foreigner permits are restricted by a quota which is rather stringent, particularly with regard to pensioners under 60 years of age. They are practically excluded from taking up residence in Switzerland. Pensioners over 60 years of age may obtain a residence permit if they have close ties to Switzerland, actually take up residence in Switzerland and have the necessary means to provide for themselves.

¶1609

¶1610   Permanent residence permit (Permit C)

One can usually apply for the permanent residence permit after ten years of continued residence in Switzerland. Switzerland has concluded residence treaties with 31 states. Under certain of these treaties the permanent residence permit may be granted after a permanent stay of five years to the citizens of the following countries:

- Belgium,
- Denmark,
- Finland,
- France,
- Germany,
- Great Britain,
- Iceland,
- Ireland,
- Italy,
- Liechtenstein,
- Luxembourg,
- the Netherlands,
- Norway,
- Sweden, and
- Spain

The permanent residence permit is valid only for the canton which granted it.

Permanent residents are subject to none of the restrictions in the laws on the exercise of gainful activity by foreigners. They may exercise, without any formalities, the profession they choose; they may take up employment or be self-employed, and change their job or profession. For practical purposes C-permit holders are legally treated like Swiss citizens, with the main exception of the right to vote and the duty to perform military service.

The permanent residence permit expires if the foreigner obtains another permit from another canton or if he is expelled by criminal or administrative measures. If foreigners leave Switzerland for more than six months they lose their permanent residence permit, but the competent cantonal authority can allow them to stay abroad for up to two years.

¶1611   Seasonal workers

Seasonal workers (*saisonniers*) are foreigners who hold a temporary residence permit, entitling them to work in an enterprise of a seasonal character such as a winter resort hotel. The seasonal permit, granted for a maximum period of nine months, cannot be extended beyond that term. The seasonal worker must thus stay abroad for at least three out of the 12 months. Every year, seasonal workers must apply for a new permit and fulfil the conditions as if they were asking for it for the first time. In consequence, seasonal workers may change their employers every season. Depending on the circumstances, change of employment may be permitted during the season. In principle, however, it is not possible to move to another canton during the same season.

If the seasonal worker has worked in Switzerland for a total of 36 months within four consecutive years, he can apply for conversion of the seasonal permit into a temporary residence permit, although he has no vested right thereto. This conversion can also be requested by a seasonal worker who has married a female foreigner with a permanent residence permit, or in cases where special circumstances require it. This conversion of permits is not subject to the regulations limiting admission, for no maximum quotas have been set.

A seasonal worker has no possibility of securing the admission of his or her family: the spouse must apply for his or her own permit.

¶1612   Border permits

Foreign workers living in the border zone of one of Switzerland's neighbours may receive a border permit for work in a defined border zone, provided the worker returns daily to his or her home abroad. To apply for the border permit, the worker must have lived in the border zone of the neighbouring country for at least six months. Border permits are, like seasonal permits, not subject to the yearly quotas and are thus more easily obtainable.

¶1613   Legal status of foreign employees

With regard to public and private labour laws, foreign workers enjoy the same status as native employees. Moreover, in principle, they may be employed only at the same salary and working conditions as native employees. It is the responsibility of the cantonal authorities (labour offices and foreigners' police) and trade unions to ensure that these principles and regulations are enforced.

The nationality of the employee has no bearing on the applicability of a collective labour agreement. Contracts may provide for certain exceptions with regard to seasonal work.

SELECTED BIBLIOGRAPHY

Christiane Brunner, Jean Michel-Bühler, Jean-Bernard Waeber, *Commentaire du contrat de travail* (Bern, 1989)

Walter H. Diggelmann, Bernhard Meyer-Hauser, Christof Schauwecker, *Swiss Work Permit Regulations 1991*, Swiss-American Chamber of Commerce (Zürich, 1991)

Kluwer Law and Taxation Publishers, *International Handbook on Contracts of Employment* (Deventer, 1988)

Christiane J. Meier-Schatz, *Arbeitsrecht* (St Gallen, 1991)

Manfred Rehbinder, *Schweizerisches Arbeitsrecht*, 10th edn (Bern, 1991)

17 Property, Immovable Property, Zoning and Environmental Protection

PRINCIPAL LEGISLATION

Code civil suisse/Zivilgesetzbuch/Federal Swiss Civil Code (CC), RS 210.

Code des obligations/Obligationenrecht/Federal Code of Obligations (CO), RS 220.

Loi fédérale sur l'acquisition d'immeubles par des personnes à l'étranger/Bundesgesetz über den Erwerb von Grundstücken durch Personem im Ausland ('Lex Friedrich')/Federal Statute on Acquisition of Immovables by Non-Residents (*'Lex Friedrich'*), RS 211.412.41.

Ordonnance sur l'acquisition d'immeubles par des personnes à l'étranger/ Verordnung über den Erwerb von Grundstücken durch Personen im Ausland/Ordinance to *'Lex Friedrich'*, RS 211.41.

Loi fédérale sur l'aménagement du territoire/Raumplanungsgesetz/Federal Zoning Statute, RS 700.

Ordonnance sur l'aménagement du territoire/Raumplanungsverordnung/Ordinance to Zoning Statute, RS 700.1.

Loi fédérale sur la protection de l'environnement/Umweltschutzgesetz/Federal Environmental Protection Statute, RS 814.01.

Loi fédérale sur la protection des eaux contre la pollution/Gewässerschutzgesetz/ Federal Water Pollution Statute, RS 814.20.

Ordonnance sur la protection de l'air/Luftreinhalteverordnung/Federal Air Pollution Ordinance, RS 814.318.142.1.

Ordonnance sur la protection contre le bruit/Lärmschutzverordnung/Federal Noise Pollution Ordinance, RS 814.41.

Ordonnance sur les substances dangereuses pour l'environnement/Stoffverordnung/ Federal Dangerous Substances Ordinance, RS 814.013.

Ordonnance relative à l'étude de l'impact sur l'environnement/ Umweltverträglichkeitsprüfungsverordnung/Federal Environmental Impact Study Ordinance, RS 814.011.

MOVABLE AND IMMOVABLE PROPERTY

¶1701   Some figures

In Switzerland, the acquisition of immovable property by non-resident aliens is restricted and requires a permit. In 1990, the aggregate market value of all immovable property purchased by non-residents under 1139 permits was approximately 1470 million Swiss Francs, about 256 million Swiss Francs being spent for condominium apartments. Most permits were granted for purchase of land situated in the cantons of Ticino (242), Valais (181) and Graubünden (93).

The market price for immovable property is high compared to most other countries. For example, in 1988, in the city of Zurich, 177 single-family homes were purchased at an average purchase price of SFr 1,108,000.

¶1702   Constitutional guarantee of property

Ownership of immovable property is expressly guaranteed in the Federal Constitution (Art. 22ter). Federal and cantonal legislation may provide for limitations on this constitutional right. They may provide for expropriation when this is warranted by the public interest, but full compensation must be paid. The constitutional guarantee applies regardless of the citizenship and residence of the owner of the immovable property.

Ownership and transfer of immovable property may be subject to taxes, such as the immovable property transfer tax (¶1012), tax on capital gains on immovable property (¶1013(4)), and inheritance tax and gift tax (¶1044 and ¶1045).

¶1703   Ownership

Ownership (*propriété/Eigentum*) is the most comprehensive legal title with regard to a given asset. Ownership includes the right to use the asset and the right to dispose of it, and is akin to a fee simple absolute in common law (Art. 641 et seq. CC).

¶1704   Immovable property

(1)   Types of immovable property

Joint property can be held in the form of either joint ownership or co-ownership. Joint ownership is based on an underlying personal relationship, such as marriage or community among heirs (Arts 652 to 654 CC). Co-ownership may exist without the element of personal relationship (Arts 646 to 651 CC); it is based on an express or implied agreement of the co-owners. Special provisions apply to the ownership of a particular floor of a building (Arts 712(a) to 712(f) CC).

Ownership of a particular floor of a building (*propriété par étage/ Stockwerkeigentum*) is co-ownership of the land, supplemented by the right to use a particular portion of the building exclusively. This concept is similar to the notion of 'condominium' in United States law. Ownership is limited by the rights of the owners of the remaining floors. The owner has not merely the right, but also the obligation to maintain his or her portion, in so far as this is needed to keep the whole house in good condition.

(2)   Servitudes

Various types of servitudes are defined in the Civil Code. For instance, the right to build on a tract of land (*droit de superficie/Baurecht*) is the right to construct on or beneath the surface of a certain piece of land belonging to another person. By granting this right to a third person, the owner of the land conveys the right to possess and enjoy the tract of land for a limited period of time. Upon the expiration of this period, the conveyed rights revert to the owner. The right to build on a tract of land is entered as a servitude in the land register (Art. 675 and 779 to 779(e) CC).

Another servitude which may be entered in the land register is the right of residence. This is the right to occupy a house or part of a house (Arts 776 to 778 CC).

(3)   Options to acquire immovable property

Parties considering the purchase of immovable property may agree on an option to buy or repurchase, or an option granting the right of pre-emption (Art. 216 CO).

(4)   Fiduciary acquisition of immovable property

Immovable property may be purchased on a fiduciary basis (ATF 71 II 99). The fiduciary purchase of land is void, however, if the parties intended to evade the law, e.g., if the fiduciary purchase is a stratagem to evade the provisions regarding acquisition of immovable property by non-resident foreigners.

(5) Mortgages

Banks routinely extend credit secured by mortgages. As of summer 1991, banks grant credits secured by mortgages on residential immovable property for amounts of up to 80 per cent of the market value of the land and building. Mortgage security may be established in the form of a mortgage or a mortgage note (Arts 824 to 874 CC). See ¶904(2) and ¶1129.

(6) 'Real estate companies'

Another beneficial interest in land may be acquired by purchasing shares or the majority of shares in a real estate share corporation. In some cantons (especially Geneva), it is quite common for land with large buildings to be owned by real estate companies. The 'economic ownership' of immovable property can be transferred simply by conveying the shares of the real estate company which owns the immovable property in question.

Another means of acquiring an indirect immovable property interest consists in buying shares in a real estate investment fund; investment funds are governed by the Investment Funds Statute (¶1147). There are investment funds which invest exclusively in Swiss immovable property.

¶1705   Movable property

Property in movable things, or ownership of a chattel, is the right exclusively to use and dispose of a certain movable asset within the provisions of the law. The owner is entitled to protect his or her property against any kind of undue influence (Art. 641 CC). It is possible to have joint ownership or co-ownership of movable objects. The most frequent example of joint ownership is the acquisition of property by several heirs following the death of the decedent (Art. 560 CC).

(1) Acquisition of movable property

Movable property is transferred by agreement of the parties and upon the acquirer's taking possession of the thing sold.

(2) Retention of title

It is possible to transfer possession but reserve ownership by registering in a special register at the domicile of the possessor the fact that title has been retained by the transferor (¶904(4)). The registration does not entail constructive notice to the public of the retention of title.

Despite registration, third parties in good faith may acquire property from the possessor who is not the owner. However, the registration of the retention of title allows the owner of goods to repossess his or her assets if the possessor goes bankrupt, or if the assets are seized or attached. The registration must be effected before bankruptcy proceedings are initiated (Arts 715 and 716 CC).

(3) Possession

Possession may be transferred either through physical transfer of the object or, where the object physically remains with the transferor, through simple declaration (*constitutum possessorium*; typically so in sale and lease-back contracts). A simple declaration of the intention to transfer possession is also sufficient when the acquirer is already in possession of the object but has not yet become the owner (*brevi manu traditio*; typically so when a lessee purchases the leased object from the lessor). The references to these concepts of Roman law indicate that modern Swiss property law is still highly influenced by Roman law.

(4) Transfer of property through documents of title

It is possible to transfer property by transferring the document which represents goods stored in a warehouse or the bill of lading (*connaissement/Konnossement*) where the goods are shipped on board a vessel (Art. 925 CC). However, if the goods are acquired by a purchaser in good faith (i.e., without the knowledge that a document of title exists), the latter's rights prevail over the conflicting rights of the holder of the document of title (*titre représentant la marchandise/Warenpapier*).

(5) Acquisition of title from the non-owner

If a buyer in good faith purchases movable property, intending and believing himself to acquire property from a party who in fact is not the owner, the following situations must be distinguished:

(a) If the true owner himself or herself has conferred possession to the seller, e.g., by leasing the object to the seller, the buyer acquires ownership even though he or she purchases from the apparent rather than from the actual owner.

(b) Lost or stolen goods may be reclaimed from any third party. However, if the goods have been sold in a public auction or by a merchant dealing in this type of goods, the original owner must reimburse the full purchase price to the buyer (Art. 934 CC).

¶1706 Notarisation of sales contracts – land register

Sales agreements and contracts on options to buy or repurchase pertaining to immovable property must be drawn up as public deeds and signed before a notary public (Art. 216(1) CO). The exact manner in which the document is authenticated is governed by cantonal law. The contract on a right of first refusal is valid if in writing (Art. 216 CO). The title in immovable property passes to the purchaser when the purchase is registered in the land register (*registre foncier/Grundbuch*). Rights over immovable property are recorded in a land register (Arts 942 to 977 CC). Whenever registration is required by law for the creation of an immovable property right, it acquires the force of a right *in rem* only when it is so registered (Art. 971 CC).

Immovable property owned by a decedent is vested with the heir(s) upon death by operation of law (Arts 560 to 579 CC). Special provisions apply to the purchase of immovable property from an owner in bankruptcy.

RESTRICTIONS ON PURCHASE AND SALE OF LAND

¶1707   Agricultural immovable property

Restrictions apply to the purchase of agricultural immovable property, i.e., land used exclusively or predominantly for farming purposes.

When agricultural land is about to be sold, the descendants, spouse or parents of the seller have an option to buy. As a rule, a tenant has the same option. The spouse or the descendants who wish to buy the immovable property for their own use may purchase it at the income value (capitalised earning power).

Under the law of inheritance, special provisions are applicable to agricultural land. As a rule, it is allocated to heirs at its income value, i.e., the capitalised average income which can be obtained under ordinary circumstances over a period of several years (Art. 617 CC). This value depends on the net profit realised and the current interest rate.

¶1708   Five-year ban on sale of non-agricultural land

Non-agricultural land may not be resold within five years from the date of acquisition. There are several exceptions to this rule, such as transfers of land by operation of inheritance law, transactions among family members, and various other special circumstances. The competent cantonal authority may permit the resale of the immovable property before the expiration of the five-year ban if:

(1) the seller does not derive a gain from the transaction;

(2) the immovable property has served as the seller's family home or place of business for at least two years; or

(3) the immovable property is acquired in order to realise a construction project for which a valid construction permit has been granted.

The purpose of the applicable statutory provisions is practical, i.e., to reduce the number of speculative immovable property deals and to limit the escalation of the price of land.

¶1709 Authorisation requirement for non-residents

On 1 January 1985, the Federal Statute on Acquisition of Immovables by Non-Residents became effective (*'Lex Friedrich'*, named after the then federal Justice Minister). The *Lex Friedrich* regulates and restricts the acquisition of immovable property by non-residents. The statute defines as non-residents, *inter alia*, foreigners, whether individuals or legal entities, who are not entitled to set up their domicile in Switzerland. Further, corporate entities controlled by such individuals are treated on the same footing as non-residents, although their domicile is in Switzerland (Arts 5 and 6 *Lex Friedrich*; see ¶1710).

As discussed below, non-residents must obtain a permit from the competent cantonal authorities before purchasing immovable property. All permits that were granted under the previous legislation (*Lex Furgler/Lex Celio/Lex von Moos*) remain in force (Art. 38 *Lex Friedrich*).

¶1710 Transactions subject to restrictions

(1) Property interest

The term 'immovable property' in the statute applies to every kind of control over, and interest in, immovable property. This includes life-interest (usufruct), rights above a building (air rights), and rights of first refusal. Fiduciary ownership in immovable property, long-term leases and loan agreements which render the owner of the immovable property dependent on a non-resident are also subject to restrictions (Art. 4(1)(a) *Lex Friedrich*).

(2) Investments in real estate companies

Investments by a non-resident in a corporation whose assets consist to a substantial extent of immovable property, may be deemed acquisition of immovable property. The following distinction is made:

On the one hand, there are corporations whose purpose, as stated in their by-laws, is to trade in immovable property or which, in fact, do so (real estate companies in the narrow sense). The purchase by a non-resident of an interest in such a company, however small, requires a permit. Similarly, a permit is required for the establishment of a new corporation with the purpose of dealing in immovable property (Art. 4(1)(d) *Lex Friedrich*; Art. 1 Ordinance to *Lex Friedrich*; ATF 109 Ib 95).

On the other hand, there is the case of foreign-controlled companies engaged in general trade that present the following characteristic: more than one-third of their assets (at fair market value) consists of Swiss immovable property (real estate companies in the broader sense). Whether non-residents have a dominant position depends on the circumstances of the case (Arts 4(1) and 6 *Lex Friedrich*). In any event, a dominant position is presumed if more than one-third of the shares are held by non-residents or if, according to a special statutory formula, the corporation has been substantially financed with foreign assistance (Art. 1 Ordinance to *Lex Friedrich*).

A 'dominant position' may also be enjoyed by holding companies, or may be brought about by merger or absorption. In a given case, very tedious inquiries are often necessary to be able to draw the line between foreign-dominated corporations and others (ATF 106 Ib 201; ATF 110 Ib 113/114; ATF 105 Ib 310). In any event, if foreign domination appears to be present, substantial evidence to the contrary is required (ATF 110 Ib 113/114).

In practice, the following cases do not present a problem: share corporations with registered shares, only if the financing of these shares by residents is shown to the authorities; registered employment-benefit foundations under the Federal Occupational Pension Plans Statute; and corporations whose Swiss character is obvious, such as major Swiss banks and large Swiss food chains (ATF 104 Ib 10).

(3) Immovable property investment funds

The purchase of even a single share in an immovable property investment fund is tantamount to acquisition of immovable property if the shares are not quoted on a stock exchange (Art. 4(1)(c) *Lex Friedrich*; Art. 19 Ordinance to *Lex Friedrich*).

(4) Persons concerned

Foreign nationals residing outside Switzerland and companies with their principal place of business outside Switzerland need a permit (Art. 5(1)(a) and (b) *Lex Friedrich*). However, citizens of foreign countries who, under a residence treaty of their country of citizenship with Switzerland, have the right to reside in Switzerland and who have obtained a residence permit, do not need a permit to acquire immovable property. See ¶1610.

Regardless of the country of their citizenship or residence, the following, *inter alia*, do not need a permit:

(a) statutory heirs, according to Swiss law, of a decedent leaving immovable property in Switzerland; and

¶1710

(b) spouses, parents, grandparents, children, and grandchildren of sellers of Swiss immovable property (for instance, non-Swiss relatives of a naturalised Swiss citizen, or a Swiss citizen's grandchildren who grew up abroad and became citizens of a foreign country).

In addition, certain acquisitions of immovable property involving very small areas are exempt from the permit requirement.

Foreign citizens married to Swiss persons, and all other non-Swiss citizens, regardless of whether they have a residence permit, need a permit if they wish to acquire immovable property in the vicinity of an important military installation (but see ¶1712 for grounds for absolute refusal of permit). Within certain limits, no permit is required for foreign states and international organisations. Moreover, the Federal Government may lift the permit requirement in special cases if it deems it to be in the public interest.

If a Swiss corporation is controlled by non-residents, it must obtain a permit. The concept of dominant position applies; foreign domination may result from participation, financing, management, or all of the foregoing.

¶1711 Right to a permit

The authorities may not exercise free discretion in granting permits. Except for vacation homes and units in hotel condominiums, there is no ceiling on permits, and permits must be granted when the statutory requirements are fulfilled (Art. 8 *Lex Friedrich*).

(1) Permanent business establishments

In practice, most permits are granted for the creation of permanent business establishments. The *Lex Friedrich* accords this term a different meaning than under the law of intercantonal and international double taxation (¶1051). A permit allows non-residents to acquire immovable property in order to conduct a business. To be eligible, the owner must be able to control the business, i.e., he or she must be an influential member of the board of directors (ATF 106 Ib 65; ATF 104 Ib 149). Moreover, the owner must be primarily engaged in his or her usual line of business. This means that a subsidiary of a foreign steel corporation may not acquire immovable property to operate, for instance, a hotel. If the line of business is a different one, a mere capital investment is insufficient to obtain a permit.

The actual permanent business establishment must be a necessary unit in size and kind. Agricultural and forestry businesses and agencies renting apartments never qualify as permanent business establishments and are not available for acquisition by foreigners (Art. 3 Ordinance to *Lex Friedrich*).

Once an acquisition permit is obtained, non-resident individuals wishing to manage a permanent business establishment in Switzerland still need a work permit. See ¶1610. The acquisition of permanent business establishments in Switzerland is, in practice, open primarily to foreign legal entities and to Swiss legal entities dominated by non-resident foreigners (Art. 8(1)(a)) *Lex Friedrich*; Art. 3 Ordinance to *Lex Friedrich*).

(2)   Insurance companies: Technical reserves

A permit may further be granted to foreign insurance companies who intend to invest in Switzerland the technical reserves pertaining to their Swiss insurance portfolio (Art. 8(1)(c) *Lex Friedrich*).

(3)   Other grounds for permits

Swiss immovable property may be acquired by non-residents for charitable purposes, or with a view to securing employment benefits granted to their employees by permanent business establishments of foreign enterprises. To qualify, the acquisitions must be tax-exempt in Switzerland (Art. 8(1)(c) *Lex Friedrich*). This category of permit is, in practice, limited to foundations.

There are three further general grounds for permits in special cases:

(a)   A foreign bank or an insurance company may acquire immovable property by enforcing a mortgage in the event of an overdue mortgage-secured loan. The property must be resold by the bank within two years (Art. 8(1)(d) *Lex Friedrich*).

(b)   The same applies to beneficiaries under a will who otherwise do not qualify for a permit (Art. 8(2) *Lex Friedrich*).

(c)   Non-residents may resell immovable property that was acquired with a permit to another non-resident if they are in a narrowly defined emergency situation (Art. 8(3) *Lex Friedrich*).

(4)   'Cantonal grounds'

There are additional grounds for a permit established by cantonal law. The *Lex Friedrich* defines their substance and their minimum scope, but they are available only if a canton adopts them expressly by enacting special cantonal laws. For instance, if housing is scarce, cantons are free to grant permits for the acquisition of immovable property with a view to the construction of subsidised housing (Art. 9(1)(c) *Lex Friedrich*; Art. 3 Ordinance to *Lex Friedrich*).

(5)   Permanent residence

Foreigners who permanently take up their main residence in Switzerland will be permitted to acquire a house or an apartment. However, in tandem with this permit, they still need a residence permit and a work permit, as the case may be. The land may not exceed 1,000 square metres; the net living area may not

¶1711

exceed 200 square metres (ATF 108 Ib 1). Many cantons have, on their own initiative, restricted this rule further by requiring a minimum duration for the foreigner's stay in Switzerland.

Finally, non-residents must sell their immovable property within two years if they no longer use it as their main residence due to a change of residence within Switzerland or a return to their home country (Arts 9(1)(b) and 14(2) *Lex Friedrich*; Arts 5 and 8 Ordinance to *Lex Friedrich*).

(6) Second homes

For the acquisition of a second home, it is strictly required that non-residents have an unusually close relationship with the place where they wish to acquire immovable property. Neither frequent stays in Switzerland, such as stays for study or health reasons, nor family members residing in Switzerland are deemed sufficient grounds for a permit (ATF 106 Ib 198).

(7) Vacation homes and condominiums

For vacation homes and hotel condominium units, there is, in addition, a federal quota system (Art. 9(2) and (3) *Lex Friedrich*). The Federal Government has assigned a quota to each canton. These quotas have been continuously reduced over the years.

¶1712 Grounds for refusal of permits

There are some absolute grounds for refusal of permits. Generally speaking, a non-resident is prohibited from making a financial investment in immovable property. As a result, it is not possible for a non-resident to acquire an apartment in order to rent it out.

A person who is found guilty of evading the law is no longer eligible for a permit for the same object, even if the legal requirements are subsequently met (Art. 12(c) *Lex Friedrich*).

If the immovable property is within one kilometre of an important military installation, no permit will be granted (Art. 12(e) *Lex Friedrich*; Arts 13 and 14 Ordinance to *Lex Friedrich*). This also applies if national interests are at stake, e.g., if a non-resident wants to acquire a landmark of national importance or a key industry. Conversely, it is possible for the Federal Government to grant a non-resident a permit to acquire immovable property for reasons of government interest, even though no other statutory grounds for a permit exist (Art. 12(f) *Lex Friedrich*).

¶1713 Conditions of permits

If permits are made subject to conditions, these conditions are entered in the land register (¶1706). The *Lex Friedrich* provides for general requirements; the authority granting the permit states the conditions in a more detailed fashion. If conditions are subsequently not fulfilled, the permit will be revoked. Permits for the acquisition of homes for individuals are accompanied by conditions on use and, depending on the cantonal and local statutory provisions, resale (Art. 14 *Lex Friedrich*).

For permanent business establishments, there is a ten-year ban on resale. Special conditions apply to the acquisition of investments in real estate companies. The deposit of shares may be required. Where non-residents have a controlling interest, the cantonal authority may require that every change of control be immediately reported. If conditions become overly onerous or can no longer be fulfilled because of changed circumstances, they can be revoked on the motion of the applicant (Arts 11 and 12 Ordinance to *Lex Friedrich*).

¶1714   Procedure for obtaining permits

(1)   Application

Applications for permits must be filed with the appropriate cantonal authority at the place where the immovable property to be acquired is situated (Art. 15 *Lex Friedrich*; Art. 16 Ordinance to *Lex Friedrich*). Preliminary decisions may be obtained if it is unclear whether a permit is required at all. Thus, a would-be investor who cannot entirely rule out the possibility that a planned transaction might fall within the ambit of the *Lex Friedrich* is well advised to seek a declaratory decision. Similarly, if there are foreign shareholders, it would be good business practice to have the authorities check whether the investments of these foreigners trigger the permit requirement (Art. 17 *Lex Friedrich*; Art. 15 Ordinance to *Lex Friedrich*).

Applicants must provide the authorities with all necessary information and submit complete supporting documentation. If they fail to co-operate, their application may be rejected (Art. 22 *Lex Friedrich*).

(2)   Permit prior to transaction

The permit must be obtained before the transaction is effected. The registrars of the land register and Register of Commerce will refuse registration if there are any doubts as to whether the transaction requires a permit (Art. 18 *Lex Friedrich*; Art. 18 Ordinance to *Lex Friedrich*). Specific rules apply to involuntary auction sales (Art. 19 *Lex Friedrich*; Art. 18 Ordinance to *Lex Friedrich*).

(3)   Validity of permits

Permits are valid for three years only; the authorised transaction must be concluded within that period of time.

¶1714

(4) Remedies
The decisions of the authorities granting (or refusing) permits are subject to review by the respective administrative judicial authorities. Ultimately, the Federal Supreme Court decides upon an administrative-law appeal of the party whose request for a permit is refused. The Federal Justice Office has standing to file an administrative law appeal against a cantonal decision in the interest of a nationally uniform application of the law (Arts 20 and 21 *Lex Friedrich*).

¶1715 Sanctions against unlawful acquisitions

(1) Voidness of the transaction
The acquisition of immovable property by a non-resident is void if no permit has been obtained. Transactions that were closed without a permit are null and void (Art. 26 *Lex Friedrich*). The considerations exchanged may be reclaimed within ten years (Art. 27 *Lex Friedrich*; ATF 111 Ib 195). These consequences ensue automatically. The cantonal authorities may sue for reinstatement of the original legal situation.

(2) Confiscation
It is possible to dissolve companies and to confiscate their assets if they were organised in order to evade the law (ATF 110 Ib 105). Immovable property that was purchased without the necessary permit may be auctioned off in a forced liquidation. Under certain conditions, the earlier actions or omissions of a representative of a legal entity that is applying for a permit may be imputed to that legal entity itself. As a result, these individuals and corporations who once circumvented the *Lex Friedrich* are precluded from doing so again by using an agent (Art. 12(c) *Lex Friedrich*; ATF 114 Ib 16).

(3) Criminal penalties
The intentional evasion of the permit requirement is punishable with imprisonment for up to three years or a fine of up to SFr 100,000. The same applies to incorrect statements made to the permit-granting authorities and to the failure to comply with imposed conditions. In the case of negligence, the punishment is a fine.

¶1716 Illustrative cases

(1) Sale from non-resident to non-resident
A non-resident purchasing immovable property is required to obtain a permit, even though the immovable property may already be owned by another non-resident (ATF 103 Ib 182). If, from a commercial point of view, it is likely that non-residents may gain control over Swiss immovable property, they are

under the permit requirement. In judging whether a transaction falls under the permit requirement, the courts review the framework of contracts as a whole (ATF 107 Ib 18).

(2) Indirect ownership
A holding company indirectly owning – through a wholly-owned subsidiary – Swiss immovable property worth more than one-third of the subsidiary's assets, qualifies as a real estate company in the broader sense. The permit-granting authority has wide discretion in assessing whether the book value is equivalent to the market value (ATF 105 Ib 310; ATF 106 Ib 71).

(3) Granting of option or right of first refusal
Not only the exercise of an option to purchase or a right of first refusal, but also the granting of this right or option, requires a permit (ATF 101 II 240).

(4) Long-term leases
A long-term lease requires a permit if the tenant may, on his or her own, remodel, upgrade, or sublet the premises without obtaining the landlord's consent (ATF 106 Ib 14; ATF 104 Ib 143; ATF 105 Ib 323). As a rule, a lease with a life of more than ten years is deemed to put the lessee in the position of a proprietor. Accordingly, such lease is subject to the permit requirements.

(5) 'Unusual financing'
The dominant position of a non-resident is assumed if there is 'unusual financing' of a company which intends to acquire immovable property. This is the case, for example, if non-residents grant mortgage credits of more than two-thirds of the market value of the immovable property (ATF 106 Ib 207; see Art. 6 *Lex Friedrich*). The conditions prevailing at the time when a non-resident obtains control over immovable property are decisive. A subsequent modification of the actual parameters is not relevant. An illegal transaction cannot be saved by such modifications (ATF 108 II 464/465; ATF 110 Ib 111/114).

(6) Personal involvement of non-resident
A non-resident must either personally manage the permanent business establishment or act through its proper officers. Foreigners may not use an essentially independent third person as an employee. They must concern themselves directly with the management. Otherwise, a mere capital investment, which is prohibited, is assumed. Undeveloped land and/or buildings which are not suited for business purposes may not be acquired for a permanent business establishment (ATF 104 Ib 147; ATF 106 Ib 291; ATF 108 Ib 449).

¶1716

(7) Time-sharing

Even when limited in time, all forms of ownership are subject to the permit requirements. Thus, time-sharing of apartments in vacation clubs requires a permit to be obtained by each stakeholder. If the non-resident acquires a condominium share or gives a financial consideration for a vacation period that is exclusively and organisationally reserved for him or her in such a way that one must equate this to the control of an owner, a permit is required.

(8) 'Exceptional cases'

In 'exceptional cases' a permit may be granted to resell immovable property, e.g., if the owner's health necessitates a sale. Financial difficulties resulting from a risky financing scheme are not sufficient to constitute an 'exceptional case' (ATF 102 Ib 333; ATF 104 Ib 19; ATF 111 Ib 179).

ZONING LAW

¶1717 Sources of law

The constitutional basis is a 1969 amendment to Art. 22^{quater} of the Federal Constitution. In 1972, federal emergency zoning measures were enacted. They limited building areas and led to a concentration of building in the centres of cities and villages. The current Federal Zoning Statute has been in effect since 1 January 1990.

¶1718 Federal zoning regulations

(1) Purpose of Zoning Statute

Federal zoning law is limited to general principles. They proclaim that the Federal Government, the cantons and the municipalities are under a general zoning obligation. Zoning is aimed at determining the use of given areas and at defining priorities and the means by which the intended use of the land can be achieved (Art. 2 Zoning Statute). The Federal Government co-ordinates activities that extend over cantonal borders. Traditionally, zoning respects the autonomy of the municipalities. The municipalities pass the planning and building regulations, taking local conditions into account.

The purpose of zoning is to make good use of land. The federal regulations postulate the protection of land, air, water, forests and scenery, and the securing of a high quality of life in cities and villages. Moreover, the regulations aim at providing a sound basis for economic activity, a balanced mix of social, economic and cultural activities and a sufficient supply of food for the country (Art. 1 Zoning Statute).

In addition, planning principles are important. In rural areas sufficient arable land must be preserved, while in cities and villages, areas for housing and working must be reasonably co-ordinated and interconnected by public transportation.

(2)   Windfall profits
A statutory provision provides for the recapture of planning windfalls (Art. 5 Zoning Statute). A landowner benefiting from government zoning measures that allow more intensive land use, and consequently increase the value of the land, is required to pay taxes or dues on land sales (¶1013(4)). In contrast, zoning losses which have an effect similar to expropriation for a landowner must be fully compensated (Art. 5(2) Zoning Statute).

(3)   Zoning procedure
Zoning must be complete and openly accessible. If it covers only certain aspects, this must be declared expressly. Further, zoning must be open in the sense that it must be reasonably flexible.

To the extent that zoning sets forth only guide-lines, the authorities have a certain leeway in applying the rules. They may, for instance, establish the precise border of a zoning area whose extent is not clearly determined. Zoning must always be co-ordinated with geographical neighbours and with the authorities in the affected area. Zoning has a minimum validity period (normally 10–15 years) but remains flexible.

Decisions regarding building outside building zones may be appealed to the Federal Supreme Court. Thus, the uniform application of zoning law is secured in all of Switzerland (Arts 33 and 34 Zoning Statute).

(4)   General zoning directives
An important instrument of federal zoning law is the general zoning directive (*plan directeur/Richtplan*). In maps and text, it indicates how a particular area shall be developed. General zoning directives contain statements of facts and trends: scenic areas that are important for recreation or preservation are set aside and future developments are allowed or prohibited (Arts 6 to 8 Zoning Law Statute).

General zoning directives are binding only on official bodies (Art. 9 Zoning Law). They tell the federal, cantonal and municipal governments what to do. Landowners are affected only when these authorities enact plans. Landowners have no remedy against general zoning directives, even though they may infer a particular development from them (ATF 107 Ia 77).

¶1718

Finally, the Federal Government may develop concepts and topical plans where it has the requisite authority, e.g., for the preservation of arable land (Art. 13 Zoning Statute; Arts 16 to 20 Ordinance). In all of Switzerland, the arable land in each agriculturally usable area must be determined. A minimum arable area of land is set aside in order to secure sufficient food production in times of threatened supplies. The federal legislature has defined the minimum area that each canton must set aside as arable land.

(5) Utilisation plans

Utilisation plans (*plans d'affectation/Nutzungspläne*) are an extension of general zoning directives. The individual landowner is directly affected by utilisation plans (Art. 21 Zoning Statute), which regulate every piece of land with respect to its permissible utilisation and purpose (Art. 14 Zoning Statute). The principal zones established by federal law are construction, agricultural and protection zones. The cantons are free to provide for further subzones (Art. 18 Zoning Statute). Moreover, there is a distinction between general utilisation zones and particular utilisation zones. A general utilisation zone must be set up in every municipality and covers the municipality's entire area. For smaller areas there often are special utilisation plans (for instance, for the realisation of a large village centre consisting of residential and commercial areas).

Each municipality must decide where to place the residential area. Usually, housing is limited to areas that have already been developed. If there are undeveloped areas left, it is decided whether they should be developed or preserved as parks or playgrounds. In rural areas where arable land is scarce, only land that for topographical reasons is difficult to cultivate will be permitted to be developed. This makes building more expensive. This side-effect may be compensated for by allowing higher density building.

According to the Zoning Statute, protective zones embrace river and lake shores and larger scenic areas. Protective zones are established for the protection of the nation's cultural heritage and the natural habitats of animals (Art. 17 Zoning Statute).

(6) Utilities

The concept of bringing utilities and roads to a plot of land is uniformly regulated by federal law (Art. 19 Zoning Statute). Building zones must be provided with proper infrastructure. This places substantial financial burdens on municipalities. For this reason, zoning sometimes occurs in stages in order to allow cost-effective building of water, energy and sewage conduits. A piece of land is basically ready to be developed if it can be connected to existing utilities nearby without substantial expense. Building land is entirely ready to be developed if there are conduits leading directly to the land, allowing for immediate connection. As for

¶1718

access by road, different provisions exist from place to place, since the cantons and municipalities have authority for zoning and building.

An important feature of the Zoning Statute is that one may no longer build anywhere without a permit (Art. 22 Zoning Statute). In order to obtain a permit (a building, conversion or change of utilisation permit), the site must be provided with utilities and must be ready to be developed. The building plans must be in conformity with zoning requirements. Further details may be regulated by the cantons.

Variances are granted only if necessary (Art. 24 Zoning Statute). According to case law, the prohibition of building outside building zones is strictly enforced. However, there are borderline cases involving small extensions, renewals or partial changes of already existing buildings. The change of utilisation of existing structures also falls into this category. In scenery protection zones it is possible to convert existing buildings that are no longer needed for agricultural use if they are not changed externally, and if the new usage does not lead to additional traffic.

¶1719   Cantonal zoning and building regulations

Zoning is implemented by cantonal authorities. In addition to the zones defined in the Zoning Statute (construction zones, agricultural zones and protection zones), cantonal law may make more detailed subdivisions of the various zones, a possibility of which the cantons usually make extensive use. The Zoning Statute required the cantons to submit general zoning directives and utilisation plans to the Federal Government. As of 1991, all cantonal general zoning directives but one had been approved by the federal authorities.

To a very large extent, substantive zoning law is cantonal law. Federal law provides only two substantive rules which affect the individual directly. The first is Art. 22(3) of the Federal Constitution, which provides that in cases of expropriation and restrictions on ownership equivalent to expropriation (*expropriation matérielle/Materielle Enteignung*), just compensation must be paid (see ¶1721). The second is Art. 24 of the Zoning Statute, which permits construction outside construction zones only under specific restrictive conditions.

Cantons implement general zoning directives through a utilisation zoning statute. Most cantonal statutes are general building and zoning statutes that regulate municipal zoning regulations, the dimension of buildings, the granting of building permits, and the installation of utilities. In addition, aesthetic regulations provide a way to prevent undesirable building.

In a typical cantonal utilisation zoning statute, zones set aside in the general zoning directives for residential areas are divided up into various building zones. Some areas may be set aside as reserve zones or potential building zones. The land affected is suitable for building but is not yet actually needed for this purpose. Landowners in a reserve zone may keep and renew existing buildings but they may not expand them or construct new buildings. They can expect their land to be included in a construction zone in due course.

Some parts of the residential area may be set aside as an undeveloped zone. Here all construction is forbidden with very few exceptions. The core construction zone encompasses the centres of villages and other densely built areas which have usually grown historically and form an organic whole.

The commercial and industrial zones are reserved for disruptive and noisy businesses. Housing in these zones is discouraged and is permitted only in exceptional cases. There are few restrictions on construction. However, even in industrial zones, there is no unfettered right to pollute: environmental protection legislation provides for noise reduction and air protection (see ¶1736 et seq.).

Residential areas are divided into several subzones. The zones differ according to the intensity of utilisation, i.e., the ratio of living space in a building to the surface of the land. A small ratio leads to lightly built areas. Often there are also restrictions on building heights and distances from the property boundaries. Businesses are allowed only if they do not cause noise or air pollution. Thus, for example, physicians and lawyers are allowed to practise in residential areas.

Particular utilisation plans include, for instance, plans on how a lot will be developed. The plans set a time frame for conduits to be constructed by the municipality. They help a landowner at the edge of a developed area to decide when to go ahead with construction. This is sometimes combined with the possibility of building certain facilities at one's own cost and of selling investments to neighbouring proprietors or to the municipality later on, once the neighbourhood has been predominantly built up.

¶1720   Municipal building codes

(1)   Policing power
Many zoning measures are eventually implemented by means of a building provision on either the cantonal or municipal level. Unless there is a provision to the contrary on the cantonal level, the municipalities have policing power over building. This body of law is mostly composed of various technical provisions which prescribe how buildings or installations must be built. These technical provisions deal with the building's safety (for instance, the use of particular building materials, minimum wall thickness), traffic safety (for example, separate access for pedestrians and automobiles, special parking lots off the street), health (for instance, minimum window area to floor area ratios, air vents in staircases and windowless bathrooms), equipment (type of heating and elevator equipment) and amenities (for instance, children's playing grounds, car parks, garbage collection facilities).

¶1720

A further group of provisions concerns building utilisation, in particular density. In addition, the position of a building within its lot may be regulated by the distance from the boundary line or other buildings, or both. The volume of a building may be restricted by prescribing a maximum length, depth and height, this last being measured (for instance) by the number of permissible floors of standard floor height. Buildings may be restricted to residential or commercial purposes, or both. In larger cities, there are additional restrictions on the extent to which houses may be put to business use, regardless of the permitted utilisation.

Finally, there are aesthetic regulations that all sorts of construction must meet. Buildings may not compromise the neighbourhood – a house in a fanciful style may be tolerated in an artistic neighbourhood but would not be permitted in a historic district. Many codes stipulate that large developments may be built only if they create a pleasing neighbourhood character. As a result, concrete buildings in drab army barrack style can rarely be built.

(2)   Construction permits

Unless details are regulated in the cantonal statute, the procedure to follow in obtaining a construction permit is governed by municipal codes. Usually, there are four steps in the construction permit issuance process. First, a request for a permit is filed with the municipal authorities (in a few cantons with the district of cantonal authorities). Secondly, a notice-and-comment period begins, during which time interested parties may lodge written objections to the issuance of the requested permit with the municipal authorities. The notice-and-comment period must be publicised in different ways: pursuant to the applicable code, through publication in a local newspaper, posting on a public bulletin board or by some other means of publication. Each announcement, as a rule, must indicate the precise location of the projected construction and, if it is a building, its ultimate use. Often, the dimension of the projected building must be made visible at the site with wooden poles.

The notice-and-comment period is closed after a short period of time. Within the time stated in the applicable code, the municipal authority must either grant or deny the construction permit. Once a permit is granted or refused, interested parties may challenge the decision before a special cantonal court for appeals of building code cases.

Detailed architectural plans indicating the use of each room must be filed with the authorities. It is not sufficient to describe a planned building verbally.

The beneficiary of a construction permit need not be the owner of the land. If the beneficiary is a third party, the landowner must grant permission in writing to seek a construction permit. A construction permit usually lapses after a period of up to three years. It may be renewed or amended or supplemented (this happens frequently during the construction process).

¶1720

Finally, on the municipal level, building and zoning law is not so much a legal as a political issue. Both the building code and the zoning code – a precise topographic map with the zones marked in colour – are regularly established by the municipal legislature, subject to approval by the constituents in a referendum or in a town meeting. Political considerations are, therefore, often as important as the legal requirements contained in federal or cantonal statutes. Whether a certain area ends up being included in or excluded from a construction zone is to a large extent decided freely by the municipality.

¶1721   Expropriation and just compensation

Article $22^{ter}(3)$ of the Federal Constitution prohibits expropriation of private property for public use without just compensation. Restrictions on property are permitted only if they have a statutory basis, are in the public interest, for example, in that they further health, welfare, safety, social, economic or aesthetic purposes, and do not go any further than necessary in order to achieve the statutory goal. If these requirements are met, the right of eminent domain, in a procedure precisely regulated by statute, may be exercised. Full compensation must be awarded.

The exercise of eminent domain is frequent in zoning law. On the one hand, there is outright expropriation (*expropriation formelle/formelle Enteignung*): if the municipality needs to remove a house in order to broaden a street, there will be a formal expropriation if the proprietor refuses to sell the premises. The owner must be paid the fair market value for the interest taken.

Of much greater practical importance is constructive expropriation (*expropriation matérielle/materielle Enteignung*). Here, the proprietor of the land remains the same, but a government measure restricts the enjoyment of the landowner's rights in such a way that the market value of the land is substantially reduced. The crucial issue is whether the government action is an expropriation that requires payment of just compensation or merely a decision taken under the general policing power that does not require compensation.

Zoning ordinances which restrict the use of property or cause a reduction in value are not expropriation if they substantially advance legitimate public interests and do not extinguish a fundamental attribute of ownership. Most challenges of regulations occur after the government reclassifies a construction zone as a construction zone with more restrictions or as an undeveloped zone.

However, decrease in the value of the immovable property as a result of government reclassification does not automatically trigger compensation. Whether compensation is due depends on how the land was used when the new zoning came into effect. If somebody owned land in a construction zone bordering on agricultural land, and never prepared architectural plans or arranged for the installation of utilities, that person will not receive any compensation. In fact, under the circumstances, the landowner is not deemed to lose an actual or imminent and legally possible utilisation. The land may continue to be utilised in an agricultural manner even though building is no longer possible. In addition, proprietors can expect zoning to change after 10 to 15 years.

Conversely, no compensation becomes due if land is not upgraded, or if construction is suspended for a limited period of time. The same is true for restrictions on construction along the border of a lot. Thus, a strip of land running along a street may remain undeveloped in order to make it possible for the street to be widened if needed.

LANDLORD AND TENANT

¶1722   Rental agreements

Under a rental agreement, the landlord leaves the use of the property to the tenant in return for payment of rent. Landlord-tenant law is particularly important, because about 60 per cent of all residents rent rather than own their apartments and houses. With effect from mid-1990, landlord-tenant law was substantially amended, especially regarding the renting of apartments. The statutory scheme aimed at protecting tenants, included rent control and the possibility for tenants to delay the effecting of a notice of termination.

The rental period may be fixed in advance or left indefinite. If it is indefinite, both landlord and tenant may terminate the contract by giving notice. Depending on the rented object, various statutory notice periods and dates apply. For apartments, local usage must be followed, for example, notice in a given area may only possibly be effective at the end of March or September. The statutory notice period is three months (Arts 266 to 266o CO).

In many places, there are associations of landlords and tenants. Some of them, especially in Zurich, Basel and Geneva, have together drafted standard rental agreements for apartments and business premises. Use of standard rental agreements is recommended, because they strike a fair balance between the interests of landlords and tenants.

Especially when renting business premises, it is important contractually to regulate in detail the consequences of the tenant's improving the premises. Since the tenant is not the proprietor of the premises, whatever is added to the premises becomes a fixture owned by the landlord. Often there is an agreement that the tenant may leave the premises as altered but receives no compensation for improvements made. Sometimes the first tenant can sell certain improvements directly to the successor tenant.

Rent is usually paid monthly or quarterly in advance. In addition to rent, costs for heating, air-conditioning and cleaning must be paid, unless the tenant rents an entire building. For business premises a price per square metre per year is used (as of summer 1991, up to SFr 1,000 in downtown Zurich).

An escalation clause or a provision for yearly automatic rent increases is valid only if the contract has a term of at least five or three years, respectively (Arts 269b to 269c CO). (For further details of rent control, see ¶1723.)

There are limitations on notice. Notice may be given only in writing and on an official form (Art. 266l CO). Spouses can give notice only in common, and the landlord must give notice to both. Notice that is not so given is null and void (Arts 366m to 366o CO). Notice violating the principle of good faith may be challenged and declared invalid by the court (Art. 271 CO).

A tenant may obtain a delay in the taking effect of a valid notice. The delay is granted if no other apartment can be found at the time when the notice becomes effective. The interest of the landlord in having the apartment vacated is taken into account by the court, but this interest is not paramount. In cases of hardship, the taking effect of the notice may be postponed for up to four years for apartments and for up to six years for business premises (Art. 272b CO).

¶1723   Rent control

Rent increases, or within certain narrow limits even the initial rent, may be challenged by the tenant. Increases can take effect on dates on which notice can be given. The rent increase must be justified by the landlord and notified on an official form. If the increase exceeds statutory limits, it can be rejected in part or in whole. If a tenant is successful in challenging a rent increase, the landlord is precluded from evicting the tenant for three years (prohibition of retaliatory eviction).

If the premises are sold, the existing leases continue with the new landlord by operation of law.

ENVIRONMENTAL PROTECTION

¶1724   The Federal Environmental Protection Statute of 1983

In 1972, the Federal Constitution was amended to give the Confederation the authority to legislate in the field of environmental protection (Art. $24^{septies}$ Federal Constitution). The Federal Environmental Protection Statute was subsequently enacted in 1983, and became effective on 1 January 1985.

This statute deals with the impact of industrial and human activities on the environment. The notion of 'environment' is understood in a broad sense to comprise every aspect of the habitat in which human beings, animals and plants exist.

The Federal Environmental Protection Statute focuses on air pollution, excessive noise, vibrations and radiation, and substances which may contaminate the soil. It sets ceilings on the quantities of undesirable substances that can be disposed of at all, and contains a comprehensive catalogue of provisions on procedure and enforcement.

The implementation of the statute is left to the cantons. The Federal Environmental Protection Office (*Office fédéral de l'environnement, des forêts et du paysage/Bundesamt für Umwelt, Wald und Landschaft*) is assigned only limited tasks of implementation of the statute. Basically, it counsels, co-ordinates and supervises.

¶1725   Other statutes in the field of environmental law

The Federal Environmental Protection Statute does not supersede or repeal previous law aimed at protecting the environment. Rather, these provisions, for example, water pollution legislation, wildlife protection and animal protection, are expressly reserved.

Other statutes promote environmentally sound technology or equipment. Increasingly, cantonal legislatures require heat insulation materials to be used in new buildings in order to reduce energy consumption, and new buildings to be equipped with devices to determine the actual consumption of heating energy in order to create an incentive for tenants to reduce energy consumption.

¶1726   Environmental protection through zoning law

As construction has a substantial impact on the environment, zoning and environmental law are closely interrelated. The promoters of large building developments are routinely required to submit environmental impact studies. Zoning law can bar the establishment of shopping centres or drive-through restaurants in order to avoid undesirable automobile traffic in a given area.

¶1727   Policies of environmental protection law

Environmental protection law is primarily concerned with man-made structures. Within the scope of environmental protection law, the term 'structures' includes buildings, parts of buildings, roads, bridges, tunnels and other permanent constructions, as well as topographic alterations such as the preparation of ski slopes in the Alps.

In the areas of air pollution, noise, vibrations and radiation, the Federal Environmental Protection Statute distinguishes between effects (*émissions/Emissionen*) and impacts (*immissions/Immissionen*) (Arts 11 to 15 Environmental Protection Statute). Measures can be taken either at the source of the pollution or at the site affected by the pollution. The law primarily aims at reducing the pollution at source. Increasingly, polluting structures are required to be equipped with the most modern devices to curtail pollution. For instance, a smoke stack releasing noxious substances must be fitted out with a state-of-the-art filter to hold back these substances.

If pollution control at the source is not feasible for technical or economic reasons, measures must be taken at the affected site.

¶1728   Measuring pollution levels

Various criteria are used to limit emissions. In the areas of air and noise pollution, the statute defines maximum emission standards (*valeurs limites d'exposition/ Belastungsgrenzwerte*) in technical or chemical formulae. For buildings and equipment, the statute provides minimum standards on how to build.

¶1729   Effects of excessive pollution levels

If emissions at the source and impacts at the target are in excess of the statutory ceilings, new buildings or structures cannot be built. Existing buildings or structures are also affected by the new legislation. Thus, if an existing structure causes an excessive environmental impact, it must be updated to bring it into compliance with the new statutory requirements (Arts 16 to 18 Federal Environmental Protection Statute).

Restrictions on pollution apply regardless of whether the surroundings of a building or structure are already polluted or not (Art. 11 Federal Environmental Protection Statute). If a business operates a noisy plant, it cannot be argued that it is in a zone where heavy industry is permitted and where noise and air pollution are already substantial. On the contrary, if the existing environmental pollution is already so high that a new business worsens the situation, the authorities may set more stringent requirements for the newcomer, even though the newcomer operates within the limits governing its specific production process.

¶1730   Polluters pay

The foremost principle of environmental law is that polluters pay (*principe du pollueur-payeur/Verursacherprinzip*). It means that those who cause pollution must bear the expenses stemming from cleaning up the pollution (Art. 20 Federal Environmental Protection Statute). If the authorities take a measure to curb or mitigate the consequences of a specific pollution, the ensuing costs must be borne by the individual or company that caused the authorities to intervene. This liability is triggered regardless of fault. While the economic feasibility of the measures is taken into consideration (Art. 17 Federal Environmental Protection Statute), the entity concerned must bear the expenses necessary to comply with the minimum statutory standards. Therefore, some industrial plants may have to change their site or change their manufacturing process altogether.

¶1731   Application of state-of-the-art technologies

A further principle is that a polluter must keep abreast of technological developments (Art. 11 Federal Environmental Protection Statute). This means that a business that creates emissions in operating its plant may not remain inactive. Rather, it is under a continuous obligation to apply technical improvements and to use state-of-the-art equipment. As a result, it is perfectly possible that, in order to receive a new construction permit, a plant will have to install newly available air filters or overflow pools although already existing comparable plants are not yet equipped with modern devices.

¶1732   Federal Water Pollution Statute of 1971

Since 1972, various regulations setting limits on waste effluents released into bodies of water have been in effect. The Water Pollution Statute of 1971 aims at diminishing water pollution, furthering the health of humans and animals, and securing a sufficient supply of water for drinking and irrigation.

Cantons and municipalities must establish a water-protection police trained for rapid intervention in cases of water pollution (Arts 5 to 8 Water Pollution Statute).

¶1733   Strict liability for water pollution

Everybody must apply the care necessary under the circumstances to avoid pollution of surface and ground water (Art. 13 Water Pollution Statute). Anyone who does not act with the required care and causes damages is liable regardless of fault. Anyone who causes water to be polluted by his own action or omission, such as by dumping liquid or solid waste in a river, is liable. Anyone who has responsibility over a structure or premises that leads to pollution is liable (Art. 36 Water Pollution Statute). Even mere negligence leading to water pollution may be punished with imprisonment or a fine of up to SFr 20,000 (Arts 37 to 43 Water Pollution Statute).

¶1734   Requirement to treat waste effluents

The Federal Water Protection Statute deals with waste effluents from homes, farms and industries (Arts 15 to 21). Cantons and municipalities are required to build waste water treatment plants and to cleanse all accruing waste water. Chemical plants producing heavily polluted waste water may be required to build their own treatment plants in order to reduce the level of pollution of the waste water so that it can be cleansed at the public plant. Only sewage that has been at least preliminarily treated may be funnelled into public waters.

In order to protect the municipality's water supply, building permits are granted only if the connection to the conduit system is secured. This requirement may entail that the applicants for a building permit must construct connecting conduits at their own expense. Public sewage systems are today part of zoning. This is so because only those areas which can be linked to a public sewage system may be classified as building zones (see ¶1720). Only in exceptional cases involving remote buildings will the authorities grant a special permit excusing the applicant from the requirement that waste water be funnelled into the public sewage system. To be eligible, the applicant must show that there is no satisfactory alternative way of disposing of the sewage.

For zoning reasons, construction permits for structures which are not part of the public sewage system are extremely difficult to obtain (Art. 24 Federal Zoning Statute). Moreover, the Water Pollution Statute requires that in all circumstances waste water must be disposed of adequately.

¶1735   Handling of noxious substances

Special statutory provisions apply to the storage, shipping and handling of noxious substances in general, and noxious liquids in particular. Almost all homeowners are affected by these provisions since they store heating fuel. Only tanks that have been approved by the authorities are permitted. Tanks must always be embedded in a concrete pool capable of containing any spill.

Beneath large parts of Switzerland, there are extensive ground water layers which serve as reservoirs for natural drinking water. They may be tapped only with official permission. Similarly, covering rivers or modifying banks of lakes by means of landfills requires a permit.

¶1736   Air Pollution Ordinance of 1985

Implementing the Federal Environmental Protection Statute, the Air Pollution Ordinance regulates details of air quality protection in over 40 articles. Annexes to the Ordinance provide standards for all pollutants that have practical importance in a modern industrial country.

Different requirements must be met, depending on whether the polluting structure (¶1727) already exists or is newly built. The Ordinance covers not only immovable structures but also vehicles and infrastructures such as highways, airports and railroad tracks (Arts 17 to 19 Air Pollution Ordinance). Heating systems and burners may be marketed only if they have passed a test (Art. 20 Air Pollution Ordinance). Fuels must be declared and may be imported and marketed within Switzerland only by registered traders (Arts 21 to 24 Air Pollution Ordinance).

¶1737   Air pollution levels

The Ordinance lists maximum pollutant levels for the various types of emission, which stationary structures may not exceed (Art. 3 Air Pollution Ordinance). In individual cases, the local environmental protection office may set even more exacting standards. Generally, emissions within the set limit must be controlled in such a way that they do not affect the neighbourhood. Heating systems are inspected at least every three years. The relevant testing procedures are precisely defined in technical and physical terms (Arts 3 to 16 Air Pollution Ordinance).

The authorities constantly monitor pollution levels in critical areas. They arrange for periodic measurement, testing and analysis of the air quality.

Precise maximum emission standards exist for the main pollutants such as carbon monoxide, ozone, sulphur dioxide, sodium dioxide, dust particles and certain heavy metals.

If there are no precise maximum levels for a specific emission, the authorities determine the admissible levels by other means. Air pollution will be deemed excessive if it does not meet any of the following criteria:

(1) there should be no threat to humans, animals and plants in their communities and habitats (empirical identification of causes of illness and epidemics);

(2) there should be no substantial impairment of the well-being of the population;

(3) no damage should be caused to buildings;

(4) the fertility of the soil, the vegetation and the water quality should not be impaired (Art. 2 Air Pollution Ordinance).

¶1738   Noise Protection Ordinance of 1986

This Ordinance details noise abating measures. It is supplemented by some annexes which contain maximum decibel levels for various types of noise.

The purpose of noise protection is to limit noise which is generated by newly built structures, and to provide for noise protection of buildings used for housing. For these purposes, noise emissions produced in whole neighbourhoods and in individual buildings are measured separately. Housing zones may be created in noisy areas only to a limited extent, and building permits in such areas may no longer be granted (Art. 1 Noise Protection Ordinance).

¶1739   Ascertaining noise levels

The Ordinance contains detailed regulations on ascertaining and assessing external noise (Arts 36 to 44 Noise Protection Ordinance). If noise pollution can be reduced at the source, this must be done. In residential areas where noise must be reduced, the emphasis is on ascertaining the impact of current noise levels on noise-sensitive rooms. The authorities must establish a noise pollution map, which is open for inspection by the public.

For particular types of noise the levels are defined in advance. There may be difficulties arising from the simple fact that several noise sources are cumulative. In such a case the maximum levels for noise and vibrations must be lowered to ensure, as far as the available technology and experience permit, that the population is not disturbed in its well-being (Art. 15 Federal Environmental Protection Statute).

¶1740   Regulatory techniques for noise protection

The Ordinance distinguishes between planning levels, maximum levels and alarm levels in the area affected by emissions (Art. 2 Noise Protection Ordinance).

It sets different ceilings on noise, depending on the area involved and the type of noise. Every source of noise must be controlled by structural and technical measures so as to diminish its impact outside and inside buildings. As for noise insulation of new buildings, the technical norms of the Swiss Association of Engineers and Architects (SIA) are referred to as minimum standards.

The rule is that noise emanating from a new structure must not exceed the statutory planning levels. Existing but substantially altered structures must observe maximum levels. Finally, existing structures may be required to be adapted if they exceed the maximum noise level. Alarm levels are an absolute ceiling and must not be exceeded.

Regarding movables such as automobiles, railroads or ships, noise emission must be reduced to the extent technically, operationally and economically feasible. For certain types of machinery, such as lawn mowers and construction machinery, special approval by the federal authorities is required. For cars, aircraft and motor boats, special statutes specify the required equipment.

¶1741   Adapting old structures to meet noise standards

Structures (¶1727) whose construction started after 1 April 1987 are considered 'new' and structures already existing at that time are considered 'old'. Old structures whose utilisation totally changed after that date are deemed to be 'new' (Arts 2, 7 and 47 Noise Protection Ordinance). Depending on the nature of the zone, the permitted ceilings or noise sensitivity levels vary as defined by the applicable planning noise levels. 'Old' structures which were substantially changed after that date must be adapted so as not to exceed the applicable noise sensitivity levels (Arts 8 and 47 Noise Protection Ordinance). Construction of a new structure or modification of an 'old' one must not lead to such an increase in traffic that the statutory maximum noise levels are exceeded (Art. 9 Noise

Protection Ordinance). Exceptions are possible only for public structures such as new highways. These structures must be accompanied by noise protection measures in neighbouring buildings, such as additional insulation or special noise protection windows (Arts 10 and 11 Noise Protection Ordinance).

'Old' structures that substantially contribute to noise in excess of the maximum level after 1 April 1987 must be modified. Noise abatement measures are meant to reduce noise emissions below the maximum level. Exceptions are permitted only if such a modification would lead to unreasonable cost or to restrictions on operation. The same applies if a national heritage object is concerned. Alarm levels may be exceeded only if a public structure is involved and noise protection measures are taken in the impact zone. The cantons are required by law to review noise levels on a street-by-street basis and to provide for noise abating measures; the Federal Government grants subsidies to cover at least part of the costs stemming from these measures (Arts 13 to 28 Noise Protection Ordinance).

¶1742   Noise control and zoning law

Noise-control regulations directly affect zoning and building law. Noise-sensitive rooms such as bedrooms, living rooms and studies that are newly built or renovated may not be exposed to maximum noise levels unless special building measures are taken for noise control. If new building zones are created in which buildings with noise-sensitive rooms are permitted, the noise planning levels must not be exceeded in these zones (Arts 29 to 31 Noise Protection Ordinance).

By 31 March 1997, every municipality must revise its building and zoning plan, based on an assessment of noise levels. The municipalities must ensure that activities triggering similar noise levels will be exercised in the same type of zone.

¶1743   Sources of the law on dangerous substances

Dangerous substances, waste disposal and soil pollution are regulated in the Federal Environmental Protection Statute. The three items are closely interrelated. Substances are deemed dangerous and subjected to regulation if they endanger human beings or their natural environment. The law relies heavily on the self-control of individuals and businesses dealing with these substances. All products containing the substances must conspicuously display consumer information that, *inter alia*, warns of possible dangers and indicates appropriate safety measures (Arts 26 to 29 Federal Environmental Protection Statute).

The implementing ordinance lists more than 100 natural and artificial substances. These may be basic substances or mixtures of substances. An 'old' substance, within the meaning of the statute, is defined as a substance referred to either in the list of dangerous substances established by the federal health authorities or in the list compiled by the European Community (EINECS). These substances must be handled with care, and they may be used only to the extent absolutely necessary.

¶1744   Testing new substances

Dangerous substances that are listed neither on the chart of the European Community nor by the federal government are considered 'new' substances unless they have been on the market for an extended period of time (Art. 5 Dangerous Substances Ordinance). Manufacturers or retailers must test 'new' substances for their environmental impact before marketing them (Arts 11 to 34 Dangerous Substances Ordinance). The results of the tests must be submitted to the Federal Environmental Protection Office. Test procedures are statutorily regulated; the law requires the use of testing methods which are reproducible and conclusive. Further testing may be imposed. Products such as textiles, dishwasher detergents and agricultural fertilisers may not be marketed at all without having previously been registered. Wood dyes and insecticides must first receive an express official approval certificate. For practical reasons, only representative samples can be tested. Alternatively, manufacturers may receive laboratory certificates which allow them to market regulated substances freely if they adhere to officially recognised testing methods and continuously employ the required qualified personnel.

¶1745   Consumer information on dangerous substances

Manufacturers are not free to decide on the consumer information that goes with the substances (Art. 35 to 41 Dangerous Substances Ordinance). All harmful substances must be accompanied by data sheets or instructions on handling. The packaging must include standard labels; pictographs must be affixed to signal substances that are toxic for fish and bees or that contaminate ground water. The same applies to special wastes and substances which must not be disposed of in the household sink.

Substances which are particularly problematic or heavily polluting because of widespread use are listed in annexes to the Ordinance. These lists are continuously updated; requirements are becoming increasingly stringent. For example, the Ordinance limits the mercury content of batteries, and sellers are required to collect and recycle used batteries. In addition, chlorofluorocarbons (cfc) must not be used as propellants in aerosol containers.

¶1746   Sources of waste disposal law

Under federal law, waste must be recycled, stabilised or destroyed. Landfills may be operated only with a permit (see below). Waste is classified according to its polluting potential. Almost without exception, household waste that is not recycled (especially glass and newspapers) or composted is burned in waste incinerators operated by the municipalities or groups of municipalities. Building waste and other materials that are stable and do not endanger soil or ground water, may be disposed of in landfills. Today, biodegradable waste is collected separately in many municipalities, composted and used as fertiliser.

On the federal level, only the management of the most dangerous waste is regulated. The Federal Government has regulated the manner in which landfills must be operated. Federal regulations require, *inter alia*, that operators of waste disposal businesses have a permit. Particular skills and facilities are required for the handling, transportation, depositing and recycling of special wastes.

¶1747   Waste recycling

Under the Federal Environmental Protection Statute, the Federal Government may issue ordinances on the separate collection of dangerous substances, glass and waste paper. It may require recycling of waste if it is economically reasonable to do so and leads to less of a burden on the environment than burning or dumping. Sellers of dangerous substances (for example, products containing mercury) or of reusable packaging may be required to take back the used product and the packaging. On 1 November 1990, an ordinance was enacted which prohibits small aluminum and plastic beverage containers unless they are taken back and recycled. In addition, it provides for a deposit for large glass bottles and requires stores to take them back and recycle them. Finally, packaging materials that lead to excessive waste volume, or that can be incinerated only with difficulty may be prohibited (Art. 32 Federal Environmental Protection Statute).

Soil fertility is of constant concern to the authorities (Arts 33 to 35 Federal Environmental Protection Statute). If a critical substance reaches an excessive concentration in a region, the source of the pollution must be ascertained. As a result, new measures curtailing the release of that substance into the air or the use or handling of the pollutant itself may be adopted.

¶1748   Sources of environmental impact study law

If new structures (see ¶1727 and ¶1741) are built or if existing structures are put to a substantially different use, the proprietor must always check whether the project is compatible with federal environmental protection laws and the provisions on the protection of nature, the nation's cultural heritage, forests and game and fishery. Although environmental impact studies have been required since the effective date of the Federal Environmental Protection Statute on 1 January 1985, an implementing ordinance containing the necessary details was enacted only on 19 October 1988, becoming effective on 1 January 1989.

Impact studies are required in order to co-ordinate construction activities. The environmental impact study is an important and necessary tool for the authorities to decide whether or not to grant a construction permit.

¶1749   Formal environmental impact studies

A formal environmental impact study is necessary for structures of a certain importance, which are contained in the applicable ordinance. They include highways, railway tracks, harbour installations on lakes, airports, power plants, refineries, pipelines, dams, large dumps, certain military installations, large recreational projects (mountain cable-cars, artificial snow machines, amusement parks, etc.) and large production units, particularly in the chemical, paper and metal industries. Large individual objects which require an environmental impact study include meat factories, animal farms, shopping centres of more than 5,000 square metres and high-capacity radio and television antennas (Arts 7 and 8 Environmental Impact Study Ordinance).

¶1750   Procedure for environmental impact study

Anyone who builds a structure or changes it substantially must undertake a preliminary study if it falls within one of the listed categories. The Federal Environmental Protection Office publishes guide-lines on how certain types of structures affect the environment. The owner must submit a written report, even though no environmental impact may be expected. If an impact is expected, the applicant, in co-operation with the environmental protection authorities, must establish a list of measures likely to reduce the impact.

This report must address the following points:

(1) conditions before the construction or the alteration begins;

(2) a description of the intended structure, including planned measures for the protection of the environment and for emergency situations;

(3) the expected permanent environmental impact;

(4) any measures which soften the environmental impact; and

(5) the cost of these measures (Art. 9(2) Federal Environmental Protection Statute; Art. 9 Environmental Impact Study Ordinance).

The authorities normally examine this report while reviewing the application for a construction permit. During the reviewing process, experts other than those already consulted by the author of the environmental study may be heard. Public hearings may also be conducted. Under all circumstances, the environmental impact study report is open to the public. Business secrets are protected.

¶1751   Remedies in environmental protection law

All environmental protection concerns may eventually be appealed by means of an administrative law complaint.

The private environmental protection organisations have the authority to file a complaint if an environmental impact study is required. To qualify, those organisations must have been in existence for at least ten years. The purpose of this requirement is to prevent associations from being created just to attack a particular project. Currently about 20 organisations have the authority to file complaints.

SELECTED BIBLIOGRAPHY

Walter Haller and Peter Karlen, *Raumplanungs- und Baurecht* (Zürich, 1990)

Alfred Kölz and Hans-Ulrich Müller-Stahel, *Kommentar zum Umweltschutzgesetz* (Zürich, 1991), looseleaf service

Peter Liver, Hans Hinderling, Paul Piotet and Henri Deschenaux, 'Sachenrecht', in *Schweizerisches Privatrecht*, vol. V (Basel, 1977/88/89)

Paul-Henri Steinauer, *Les droits réels*, 2 vols. (Bern, 1990)

Peter Tuor and Bernhard Schnyder, *Das Schweizerische Zivilgesetzbuch*, 10th edn (Zürich, 1986)

¶1751

18 Criminal Law and Judicial Assistance in Criminal Matters

PRINCIPAL LEGISLATION

Code pénal suisse/Strafgesetzbuch/Federal Penal Code (PC), RS 311.0.

Loi fédérale sur l'entraide internationale en matière pénale/Rechtshilfegesetz/ Federal Statute on International Judicial Assistance in Criminal Matters, RS 351.1.

Convention de sauvegarde des droits de l'homme et des libertés fondamentales/ Europäische Menschenrechtskonvention/European Convention on Human Rights and Fundamental Liberties, RS 0.101.

SOURCES OF LAW

¶1801   International law – Federal Constitution – statutes

The Federal Constitution contains substantive and procedural rules of criminal law. The European Convention for the Protection of Human Rights and Fundamental Freedoms (especially in its Arts 5 and 6) contains law which is deemed to be at the constitutional level and which is directly applicable in the criminal courts. The Penal Code contains the most important part of substantive criminal law and basic rules of intercantonal and international jurisdiction. In addition, numerous federal and cantonal statutes (the cantonal statutes based on the delegation clause in Art. 335 PC) define criminal offences that are related to the particular field of law regulated in the respective statute. The most prominent of these statutes are the Road Traffic Statute (RS 741.01), the Narcotics Statute (RS 812.121) and various statutes concerning social security, unfair competition, and federal and cantonal taxes.

¶1801

¶1802   Constitutional standards

Article 64bis of the Federal Constitution divides the law-making power among cantonal and federal legislatures as far as criminal law is concerned. It authorises the Federal Parliament to legislate in the field of substantive criminal law, while criminal procedure and organisation of the courts remain cantonal.

Despite this rule, many constitutional standards applicable in criminal law are inferred from Art. 4 of the Federal Constitution, e.g., the principle of legality (see Art. 1 PC), the exclusion of retroactively declaring illegal certain activities and the prohibition of arbitrariness. This results in the application of certain standards of rationality and reasonableness with which the law-enforcing and judicial authorities must comply. The principle of personal integrity, which has been deduced by the Federal Supreme Court from the broad wording of Art. 4 of the Federal Constitution, must be observed in preventive detention and during imprisonment. Article 4 of the Constitution has further been interpreted to guarantee the procedural rights to be heard and defended by an attorney in court and to have an interpreter if necessary. It also protects certain aspects of the attorney-client relationship.

Some standards are fixed in Arts 5 and 6 of the European Convention on Human Rights, or are dealt with in the Penal Code itself.

FEDERAL PENAL CODE

¶1803   Enactment and recent revisions

The Federal Penal Code became effective on 1 January 1942 and has since been revised several times. For example, revisions took place in the areas of juvenile criminality, security measures and the suspended execution of criminal sentences in order to impose the protection of privacy (Arts. 179bis to 179^{octies} PC). The Code was further revised to reinforce the criminal sanctions against hostage-taking (Art. 260bis PC). Most recently, provisions on criminal insider trading (Art. 161 PC) and money laundering (Art. 305bis PC) have been adopted. The provisions regarding economic crimes are being revised as of the summer of 1991. For further details, see ¶1041 and ¶1042.

¶1804   Principle of legality

The Penal Code is based on the principle of legality, viz. *nullum crimen, nulla poena sine lege*: no crime, no punishment without a specific provision of the law (Art. 1 PC). In addition, a given conduct may not retroactively be defined as a criminal offence.

¶1805 Intent and negligence

According to Art. 18 PC, and unless otherwise specifically stated in the Code, criminal sanctions may be imposed only if the offence was committed intentionally.

Intent, as a precondition for rendering persons criminally accountable for their behaviour, means that the action (or omission) has been committed knowingly and willingly.

The requirement of intent is met by *dolus eventualis*, a form of recklessness approximating intent. However, the categories of fault do not correspond exactly with those known in common law.

Some offences are punishable even when committed through negligence.

¶1806 Policies of criminal law

(1) Educating effect of detention
Article 37 PC states the ambitious goal that criminal detention should have an educating effect upon prisoners and should prepare them for their re-entry into social life. Accordingly, the penitentiaries are divided into prisons for first-time and recidivist offenders; 'half freedom' is possible after a part of the prison sentence has been served. Social and psychiatric counselling are available.

(2) No death penalty
The Penal Code does not provide for the death penalty, although under the Federal Constitution the death penalty is prohibited only for political crimes (Art. 65 Federal Constitution).

(3) Release on probation
When two-thirds of the prison sentence has been served, the authorities, usually the cantonal Justice Department, may order the release of a prisoner on probation if the prisoner's behaviour supports the conclusion that no new offences will be committed.

(4) Security and preventive measures
Besides the penalties of detention and fines, the Penal Code provides for other sanctions and measures which may be applied to alcoholics, drug addicts, habitual offenders, etc. Some of these measures may be taken even if the accused cannot be convicted of the crime itself because of lack of fault or intent.

(5) Juvenile criminals
The Penal Code does not apply to children below the age of seven, and contains special rules for children aged from seven to 15 and for juveniles from 15 to 18

years of age. Young adults (18 to 25) are still treated differently as far as the mode of detention is concerned.

(6) Confiscation
The proceeds of a criminal offence are confiscated and primarily used to compensate the victim for the losses suffered.

¶1807   Scope of application of Penal Code

The Code applies to all offences committed or having their effects in the territory of Switzerland. Crimes committed abroad against Swiss nationals and crimes perpetrated by Swiss nationals abroad are judged under the Penal Code unless the foreign applicable law is more favourable to the accused than Swiss law, in which case it is applied. If the accused has been found not guilty, or has been sentenced by a competent foreign court and the sentence has been executed or remitted or has long become time-barred, the accused need not stand trial again in Switzerland. Where the effect of a criminal action lies in Switzerland, e.g., when a fraudulent money transfer abroad results in a Swiss bank account being credited with the proceeds of the crime, the Swiss prosecution and judiciary authorities have jurisdiction and can apply their own substantive and procedural laws (Arts. 3, 7, and 346 PC; ATF 109 IV 1).

¶1808   Penalties

The Penal Code defines three types of punishable offences:

   (1) *Felony* (Art. 9(1) PC), sanctioned with imprisonment from one to 20 years or life.

   (2) *Misdemeanor* (Art. 9(2) PC), sanctioned with imprisonment from three days to three years.

   (3) *Contravention* (Art. 101 PC), sanctioned with detention from one day to three months or with a fine.

Fines may be combined with imprisonment if the specific provision allows for alternative or cumulative penalties. They may range from SFr 1 to 40,000. There is no maximum amount if the person who is being sentenced acted out of greed (Art. 48 PC). The provisions defining specific offences usually allow for a wide range of judicial discretion as far as the duration of the prison term and the amount of the fine are concerned.

As a matter of principle, the penalty should reflect, and be in proportion to, the fault of the offender (Art. 63 PC). Unless specifically stated grounds for mitigating or aggravating the fault are present, the court is bound by the minimum and maximum punishment as stated in the provision dealing with the particular offence(s).

The court may issue a milder sentence if (Arts 64 and 65 PC):

(a) the accused acted under the influence of a severe threat;

(b) the offender has shown sincere and active repentance; or

(c) a long period of time, during which the offender has not committed any further offences, has passed since the offence for which the accused stands trial.

For recidivist criminals the detention terms may be prolonged in accordance with Art. 67 PC.

If several criminal offences have been committed, they are judged in the same trial, and the range of the penalty that may be imposed is increased by half of the maximum detention period applicable to the most serious crime committed.

¶1809 Conditions for suspending execution of sentences

The execution of the penalty may be suspended and the offender may be put on probation if *all* of the following conditions are fulfilled:

(1) The offender has not served a term of more than three months of detention during the last five years before the offence was judged.

(2) The offender has reasonably good prospects of successfully completing a period of probation from two to five years (the duration being largely within the court's discretion).

(3) The penalty to be handed down does not exceed 18 months of detention.

(4) The victim has been recompensed as far as is reasonably possible.

It should be noted that it is not the sentence itself which is suspended, but only its execution (Art. 41 PC).

¶1810 Statute of Limitations

The Penal Code lists various time limits for the prosecution of offences (Art. 70 PC) and the execution of sanctions that have already been imposed (Art. 73 PC). The Statute of Limitations of prosecutions begins to run on the day the offence was committed or terminated, whichever comes later. It is suspended if the offender is detained abroad; it is interrupted by any action of the prosecuting authorities or courts against the accused. After each interruption, the Statute of Limitations begins to run anew, up to the maximum of one and a half times the original time limit. The limitation periods range from two years (e.g., libel) to 30 years (murder or the taking of hostages). Article 75bis PC defines particularly hideous crimes, such as genocide, which are not subject to time limit at all.

The time limits are as follows (examples):

- *ten years*: the prosecution of felonies such as simple homicide (Art. 113 PC), theft (Art. 137 PC), fraud (Art. 148 PC), coercion (Art. 156 PC), and money laundering in a criminal organisation (Art. 305bis (2)),

- *five years*: the prosecution of offences such as illicit recording of private conversations (Arts 179bis to 179^{quater} PC), negligent and simple assault (Arts 123 and 125 PC), embezzlement (Art. 140 PC), insider trading (Art. 161 PC), illegal actions for a foreign state (Art. 271 PC) and money laundering (Art. 305bis PC), and

- *two years*: illegal abortion (Art. 118 PC), or slander (Arts 173 to 178 PC).

¶1811   Specific offences

The second part of the Penal Code lists specific criminal offences. In the present context, it is impossible to enter into the details of these numerous provisions. In general, the Code groups qualifying criteria which may lead to either severer or lighter penalties around a basic fact pattern. For example, the penalty for intentional manslaughter is five to 20 years of imprisonment (Art. 111 PC), but if the killing took place under circumstances showing an especially dangerous or depraved state of mind, the sanction is imprisonment for life (Art. 112 PC). If the killing was the result of strong emotions which, under the circumstances, were excusable, the sanction is imprisonment for one to ten years (Art. 113 PC).

A few examples of sanctions imposed: the sanction for fraud, money laundering within the framework of organised crime (see ¶1141 for details), embezzlement and coercion is up to five years' imprisonment; for insider trading (for details see ¶1140), the maximum is three years' imprisonment; in the case of illicit actions for a foreign state that could be taken only by the Swiss authorities (Art. 271 PC) or the illicit provision of economic information (Art. 273 PC), the maximum penalty is three years' imprisonment.

CRIMINAL PROCEDURE

¶1812   Sources of law

Criminal procedure is mostly a matter of cantonal legislation. However, the Federal Penal Code reserves federal jurisdiction for particular crimes (Art. 112 of the Federal Constitution; Arts 340 to 342 PC).

¶1813   Jurisdiction

Cantonal authorities prosecute and adjudicate, according to their own cantonal procedural law, all criminal offences not expressly reserved to federal criminal jurisdiction (Art. 64*bis* of the Federal Constitution; Art. 343 PC). Further, the Federal Government makes frequent use of its power to delegate matters of federal criminal jurisdiction to the cantonal courts (Art. 18 of the Federal Code of Criminal Procedure).

As a rule, the authorities of the place where the crime was perpetrated (*locus delicti*) or where it had its effect have jurisdiction to prosecute and to judge (see Arts 3, 7 and 346 PC; ATF 109 IV 1). Articles 344 to 351 PC contain detailed rules determining the competent jurisdiction. If a person is prosecuted for several crimes, jurisdiction lies in the canton where the most severely sanctioned crime was committed (Art. 350 PC). If the same offence was committed in the territory of several cantons, the canton in which the prosecution is first initiated is competent to adjudicate (*forum preventionis*, Art. 346 PC).

¶1814   Criminal prosecution and court organisation

(1)   Prosecution

The organisational structures of criminal prosecution and the courts organisation vary greatly among the cantons.

A criminal prosecution is usually conducted by the district attorney (in Zurich: *Bezirksanwalt*; in Geneva: *juge d'instruction*) in co-operation with the police. Often, the district attorney has the power to issue a first order of detention. The detainee may appeal to a judicial authority which decides about the maintenance and/or duration of the detention pending trial. The provisional measures which prosecutors may take include:

- detention pending trial,
- search of persons and property,
- seisure, confiscation, attachment,
- observation of telephone lines, mail, etc.

(2)   Sentencing by the prosecutor

In many cantons, a district attorney other than the one conducting the investigation may impose a penalty if the accused confesses to the material facts, and only a short term of imprisonment or fines are imposed. If the accused disagrees with the order issued by the prosecutor, the accused may – by a simple request – obtain a hearing before, and decision by, a court.

(3) Trial by courts and juries

If the prosecutor calls for a short-term prison sentence (i.e., up to three months), the trial is usually conducted and the decision rendered by a single judge. If a long-term prison sentence is requested, a panel of three judges regularly hears the case and renders the judgment.

Some codes of criminal procedure provide for specific crimes to be judged directly by the superior courts (i.e., Court of Appeals). Only a few cantons, including Zurich, provide for jury trials at all. In 1952, the Federal Supreme Court decided that all criminal judgments must give the reasons why a certain verdict was reached (*ratio decidendi*). The common-law type of jury trial has largely been replaced either by courts consisting of judges or by panels made up of a combination of jurors and judges who render the verdict.

If federal administrative law is violated and the violations are sanctioned with criminal penalties, the competent administrative agency itself sets the penalty, except if the sanction is imprisonment, in which case the courts are competent. This applies, for example, in the areas of customs law and wholesale tax law.

¶1815   Principles of criminal procedure

(1) Discretion in prosecuting

The principle of legality (¶1804), which is at the basis of substantive criminal law, contrasts with the wide discretion which criminal prosecutors have in initiating and pursuing the prosecution of a specific crime. Prosecutors do not have formal bargaining authority in dealing with criminals who are potential witnesses for the conviction of other criminals.

(2) Public trials

In principle, court hearings are open to the public. Restrictions may apply if public morality or security is in danger.

(3) Access to evidence

In principle, the accused has access to the documentation and evidence regarding his or her case after formal proceedings have been initiated (in Zurich) or when the indictment is rendered (in Geneva). Likewise, the injured party is entitled to consult the documents and evidence so as to be able to recover the damages suffered.

(4) Free weighing of evidence

The court's aim is to discover the truth. It has the power to evaluate the evidence presented without restraints regarding the value of certain types of evidence. The court may not base a conviction solely on the confession of the accused.

(5) Pretrial disclosure and right to defence

The accused has the right to a fair trial: that is, the accused has the right to be heard and the right to be confronted with the evidence. Because criminal procedure is mostly a matter of cantonal legislation, the procedural rights and duties of the accused and injured parties vary. For example, in Geneva, the preliminary procedures and the hearing of evidence are secret and not open to the parties before the formal indictment is rendered (Arts 131 and 138 Geneva Code of Criminal Procedure). In Zurich, the accused may have access to the documentary evidence and transcripts of interrogations, and may request disclosure to the extent that the purpose of the investigation is not hindered by the disclosure (Art. 17 Zurich Code of Criminal Procedure). Disclosure in matters of federal administrative criminal law can be requested only after the final record of the investigation is established by the administrative authorities. Further, the accused and the injured party are entitled to comment on the evidence presented and to take part in the procedures leading to the administration of evidence, especially the examination of witnesses, whom they may question. They may request that additional evidence be admitted. They are entitled to a reasoned judgment.

(6) Right to counsel

The accused have the right to a private attorney of their choice or a court-appointed public defence attorney. Switzerland made a reservation to Art. 6 of the European Human Rights Convention regarding the costs of the public defence attorney. In some circumstances, these costs may be obtained from the accused at a later stage after the trial.

(7) Testimony

Anybody can be called to testify in a criminal trial. However, close relatives, doctors, attorneys, notaries public, and clergymen may refuse to testify in court. Bank officers and bank employees cannot refuse to testify or produce documentation on their clients in a criminal trial (see ¶1138).

(8) Civil damages in criminal proceedings

Civil damages may be claimed and adjudicated in the criminal trial if they do not disproportionately lengthen the proceedings. In complicated cases, the criminal court will usually refer civil damage claims to a civil court.

¶1816 Appeals to the Federal Supreme Court in criminal matters

Each canton has its own system of criminal jurisdiction. Of course, all orders issued by prosecution authorities which impose criminal penalties may be challenged by a simple request for a court hearing. In many cases, an appeal is possible to a superior prosecution or judiciary authority, depending on the stage of the criminal trial. An appeal to the Federal Supreme Court may be filed within ten days after the judgment is rendered. The motivation of the appeal must be filed within 20 days after the written decision of the cantonal court is received (Art. 272 of the Federal Criminal Procedure Statute).

If constitutional rights are violated in a canton's criminal procedure or in the final judgment by a cantonal court, a constitutional complaint may be filed at the Federal Supreme Court (Arts 83 to 96 of the Federal Statute on the Organisation of the Judiciary).

¶1817   Criminal register

The Federal Office of Police keeps a criminal register. All criminal sentences involving imprisonment or fines of at least SFr 500 are registered. Those registrations have, *inter alia*, the effect of leading to heavier penalties if the registered person commits new offences before the expiration of the time limits stated in Art. 80 PC. Suspended sentences are deleted from the criminal register if, during the probation period, the suspension has not been withdrawn and the sentence has not been executed.

Private persons may request an excerpt of the criminal register only for themselves. Even deleted registrations may be communicated to prosecuting authorities and criminal courts.

DOMESTIC JUDICIAL ASSISTANCE IN CRIMINAL MATTERS

¶1818   Sources of law

In criminal matters in which the Penal Code or another federal statute is applicable, the federal and cantonal authorities must provide each other with judicial assistance. Arrest warrants are executed by the competent local authorities anywhere in the territory of Switzerland (Art. 352(1) PC). For criminal matters involving the press or political issues, cantonal authorities may refuse to turn over an accused person to the requesting canton's authorities. In this case the refusing canton must conduct the court trial itself (Art. 352(2)).

In intercantonal judicial assistance the authorities contact each other directly when they need help. Officers of the different cantonal police forces co-operate without explicit requests in matters of judicial aid (Art. 353 PC).

Except for scientific or technical expert reports, no costs may be charged to the canton asking for judicial assistance. If a party to the procedure is ordered

¶1817

to pay the costs of the proceedings, that party pays the costs of judicial assistance (Art. 354 PC).

Criminal prosecution authorities may pursue prosecutions in the territory of another canton only with the express permission of that canton's authorities. The procedural rules of the canton in which the prosecution is taking place are applicable (Art. 355 PC).

The Federal Supreme Court resolves any conflicts arising among various cantonal authorities or cantonal and federal authorities. Until a decision is rendered, provisional measures taken by the cantonal or federal authorities remain in force (Art. 357 PC).

INTERNATIONAL JUDICIAL ASSISTANCE IN CRIMINAL MATTERS

¶1819　Sources of law

The most important sources of law for international judicial assistance in criminal matters are the European Convention on Judicial Assistance in Criminal Matters of 20 April 1959 (RS 0.351.1), the treaty between Switzerland and the United States of America on Mutual Assistance in Criminal Matters of 25 May 1973 (see ¶112(4)), and the Federal Statute on International Judicial Assistance in Criminal Matters (RS 351.1; Federal Judicial Assistance Statute).

The Federal Office of Police has published an unofficial English text of the Federal Judicial Assistance Statute and guide-lines in English for the general information of interested individuals and foreign authorities (7th edn, July 1990). The countries with which Switzerland has concluded multilateral or bilateral treaties regarding international judicial assistance in criminal matters and/or extradition include:

- Argentina,

- Austria,

- Australia (only declarations of reciprocity on a case-by-case basis),
- Belgium,
- Brazil,
- Denmark,
- Ecuador,
- El Salvador,
- Germany,

- Finland,
- France,
- Greece,
- Hungary,
- Iceland,
- Israel,
- Italy,
- Japan,
- Liechtenstein,
- Luxembourg,
- Monaco,
- the Netherlands,
- Norway,
- Paraguay,
- Poland,
- Portugal,
- Rwanda,
- Spain,
- Sweden,
- Turkey,
- the United States of America,
- Uruguay, and
- Yugoslavia.

The federal authorities in charge of judicial assistance in criminal matters have neither their own police force nor a large number of federal prosecutors. They rely instead on the cantonal authorities. The cantonal codes of criminal procedure designate the competent authorities and their methods of prosecution. Exceptionally, and only upon explicit request by the foreign state, foreign procedural law may be applied if it does not result in substantial prejudice to the persons affected (Art. 65(c) Federal Judicial Assistance Statute).

¶1820 Requests for international judicial assistance

The Federal Office of Police receives requests for assistance in criminal matters from abroad, usually through diplomatic channels. German, French, and Austrian Ministries of Justice, courts and prosecutors may request judicial assistance directly from their Swiss counterparts. Italian superior courts may also request judicial assistance directly. All other member states of the European Convention on Judicial Assistance, except Sweden, transmit their requests for judicial assistance through their respective Ministries of Justice. In urgent cases, the requesting authority may contact the appropriate authorities directly or through Interpol, as long as the regular means of transmission is used at the same time. The same procedures are followed in judicial assistance between Switzerland and the United States.

All other states forward their requests for judicial assistance through diplomatic channels. In urgent cases, the competent prosecuting authorities may be contacted directly, with copies of that request following through diplomatic channels.

Requests by foreign authorities must contain the 'Reservation of Specialty', i.e., a declaration that the information requested will be used to prosecute only the crimes mentioned in the request for judicial assistance. If the 'Reservation of Specialty' is not contained in the request, the Swiss authorities will usually contact the requesting authorities regarding this matter and obtain confirmation of the acceptance of the 'Reservation of Specialty'.

A request for judicial assistance which aims at obtaining evidence within Switzerland must be submitted in one of the three official languages of Switzerland, i.e., German, French or Italian, except where a bilateral treaty states otherwise. Requests in another language must be translated by the requesting state.

¶1821 Decisions on admissibility of judicial assistance

(1) Federal supervision and preliminary measures
Upon receipt of the request from the foreign state, the Federal Office of Police summarily examines its formal aspects. The Office may take the necessary action for co-ordinating execution of the request; it is responsible for obtaining the declaration of reciprocity from the requesting state (Arts 8(1) and 17(3)(a) Federal Judicial Assistance Statute). It also examines whether the actions for which judicial assistance is requested are criminal offences under Swiss law. Because of the introduction of rules against money laundering and insider trading, it is possible for foreign states to request judicial assistance in these matters. The Federal Office of Police may order preliminary measures. The Federal Justice Department is competent to decide whether judicial assistance in a given case may conflict with Swiss sovereignty, security or other substantial interests, in which case judicial assistance would be denied.

(2) Cantonal decisions
After the request for judicial assistance has been forwarded by the Federal Office of Police to the respective cantonal authorities, the cantonal authorities decide

on the basis of Arts 79(1) and 16(1) Federal Judicial Assistance Statute whether the prerequisites of the law are met and whether judicial assistance is to be granted. In cases which would fall under the jurisdiction of the Federal Supreme Court (see Art. 340 PC), the cantonal authorities decide in co-operation with the Federal Prosecutor.

(3) Condition for granting judicial assistance

If no treaty exists between the requesting state and Switzerland, judicial assistance may be granted by Swiss authorities only if the requesting state declares that it is prepared to do the same in a comparable situation (declaration of reciprocity; Art. 8 Federal Judicial Assistance Statute). According to ATF 110 Ib 176, a declaration of reciprocity may not be necessary, depending on the type of offence which is being prosecuted and the necessity of eliminating the crimes; the cited case involved fraud in the amount of US\$ 28 million. A declaration of reciprocity should not be necessary when, for example, prosecuting and investigating terrorism.

The declaration of reciprocity is usually contained in a diplomatic note.

(4) Reasons for denying judicial assistance

Judicial assistance is not granted for the prosecution of political offences and actions related thereto (Art. 2(a) European Convention on Judicial Assistance in Criminal Matters; Art. 3(1) Federal Judicial Assistance Statute).

If the foreign prosecuting authorities violate the European Convention on Human Rights and Fundamental Liberties, judicial assistance will be denied. Especially serious violations of Art. 5 of the Convention for the Protection of Human Rights and Fundamental Freedoms will lead to a denial. If persons are prosecuted because of their race, religion, ethnic origin, or membership of a political association, judicial assistance will be denied.

Judicial assistance will also be denied if Swiss authorities are conducting or have conducted a criminal prosecution against the accused themselves, or if the competent authorities at the place where the crime was committed (*locus delicti*) have already adjudicated the case and the accused has either served his sentence or was found not guilty.

¶1822   Judicial assistance in fiscal matters

Judicial assistance will not be granted in fiscal matters, i.e., taxation, customs, or currency exchange regulations (Art. 3(3) Federal Judicial Assistance Statute). This restriction does not apply if the fiscal offence involves falsification of documents, except for forgeries exclusively used for the purpose of reducing the amount of fiscal duties (ATF 103 Ia 221; 108 IV 30). In the case of serious tax fraud (as opposed to mere tax evasion), judicial assistance may be granted even if the tax fraud was not committed by means of forgery; fraud alone suffices to make judicial assistance possible, even when the only goal was to reduce taxes or duties owed to a foreign state (ATF 111 Ib 249). For violations of high-tech export regulations, judicial assistance may be granted to member states of the European Convention on Judicial Assistance in Criminal Matters and to the United States (ATF 110 Ib 82; 112 Ib 212). Whether or not a specific request for judicial assistance regards fiscal matters does not depend on the classification under foreign law but, rather, is defined by Swiss law.

Judicial assistance in fiscal matters is granted by way of exception:

(1) if the evidence to be obtained is requested in favour of the accused (Art. 63(5) Federal Judicial Assistance Statute);

(2) if the request for judicial assistance is made by United States authorities who are prosecuting leaders of organised crime; or

(3) if the offence is characterised as fraud under Swiss law, which is the case if the offender has deceived the fiscal authorities with malicious intent (ATF 111 Ib 249 f).

See ¶1071 and ¶1038(2)(b).

¶1823 Parties affected by judicial assistance

(1) Third parties and banks

The protection of third parties (Art. 82 Federal Judicial Assistance Statute) and the importance of the bank secrecy law have been somewhat reduced by the Federal Supreme Court's recent case law (see, e.g., ATF 115 Ib 68). The cantonal authorities involved with the case have wide discretion to decide directly whether certain documents could be of significance and constitute evidence pertinent to the criminal investigation concluded abroad (see ATF 115 Ib 82). For the involvement of banks in international judicial assistance, see ¶1138.

(2) The injured party's access to information

The injured party, as a person indirectly affected by the international judicial assistance proceedings, has the right to obtain information about these proceedings. The extent of access to the information and file depends upon cantonal and criminal procedure law.

¶1824 Appeal against orders granting judicial assistance

Each order granting judicial assistance must state in detail which form of complaint may be filed and what time limit must be observed in order to quash the order itself (Art. 22 Federal Judicial Assistance Statute). As a rule, this remedy is possible in all cases based on the Judicial Assistance Statute, except requests from the United States. The complaint is based on cantonal procedural law and must usually be addressed either to the Superior Court or to the cantonal Attorney-General within five to ten days. Orders issued by the Federal Office of Police on requests for judicial assistance by United States authorities may be appealed within ten days (Art. 16 Federal Statute Regarding the Treaty Between the United States of America and Switzerland on Mutual Judicial Assistance In Criminal Matters, RS 351.93). Final decisions by the cantonal authorities or the Federal Office of Police may be appealed by means of an administrative law complaint to the Federal Supreme Court, or may be reviewed by the Federal Justice Department (Arts 25 and 26 Federal Judicial Assistance Statute; Arts 17 and 18(2) Federal Statute Regarding the Swiss/United States Treaty).

SELECTED BIBLIOGRAPHY

André Panchaud, Denys Ochsenbein and Vésale van Ruymbeke, *Code pénal suisse annoté* (Lausanne, 1989)

Gérard Piquerez, *Précis de procédure pénale suisse* (Lausanne, 1987)

Niklaus Schmid, *Strafprozessrecht – Eine Einführung auf der Grundlage des Strafprozessrechts des Kantons Zürich und des Bundes* (Zürich, 1989)

Schultz Hans, *Einführung in den allgemeinen Teil des Strafrechts*, 2 vols, 3rd/4th edn (Bern, 1982)

Günther Stratenwerth, *Strafrecht Allgemeiner Teil*, 2 vols (Bern, 1982, 1989), *Strafrecht, Besonderer Teil*, 2 vols (Bern, 1983, 1984)

Stefan Trechsel, *Schweizerisches Strafgesetzbuch*, Kurzkommentar (Zürich, 1989)

¶1824

19 Choice of Law, Jurisdiction and Enforcement of Foreign Decisions

PRINCIPAL LEGISLATION

Loi fédérale sur le droit international privé/Gesetz über das internationale Privatrecht/Federal Private International Law Statute (PIL Statute), RS 291.

UNIFORM LAW

¶1901 Types of uniform law

(1) Historical reasons
For historical reasons Switzerland's substantive law is in many cases the same as that of other countries, particularly its larger neighbours: Germany, France, Italy and Austria.

(2) International treaties for uniform law
According to Swiss views, the law of nations ('international law') is the law of the land in Switzerland, and there is no need for implementing statutes once a treaty has been ratified by Switzerland, except where the treaty is not capable of direct application ('non-self-executing'). As a source of law, the law of nations is second only to federal constitutional law. It takes precedence over federal statutes such as the PIL Statute (¶105).

By virtue of international treaties, Switzerland's substantive law is uniform with that of its neighbouring and other countries in the following areas:

(a) Air transportation
With some 110 countries: *Convention du 7 décembre 1944 relative à l'aviation civile internationale* – RS 0.748.0. With some 40 countries: *Convention du 19*

juin 1948 relative à la reconnaissance internationale des droits sur aéronef – RS 0.748.217.1. With more than 100 countries: (Warsaw) *Convention du 12 octobre 1929 pour l'unification de certaines règles relatives au transport aérien international (avec protocole additionnel)* – RS 0.748.410. Also later additional treaties, most recently the *Convention du 18 septembre 1961, complémentaire à la convention de Varsovie, pour l'unification de certaines règles relatives au transport aérien international effectué par une personne autre que le transporteur contractuel* – RS 0.748.410.2.

(b)   Sea transportation
With some 20 countries: *Convention internationale du 10 avril 1926 pour l'unification de certaines règles relatives aux privilèges et hypothèques maritimes (avec protocole de signature)* – RS 0.747.322.2; (Brussels) *Convention internationale du 29 avril 1961 pour l'unification de certaines règles en matière de transport de passagers par mer (avec protocole)* – RS 0.747.355.1.

(c)   Rail transportation
With some 25 countries: *(COTIF) Convention du 9 mai 1980 relative aux transports internationaux ferroviaires (COTIF) (avec protocole)* – RS 0.742.403.1.

(d)   Road transportation
With some 20 countries: *Convention du 19 mai 1956 relative au contrat de transport international de marchandises par route (CMR) (avec protocole de signature)* – RS 0.741.611.

(e)   Bills and notes
(Geneva) *Convention du 7 juin 1930 portant loi uniforme sur les lettres de change et billets à ordre (avec annexes et protocole)* – RS 0.221.554.1; *Convention du 7 juin 1930 relative au droit de timbre en matière de lettres de change et de billets à ordre (avec protocole)* – RS 0.221.554.3; *Acte final de la Conférence de Genève pour l'unification du droit en matière de lettres de change et de billets à ordre, du 7 juin 1930* – RS 0.221.554.4; *Convention du 19 mars 1931 portant loi uniforme sur les chèques (avec annexes et protocole)* – RS 0.221.555.1; *Convention du 19 mars 1931 relative au droit de timbre en matière de chèques (avec protocole)* – RS 0.221.555.3; *Acte final de la Conférence de Genève pour l'unification du droit en matière de chèques, du 19 mars 1931* – RS 0.221.555.4.

(f)   International sales
Since 1 March 1991, (Vienna) Convention on International Sales. In international sales, as there defined, the Vienna Convention applies rather than the Federal Code of Obligations. See ¶213(1).

¶1901

(g) Nuclear liability
Switzerland is not a member of the Geneva and Brussels Conventions.

(3) Uniform international practice
Uniform international practices are followed in many industries. An example is the International Chamber of Commerce's Uniform Rules on Letters of Credit.

TREATIES

¶1902 Multinational treaties of universal application

(1) International jurisdiction: Collision at sea
Convention internationale du 10 mai 1952 pour l'unification de certaines règles relatives à la compétence civile en matière d'abordage – RS 0.747.313.24.

(2) Private international law

(a) Bills and notes
(Geneva) *Convention du 7 juin 1930 destinée à régler certains conflits de lois en matière de lettres de change et de billets à ordre (avec protocole)* – RS 0.221.554.2; *Convention du 19 mars 1931 destinée à régler certains conflits de lois en matière de chèques (avec protocole)* – RS 0.221.555.2. Substantive law is unified as well.

(b) International sales
Convention du 15 juin 1955 sur la loi applicable aux ventes à caractère international d'objets mobiliers corporels – RS 0.221.211.4, *loi uniforme*, declared universally applicable by Art. 118 PIL Statute. There are no special rules for sales at a trade fair, auction or stock exchange.

(c) Traffic accidents
With seven countries: (Hague) *Convention du 4 mai 1971 sur la loi applicable en matière d'accidents de la circulation routière* – RS 0.741.31, declared universally applicable by Art. 134 PIL Statute.

(3) International arbitration
With some 70 countries: (New York) *Convention du 10 juin 1958 pour la reconnaissance et l'exécution des sentences arbitrales étrangères* – RS 0.277.12. The prior reservation has been dropped in effect, Art. 194 PIL Statute. With some 30 countries: (Geneva) *Protocole du 24 septembre 1923 relatif aux clauses*

d'arbitrage – RS 0.277.11. With some 10 countries: (Geneva) *Convention du 26 septembre 1927 pour l'exécution des sentences arbitrales étrangères* – RS 0.277.111. With some 80 countries: (Washington) *Convention du 18 mars 1965 pour le règlement des différends relatifs aux investissements entre Etats et ressortissants d'autres Etats*, 1968 – RS 0.975.1. See ¶2120.

¶1903   Multinational treaties of limited application

Some multilateral treaties remain of non-universal application. These are not mentioned in the PIL Statute, but they retain precedence over the PIL Statute (Art. 1 PIL Statute).

These treaties include the following:

(1)   Diplomatic missions
With most countries: *Convention de Vienne du 18 avril 1961 sur les relations diplomatiques*, Arts 30 to 41 – RS 0.191.01; *Convention de Vienne du 24 avril 1963 sur les relations consulaires*, Arts 43 and 53 – RS 0.191.02. With Austria, Belgium, the UK and Cyprus: also *Convention européenne du 16 mai 1972 sur l'immunité des Etats (avec annexe)*, Arts 1 to 15 – RS 0.273.1.

(2)   International organisations
In general – RS 0.192.11 et seq.

(3)   Conflict of jurisdictions; recognition and enforcement
With all EC and EFTA countries, Switzerland has signed the Lugano Convention, which extends many features of the Brussels Convention to a large area of Europe. The Convention will become effective for Switzerland on 1 January 1992. See ¶1919.

(4)   Civil procedure
With Austria, Belgium, Denmark, Finland, France, Germany, Hungary, Israel, Italy, Luxembourg, the Netherlands, Norway, Poland, Portugal, Spain, Sweden and Turkey: (Hague) *Convention du 1er mars 1954 relative à la procédure civile*, Art. 18 et seq. – RS 0.274.12. With Iceland: (Hague) *Convention du 17 juillet 1905 relative à la procédure civile*, Art. 18 et seq. – RS 0.274.11. Switzerland is not a member of the Brussels/European Convention of 27 September 1968.

(5)   Copyright
With some 70 countries: *Convention de Berne* (1886) *du 13 novembre 1908, revisée pour la protection des oeuvres littéraires et artistiques (texte de Berlin)* – RS 0.231.11; and later conventions, most recently the *Convention de Berne pour la protection des oeuvres littéraires et artistiques, revisée à Stockholm le*

14 juillet 1967 (avec protocole relatif aux pays en voie de développement) – RS 0.231.14; (Geneva) *Convention universelle du 6 septembre 1952 sur le droit d'auteur* – RS 0.231.0. See ¶1315.

(6) Design
With some 20 countries: *Arrangement de La Haye concernant le dépôt international des dessins ou modèles industriels, revisé à Londres le 2 juin 1934* – RS 0.232.121.1. See ¶1304.

(7) Patents
With some 90 countries: *Convention d'Union de Paris pour la protection de la propriété industrielle (1893), revisée à La Haye le 6 novembre 1925* – RS 0.232.01; and later conventions, most recently the *Convention de Paris pour la protection de la propriété industrielle, revisée à Stockholm le 14 juillet 1967* – RS 0.232.04. See ¶1301 and ¶1303.

(8) Trade marks
With some 20 countries: *Arrangement de Madrid (1891) concernant l'enregistrement international des marques, revisé à Stockholm le 14 juillet 1967* – RS 0.232.112.3. See ¶1307.

(9) Plant varieties
With some 10 countries: *Convention internationale du 2 décembre 1961 pour la protection des obtentions végétales (avec annexe)* – RS 0.232.161. See ¶1324.

(10) Nuclear energy
With the International Atomic Energy Agency: *Accord du 6 septembre 1978 entre la Confédération suisse et l'Agence internationale de l'énergie atomique relatif à l'application de garanties dans le cadre du traité sur la non-prolifération des armes nucléaires*, Art. 16 – RS 0.515.031.

(11) Ship mortgages
With some 20 countries: *Convention internationale du 10 avril 1926 pour l'unification de certaines règles relatives aux privilèges et hypothèques maritimes (avec protocole de signature)* – RS 0.747.322.2.

(12) Aircraft mortgages
With some 110 countries: *Convention du 7 décembre 1944 relative à l'aviation civile internationale* – RS 0.748.0. With some 40 countries: *Convention du 19 juin 1948 relative à la reconnaissance internationale des droits sur aéronef* – RS 0.748.217.1.

¶1903

¶1904   Bilateral treaties

Bilateral treaties retain precedence over federal statutes such as the PIL Statute. Those marked with an asterisk (*) will be superseded by the Lugano Convention (¶1903(3) and ¶1919). The most important bilateral treaties are those with the United States (1850) and with *France (1869).

With Austria
Accord du 26 août 1968 entre la Confédération suisse et la République d'Autriche visant à compléter la convention de La Haye du 1ᵉʳ mars 1954 sur la procédure civile – RS 0.274.181.631; *Convention du 16 décembre 1960 entre la Confédération suisse et la République d'Autriche relative à la reconnaissance et à l'exécution de décisions judiciaires* – RS 0.276.191.632.

With the Bahamas
Echange de lettres des 3 mars/3 mai 1977 concernant l'application entre la Suisse et les Bahamas de la convention conclue le 3 décembre 1937 par la Suisse et la Grande-Bretagne en matière de procédure civile – RS 0.274.181.641.

With Belgium
Déclaration du 29 novembre 1900 entre la Suisse et la Belgique concernant la transmission directe des actes judiciaires, etc. – RS 0.274.181.721; *Convention du 9 décembre 1886 entre la Suisse et la Belgique sur l'assistance judiciaire devant les tribunaux (bénéfice du pauvre)* – RS 0.274.181.722; *Convention du 29 avril 1959 entre la Suisse et la Belgique sur la reconnaissance et l'exécution de décisions judiciaires et de sentences arbitrales* – RS 0.276.191.721.

With Czechoslovakia
Accord du 21 décembre 1926 entre la Suisse et la République tchécoslovaque concernant l'assistance judiciaire réciproque en matière civile et commerciale (avec protocole additionnel) – RS 0.274.187.411; *Convention du 21 décembre 1926 entre la Suisse et la République tchécoslovaque relative à la reconnaissance et à l'exécution de décisions judiciaires (avec protocole additionnel)* – RS 0.276.197.411.

With Estonia
Déclaration du 29 octobre 1926 entre la Suisse et l'Estonie concernant l'application réciproque de la Convention de La Haye relative à la procédure civile – RS 0.274.181.341.

With France
Convention du 15 juin 1869 entre la Suisse et la France sur la compétence judiciaire et l'exécution des jugements en matière civile (avec protocole explicatif) – RS 0.276.193.491. *Déclaration du 1ᵉʳ février 1913 entre la Suisse et la France relative à la transmission des actes judiciaires et extrajudiciaires*

et des commissions rogatoires en matière civile et commerciale (avec annexe) – RS 0.274.181.491.

With Germany
Déclaration du 1er/13 décembre 1878 entre la Suisse et l'Empire allemand au sujet de la correspondance directe entre les autorités judiciaires des deux pays – RS 0.274.181.361; **Convention du 2 novembre 1929 entre la Confédération suisse et le Reich allemand relative à la reconnaissance et l'exécution de décisions judiciaires et de sentences arbitrales* – RS 0.276.191.361. Boards of Directors of Border Water Power Plants, *Accord du 6 décembre 1955 entre la Confédération suisse et la République fédérale d'Allemagne au sujet du règlement de questions concernant les conseils d'administration des sociétés anonymes constituées en République fédérale d'Allemagne en vue d'exploiter les usines hydroélectriques frontières du Rhin* – RS 0.221.333.213.6.

With Greece
Convention du 30 mars 1934 réglant l'entraide judiciaire en matière civile et commerciale entre la Suisse et la Grèce – RS 0.274.183.721; *Convention d'établissement et de protection juridique du 1er décembre 1927 entre la Suisse et la Grèce,* Art. 11(1) – RS 0.142.113.721.

With Hungary
Echange de notes du 20 octobre 1972 entre la Suisse et la Hongrie concernant la transmission d'actes judiciaires et extrajudiciaires et de commissions rogatoires – RS 0.274.184.181.

With Iran
Convention d'établissement du 25 avril 1934 entre la Confédération suisse et l'Empire de Perse (Iran) (avec annexe), Art. 8 – RS 0.142.114.362.

With Italy
Accord avec l'Italie sur la compétence judiciaire; Convention d'établissement et consulaire du 22 juillet 1868 entre la Suisse et l'Italie (avec décl.), Arts 1, 2, and 8 – RS 0.142.114.541; *Protocole du 1er mai 1869 concernant l'exécution des conventions conclues et signées à Berne et à Florence entre la Suisse et l'Italie le 22 juillet 1868,* Art. IV – RS 0.142.114.541.1; **Convention du 3 janvier 1933 entre la Suisse et l'Italie sur la reconnaissance et l'exécution de décisions judiciaires,* Art. 8 – RS 0.276.194.541.

With Kenya
Echange de notes des 19 mai/21 septembre 1965 entre la Suisse et le Kenya concernant le maintien en vigueur dans leurs rapports de la convention du 3 décembre 1937 entre la Suisse et la Grand-Bretagne en matière de procédure civile – RS 0.274.184.721.

¶1904

With Liechtenstein
Convention du 25 avril 1968 entre la Confédération suisse et la Principauté de Liechtenstein sur la reconnaissance et l'exécution de décisions judiciaires et de sentences arbitrales en matière civile – RS 0.276.195.141.

With Luxembourg
Echange de lettres des 12/15 février 1979 entre la Suisse et le Grand-Duché de Luxembourg sur l'acheminement des actes judiciaires et extrajudiciaires en matière civile et commerciale (avec annexe) – RS 0.274.185.181.

With Nauru
Echange de notes des 23 août 1978/10 janvier 1979 concernant l'application entre la Suisse et la République de Nauru de la convention du 3 décembre 1937 conclue entre la Suisse et la Grande-Bretagne en matière de procédure civile – RS 0.274.185.761.

With Pakistan
Echange de lettres des 12 mai/7 juillet 1960 entre la Suisse et le Pakistan concernant l'entraide judiciaire en matière civile – RS 0.274.186.231.

With Poland
Echange de notes des 15 mars/18 août 1928 entre la Suisse et la Pologne concernant l'application de la Convention de La Haye relative à la procédure civile – RS 0.274.186.491.

With the Soviet Union
Traité de commerce du 17 mars 1948 entre la Confédération suisse et l'Union des Républiques soviétiques socialistes, 1948, Art. 10 – RS 0.946.297.721.

With Spain
Accord avec l'Espagne sur la transmission des actes judiciaires – RS 0.274.183.321; **Traité du 19 novembre 1896 entre la Suisse et l'Espagne sur l'exécution réciproque des jugements ou arrêts en matière civile et commerciale (avec protocole additionnel)* – RS 0.276.193.321.

With Swaziland
Echange de notes des 20 juillet/24 septembre 1971 concernant l'application entre la Suisse et le Royaume du Swaziland de la convention du 3 décembre 1937 conclue entre la Suisse et la Grande-Bretagne en matière de procédure civile – RS 0.274.187.231.

With Sweden
*Convention du 15 janvier 1936 entre la Suisse et la Suède relative à la reconnaissance et l'exécution de décisions judiciaires et de sentences arbitrales – RS 0.276.197.141.

¶1904

With Tanzania
Echange de notes des 2 décembre 1963/30 janvier 1964 entre la Suisse et le Tanganyika concernant le maintien en vigueur, dans leurs rapports, de la convention du 3 décembre 1937 entre la Suisse et la Grande-Bretagne en matière de procédure civile – RS 0.274.187.321.

With Tonga
Echange de lettres des 6 juin/20 août 1973 concernant l'application entre la Suisse et Tonga de la convention conclue le 3 décembre 1937 par la Suisse et la Grande-Bretagne en matière de procédure civile – RS 0.274.187.521.

With Turkey
Convention du 1er juin 1933 réglant les rapports judiciaires en matière civile et commerciale entre la Suisse et la Turquie – RS 0.274.187.631.

With Uganda
Echange de notes des 24 mars/26 mai 1965 entre la Suisse et l'Ouganda concernant le maintien en vigueur dans leurs rapports de la convention du 3 décembre 1937 entre la Suisse et la Grande-Bretagne en matière de procédure civile – RS 0.274.186.181.

With the United Kingdom
Convention du 3 décembre 1937 entre la Suisse et la Grande-Bretagne en matière de procédure civile – RS 0.274.183.671. For former colonies, see the independent countries.

With Yugoslavia
Traité de commerce du 27 septembre 1948 entre la Confédération suisse et la République fédérative populaire de Yougoslavie, Art. 10 – RS 0.946.298.181.

LEGISLATION

¶1905   PIL Statute

(1)   Codification of private international law
Private international law is codified in the PIL Statute of 1989. The Statute stands alone as a separate piece of legislation. It is not integrated into the Federal Civil Code and the Federal Code of Obligations, but the system upon which the Statute is built loosely follows both codes. With the exception of the entirely separate law of negotiable instruments (see ¶1902(2)), it is a civil law-type code. The chapter on international arbitration essentially stands apart.

(2) Overview of the PIL Statute

The PIL Statute deals with international conflict of laws, but related areas, including intellectual property, bankruptcy and international arbitration, are also covered. The PIL Statute also addresses international conflict of jurisdictions, and the recognition and enforcement of foreign decisions.

Table 19.1, simplified and limited to business law, illustrates the overall structure of the PIL Statute with its 'three-part harmony'.

Table 19.1: Private International Law Statute Articles

	Jurisdiction	*Applicable Law*	*Recognition and Enforcement*
First chapter: General Provisions	2 – 12	13–19	25 – 32
Seventh chapter: Real Rights	97 – 98	99–107	108
Eighth chapter: Intellectual Property	109	110	111
Ninth chapter: Obligations			
First Section: Contracts	112 – 115	116 – 126 143 – 148	149
Second Section: Unjust Enrichment	127	128 143 – 148	149
Third Section: Unlawful Acts	129 – 131	132 – 142 143 – 148	149
Tenth chapter: Companies	151 – 153	154 – 164	165

¶1906   Special statute: Bills and notes

The private international law of bills and notes/negotiable instruments remains outside the scope of the PIL Statute and is regulated by special provisions in the Federal Code of Obligations. See Arts 1086 to 1095 and 1138 to 1142 CO, corresponding to the Geneva Convention on Drafts (RS 0.215.551.2), and the Geneva Convention on Cheques (RS 0.211.555.2).

INTERNATIONAL JURISDICTION

¶1907   Choice of jurisdiction

(1)   Freedom
Under the PIL Statute, the parties are normally free to make an express choice of jurisdiction (or an arbitration agreement) for an existing or future dispute of financial interest arising from a specific legal relationship.

(2)   Formal requirements
The agreement may be made in writing, by telegram, by telex, by telecopier, or by any other means of communication which permits it to be evidenced by a text.

Likewise, an unconditional appearance gives jurisdiction to the Swiss court or to an arbitral tribunal having its seat in Switzerland (Arts 5(3), 6, 7 and 186(2) PIL Statute). An appearance is conditional if the party states prior to or in its answer that it does not recognise the jurisdiction of the court.

(3)   Binding effect upon Swiss *'forum prorogatum'*
The Swiss court chosen may not decline jurisdiction if one of the parties has its registered seat, domicile, habitual residence or business establishment in the canton of the chosen court, if the parties have expressly declared Swiss law applicable, or if Swiss law applies pursuant to the private international law rules of the PIL Statute (Art. 5(3) PIL Statute). Previous cantonal law to the contrary no longer applies.

(4)   Exclusiveness
Unless otherwise provided by the agreement, the choice of jurisdiction is exclusive.

(5)   Mandatory jurisdiction
Occasionally, the choice of jurisdiction is limited or even excluded. Thus, if a consumer sues on a contract concerning consumer goods in a non-business context, jurisdiction lies mandatorily (Art. 114(2) PIL Statute) with the Swiss courts at the consumer's domicile or habitual residence (Art. 114(1)(a) PIL Statute). However, the consumer may also sue the merchant at the merchant's seat or domicile or, if there is none, at the merchant's habitual residence.

¶1908   Main rule: Jurisdiction at domicile of defendant
In the absence of a choice of jurisdiction, the basic rule governing conflict of jurisdictions remains Art. 59 of the Federal Constitution, which Switzerland took

care to reserve in all its treaty law: a solvent debtor having a domicile in Switzerland must be sued in Switzerland.

This is also applied internationally by Switzerland to protect Swiss companies owned or controlled by non-Swiss persons. Thus, as a rule, Swiss companies can be sued only in Switzerland. The Lugano Convention will change this substantially, since the main rule will be that the courts at the place of performance have jurisdiction (see ¶1919).

Partly as mandated by Art. 59 of the Federal Constitution, provisions on conflict of jurisdictions in the PIL Statute secure jurisdiction at the (last) domicile or seat of the defendant (Arts 2, 33, 38, 46, 57, 75, 84, 98, 109, 112, 127, 129 and 151 PIL Statute).

For persons without a domicile but with habitual residence in Switzerland, particularly children, many provisions secure jurisdiction at the place of habitual residence.

¶1909   Special places of jurisdiction

Exceptions to the main rule include cases where the Private International Law Statute provides for special places of jurisdiction deemed compatible with the principle of Art. 59 of the Federal Constitution.

(1)   Real rights in movable goods
If the defendant has neither a seat, domicile nor a habitual residence in Switzerland, jurisdiction for lawsuits on real rights in movable goods lies with the Swiss courts at the location of the goods (Art. 98(2) PIL Statute).

(2)   Protection of intellectual property rights
If the defendant does not have a seat, domicile, or habitual residence in Switzerland, lawsuits on the protection of intellectual property rights are subject to jurisdiction at the place where protection is sought. If the defendant is not domiciled in Switzerland, jurisdiction for lawsuits on the validity or registration of intellectual property rights in Switzerland lies with the Swiss courts at the seat of the registered agent or, if there is none, at the seat of the Swiss registration authority (Art. 109(1) and (3) PIL Statute).

(3)   Disputes involving corporate law
Disputes involving corporate law, and lawsuits against the company, the members of the company or the persons liable according to corporate law, are subject to the jurisdiction of the Swiss courts at the seat of the company involved (Art. 151(1) PIL Statute).

¶1909

(4) Business establishment
Lawsuits based on the activity of a business establishment in Switzerland are also subject to the jurisdiction of the courts at the place of the business establishment (Art. 112(2) PIL Statute).

(5) Public issues of shares and bonds
Lawsuits for responsibility arising from the public issue of shares and bonds are also subject to the jurisdiction of the Swiss courts at the place of issue. This jurisdiction cannot be waived by a choice of jurisdiction (Art. 151(3) PIL Statute).

(6) Unjust enrichment and torts
Lawsuits alleging unjust enrichment and lawsuits based on unlawful acts (torts), are subject to the jurisdiction of the Swiss courts at the place of the business establishment of the defendant if he or she has no seat, domicile or habitual residence in Switzerland. For lawsuits based on unlawful acts (torts), jurisdiction also lies with the Swiss court where the act occurred or where it had its effect.

(7) Special jurisdiction for provisional measures
The Swiss judicial or administrative authorities may order provisional measures even if they have no jurisdiction to render a decision on the merits. (Arts 10 and 183 PIL Statute).

¶1910 Jurisdictionally improper forum – *'forum arresti'*

Federal law on collection of debt provides for the possibility of attaching the assets of non-Swiss persons in Switzerland, including receivables from Swiss debtors such as bank accounts in Swiss banks (for this, one must know in which branch of which bank the account is maintained). This will remain possible without exception, even after the Lugano Convention comes into force in Switzerland (see ¶1919).

In the absence of a choice of jurisdiction clause, and in the absence of international treaty provisions to the contrary (which Switzerland already has with France, and which it will have with numerous countries in Europe under the Lugano Convention), there is an internationally improper *forum arresti* in Switzerland (Art. 4 PIL Statute). See ¶910 and ¶2014.

¶1911 International jurisdiction – exceptions

A choice of jurisdiction is ineffective if a party is abusively deprived of protection at a place of jurisdiction provided by Swiss law (Art. 5(2) PIL Statute).

The Swiss courts may assume jurisdiction in cases not already pending elsewhere to avoid a denial of justice. If proceedings abroad are impossible or highly impracticable, jurisdiction lies at the place which has a sufficient connection with the case (Art. 3 PIL Statute).

PRIVATE INTERNATIONAL LAW

¶1912   Structure

The PIL Statute begins in typical civil-law code fashion with a first chapter of general provisions, but the importance of these can easily be overestimated. There are no provisions on characterisation (characterisation should be autonomous according to the majority of legal writers), preliminary question, *fraus legis*, or *conflit mobile*.

In its later chapters, the PIL Statute is not limited to general rules. Rather, it spells out the specific rules and exceptions in considerable detail.

The PIL Statute's conflict rules are in the traditional form: for a particular legal issue they designate the applicable law by means of a *point de rattachement*.

Most conflict of law rules are worded as rules that conceivably could appear, worded the same way, in the legislation of other countries (e.g., Art. 68 PIL Statute). By contrast, most conflict of jurisdiction rules, and all recognition and enforcement rules, state only what Switzerland will or will not do (e.g., Arts 66 and 70 PIL Statute).

As in the more recent Hague Conventions, the conflict rules use non-technical autonomous concepts such as 'habitual residence', rather than the technical terms appearing in other Swiss statutes. Some statutory definitions are provided.

- *Domicile of an individual.* This is the place where the individual's personal relationships are centered. No individual can be domiciled in more than one place at the same time. If an individual has no domicile, his habitual residence serves to replace domicile (Art. 20(2) PIL Statute).

- *Companies* (defined in Art. 150 PIL Statute) *are domiciled* at *their seat.* The seat of a company is at the place designated in the Articles or the Contract of Association. If there is no such designation, the seat is at the place where the company is in fact administered (Art. 21 PIL Statute).

Where the Statute refers to a foreign 'law', the reference encompasses all provisions that are applicable to the case according to that law. This would include foreign conflict of laws rules, but in the area of business law, *renvoi* is expressly excluded (Art. 14(1) PIL Statute). A foreign provision is not inapplicable for the sole reason that it is characterised as public law (Art. 13 PIL Statute).

¶1913   Permissible choice of law

(1)   Freedom of choice

In a wide area of private international law, the parties are free to choose the applicable law, but the choice of law must be explicit or be clearly evident from the agreement or from the circumstances. Moreover, it is governed by the chosen law (Art. 116(2) PIL Statute, of general application).

(2)   Movable goods

The parties may subject the acquisition and loss of rights in movable goods to the law of the country of dispatch or destination of the goods, or to the law governing the underlying legal transaction, but this choice of law cannot be invoked against third parties (Art. 104 PIL Statute).

(3)   Contracts

Contracts are governed by the law chosen by the parties (Art. 116(1) PIL Statute).

(4)   Torts

As far as torts are concerned, the parties may always agree after the damage occurs that the law of the place of the court applies (Art. 132 PIL Statute).

(5)   Corporations

Corporations are subject to the law of the country according to which they are organised, provided they meet its provisions on publicity or registration or, if no such provisions exist, if they organise themselves according to the law of that country. If a company does not meet these conditions, it is governed by the law of the country where it is in fact administered (Art. 154 PIL Statute).

¶1914   Special rules when no choice of law

In the absence of a permissible choice of law by the parties, the Private International Law Statute provides specific rules for various situations.

(1)   'Lex rei sitae'

In the area of rights in movable goods, commercial paper, and the pledge of receivables, the principle of *lex rei sitae* is supplemented by special rules (Arts 100 to 107 PIL Statute).

(2)   Intellectual property rights

Rights in intellectual property are governed by the law of the country for which protection of those rights is sought (Art. 110(1) PIL Statute).

(3) Contract type formula

For contracts, the PIL Statute generally follows the contract type formula: a contract is governed by the law of the country most closely connected with it, which is presumed to be the country where the party which must make the characteristic performance has its habitual residence, or, if the contract is based on a business activity, its business establishment (Art. 117(2) PIL Statute).

The characteristic performance is, in particular:

(a) in contracts to pass title, the performance of the transferor (for sales, the Hague Convention of 1955 applies: Art. 118(1) PIL Statute);

(b) in contracts to grant the use of a thing or a right, the performance of the party that grants the use;

(c) in mandates, construction contracts, and similar contracts for services, the service;

(d) in contracts for storage, the performance of the keeper;

(e) in guarantee and suretyship contracts, the performance of the guarantor or surety (Art. 117(3) PIL Statute).

(4) Special types of contracts

The contract type formula does not apply to special types of contracts, such as barter contracts, contracts with consumers (Art. 120 PIL Statute), employment contracts (Art. 121 PIL Statute), and contracts concerning intellectual property (Art. 122 PIL Statute).

¶1915 General exceptions

(1) Built-in flexibilities

Many rules have built-in flexibility, for instance the contract type formula. Because of the flexibility built into Art. 117 of the PIL Statute, there is no need to resort to the general provision on '*Näherberechtigung*', Art. 15(1) PIL Statute, according to which the law designated by the Statute is, by way of exception, not applicable if, under all the circumstances, the case clearly has only a slight connection with the designated law, and has much closer connection with another law.

(2) Treble damages, and other excessive damages awards

Some provisions build in protection, particularly of Swiss-domiciled defendants against foreign (mainly American) law that provides for exemplary damages, treble damages, and excessive damages. Accordingly, there is no need to resort to the general public policy exception in Art. 17 PIL Statute (see ¶1916).

¶1915

For example, product liability claims are governed, at the option of the injured party, by a whole series of laws: the law of the country where the tortfeasor has its business establishment or, if it has none, its habitual residence, or the law of the country where the product was acquired, unless the tortfeasor proves that it came to the market in that country without its assent (Art. 135(1) PIL Statute).

No damages can be awarded in Switzerland beyond those that would be awarded under Swiss law for such an injury (Art. 135(2) PIL Statute).

Likewise, if claims of restraint of competition are governed by foreign law, no damages can be awarded in Switzerland beyond those that would be awarded under Swiss law in the case of an unlawful restraint of competition (Art. 137(2) PIL Statute).

¶1916   Public policy exceptions

An ordinary Swiss court will look to the provisions of the general part of the PIL Statute, which have not yet been discussed here, only after the outcome of the case has been determined according to the rules found in the special part of the PIL Statute. The public policy exceptions are therefore of limited application. There are three such exceptions in the area of private international law:

(1) Swiss public policy
Article 17 of the PIL Statute is the classic exclusion clause, according to which the application of provisions of a foreign law is excluded if the outcome is incompatible with Swiss public policy.

(2) *'Lois d'ordre public'*
Provisions of Swiss law which, in view of their special policy, must be applied without regard to the law designated by the PIL Statute (*lois d'ordre public*) remain reserved (Art. 18 PIL Statute).

(3) Mandatory provisions of foreign law
Finally, there is a special provision, Art. 19 PIL Statute, on taking into account mandatory provisions of foreign law if the following prerequisites are met:

- According to their policy, the other provisions must be meant to be applied mandatorily.
- The foreign provisions are taken into account; they do not replace the otherwise applicable law.
- This is optional, not mandatory.
- This is permitted only if there is a close connection with the other law, which will hardly exist if there is choice of law.

¶1916

- This is permitted only if legitimate and clearly overriding interests exist.
- This must be in the interest of a party, not some foreign state (disputed).
- The only way to safeguard these interests is to take them into account; they cannot be safeguarded in another way.
- All this must be assessed according to Swiss views of what is fair.

(4)   Public policy in international arbitration
The conflict of laws concept of Swiss public policy just discussed is not applicable in international arbitration (Arts 187 and 190(2)(e) PIL Statute).

RECOGNITION AND ENFORCEMENT OF FOREIGN DECISIONS

¶1917   Policy in favour of recognition

The general policy is to grant recognition to foreign decisions (*favor recognitionis*), provided:

(1) jurisdiction lay with the judicial or administrative authorities of the country in which the decision was rendered;

(2) an ordinary judicial remedy can no longer be brought against the decision (i.e., the decision is final); and

(3) no special ground for non-recognition under Art. 27 PIL Statute exists.

There are special provisions on recognition and enforcement of foreign decisions in particular areas of law.

¶1918   Exceptions

Under Art. 27 PIL Statute, a foreign decision will not be recognised in Switzerland if its recognition would be clearly incompatible with Swiss public policy or if a party proves:

(1) that neither according to the law of its domicile nor according to the law of its habitual residence was the party properly served with process, unless the party entered an unconditional appearance in the proceedings;

(2) that the judgment was rendered in violation of essential principles of Swiss procedural law, such as the right of a party to be heard;

(3) that a lawsuit between the same parties concerning the same case was first commenced or decided in Switzerland, or was first decided in a third

country, provided that the prerequisites for the recognition of that decision are met.

The foreign decision may not be reviewed on the merits in any other respect.

OUTLOOK

¶1919   Lugano Convention of 1988

Switzerland ratified the Lugano Convention of 16 September 1988. It will become effective on 1 January 1992. For the EC and EFTA countries, the Lugano Convention parallels the Brussels Convention of 27 September 1968 between the EC countries on jurisdiction and the enforcement of judgments in civil and commercial matters, as amended by the three Accession Conventions of 1978, 1982 and 1989.

This means that soon the federal statutory provision on conflict of jurisdictions will apply only against persons not domiciled (in the sense of the Lugano Convention) in one of the Lugano Convention countries, and only to the extent that Switzerland has no bilateral treaties with the country of domicile. On the other hand, through Art. 4 of the Lugano Convention these statutory provisions will apply against persons not domiciled in a Lugano Convention country to the benefit of any person domiciled in any Lugano Convention country.

The Lugano Convention, Art. 5(1), provides for the jurisdiction of the courts at the place of performance of the obligation in matters relating to the contract. This is at odds with the principle of Art. 59 of the Federal Constitution. Switzerland did not wish to enter into an international treaty conflicting with a provision of its Federal Constitution. Therefore, Switzerland reserved Art. 59 of the Federal Constitution in Art. Ia of Protocol No. 1 to the Lugano Convention. The Swiss reservation will, however, cease to have effect on 31 December 1999. How the conflict will be finally resolved is an open question.

In relation to parties domiciled in Lugano Convention countries, Switzerland gives up its jurisdictionally improper *forum arresti* (¶910, ¶1910 and ¶2014) for the validation of attachments (as it had already done in its bilateral treaty with France (¶1904): see Art. 3, Lugano Convention). Thus, many Swiss attachments will have to be validated abroad. The time limit to validate an attachment is relatively short. However, meeting the deadline is facilitated by a special provision: if a person abroad must observe a time limit before Swiss judicial or administrative authorities, it is sufficient for the submission to arrive on the last day of the time limit at a Swiss diplomatic or consular mission (Art. 12 PIL Statute).

SELECTED BIBLIOGRAPHY

Bernard Dutoit, François Knoepfler, Pierre Lalive and Pierre Mercier, *Répertoire de droit international privé suisse* (Bern, 1982)

Anne-Catherine Imhoff-Scheier and Paolo Michele Patocchi, *Torts and Unjust Enrichment in the New Swiss Conflict of Laws* (Zürich, 1990)

Pierre A. Karrer and Karl W. Arnold, *Switzerland's Private International Law Statute* (Deventer, Netherlands, 1989)

Max Keller and Kurt Siehr, *Allgemeine Lehren des internationalen Privatrechts* (Zürich, 1986)

François Knoepfler and Philippe Schweizer, *Précis de droit international privé suisse* (Bern, 1990)

Hans Ulrich Walder, *Einführung in das internationale Zivilprozessrecht der Schweiz* (Zürich, 1989)

20 Civil Litigation and Judicial Assistance in Civil Matters

PRINCIPAL LEGISLATION

Federal Procedure: *Loi fédérale sur le droit international privé/Bundesgesetz über das internationale Privatrecht*/Swiss Private International Law Statute (PIL Statute), RS 291.

Zurich Procedure: *Gesetz über den Zivilprozess/Zivilprozessordnung*/(Zurich) Code of Civil Procedure.

Zurich Court Organisation: *Gerichtsverfassungsgesetz*/(Zurich) Court Organisation Statute.

Geneva Procedure: *Loi de procédure civile*/(Geneva) Code of Civil Procedure.

Geneva Court Organisation: *Loi sur l'organisation judiciaire*/(Geneva) Court Organisation Statute.

SOURCES OF LAW

¶2001 Procedural law mainly cantonal

While substantive law is mainly federal, the law of civil procedure is mainly cantonal. Each of the 26 cantons has a code of civil procedure and a statute on judicial organisation. The Federal Code of Civil Procedure applies to those few matters where the Federal Supreme Court has exclusive jurisdiction, or where it has authority to decide appeals and complaints against cantonal decisions.

Article 4 of the Federal Constitution provides that all Swiss citizens are equal before the law. The Federal Supreme Court has declared that any application of the law, including cantonal procedural law, which is manifestly erroneous or arbitrary is tantamount to inequality before the law and constitutes a violation of Art. 4 of the Federal Constitution.

A number of provisions for civil procedure can be found in federal statutes, mainly the Civil Code (CC) and the Code of Obligations (CO). These provisions of federal law have priority over any cantonal procedural law.

COURT ORGANISATION

¶2002   Organisation of cantonal courts

(1)   Different systems in different cantons
The organisation of the courts differs from canton to canton. The systems and the names of the courts are quite diverse. Smaller cantons have only one court at the trial level, while larger cantons have several courts of first instance of general jurisdiction, one for each district.

(2)   Cantonal courts of general jurisdiction
Most trial courts are composed of three or more members. Cases where small amounts of money are at stake or which are subject to summary judgment are usually adjudicated by a single judge.

In addition to courts of general jurisdiction, some cantons have specialised courts, e.g., commercial courts, labour courts, and landlord-tenant courts.

Jurisdiction may depend upon the amount in dispute (see (4) and (5) below).

In general, a plaintiff cannot bring an action without first going to a justice of the peace (*conciliateur/Vermittler, Friedensrichter* in Zurich), that is, to an official mediator who will try to settle the dispute. These mediators usually have no legal training. For small claims, the mediators may render judgment.

In most cantons, cases involving larger amounts are heard by the trial courts (the cantonal district courts – *tribunal de district/arrondissement/Bezirksgericht* in Zurich). Appeals from the judgments of such courts are normally made by filing an appeal in the cantonal appellate courts (*tribunal cantonal/ Kantonsgericht, Obergericht* in Zurich).

In several cantons, gross procedural errors made by the cantonal appellate courts may be grounds for a complaint to the cantonal superior court. In general, if the complaint is granted, the case will be vacated and remanded to the original lower court but will be heard by a different panel of judges.

A further appeal may be filed with the Federal Supreme Court on the ground that federal substantive law was violated by the cantonal court. The Federal Supreme Court can hear complaints that the Federal Constitution was violated (constitutional complaint: *recours de droit public/Staatsrechtliche Beschwerde*).

(3) Specialised cantonal courts

Many cantons have special courts which have limited jurisdiction to deal with certain types of disputes, such as employment contracts, lease contracts or commercial matters in general. This specialisation is said to contribute to the speedy and efficient handling of disputes, because the judges have expert knowledge in a given field and the parties therefore have greater confidence in these judges. Not all cantons have set up these special courts.

The labour court adjudicates disputes between employers and employees that arise from employment situations. This court usually consists of one professional judge, one employer representative and one employee representative.

The commercial court (*Handelsgericht* in Zurich) adjudicates disputes concerning trade and commerce. This court may consist of one or more professional judges and several associate judges, who are often local businessmen. Its jurisdiction depends on a minimum amount in dispute and, in addition, on the registration of one or both of the parties in the Register of Commerce.

The landlord-tenant court adjudicates disputes which arise out of rental arrangements. The court includes landlord and tenant representatives.

(4) Example: Geneva court organisation

The canton of Geneva is not divided into districts for jurisdictional purposes. All of the canton's courts have their seat in the city of Geneva.

(a) Justice of the peace

When the amount in dispute is SFr 2,000 or less, the justice of the peace decides the case. If the amount in dispute is between SFr 2,000 and SFr 8,000, the justice of the peace acts as a mediator; if it is impossible to reach a settlement, the case then goes to the Trial Court.

(b) Trial Court

The Trial Court (*Tribunal de première instance*) can hear all cases of financial interest where the amount in dispute exceeds SFr 2,000. When this amount exceeds SFr 8,000, the conciliatory task is exercised by the Chamber of Conciliation of this court, not by the justice of the peace. Judgments of this court may be appealed to the Court of Appeals.

(c) Court of Appeals

The Court of Appeals (*Cour de Justice*) has different functions. It is the appellate court for judgments rendered by the Trial Court when the amount in dispute exceeds SFr 8,000. In addition, the Court of Appeals can hear cases when the parties agree to bypass the Trial Court and to go directly to the Court of Appeals.

¶2002

The Court of Appeals has other special functions which are mainly based on federal law: for example, it decides unfair competition cases.

In addition to these customary civil courts, the Canton of Geneva has courts of special jurisdiction: the Labour Law Court (*Tribunal des prud'hommes*) and the Landlord-Tenant Court (*Tribunal des baux*).

(5) Example: Zurich court organisation

The canton of Zurich is divided into 11 districts. The district courts, which are generally trial courts, have their seat in the capital of the district.

(a) Justice of the peace

Every municipality has a justice of the peace (*Friedensrichter*). He decides the case if the amount in dispute does not exceed SFr 300. If the amount is more than SFr 300, the justice of the peace acts as a mediator. If a settlement is not reached, the plaintiff can file an action in the District Court.

(b) District Court

If the amount in dispute ranges from SFr 8,000 to SFr 12,000, the District Court (*Bezirksgericht*) has final jurisdiction. It acts as a trial court if the amount in dispute exceeds SFr 12,000. The president or other members of the District Court may sit as single judges. The single judge has final jurisdiction over disputes if the amount in dispute ranges from SFr 300 to SFr 8,000.

(c) Court of Appeals

The Court of Appeals (*Obergericht*) acts as an appellate court (examining both the facts and the law) if the amount in dispute exceeds SFr 12,000 and as a court of errors to hear pleas in nullity to redress reversible errors of law if the amount in dispute ranges from SFr 300 to SFr 12,000. The parties can agree to go directly to the Court of Appeals instead of the District Court. The Court of Appeals decides cases of copyright law.

(d) Specialised courts

The Canton of Zurich has courts of special jurisdiction besides the customary civil courts: the Labour Law Court (*Arbeitsgericht*), the Landlord-Tenant Court (*Mietgericht*) and the Commercial Court (*Handelsgericht*). The Commercial Court decides civil procedures between parties which are entered into the Register of Commerce, if the dispute concerns the business of one of the parties or commercial relations in general, and if the amount in dispute reaches the minimum amount which allows one to file an appeal with the Federal Supreme Court (SFr 8,000). A decision of the Commercial Court may be challenged by an appeal to the Federal Supreme Court.

¶2002

¶2003   Federal Supreme Court

The Federal Supreme Court (*Tribunal fédéral suisse/Schweizerisches Bundesgericht*) with its seat in Lausanne and the Federal Insurance Court (*Tribunal fédéral des assurances/Eidgenössisches Versicherungsgericht*) with seat in Lucerne are judicial bodies which have (mostly appellable) jurisdiction in disputes arising in all of the 26 cantons. The Federal Constitution of 1874 established the Federal Supreme Court which we know today.

The Federal Supreme Court presently consists of 30 ordinary and 30 extraordinary judges. They are elected by both houses of the Federal Parliament for a term of six years and may be re-elected. Any Swiss citizen who is not a member of the clergy may be elected. There are no further requirements, although in reality only lawyers, who are frequently judges from cantonal appellate courts, are chosen.

The President and Vice-President of the Federal Supreme Court are elected for a term of two years by the Federal Parliament (¶103(3)).

The Federal Supreme Court has original jurisdiction for disputes between the Federal and cantonal governments, disputes between cantons, claims by private individuals or corporations against the federal government, and disputes in which a minimum amount is being contested and the parties agree that the sole forum for adjudication shall be the Federal Supreme Court.

The Federal Supreme Court has appellate jurisdiction for federal questions and for cases in which a party requests annulment of a lower court's decision. The Federal Insurance Court has appellate jurisdiction for disputes involving social security and some litigation involving insurance matters.

¶2004   Appointment of judges

The appointment of judges is a political choice. A parliamentary or public vote determines which candidates from which political parties will become judges.

Usually, the voters of the district concerned elect the justices of the peace and the judges of the trial courts. The judges of the cantonal appellate courts are elected by the cantonal parliaments. It is left to cantonal courts to choose their presidents. The justices of the Federal Supreme Court are elected by the Federal Assembly (House and Senate in joint session) (¶103(3)). The judges need not have a formal legal education. Lay judges are thoroughly integrated into the lower court system. Judges are usually elected by majority vote, although in two cantons (Zug and Ticino) judges are appointed in proportion to the representation in Parliament of their respective political parties. No judge is appointed for a life term in any canton.

There are strict requirements concerning the impartiality of judges. A judge must refrain from handling a case where a close relative or the judge's spouse is concerned, or where the judge had previously adjudicated in the lower courts or had represented one of the parties. In general, judges may be rejected if circumstances could make them biased in any way.

CIVIL PROCEDURE

¶2005 Sources of law

A number of basic principles of civil procedure can be found in the cantonal codes of civil procedure (*Code de procédure civile*, CPC/*Zivilprozessordnung*, ZPO). For example, each party is required to assist the court in finding the relevant facts, provide a defence, and submit evidence; the court may, and in some cases must, question insufficient or unclear allegations filed by the parties; the parties have the right to be heard; the judge is in charge of conducting the proceedings; the court must not award an amount larger than that claimed by a party.

The court must, on its own initiative, determine the law(s) applicable in each particular case, i.e., the parties may, but do not have to, argue the law embodied in statutes or precedents. Even the content of the applicable foreign law must be established by the court (Art. 16 PIL Statute). For this purpose, the court may request the assistance of the parties. For claims involving financial interests (and to a lesser degree in family law cases), the parties may be required to supply proof of the applicable law. If the court cannot ascertain the content of the foreign law it will apply Swiss law.

The court summons the parties to the proceedings, sets time-limits for written petitions or the fulfilment of other obligations, and issues interlocutory decrees until it renders the final judgment. The summonses, decrees, interlocutory decrees and final judgments must be served on the parties by the court in accordance with the rules of the applicable code of civil procedure.

¶2006 Time limits

Special rules apply to time limits set by courts or other government bodies. Thus, various cantonal rules of civil procedure contain provisions extending the time periods within which an act must be performed. Such extensions mostly occur in the holiday seasons (courts' recess). According to Art. 140 of the Zurich Law on the Organisation of the Judiciary, no hearings are held and the statutory and judicial time periods do not run between 10 July and 20 August, and between 20 December and 8 January. Similarly, the time from 10 July to 20 August, and from 8 December to 20 January is not taken into consideration for the purpose of computation of time limits. However, these rules do not apply to certain kinds of proceedings, and not all time periods are affected. Similar rules apply in other cantons and at the federal level.

In contrast, papers to be filed with a court or another government body within a certain period of time are deemed to have been filed in a timely manner if a Swiss postal office receives them prior to the expiration of the period. Thus, in Switzerland dispatch, and not receipt, prevails. In order to secure proof of timely filing, it is advisable to register the mailed items.

¶2007 Service of process

Summonses, notices of deadlines, interlocutory decrees and final judgments must be delivered to the parties and witnesses as official documents in order to have effect.

A summons is usually delivered in writing; an oral summons is allowed under special circumstances.

The summons must contain the address of the party for whom it is intended. It should describe the manner in which one is summonsed, the object of the dispute, the time and place of the required appearance, and the signature of the person issuing the summons. Usually, printed forms are used for summonses.

The documents are usually sent by mail or delivered by the court bailiff. A party who does not live in Switzerland may be ordered to appoint an agent to receive service of process. The same applies to a party who does not live in the particular canton where the civil proceedings are being conducted.

If the whereabouts of a party to be served are unknown, service of legal documents is effected by means of publication in the official gazette. However, reasonable efforts must be made to discover the address of the party in question. Service on parties in foreign countries is effected in accordance with the provisions of the various international treaties to which Switzerland is a party (see ¶1903(3) and (4), ¶1904 and ¶1919). The summonses and decrees to be served are deemed sovereign acts; their delivery must be approved by competent foreign officials.

¶2008 Presenting facts and arguments

Generally speaking, a legal action is commenced by filing a complaint (*demande/Klage*) containing a statement of facts, together with any specific requests to be considered. The facts must be explained in detail. The plaintiff may request a declaratory judgment or the award of a specific amount of money. In the first or subsequent briefs, the plaintiff must list the available evidence.

As a rule, the court then orders the defendant to submit an answer in writing (*réponse/Klageantwort*). The defendant must present his own statement of facts and/or deny the facts alleged by the plaintiff; he may present new evidence.

Quite often, the plaintiff is then ordered to file a written reply (*réplique/Replik*), and the defendant to file a written rejoinder (*duplique/Duplik*). The court may order oral presentation of reply and rejoinder.

In all cantons, the pleadings must be specific, i.e., they must assert the relevant facts in detail, or deny in detail the facts asserted by the other party or the relevance of those facts.

The court may invite the parties to an informal hearing (*Referentenaudienz*). During the hearing, the judge in charge of the file will discuss his prima facie impression of the facts and the law with the parties, and try to convince them to reach a settlement.

¶2009   Presenting evidence

(1)   Federal law on burden of proof

Article 8 CC reads: 'Where the law does not provide otherwise, the burden of proving an alleged fact rests on the party who bases his claim on that fact.' This rule means that factual assertions which call for affirmative legal action by the court must be asserted and proved in order to demonstrate that a legal relationship exists or that a legal rule applies: for example, the making of a loan contract or an injury resulting from the conduct of the defendant.

Factual assertions which call for the forbearance of the court in the matter must be proved: for example, the repayment of a loan or the interruption of a chain of causation due to contributory negligence.

Where the law requires the proof of certain negative facts to establish liability, the party who bears the burden of proving the facts must demonstrate some conditions from which the negative fact may naturally follow, so as to make a prima facie case: an example is an action against the seller for breach of warranty because the goods sold do not have the promised qualities.

The burden of proof shifts to the party that initially did not have this burden if he or she frustrates, or renders more difficult, the discharge of the burden by the counter-party. The same occurs if there are legal presumptions. These presumptions are conclusions that certain results arise from the normal course of events. Presumptions of fact may concern external conditions (e.g., that the buyer had received the products in good condition) or an internal state of mind (e.g., that the parties do not wish to be bound by a contract unless they comply with a specific form that they previously agreed upon). Presumptions of law are conclusions pertaining to the existence or absence of certain legal relationships, given certain facts. For example, the conclusion of ownership (title) derives from possession. The person having the benefit of a presumption must prove the basis for its application (e.g., that he has a thing under his control). For the conclusion, the burden of proof is shifted in this manner. The opposing party must then overturn the presumption by proving the opposite.

(2) Means of proof

Direct proof covers a fact which needs to be proved, e.g., that the witness was present when the contract was signed. Indirect proof or circumstantial evidence allows conclusions about a fact which needs to be proved; e.g., circumstances can show that a written contract was waived.

The 'main proof' is that which the party with the burden of proof is obliged to demonstrate. The 'corroborating proof' is used by the other party to challenge or weaken the factual assertions made by the first party. The opposing party only has to cast a reasonable doubt on these factual assertions to cause the 'main proof' to fail.

In certain cases (e.g., summary procedures), the law requires only prima facie evidence. The rules concerning the burden of proof specify the consequences if sufficient proof is not supplied: the court will decide against the party who had the burden of proof.

The following is generally admissible evidence: documents, witnesses, local inspections, experts, and, rarely, oaths taken by the parties. In practice, the most important means of proof are documents.

(3) Witnesses and experts

Every person has a duty to appear as a witness in legal proceedings if directed to do so by a court. The parties to the proceedings may not act as witnesses.

Some persons may be excluded as witnesses according to the law: for example, mentally ill or mentally deficient persons, children who have not reached the age of majority, persons convicted of criminal offences, and close relatives.

A witness is obliged to appear only in the canton of his or her domicile. However, according to Art. 7 of the Intercantonal Legal Assistance Concordat, a witness must comply with the summons order of another canton to which the Concordat applies.

The general duty to testify as a witness may be lifted in the event of a conflict of interests recognised by statutory immunity rules. Most cantonal codes of civil procedure grant general immunity to a party's spouse and close relatives.

Other statutory rules allow a witness to refuse to answer certain types of questions, e.g., if the answer might directly prejudice or disadvantage the witness or a close relative. A witness does not have to testify about confidential matters or business secrets. Certain professionals (attorneys, physicians, social workers, marriage counsellors, psychologists) may refuse to answer questions about their clients or patients. A court may allow immunity to be lifted if one party's interest

¶2009

in keeping the matter confidential is outweighed by the other party's interest in proving his case.

All witnesses must appear personally before the court and give their testimony orally. This also applies to witnesses who are permitted by law to refuse to testify, since they must explain their refusal. Any witness who does not appear may be fined or arrested.

Court-appointed experts must be neutral and impartial persons. Since they assist the court, the statutory rules regarding refusal of testimony are applicable to them. Only individuals, not corporations, may act as experts. In specialised courts such as commercial courts, the judges may themselves be experts.

An expert only answers questions within his field of expertise – the expert does not make the decision. This is the duty of the court.

Experts are appointed by the court, although parties may suggest individuals whom they prefer. The questioning of experts is done by the court, although the parties may propose supplementary questions which they wish to be asked. An expert's opinion may be supplied orally or in writing.

¶2010   Court decisions

A court may issue procedural rulings, such as ordering bonds to be posted and deciding whether the parties are to plead orally or in writing.

A judgment on the merits of the case is issued as a final judgment, or as a preliminary or interim judgment. Questions of substantive law (e.g., standing to sue or be sued, time limitations of claims) may be decided in an interim judgment on part of the claim. The judgment on the litigated issue is based on the court's own findings, the parties' express statements (e.g., regarding settlement in court), or the parties' stipulations.

A judgment may be a final judgment if a procedural requirement is not met (e.g., the court does not hear the case), or an interlocutory judgment if the argument requesting an interlocutory decision is rejected. The judgments are based either on the court's own legal findings or, exceptionally, on the parties' statements (e.g., voluntary withdrawal of the claims with or without prejudice). A judgment pertains to the facts as established at the time when the judgment is rendered, not when the claim was initiated.

¶2011   Appeals

Whether or not a party may appeal a judgment depends largely upon the type of claim and the value in dispute. For claims involving financial interests, judgments made by a justice of the peace or mediator, and those of the courts of first instance for less than a specified amount, are considered final and ordinarily may not be appealed. Cases where this specified amount is exceeded may be appealed to a cantonal court. Since an appeal may be filed with the

Federal Supreme Court only when the amount in dispute is greater than SFr 8,000, judgments made by a cantonal appellate court for smaller amounts are final.

In other cases, an extraordinary appeal (action of nullity) may be available against judgments or interlocutory decisions. In this procedure errors in fact finding (which is within the court's discretion) and incorrect application of the law (if the court may follow one of several possible interpretations of the law) cannot be appealed. However, a party need not accept gross errors should they occur.

¶2012   Example: Civil procedure in Geneva

A case is normally initiated by sending a claim in writing to the conciliatory judge. The claim must contain the name of the court, the names and addresses of the parties, the facts and the requests (Art. 7 Code of Civil Procedure). It is possible for the plaintiff to develop his arguments at a later stage.

If the conciliation is of no avail (as it usually is), the plaintiff receives a notice within ten days granting leave to bring his claim before the court of first instance or, in some cases, before the Court of Appeals. A hearing is scheduled immediately. The court decides at this hearing whether an investigation of the case is necessary before the pleadings are introduced. Normally, an investigation will not be made if the case is urgent or if an investigation does not seem to be required by the circumstances.

If the court determines that an investigation must take place, it will set a time limit by which the defendant must submit a reply brief, and a date for the oral pleadings. At this stage, the court can decide to make further inquiries, even if the parties do not specifically request it.

Other hearings related to the needs of the case can be scheduled by the court. It will hear the parties but is not bound by their statements.

The pleadings take place during the last hearing. Before pleading, the parties communicate their conclusions to the court in writing. If an investigation has taken place, its conclusions do not normally differ from those reached in the proceedings. The plaintiff pleads and the defendant answers. The court is free to allow further pleadings if it deems them necessary.

It is the duty of each party to prove the facts of its argument. The court may compel a party to produce documents which it considers relevant, even if the party does not bear the burden of proof.

Unless otherwise ordered, the procedure for hearing evidence is limited to the contested facts. The court can refuse to hear evidence if it is of the opinion that this will require too much time or that the evidence is only intended to delay the judgment. The court has broad discretion to weigh evidence.

The court can hear parties, witnesses and experts, or order other measures which are useful to determine the truth. However, the court is not bound by its orders or their consequences.

A witness who holds a secret (e.g., an attorney, a physician, or a bank officer (see ¶1138(1)) can refuse to answer the questions asked by the court. A witness who testifies must swear or promise to tell the truth.

The court can order an expert to give either an oral opinion or a written report. The court designates the expert and the nature of his task. Normally only one expert is designated, unless the complexity of the case requires three experts. When no written report is required, the expert may be heard at the hearing.

¶2013   Example: Civil procedure in Zurich

A case is generally initiated by a conciliation hearing with the justice of the peace. The request to the justice of the peace to organise a conciliation hearing can be made orally or in writing. The justice of the peace summons the parties to a hearing. In this hearing the parties indicate the amount in dispute, state the facts and submit the evidence that is already available. The justice of the peace acts as a mediator.

If the conciliation hearing is of no avail, the plaintiff receives a notice granting leave to bring the claim before the trial court. The plaintiff must send this notice to the court within three months of the date of its issuance. If the time-limit expires, the plaintiff must request a new conciliation hearing. The plaintiff formulates an oral or written request to the court, indicating the parties, their representatives and the amount in dispute.

The first stage of the procedure, the main procedure (*Hauptverfahren*), is oral if a single judge or the labour court decides, if the lawsuit concerns family law, and, generally, if the amount in dispute does not exceed SFr 12,000. In oral proceedings, every party has the right to two statements: complaint and reply (plaintiff) and answer and rejoinder (defendant). The facts must be presented specifically and in detail. The defendant gives his or her own statement of facts and/or denies the facts alleged by the plaintiff. Both parties indicate the evidence and submit the evidence available to them. If the main procedure is in writing, the plaintiff submits the complaint which contains all the facts and a list of the evidence. The court then sets a time-limit for the defendant to answer the complaint. Reply and rejoinder may be given orally or in writing if the case is complicated.

After the main procedure has finished, the court administers the evidence in the evidentiary procedure (*Beweisverfahren*) by a court order (*Beweis-auflagebeschluss*), saying which facts must be proved by which party and indicating the time limit by which the parties must list the evidence and send the documents of evidence (*Beweismittel*) that are available to the parties (*Beweisantretungsschrift*). The procedure for hearing evidence is limited to the contested facts.

After the parties have sent their lists of evidence and documents of evidence that are already available to the court, the court decides which evidence will be accepted (*Beweisabnahme*). The court may hear parties, witnesses and experts. The court may order inspections (*Augenschein*) or expert testimonies (*Gutachten*). A witness who holds a secret can, or must, refuse to answer the questions asked by the court. After the termination of this stage of the proceedings, the parties have the right to express their opinions (orally or in writing) on the result of the evidentiary procedure.

Finally, the court decides the case and provides the parties with the written judgment. The judgment contains the facts and the legal grounds; it indicates whether the parties have a right to challenge the judgment by an appeal or only by a plea in nullity.

¶2014 Attachment as a basis of jurisdiction

Assets located in Switzerland and owned by debtors who do not have a domicile in Switzerland may be subject to attachment. Claims secured by a mortgage or by a pledge cannot be attached. The creditor seeking an attachment must send a request for attachment to the court (usually a single judge) at the site of the property to be attached. The attaching creditor must provide prima facie evidence supporting the existence of the claim and the assets to be attached. Then, in most cantons, the court issues an order of attachment in summary, ex parte proceedings. If the court determines that the claim appears to be weak, or if the attachment is likely to harm the debtor, it may require the attaching creditor to post a bond, usually 10 per cent of the claim to be secured by the attachment. 'Fishing expeditions' (attachment of all banks where assets are suspected) are not allowed. After execution of the attachment by the local office of debt collection, the debtor – who as a result of the execution learns for the first time that his assets are subject to attachment – may ask the court to set aside the order. He may also sue the creditor for damages caused by an unjustified attachment.

If the creditor has not previously instituted legal or execution proceedings for his claim, he must institute execution proceedings within ten days after receiving a document confirming that an attachment has been effected. If the debtor contests the claim in execution proceedings, the creditor must initiate court action again within ten days. The creditor has the option of bringing an action against a non-resident debtor at the location where the assets were attached or at any other court that has jurisdiction over the debtor (*forum arresti*, Art. 4 PIL). For the Lugano Convention, see ¶1919.

RECOGNITION AND ENFORCEMENT OF DECISIONS

¶2015   Swiss and non-Swiss judgments distinguished

Judgments rendered by a Swiss court in civil actions are recognised and enforced in all cantons and have *res judicata* effect, provided that they have been rendered by a competent court, that the defendant has been duly notified, and that the judgment has become final.

Foreign judgments in matters of private law are recognised and enforced in Switzerland in accordance with bilateral international treaties signed by Switzerland with other countries such as Italy, France and Germany. Otherwise, they are recognised and enforced under the Private International Law Statute.

In general, foreign decisions are recognised in Switzerland if the foreign court had jurisdiction (pursuant to Swiss law) to render a decision, the court order has become final, and the order is not in violation of public policy. Violation of public policy may exist, for example, if the defendant was denied the right to be heard, if legal proceedings between the same parties concerning the same case had already been initiated or decided in Switzerland, or if the foreign court was improperly seized of the matter and the party to be charged did not enter an unconditional appearance.

Under Swiss law, jurisdiction lies with a foreign court if the defendant has his domicile in the country where the judgment was rendered, or if a specific provision of Swiss law provides for the jurisdiction of the foreign court. Foreign jurisdiction also lies with a foreign court if the parties involved in a dispute of financial interest agreed to subject themselves to the jurisdiction of the foreign court which rendered the judgment, if the defendant entered an unconditional appearance, or if a counterclaim related to the principal claim was dealt with in the judgment.

A judgment recognisable under Swiss law is declared enforceable upon application by the party who stands to benefit from it.

INTERNATIONAL JUDICIAL ASSISTANCE IN CIVIL MATTERS

¶2016   Sources of the law

In the absence of any treaty provisions to the contrary, testimony or service of process in civil matters can be obtained in Switzerland through 'letters rogatory' (see ¶2017). This is true regardless of the nationality of the witness or person to be served, and regardless of whether he or she agrees to be examined as a witness or to be served. In addition, under the Swiss Penal Code (Art. 271) attorneys seeking to obtain statements from witnesses (depositions) or to serve process in Switzerland without involvement of the competent Swiss court, are subject to criminal charges (ATF 114 IV 128).

Switzerland is a member of the 1954 Hague Convention on Civil Procedure. In contrast, Switzerland has neither signed nor ratified the 1965 Hague Convention on Service Abroad of Judicial and Extrajudicial Documents, or the 1970 Hague Convention on the Taking of Evidence Abroad in Civil and Commercial Matters. Switzerland has, however, signed a number of bilateral treaties. Thus, with respect to some countries, requests for civil assistance may be granted on the basis of comity and reciprocity. This assistance is granted only in civil matters. The Swiss definition of 'civil' differs from that of most common law countries. Civil assistance can be allowed, for instance, whenever a private entity sues another private entity for violation of cartel law, but not when a foreign court seeks the assistance of the Swiss authorities in a tax matter.

¶2017 Procedure for letters rogatory

A letter rogatory is a request from a foreign court to a corresponding court in Switzerland. The letter of request may be addressed to 'the appropriate judicial authority in Switzerland', and must be issued and signed by the responsible foreign court. The request should contain a summary of the reasons for the action brought before the foreign court and clearly describe the nature of the assistance requested, in terms understandable to court officers and judges in Switzerland. The Swiss court will decide whether to proceed with the letter rogatory based on its understanding of the facts of the case. The letter rogatory must be translated into the official language of the receiving canton (for instance, into German for Zurich, Berne or Basel; into French for Geneva or Lausanne; or into Italian for Ticino).

Letters rogatory issued by a United States court should be sent, together with a translation, to the Department of State, Washington, DC. The State Department will then forward these documents to the United States embassy in Berne, Switzerland. In turn, the embassy will forward the documents to the (Swiss) Ministry of Justice, which will transmit them to the appropriate court in Switzerland. After the request has been executed, the documents are returned to the embassy via the same chain of Swiss authorities. The embassy will return the envelope to the Department of State, which will forward the documents to the appropriate court.

The cantonal authorities, who receive the request from the Federal Office of Police, will apply their own cantonal code of civil procedure.

When the foreign litigation is of an administrative nature as defined by Swiss law, the issue becomes complex. A number of treaties, such as those on avoidance of double taxation or social security, provide for a certain amount of co-operation between the signatories. In addition, there is a certain amount of informal co-operation between supervisory authorities, such as banking authorities. When there is no treaty, judicial assistance in administrative matters may be granted on a case-by-case basis. Once again, it should be stressed that some administrative matters in Switzerland are considered civil matters in common law countries, and vice versa.

¶2018   Swiss secrecy laws – obtaining evidence from Switzerland

Swiss secrecy laws are sometimes considered an obstacle to the administration of justice. In Switzerland the basis for secrecy lies in the law of contracts. In addition, in many cases secrecy is protected by penal law. Banking secrecy is protected under Art. 47 of the Federal Banking Statute. Business and manufacturing secrets are protected under Art. 162 of the Swiss Penal Code. For a foreign party who wishes to obtain evidence within Switzerland, Art. 47 of the Federal Banking Statute and Arts 162 and 273 of the Swiss Penal Code are of particular interest.

Whenever a party is requested to testify at a hearing or hand over documents to a court, there are certain limitations when the information requested by the other party is considered a business or manufacturing secret. Federal and cantonal law provides that evidence disclosed by one party may be rendered accessible to the other party only to the extent compatible with the preservation of any secrets contained therein. Business secrets must be disclosed only if it is necessary to do so.

A party who requests documents must tell the judge its reasons for requesting the documents. If a third party is examined as a witness or requested to produce documents, a legal privilege may be invoked with regard to the hearing of evidence. Some cantonal codes of civil procedure grant immunity from testifying for reasons of professional secrecy, irrespective of the witness's profession. Most cantonal codes of civil procedure stipulate that there is an obligation to produce a document in so far as the document may be useful in proving a fact which is relevant to the case being heard.

There is no statutory definition of banking secrecy. Legal writers think that rules of non-disclosure cover all contracts between banks and their customers, any information given by customers concerning their economic situation, and other information on their transactions with the bank.

The banking secrecy rules cover the identity of third parties with whom the customer transacts business. A bank is not even permitted to say whether or not a certain individual has an account with the bank. Bank customers may waive their right to confidentiality if they so desire.

Pursuant to Art. 273 of the Penal Code, anyone who makes a Swiss banking, manufacturing or business secret available to a foreign authority may be punished. This article is designed to protect Swiss sovereignty and to safeguard the security of the Swiss economy at large. Article 273 applies only when the information has a sufficient domestic connection. The prevailing view is that a person giving information must decide whether it should be disclosed. He needs to consider whether the information concerns facts which only he has an interest in not disclosing.

Article 273 of the Penal Code makes it an offence to furnish financial information to foreign entities when there is a direct and general Swiss interest in its non-disclosure, or when a third party who has not submitted a formal request to disclose has a legitimate interest in non-disclosure. If a foreign court orders a Swiss company to provide confidential information, the company may ask third parties who are involved whether they agree to the disclosure. If no agreement is given, or if Swiss interests are at stake, the company may not furnish that information. The only way in which a foreign court may overcome this barrier is to request international judicial assistance from the Swiss judicial authorities.

Direct service of process by mail from abroad is improper and illegal under Art. 271 of the Penal Code. In addition, improper service may render any judgment made by a foreign court unenforceable in Switzerland.

In many countries, evidence may be gathered without restrictions by foreign parties to a civil action. However, in Switzerland the gathering of evidence for use in a foreign proceeding may be considered an official act within the meaning of Art. 271 of the Penal Code (¶2016). Permission is granted by the Federal Department of Justice if there are compelling reasons for the foreign officials or attorneys to gather evidence or examine witnesses in Switzerland.

SELECTED BIBLIOGRAPHY

Bernard Bertossa, Louis Gaillard and Jacques Guyet, *Commentaire de la loi de la procédure civile de Genève du 10 avril 1987* (Genève 1989)

Hans Giger, *Handbuch der Schweizerischen Zivilrechtspflege* (Zürich, 1990)

Max Guldener, *Schweizerisches Zivilprozessrecht*, 3rd edn (Zürich, 1979)

Walther J. Habscheid, *Droit judiciaire privé suisse*, 2nd edn (Genève, 1981)

Jean-René H. Mermoud, *Loi de procédure civile genevoise annotée* (Genève, 1988)

Jean-François Poudret, *Commentaire de la loi fédérale d'organisation judiciaire* (Bern, 1990), Articles 1 to 74

Suzette Sandoz-Monod, *Commentaire de la loi fédérale d'organisation judiciaire* (Bern, 1990), Articles 75 to 82

Hans Sträuli and Georg Messmer, *Kommentar zur Zürcherischen Zivilprozessordnung*, 2nd edn (Zürich, 1982)

Oscar Vogel, *Grundriss des Zivilprozessrechts*, 2nd edn (Bern, 1988)

¶2018

21 International and Domestic Arbitration

PRINCIPAL LEGISLATION

Loi fédérale sur le droit international privé/Gesetz über das internationale Privatrecht/Swiss Private International Law Statute, RS 291 (translated by Pierre A. Karrer and Karl W. Arnold, *Switzerland's Private International Statute 1987*, (Deventer, 1989)).

Convention pour la reconnaissance et l'exécution des sentences arbitrales étrangères (conclue à New York le 10 juin 1958) Convention on the Recognition and Enforcement of Foreign Arbitral Awards (New York Convention), RS 0.277.12.

Concordat sur l'arbitrage/Konkordat über die Schiedsgerichtsbarkeit/Swiss Intercantonal Concordat on Arbitration, RS 279 (translated by Pierre A. Karrer and Karl W. Arnold, *Switzerland's Private International Statute 1987* (Deventer, 1989)).

INTRODUCTION

¶2101 Types of arbitration

(1) International arbitration
Switzerland is a popular place for international arbitration between non-Swiss parties, and has been for a long time. The reasons are numerous. First, in many international contracts, the parties have chosen Swiss law to govern the contract, quite often because they feel that the contract should be governed by the law of a country which has no close connection to either of the parties to the contract. In these cases, it appears logical for the resolution of any dispute to take place in the country whose law governs the contract. Secondly, Switzerland is a place which can provide excellent logistical support for international arbitration, such as experienced arbitrators and staff with multilingual capabilities, flexible

arbitration rules, and advanced telecommunications. The intervention of local courts is limited or can be excluded. In addition, the positive impact of the Private International Law Statute, which governs international arbitration and provides a favourable environment for international dispute resolution, makes Switzerland a suitable place for international arbitration for practical, legal and psychological reasons.

(2) Domestic arbitration
In the Private International Law Statute, which came into effect on 1 January 1989, domestic arbitration (between parties registered or domiciled in Switzerland) is distinguished from international arbitration.

To a large extent, the cantonal law on domestic arbitration is now unified. All cantons, with the exception of Lucerne, have adopted the same arbitration legislation, the intercantonal Arbitration Convention of 27 March 1969, hereinafter referred to as the 'Concordat'.

(3) Role of Chambers of Commerce
A number of Chambers of Commerce offer services and arbitration rules which are designed for the needs of international and domestic arbitration. The most important of them are as follows:

Bern Chamber of Commerce, Bundesgasse 32, 3011 Bern

Geneva Chamber of Commerce and Industry, 4, Boulevard du Théâtre, 1204 Genève

Zurich Chamber of Commerce, Bleicherweg 5, 8001 Zürich

INTERNATIONAL ARBITRATION

¶2102 International and domestic arbitration distinguished: Seat of arbitration

(1) Principle
International arbitration in Switzerland is governed by the new provisions of Chapter 12 of the Swiss Private International Law Statute (PIL Statute). Unless stated otherwise, all Articles mentioned in this chapter are from this statute.

Article 176 of the PIL Statute states that Chapter 12 applies to arbitration if the seat of the arbitral tribunal is in Switzerland and at least one of the parties had neither its domicile nor its habitual residence in Switzerland when the arbitration agreement was concluded.

Under the PIL Statute, the domicile of an individual is in the country in which he or she is living with the intention of residing permanently (Art. 20). A person has his or her habitual residence at the place where he or she is living for a certain time, even if this time is limited from the outset (Art. 20 PIL Statute). Companies are domiciled at their seat. The seat of a company is designated by its Articles of Incorporation or, in the absence of a designation, at the place where the company is managed (Art. 21 PIL Statute).

Article 176(2) of the PIL Statute allows parties to exclude the application of Chapter 12 altogether. If the parties wish to arbitrate under the Concordat, they must simultaneously and expressly (a) exclude Chapter 12 and (b) stipulate the applicability of the Concordat in the arbitration clause or in the agreement (see ATF 115 II 393).

A dispute between two Swiss companies on an international project outside Switzerland is not considered an international arbitration.

(2) Seat of arbitration

The seat of the arbitral tribunal is determined by the parties, the arbitral institution designated by them, or, failing both, by the arbitral tribunal (Art. 176(3) PIL Statute). The ordinary court at the seat of the arbitration may appoint arbitrators where the full tribunal has not been nominated and decide on challenges of arbitrators where the parties have not provided for an arbitral institution to do so. It may also provide various types of assistance to the arbitral tribunal, e.g., for interlocutory injunctions or letters rogatory for the hearing of evidence. The seat of the arbitration determines the remedies, if any, against arbitral awards.

The determination of the seat of the arbitral tribunal does not prevent the arbitral tribunal from meeting in other places that are more convenient or appropriate.

¶2103   Arbitrability

Any dispute involving financial interests may be arbitrated. Article 177 of the PIL Statute reflects a broad concept of arbitrability. Arbitration is not limited to 'commercial' disputes; rather, any dispute of a financial nature can be the object of arbitration, whether or not it arises from private or public law (for the distinction see ¶107), or from a domestic or international law relationship. For instance, claims for patents and trade marks are arbitrable under Swiss law. Likewise, creditors' claims in bankruptcy procedures are arbitrable.

A state or state-controlled enterprise may not invoke its own law to override its promise to arbitrate on the grounds of sovereign immunity or lack of arbitrability of the dispute (Art. 177(2) PIL Statute). This clause spells out the principle that it would constitute contradictory, and hence abusive, behaviour to sign a contract containing the arbitration clause and thereafter invoke sovereign immunity.

¶2104 Arbitration agreements

(1) Validity of arbitration agreement and clauses

An arbitration agreement, be it an arbitration clause in a contract or an agreement to submit an already existing dispute to arbitration, is valid if made in writing, by telegram, telex, fax or by any other form of communication which permits it to be evidenced by a text. Furthermore, an arbitration agreement is valid if it conforms either to the law chosen by the parties, the law governing the subject matter of the dispute (e.g., the main contract), or Swiss law. The validity of an arbitration agreement cannot be contested on the grounds that the main contract is invalid or that the arbitration agreement concerns a dispute which has not yet arisen. It is essential to state a specific geographical location (for instance, Basel, Geneva or Zurich) as the seat of the arbitral tribunal, or to refer to an arbitration institution such as the previously-mentioned Chambers of Commerce.

Examples of suitable arbitration clauses are shown in (2) to (5) below:

(2) Clause for '*ad hoc*' arbitration

'Any disputes between the parties arising out of or in connection with this agreement, in particular as to its conclusion, existence, validity, interpretation, performance or non-performance, breach, termination or assessment of damages, whether arising before or after the termination of the agreement, shall be referred to, and determined by an *ad hoc* arbitral tribunal consisting of three arbitrators. The arbitral tribunal will have its seat in Zurich, Switzerland.'

(3) Clause recommended by the International Chamber of Commerce (ICC):

'All disputes arising in connection with the present contract shall be finally settled under the Rules of Conciliation and Arbitration of the International Chamber of Commerce by one or more arbitrators appointed in accordance with the said Rules.'

(4)   Clauses recommended by the Zurich Chamber of Commerce:

(a)   Clause providing for appointment of all three arbitrators by the Zurich Chamber of Commerce

'All disputes arising out of or in connection with the present agreement, including disputes on its conclusion, binding effect, amendment and termination, shall be resolved, to the exclusion of the ordinary courts, by a three-person Arbitral Tribunal in accordance with the International Arbitration Rules of the Zurich Chamber of Commerce. (Optional: The decision of the Arbitral Tribunal shall be final, and the parties waive all challenge of the award in accordance with Article 192 of the Private International Law Statute.)'

(b)   Clause providing for appointment of arbitrators by the parties

'All disputes arising out of or in connection with the present agreement, including disputes on its conclusion, binding effect, amendment and termination, shall be resolved, to the exclusion of the ordinary courts, by a three-person Arbitral Tribunal in accordance with the International Arbitration Rules of the Zurich Chamber of Commerce. If there are not more than two parties involved in the procedure, each party nominates an arbitrator. (Optional: The decision of the Arbitral Tribunal shall be final, and the parties waive all challenge of the award in accordance with Article 192 of the Private International Law Statute.)'

(5)   Clause recommended by the Geneva Chamber of Commerce and Industry

'Any dispute arising in connection with the present contract which the parties are unable to settle by mutual agreement shall be finally settled by an Arbitral Tribunal composed of three arbitrators and constituted by the Geneva Chamber of Commerce and Industry in accordance with the Arbitration Directives.'

(6)   Optional elements of an arbitration clause

The parties may agree on the method for appointing the arbitrators. For instance, they may agree on the nationality or professional background of the arbitrators to be appointed by the parties, or the authority who will appoint them.

The parties may wish to determine the language of the proceedings. They may do so as follows in the arbitration clause:

'The arbitral proceedings shall be conducted in the . . . language. However, documents may also be filed or submitted in the following languages without a translation: . . . Witnesses and experts may be examined without simultaneous translation in the following languages: . . .'

If both parties have their domiciles or seats outside Switzerland, the parties may expressly agree to exclude an action for annulment. They may do so as follows:

'The arbitral award shall be final; in the sense of Article 192(1) of the Private International Law Statute, the parties exclude any and all actions for annulment of the award.'

If the contract is concluded with a state or a state-controlled organisation, the arbitration clause may include a waiver of sovereign immunity so as to facilitate enforcement outside Switzerland.

¶2105   Setting up the arbitral tribunal

The arbitrators are appointed in accordance with the agreement of the parties (Art. 179 PIL Statute). In the absence of an agreement, the court where the tribunal has its seat may be charged with the appointment of the arbitrators. If a court has been designated as the authority responsible for appointing an arbitrator, it shall make the appointment unless a cursory examination shows that no arbitration agreement exists between the parties.

In the case of an ICC arbitration, the International Court of Arbitration of the ICC does not itself settle disputes; rather, it appoints and confirms the appointment of arbitrators if the parties do not provide otherwise. The parties may nominate one or more arbitrators for confirmation by the International Court of Arbitration of the ICC. When three arbitrators are required, each party nominates its own arbitrator, and the International Court of Arbitration of the ICC appoints the third arbitrator, possibly on the proposal of the two appointed arbitrators. If the parties fail to nominate an arbitrator within a specified period of time, the International Court of Arbitration of the ICC may appoint one.

If arbitration is referred to the Zurich Chamber of Commerce and if the parties have not expressly agreed on the number of arbitrators, the President of the Chamber decides whether a sole arbitrator or a three-person arbitral tribunal shall be appointed, independently of any nomination of an arbitrator by the claimant. If the value of a litigation exceeds SFr 1,000,000 and the parties have not expressly provided for a sole arbitrator, a three-person arbitral tribunal is appointed. For multi-party arbitration, a three-person arbitral tribunal is appointed. The Board of the Zurich Chamber of Commerce appoints eight or more experienced lawyers and/or judges as permanent chairmen of the arbitral tribunal. For each arbitration, the President of the Chamber of Commerce appoints one of the permanent chairmen as chairman or sole arbitrator. In special cases, the President of the Zurich Chamber of Commerce may appoint another suitable person as chairman of the Arbitral Tribunal or as sole arbitrator. If there are multiple parties, or if the parties did not provide that they would themselves appoint the arbitrators, the chairman of the arbitral tribunal appoints co-arbitrators from a list of four or more names submitted to him or her by the President of the Chamber of Commerce.

¶2106 Challenge of an arbitrator

An arbitrator can be challenged only if the arbitral tribunal is notified of the grounds for challenge without delay (Art. 180 PIL Statute). The procedure for challenging an arbitrator is governed in the first place by the parties' agreement. In the case of an ICC arbitration, the ICC has jurisdiction to rule on a challenge of an arbitrator. Pursuant to the International Arbitration Rules of the Zurich Chamber of Commerce, an arbitral supervisory commission has the final right of decision if an arbitrator contests the challenge.

¶2107 Decision on jurisdiction

The arbitral tribunal decides on its own jurisdiction. The validity of an arbitration agreement cannot be contested on the grounds that the main contract may be invalid (principle of severability of the arbitration clause, Art. 178 PIL Statute). Any objections to the tribunal's jurisdiction must be raised prior to any defence on the merits of the case. The arbitral tribunal will, as a rule, decide on its jurisdiction by a preliminary award. Whenever an arbitration agreement exists prima facie, the arbitral tribunal has the authority to decide on its own jurisdiction. If the arbitral tribunal decides its jurisdiction by a preliminary award, any action for annulment of its verdict must be instituted immediately (Art. 190 PIL Statute).

If there is no arbitration agreement, a respondent is deemed to have entered an unconditional appearance unless it pleads lack of jurisdiction prior to any defence on the merits of the case.

¶2108 *'Lis pendens'* in arbitration

There is *'lis pendens'* when one of the parties submits its request to the arbitrator or initiates the procedure for the constitution of the arbitral tribunal.

¶2109 Procedure before the arbitral tribunal

The parties have ample authority to determine the arbitral procedure.

To the extent that the parties have not determined the procedure themselves, it is determined by the arbitral tribunal (principle of liberty of the arbitral tribunal). The arbitral tribunal is in no way required to apply local procedural law. The arbitral tribunal will determine, for instance, the number of written submissions which each party may file, the number of hearings and pleadings, and the presence or absence of evidence at the proceedings. It will also determine the presentation of witnesses, written affidavits of witnesses, the appointment of experts, the language in which documents may be filed without translation, and the means by which the parties and the arbitral tribunal may communicate.

Whichever rules are applicable, the principle of equal treatment of the parties and the right of both parties to be heard must be respected.

The arbitral tribunal may, at the request of a party, order provisional or conservatory measures. If a party does not comply voluntarily with the order, the arbitral tribunal may request the assistance of the local court (Art. 183 PIL Statute). The arbitral tribunal does not have exclusive competence to issue provisional and conservatory measures: the petitioner may seek appropriate measures from any court. A request for the measures addressed to a court is not a violation of the arbitration agreement.

The taking of evidence is conducted by the arbitral tribunal. Where the assistance of state courts is needed for the taking of evidence, the arbitral tribunal may request the assistance of the court at the seat of the arbitral tribunal. Evidence may be taken in the way deemed most suitable by the parties and the arbitral tribunal. The parties may be requested to produce written witness statements; the arbitral tribunal may examine witnesses or allow examination and cross-examination by the parties.

¶2110　Decision on the merits

The arbitral tribunal primarily decides the case according to the law chosen by the parties. Swiss arbitration law recognises the choice of law made by the parties without limitation.

In the absence of a choice, Swiss international arbitration law states a conflict of laws rule. The arbitral tribunal must decide the matter according to the rules of law with which the case has the closest connection. The first eleven chapters of the PIL Statute do not apply.

The parties may authorise the arbitral tribunal to decide *ex aequo et bono* (Art. 187(2) PIL Statute).

If the parties reach settlement, this is usually formalised in a consent award. Unless the parties have agreed otherwise, the arbitral tribunal may render partial awards (Art. 188 PIL Statute). A partial award is, in a large sense, an award which adjudicates a portion of the claims or counterclaims submitted to the arbitral tribunal; it can be a decision with respect to a factual or legal issue.

The arbitral award is rendered according to the rules of procedure agreed upon by the parties. In the absence of an agreement, the arbitral award is rendered by a majority decision or, in the absence of a majority, by the chairman alone. It is made in writing, supported by articulated reasons, dated and signed (Art. 189 PIL Statute). The parties may waive their right to a reasoned award. It is generally admitted that an arbitrator may render a dissenting opinion.

The award includes a statement of the arbitrators' costs and the fees charged to each party. In accordance with Swiss practice, the arbitral tribunal will impose costs on the losing party and grant legal expenses to the winning party.

¶2111   Remedies against the award in international arbitration

The award or partial award in its final form is communicated to the parties.

Parties to an international arbitration who are neither domiciled nor have a business establishment in Switzerland may exclude any action for annulment before the Swiss courts by an express stipulation in the arbitration agreement or a subsequent agreement (Art. 192(1) PIL Statute).

If no exclusion has been stipulated, an award may be set aside upon action for annulment only for the following reasons:

(1) the sole arbitrator has not been properly appointed;

(2) the arbitral tribunal has not been properly constituted;

(3) the arbitral tribunal has wrongly accepted or declined jurisdiction;

(4) the award has gone beyond the claims submitted to the arbitral tribunal;

(5) the tribunal has failed to decide one of the claims;

(6) the principle of equal treatment of the parties or the right to be heard in adversary proceedings has not been observed; or

(7) the award is contrary to public policy.

The time-limit for bringing any action for annulment is 30 days from the time of the communication of the award; this deadline cannot be extended. Communication is effected upon delivery of the award to the party.

An action for annulment of a partial award does not suspend the arbitral proceedings.

¶2112   Zurich Chamber of Commerce international arbitration

(1)   General provisions of Zurich rules of arbitration

The Zurich Chamber of Commerce traditionally provides arbitration facilities to both Swiss and foreign parties. The International Arbitration Rules of 1 January 1989 ('Zurich Rules') contain a complete guide to procedure in 60 articles and a separate schedule of arbitration costs.

The Zurich Rules apply if at least one of the parties had either its registered or actual seat, his or her domicile or habitual residence outside Switzerland when the arbitration agreement was signed (Art. 1 Zurich Rules).

The arbitral tribunal decides the case according to the substantive law declared applicable by the parties. If the parties have not chosen an applicable law, the arbitral tribunal decides the case according to the law that applies pursuant to the rules of the Private International Law Statute. If the application of the private international law at the seat, domicile or habitual residence of all parties leads to a different result, the case must be decided on the motion of one of the parties.

The seat of the arbitral tribunal is Zurich, but the President of the Zurich Chamber of Commerce may designate another venue if this is required or deemed desirable. The tribunal may conduct meetings and hearings in places other than the venue.

The parties may empower the arbitral tribunal to make its award *ex aequo et bono*.

As previously discussed, there are exhaustive rules concerning the setting up of the arbitral tribunal (¶2105) (Art. 10 et seq. Zurich Rules).

(2) Procedure before the arbitral tribunal

After hearing the parties, the sole arbitrator or the arbitral tribunal issues an initial order specifying some procedural details, such as the form and number of briefs and documents to be submitted by the parties, the language(s) for the proceedings, and a deadline by which the claimant must submit a detailed complaint with exhibits or, if a detailed complaint already exists, a deadline for the respondent to submit a written answer with exhibits. In addition, the order may provide for a time-limit by which the parties must pay advances and the consequences of non-compliance (Art. 20 Zurich Rules).

The chairman leads the arbitration. He or she may direct the parties to make cash deposits, call meetings, and set or extend time-limits. He or she represents the arbitral tribunal *vis-à-vis* the courts, the authorities, and the Zurich Chamber of Commerce.

The arbitral tribunal determines the languages that must be used in written communications and in hearings. Usually proceedings are conducted in the language of the arbitration agreements; the parties may arrange at their own risk and expense for their own translators and interpreters.

Parties may be represented or counselled before the arbitral tribunal by practising lawyers and other individuals. In the case of a difficult or time-consuming notification, the tribunal may order a party to appoint an authorised representative for notification at a suitable place.

A plea that the arbitral tribunal lacks jurisdiction must be raised at the latest in the respondent's answer on the merits (Art. 25 Zurich Rules). The arbitral tribunal decides – usually by interim award – on its own jurisdiction after hearing the party. Counterclaims must generally be raised in the answer. With the agreement of the claimant, they may be raised at a later date (Art. 26 Zurich Rules).

If not expressly excluded by the parties, the arbitral tribunal may order, on the motion of a party, provisional or conservatory measures in accordance with Article 183 of the Private International Law Statute (Art. 28 Zurich Rules).

The complaint and the answer (as well as the counterclaim and the answer to the counterclaim, if any) must be in writing. In the complaint, the prayers for relief and the amount of the claim must be specified, and all factual and legal grounds must be given in detail. In the answer, the respondent must respond in detail to the claims made against him. Evidence must be offered with precision, witnesses must be identified by name, and the documents available must be submitted with the required number of copies, together with a schedule of documents. As a rule, after these briefs have been submitted, the tribunal holds an informal hearing and discusses further proceedings with the parties.

The arbitral tribunal can set deadlines. Requests for extensions of deadlines must be submitted before the deadline in question has expired. The party should specify the length of the requested extension. If a party fails to submit a brief before the deadline expires, or fails to appear at the hearing without adequate excuse, the arbitral tribunal may restore the deadline, set a new deadline, or call a new hearing and specify the consequence of failure to comply (Art. 32 Zurich Rules). If a party fails to comply once more, the tribunal may deem the factual allegations of the other party to be undisputed or may investigate the matter on its own.

To continue the main proceedings, the chairman sets a deadline for reply and rejoinder, and for reply and rejoinder on the counterclaim, if any; he or she can call a hearing with the parties. For special reasons, further exchanges of briefs or a hearing may be ordered (Art. 33 Zurich Rules). The main proceedings are concluded with the receipt of the last brief or with the last oral pleading. New or modified motions, allegations of fact, defences and denials are no longer admissible (Art. 34 Zurich Rules). At a later date, new motions, allegations of fact, defences and/or denials can be brought before the tribunal for special reasons only; or, exceptionally, new or amended claims can be admitted if the legal position of the other party is not appreciably worsened, and the proceedings are not unnecessarily lengthened.

The arbitral tribunal makes its findings of fact in adversary proceedings (Art. 35 et seq. Zurich Rules). Usually, it administers proof after the main proceedings are concluded. The arbitral tribunal may order oral testimony by witnesses (Art. 36 et seq. Zurich Rules) or make a local inspection to ascertain relevant facts. Parties may submit experts' written reports. The arbitral tribunal may, on its own initiative or on the motion of one party, question one or more experts orally or in writing. The parties are given an opportunity to raise

¶2112

objections against the persons proposed as experts and may pose questions to an expert (Art. 40 Zurich Rules). The parties and persons who have been appointed as experts by the tribunal or who have been proposed as such, may not communicate directly with each other. Each party may call upon the other to supply the arbitral tribunal with specified documents relevant to the dispute between the parties (Art. 42 Zurich Rules).

The arbitral tribunal may, in case of refusal or on its own motion, order the production of documents.

The parties are given the opportunity to comment on the evidence (Art. 43 Zurich Rules). The tribunal is free to assess the evidence. It takes into consideration the conduct of the parties during the procedure, especially any refusals to co-operate in giving evidence.

(3) Award

The arbitral tribunal deliberates in closed chambers and decides by a simple majority vote. If no majority can be found, the chairman decides alone; he or she may not award more than the highest motion of the other arbitrators, nor less than the lowest (Art. 46 Zurich Rules).

The award must be made in writing and contain reasons, unless the parties have expressly waived this requirement (Art. 47 Zurich Rules). The arbitral award is issued by notification to the parties and becomes final immediately. The award may not be challenged if the parties who do not reside in Switzerland have, by an express declaration in the arbitration agreement or in a later written agreement, excluded all challenges to the award (see Art. 192 PIL Statute). Otherwise, the award may be challenged only on the grounds enumerated in Art. 190 of the Private International Law Statute.

A copy of the award and the record shall be kept for at least ten years by the Zurich Chamber of Commerce, unless the record is given to the parties (Art. 50 Zurich Rules). All participants in the proceedings must keep the proceedings and the award confidential from uninvolved third parties and the public in general.

¶2113   Arbitration fees

Normally, the arbitral tribunal determines the arbitrators' fees.

(1) Fees in ICC arbitration

For arbitrations under ICC rules, the fee is determined by the ICC Court of Arbitration, not by the arbitral tribunal.

For ICC arbitrations to be decided by one arbitrator and involving an amount in dispute of US$ 100,000, the ICC administrative fee and the arbitrator's fee will be up to US$ 11,500. For an arbitration with a panel of three arbitrators involving an amount in dispute of US$ 1,000,000, the ICC administrative fee and the arbitrators' fee will be up to US$ 105,000. This maximum will rise to about US$ 265,000 for cases where the amount in dispute is US$ 10,000,000.

(2)   Fees in Zurich Chamber of Commerce arbitration
For Zurich Chamber of Commerce arbitrations, where the amount in dispute is US$ 70,000 and is to be decided by one arbitrator, the fee (registration fee and arbitration fee) will be up to US$ 9,000. For an arbitration where the amount in dispute is US$ 700,000 and is to be decided by a panel of three arbitrators, the fee will be up to US$80,000. For an arbitration where the amount in dispute is US$ 7,000,000 and is to be decided by panel of three arbitrators, the fee will be up to about US$ 80,000.

DOMESTIC ARBITRATION

¶2114   Source of law: Concordat

The intercantonal Concordat (*Concordat sur l'arbitrage/Konkordat über die Schiedsgerichtsbarkeit*: see ¶2101(2)) applies to arbitration proceedings before any arbitral tribunal with its seat in any canton, except for Lucerne, provided that none of the parties involved has its seat or his or her domicile outside Switzerland. Although the Concordat, an agreement entered into by all cantons except Lucerne, is applicable uniformly in most of Switzerland, it is cantonal, not federal, law.

The most important part of the Concordat concerns the organisation of domestic arbitration. There are some basic procedural rules, but they are not an exhaustive procedural ordinance.

¶2115   Appointment and removal of arbitrators

The seat of the arbitral tribunal is at the place chosen by agreement between the parties, by a decision of the body designated by them or by decision of the arbitrators. Any right at the free disposal of the parties is arbitrable. The agreement to arbitrate an already existing or a future dispute must be in writing, which means that it must be signed. If the validity or content of the agreement to arbitrate is challenged before the arbitral tribunal, the tribunal decides on its own jurisdiction by an interim or final award. A plea of lack of jurisdiction must be raised prior to any défence on the merits (Art. 8 Concordat).

The arbitral tribunal consists of three arbitrators, unless the parties have agreed on a different number (which must be odd, not even) or on a sole arbitrator. The parties may designate the arbitrator or arbitrators by common consent. They may specify that the arbitrator(s) be designated by a body of their choice, such as the Zurich or Geneva Chamber of Commerce. If the parties cannot agree on the designation of a sole arbitrator, the supreme court of the canton in which the seat of the arbitration is located will make the appointment. The parties may challenge an arbitrator on any of the grounds that are provided in the federal law for the challenge and withdrawal of federal judges. An arbitrator may be removed by written agreement of the parties.

¶2116   Procedure before the arbitral tribunal

The procedural rules for an arbitration are determined by agreement between the parties or, if there is no agreement, by decision of the arbitral tribunal. The Federal Code of Civil Procedure (*loi fédérale de procédure civile fédérale/ Bundesgesetz über den Bundeszivilprozess* – RS 273) applies to fill gaps. The procedural rules selected must always respect the principle of equality of the parties. The rules must allow the parties sufficient time to review the relevant files, exercise their rights, present their factual and legal arguments, participate in the hearings for the taking of evidence, and be represented or assisted by a representative of their choice. All these terms are fulfilled if the parties wish to proceed under the Conciliation and Arbitration Rules of the Zurich Chamber of Commerce, which have been in effect since 1 January 1977.

The arbitral tribunal hears the evidence. If necessary, the arbitral tribunal may request the assistance of the courts. The ordinary courts alone have jurisdiction to make provisional orders.

The impleader of a third party is allowed only if provided for by an agreement to arbitrate between the third party and the parties in dispute.

Where one of the parties pleads a set-off on the basis of a legal relationship over which the arbitral tribunal lacks jurisdiction, the proceedings are stayed to the extent (only) set-off is claimed and a reasonable time is allowed for the party claiming the set-off to establish it before the court having jurisdiction ATF 116 Ia 154.

Unless the parties agree otherwise, the arbitral tribunal may make a partial award.

The arbitral award announces the decision on the merits, specifies the factual and legal reasons for the decision (unless the parties expressly waive this requirement), and specifies the amount and burden of costs.

¶2117   Remedies against the award in domestic arbitration

Action for the annulment of the arbitral award may be brought before the high court of the canton where the seat of the arbitration is located. Grounds for annulment are the following:

(a) that the arbitral tribunal was not properly constituted;

(b) that the arbitral tribunal mistakenly accepted or declined jurisdiction;

(c) that the arbitral tribunal decided points which were not submitted, or failed to make a determination on one of the items in the claim;

(d) that there was a breach of one of the mandatory procedural rules;

(e) that the arbitral tribunal awarded to one of the parties more or less than the amount claimed;

(f) that the award is arbitrary, in that it was based on findings which were clearly contrary to the facts appearing on the record, or that it constitutes a clear violation of law or fairness;

(g) that the arbitral tribunal made its award after the expiration of the time-limit imposed upon it for accomplishing its purpose;

(h) that the order is unintelligible or contradictory;

(i) that the fees of the arbitrators fixed by the arbitral tribunal are manifestly excessive.

RECOGNITION AND ENFORCEMENT

¶2118 By the parties

In practice, most arbitral awards are voluntarily complied with by the parties. As a result, these awards need not be enforced by an outside authority.

¶2119 Enforcement of Swiss international arbitral awards

The Federal Private International Law Statute standardises preconditions for the recognition and enforcement of international arbitral awards in Switzerland. For final awards made in Switzerland, Art. 193(1) of the PIL Statute allows parties to file a copy of the award, at their own expense, with the local court at the seat of the arbitral tribunal. At the request of a party, the state court will certify the enforceability of the award (*certificat de force exécutoire/Vollstreckbarkeits-bescheinigung*: Art. 193(2) PIL Statute). Furthermore, the arbitral tribunal will certify, at the request of a party, that the award was rendered pursuant to the provisions of the Statute (Art. 193(3) PIL Statute); this certification has the same effect as the filing of the award.

The Private International Law Statute does not contain any further rules concerning enforcement procedures. If the enforcement is to take place in Switzerland, subsequent steps depend on whether the claim is for a sum of money. Awards that order the payment of a certain amount of money (or the posting of some security) can be enforced, like other monetary claims, according to the rules of the Federal Statute on Debt Collection and Bankruptcy. This federal statute does not apply to non-monetary claims. Such awards must be brought to the cantonal court or to the competent authority which has jurisdiction to order their execution.

If both parties have fully waived their right to demand an annulment in the sense of Art. 192(1) of the Private International Law Statute, and if the award is to be enforced in Switzerland, the New York Convention applies by analogy (Art. 192(2) PIL Statute).

¶2120 Enforcement of foreign arbitral awards in Switzerland

Whether or not the award involves money, enforcement of Swiss awards and enforcement of foreign awards are subject to different rules. Pursuant to Art. 194 of the Private International Law Statute, recognition and enforcement of a foreign arbitral award are governed by the New York Convention of 10 June 1958. Despite the fact that Switzerland made a reservation in this respect, the New York Convention applies even if the other state is not a party to the Convention.

The New York Convention (¶1902(3)) in effect supersedes the bilateral treaties between Switzerland and, *inter alia*, Austria, Belgium, France, Italy, Spain and Sweden.

A party applying for recognition and enforcement must, at the time of application, supply both the duly authenticated original award (or a duly certified copy) and the original arbitral agreement (or a duly certified copy), according to Art. IV of the New York Convention. If the award or agreement is not made in an official language of the canton in which enforcement of the award is sought, the party must produce a translation of these documents into the official language. This translation must be certified by an official or sworn translator, or a diplomatic or consular agent. Recognition and enforcement may be refused only on specific grounds as set down in Art. V of the New York Convention. If an award can be enforced in Switzerland, the relevant procedural rules are approximately the same as those for the enforcement of monetary and non-monetary judgments.

¶2121 Declaration of enforceability of domestic arbitral awards

Upon petition by one of the parties, the competent cantonal judicial authority will declare any arbitral award enforceable if one of the reasons designated in Article 44 of the Concordat is fulfilled. The reasons are:

- that the terms of the award have been formally accepted by the parties, or

- that no action for an annulment has been brought forward within the time limit, or

- that an action for annulment has been brought forward in due time, but no order causing the award to be suspended has been granted, or

- that an action for annulment has been dismissed.

The declaration of enforceability may be refused if the award is contrary to Art. 5 of the Concordat. An enforceable arbitral award is entitled to the same full faith and credit as a judgment by a cantonal court. See Art. 61 of the Federal Constitution and can be executed in the same manner as other monetary and non-monetary claims.

SELECTED BIBLIOGRAPHY

Marc Blessing, 'The New International Arbitration Law in Switzerland', in *Journal of International Arbitration*, vol. 5, No. 2 (June, 1988)

Robert Briner, 'Switzerland', in *International Handbook on Commercial Arbitration* (Deventer, 1984); also Supplement 9 of September 1988

Andreas Bucher and Pierre-Yves Tschanz, *International Arbitration in Switzerland* (Basel, 1988)

Pierre Jolidon, *Commentaire du Concordat suisse sur l'arbitrage* (Bern, 1984)

Pierre Lalive, Jean-François Poudret and Claude Reymond, *Le droit de l'arbitrage interne et international en Suisse* (Lausanne, 1989)

Claude Reymond and Eugène Bucher, eds, *Swiss Essays on International Arbitration* (ICCA Congress Lausanne 1984) (Zürich, 1984)

The Swiss Arbitration Association, *The New Swiss Law on International Arbitration* (Basel, 1990)

Glossary of Terms

E English, *F* French, *G* German

Abgabebetrug *G*, Fiscal fraud *E*, Escroquerie en matière de prestations et de contributions *F*

Ablehnung eines Schiedsrichters *G*, Challenge of an arbitrator *E*, Récusation d'un arbitre *F*

Above par *E*, Au-dessus du pair *F*, Ueber pari *G*

Abschreibung *G*, Depreciation *E*, Amortissement *F*

Abtretung *G*, Assignment *E*, Cession *F*

Abuse Decree *E*, Arrêté relatif aux abus *F*, Missbrauchsbeschluss *G*

Abusif *F*, Abusive *E*, Missbräuchlich *G*

Abusive *E*, Abusif *F*, Missbräuchlich *G*

Accounting *E*, Comptabilité *F*, Buchhaltung *G*

Accréditif *F*, Letter of credit, L/C *E*, Akkreditiv *G*

Acte de défaut de biens *F*, Certificate of loss *E*, Verlustschein *G*

Acte illicite *F*, Tort *E*, Unerlaubte Handlung *G*

Acte juridique *F*, Legal transaction *E*, Rechtsgeschäft *G*

Actif circulant *F*, Current asset *E*, Umlaufvermögen *G*

Actifs *F*, Assets *E*, Aktiven *G*

Acting without authority *E*, Gestion d'affaires *F*, Geschäftsführung ohne Auftrag *G*

Action *F*, Share *E*, Aktie *G*

Action for annulment *E*, Annulation *F*, Anfechtung *G*

Action for undue preference *E*, Action révocatoire *F*, Paulianische Anfechtungsklage *G*

Action gratuite *F*, Stock dividend *E*, Gratisaktie *G*

Action nominative *F*, Registered share *E*, Namenaktie *G*

Action privilégiée *F*, Preferred share *E*, Vorzugsaktie *G*

Action révocatoire *F*, Action for undue preference *E*, Paulianische Anfechtungsklage *G*

Administrateur *F*, Member of the board of directors, Director *E*, Verwaltungsratsmitglied *G*

Administration de faillite *F*, Receiver in bankruptcy *E*, Konkursverwaltung *G*

Administration des preuves *F*, Taking of evidence *E*, Beweisaufnahme *G*

Administration fédérale des contributions (AFC) *F*, Federal Tax Administration *E*, Eidgenössische Steuerverwaltung (EStV) *G*

Administration fédérale des douanes (AFD) *F*, Federal Customs Administration *E*, Eidgenössische Zollverwaltung (EZV) *G*

Administrative assistance *E*, Entraide administrative *F*, Amtshilfe *G*

Administrative court *E*, Tribunal administratif *F*, Verwaltungsgericht *G*

Administrative law complaint *E*, Recours de droit administratif *F*, Verwaltungsgerichtsbeschwerde *G*

Admission to stock exchange dealing *E*, Introduction en bourse *F*, Börseneinführung *G*

Advance share *E*, Préciput *F*, Vorausabzug, Praecipuum *G*

After market *E*, Après bourse *F*, Nachbörse *G*

Agence *F*, Commercial agency *E*, Agentur *G*

Agent *E*, Représentant *F*, Vertreter *G*

Agentur *G*, Commercial agency *E*, Agence *F*

Agio *F*, *G*, Share premium *E*

Akkreditiv *G*, Letter of credit, L/C *E*, Accréditif *F*

Aktie *G*, Share *E*, Action *F*

Aktiengesellschaft (AG) *G*, Share corporation *E*, Société anonyme (SA) *F*

Aktienmantel *G*, Bare shell *E*, Manteau d'actions *F*

Aktiven *G*, Assets *E*, Actifs *F*

Aktiver Veredlungsverkehr *G*, Inward processing *E*, Trafic de perfectionnement actif *F*

Alleinvertriebssvertrag *G*, Exclusive distributorship agreement *E*, Concession exclusive de vente *F*

Allgemein anerkannte Buchführungsgrundsätze *G*, Generally accepted accounting principles *E*, Principes de comptabilité généralement admis *F*

Allgemeine Geschäftsbedingungen (AGB) *G*, General conditions *E*, Conditions générales (CG) *F*

Allocation *E*, Attribution *F*, Zuteilung *G*

Amortissement *F*, Depreciation *E*, Abschreibung *G*

Amtshilfe *G*, Administrative assistance *E*, Entraide administrative *F*

Anfechtung *G*, Action for annulment *E*, Annulation *F*

Anlagefonds *G*, Investment fund *E*, Fonds de placement *F*

Anlagevermögen *G*, Fixed assets *E*, Capital investi *F*

Anleihensobligation *G*, Bond *E*, Emprunt par obligation *F*

Annulation *F*, Action for annulment *E*, Anfechtung *G*

Answer to the complaint *E*, Réponse *F*, Klageantwort *G*

Anticipatory tax *E*, Impôt anticipé *F*, Verrechnungssteuer *G*

Anweisung *G*, Payment order *E*, Assignation *F*

Anwendbares Recht *G*, Applicable law *E*, Droit applicable *F*

Appeal *E*, Recours en réforme *F*, Berufung *G*

Applicable law *E*, Droit applicable *F*, Anwendbares Recht *G*
Après bourse *F*, After market *E*, Nachbörse *G*
Arbitrabilité *F*, Arbitrability *E*, Schiedsfähigkeit *G*
Arbitrability *E*, Arbitrabilité *F*, Schiedsfähigkeit *G*
Arbitrage *F*, Arbitration *E*, Schiedsgerichtsbarkeit *G*
Arbitral tribunal *E*, Tribunal arbitral *F*, Schiedsgericht *G*
Arbitration *E*, Arbitrage *F*, Schiedsgerichtsbarkeit *G*
Arbitration agreement *E*, Convention d'arbitrage *F*, Schiedsvereinbarung *G*
Arbitration clause *E*, Clause d'arbitrage *F*, Schiedsklausel *G*
Arbitration rules *E*, Règlement d'arbitrage *F*, Schiedsordnung *G*
Arglist *G*, Fraudulent behaviour *E*, Astuce *F*
Arrest *G*, Attachment *E*, Séquestre *F*
Arrestprosequierung *G*, Validation of attachment *E*, Validation du séquestre *F*
Arrêt du Tribunal fédéral (ATF) *F*, Judgment of the Federal Supreme Court (ATF) *E*, Bundesgerichtsentscheid (BGE) *G*
Arrêté du Conseil fédéral (ACF) *F*, Decree of the Federal Government *E*, Bundesratsbeschluss (BRB) *G*
Arrêté du Conseil fédéral instituant des mesures contre l'utilisation sans cause légitime des conventions conclues par la Confédération en vue d'éviter les doubles impositions ('arrêté relatif aux abus') *F*, Bundesratsbeschluss betreffend Massnahmen gegen die ungerechtfertigte Inanspruchnahme von Doppelbesteuerungsabkommen des Bundes ('Missbrauchsbeschluss') *G*, Federal Decree regarding measures against improper use of double taxation conventions entered into by the Confederation ('Abuse Decree') *E*
Arrêté du Conseil fédéral instituant un impôt sur le chiffre d'affaires (AChA) *F*, Federal Wholesale Tax Decree *E*, Bundesratsbeschluss über die Warenumsatzsteuer (WUB) *G*
Arrêté du Conseil fédéral sur la perception d'un impôt fédéral direct (AIFD) *F*, Federal Income Tax Decree (FITD) *E*, Bundesratsbeschluss über die Erhebung einer direkten Bundessteuer (BdBSt) *G*
Arrêté fédéral (AF) *F*, Federal Decree *E*, Bundesbeschluss (BB) *G*
Arrêté relatif aux abus *F*, Abuse Decree *E*, Missbrauchsbeschluss *G*
Articles of Incorporation *E*, Statuts *F*, Statuten *G*
Assemblée générale *F*, General meeting *E*, Generalversammlung *G*
Assets *E*, Actifs *F*, Aktiven *G*
Assignation *F*, Payment order *E*, Anweisung *G*
Assignee *E*, Cessionnaire *F*, Zessionar *G*
Assignment *E*, Cession *F*, Abtretung *G*
Assignor *E*, Cédant *F*, Zedent *G*
Association *E*, *F*, Verein *G*
Association des Bourses Suisses *F*, Association of Swiss Stock Exchanges *E*, Vereinigung der Schweizer Börsen *G*

Association of Swiss Stock Exchanges *E*, Association des Bourses Suisses *F*, Vereinigung der Schweizer Börsen *G*

Association Suisse des Banquiers *F*, Swiss Bankers Association *E*, Schweizerische Bankiervereinigung *G*

Assurance immobilière *F*, Building insurance *E*, Gebäudeversicherung *G*

Astuce *F*, Fraudulent behaviour *E*, Arglist *G*

Attachment *E*, Séquestre *F*, Arrest *G*

Attorney-General's Office *E*, Ministère public *F*, Staatsanwaltschaft *G*

Attorney-at-law *E*, Avocat (av.) *F*, Rechtsanwalt (RA) *G*

Attribution *F*, Allocation *E*, Zuteilung *G*

Au-dessous du pair *F*, Below par *E*, Unter pari *G*

Au-dessus du pair *F*, Above par *E*, Ueber pari *G*

Aufsichtsbehörde *G*, Supervisory authority *E*, Autorité de surveillance *F*

Auftrag *G*, Mandate *E*, Mandat *F*

Ausländische Entscheidung *G*, Foreign decision *E*, Décision étrangère *F*

Ausservertragliche Haftung *G*, Liability in tort *E*, Responsabilité aquilienne *F*

Autorité de surveillance *F*, Supervisory authority *E*, Aufsichtsbehörde *G*

Avocat (av.) *F*, Attorney-at-law *E*, Rechtsanwalt (RA) *G*

Balance sheet *E*, Bilan *F*, Bilanz *G*

Bank-like finance company *E*, Société financière à caractère bancaire *F*, Bankähnliche Finanzgesellschaft *G*

Bankähnliche Finanzgesellschaft *G*, Bank-like finance company *E*, Société financière à caractère bancaire *F*

Bankgeheimnis *G*, Bank secrecy *E*, Secret bancaire *F*

Banking secrecy *E*, Secret bancaire *F*, Bankgeheimnis *G*

Bankruptcy *E*, Faillite *F*, Konkurs *G*

Bankruptcy office *E*, Office des faillites *F*, Konkursamt *G*

Banque cantonale *F*, Cantonal bank *E*, Kantonalbank *G*

Banque chef de file *F*, Lead manager *E*, Federführende Bank *G*

Banque Nationale Suisse (BNS) *F*, Swiss National Bank *E*, Schweizerische Nationalbank (SNB) *G*

Banque privée *F*, Private bank *E*, Privatbank *G*

Bare shell *E*, Manteau d'actions *F*, Aktienmantel *G*

Baurecht *G*, Right to build *E*, Droit de superficie *F*

Beklagter *G*, Defendant, Respondent *E*, Défendeur *F*

Belastungsgrenzwert *G*, Maximum emission or immission standard *E*, Valeur limite d'exposition *F*

Below par *E*, Au-dessous du pair *F*, Unter pari *G*

Bénéfice *F*, Profit *E*, Gewinn *G*

Benefit of a financial nature *E*, Prestation appréciable en argent *F*, Geldwerte Leistung *G*

Berufung *G*, Appeal *E*, Recours en réforme *F*

Beschwerde *G*, Complaint *E*, Recours *F*
Beteiligung *G*, Investment in companies *E*, Participation *F*
Betreibung *G*, Debt collection *E*, Poursuite *F*
Betreibungsamt *G*, Debt collection office *E*, Office des poursuites *F*
Betreibungsbegehren *G*, Request for order to pay *E*, Réquisition de poursuite *F*
Betriebsstätte *G*, Permanent establishment *E*, Etablissement permanent *F*
Betriebsvermögen *G*, Current assets *E*, Capital d'exploitation *F*
Betrug *G*, Fraud *E*, Escroquerie *F*
Beweisaufnahme *G*, Taking of evidence *E*, Administration des preuves *F*
Bezirksgericht *G*, Trial court *E*, Tribunal de première instance, Tribunal de district, Tribunal d'arrondissement *F*
Bilan *F*, Balance sheet *E*, Bilanz *G*
Bilan consolidé *F*, Consolidated balance sheet *E*, Konsolidierte Bilanz *G*
Bilanz *G*, Balance sheet *E*, Bilan *F*
Bill of exchange, draft *E*, Effet de change *F*, Wechsel *G*
Bill of lading, B/L *E*, Connaissement *F*, Konnossement *G*
Billet à ordre *F*, Promissory note *E*, Eigenwechsel *G*
Board of tax appeals *E*, Commission de recours *F*, Rekurskommission *G*
Bon de jouissance *F*, Dividend-right certificate *E*, Genussschein *G*
Bon de participation *F*, Participation certificate *E*, Partizipationsschein *G*
Bond *E*, Emprunt par obligation *F*, Anleihensobligation *G*
Bond issue with warrants attached *E*, Emprunt à option *F*, Optionsanleihe *G*
Börseneinführung *G*, Admission to stock exchange dealing *E*, Introduction en bourse *F*
Börsenkapitalisierung *G*, Market capitalisation *E*, Capitalisation boursière *F*
Botschaft des Bundesrates *G*, Federal Government accompanying report on proposed legislation *E*, Message du Conseil fédéral *F*
Branch office *E*, Succursale *F*, Zweigniederlassung *G*
Brevet *F*, Patent *E*, *G*
Broker *E*, Courtier *F*, Mäkler *G*
Brokerage *E*, Courtage *F*, *G*
Brokerage agreement *E*, Contrat de courtage *F*, Mäklervertrag *G*
Brokerage fee *E*, Salaire du courtier *F*, Mäklerlohn *G*
Buchhaltung *G*, Accounting *E*, Comptabilité *F*
Building insurance *E*, Assurance immobilière *F*, Gebäudeversicherung *G*
Bundesamt für Aussenwirtschaft (BAWI) *G*, Federal Office for Foreign Economic Affairs *E*, Office fédéral des affaires économiques extérieures (OFAEE) *F*
Bundesamt für geistiges Eigentum (BAGE) *G*, Federal Intellectual Property Office *E*, Office fédéral de la propriété intellectuelle (OFPI) *F*
Bundesamt für Gesundheitswesen (BAG) *G*, Federal Public Health Office *E*, Office fédéral de la santé publique (OFSP) *F*

Bundesamt für Industrie, Gewerbe und Arbeit (BIGA) *G*, Federal Office of Industry, Trade and Labour *E*, Office fédéral de l'industrie, des arts et métiers et du travail (OFIAMT) *F*

Bundesamt für Justiz (BJ) *G*, Federal Justice Office *E*, Office fédéral de la justice (OFJ) *F*

Bundesamt für Polizeiwesen (BAP) *G*, Federal Office of Police *E*, Office fédéral de la police (OFP) *F*

Bundesamt für Privatversicherungswesen (BPV) *G*, Federal Insurance Office *E*, Office fédéral des assurances privées (OFAP) *F*

Bundesamt für Sozialversicherung (BSV) *G*, Federal Social Security Office *E*, Office fédéral des assurances sociales (OFAS) *F*

Bundesamt für Umwelt, Wald und Landschaft (BUWAL) *G*, Federal Environmental Protection Office *E*, Office fédéral de l'environnement, des fôrets et du paysage (OFEFP) *F*

Bundesamt für Zivilluftfahrt (BAZL) *G*, Federal Civil Aviation Office *E*, Office fédéral de l'aviation civile (OFAC) *F*

Bundesanwalt *G*, Federal Prosecutor *E*, Procureur de la Confédération *F*

Bundesbeschluss (BB) *G*, Federal Decree *E*, Arrêté fédéral (AF) *F*

Bundesblatt (BBl.) *G*, Federal Register *E*, Feuille fédérale (FF) *F*

Bundesgericht (BGer) *G*, Federal Supreme Court *E*, Tribunal fédéral (TF) *F*

Bundesgerichtsentscheid (BGE) *G*, Judgment of the Federal Supreme Court (ATF) *E*, Arrêt du Tribunal fédéral (ATF) *F*

Bundesgesetz (BG) *G*, Federal statute *E*, Loi fédérale (LF) *F*

Bundesgesetz betreffend das Urheberrecht an Werken der Literatur und Kunst (URG) *G*, Federal Statute on Copyrights of Works of Literature and Art *E*, Loi fédérale concernant le droit d'auteurs sur les oeuvres littéraires et artistiques (LDA) *F*

Bundesgesetz betreffend den Schutz der Fabrik- und Handelsmarken (MSchG) *G*, Federal Statute on Protection of Trade Marks *E*, Loi fédérale concernant la protection des marques de fabrique et de commerce (LMF) *F*

Bundesgesetz betreffend die Erfindungspatente (PatG) *G*, Federal Patent Statute *E*, Loi fédérale sur les brevets d'invention (LBI) *F*

Bundesgesetz über das Verwaltungsstrafrecht (VStrR) *G*, Federal Statute on Administrative Criminal Law *E*, Loi fédérale sur le droit pénal administratif (DPA) *F*

Bundesgesetz über den Erwerb von Grundstücken durch Personen im Ausland (BewG; Lex Friedrich) *G*, Federal Statute on Acquisition of Immovables by Non-Residents (Lex Friedrich) *E*, Loi fédérale sur l'acquisition d'immeubles par des personnes à l'étranger (LFAIE; Lex Friedrich) *F*

Bundesgesetz über den unlauteren Wettbewerb (UWG) *G*, Federal Unfair Competition Statute *E*, Loi fédérale sur la concurrence déloyale (LCD) *F*

Bundesgesetz über die Alters- und Hinterlassenenversicherung (AHVG) *G*, Federal Statute on Old-Age and Survivors Insurance *E*, Loi fédérale sur l'assurance-vieillesse et survivants (LAVS) *F*

Bundesgesetz über die Anlagefonds (AFG) *G*, Federal Investment Funds Statute *E*, Loi fédérale sur les fonds de placement (LFP) *F*

Bundesgesetz über die Arbeit in Industrie, Gewerbe und Handel (ArG) *G*, Federal Labour Statute *E*, Loi fédérale sur le travail dans l'industrie, l'artisanat et le commerce (LTr) *F*

Bundesgesetz über die Banken und Sparkassen (BankG) *G*, Federal Banking Statute *E*, Loi fédérale sur les banques et les caisses d'épargne (LB) *F*

Bundesgesetz über die berufliche Alters-, Hinterlassenen- und Invalidenvorsorge (BVG) *G*, Federal Statute on Occupational Pension Plans *E*, Loi fédérale sur la prévoyance professionnelle vieillesse, survivants et invalidité (LPP) *F*

Bundesgesetz über die direkte Bundessteuer (DBG) *G*, Federal Income Tax Statute *E*, Loi fédérale sur l'impôt fédéral direct (LIFD) *F*

Bundesgesetz über die Harmonisierung der direkten Steuern der Kantone und Gemeinden (StHG) *G*, Federal Statute on Harmonisation of Cantonal and Municipal Income Taxes *E*, Loi fédérale sur l'harmonisation des impôts directs des cantons et des communes (LHID) *F*

Bundesgesetz über die Invalidenversicherung (IVG) *G*, Federal Disability Insurance Statute *E*, Loi fédérale sur l'assurance-invalidité (LAI) *F*

Bundesgesetz über die Krankenversicherung (KUVG) *G*, Federal Health Insurance Statute *E*, Loi fédérale sur l'assurance-maladie (LAMA) *F*

Bundesgesetz über die Organisation der Bundesrechtspflege (OG) *G*, Federal Statute on the Organisation of the Judiciary *E*, Loi fédérale d'organisation judiciaire (OJ) *F*

Bundesgesetz über die Stempelabgaben (StG) *G*, Federal Stamp Tax Statute (FSTS) *E*, Loi fédérale sur les droits de timbre (LT) *F*

Bundesgesetz über die Unfallversicherung (UVG) *G*, Federal Accident Insurance Statute *E*, Loi fédérale sur l'assurance-accidents (LAA) *F*

Bundesgesetz über die Verrechnungssteuer (VStG) *G*, Federal Anticipatory Tax Statute (FATS) *E*, Loi fédérale sur l'impôt anticipé (LIA) *F*

Bundesgesetz über internationale Rechtshilfe in Strafsachen (IRSG) *G*, Federal Statute on International Judicial Assistance in Criminal Matters *E*, Loi fédérale sur l'entraide internationale en matière pénale (EIMP) *F*

Bundesgesetz über Kartelle und ähnliche Organisationen (KG) *G*, Federal Cartel Statute *E*, Loi fédérale sur les cartels et organisations analogues (LCart) *F*

Bundesgesetz über Schuldbetreibung und Konkurs (SchKG) *G*, Federal Statute on Debt Collection and Bankruptcy *E*, Loi fédérale sur la poursuite pour dettes et la faillite (LP) *F*

Bundesgesetz zum Staatsvertrag mit den Vereinigten Staaten von Amerika über gegenseitige Rechtshilfe in Strafsachen (BG RVUS) *G*, Federal Statute

Regarding the Treaty with the United States of America on International Judicial Assistance in Criminal Matters *E*, Loi fédérale relative au traité conclu avec les Etats-Unis d'Amérique sur l'entraide judiciaire en matière pénale (LTEJUS) *F*

Bundesrat (BR) *G*, Federal Government *E*, Conseil fédéral (CF) *F*

Bundesratsbeschluss (BRB) *G*, Decree of the Federal Government *E*, Arrêté du Conseil fédéral (ACF) *F*

Bundesratsbeschluss betreffend Massnahmen gegen die ungerechtfertigte Inanspruchnahme von Doppelbesteuerungsabkommen des Bundes ('Missbrauchsbeschluss') *G*, Federal Decree regarding measures against improper use of double taxation conventions entered into by the Confederation ('Abuse Decree') *E*, Arrêté du Conseil fédéral instituant des mesures contre l'utilisation sans cause légitime des conventions conclues par la Confédération en vue d'éviter les doubles impositions ('arrêté relatif aux abus') *F*

Bundesratsbeschluss über die Erhebung einer direkten Bundessteuer (BdBSt) *G*, Federal Income Tax Decree (FITD) *E*, Arrêté du Conseil fédéral sur la perception d'un impôt fédéral direct (AIFD) *F*

Bundesratsbeschluss über die Warenumsatzsteuer (WUB) *G*, Federal Wholesale Tax Decree *E*, Arrêté du Conseil fédéral instituant un impôt sur le chiffre d'affaires (AChA) *F*

Bundesverfassung der Schweizerischen Eidgenossenschaft (BV) *G*, Federal Constitution *E*, Constitution fédérale de la Confédération suisse (Cst.) *F*

Bürgerrecht *G*, Citizenship *E*, Droit de cité *F*

Bürgschaft *G*, Suretyship *E*, Cautionnement *F*

Business establishment *E*, Etablissement *F*, Niederlassung *G*

Caisse nationale suisse d'assurances en cas d'accident (CNA) *F*, Federal Accident Insurance Company *E*, Schweizerische Unfallversicherungsanstalt (SUVA) *G*

Cantonal bank *E*, Banque cantonale *F*, Kantonalbank *G*

Cantonal government *E*, Conseil d'Etat *F*, Regierungsrat *G*

Capital d'exploitation *F*, Current assets *E*, Betriebsvermögen *G*

Capital de dotation *F*, Deemed equity of branch *E*, Dotationskapital *G*

Capital gain *E*, Gain en capital *F*, Kapitalgewinn *G*

Capital investi *F*, Fixed assets *E*, Anlagevermögen *G*

Capitalisation boursière *F*, Market capitalisation *E*, Börsenkapitalisierung *G*

Capitalised income value *E*, Valeur de rendement *F*, Ertragswert *G*

Cause *E*, Juste motif *F*, Wichtiger Grund *G*

Cautionnement *F*, Suretyship *E*, Bürgschaft *G*

Cédant *F*, Assignor *E*, Zedent *G*

Cédule hypothécaire *F*, Mortgage note *E*, Schuldbrief *G*

Certificat d'origine *F*, Certificate of origin *E*, Ursprungszeugnis *G*

Certificat de dépôt *F*, Medium-term note *E*, Kassaobligation *G*

Certificat de force exécutoire *F*, Certificate of enforceability *E*, Vollstreckbarkeitsbescheinigung *G*
Certificate of enforceability *E*, Certificat de force exécutoire *F*, Vollstreckbarkeitsbescheinigung *G*
Certificate of loss *E*, Acte de défaut de biens *F*, Verlustschein *G*
Certificate of origin *E*, Certificat d'origine *F*, Ursprungszeugnis *G*
Cession *F*, Assignment *E*, Abtretung *G*
Cessionnaire *F*, Assignee *E*, Zessionar *G*
Challenge of an arbitrator *E*, Récusation d'un arbitre *F*, Ablehnung eines Schiedsrichters *G*
Characteristic performance *E*, Prestation caractéristique *F*, Charakteristische Leistung *G*
Charakteristische Leistung *G*, Characteristic performance *E*, Prestation caractéristique *F*
Chemins de fer fédéraux (CFF) *F*, Federal Railway System *E*, Schweizerische Bundesbahnen (SBB) *G*
Chèque barré *F*, Crossed cheque *E*, Gekreuzter Check *G*
Circulaire *F*, Circular letter *E*, Kreisschreiben *G*
Circular letter *E*, Circulaire *F*, Kreisschreiben *G*
Citizenship *E*, Droit de cité *F*, Bürgerrecht *G*
Civil Code (CC) *E*, Code civil suisse (CC) *F*, Zivilgesetzbuch (ZGB) *G*
Claim *E*, Créance *F*, Forderung *G*
Claimant *E*, Demandeur *F*, Kläger *G*
Clause d'arbitrage *F*, Arbitration clause *E*, Schiedsklausel *G*
Co-ownership *E*, Copropriété *F*, Miteigentum *G*
Code civil suisse (CC) *F*, Civil Code (CC) *E*, Zivilgesetzbuch (ZGB) *G*
Code de procédure pénale (CPP) *F*, Code of criminal procedure *E*, Strafprozessordnung (StPO) *G*
Code des obligations (CO) *F*, Code of Obligations (CO) *E*, Obligationenrecht (OR) *G*
Code of criminal procedure *E*, Code de procédure pénale (CPP) *F*, Strafprozessordnung (StPO) *G*
Code of Obligations (CO) *E*, Code des obligations (CO) *F*, Obligationenrecht (OR) *G*
Code pénal suisse (CP) *F*, Federal Penal Code (PC) *E*, Strafgesetzbuch (StGB) *G*
Code suisse des offres publiques d'achat *F*, Swiss Take-Over Code *E*, Schweizerischer Uebernahme-Kodex *G*
Collective labour agreement *E*, Convention collective de travail *F*, Gesamtarbeitsvertrag *G*
Commandement de payer *F*, Order to pay *E*, Zahlungsbefehl *G*

Commerçant de titre *F*, Securities dealer *E*, Wertschriftenhändler, Effektenhändler *G*

Commercial Agency *E*, Agence *F*, Agentur *G*

Commercial representative *E*, Mandataire commercial *F*, Handlungsbevollmächtigter *G*

Commission *E*, Provision *F*, Provision *G*

Commission agent *E*, Commissionnaire *F*, Kommissionär *G*

Commission de recours *F*, Board of tax appeals *E*, Rekurskommission *G*

Commission fédérale des banques (CFB) *F*, Federal Banking Commission *E*, Eidgenössische Bankenkommission (EBK) *G*

Commission fédérale des cartels *F*, Federal Cartel Commission *E*, Eidgenössische Kartellkommission *G*

Commissionnaire *F*, Commission agent *E*, Kommissionär *G*

Compensation *F*, Set-off *E*, Verrechnung *G*

Complaint *E*, Demande, Recours *F*, Klage, Beschwerde *G*

Composition *E*, Concordat *F*, Nachlassvertrag *G*

Comptabilité *F*, Accounting *E*, Buchhaltung *G*

Compte de pertes et profits *F*, Profit and loss account *E*, Gewinn- und Verlustrechnung *G*

Compte-joint *F*, Joint account *E*, Gemeinschaftskonto *G*

Compte numérique *F*, Numbered account *E*, Nummernkonto *G*

Compte-courant *F*, Current account *E*, Kontokorrent *G*

Concession exclusive de vente *F*, Exclusive distributorship agreement *E*, Alleinvertriebssvertrag *G*

Conciliation proceedings *E*, Procédure de conciliation *F*, Sühneverfahren *G*

Concordat *F*, Composition *E*, Nachlassvertrag *G*

Concurrence déloyale *F*, Unfair competition *E*, Unlauterer Wettbewerb *G*

Conditions générales (CG) *F*, General conditions *E*, Allgemeine Geschäftsbedingungen (AGB) *G*

Confédération suisse *F*, Swiss Confederation *E*, Schweizerische Eidgenossenschaft *G*

Conflict of laws *E*, Droit international privé *F*, Internationales Privatrecht *G*

Conflict-of-law rules *E*, Règles de droit international privé *F*, Kollisionsrecht *G*

Connaissement *F*, Bill of lading, B/L *E*, Konnossement *G*

Conseil d'Etat *F*, Cantonal government *E*, Regierungsrat *G*

Conseil des Etats *F*, Senate *E*, Ständerat *G*

Conseil fédéral (CF) *F*, Federal Government *E*, Bundesrat (BR) *G*

Conseil national *F*, House *E*, Nationalrat *G*

Conservatory measures *E*, Mesures conservatoires *F*, Sichernde Massnahmen *G*

Consolidated balance sheet *E*, Bilan consolidé *F*, Konsolidierte Bilanz *G*

Constitution fédérale de la Confédération suisse (Cst.) *F*, Federal Constitution *E*, Bundesverfassung der Schweizerischen Eidgenossenschaft (BV) *G*

Constitutional complaint *E*, Recours de droit public *F*, Staatsrechtliche Beschwerde *G*

Constructive dividend *E*, Distribution de bénéfices dissimulée *F*, Verdeckte Gewinnausschüttung *G*

Constructive expropriation *E*, Expropriation matérielle *F*, Materielle Enteignung *G*

Contemporaneous performance *E*, Trait par trait *F*, Zug um Zug *G*

Contingent liability *E*, Engagement conditionnel *F*, Eventualverpflichtung *G*

Contract *E*, Contrat *F*, Vertrag *G*

Contract penalty *E*, Peine conventionnelle *F*, Vertragsstrafe *G*

Contractual liability *E*, Responsabilité contractuelle *F*, Vertragliche Haftung *G*

Contrat *F*, Contract *E*, Vertrag *G*

Contrat de courtage *F*, Brokerage agreement *E*, Mäklervertrag *G*

Contrat-type de travail *F*, Standard-provision contract *E*, Normalarbeitsvertrag *G*

Contravention fiscale *F*, Tax contravention *E*, Steuerwiderhandlung *G*

Convention collective de travail *F*, Collective labour agreement *E*, Gesamtarbeitsvertrag *G*

Convention contre la double imposition *F*, Double taxation convention *E*, Doppelbesteuerungsabkommen *G*

Convention d'arbitrage *F*, Arbitration agreement *E*, Schiedsvereinbarung *G*

Convention de diligence *F*, Due Diligence Convention *E*, Sorgfaltspflicht-vereinbarung *G*

Convention européenne des droits de l'homme et des libertés fondamentales (CEDH) *F*, European Convention on Human Rights and Fundamental Liberties *E*, Europäische Konvention zum Schutz der Menschenrechte und Grundfreiheiten (EMRK) *G*

Convertible bond *E*, Obligation convertible *F*, Wandelobligation *G*

Copropriété *F*, Co-ownership *E*, Miteigentum *G*

Counterclaim *E*, Demande reconventionnelle *F*, Widerklage *G*

Country *E*, Etat *F*, Staat *G*

Cour de justice de Genève *F*, Geneva Supreme Court *E*, Genfer Kantonsgericht *G*

Court *E*, Tribunal *F*, Gericht *G*

Courtage *F*, *G*, Brokerage *E*

Courtier *F*, Broker *E*, Mäkler *G*

Covered warrant *E*, Option couverte *F*, Stillhalteroption, gedeckte Option *G*

Créance *F*, Claim *E*, Forderung *G*

Créance comptable à court terme *F*, Money-market book claim *E*, Geldmarkt-buchforderung *G*

Crédit d'escompte *F*, Discount credit *E*, Diskontkredit *G*

Crédit documentaire *F*, Documentary credit *E*, Dokumentenakkreditiv *G*

Crossed cheque *E*, Chèque barré *F*, Gekreuzter Check *G*
Current account *E*, Compte-courant *F*, Kontokorrent *G*
Current assets *E*, Capital d'exploitation *F*, Betriebsvermögen *G*
Customs *E*, Douane *F*, Zoll *G*
Darlehen *G*, Loan *E*, Prêt *F*
Débiteurs *F*, Receivables *E*, Debitoren *G*
Debitoren *G*, Receivables *E*, Débiteurs *F*
Debt *E*, Fond de tiers *F*, Fremdkapital *G*
Debt collection *E*, Poursuite *F*, Betreibung *G*
Debt collection office *E*, Office des poursuites *F*, Betreibungsamt *G*
Decedent *E*, De cujus *F*, Erblasser *G*
Decedent's estate *E*, Succession *F*, Nachlass *G*
Décision étrangère *F*, Foreign decision *E*, Ausländische Entscheidung *G*
Déclaration de grossiste *F*, Wholesaler's declaration *E*, Grossistenerklärung *G*
Déclaration fiscale *F*, Tax return *E*, Steuererklärung *G*
Decree of the Federal Government *E*, Arrêté du Conseil fédéral (ACF) *F*,
     Bundesratsbeschluss (BRB) *G*
De cujus *F*, Decedent *E*, Erblasser *G*
Deemed equity of branch *E*, Capital de dotation *F*, Dotationskapital *G*
Default of obligee *E*, Demeure du créancier *F*, Gläubigerverzug *G*
Default of obligor *E*, Demeure du débiteur *F*, Schuldnerverzug *G*
Defendant, Respondent *E*, Défendeur *F*, Beklagter *G*
Défendeur *F*, Defendant, Respondent *E*, Beklagter *G*
Definitive removal of opposition *E*, Mainlevée définitive d'opposition *F*,
     Definitive Rechtsöffnung *G*
Definitive Rechtsöffnung *G*, Definitive removal of opposition *E*, Mainlevée
     définitive d'opposition *F*
Délai *F*, Time limit *E*, Frist *G*
Delcredere *G*, Provisions for doubtful debts *E*, Réserve pour débiteurs
     douteux *F*
Demande *F*, Complaint *E*, Klage *G*
Demande reconventionnelle *F*, Counterclaim *E*, Widerklage *G*
Demandeur *F*, Plaintiff, Claimant *E*, Kläger *G*
Demeure du créancier *F*, Default of obligee *E*, Gläubigerverzug *G*
Demeure du débiteur *F*, Default of obligor *E*, Schuldnerverzug *G*
Département des affaires étrangères (DFAE) *F*, Federal Department of Foreign
     Affairs *E*, Eidgenössisches Departement für auswärtige Angelegenheiten
     (EDA) *G*
Département fédéral de justice et police (DJP) *F*, Federal Justice Department *E*,
     Eidgenössisches Justiz- und Polizeidepartement (EJPD) *G*
Département fédéral de l'économie publique (DFEP) *F*, Federal Department of
     National Economy *E*, Eidgenössisches Volkswirtschaftsdepartement (EVD) *G*

Département fédéral de l'intérieur (DFI) *F*, Federal Department of the Interior *E*, Eidgenössisches Departement des Innern (EDI) *G*

Département fédéral des finances (DFF) *F*, Federal Finance Department *E*, Eidgenössisches Finanzdepartement (EFD) *G*

Dépôt à terme *F*, Time deposit *E*, Festgeld *G*

Depreciation *E*, Amortissement *F*, Abschreibung *G*

Design *E*, Modèle déposé *F*, Gebrauchsmuster *G*

Devisen *G*, Foreign exchange *E*, Devises *F*

Devises *F*, Foreign exchange *E*, Devisen *G*

Directeur *F*, Manager *E*, Direktor *G*

Director, member of the board of directors *E*, Administrateur *F*, Verwaltungsratsmitglied *G*

Direkte Bundessteuer *G*, Federal income tax *E*, Impôt fédéral direct *F*

Direktor *G*, Manager *E*, Directeur *F*

Discount credit *E*, Crédit d'escompte *F*, Diskontkredit *G*

Diskontkredit *G*, Discount credit *E*, Crédit d'escompte *F*

Distribution de bénéfices dissimulée *F*, Constructive dividend *E*, Verdeckte Gewinnausschüttung *G*

Dividend *E*, Dividende *G*, *F*

Dividend-right certificate *E*, Bon de jouissance *F*, Genussschein *G*

Dividende *G*, *F* Dividend *E*

Document of title *E*, Titre représentant la marchandise *F*, Warenpapier *G*

Documentary credit *E*, Crédit documentaire *F*, Dokumentenakkreditiv *G*

Dokumentenakkreditiv *G*, Documentary credit *E*, Crédit documentaire *F*

Doppelbesteuerung *G*, Double taxation *E*, Double imposition *F*

Doppelbesteuerungsabkommen *G*, Double taxation convention *E*, Convention contre la double imposition *F*

Dotationskapital *G*, Deemed equity of branch *E*, Capital de dotation *F*

Douane *F*, Customs *E*, Zoll *G*

Double imposition *F*, Double taxation *E*, Doppelbesteuerung *G*

Double taxation *E*, Double imposition *F*, Doppelbesteuerung *G*

Double taxation convention *E*, Convention contre la double imposition *F*, Doppelbesteuerungsabkommen *G*

Draft *E*, Effet de change *F*, Wechsel *D*

Droit applicable *F*, Applicable law *E*, Anwendbares Recht *G*

Droit de cité *F*, Citizenship *E*, Bürgerrecht *G*

Droit de la propriété intellectuelle *F*, Industrial (intellectual) property law *E*, Immaterialgüterrecht *G*

Droit de la responsabilité civile (RC) *F*, Law of torts *E*, Haftpflichtrecht *G*

Droit de préemption *F*, Right of first refusal *E*, Vorkaufsrecht *G*

Droit de superficie *F*, Right to build *E*, Baurecht *G*

Droit de timbre d'émission *F*, Issuance stamp tax *E*,
Emissionsstempelabgabe *G*
Droit de timbre de négociation *F*, Securities turnover stamp tax *E*,
Umsatzstempelabgabe *G*
Droit de timbre *F*, Stamp tax *E*, Stempelabgabe *G*
Droit international privé *F*, Conflict of laws *E*, Internationales Privatrecht *G*
Due date *E*, Echéance *F*, Fälligkeit *G*
Due Diligence Convention *E*, Convention de diligence *F*, Sorgfaltspflicht-
vereinbarung *G*
Duplik *G*, Rejoinder *E*, Duplique *F*
Duplique *F*, Rejoinder *E*, Duplik *G*
Durchgriff *G*, Piercing the corporate veil *E*, Non-reconnaissance de la personne
morale *F*
Easement *E*, Servitude foncière *F*, Grunddienstbarkeit *G*
Echéance *F*, Due date *E*, Fälligkeit *G*
Effektenhändler *G*, Securities dealer *E*, Commerçant de titres *F*
Effet de change *F*, Bill of exchange, draft *E*, Wechsel *G*
Eidgenössisch (Eidg.) *G*, Federal *E*, Fédéral (féd.) *F*
Eidgenössische Bankenkommission (EBK) *G*, Federal Banking Commission *E*,
Commission fédérale des banques (CFB) *F*
Eidgenössische Drucksachen- und Materialzentrale (EDMZ) *G*, Federal Central
Office for Printed Matters and Materials *E*, Office central fédéral des imprimés
et du matériel (UCFIM) *F*
Eidgenössische Kartellkommission *G*, Federal Cartel Commission *E*,
Commission fédérale des cartels *F*
Eidgenössische Steuerverwaltung (EStV) *G*, Federal Tax Administration *E*,
Administration fédérale des contributions (AFC) *F*
Eidgenössische Zollverwaltung (EZV) *G*, Federal Customs Administration *E*,
Administration fédérale des douanes (AFD) *F*
Eidgenössisches Departement des Innern (EDI) *G*, Federal Department of the
Interior *E*, Département fédéral de l'intérieur (DFI) *F*
Eidgenössisches Departement für auswärtige Angelegenheiten (EDA) *G*, Federal
Department of Foreign Affairs *E*, Département des affaires étrangères
(DFAE) *F*
Eidgenössisches Finanzdepartement (EFD) *G*, Federal Finance Department *E*,
Département fédéral des finances (DFF) *F*
Eidgenössisches Justiz- und Polizeidepartement (EJPD) *G*, Federal Justice
Department *E*, Département fédéral de justice et police (DJP) *F*
Eidgenössisches Volkswirtschaftsdepartement (EVD) *G*, Federal Department of
National Economy *E*, Département fédéral de l'économie publique (DFEP) *F*
Eigentumsvorbehalt (EV) *G*, Retention of title *E*, Pacte de réserve de
propriété *F*

Eigenwechsel *G*, Promissory note *E*, Billet à ordre *F*

Einfache Gesellschaft *G*, Ordinary partnership *E*, Société simple *F*

Einführungsprospekt *G*, Prospectus *E*, Prospectus d'introduction à la bourse *F*

Einkommenssteuer *G*, Income tax *E*, Impôt sur le revenu *F*

Einsprache *G*, Motion to reconsider *E*, Opposition *F*

Einstweilige Verfügung *G*, Interlocutory injunction *E*, Mesure provisionnelle *F*

Emission *G*, *F*, Issue *E*

Emissionsstempelabgabe *G*, Issuance stamp tax *E*, Droit de timbre d'émission *F*

Emprunt à option *F*, Bond issue with warrants attached *E*, Optionsanleihe *G*

Emprunt de rang postérieur *F*, Subordinated issue *E*, Nachrangige Anleihe *G*

Emprunt par obligation *F*, Bond *E*, Anleihensobligation *G*

Endossement *F*, Indorsement *E*, Indossament *G*

Engagement conditionnel *F*, Contingent liability *E*, Eventualverpflichtung *G*

Enrichissement illégitime *F*, Unjust enrichment *E*, Ungerechtfertigte Bereicherung *G*

Entraide administrative *F*, Administrative assistance *E*, Amtshilfe *G*

Entraide judiciaire *F*, Judicial assistance *E*, Rechtshilfe *G*

Entreprise des postes, téléphones et télégraphes (PTT) *F*, Federal Postal Service *E*, Post- Telephon- und Telegraphenbetriebe (PTT) *G*

Entreprise en participation *F*, Joint venture *E*, Gemeinschaftsunternehmen *G*

Erblasser *G*, Decedent *E*, De cujus *F*

Erbschaftssteuer *G*, Inheritance tax *E*, Impôt sur les successions *F*

Ertragswert *G*, Capitalised income value *E*, Valeur de rendement *F*

Escroquerie *F*, Fraud *E*, Betrug *G*

Escroquerie en matière de prestations et de contributions *F*, Fiscal fraud *E*, Abgabebetrug *G*

Establishment *E*, Fondation *F*, Gründung *G*

Etablissement *F*, Business establishment *E*, Niederlassung *G*

Etablissement permanent *F*, Permanent establishment *E*, Betriebsstätte *G*

Etat *F*, Country *E*, Staat *G*

Etat de collocation *F*, Schedule of claims *E*, Kollokationsplan *G*

Europäische Konvention zum Schutz der Menschenrechte und Grundfreiheiten (EMRK) *G*, European Convention on Human Rights and Fundamental Liberties *E*, Convention européenne des droits de l'homme et des libertés fondamentales (CEDH) *F*

European Convention on Human Rights and Fundamental Liberties *E*, Convention européenne des droits de l'homme et des libertés fondamentales (CEDH) *F*, Europäische Konvention zum Schutz der Menschenrechte und Grundfreiheiten (EMRK) *G*

Evasion fiscale *F*, Tax evasion *E*, Steuerumgehung *G*

Eventualverpflichtung *G*, Contingent liability *E*, Engagement conditionnel *F*

Exclusive distributorship agreement *E*, Concession exclusive de vente *F*, Alleinvertriebssvertrag *G*

Exécution des obligations contractuelles *F*, Performance of contract *E*, Vertragserfüllung *G*

Export risk guarantee *E*, Garantie des risques à l'exportation *F*, Exportrisikogarantie *G*

Exportrisikogarantie *G*, Export risk guarantee *E*, Garantie des risques à l'exportation *F*

Expropriation formelle *F*, Formal expropriation *E*, Formelle Enteignung *G*

Expropriation matérielle *F*, Constructive expropriation *E*, Materielle Enteignung *G*

Extract from the Register of Commerce *E*, Extrait du registre du commerce *F*, Handelsregisterauszug *G*

Extrait du registre du commerce *F*, Extract from the Register of Commerce *E*, Handelsregisterauszug *G*

Extrait du registre foncier *F*, Land register extract *E*, Grundbuchauszug *G*

Faillite *F*, Bankruptcy *E*, Konkurs *G*

Fälligkeit *G*, Due date *E*, Echéancc *F*

Faustpfand *G*, Pledge *E*, Nantissement *F*

Fédéral (féd.) *F*, Federal *E*, Eidgenössisch (Eidg.) *G*

Federal *E*, Fédéral (féd.) *F*, Eidgenössisch (Eidg.) *G*

Federal Accident Insurance Company *E*, Caisse nationale suisse d'assurances en cas d'accident (CNA) *F*, Schweizerische Unfallversicherungsanstalt (SUVA) *G*

Federal Accident Insurance Statute *E*, Loi fédérale sur l'assurance-accidents (LAA) *F*, Bundesgesetz über die Unfallversicherung (UVG) *G*

Federal Anticipatory Tax Statute (FATS) *E*, Loi fédérale sur l'impôt anticipé (LIA) *F*, Bundesgesetz über die Verrechnungssteuer (VStG) *G*

Federal Banking Commission *E*, Commission fédérale des banques (CFB) *F*, Eidgenössische Bankenkommission (EBK) *G*

Federal Banking Ordinance *E*, Ordonnance sur les banques et les caisses d'épargne (OB) *F*, Verordnung zum Bankengesetz (BankV) *G*

Federal Banking Statute *E*, Loi fédérale sur les banques et les caisses d'épargne (LB) *F*, Bundesgesetz über die Banken und Sparkassen (BankG) *G*

Federal Cartel Commission *E*, Commission fédérale des cartels *F*, Eidgenössische Kartellkommission *G*

Federal Cartel Statute *E*, Loi fédérale sur les cartels et organisations analogues (LCart) *F*, Bundesgesetz über Kartelle und ähnliche Organisationen (KG) *G*

Federal Central Office for Printed Matters and Materials *E*, Office central fédéral des imprimés et du matériel (UCFIM) *F*, Eidgenössische Drucksachen- und Materialzentrale (EDMZ) *G*

Federal Civil Aviation Office *E*, Office fédéral de l'aviation civile (OFAC) *F*, Bundesamt für Zivilluftfahrt (BAZL) *G*

Federal Constitution *E*, Constitution fédérale de la Confédération suisse (Cst.)
F, Bundesverfassung der Schweizerischen Eidgenossenschaft (BV) *G*
Federal Customs Administration *E*, Administration fédérale des douanes (AFD)
F, Eidgenössische Zollverwaltung (EZV) *G*
Federal Customs Statute *E*, Loi sur les douanes (LD) *F*, Zollgesetz (ZG) *G*
Federal Decree *E*, Arrêté fédéral (AF) *F*, Bundesbeschluss (BB) *G*
Federal Decree regarding measures against improper use of double taxation
conventions entered into by the Confederation ('Abuse Decree') *E*, Arrêté du
Conseil fédéral instituant des mesures contre l'utilisation sans cause légitime
des conventions conclues par la Confédération en vue d'éviter les doubles
impositions ('arrêté relatif aux abus') *F*, Bundesratsbeschluss betreffend
Massnahmen gegen die ungerechtfertigte Inanspruchnahme von
Doppelbesteuerungsabkommen des Bundes ('Missbrauchsbeschluss') *G*
Federal Department of Foreign Affairs *E*, Département des affaires étrangères
(DFAE) *F*, Eidgenössisches Departement für auswärtige Angelegenheiten
(EDA) *G*
Federal Department of National Economy *E*, Département fédéral de l'économie
publique (DFEP) *F*, Eidgenössisches Volkswirtschaftsdepartement (EVD) *G*
Federal Department of the Interior *E*, Département fédéral de l'intérieur (DFI)
F, Eidgenössisches Departement des Innern (EDI) *G*
Federal Disability Insurance Statute *E*, Loi fédérale sur l'assurance-invalidité
(LAI) *F*, Bundesgesetz über die Invalidenversicherung (IVG) *G*
Federal Environmental Protection Office *E*, Office fédéral de l'environnement,
des forêts et du paysage (OFEFP) *F*, Bundesamt für Umwelt, Wald und
Landschaft (BUWAL) *G*
Federal Finance Department *E*, Département fédéral des finances (DFF) *F*,
Eidgenössisches Finanzdepartement (EFD) *G*
Federal Government accompanying report on proposed legislation *E*, Message
du Conseil fédéral *F*, Botschaft des Bundesrates *G*
Federal Government *E*, Conseil fédéral (CF) *F*, Bundesrat (BR) *G*
Federal Health Insurance Statute *E*, Loi fédérale sur l'assurance-maladie (LAMA)
F, Bundesgesetz über die Krankenversicherung (KUVG) *G*
Federal Income Tax Decree (FITD) *E*, Arrêté du Conseil fédéral sur la perception
d'un impôt fédéral direct (AIFD) *F*, Bundesratsbeschluss über die Erhebung
einer direkten Bundessteuer (BdBSt) *G*
Federal income tax *E*, Impôt fédéral direct *F*, Direkte Bundessteuer *G*
Federal Income Tax Statute *E*, Loi fédérale sur l'impôt fédéral direct (LIFD) *F*,
Bundesgesetz über die direkte Bundessteuer (DBG) *G*
Federal Insurance Office *E*, Office fédéral des assurances privées (OFAP) *F*,
Bundesamt für Privatversicherungswesen (BPV) *G*
Federal Intellectual Property Office *E*, Office fédéral de la propriété intellectuelle
(OFPI) *F*, Bundesamt für geistiges Eigentum (BAGE) *G*

Federal Investment Funds Statute *E*, Loi fédérale sur les fonds de placement (LFP) *F*, Bundesgesetz über die Anlagefonds (AFG) *G*

Federal Justice Department *E*, Département fédéral de justice et police (DJP) *F*, Eidgenössisches Justiz- und Polizeidepartement (EJPD) *G*

Federal Justice Office *E*, Office fédéral de la justice (OFJ) *F*, Bundesamt für Justiz (BJ) *G*

Federal Labour Statute *E*, Loi fédérale sur le travail dans l'industrie, l'artisanat et le commerce (LTr) *F*, Bundesgesetz über die Arbeit in Industrie, Gewerbe und Handel (ArG) *G*

Federal Office for Foreign Economic Affairs *E*, Office fédéral des affaires économiques extérieures (OFAEE) *F*, Bundesamt für Aussenwirtschaft (BAWI) *G*

Federal Office of Industry, Trade and Labour *E*, Office fédéral de l'industrie, des arts et métiers et du travail (OFIAMT) *F*, Bundesamt für Industrie, Gewerbe und Arbeit (BIGA) *G*

Federal Office of Police *E*, Office fédéral de la police (OFP) *F*, Bundesamt für Polizeiwesen (BAP) *G*

Federal Patent Statute *E*, Loi fédérale sur les brevets d'invention (LBI) *F*, Bundesgesetz betreffend die Erfindungspatente (PatG) *G*

Federal Penal Code (PC) *E*, Code pénal suisse (CP) *F*, Strafgesetzbuch (StGB) *G*

Federal Postal Service *E*, Entreprise des postes, téléphones et télégraphes (PTT) *F*, Post-, Telephon- und Telegraphenbetriebe (PTT) *G*

Federal Prosecutor *E*, Procureur de la Confédération *F*, Bundesanwalt *G*

Federal Public Health Office *E*, Office fédéral de la santé publique (OFSP) *F*, Bundesamt für Gesundheitswesen (BAG) *G*

Federal Railway System *E*, Chemins de fer fédéraux (CFF) *F*, Schweizerische Bundesbahnen (SBB) *G*

Federal Register *E*, Feuille fédérale (FF) *F*, Bundesblatt (BBl.) *G*

Federal Social Security Office *E*, Office fédéral des assurances sociales (OFAS) *F*, Bundesamt für Sozialversicherung (BSV) *G*

Federal Stamp Tax Statute (FSTS) *E*, Loi fédérale sur les droits de timbre (LT) *F*, Bundesgesetz über die Stempelabgaben (StG) *G*

Federal statute *E*, Loi fédérale (LF) *F*, Bundesgesetz (BG) *G*

Federal Statute on Acquisition of Immovables by Non-Residents (Lex Friedrich) *E*, Loi fédérale sur l'acquisition d'immeubles par des personnes à l'étranger (LFAIE; Lex Friedrich) *F*, Bundesgesetz über den Erwerb von Grundstücken durch Personen im Ausland (BewG; Lex Friedrich) *G*

Federal Statute on Administrative Criminal Law *E*, Loi fédérale sur le droit pénal administratif (DPA) *F*, Bundesgesetz über das Verwaltungsstrafrecht (VStrR) *G*

Federal Statute on Copyrights of Works of Literature and Art *E*, Loi fédérale concernant le droit d'auteurs sur les oeuvres littéraires et artistiques (LDA) *F*,

Bundesgesetz betreffend das Urheberrecht an Werken der Literatur und Kunst (URG) *G*

Federal Statute on Debt Collection and Bankruptcy *E*, Loi fédérale sur la poursuite pour dettes et la faillite (LP) *F*, Bundesgesetz über Schuldbetreibung und Konkurs (SchKG) *G*

Federal Statute on Harmonisation of Cantonal and Municipal Income Taxes *E*, Loi fédérale sur l'harmonisation des impôts directs des cantons et des communes (LHID) *F*, Bundesgesetz über die Harmonisierung der direkten Steuern der Kantone und Gemeinden (StHG) *G*

Federal Statute on International Judicial Assistance in Criminal Matters *E*, Loi fédérale sur l'entraide internationale en matière pénale (EIMP) *F*, Bundesgesetz über internationale Rechtshilfe in Strafsachen (IRSG) *G*

Federal Statute on Occupational Pension Plans *E*, Loi fédérale sur la prévoyance professionnelle vieillesse, survivants et invalidité (LPP) *F*, Bundesgesetz über die berufliche Alters-, Hinterlassenen- und Invalidenvorsorge (BVG) *G*

Federal Statute on Old-Age and Survivors Insurance *E*, Loi fédérale sur l'assurance-vieillesse et survivants (LAVS) *F*, Bundesgesetz über die Alters- und Hinterlassenenversicherung (AHVG) *G*

Federal Statute on Protection of Trade Marks *E*, Loi fédérale concernant la protection des marques de fabrique et de commerce (LMF) *F*, Bundesgesetz betreffend den Schutz der Fabrik- und Handelsmarken (MSchG) *G*

Federal Statute on the Organisation of the Judiciary *E*, Loi fédérale d'organisation judiciaire (OJ) *F*, Bundesgesetz über die Organisation der Bundesrechtspflege (OG) *G*

Federal Statute Regarding the Treaty with the United States of America on International Judicial Assistance in Criminal Matters *E*, Loi fédérale relative au traité conclu avec les Etats-Unis d'Amérique sur l'entraide judiciaire en matière pénale (LTEJUS) *F*, Bundesgesetz zum Staatsvertrag mit den Vereinigten Staaten von Amerika über gegenseitige Rechtshilfe in Strafsachen (BG-RVUS) *G*

Federal Supreme Court *E*, Tribunal fédéral (TF) *F*, Bundesgericht (BGer) *G*

Federal Tax Administration *E*, Administration fédérale des contributions (AFC) *F*, Eidgenössische Steuerverwaltung (EStV) *G*

Federal Unfair Competition Statute *E*, Loi fédérale sur la concurrence déloyale (LCD) *F*, Bundesgesetz über den unlauteren Wettbewerb (UWG) *G*

Federal Wholesale Tax Decree *E*, Arrêté du Conseil fédéral instituant un impôt sur le chiffre d'affaires (AChA) *F*, Bundesratsbeschluss über die Warenumsatzsteuer (WUB) *G*

Federführende Bank *G*, Lead manager *E*, Banque chef de file *F*

Festgeld *G*, Time deposit *E*, Dépôt à terme *F*

Festübernahme *G*, Firm underwriting *E*, Prise ferme *F*

Feuille fédérale (FF) *F*, Federal Register *E*, Bundesblatt (BBl.) *G*

Feuille officielle suisse du commerce (FOSC) *F*, Swiss Official Journal of Commerce *E*, Schweizerisches Handelsamtsblatt (SHAB) *G*

Fiduciary transaction *E*, Opération fiduciaire *F*, Treuhandgeschäft *G*

Firm underwriting *E*, Prise ferme *F*, Festübernahme *G*

Fiscal fraud *E*, Escroquerie en matière de prestations et de contributions *F*, Abgabebetrug *G*

Fixed assets *E*, Capital investi *F*, Anlagevermögen *G*

Fondation *F*, Establishment *E*, Gründung *G*

Fondation *F*, Foundation *E*, Stiftung *G*

Fonds de placement *F*, Investment fund *E*, Anlagefonds *G*

Fonds de tiers *F*, Debt *E*, Fremdkapital *G*

For judiciaire *F*, Place of jurisdiction *E*, Gerichtsstand *G*

Forderung *G*, Claim *E*, Créance *F*

Foreign decision *E*, Décision étrangère *F*, Ausländische Entscheidung *G*

Foreign exchange *E*, Devises *F*, Devisen *G*

Foreign tax credit *E*, Imputation forfaitaire d'impôt *F*, Pauschale Steueranrechnung *G*

Formal expropriation *E*, Expropriation formelle *F*, Formelle Enteignung *G*

Formelle Enteignung *G*, Formal expropriation *E*, Expropriation formelle *F*

Fortsetzungsbegehren *G*, Request to continue collection proceedings *E*, Réquisition de continuer la poursuite *F*

Foundation *E*, Fondation *F*, Stiftung *G*

Fraud *E*, Escroquerie *F*, Betrug *G*

Fraude fiscale *F*, Tax fraud *E*, Steuerbetrug *G*

Fraudulent behaviour *E*, Astuce *F*, Arglist *G*

Fremdkapital *G*, Debt *E*, Fonds de tiers *F*

Frist *G*, Time limit *E*, Délai *F*

Fusion *F*, *G*, Merger *E*

Gain en capital *F*, Capital gain *E*, Kapitalgewinn *G*

Garantie des risques à l'exportation *F*, Export risk guarantee *E*, Exportrisikogarantie *G*

Garantievertrag *G*, Guarantee *E*, Porte-fort *F*

Gebäudeversicherung *G*, Building insurance *E*, Assurance immobilière *F*

Gebrauchsmuster *G*, Design *E*, Modèle déposé *F*

Gedeckte Option, Stillhalteroption *G*, Covered warrant *E*, Option couverte *F*

Gekreuzter Check *G*, Crossed cheque *E*, Chèque barré *F*

Geldmarkt *G*, Money market *E*, Marché de l'argent *F*

Geldmarktbuchforderung *G*, Money-market book claim *E*, Créance comptable à court terme *F*

Geldmarktpapier *G*, Money-market paper *E*, Papier monétaire *F*

Geldwäscherei *G*, Money laundering *E*, Recyclage d'argent *F*

Geldwerte Leistung *G*, Benefit of a financial nature *E*, Prestation appréciable en argent *F*

Gemeinschaftskonto *G*, Joint account *E*, Compte-joint *F*

Gemeinschaftsunternehmen *G*, Joint venture *E*, Entreprise en participation *F*

General conditions *E*, Conditions générales (CG) *F*, Allgemeine Geschäftsbedingungen (AGB) *G*

General meeting *E*, Assemblée générale *F*, Generalversammlung *G*

General partnership *E*, Société en nom collectif *F*, Kollektivgesellschaft *G*

General power of attorney *E*, Procuration générale *F*, Generalvollmacht *G*

Generally accepted accounting principles *E*, Principes de comptabilité généralement admis *F*, Allgemein anerkannte Buchführungsgrundsätze *G*

Generalversammlung *G*, General meeting *E*, Assemblée générale *F*

Generalversammlungsvollmacht *G*, Proxy *E*, Procuration pour l'assemblée générale *F*

Generalvollmacht *G*, General power of attorney *E*, Procuration générale *F*

Geneva Supreme Court *E*, Cour de justice de Genève *F*, Genfer Kantonsgericht *G*

Genussschein *G*, Dividend-right certificate *E*, Bon de jouissance *F*

Gérant de fortune *F*, Portfolio manager *E*, Vermögensverwalter *G*

Gericht *G*, Court *E*, Tribunal *F*

Gerichtsschreiber *G*, Secretary of the court *E*, Greffier *F*

Gerichtsstand *G*, Place of jurisdiction *E*, For judiciaire *F*

Gesamtarbeitsvertrag *G*, Collective labour agreement *E*, Convention collective de travail *F*

Gesamteigentum *G*, Joint property *E*, Propriété commune *F*

Geschäftsführung ohne Auftrag *G*, Acting without authority *E*, Gestion d'affaires *F*

Gesellschaft mit beschränkter Haftung (GmbH) *G*, Limited liability company *E*, Société à responsabilité limitée (Sàrl) *F*

Gesetzliche Reserven *G*, Legal reserves *E*, Réserve légale *F*

Gestion d'affaires *F*, Acting without authority *E*, Geschäftsführung ohne Auftrag *G*

Gewinn *G*, Profit *E*, Bénéfice *F*

Gewinn- und Verlustrechnung *G*, Profit and loss account *E*, Compte de pertes et profits *F*

Gift tax *E*, Impôt sur les donations *F*, Schenkungssteuer *G*

Gläubigerverzug *G*, Default of obligee *E*, Demeure du créancier *F*

Gratisaktie *G*, Stock dividend *E*, Action gratuite *F*

Greffier *F*, Secretary of the court *E*, Gerichtsschreiber *G*

Grossist *G*, Wholesaler *E*, Grossiste *F*

Grossiste *F*, Wholesaler *E*, Grossist *G*

Grossistenerklärung *G*, Wholesaler's declaration *E*, Déclaration de grossiste *F*

Grundbuch *G*, Land register *E*, Registre foncier *F*

Grundbuchauszug *G*, Land register extract *E*, Extrait du registre foncier *F*
Grunddienstbarkeit *G*, Easement *E*, Servitude foncière *F*
Gründeranteilschein *G*, Incorporator's certificate *E*, Part de fondateur *F*
Grundpfandverschreibung *G*, Mortgage *E*, Hypothèque *F*
Grundstückgewinnsteuer *G*, Immovable property capital gains tax *E*, Impôt sur
  les gains immobiliers *F*
Gründung *G*, Establishment *E*, Fondation *F*
Guarantee *E*, Porte-fort *F*, Garantievertrag *G*
Haftpflichtrecht *G*, Law of torts *E*, Droit de la responsabilité civile (RC) *F*
Haftung *G*, Liability *E*, Responsabilité civile (RC) *F*
Handelsregister (HR) *G*, Register of Commerce *E*, Registre du commerce
  (RC) *F*
Handelsregisterauszug *G*, Extract from the Register of Commerce *E*, Extrait du
  registre du commerce *F*
Handlungsbevollmächtigter *G*, Commercial representative *E*, Mandataire
  commercial *F*
House *E*, Conseil national *F*, Nationalrat *G*
Hypothèque *F*, Mortgage *E*, Grundpfandverschreibung *G*
Immaterialgüterrecht *G*, Industrial (intellectual) property law *E*, Droit de la
  propriété intellectuelle *F*
Immovable property capital gains tax *E*, Impôt sur les gains immobiliers *F*,
  Grundstückgewinnsteuer *G*
Implementing   ordinance   *E*,   Ordonnance   d'exécution   (Od'ex.)   *F*,
  Vollzugsverordnung (VV) *G*
Imposition forfaitaire *F*, Lump-sum taxation *E*, Pauschalbesteuerung *G*
Imposition selon la réalité économique *F*, Substance over form *E*, Wirtschaftliche
  Betrachtungsweise *G*
Impôt *F*, Tax *E*, Steuer *G*
Impôt à la source *F*, Withholding tax *E*, Quellensteuer *G*
Impôt anticipé *F*, Anticipatory tax *E*, Verrechnungssteuer *G*
Impôt fédéral direct *F*, Federal income tax *E*, Direkte Bundessteuer *G*
Impôt sur la fortune *F*, Net-worth tax *E*, Vermögenssteuer *G*
Impôt sur le chiffre d'affaires *F*, Wholesale tax *E*, Warenumsatzsteuer *G*
Impôt sur le revenu *F*, Income tax *E*, Einkommenssteuer *G*
Impôt sur les donations *F*, Gift tax *E*, Schenkungssteuer *G*
Impôt sur les gains immobiliers *F*, Immovable property capital gains tax *E*,
  Grundstückgewinnsteuer *G*
Impôt sur les successions *F*, Inheritance tax *E*, Erbschaftssteuer *G*
Imputation   forfaitaire   d'impôt   *F*,   Foreign   tax   credit   *E*,   Pauschale
  Steueranrechnung *G*
Income tax *E*, Impôt sur le revenu *F*, Einkommenssteuer *G*
Incorporator's certificate *E*, Part de fondateur *F*, Gründeranteilschein *G*

Individual *E*, Personne physique *F*, Natürliche Person *G*
Indorsement *E*, Endossement *F*, Indossament *G*
Indossament *G*, Indorsement *E*, Endossement *F*
Industrial (intellectual) property law *E*, Droit de la propriété intellectuelle *F*,
    Immaterialgüterrecht *G*
Inexécution des obligations contractuelles *F*, Non-performance of contract *E*,
    Nichterfüllung des Vertrages *G*
Inflationary shift into higher tax brackets *E*, Progression à froid *F*, Kalte
    Progression *G*
Inheritance tax *E*, Impôt sur les successions *F*, Erbschaftssteuer *G*
Insider trading *E*, Opération d'initiés *F*, Insiderhandel *G*
Insiderhandel *G*, Insider trading *E*, Opération d'initiés *F*
Insolvabilité *F*, Insolvency *E*, Zahlungsunfähigkeit *G*
Insolvency *E*, Insolvabilité *F*, Zahlungsunfähigkeit *G*
Instruction *E*, *F*, Wegleitung *G*
Intérêt négatif *F*, Reliance interest *E*, Negatives Interesse *G*
Intérêt positif *F*, Performance interest *E*, Positives Interesse *G*
Interlocutory injunction *E*, Mesure provisionnelle *F*, Einstweilige Verfügung *G*
Internationales Privatrecht *G*, Conflict of laws *E*, Droit international privé *F*
Introduction en bourse *F*, Admission to stock exchange dealing *E*,
    Börseneinführung *G*
Investment fund *E*, Fonds de placement *F*, Anlagefonds *G*
Investment in companies *E*, Participation *F*, Beteiligung *G*
Inward processing *E*, Trafic de perfectionnement actif *F*, Aktiver
    Veredlungsverkehr *G*
Issuance stamp tax *E*, Droit de timbre d'émission *F*,
    Emissionsstempelabgabe *G*
Issue *E*, Emission *G*, *F*
Joint account *E*, Compte-joint *F*, Gemeinschaftskonto *G*
Joint and several *E*, Solidaire *F*, Solidarisch *G*
Joint property *E*, Propriété commune *F*, Gesamteigentum *G*
Joint venture *E*, Entreprise en participation *F*, Gemeinschaftsunternehmen *G*
Judgment of the Federal Supreme Court (ATF) *E*, Arrêt du Tribunal fédéral
    (ATF) *F*, Bundesgerichtsentscheid (BGE) *G*
Judicial assistance *E*, Entraide judiciaire *F*, Rechtshilfe *G*
Juristische Person *G*, Legal entity *E*, Personne morale *F*
Juste motif *F*, Cause *E*, Wichtiger Grund *G*
Kalte Progression *G*, Inflationary shift into higher tax brackets *E*, Progression à
    froid *F*
Kantonalbank *G*, Cantonal bank *E*, Banque cantonale *F*
Kapitalgewinn *G*, Capital gain *E*, Gain en capital *F*
Kassaobligation *G*, Medium-term note *E*, Certificat de dépôt *F*

Klage *G*, Complaint *E*, Demande *F*

Klageantwort *G*, Answer to the complaint *E*, Réponse *F*

Kläger *G*, Plaintiff, Claimant *E*, Demandeur *F*

Kollektivgesellschaft *G*, General partnership *E*, Société en nom collectif *F*

Kollisionsrecht *G*, Conflict-of-law rules *E*, Règles de droit international privé *F*

Kollokationsplan *G*, Schedule of claims *E*, Etat de collocation *F*

Kommanditaktiengesellschaft *G*, Limited partnership with shares *E*, Société en commandite par actions *F*

Kommanditgesellschaft *G*, Limited partnership *E*, Société en commandite *F*

Kommissionär *G*, Commission agent *E*, Commissionnaire *F*

Konkurs *G*, Bankruptcy *E*, Faillite *F*

Konkursamt *G*, Bankruptcy office *E*, Office des faillites *F*

Konkursprivileg *G*, Preferred claim under bankruptcy *E*, Privilège en cas de faillite *F*

Konkursverwaltung *G*, Receiver in bankruptcy *E*, Administration de faillite *F*

Konnossement *G*, Bill of lading, B/L *E*, Connaissement *F*

Konsolidierte Bilanz *G*, Consolidated balance sheet *E*, Bilan consolidé *F*

Kontokorrent *G*, Current account *E*, Compte-courant *F*

Kreisschreiben *G*, Circular letter *E*, Circulaire *F*

L/C, Letter of credit *E*, Accréditif *F*, Akkreditiv *G*

Land register *E*, Registre foncier *F*, Grundbuch *G*

Land register extract *E*, Extrait du registre foncier *F*, Grundbuchauszug *G*

Law of torts *E*, Droit de la responsabilité civile (RC) *F*, Haftpflichtrecht *G*

Lead manager *E*, Banque chef de file *F*, Federführende Bank *G*

Legal entity *E*, Personne morale *F*, Juristische Person *G*

Legal reserves *E*, Réserve légale *F*, Gesetzliche Reserven *G*

Legal transaction *E*, Acte juridique *F*, Rechtsgeschäft *G*

Liabilities *E*, Passifs *F*, Passiven *G*

Liability *E*, Responsabilité civile (RC) *F*, Haftung *G*

Liability in tort *E*, Responsabilité aquillienne *F*, Ausservertragliche Haftung *G*

Lieu de règlement *F*, Place of performance *E*, Zahlungsort *G*

Life-interest, usufruct *E*, Usufruit *F*, Nutzniessung *G*

Limited partnership *E*, Société en commandite *F*, Kommanditgesellschaft *G*

Limited partnership with shares *E*, Société en commandite par actions *F*, Kommanditaktiengesellschaft *G*

Limited liability company *E*, Société à responsabilité limitée (Sàrl) *F*, Gesellschaft mit beschränkter Haftung (GmbH) *G*

Lis pendens *E*, Litispendance *F*, Rechtshängigkeit *G*

Litispendance *F*, Lis pendens *E*, Rechtshängigkeit *G*

Lizenzgebühr *G*, Royalty *E*, Redevance de licence *F*

Loan *E*, Prêt *F*, Darlehen *G*

Local customs *E*, Usages locaux *F*, Ortsgebrauch *G*

Loi fédérale (LF) *F*, Federal statute *E*, Bundesgesetz (BG) *G*

Loi fédérale concernant la protection des marques de fabrique et de commerce (LMF) *F*, Federal Statute on Protection of Trade Marks *E*, Bundesgesetz betreffend den Schutz der Fabrik- und Handelsmarken (MSchG) *G*

Loi fédérale concernant le droit d'auteurs sur les oeuvres littéraires et artistiques (LDA) *F*, Federal Statute on Copyrights of Works of Literature and Art *E*, Bundesgesetz betreffend das Urheberrecht an Werken der Literatur und Kunst (URG) *G*

Loi fédérale d'organisation judiciaire (OJ) *F*, Federal Statute on the Organisation of the Judiciary *E*, Bundesgesetz über die Organisation der Bundesrechtspflege (OG) *G*

Loi fédérale relative au traité conclu avec les Etats-Unis d'Amérique sur l'entraide judiciaire en matière pénale (LTEJUS) *F*, Federal Statute Regarding the Treaty with the United States of America on International Judicial Assistance in Criminal Matters *E*, Bundesgesetz zum Staatsvertrag mit den Vereinigten Staaten von Amerika über gegenseitige Rechtshilfe in Strafsachen (BG-RVUS) *G*

Loi fédérale sur l'acquisition d'immeubles par des personnes à l'étranger (LFAIE; Lex Friedrich) *F*, Federal Statute on Acquisition of Immovables by Non-Residents (Lex Friedrich) *E*, Bundesgesetz über den Erwerb von Grundstücken durch Personen im Ausland (BewG; Lex Friedrich) *G*

Loi fédérale sur l'assurance-accidents (LAA) *F*, Federal Accident Insurance Statute *E*, Bundesgesetz über die Unfallversicherung (UVG) *G*

Loi fédérale sur l'assurance-invalidité (LAI) *F*, Federal Disability Insurance Statute *E*, Bundesgesetz über die Invalidenversicherung (IVG) *G*

Loi fédérale sur l'assurance-maladie (LAMA) *F*, Federal Health Insurance Statute *E*, Bundesgesetz über die Krankenversicherung (KUVG) *G*

Loi fédérale sur l'assurance-vieillesse et survivants (LAVS) *F*, Federal Statute on Old-Age and Survivors Insurance *E*, Bundesgesetz über die Alters- und Hinterlassenenversicherung (AHVG) *G*

Loi fédérale sur l'entraide internationale en matière pénale (EIMP) *F*, Federal Statute on International Judicial Assistance in Criminal Matters *E*, Bundesgesetz über internationale Rechtshilfe in Strafsachen (IRSG) *G*

Loi fédérale sur l'harmonisation des impôts directs des cantons et des communes (LHID) *F*, Federal Statute on Harmonisation of Cantonal and Municipal Income Taxes *E*, Bundesgesetz über die Harmonisierung der direkten Steuern der Kantone und Gemeinden (StHG) *G*

Loi fédérale sur l'impôt anticipé (LIA) *F*, Federal Anticipatory Tax Statute (FATS) *E*, Bundesgesetz über die Verrechnungssteuer (VStG) *G*

Loi fédérale sur l'impôt fédéral direct (LIFD) *F*, Federal Income Tax Statute *E*, Bundesgesetz über die direkte Bundessteuer (DBG) *G*

Loi fédérale sur la concurrence déloyale (LCD) *F*, Federal Unfair Competition Statute *E*, Bundesgesetz über den unlauteren Wettbewerb (UWG) *G*

Loi fédérale sur la poursuite pour dettes et la faillite (LP) *F*, Federal Statute on Debt Collection and Bankruptcy *E*, Bundesgesetz über Schuldbetreibung und Konkurs (SchKG) *G*

Loi fédérale sur la prévoyance professionnelle vieillesse, survivants et invalidité (LPP) *F*, Federal Statute on Occupational Pension Plans *E*, Bundesgesetz über die berufliche Alters-, Hinterlassenen- und Invalidenvorsorge (BVG) *G*

Loi fédérale sur le droit pénal administratif (DPA) *F*, Federal Statute on Administrative Criminal Law *E*, Bundesgesetz über das Verwaltungsstrafrecht (VStrR) *G*

Loi fédérale sur le travail dans l'industrie, l'artisanat et le commerce (LTr) *F*, Federal Labour Statute *E*, Bundesgesetz über die Arbeit in Industrie, Gewerbe und Handel (ArG) *G*

Loi fédérale sur les banques et les caisses d'épargne (LB) *F*, Federal Banking Statute *E*, Bundesgesetz über die Banken und Sparkassen (BankG) *G*

Loi fédérale sur les brcvets d'invention (LBI) *F*, Federal Patent Statute *E*, Bundesgesetz betreffend die Erfindungspatente (PatG) *G*

Loi fédérale sur les cartels et organisations analogues (LCart) *F*, Federal Cartel Statute *E*, Bundesgesetz über Kartelle und ähnliche Organisationen (KG) *G*

Loi fédérale sur les droits de timbre (LT) *F*, Federal Stamp Tax Statute (FSTS) *E*, Bundesgesetz über die Stempelabgaben (StG) *G*

Loi fédérale sur les fonds de placement (LFP) *F*, Federal Investment Funds Statute *E*, Bundesgesetz über die Anlagefonds (AFG) *G*

Loi sur les douanes (LD) *F*, Federal Customs Statute *E*, Zollgesetz (ZG) *G*

Lump-sum taxation *E*, Imposition forfaitaire *F*, Pauschalbcsteuerung *G*

Mainlevée définitive d'opposition *F*, Definitive removal of opposition *E*, Definitve Rechtsöffnung *G*

Mainlevée provisoire *F*, Provisional removal of opposition *E*, Provisorische Rechtsöffnung *G*

Mäkler *G*, Broker *E*, Courtier *F*

Mäklerlohn *G*, Brokerage fee *E*, Salaire du courtier *F*

Mäklervertrag *G*, Brokerage agreement *E*, Contrat de courtage *F*

Management authority *E*, Mandat de gestion *F*, Verwaltungsvollmacht *G*

Manager *E*, Directeur *F*, Direktor *G*

Mandat *F*, Mandate *E*, Auftrag *G*

Mandataire commercial *F*, Commercial representative *E*, Handlungsbevollmächtigter *G*

Mandat de gestion *F*, Management authority *E*, Verwaltungsvollmacht *G*

Mandate *E*, Mandat *F*, Auftrag *G*

Manteau d'actions *F*, Bare shell *E*, Aktienmantel *G*

Marché de l'argent *F*, Money market *E*, Geldmarkt *G*

Market capitalisation *E*, Capitalisation boursière *F*, Börsenkapitalisierung *G*
Market value *E*, Valeur vénale *F*, Verkehrswert *G*
Marque déposée *F*, Trade mark *E*, Warenzeichen *G*
Materielle Enteignung *G*, Constructive expropriation *E*, Expropriation matérielle *F*
Maximum emission or immission standard *E*, Valeur limite d'exposition *F*, Belastungsgrenzwert *G*
Medium-term note *E*, Certificat de dépôt *F*, Kassaobligation *G*
Member of the board of directors, Director *E*, Administrateur *F*, Verwaltungsratsmitglied *G*
Merger *E*, Fusion *F*, *G*
Merkblatt *G*, Notice *E*, Note *F*
Message du Conseil fédéral *F*, Federal Government accompanying report on proposed legislation *E*, Botschaft des Bundesrates *G*
Mesure provisionelle *F*, Interlocutory injunction *E*, Einstweilige Verfügung *G*
Mesures conservatoires *F*, Conservatory measures *E*, Sichernde Massnahmen *G*
Ministère public *F*, Attorney-General's Office *E*, Staatsanwaltschaft *G*
Missbräuchlich *G*, Abusive *E*, Abusif *F*
Missbrauchsbeschluss *G*, Abuse Decree *E*, Arrêté relatif aux abus *F*
Miteigentum *G*, Co-ownership *E*, Copropriété *F*
Modèle déposé *F*, Design *E*, Gebrauchsmuster *G*
Money laundering *E*, Recyclage d'argent *F*, Geldwäscherei *G*
Money market *E*, Marché de l'argent *F*, Geldmarkt *G*
Money-market book claim *E*, Créance comptable à court terme *F*, Geldmarktbuchforderung *G*
Money-market paper *E*, Papier monétaire *F*, Geldmarktpapier *G*
Money-transfer order *E*, Ordre de paiement *F*, Zahlungsauftrag *G*
Mortgage *E*, Hypothèque *F*, Grundpfandverschreibung *G*
Mortgage note *E*, Cédule hypothécaire *F*, Schuldbrief *G*
Motion to reconsider *E*, Opposition *F*, Einsprache *G*
Nachbörse *G*, After market *E*, Après bourse *F*
Nachlass *G*, Decedent's estate *E*, Succession *F*
Nachlassvertrag *G*, Composition *E*, Concordat *F*
Nachrangige Anleihe *G*, Subordinated issue *E*, Emprunt de rang postérieur *F*
Namenaktie *G*, Registered share *E*, Action nominative *F*
Nantissement *F*, Pledge *E*, Faustpfand *G*
Nationalrat *G*, House *E*, Conseil national *F*
Natürliche Person *G*, Individual *E*, Personne physique *F*
Negatives Interesse *G*, Reliance interest *E*, Intérêt négatif *F*
Negotiable instrument, security *E*, Papier-valeur *F*, Wertpapier *G*
Nennwert *G*, Par value *E*, Valeur nominale *F*
Net-worth tax *E*, Impôt sur la fortune *F*, Vermögenssteuer *G*

Office fédéral des affaires économiques extérieures (OFAEE) *F*, Federal Office for Foreign Economic Affairs *E*, Bundesamt für Aussenwirtschaft (BAWI) *G*
Office fédéral des assurances privées (OFAP) *F*, Federal Insurance Office *E*, Bundesamt für Privatversicherungswesen (BPV) *G*
Office fédéral des assurances sociales (OFAS) *F*, Federal Social Security Office *E*, Bundesamt für Sozialversicherung (BSV) *G*
Open reserves, pretaxed earnings *E*, Réserves ouvertes *F*, Offene Reserven *G*
Opération d'initiés *F*, Insider trading *E*, Insiderhandel *G*
Opération fiduciaire *F*, Fiduciary transaction *E*, Treuhandgeschäft *G*
Opposition *F*, Motion to reconsider *E*, Einsprache *G*
Option couverte *F*, Covered warrant *E*, Stillhalteroption, gedeckte Option *G*
Optionsanleihe *G*, Bond issue with warrants attached *E*, Emprunt à option *F*
Order to pay *E*, Commandement de payer *F*, Zahlungsbefehl, *G*
Ordinance *E*, Ordonnance *F*, Verordnung *G*
Ordinary partnership *E*, Société simple *F*, Einfache Gesellschaft *G*
Ordonnance *F*, Ordinance *E*, Verordnung *G*
Ordonnance d'exécution (Od'ex.) *F*, Implementing ordinance *E*, Vollzugsverordnung (VV) *G*
Ordonnance sur les banques et les caisses d'épargne (OB) *F*, Federal Banking Ordinance *E*, Verordnung zum Bankengesetz (BankV) *G*
Ordre de paiement *F*, Money-transfer order *E*, Zahlungsauftrag *G*
Ortsgebrauch *G*, Local customs *E*, Usages locaux *F*
Outward processing *E*, Trafic de perfectionnement passif *F*, Passiver Veredlungsverkehr *G*
Pacte de réserve de propriété *F*, Retention of title *E*, Eigentumsvorbehalt (EV) *G*
Papier monétaire *F*, Money-market paper *E*, Geldmarktpapier *G*
Papier-valeur, titre *F*, Security, negotiable instrument *E*, Wertpapier *G*
Par value *E*, Valeur nominale *F*, Nennwert *G*
Part de fondateur *F*, Incorporator's certificate *E*, Gründeranteilschein *G*
Participation *F*, Investment in companies *E*, Beteiligung *G*
Participation certificate *E*, Bon de participation *F*, Partizipationsschein *G*
Partizipationsschein *G*, Participation certificate *E*, Bon de participation *F*
Passifs *F*, Liabilities *E*, Passiven *G*
Passiven *G*, Liabilities *E*, Passifs *F*
Passiver Veredlungsverkehr *G*, Outward processing *E*, Trafic de perfectionnement passif *F*
Patent *E*, Brevet *F*, Patent *G*
Patent *E*, *G*, Brevet *F*
Paulianische Anfechtungsklage *G*, Action for undue preference *E*, Action révocatoire *F*
Pauschalbesteuerung *G*, Lump-sum taxation *E*, Imposition forfaitaire *F*

Pauschale Steueranrechnung *G*, Foreign tax credit *E*, Imputation forfaitaire d'impôt *F*

Payment order *E*, Assignation *F*, Anweisung *G*

Peine conventionnelle *F*, Contract penalty *E*, Vertragsstrafe *G*

Performance interest *E*, Intérêt positif *F*, Positives Interesse *G*

Performance of contract *E*, Exécution des obligations contractuelles *F*, Vertragserfüllung *G*

Permanent establishment *E*, Etablissement permanent *F*, Betriebsstätte *G*

Personne morale *F*, Legal entity *E*, Juristische Person *G*

Personne physique *F*, Individual *E*, Natürliche Person *G*

Piercing the corporate veil *E*, Non reconnaissance de la personne morale *F*, Durchgriff *G*

Place of jurisdiction *E*, For judiciaire *F*, Gerichtsstand *G*

Place of performance *E*, Lieu de règlement *F*, Zahlungsort *G*

Placement privé *F*, Private placement *E*, Privatplazierung *G*

Plaintiff, Claimant *E*, Demandeur *F*, Kläger *G*

Plan d'affectation *F*, Utilisation plan *E*, Nutzungsplan *G*

Plan directeur *F*, Zoning directive *E*, Richtplan *G*

Plan social *F*, Severance compensation plan *E*, Sozialplan *G*

Pledge *E*, Nantissement *F*, Faustpfand *G*

Porte-fort *F*, Guarantee *E*, Garantievertrag *G*

Portfolio manager *E*, Gérant de fortune *F*, Vermögensverwalter *G*

Positives Interesse *G*, Performance interest *E*, Intérêt positif *F*

Post-, Telephon- und Telegraphenbetriebe (PTT) *G*, Federal Postal Service *E*, Entreprise des postes, téléphones et télégraphes (PTT) *F*

Poursuite *F*, Debt collection *E*, Betreibung *G*

Power of attorney, proxy *E*, Procuration *F*, Vollmacht *G*

Préciput *F*, Advance share *E*, Vorausabzug, Praecipuum *G*

Preferred claim under bankruptcy *E*, Privilège en cas de faillite *F*, Konkursprivileg *G*

Preferred share *E*, Action privilégiée *F*, Vorzugsaktie *G*

Prescription *F*, Statute of Limitations, time bar *E*, Verjährung *G*

Prestation appréciable en argent *F*, Benefit of a financial nature *E*, Geldwerte Leistung *G*

Prestation caractéristique *F*, Characteristic performance *E*, Charakteristische Leistung *G*

Prêt *F*, Loan *E*, Darlehen *G*

Pretaxed earnings, open reserves *E*, Réserves ouvertes *F*, Offene Reserven *G*

Principe du pollueur-payeur *F*, Principle that polluters pay *E*, Verursacherprinzip *G* ˙

Principes de comptabilité généralement admis *F*, Generally accepted accounting principles *E*, Allgemein anerkannte Buchführungsgrundsätze *G*

Principle that polluters pay *E*, Principe du pollueur-payeur *F*, Verursacherprinzip *G*
Prise ferme *F*, Firm underwriting *E*, Festübernahme *G*,
Privatbank *G*, Private bank *E*, Banque privée *F*
Private bank *E*, Banque privée *F*, Privatbank *G*
Private placement *E*, Placement privé *F*, Privatplazierung *G*
Privatplazierung *G*, Private placement *E*, Placement privé *F*
Privilège en cas de faillite *F*, Preferred claim under bankruptcy *E*, Konkursprivileg *G*
Procédure de conciliation *F*, Conciliation proceedings *E*, Sühneverfahren *G*
Procuration *F*, Power of attorney, proxy *E*, Vollmacht *G*
Procuration générale *F*, General power of attorney *E*, Generalvollmacht *G*
Procuration pour l'assemblée générale *F*, Proxy *E*, Generalversammlungs-vollmacht *G*
Procureur de la Confédération *F*, Federal Prosecutor *E*, Bundesanwalt *G*
Procureur du district de Zurich *F*, Zurich District Attorney *E*, Zürcher Bezirksanwaltschaft (BAZ) *G*
Product liability *E*, Responsabilité du fait d'un produit *F*, Produktehaftung *G*
Produktehaftung *G*, Product liability *E*, Responsabilité du fait d'un produit *F*
Profit *E*, Bénéfice *F*, Gewinn *G*
Profit and loss account *E*, Compte de pertes et profits *F*, Gewinn- und Verlustrechnung *G*
Progression à froid *F*, Inflationary shift into higher tax brackets *E*, Kalte Progression *G*
Promissory note *E*, Billet à ordre *F*, Eigenwechsel *G*
Propriété commune *F*, Joint property *E*, Gesamteigentum *G*
Prospectus *E*, *F*, Prospekt *G*
Prospectus *E*, Prospectus d'introduction à la bourse *F*, Einführungsprospekt *G*
Prospectus d'introduction à la bourse *F*, Prospectus *E*, Einführungsprospekt *G*
Prospekt *G*, Prospectus *E*, *F*
Provision *E*, *F*, Rückstellung *G*
Provision *F*, *E*, Rückstellung *G*
Provision *G*, *F*, Commission *E*
Provisional removal of opposition *E*, Mainlevée provisoire *F*, Provisorische Rechtsöffnung *G*
Provisions for doubtful debts *E*, Réserve pour débiteurs douteux *F*, Delcredere *G*
Provisorische Rechtsöffnung *G*, Provisional removal of opposition *E*, Mainlevée provisoire *F*
Proxy *E*, Procuration pour l'assemblée générale *F*, Generalversammlungs-vollmacht *G*
Quellensteuer *G*, Withholding tax *E*, Impôt à la source *F*
Rangrücktritt *G*, Subordination *E*, *F*

Receivables *E*, Débiteurs *F*, Debitoren *G*

Receiver in bankruptcy *E*, Administration de faillite *F*, Konkursverwaltung *G*

Rechtsanwalt (RA) *G*, Attorney-at-law *E*, Avocat (av.) *F*

Rechtsgeschäft *G*, Legal transaction *E*, Acte juridique *F*

Rechtshängigkeit *G*, Lis pendens *E*, Litispendance *F*

Rechtshilfe *G*, Judicial assistance *E*, Entraide judiciaire *F*

Recours *F*, Complaint *E*, Beschwerde *G*

Recours de droit administratif *F*, Administrative law complaint *E*, Verwaltungs-gerichtsbeschwerde *G*

Recours de droit public *F*, Constitutional complaint *E*, Staatsrechtliche Beschwerde *G*

Recours en réforme *F*, Appeal *E*, Berufung *G*

Recueil systématique du droit fédéral (RS) *F*, Systematic Collection of Swiss Federal Law (RS) *E*, Systematische Sammlung des Bundesrechtes (SR) *G*

Récusation d'un arbitre *F*, Challenge of an arbitrator *E*, Ablehnung eines Schiedsrichters *G*

Recyclage d'argent *F*, Moncy laundering *E*, Geldwäscherei *G*

Redevance de licence *F*, Royalty *E*, Lizenzgebühr *G*

Regierungsrat *G*, Cantonal government *E*, Conseil d'Etat *F*

Register of Commerce *E*, Registre du commerce (RC) *F*, Handelsregister (HR) *G*

Registered share *E*, Action nominative *F*, Namenaktie *G*

Registre du commerce (RC) *F*, Register of Commerce *E*, Handelsregister (HR) *G*

Registre foncier *F*, Land register *E*, Grundbuch *G*

Règlement d'arbitrage *F*, Arbitration rules *E*, Schiedsordnung *G*

Règles de droit international privé *F*, Conflict-of-law rules *E*, Kollisionsrecht *G*

Rejoinder *E*, Duplique *F*, Duplik *G*

Rekurskommission *G*, Board of tax appeals *E*, Commission de recours *F*

Reliance interest *E*, Intérêt négatif *F*, Negatives Interesse *G*

Replik *G*, Reply *E*, Réplique *F*

Réplique *F*, Reply *E*, Replik *G*

Reply *E*, Réplique *F*, Replik *G*

Réponse *F*, Answer to the complaint *E*, Klageantwort *G*

Représentant *F*, Agent *E*, Vertreter *G*

Request for order to pay *E*, Réquisition de poursuite *F*, Betreibungsbegehren *G*

Request to continue collection proceedings *E*, Réquisition de continuer la poursuite *F*, Fortsetzungsbegehren *G*

Request to realise seized assets *E*, Réquisition de vente *F*, Verwertungsbegehren *G*

Réquisition de continuer la poursuite *F*, Request to continue collection proceedings *E*, Fortsetzungsbegehren *G*

Réquisition de poursuite *F*, Request for order to pay *E*, Betreibungsbegehren *G*
Réquisition de vente *F*, Request to realise seized assets *E*,
   Verwertungsbegehren *G*
Réserve légale *F*, Legal reserves *E*, Gesetzliche Reserven *G*
Réserve pour débiteurs douteux *F*, Provisions for doubtful debts *E*,
   Delcredere *G*
Réserves latentes *F*, Undisclosed reserves *E*, Stille Reserven *G*
Réserves ouvertes *F*, Open reserves, pretaxed earnings *E*, Offene Reserven *G*
Respondent, Defendant *E*, Défendeur *F*, Beklagter *G*
Responsabilité aquilienne *F*, Liability in tort *E*, Ausservertragliche Haftung *G*
Responsabilité civile (RC) *F*, Liability *E*, Haftung *G*
Responsabilité contractuelle *F*, Contractual liability *E*, Vertragliche Haftung *G*
Responsabilité du fait d'un produit *F*, Product liability *E*, Produktehaftung *G*
Restricted transferability of shares *E*, Restrictions de transfert d'actions *F*,
   Vinkulierung von Aktien *G*
Restrictions de transfert d'actions *F*, Restricted transferability of shares *E*,
   Vinkulierung von Aktien *G*
Retention of title *E*, Pacte de réserve de propriété *F*, Eigentumsvorbehalt
   (EV) *G*
Richtplan *G*, Zoning directive *E*, Plan directeur *F*
Right of first refusal *E*, Droit de préemption *F*, Vorkaufsrecht *G*
Right to build *E*, Droit de superficie *F*, Baurecht *G*
Royalty *E*, Redevance de licence *F*, Lizenzgebühr *G*
Rückstellung *G*, Provision *E*, *F*
Salaire du courtier *F*, Brokerage fee *E*, Mäklerlohn *G*
Sale *E*, Vente *F*, Verkauf *G*
Schedule of claims *E*, Etat de collocation *F*, Kollokationsplan *G*
Schenkungssteuer *G*, Gift tax *E*, Impôt sur les donations *F*
Schiedsfähigkeit *G*, Arbitrability *E*, Arbitrabilité *F*
Schiedsgericht *G*, Arbitral tribunal *E*, Tribunal arbitral *F*
Schiedsgerichtsbarkeit *G*, Arbitration *E*, Arbitrage *F*
Schiedsklausel *G*, Arbitration clause *E*, Clause d'arbitrage *F*
Schiedsordnung *G*, Arbitration rules *E*, Règlement d'arbitrage *F*
Schiedsvereinbarung *G*, Arbitration agreement *E*, Convention d'arbitrage *F*
Schuldbrief *G*, Mortgage note *E*, Cédule hypothécaire *F*
Schuldnerverzug *G*, Default of obligor *E*, Demeure du débiteur *F*
Schweizerische Bankiervereinigung *G*, Swiss Bankers Association *E*,
   Association Suisse des Banquiers *F*
Schweizerische Bundesbahnen (SBB) *G*, Federal Railroad System *E*, Chemins
   de fer fédéraux (CFF) *F*
Schweizerische Eidgenossenschaft *G*, Swiss Confederation *E*, Confédération
   suisse *F*

Schweizerische Nationalbank (SNB) *G*, Swiss National Bank *E*, Banque Nationale suisse (BNS) *F*

Schweizerische Unfallversicherungsanstalt (SUVA) *G*, Federal Accident Insurance Company *E*, Caisse nationale suisse d'assurances en cas d'accident (CNA) *F*

Schweizerischer Uebernahme-Kodex *G*, Swiss Take-Over Code *E*, Code suisse des offres publiques d'achat *F*

Schweizerisches Handelsamtsblatt (SHAB) *G*, Swiss Official Journal of Commerce *E*, Feuille officielle suisse du commerce (FOSC) *F*

Seat *E*, Siège *F*, Sitz *G*

Secret bancaire *F*, Bank secrecy *E*, Bankgeheimnis *G*

Secretary of the court *E*, Greffier *F*, Gerichtsschreiber *G*

Securities dealer *E*, Commerçant de titre *F*, Wertschriftenhändler, Effektenhändler *G*

Securities turnover stamp tax *E*, Droit de timbre de négociation *F*, Umsatzstempelabgabe *G*

Security, negotiable instrument *E*, Papier-valeur, titre *F*, Wertpapier *G*

SEGA Schweizerische Effekten-Giro AG (SEGA) *G*, Swiss Securities Clearing Corporation (SEGA) *E*, SEGA Société suisse pour le virement de titres SA (SEGA) *F*

SEGA Société suisse pour le virement de titres SA (SEGA) *F*, Swiss Securities Clearing Corporation (SEGA) *E*, SEGA Schweizerische Effekten-Giro AG (SEGA) *G*

Senate *E*, Conseil des Etats *F*, Ständerat *G*

Séquestre *F*, Attachment *E*, Arrest *G*

Servitude foncière *F*, Easement *E*, Grunddienstbarkeit *G*

Set-off *E*, Compensation *F*, Verrechnung *G*

Settlement *E*, Transaction *F*, Vergleich *G*

Severance compensation plan *E*, Plan social *F*, Sozialplan *G*

Share *E*, Action *F*, Aktie *G*

Share corporation *E*, Société anonyme (SA) *F*, Aktiengesellschaft (AG) *G*

Share premium *E*, Agio *F*, *G*,

Sichernde Massnahmen *G*, Conservatory measures *E*, Mesures conservatoires *F*

Siège *F*, Seat *E*, Sitz *G*

Sitz *G*, Seat *E*, Siège *F*

Société à responsabilité limitée (Sàrl) *F*, Limited liability company *E*, Gesellschaft mit beschränkter Haftung (GmbH) *G*

Société anonyme (SA) *F*, Share corporation *E*, Aktiengesellschaft (AG) *G*

Société en commandite *F*, Limited partnership *E*, Kommanditgesellschaft *G*

Société en commandite par actions *F*, Limited partnership with shares *E*, Kommanditaktiengesellschaft *G*

Société en nom collectif *F*, General partnership *E*, Kollektivgesellschaft *G*

Société financière à caractère bancaire *F*, Bank-like finance company *E*, Bankähnliche Finanzgesellschaft *G*

Société simple *F*, Ordinary partnership *E*, Einfache Gesellschaft *G*

Solidaire *F*, Joint and several *E*, Solidarisch *G*

Solidarisch *G*, Joint and several *E*, Solidaire *F*

Solvabilité *F*, Solvency *E*, Zahlungsfähigkeit *G*

Solvency *E*, Solvabilité *F*, Zahlungsfähigkeit *G*

Sorgfaltspflichtvereinbarung *G*, Due Diligence Convention *E*, Convention de diligence *F*

Sous-participation *F*, Sub-participation *E*, Unterbeteiligung *G*

Sozialplan *G*, Severance compensation plan *E*, Plan social *F*

Staat *G*, Country *E*, Etat *F*

Staatsanwaltschaft *G*, Attorney-General's Office *E*, Ministère public *F*

Staatsrechtliche Beschwerde *G*, Constitutional complaint *E*, Recours de droit public *F*

Staatsvertrag zwischen der Schweizerischen Eidgenossenschaft und den Vereinigten Staaten von Amerika über gegenseitige Rechtshilfe in Strafsachen (RVUS) *G*, Treaty between the Swiss Confederation and the United States of America on International Judicial Assistance in Criminal Matters *E*, Traité entre la Confédération suisse et les Etats-Unis d'Amérique sur l'entraide judiciaire en matière pénale (TEJUS) *F*

Stamp tax *E*, Droit de timbre *F*, Stempelabgabe *G*

Standard-provision contract *E*, Contrat-type de travail *F*, Normalarbeitsvertrag *G*

Ständerat *G*, Senate *E*, Conseil des Etats *F*

Statute of Limitations, time bar *E*, Prescription *F*, Verjährung *G*

Statuten *G*, Articles of Incorporation *E*, Statuts *F*

Statuts *F*, Articles of Incorporation *E*, Statuten *G*

Stempelabgabe *G*, Stamp tax *E*, Droit de timbre *F*

Steuer *G*, Tax *E*, Impôt *F*

Steuerbetrug *G*, Tax fraud *E*, Fraude fiscale *F*

Steuererklärung *G*, Tax return *E*, Déclaration fiscale *F*

Steuerhinterziehung *G*, Tax evasion *E*, Soustraction fiscale *F*

Steuerumgehung *G*, Tax avoidance *E*, Evasion fiscale *F*,

Steuerwiderhandlung *G*, Tax contravention *E*, Contravention fiscale *F*

Stiftung *G*, Foundation *E*, Fondation *F*

Stille Reserven *G*, Undisclosed reserves *E*, Réserves latentes *F*

Stillhalteroption, gedeckte Option *G*, Covered warrant *E*, Option couverte *F*

Stock dividend *E*, Action gratuite *F*, Gratisaktie *G*

Strafgesetzbuch (StGB) *G*, Federal Penal Code (PC) *E*, Code pénal suisse (CP) *F*

Strafprozessordnung (StPO) *G*, Code of criminal procedure *E*, Code de procédure pénale (CPP) *F*

Sub-participation *E*, Sous-participation *F*, Unterbeteiligung *G*

Subordinated issue *E*, Emprunt de rang postérieur *F*, Nachrangige Anleihe *G*

Subordination *E*, *F*, Rangrücktritt *G*

Substance over form *E*, Imposition selon la réalité économique *F*, Wirtschaftliche Betrachtungsweise *G*

Succession *F*, Decedent's estate *E*, Nachlass *G*

Succursale *F*, Branch office *E*, Zweigniederlassung *G*

Sühneverfahren *G*, Conciliation proceedings *E*, Procédure de conciliation *F*

Supervisory authority *E*, Autorité de surveillance *F*, Aufsichtsbehörde *G*

Suretyship *E*, Cautionnement *F*, Bürgschaft *G*

Swiss Bankers Association *E*, Association Suisse des Banquiers *F*, Schweizerische Bankiervereinigung *G*

Swiss Confederation *E*, Confédération suisse *F*, Schweizerische Eidgenossenschaft *G*

Swiss National Bank *E*, Banque Nationale suisse (BNS) *F*, Schweizerische Nationalbank (SNB) *G*

Swiss Official Journal of Commerce *E*, Feuille officielle suisse du commerce (FOSC) *F*, Schweizerisches Handelsamtsblatt (SHAB) *G*

Swiss Securities Clearing Corporation (SEGA) *E*, SEGA Société suisse pour le virement de titres SA (SEGA) *F*, SEGA Schweizerische Effekten-Giro AG (SEGA) *G*

Swiss Take-Over Code *E*, Code suisse des offres publiques d'achat *F*, Schweizerischer Uebernahme-Kodex *G*

Systematic Collection of Swiss Federal Law (RS) *E*, Recueil systématique du droit fédéral (RS) *F*, Systematische Sammlung des Bundesrechtes (SR) *G*

Systematische Sammlung des Bundesrechtes (SR) *G*, Systematic Collection of Swiss Federal Law (RS) *E*, Recueil systématique du droit fédéral (RS) *F*

Taking of evidence *E*, Administration des preuves *F*, Beweisaufnahme *G*

Tax *E*, Impôt *F*, Steuer *G*

Tax assessment *E*, Taxation *F*, Veranlagung *G*

Tax avoidance *E*, Evasion fiscale *F*, Steuerumgehung *G*

Tax contravention *E*, Contravention fiscale *F*, Steuerwiderhandlung *G*

Tax evasion *E*, Soustraction fiscale *F*, Steuerhinterziehung *G*

Tax fraud *E*, Fraude fiscale *F*, Steuerbetrug *G*

Tax return *E*, Déclaration fiscale *F*, Steuererklärung *G*

Taxation *F*, Tax assessment *E*, Veranlagung *G*

Time deposit *E*, Dépôt à terme *F*, Festgeld *G*

Time limit *E*, Délai *F*, Frist *G*

Titre représentant la marchandise *F*, Document of title *E*, Warenpapier *G*

Tort *E*, Acte illicite *F*, Unerlaubte Handlung *G*

Trade mark *E*, Marque déposée *F*, Warenzeichen *G*

Trafic de perfectionnement actif *F*, Inward processing *E*, Aktiver Veredlungsverkehr *G*

Trafic de perfectionnement passif *F*, Outward processing *E*, Passiver Veredlungsverkehr *G*

Trait par trait *F*, Contemporaneous performance *E*, Zug um Zug *G*

Traité entre la Confédération suisse et les Etats-Unis d'Amérique sur l'entraide judiciaire en matière pénale (TEJUS) *F*, Treaty between the Swiss Confederation and the United States of America on International Judicial Assistance in Criminal Matters *E*, Staatsvertrag zwischen der Schweizerischen Eidgenossenschaft und den Vereinigten Staaten von Amerika über gegenseitige Rechtshilfe in Strafsachen (RVUS) *G*

Transaction *F*, Settlement *E*, Vergleich *G*

Treaty between the Swiss Confederation and the United States of America on International Judicial Assistance in Criminal Matters *E*, Traité entre la Confédération suisse et les Etats-Unis d'Amérique sur l'entraide judiciaire en matière pénale (TEJUS) *F*, Staatsvertrag zwischen der Schweizerischen Eidgenossenschaft und den Vereinigten Staaten von Amerika über gegenseitige Rechtshilfe in Strafsachen (RVUS) *G*

Treaty shopping *E*, Utilisation sans cause légitime des conventions dc double imposition *F*, Ungerechtfertigte Inanspruchnahme von Doppelbesteuerungsabkommen *G*

Treuhandgeschäft *G*, Fiduciary transaction *E*, Opération fiduciaire *F*

Trial court *E*, Tribunal de première instance, Tribunal de district, Tribunal d'arrondissement *F*, Bezirksgericht *G*

Tribunal *F*, Court *E*, Gericht *G*

Tribunal administratif *F*, Administrative court *E*, Verwaltungsgericht *G*

Tribunal arbitral *F*, Arbitral tribunal *E*, Schiedsgericht *G*

Tribunal cantonal de Zurich *F*, Zurich Supreme Court *E*, Zürcher Obergericht (OG) *G*

Tribunal d'arrondissement *F*, Trial court *E*, Bezirksgericht *G*

Tribunal de cassation de Zurich *F*, Zurich Court of Errors *E*, Zürcher Kassationsgericht (Kass.Ger.) *G*

Tribunal de district *F*, Trial court *E*, Bezirksgericht *G*

Tribunal de première instance *F*, Trial court *E*, Bezirksgericht *G*

Tribunal fédéral (TF) *F*, Federal Supreme Court *E*, Bundesgericht (BGer) *G*

Ueber pari *G*, Above par *E*, Au-dessus du pair *F*

Umlaufvermögen *G*, Current asset *E*, Actif circulant *F*

Umsatzstempelabgabe *G*, Securities turnover stamp tax *E*, Droit de timbre de négociation *F*

Undisclosed reserves *E*, Réserves latentes *F*, Stille Reserven *G*

Unerlaubte Handlung *G*, Tort *E*, Acte illicite *F*

Unfair competition *E*, Concurrence déloyale *F*, Unlauterer Wettbewerb *G*
Ungerechtfertigte Bereicherung *G*, Unjust enrichment *E*, Enrichissement illégitime *F*
Ungerechtfertigte Inanspruchnahme von Doppelbesteuerungsabkommen *G*, Treaty shopping *E*, Utilisation sans cause légitime des conventions de double imposition *F*
Unjust enrichment *E*, Enrichissement illégitime *F*, Ungerechtfertigte Bereicherung *G*
Unlauterer Wettbewerb *G*, Unfair competition *E*, Concurrence déloyale *F*
Unter pari *G*, Below par *E*, Au-dessous du pair *F*
Unterbeteiligung *G*, Sub-participation *E*, Sous-participation *F*
Ursprungszeugnis *G*, Certificate of origin *E*, Certificat d'origine *F*
Usages locaux *F*, Local customs *E*, Ortsgebrauch *G*
Usufruct, life-interest *E*, Usufruit *F*, Nutzniessung *G*
Usufruit *F*, Usufruct, life-interest *E*, Nutzniessung *G*
Utilisation sans cause légitime des conventions de double imposition *F*, Treaty shopping *E*, Ungerechtfertigte Inanspruchnahme von Doppelbesteuerungsabkommen *G*
Utilisation plan *E*, Plan d'affectation *F*, Nutzungsplan *G*
Valeur de rendement *F*, Capitalised income value *E*, Ertragswert *G*
Valeur limite d'exposition *F*, Maximum emission or immission standard *E*, Belastungsgrenzwert *G*
Valeur nominale *F*, Par value *E*, Nennwert *G*
Valeur vénale *F*, Market value *E*, Verkehrswert *G*
Validation du séquestre *F*, Validation of attachment *E*, Arrestprosequierung *G*
Validation of attachment *E*, Validation du séquestre *F*, Arrestprosequierung *G*
Vente *F*, Sale *E*, Verkauf *G*
Veranlagung *G*, Tax assessment *E*, Taxation *F*
Verdeckte Gewinnausschüttung *G*, Constructive dividend *E*, Distribution de bénéfices dissimulée *F*
Verein *G*, Association *F*, *E*
Vereinigung der Schweizer Börsen *G*, Association of Swiss Stock Exchanges *E*, Association des Bourses Suisses *F*
Vergleich *G*, Settlement *E*, Transaction *F*
Verjährung *G*, Statute of Limitations, time bar *E*, Prescription *F*
Verkauf *G*, Sale *E*, Vente *F*
Verkehrswert *G*, Market value *E*, Valeur vénale *F*
Verlustschein *G*, Certificate of loss *E*, Acte de défaut de biens *F*
Vermögenssteuer *G*, Net-worth tax *E*, Impôt sur la fortune *F*
Vermögensverwalter *G*, Portfolio manager *E*, Gérant de fortune *F*
Verordnung *G*, Ordinance *E*, Ordonnance *F*

Verordnung zum Bankengesetz (BankV) *G*, Federal Banking Ordinance *E*, Ordonnance sur les banques et les caisses d'épargne (OB) *F*
Verrechnung *G*, Set-off *E*, Compensation *F*
Verrechnungssteuer *G*, Anticipatory tax *E*, Impôt anticipé *F*
Vertrag *G*, Contract *E*, Contrat *F*
Vertragliche Haftung *G*, Contractual liability *E*, Responsabilité contractuelle *F*
Vertragserfüllung *G*, Performance of contract *E*, Exécution des obligations contractuelles *F*
Vertragsstrafe *G*, Contract penalty *E*, Peine conventionnelle *F*
Vertreter *G*, Agent *E*, Représentant *F*
Verursacherprinzip *G*, Principle that polluters pay *E*, Principe du pollueur-payeur *F*
Verwaltungsgericht *G*, Administrative court *E*, Tribunal administratif *F*
Verwaltungsgerichtsbeschwerde *G*, Administrative-law complaint *E*, Recours de droit administratif *F*
Verwaltungsratsmitglied *G*, Member of the board of directors, Director *E*, Administrateur *F*
Verwaltungsvollmacht *G*, Management authority *E*, Mandat de gestion *F*
Verwertungsbegehren *G*, Request to realise seized assets *E*, Réquisition de vente *F*
Vinkulierung von Aktien *G*, Restricted transferability of shares, *E*, Restrictions de transfert d'actions *F*
Vollmacht *G*, Power of attorney, proxy *E*, Procuration *F*
Vollstreckbarkeitsbescheinigung *G*, Certificate of enforceability *E*, Certificat de force exécutoire *F*
Vollzugsverordnung (VV) *G*, Implementing ordinance *E*, Ordonnance d'exécution (Od'ex.) *F*
Vorausabzug, Praecipuum *G*, Advance share *E*, Préciput *F*
Vorkaufsrecht *G*, Right of first refusal *E*, Droit de préemption *F*
Vorzugsaktie *G*, Preferred share *E*, Action privilégiée *F*
Wandelobligation *G*, Convertible bond *E*, Obligation convertible *F*
Warenpapier *G*, Document of title *E*, Titre représentant la marchandise *F*
Warenumsatzsteuer *G*, Wholesale tax *E*, Impôt sur le chiffre d'affaires *F*
Warenzeichen *G*, Trade mark *E*, Marque déposée *F*
Wechsel *G*, Bill of exchange, draft *E*, Effet de change *F*
Wegleitung *G*, Instruction *E*, *F*
Wertpapier *G*, Security, negotiable instrument *E*, Papier-valeur, titre *F*
Wertschriftenhändler *G*, Securities dealer *E*, Commerçant de titre *F*
Wholesale tax *E*, Impôt sur le chiffre d'affaires *F*, Warenumsatzsteuer *G*
Wholesaler *E*, Grossiste *F*, Grossist *G*
Wholesaler's declaration *E*, Déclaration de grossiste *F*, Grossistenerklärung *G*
Wichtiger Grund *G*, Cause *E*, Juste motif *F*

Widerklage *G*, Counterclaim *E*, Demande reconventionnelle *F*

Wirtschaftliche Betrachtungsweise *G*, Substance over form *E*, Imposition selon la réalité économique *F*

Withholding tax *E*, Impôt à la source *F*, Quellensteuer *G*

Zahlungsauftrag *G*, Money-transfer order *E*, Ordre de paiement *F*

Zahlungsbefehl *G*, Order to pay *E*, Commandement de payer *F*

Zahlungsfähigkeit *G*, Solvency *E*, Solvabilité *F*

Zahlungsort *G*, Place of performance *E*, Lieu de règlement *F*

Zahlungsunfähigkeit *G*, Insolvency *E*, Insolvabilité *F*

Zedent *G*, Assignor *E*, Cédant *F*

Zessionar *G*, Assignee *E*, Cessionnaire *F*

Zivilgesetzbuch (ZGB) *G*, Civil Code (CC) *E*, Code civil suisse (CC) *F*

Zoll *G*, Customs *E*, Douane *F*

Zollgesetz (ZG) *G*, Federal Customs Statute *E*, Loi sur les douanes (LD) *F*

Zoning directive *E*, Plan directeur *F*, Richtplan *G*

Zug um Zug *G*, Contemporaneous performance *E*, Trait par trait *F*

Zürcher Bezirksanwaltschaft (BAZ) *G*, Zurich District Attorney *E*, Procureur du district de Zurich *F*

Zürcher Kassationsgericht (Kass.Ger.) *G*, Zurich Court of Errors *E*, Tribunal de cassation de Zurich *F*

Zürcher Obergericht (OG) *G*, Zurich Supreme Court *E*, Tribunal cantonal de Zurich *F*

Zurich Court of Errors *E*, Tribunal de cassation de Zurich *F*, Zürcher Kassationsgericht (Kass.Ger.) *G*

Zurich District Attorney *E*, Procureur du district de Zurich *F*, Zürcher Bezirksanwaltschaft (BAZ) *G*

Zurich Supreme Court *E*, Tribunal cantonal de Zurich *F*, Zürcher Obergericht (OG) *G*

Zuteilung *G*, Allocation *E*, Attribution *F*

Zweigniederlassung *G*, Branch office *E*, Succursale *F*

Index

References are to paragraph numbers